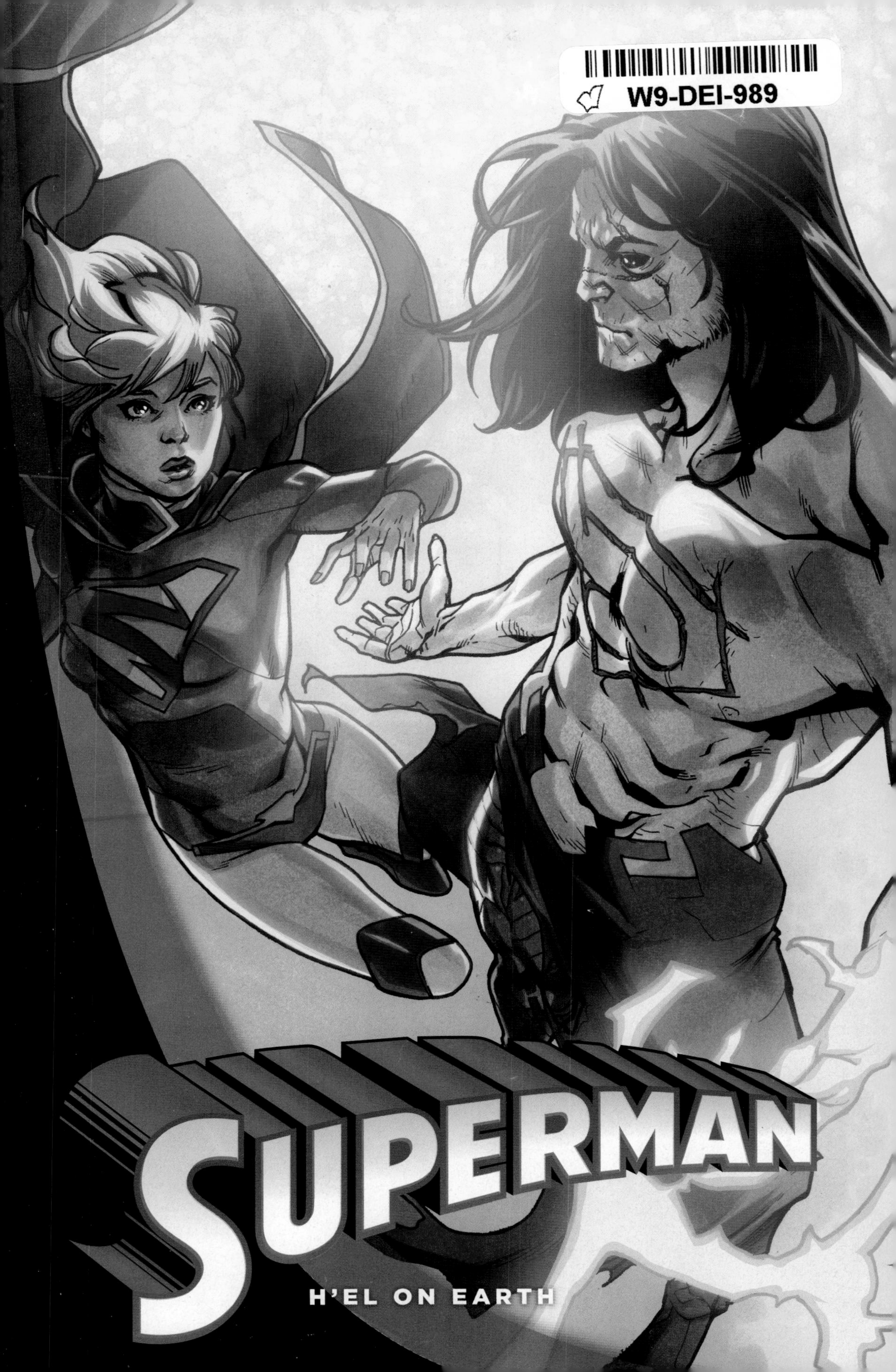
SUPERMAN
H'EL ON EARTH

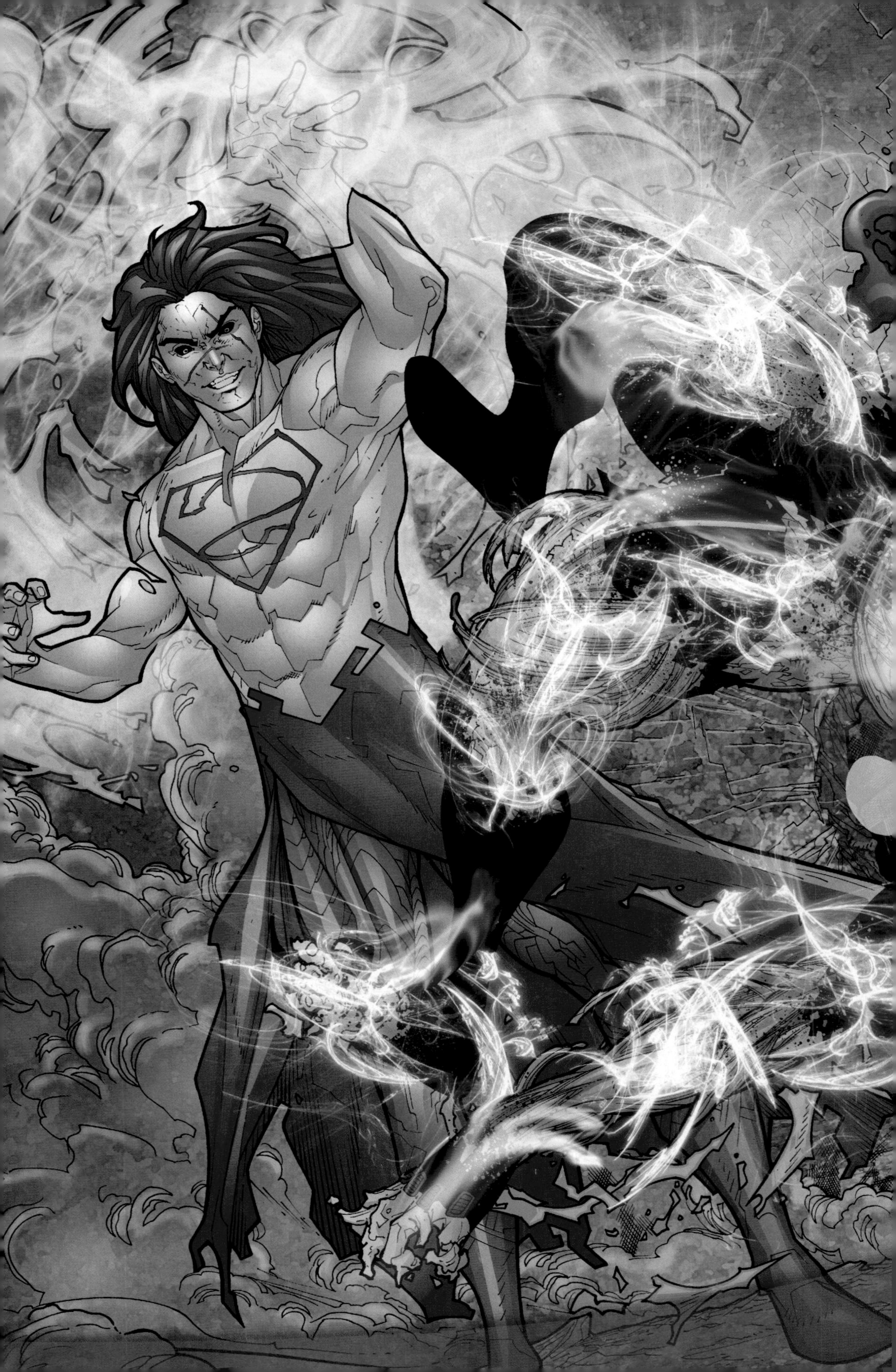

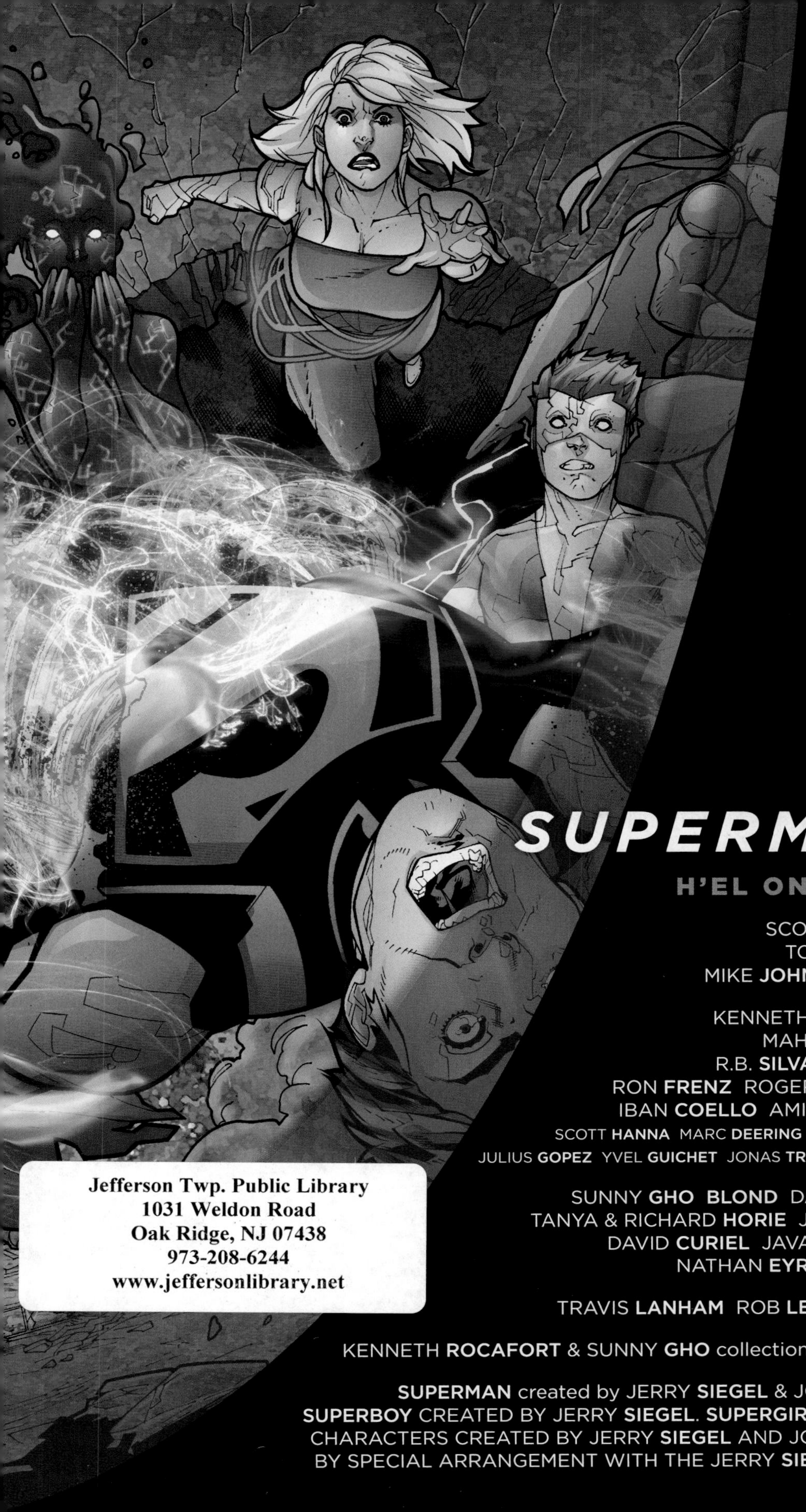

SUPERMAN

H'EL ON EART

SCOTT LOBDE
TOM DEFALC
MIKE JOHNSON write

KENNETH ROCAFO
MAHMUD ASRA
R.B. SILVA ROB LEA
RON FRENZ ROGER ROBINSO
IBAN COELLO AMILCAR PINN
SCOTT HANNA MARC DEERING TOM DEREN
JULIUS GOPEZ YVEL GUICHET JONAS TRINDADE artis

SUNNY GHO BLOND DAVE MCCA
TANYA & RICHARD HORIE JEROMY C
DAVID CURIEL JAVA TARTAGL
NATHAN EYRING coloris

TRAVIS LANHAM ROB LEIGH lettere

KENNETH ROCAFORT & SUNNY GHO collection cover arti

SUPERMAN created by JERRY SIEGEL & JOE SHUST
SUPERBOY CREATED BY JERRY SIEGEL. SUPERGIRL BASED
CHARACTERS CREATED BY JERRY SIEGEL AND JOE SHUSTE
BY SPECIAL ARRANGEMENT WITH THE JERRY SIEGEL FAMI

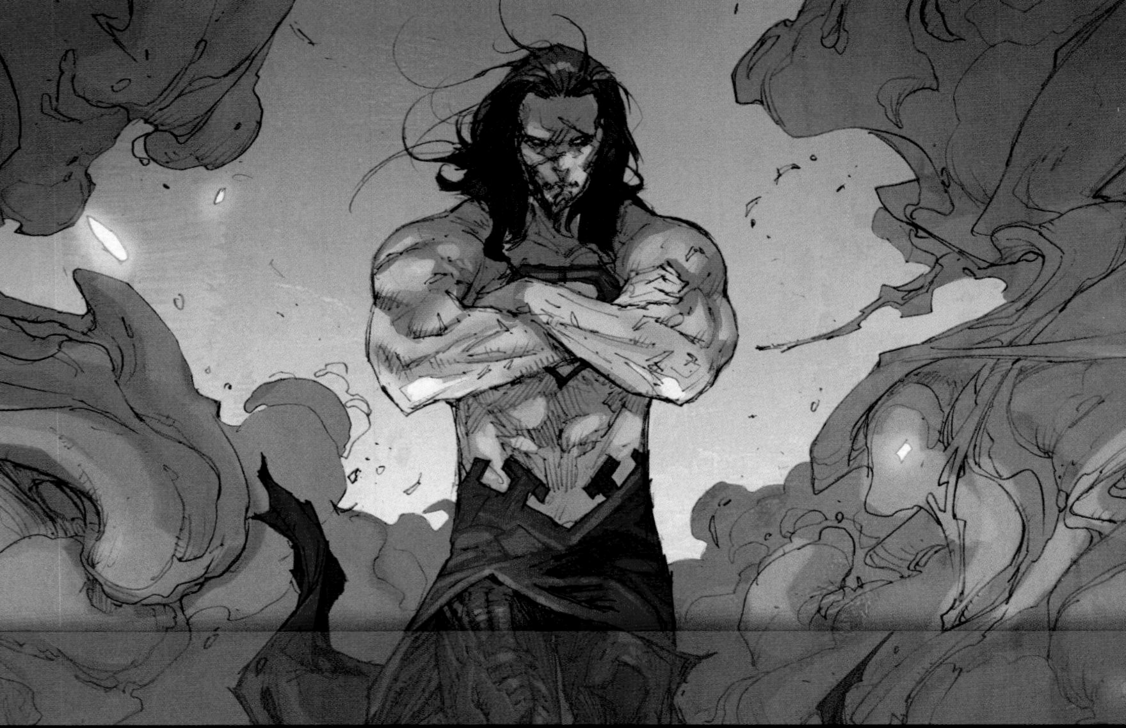

EDDIE BERGANZA WIL MOSS CHRIS CONROY Editors – Original Series
DARREN SHAN ANTHONY MARQUES Assistant Editors – Original Series RACHEL PINNELAS Editor
ROBBIN BROSTERMAN Design Director – Books ROBBIE BIEDERMAN Publication Design

BOB HARRAS Senior VP – Editor-in-Chief, DC Comics

DIANE NELSON President DAN DIDIO and JIM LEE Co-Publishers GEOFF JOHNS Chief Creative Officer
JOHN ROOD Executive VP – Sales, Marketing and Business Development AMY GENKINS Senior VP – Business and Legal Affairs
NAIRI GARDINER Senior VP – Finance JEFF BOISON VP – Publishing Planning
MARK CHIARELLO VP – Art Direction and Design JOHN CUNNINGHAM VP – Marketing
TERRI CUNNINGHAM VP – Editorial Administration ALISON GILL Senior VP – Manufacturing and Operations
HANK KANALZ Senior VP – Vertigo & Integrated Publishing JAY KOGAN VP – Business & Legal Affairs, Publishing
JACK MAHAN VP – Business Affairs, Talent NICK NAPOLITANO VP – Manufacturing Administration
SUE POHJA VP – Book Sales COURTNEY SIMMONS Senior VP – Publicity BOB WAYNE Senior VP – Sales

SUPERMAN: H'EL ON EARTH

DC Comics, 1700 Broadway, New York, NY 10019. A Warner Bros. Entertainment Company.
Printed by RR Donnelley, Salem, VA, USA. 5/16/14. First Printing.
SC ISBN: 978-1-4012-4612-9

Library of Congress Cataloging-in-Publication Data

Lobdell, Scott.
Superman : H'El on Earth / Scott Lobdell.
pages cm. -- (The New 52!)
Summary: "H'El has come to Earth! A figure from Krypton's past has come to Earth, hoping to revive the dead planet--in place of this one. uperman, Superboy, Supergirl and the Justice League stand ready to fight, but whose side is everyone on? As hero fights against hero, will he Kryptonians be able to defeat H'El, who is their equal in every way? The first Super-crossover in the New 52 is here in SUPERMAN: H'EL ON EARTH, written by Scott Lobdell, Mike Johnson and Tom DeFalco, with art by Kenneth Rocafort, Mahmud Asrar, RB Silva and more. Collects SUPERMAN #13-17, SUPERBOY ANNUAL #1, SUPERBOY #14-17 and SUPERGIRL #14-17"— Provided by publisher.
"Superman created by Jerry Siegel and Joe Shuster."
ISBN 978-1-4012-4319-7 (hardback)
1. Graphic novels. I. Title. II. Title: H'El on Earth.
PN6728.S9P47 2012
741.5'973—dc23
2012029951

SUSTAINABLE FORESTRY INITIATIVE
Certified Chain of Custody
At Least 20% Certified Forest Content
www.sfiprogram.org
SFI-01042
APPLIES TO TEXT STOCK ONLY

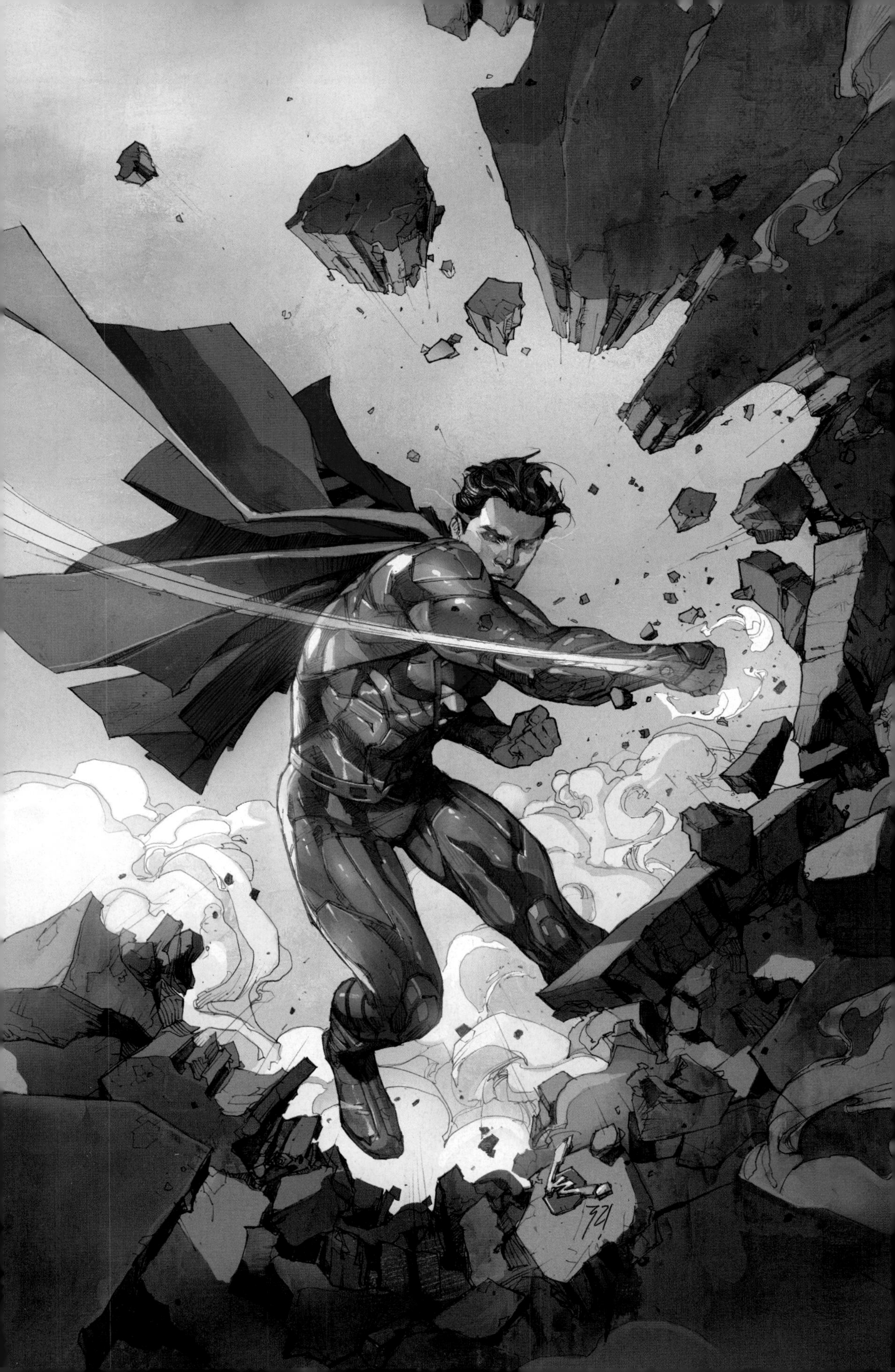

THEY WILL JOIN YOU IN THE SUN

SCOTT LOBDELL writer **KENNETH ROCAFORT** artist cover art by **KENNETH ROCAFORT & SUNNY GHO**

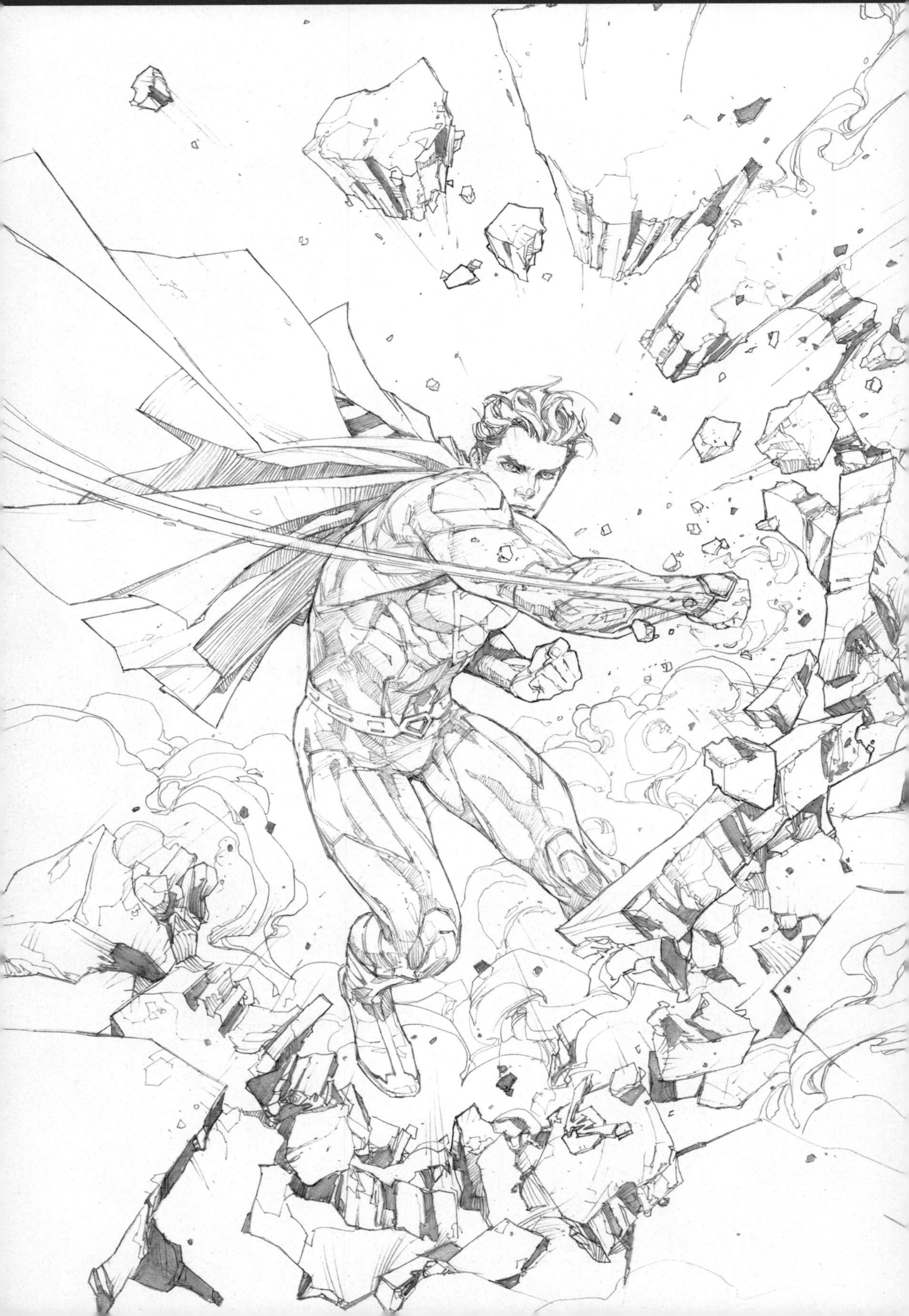

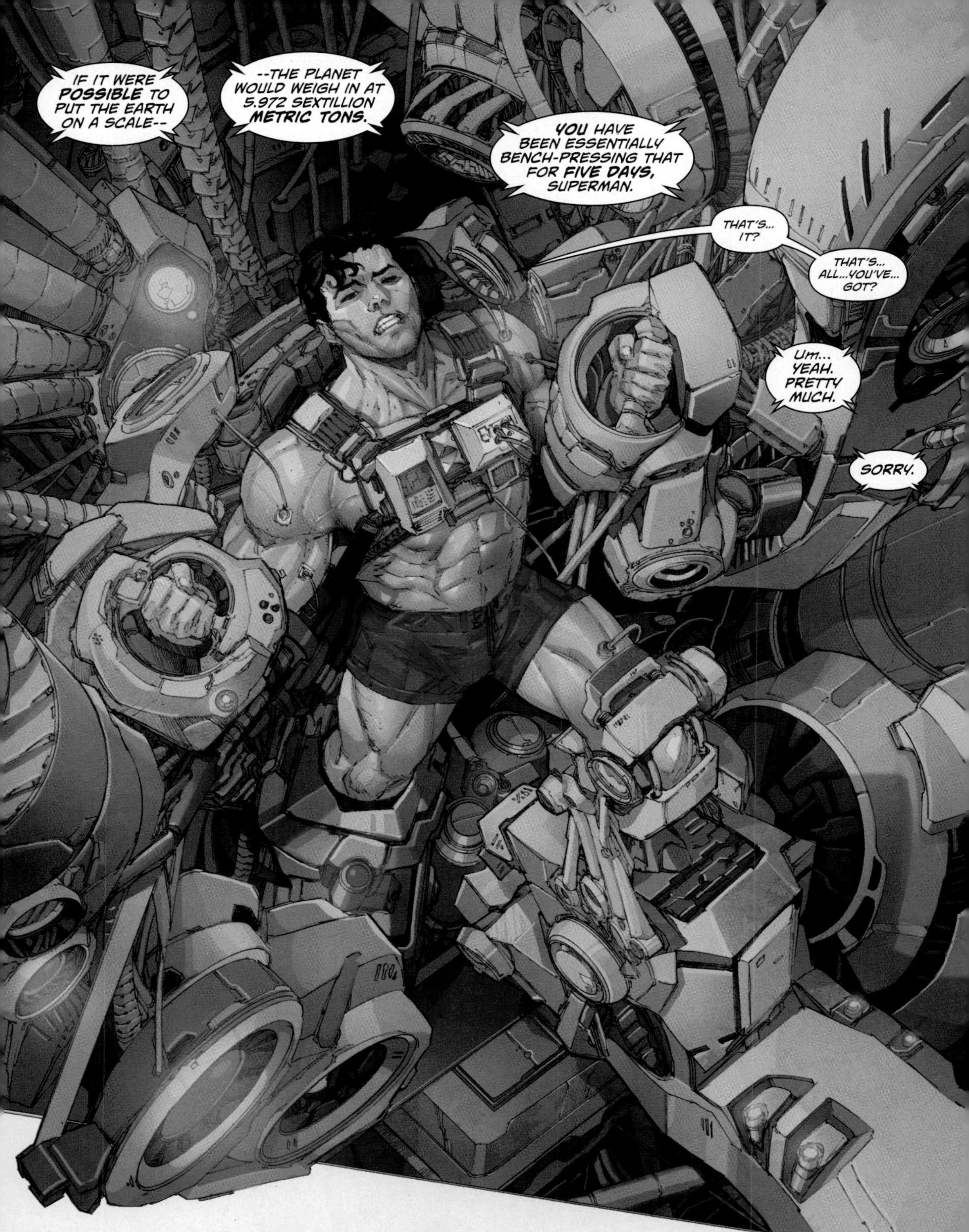
IF IT WERE POSSIBLE TO PUT THE EARTH ON A SCALE--
--THE PLANET WOULD WEIGH IN AT 5.972 SEXTILLION METRIC TONS.
YOU HAVE BEEN ESSENTIALLY BENCH-PRESSING THAT FOR FIVE DAYS, SUPERMAN.
THAT'S... IT?
THAT'S... ALL...YOU'VE... GOT?
Um... YEAH. PRETTY MUCH.
SORRY.

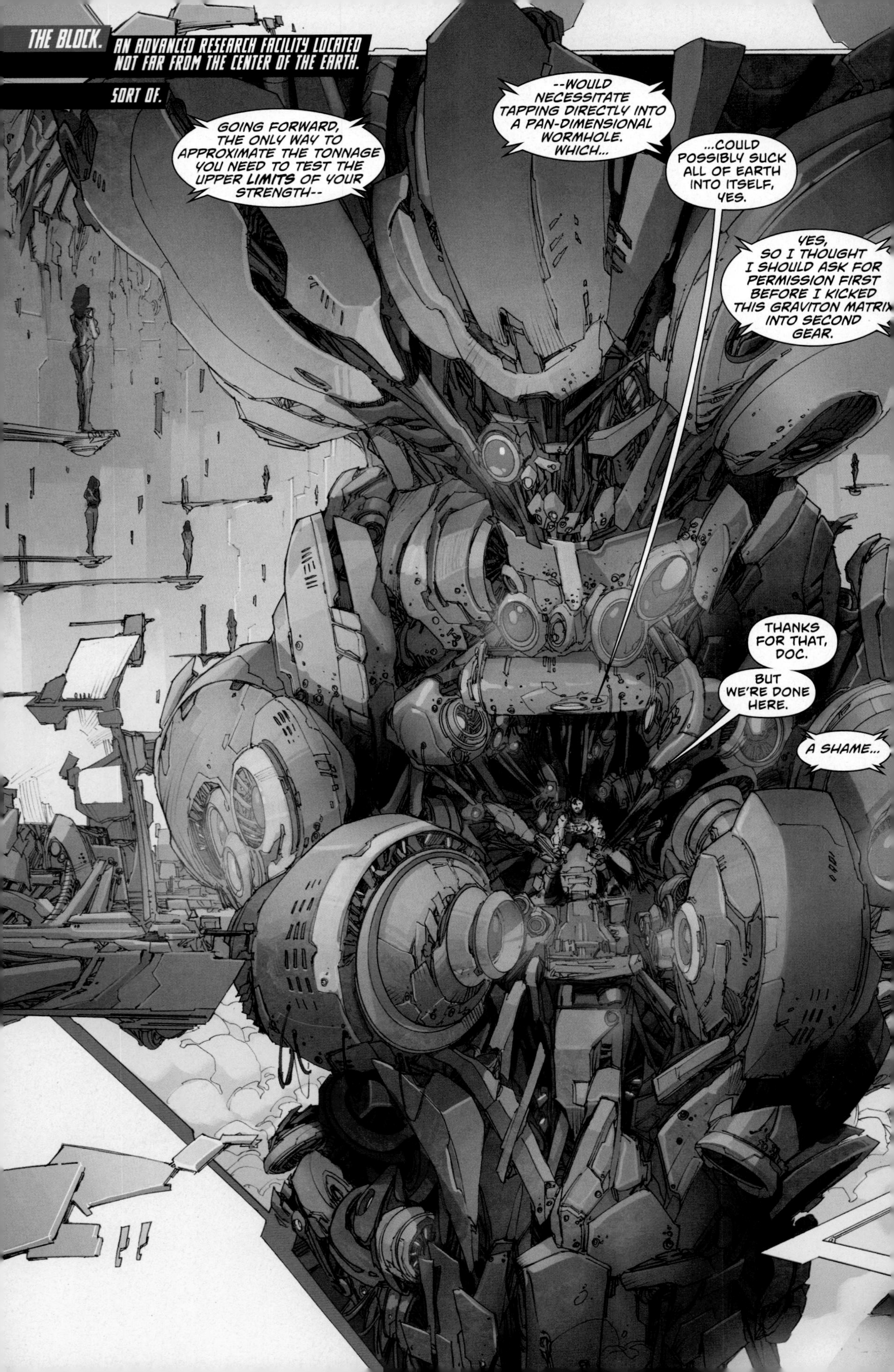
THE BLOCK. AN ADVANCED RESEARCH FACILITY LOCATED NOT FAR FROM THE CENTER OF THE EARTH.
SORT OF.
GOING FORWARD, THE ONLY WAY TO APPROXIMATE THE TONNAGE YOU NEED TO TEST THE UPPER LIMITS OF YOUR STRENGTH--
--WOULD NECESSITATE TAPPING DIRECTLY INTO A PAN-DIMENSIONAL WORMHOLE. WHICH...
...COULD POSSIBLY SUCK ALL OF EARTH INTO ITSELF, YES.
YES, SO I THOUGHT I SHOULD ASK FOR PERMISSION FIRST BEFORE I KICKED THIS GRAVITON MATRIX INTO SECOND GEAR.
THANKS FOR THAT, DOC.
BUT WE'RE DONE HERE.
A SHAME...

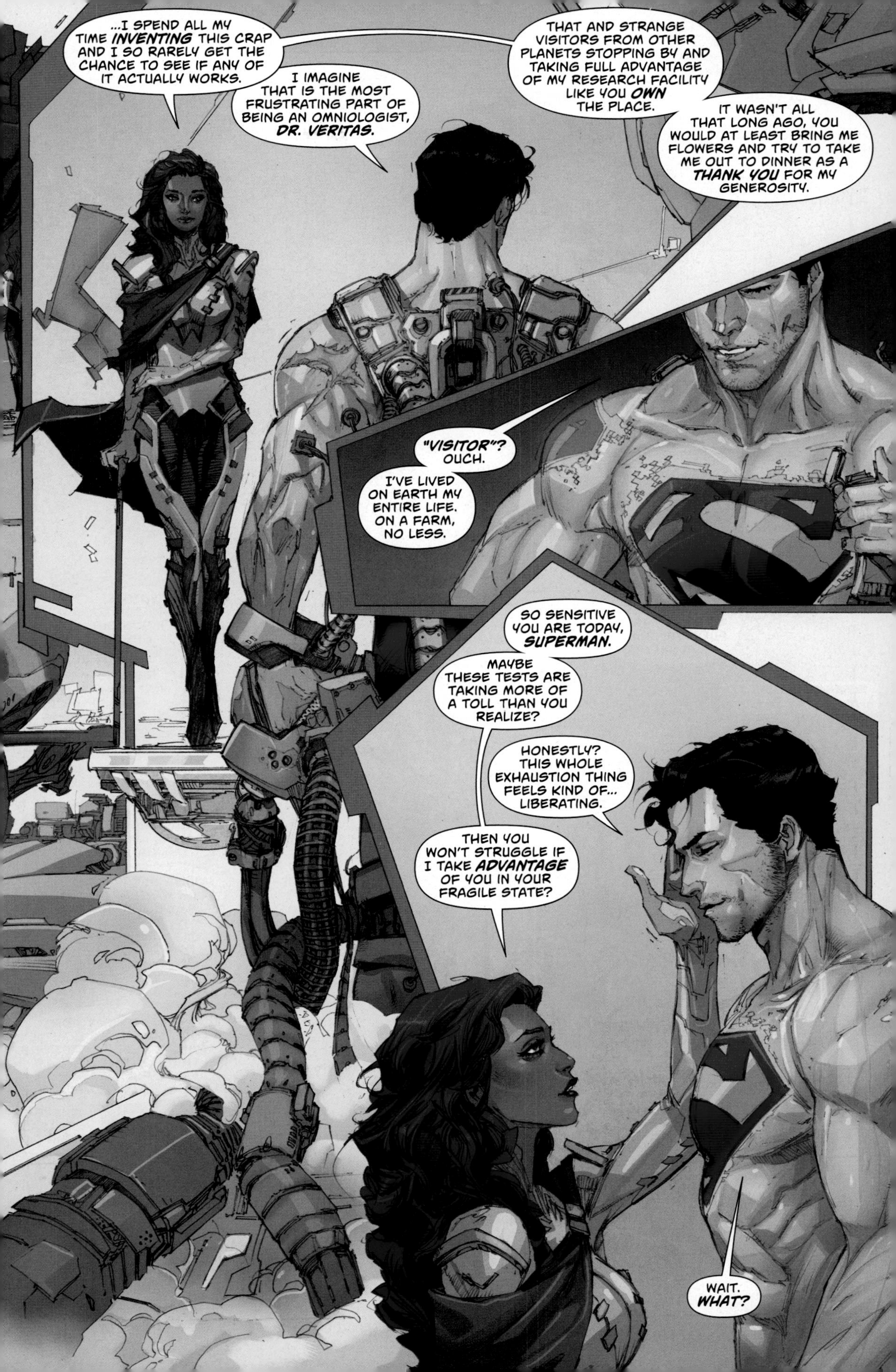
...I SPEND ALL MY TIME *INVENTING* THIS CRAP AND I SO RARELY GET THE CHANCE TO SEE IF ANY OF IT ACTUALLY WORKS.
I IMAGINE THAT IS THE MOST FRUSTRATING PART OF BEING AN OMNIOLOGIST, ***DR. VERITAS.***
THAT AND STRANGE VISITORS FROM OTHER PLANETS STOPPING BY AND TAKING FULL ADVANTAGE OF MY RESEARCH FACILITY LIKE YOU *OWN* THE PLACE.
IT WASN'T ALL THAT LONG AGO, YOU WOULD AT LEAST BRING ME FLOWERS AND TRY TO TAKE ME OUT TO DINNER AS A ***THANK YOU*** FOR MY GENEROSITY.
"VISITOR"? OUCH.
I'VE LIVED ON EARTH MY ENTIRE LIFE. ON A FARM, NO LESS.
SO SENSITIVE YOU ARE TODAY, ***SUPERMAN.***
MAYBE THESE TESTS ARE TAKING MORE OF A TOLL THAN YOU REALIZE?
HONESTLY? THIS WHOLE EXHAUSTION THING FEELS KIND OF... LIBERATING.
THEN YOU WON'T STRUGGLE IF I TAKE ***ADVANTAGE*** OF YOU IN YOUR FRAGILE STATE?
WAIT. ***WHAT?***

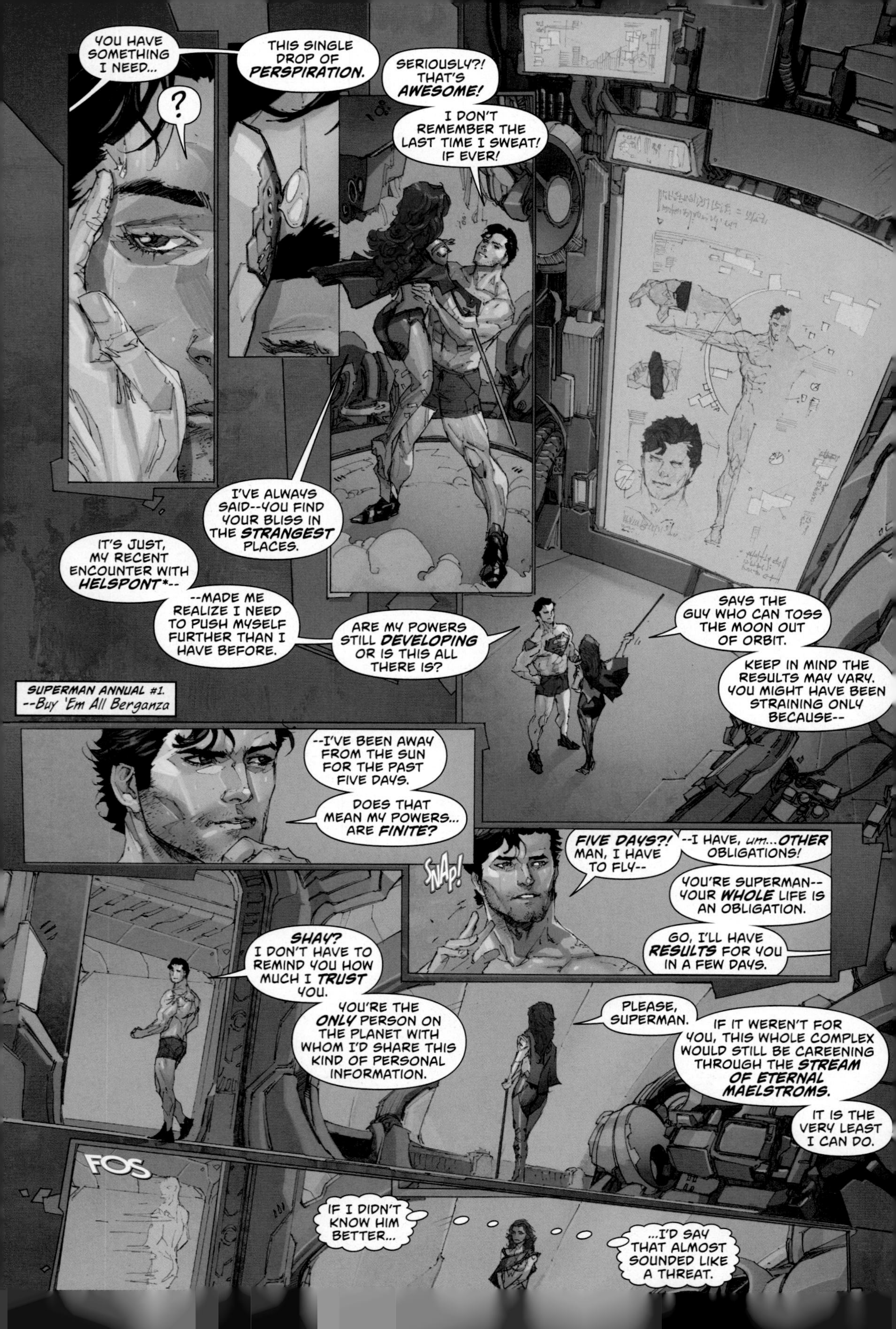
YOU HAVE SOMETHING I NEED...
THIS SINGLE DROP OF PERSPIRATION.
?
SERIOUSLY?! THAT'S AWESOME!
I DON'T REMEMBER THE LAST TIME I SWEAT! IF EVER!
I'VE ALWAYS SAID--YOU FIND YOUR BLISS IN THE STRANGEST PLACES.
IT'S JUST, MY RECENT ENCOUNTER WITH HELSPONT*--
--MADE ME REALIZE I NEED TO PUSH MYSELF FURTHER THAN I HAVE BEFORE.
ARE MY POWERS STILL DEVELOPING OR IS THIS ALL THERE IS?
SAYS THE GUY WHO CAN TOSS THE MOON OUT OF ORBIT.
KEEP IN MIND THE RESULTS MAY VARY. YOU MIGHT HAVE BEEN STRAINING ONLY BECAUSE--
*SUPERMAN ANNUAL #1. --Buy 'Em All Berganza
--I'VE BEEN AWAY FROM THE SUN FOR THE PAST FIVE DAYS.
DOES THAT MEAN MY POWERS... ARE FINITE?
SNAP!
FIVE DAYS?! MAN, I HAVE TO FLY--
--I HAVE, um...OTHER OBLIGATIONS!
YOU'RE SUPERMAN-- YOUR WHOLE LIFE IS AN OBLIGATION.
GO, I'LL HAVE RESULTS FOR YOU IN A FEW DAYS.
SHAY? I DON'T HAVE TO REMIND YOU HOW MUCH I TRUST YOU.
YOU'RE THE ONLY PERSON ON THE PLANET WITH WHOM I'D SHARE THIS KIND OF PERSONAL INFORMATION.
PLEASE, SUPERMAN.
IF IT WEREN'T FOR YOU, THIS WHOLE COMPLEX WOULD STILL BE CAREENING THROUGH THE STREAM OF ETERNAL MAELSTROMS.
IT IS THE VERY LEAST I CAN DO.
FOS
IF I DIDN'T KNOW HIM BETTER...
...I'D SAY THAT ALMOST SOUNDED LIKE A THREAT.

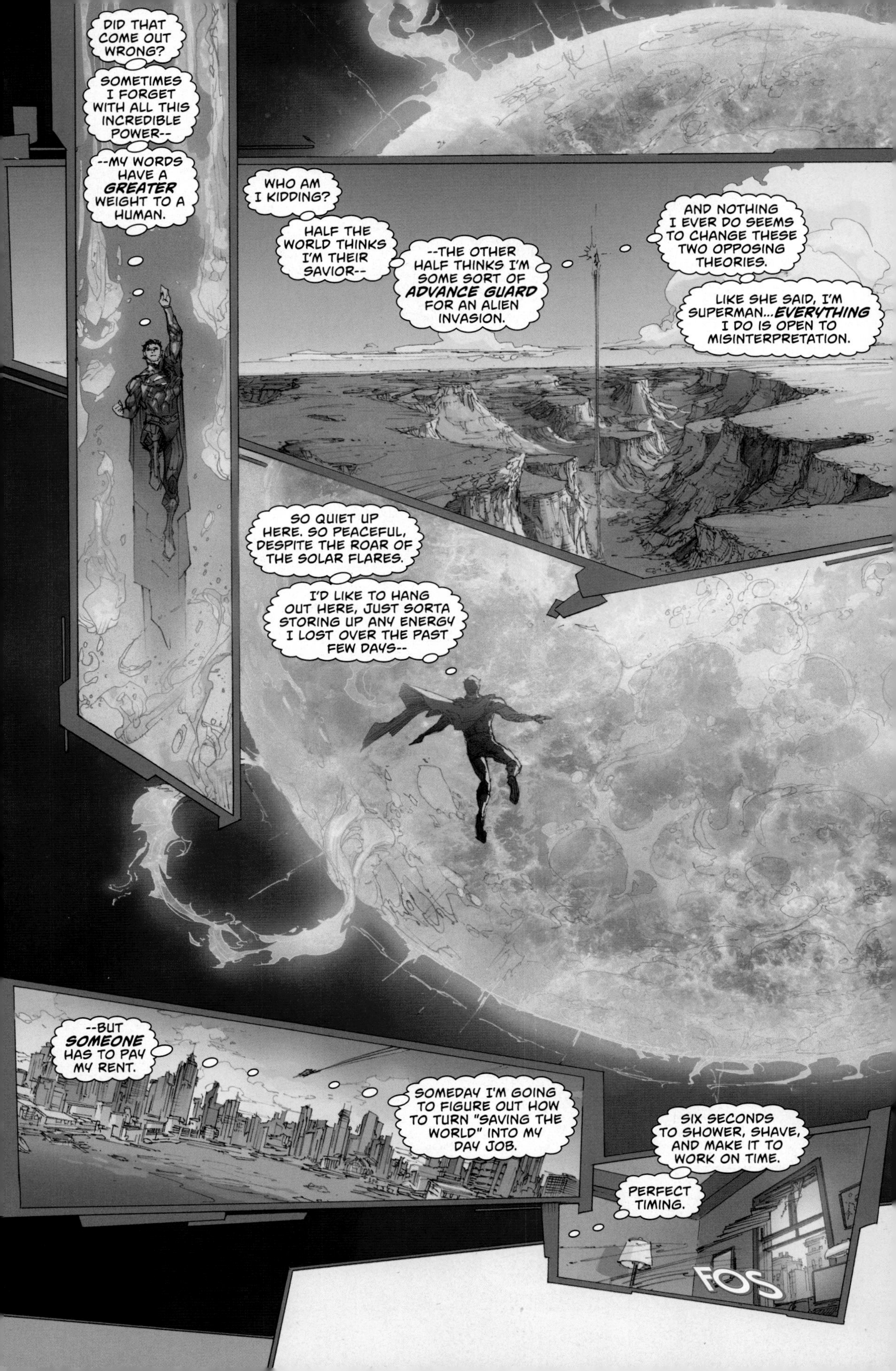
DID THAT COME OUT WRONG?
SOMETIMES I FORGET WITH ALL THIS INCREDIBLE POWER--
--MY WORDS HAVE A GREATER WEIGHT TO A HUMAN.
WHO AM I KIDDING?
HALF THE WORLD THINKS I'M THEIR SAVIOR--
--THE OTHER HALF THINKS I'M SOME SORT OF ADVANCE GUARD FOR AN ALIEN INVASION.
AND NOTHING I EVER DO SEEMS TO CHANGE THESE TWO OPPOSING THEORIES.
LIKE SHE SAID, I'M SUPERMAN...EVERYTHING I DO IS OPEN TO MISINTERPRETATION.
SO QUIET UP HERE. SO PEACEFUL, DESPITE THE ROAR OF THE SOLAR FLARES.
I'D LIKE TO HANG OUT HERE, JUST SORTA STORING UP ANY ENERGY I LOST OVER THE PAST FEW DAYS--
--BUT SOMEONE HAS TO PAY MY RENT.
SOMEDAY I'M GOING TO FIGURE OUT HOW TO TURN "SAVING THE WORLD" INTO MY DAY JOB.
SIX SECONDS TO SHOWER, SHAVE, AND MAKE IT TO WORK ON TIME.
PERFECT TIMING.
FOS

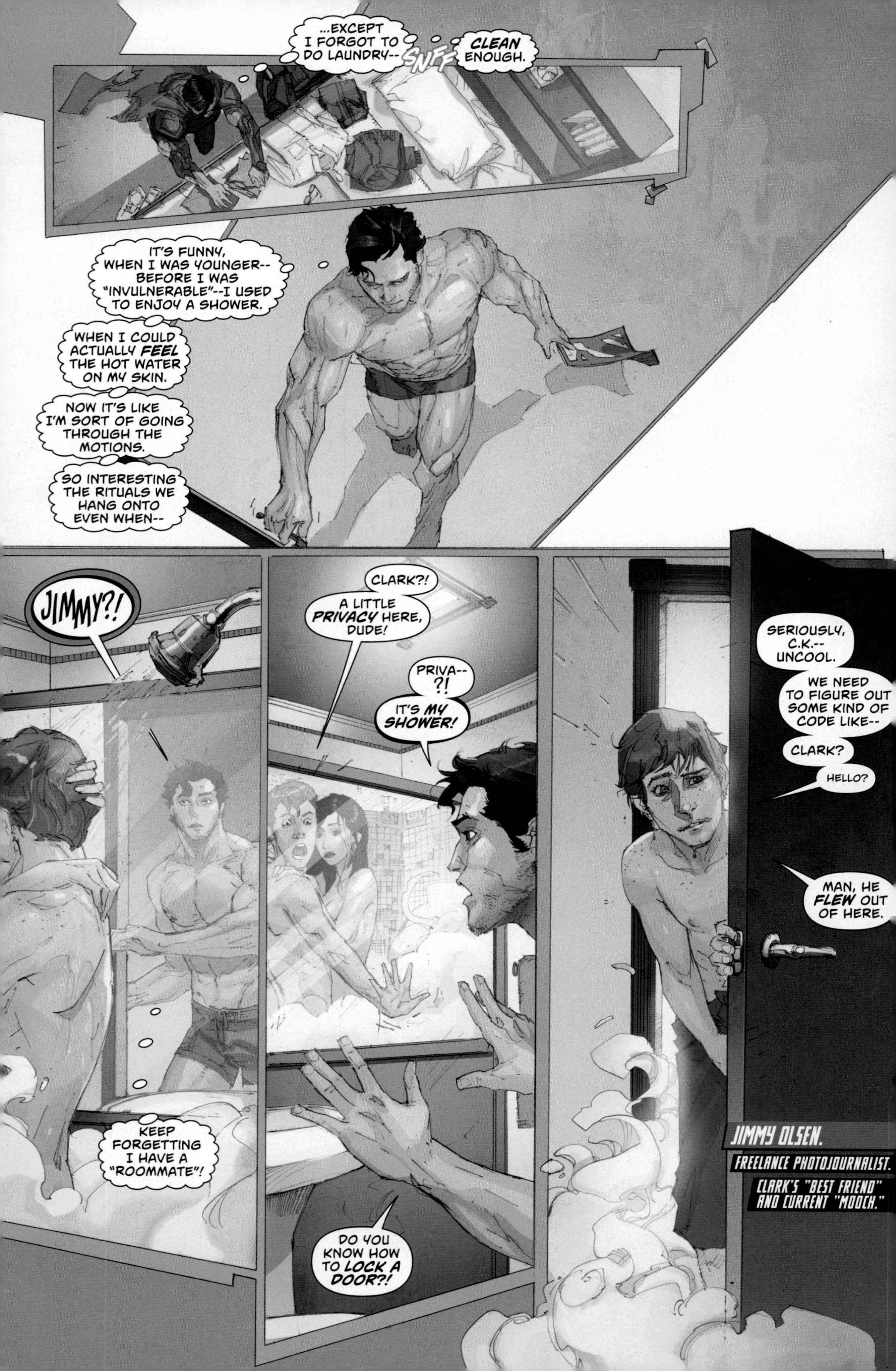

...EXCEPT I FORGOT TO DO LAUNDRY--
SNFF
CLEAN ENOUGH.
IT'S FUNNY, WHEN I WAS YOUNGER-- BEFORE I WAS "INVULNERABLE"--I USED TO ENJOY A SHOWER.
WHEN I COULD ACTUALLY FEEL THE HOT WATER ON MY SKIN.
NOW IT'S LIKE I'M SORT OF GOING THROUGH THE MOTIONS.
SO INTERESTING THE RITUALS WE HANG ONTO EVEN WHEN--
JIMMY?!
KEEP FORGETTING I HAVE A "ROOMMATE"!
CLARK?!
A LITTLE PRIVACY HERE, DUDE!
PRIVA-- ?!
IT'S MY SHOWER!
DO YOU KNOW HOW TO LOCK A DOOR?!
SERIOUSLY, C.K.-- UNCOOL.
WE NEED TO FIGURE OUT SOME KIND OF CODE LIKE--
CLARK?
HELLO?
MAN, HE FLEW OUT OF HERE.
JIMMY OLSEN.
FREELANCE PHOTOJOURNALIST.
CLARK'S "BEST FRIEND" AND CURRENT "MOOCH."

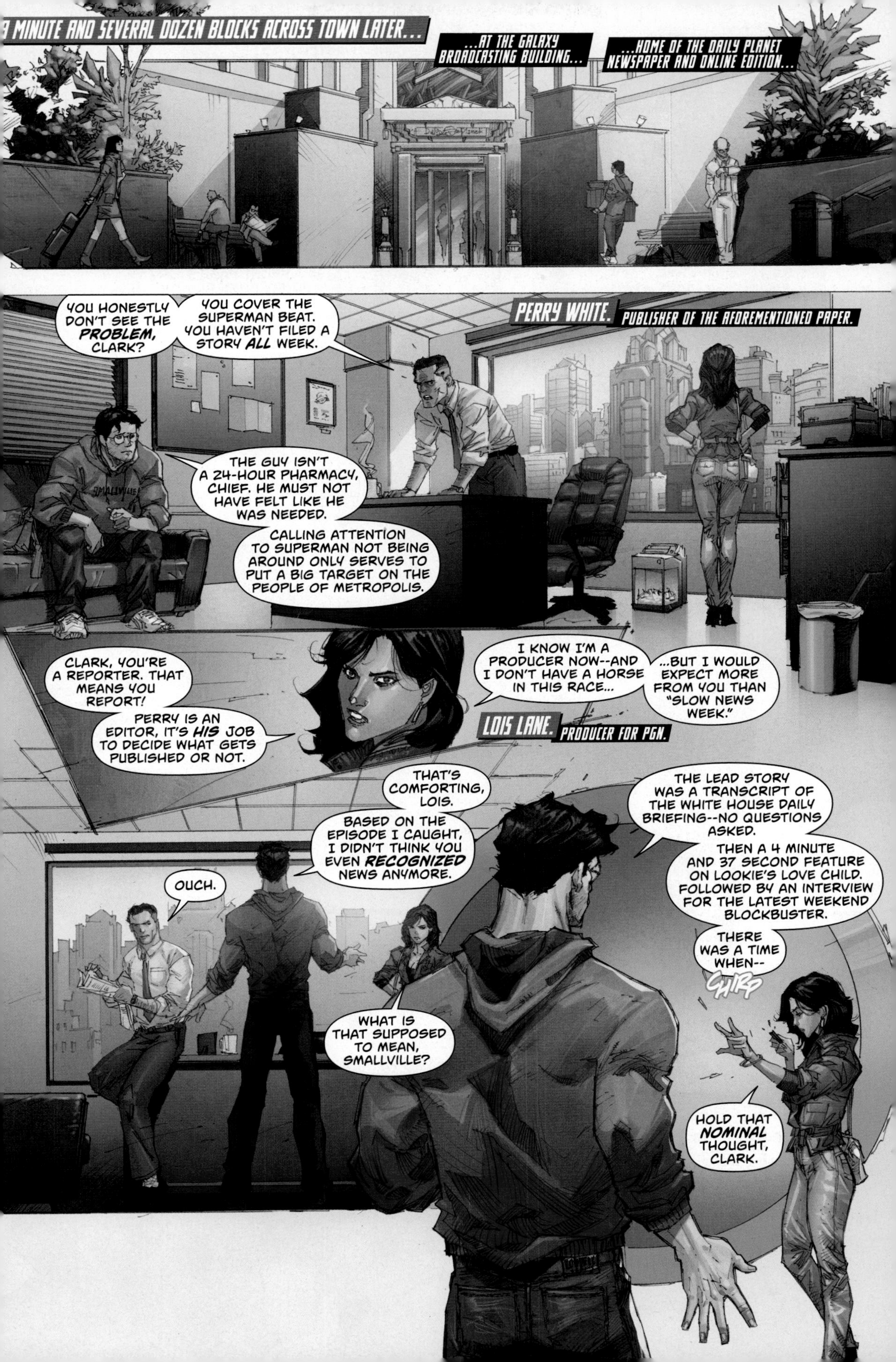

MINUTE AND SEVERAL DOZEN BLOCKS ACROSS TOWN LATER...
...AT THE GALAXY BROADCASTING BUILDING...
...HOME OF THE DAILY PLANET NEWSPAPER AND ONLINE EDITION...
YOU HONESTLY DON'T SEE THE PROBLEM, CLARK?
YOU COVER THE SUPERMAN BEAT. YOU HAVEN'T FILED A STORY ALL WEEK.
PERRY WHITE. PUBLISHER OF THE AFOREMENTIONED PAPER.
THE GUY ISN'T A 24-HOUR PHARMACY, CHIEF. HE MUST NOT HAVE FELT LIKE HE WAS NEEDED.
CALLING ATTENTION TO SUPERMAN NOT BEING AROUND ONLY SERVES TO PUT A BIG TARGET ON THE PEOPLE OF METROPOLIS.
CLARK, YOU'RE A REPORTER. THAT MEANS YOU REPORT!
PERRY IS AN EDITOR, IT'S HIS JOB TO DECIDE WHAT GETS PUBLISHED OR NOT.
I KNOW I'M A PRODUCER NOW--AND I DON'T HAVE A HORSE IN THIS RACE...
...BUT I WOULD EXPECT MORE FROM YOU THAN "SLOW NEWS WEEK."
LOIS LANE. PRODUCER FOR PGN.
THAT'S COMFORTING, LOIS.
BASED ON THE EPISODE I CAUGHT, I DIDN'T THINK YOU EVEN RECOGNIZED NEWS ANYMORE.
OUCH.
WHAT IS THAT SUPPOSED TO MEAN, SMALLVILLE?
THE LEAD STORY WAS A TRANSCRIPT OF THE WHITE HOUSE DAILY BRIEFING--NO QUESTIONS ASKED.
THEN A 4 MINUTE AND 37 SECOND FEATURE ON LOOKIE'S LOVE CHILD. FOLLOWED BY AN INTERVIEW FOR THE LATEST WEEKEND BLOCKBUSTER.
THERE WAS A TIME WHEN--
CHIRP
HOLD THAT NOMINAL THOUGHT, CLARK.

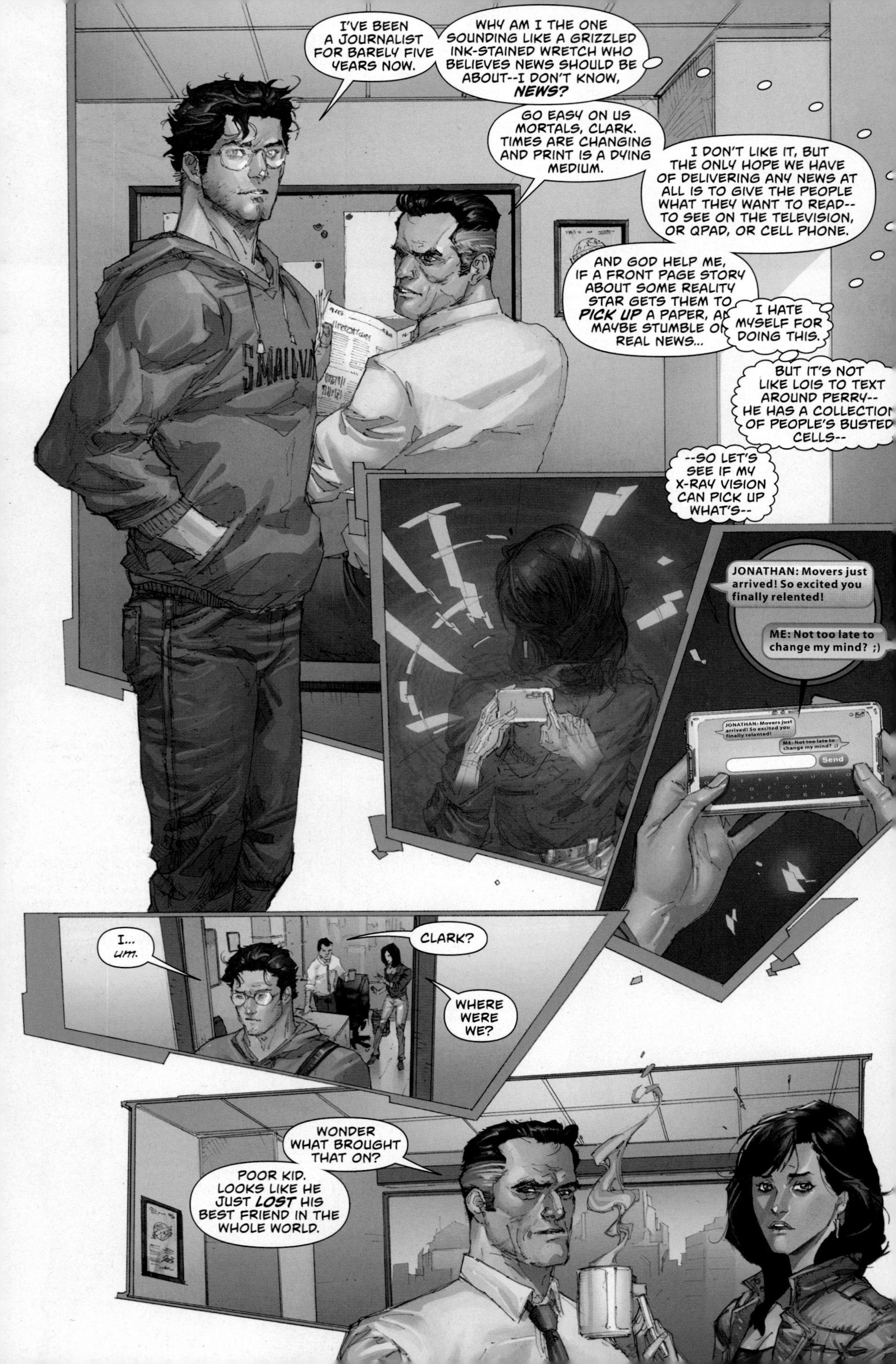
I'VE BEEN A JOURNALIST FOR BARELY FIVE YEARS NOW.
WHY AM I THE ONE SOUNDING LIKE A GRIZZLED INK-STAINED WRETCH WHO BELIEVES NEWS SHOULD BE ABOUT--I DON'T KNOW, NEWS?
GO EASY ON US MORTALS, CLARK. TIMES ARE CHANGING AND PRINT IS A DYING MEDIUM.
I DON'T LIKE IT, BUT THE ONLY HOPE WE HAVE OF DELIVERING ANY NEWS AT ALL IS TO GIVE THE PEOPLE WHAT THEY WANT TO READ-- TO SEE ON THE TELEVISION, OR QPAD, OR CELL PHONE.
AND GOD HELP ME, IF A FRONT PAGE STORY ABOUT SOME REALITY STAR GETS THEM TO PICK UP A PAPER, AN MAYBE STUMBLE ON REAL NEWS...
I HATE MYSELF FOR DOING THIS.
BUT IT'S NOT LIKE LOIS TO TEXT AROUND PERRY-- HE HAS A COLLECTION OF PEOPLE'S BUSTED CELLS--
--SO LET'S SEE IF MY X-RAY VISION CAN PICK UP WHAT'S--
JONATHAN: Movers just arrived! So excited you finally relented!
ME: Not too late to change my mind? ;)
JONATHAN: Movers just arrived! So excited you finally relented!
ME: Not too late to change my mind? ;)
Send
I... UM.
CLARK?
WHERE WERE WE?
WONDER WHAT BROUGHT THAT ON?
POOR KID. LOOKS LIKE HE JUST LOST HIS BEST FRIEND IN THE WHOLE WORLD.

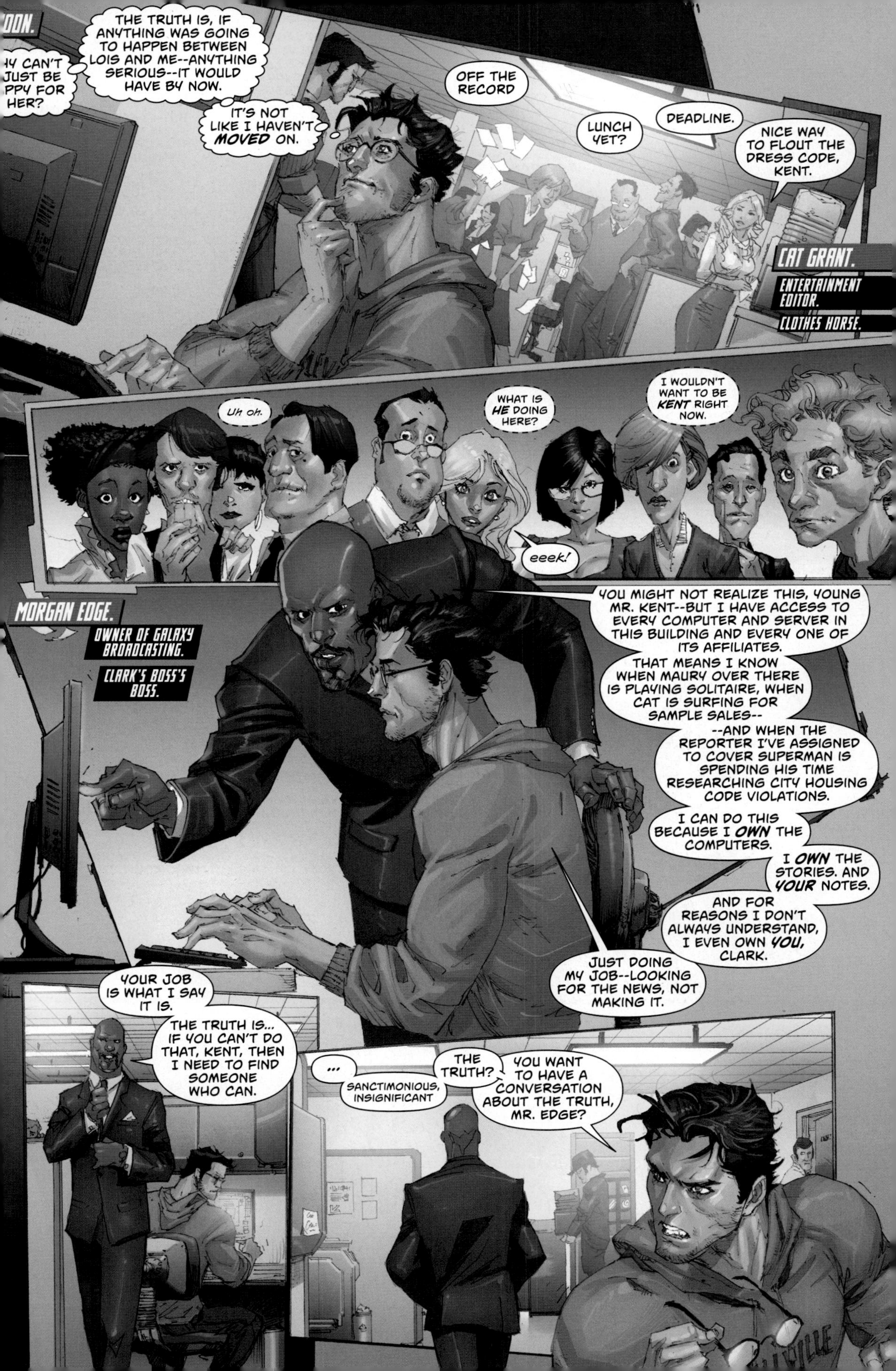
THE TRUTH IS, IF ANYTHING WAS GOING TO HAPPEN BETWEEN LOIS AND ME--ANYTHING SERIOUS--IT WOULD HAVE BY NOW.
IT'S NOT LIKE I HAVEN'T *MOVED* ON.
OFF THE RECORD
LUNCH YET?
DEADLINE.
NICE WAY TO FLOUT THE DRESS CODE, KENT.
CAT GRANT.
ENTERTAINMENT EDITOR.
CLOTHES HORSE.
Uh oh.
WHAT IS *HE* DOING HERE?
I WOULDN'T WANT TO BE *KENT* RIGHT NOW.
eeek!
MORGAN EDGE.
OWNER OF GALAXY BROADCASTING.
CLARK'S BOSS'S BOSS.
YOU MIGHT NOT REALIZE THIS, YOUNG MR. KENT--BUT I HAVE ACCESS TO EVERY COMPUTER AND SERVER IN THIS BUILDING AND EVERY ONE OF ITS AFFILIATES.
THAT MEANS I KNOW WHEN MAURY OVER THERE IS PLAYING SOLITAIRE, WHEN CAT IS SURFING FOR SAMPLE SALES--
--AND WHEN THE REPORTER I'VE ASSIGNED TO COVER SUPERMAN IS SPENDING HIS TIME RESEARCHING CITY HOUSING CODE VIOLATIONS.
I CAN DO THIS BECAUSE I *OWN* THE COMPUTERS.
I *OWN* THE STORIES. AND *YOUR* NOTES.
AND FOR REASONS I DON'T ALWAYS UNDERSTAND, I EVEN OWN *YOU,* CLARK.
JUST DOING MY JOB--LOOKING FOR THE NEWS, NOT MAKING IT.
YOUR JOB IS WHAT I SAY IT IS.
THE TRUTH IS... IF YOU CAN'T DO THAT, KENT, THEN I NEED TO FIND SOMEONE WHO CAN.
...
SANCTIMONIOUS, INSIGNIFICANT
THE TRUTH?
YOU WANT TO HAVE A CONVERSATION ABOUT THE TRUTH, MR. EDGE?

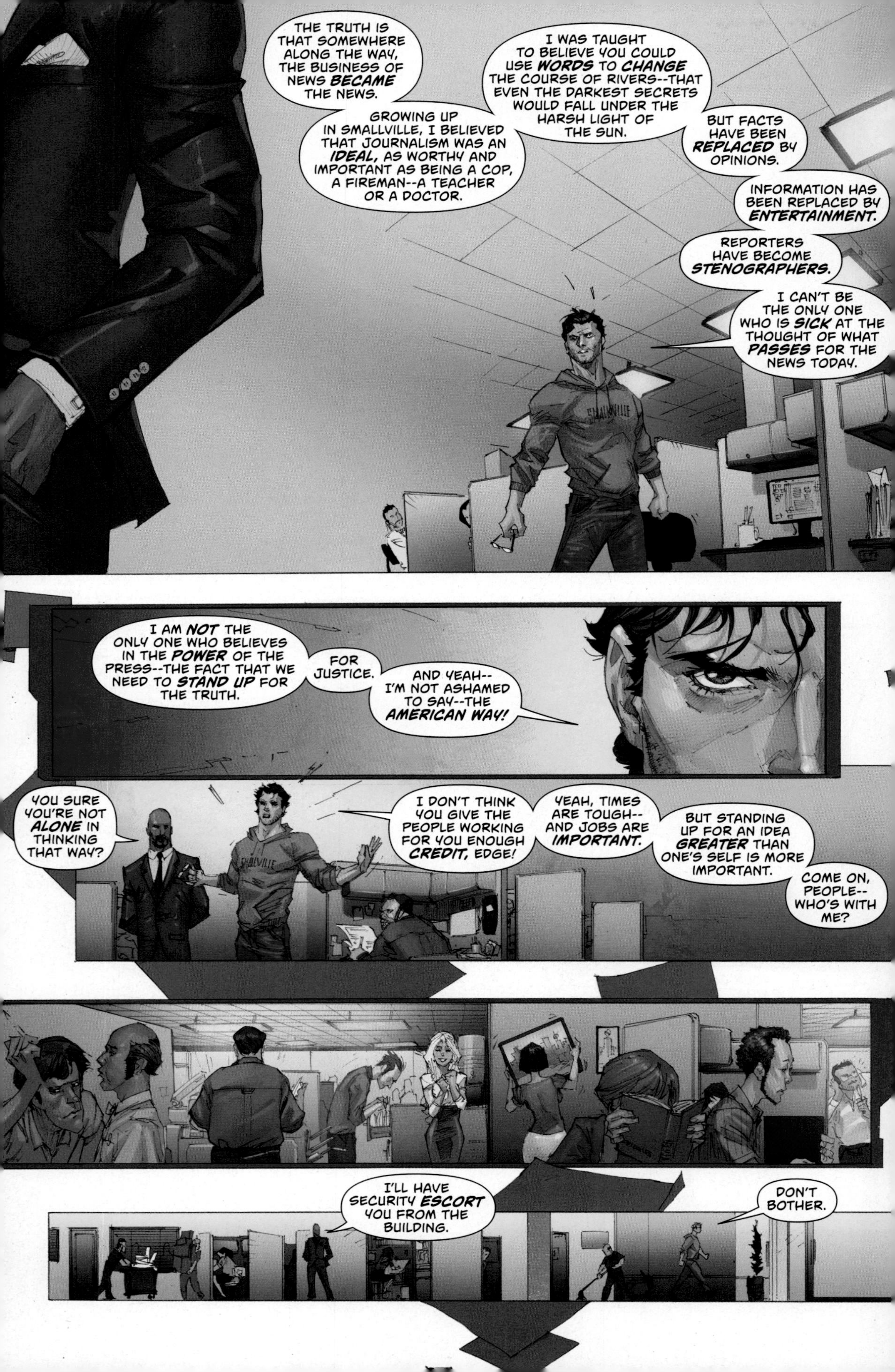
THE TRUTH IS THAT SOMEWHERE ALONG THE WAY, THE BUSINESS OF NEWS BECAME THE NEWS.
GROWING UP IN SMALLVILLE, I BELIEVED THAT JOURNALISM WAS AN IDEAL, AS WORTHY AND IMPORTANT AS BEING A COP, A FIREMAN--A TEACHER OR A DOCTOR.
I WAS TAUGHT TO BELIEVE YOU COULD USE WORDS TO CHANGE THE COURSE OF RIVERS--THAT EVEN THE DARKEST SECRETS WOULD FALL UNDER THE HARSH LIGHT OF THE SUN.
BUT FACTS HAVE BEEN REPLACED BY OPINIONS.
INFORMATION HAS BEEN REPLACED BY ENTERTAINMENT.
REPORTERS HAVE BECOME STENOGRAPHERS.
I CAN'T BE THE ONLY ONE WHO IS SICK AT THE THOUGHT OF WHAT PASSES FOR THE NEWS TODAY.
I AM NOT THE ONLY ONE WHO BELIEVES IN THE POWER OF THE PRESS--THE FACT THAT WE NEED TO STAND UP FOR THE TRUTH.
FOR JUSTICE.
AND YEAH-- I'M NOT ASHAMED TO SAY--THE AMERICAN WAY!
YOU SURE YOU'RE NOT ALONE IN THINKING THAT WAY?
I DON'T THINK YOU GIVE THE PEOPLE WORKING FOR YOU ENOUGH CREDIT, EDGE!
YEAH, TIMES ARE TOUGH-- AND JOBS ARE IMPORTANT.
BUT STANDING UP FOR AN IDEA GREATER THAN ONE'S SELF IS MORE IMPORTANT.
COME ON, PEOPLE-- WHO'S WITH ME?
I'LL HAVE SECURITY ESCORT YOU FROM THE BUILDING.
DON'T BOTHER.

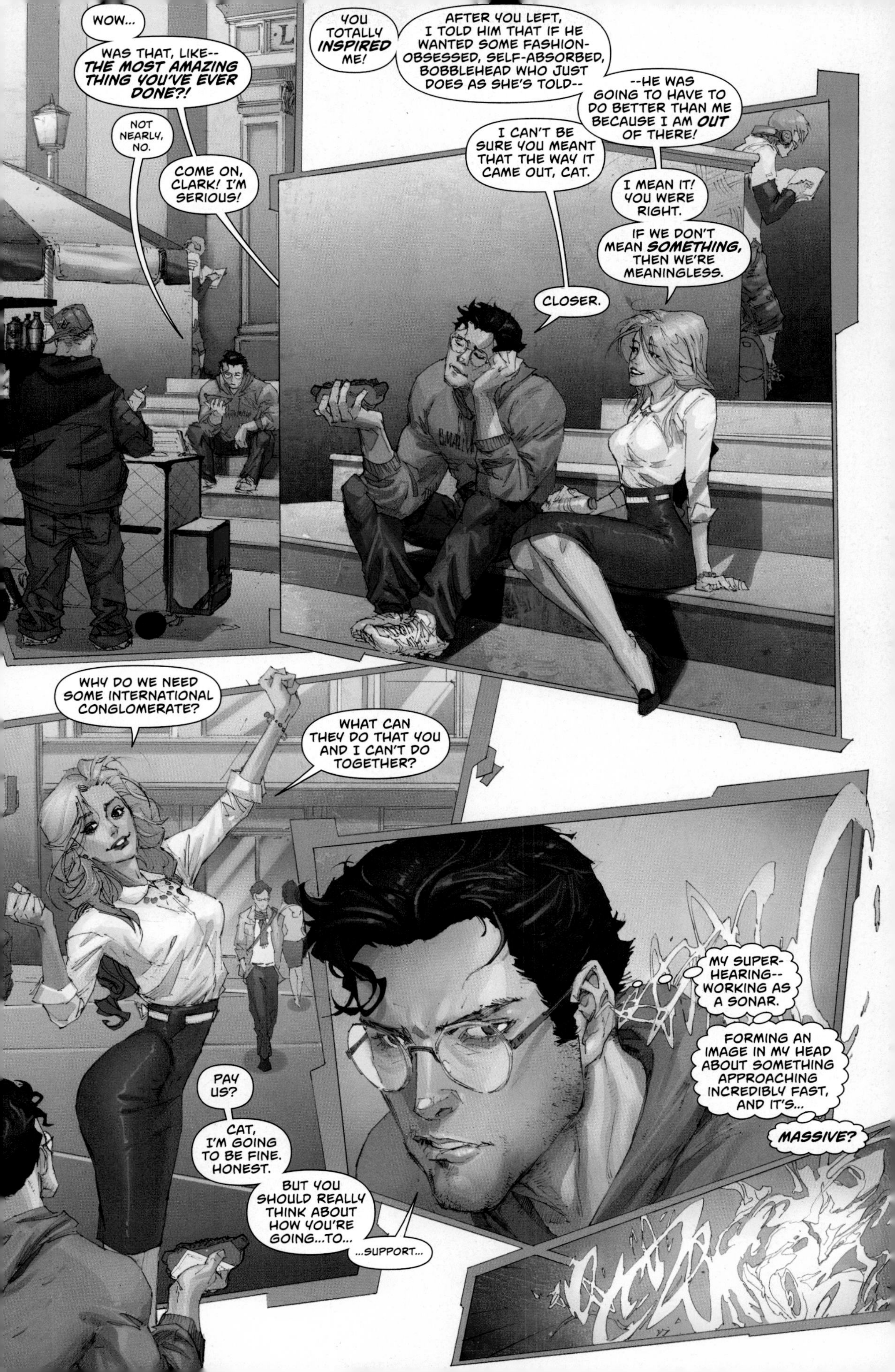
WOW...
WAS THAT, LIKE-- THE MOST AMAZING THING YOU'VE EVER DONE?!
NOT NEARLY, NO.
COME ON, CLARK! I'M SERIOUS!
YOU TOTALLY INSPIRED ME!
AFTER YOU LEFT, I TOLD HIM THAT IF HE WANTED SOME FASHION-OBSESSED, SELF-ABSORBED, BOBBLEHEAD WHO JUST DOES AS SHE'S TOLD--
--HE WAS GOING TO HAVE TO DO BETTER THAN ME BECAUSE I AM OUT OF THERE!
I CAN'T BE SURE YOU MEANT THAT THE WAY IT CAME OUT, CAT.
I MEAN IT! YOU WERE RIGHT.
IF WE DON'T MEAN SOMETHING, THEN WE'RE MEANINGLESS.
CLOSER.
WHY DO WE NEED SOME INTERNATIONAL CONGLOMERATE?
WHAT CAN THEY DO THAT YOU AND I CAN'T DO TOGETHER?
PAY US?
CAT, I'M GOING TO BE FINE. HONEST.
BUT YOU SHOULD REALLY THINK ABOUT HOW YOU'RE GOING...TO...
...SUPPORT...
MY SUPER-HEARING-- WORKING AS A SONAR.
FORMING AN IMAGE IN MY HEAD ABOUT SOMETHING APPROACHING INCREDIBLY FAST, AND IT'S...
MASSIVE?

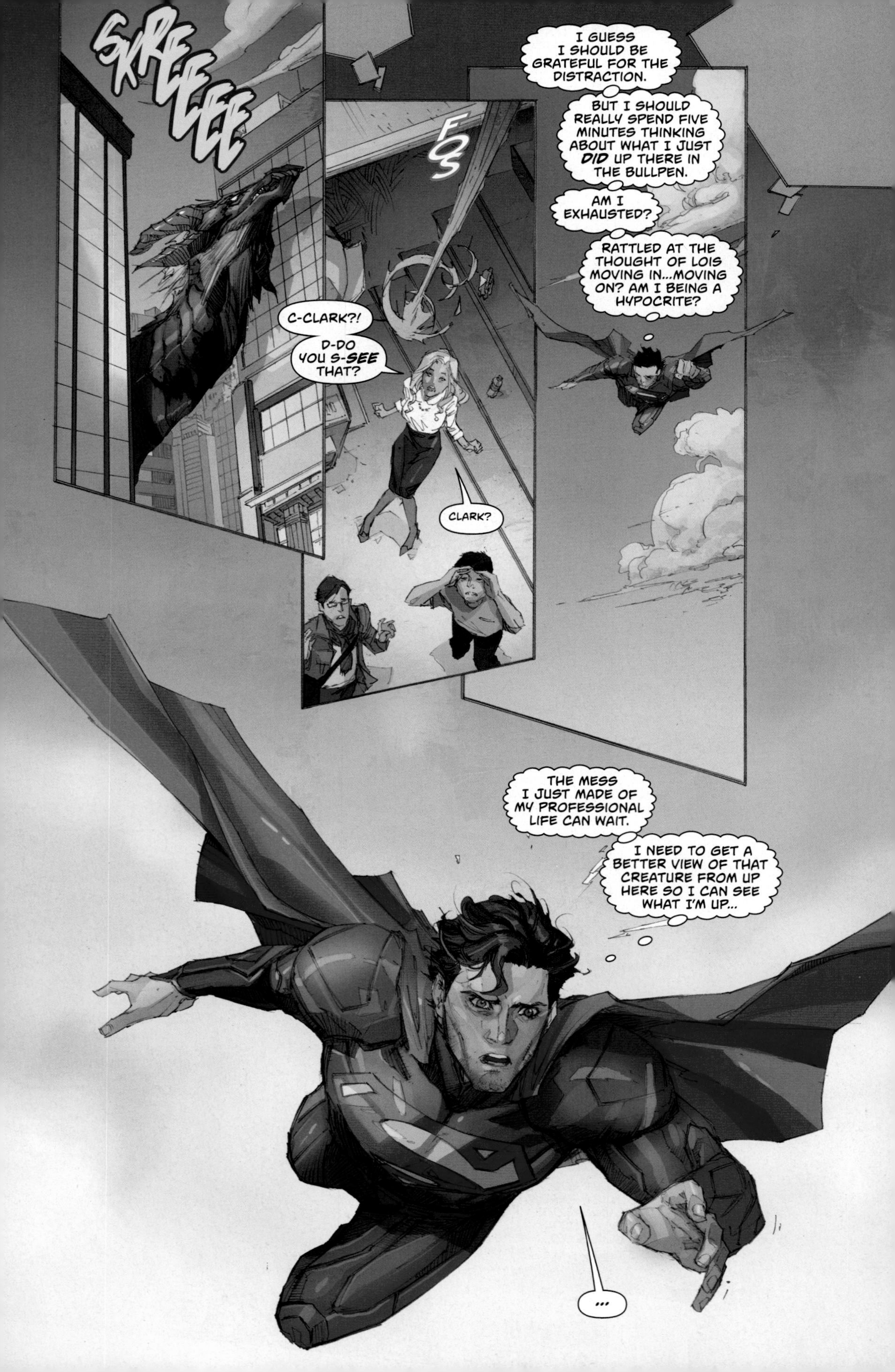
SKREEEEE
FOS
I GUESS I SHOULD BE GRATEFUL FOR THE DISTRACTION.
BUT I SHOULD REALLY SPEND FIVE MINUTES THINKING ABOUT WHAT I JUST DID UP THERE IN THE BULLPEN.
AM I EXHAUSTED?
RATTLED AT THE THOUGHT OF LOIS MOVING IN...MOVING ON? AM I BEING A HYPOCRITE?
C-CLARK?!
D-DO YOU S-SEE THAT?
CLARK?
THE MESS I JUST MADE OF MY PROFESSIONAL LIFE CAN WAIT.
I NEED TO GET A BETTER VIEW OF THAT CREATURE FROM UP HERE SO I CAN SEE WHAT I'M UP...
...

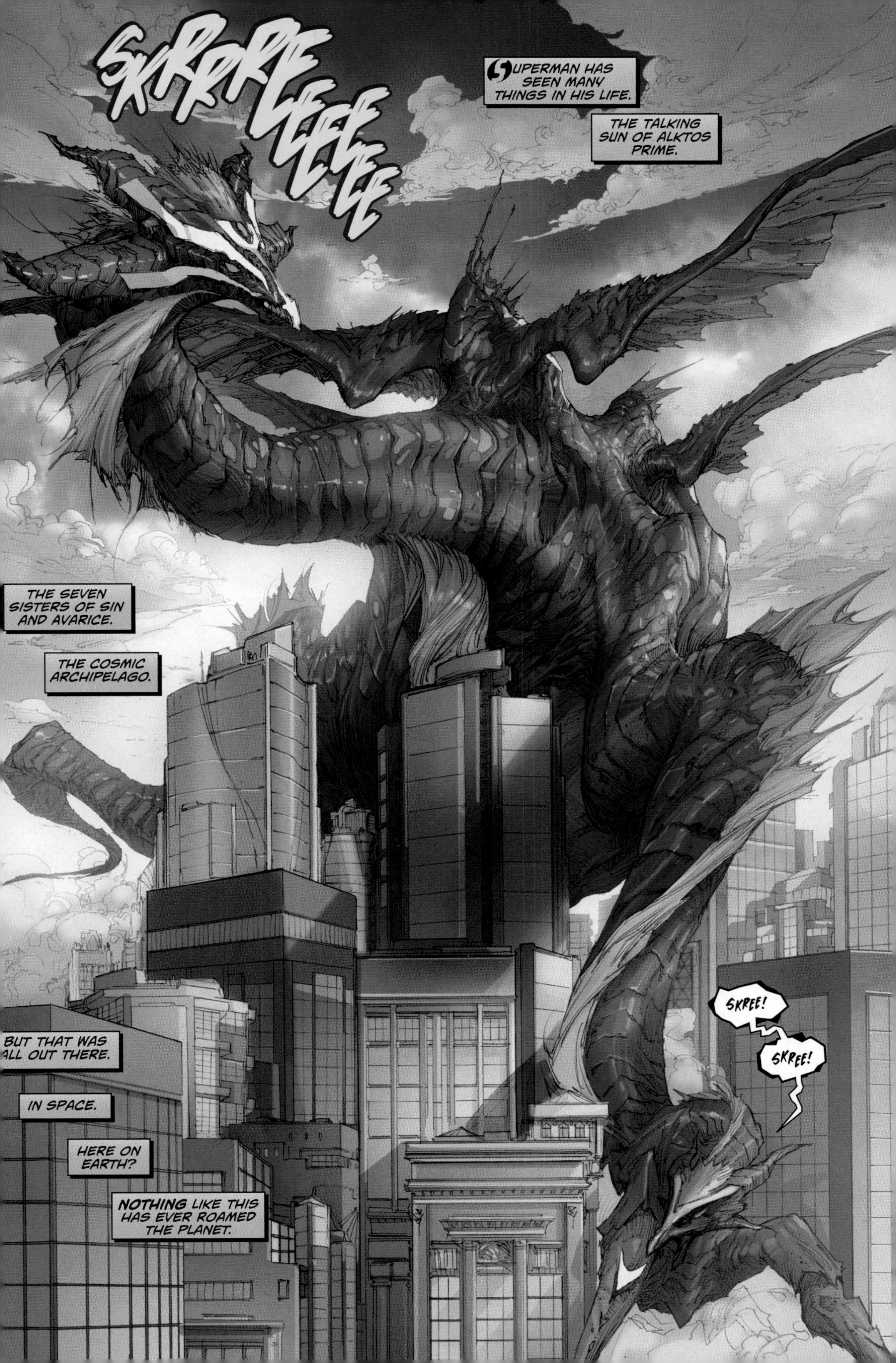
SKRRREEEEEEEE
SUPERMAN HAS SEEN MANY THINGS IN HIS LIFE.
THE TALKING SUN OF ALKTOS PRIME.
THE SEVEN SISTERS OF SIN AND AVARICE.
THE COSMIC ARCHIPELAGO.
BUT THAT WAS ALL OUT THERE.
IN SPACE.
HERE ON EARTH?
NOTHING LIKE THIS HAS EVER ROAMED THE PLANET.
SKREE!
SKREE!

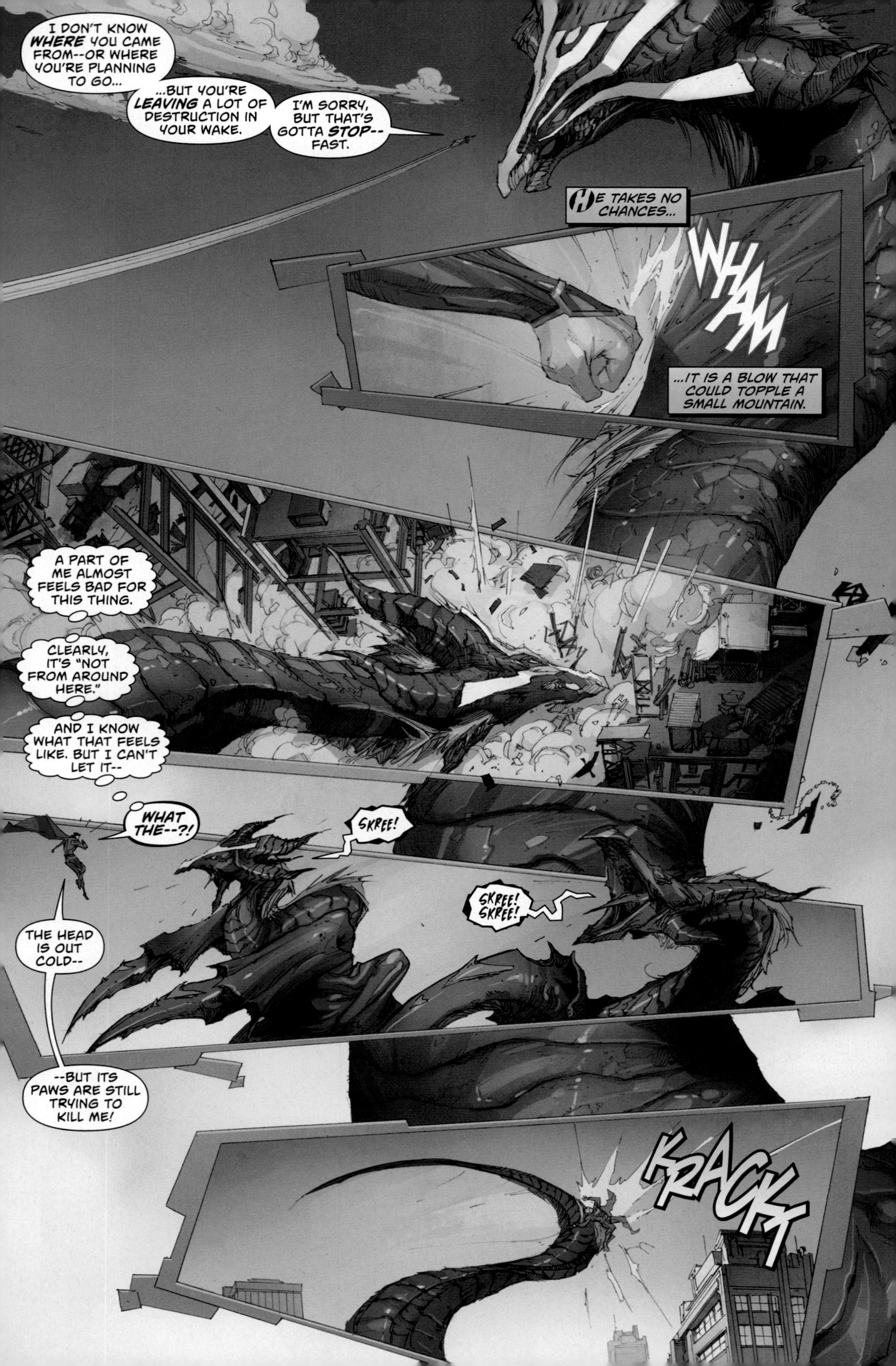
I DON'T KNOW WHERE YOU CAME FROM--OR WHERE YOU'RE PLANNING TO GO...
...BUT YOU'RE LEAVING A LOT OF DESTRUCTION IN YOUR WAKE.
I'M SORRY, BUT THAT'S GOTTA STOP--FAST.
HE TAKES NO CHANCES...
WHAM
...IT IS A BLOW THAT COULD TOPPLE A SMALL MOUNTAIN.
A PART OF ME ALMOST FEELS BAD FOR THIS THING.
CLEARLY, IT'S "NOT FROM AROUND HERE."
AND I KNOW WHAT THAT FEELS LIKE. BUT I CAN'T LET IT--
WHAT THE--?!
SKREE!
SKREE! SKREE!
THE HEAD IS OUT COLD--
--BUT ITS PAWS ARE STILL TRYING TO KILL ME!
KRACK

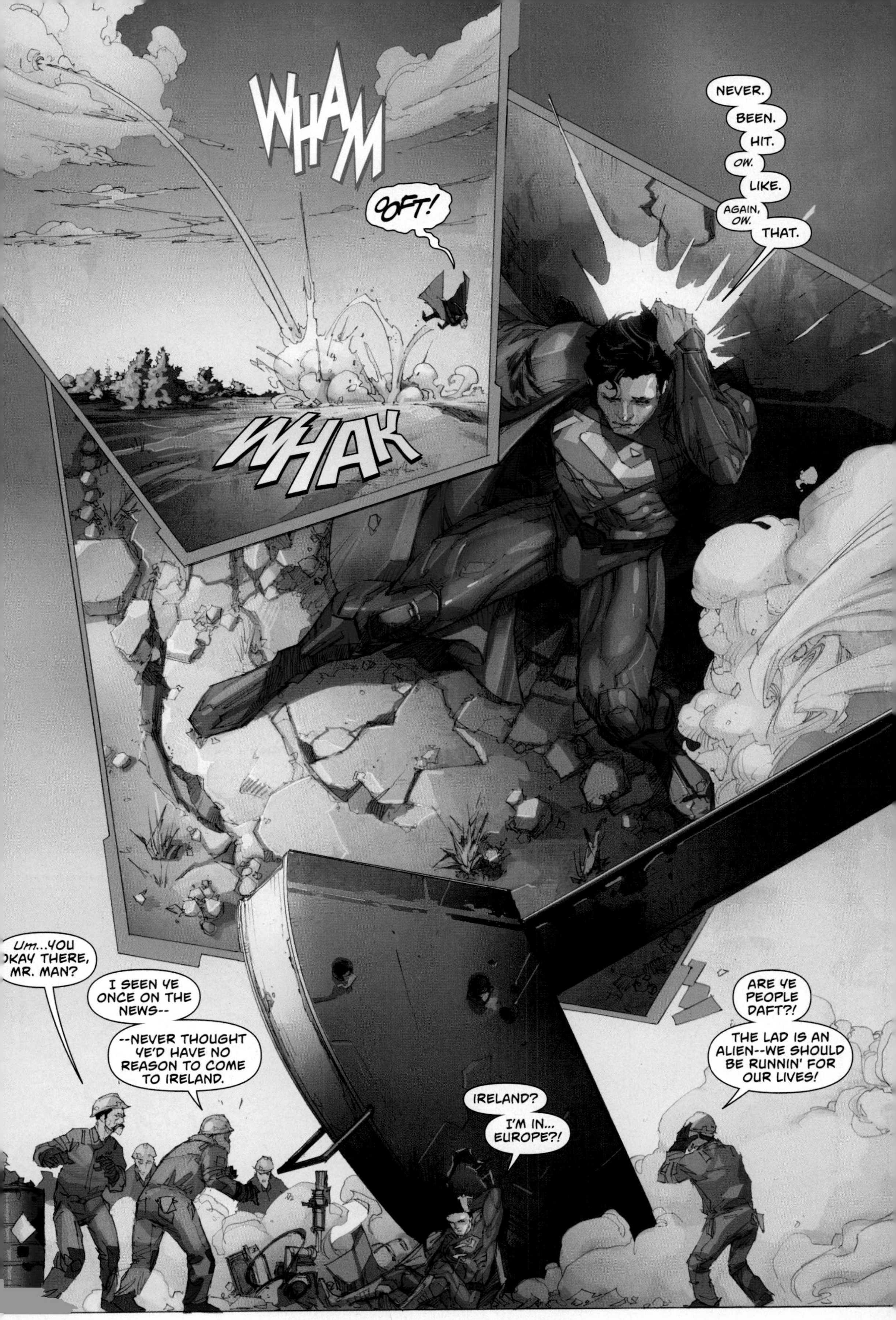
WHAM
OOFT!
NEVER.
BEEN.
HIT.
OW.
LIKE.
AGAIN, OW.
THAT.
WHAK
Um...YOU OKAY THERE, MR. MAN?
I SEEN YE ONCE ON THE NEWS--
--NEVER THOUGHT YE'D HAVE NO REASON TO COME TO IRELAND.
IRELAND?
I'M IN... EUROPE?!
ARE YE PEOPLE DAFT?!
THE LAD IS AN ALIEN--WE SHOULD BE RUNNIN' FOR OUR LIVES!

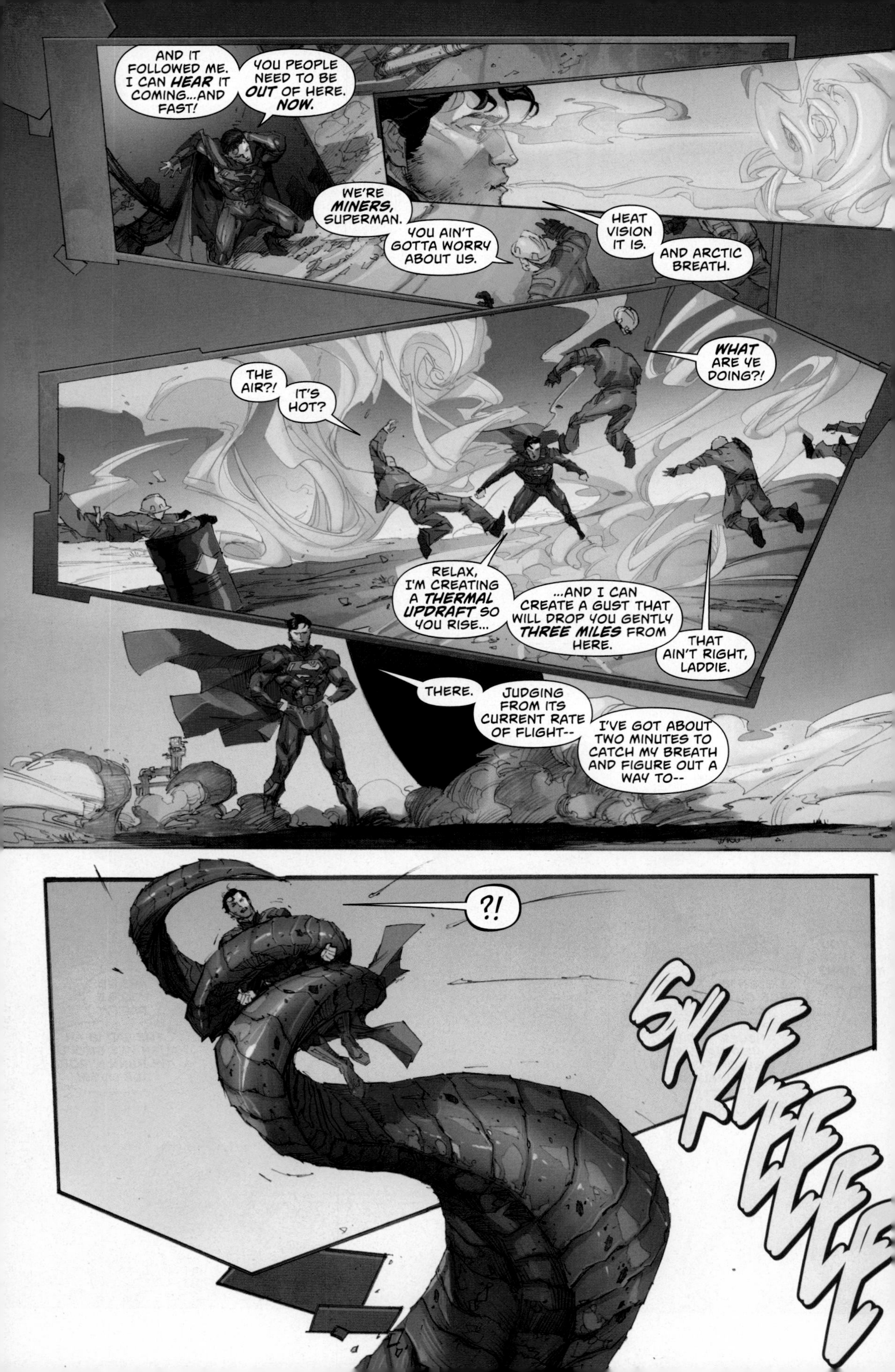
AND IT FOLLOWED ME. I CAN HEAR IT COMING...AND FAST!
YOU PEOPLE NEED TO BE OUT OF HERE. NOW.
WE'RE MINERS, SUPERMAN.
YOU AIN'T GOTTA WORRY ABOUT US.
HEAT VISION IT IS.
AND ARCTIC BREATH.
THE AIR?!
IT'S HOT?
WHAT ARE YE DOING?!
RELAX, I'M CREATING A THERMAL UPDRAFT SO YOU RISE...
...AND I CAN CREATE A GUST THAT WILL DROP YOU GENTLY THREE MILES FROM HERE.
THAT AIN'T RIGHT, LADDIE.
THERE.
JUDGING FROM ITS CURRENT RATE OF FLIGHT--
I'VE GOT ABOUT TWO MINUTES TO CATCH MY BREATH AND FIGURE OUT A WAY TO--
?!
SKREEEEE

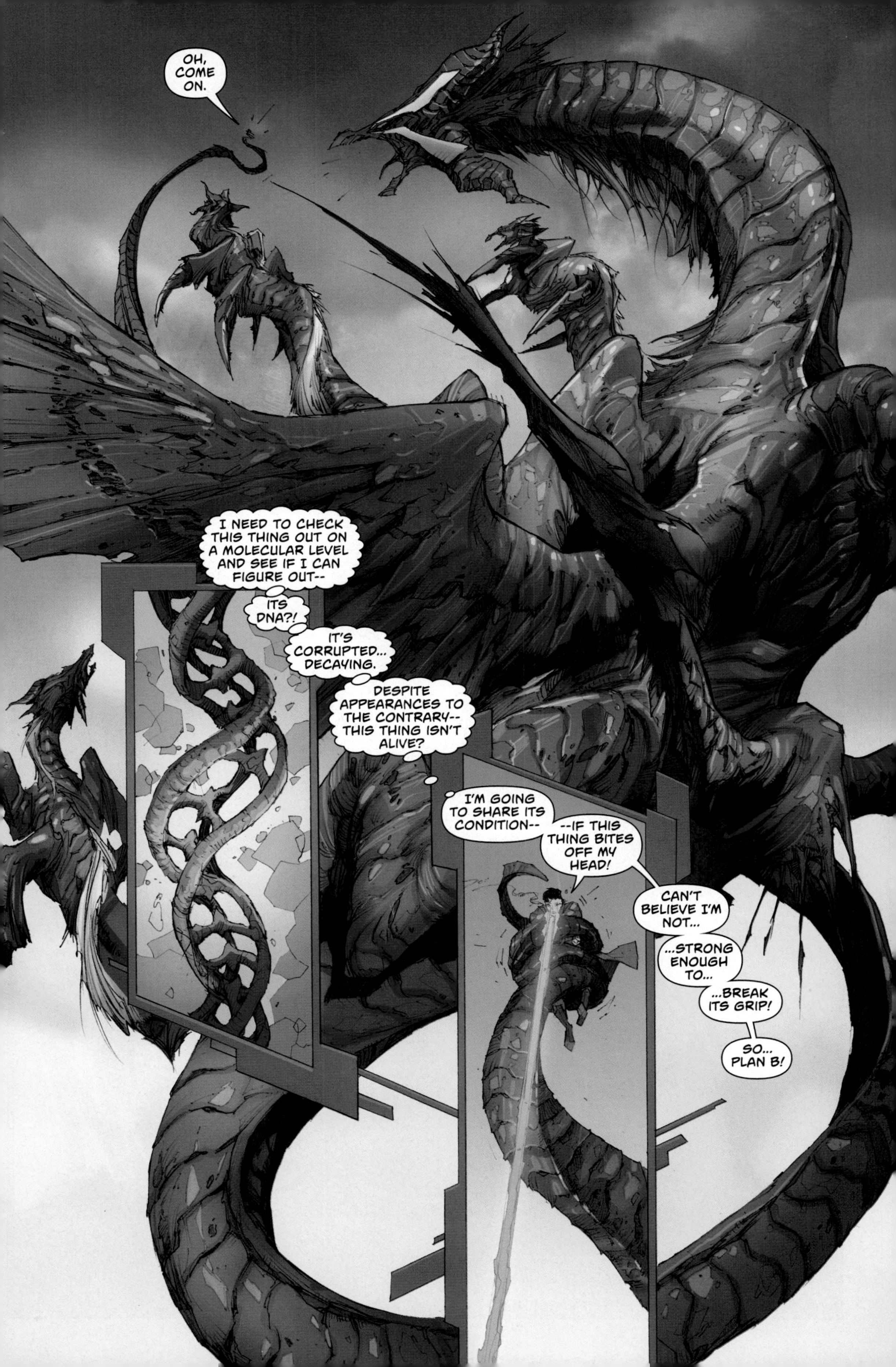
OH, COME ON.
I NEED TO CHECK THIS THING OUT ON A MOLECULAR LEVEL AND SEE IF I CAN FIGURE OUT--
ITS DNA?!
IT'S CORRUPTED... DECAYING.
DESPITE APPEARANCES TO THE CONTRARY-- THIS THING ISN'T ALIVE?
I'M GOING TO SHARE ITS CONDITION--
--IF THIS THING BITES OFF MY HEAD!
CAN'T BELIEVE I'M NOT...
...STRONG ENOUGH TO...
...BREAK ITS GRIP!
SO... PLAN B!

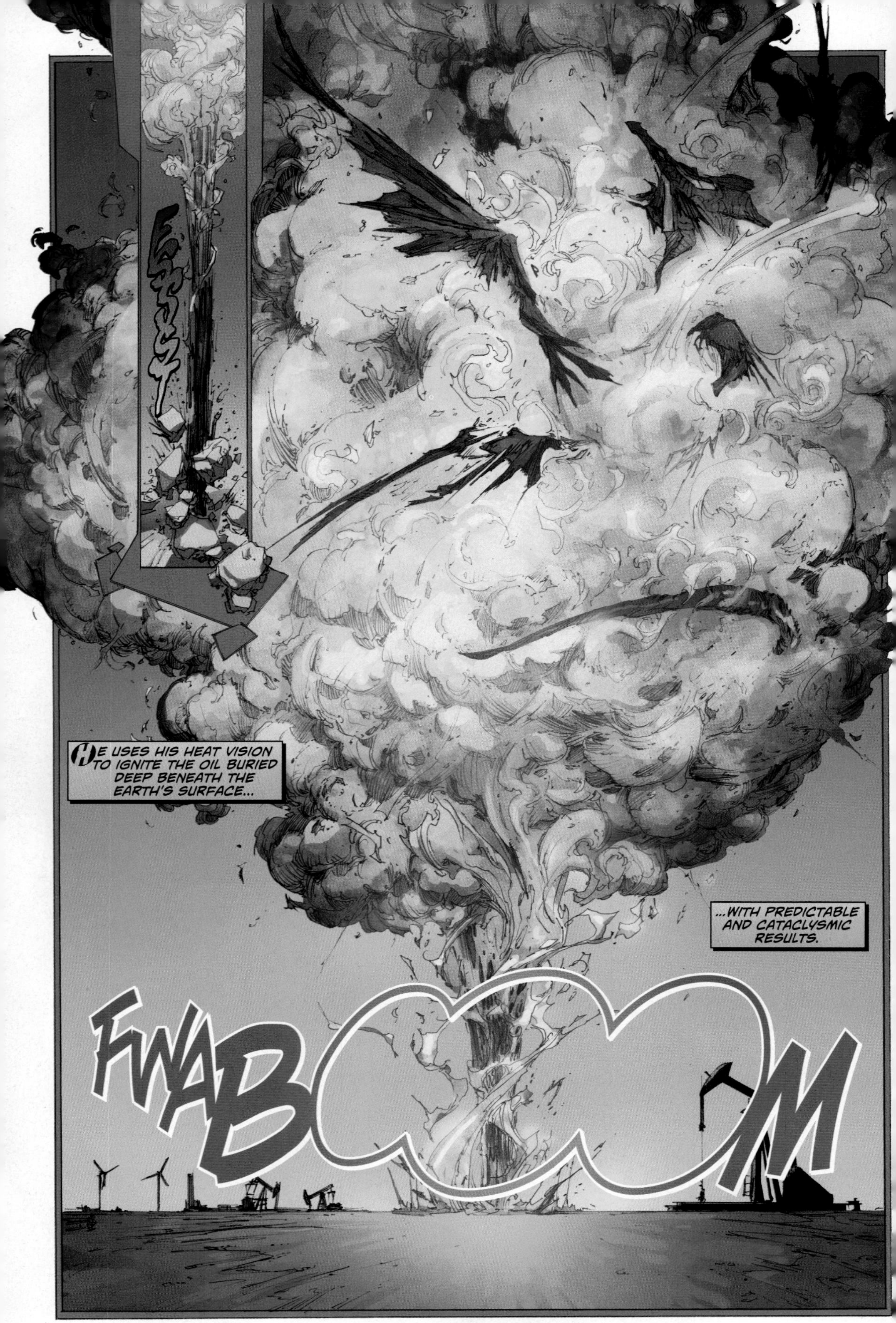
FSSSST
HE USES HIS HEAT VISION TO IGNITE THE OIL BURIED DEEP BENEATH THE EARTH'S SURFACE...
...WITH PREDICTABLE AND CATACLYSMIC RESULTS.
FWABOOOM

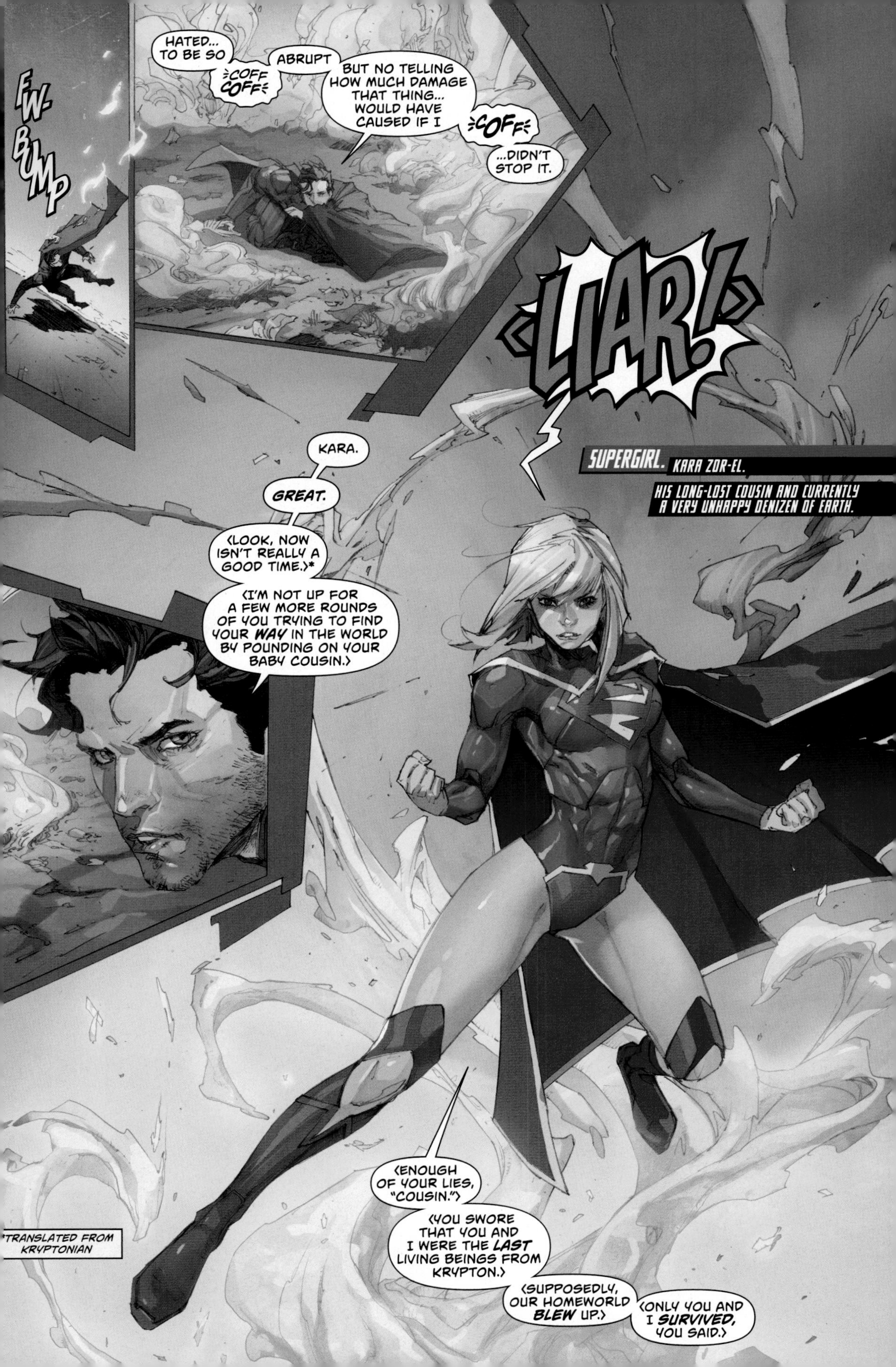
FW-BUMP
HATED... TO BE SO
COFF COFF
ABRUPT
BUT NO TELLING HOW MUCH DAMAGE THAT THING... WOULD HAVE CAUSED IF I
COFF
...DIDN'T STOP IT.
LIAR!
SUPERGIRL. KARA ZOR-EL.
HIS LONG-LOST COUSIN AND CURRENTLY A VERY UNHAPPY DENIZEN OF EARTH.
KARA.
GREAT.
‹LOOK, NOW ISN'T REALLY A GOOD TIME.›*
‹I'M NOT UP FOR A FEW MORE ROUNDS OF YOU TRYING TO FIND YOUR WAY IN THE WORLD BY POUNDING ON YOUR BABY COUSIN.›
‹ENOUGH OF YOUR LIES, "COUSIN."›
‹YOU SWORE THAT YOU AND I WERE THE LAST LIVING BEINGS FROM KRYPTON.›
‹SUPPOSEDLY, OUR HOMEWORLD BLEW UP.›
‹ONLY YOU AND I SURVIVED, YOU SAID.›
*TRANSLATED FROM KRYPTONIAN

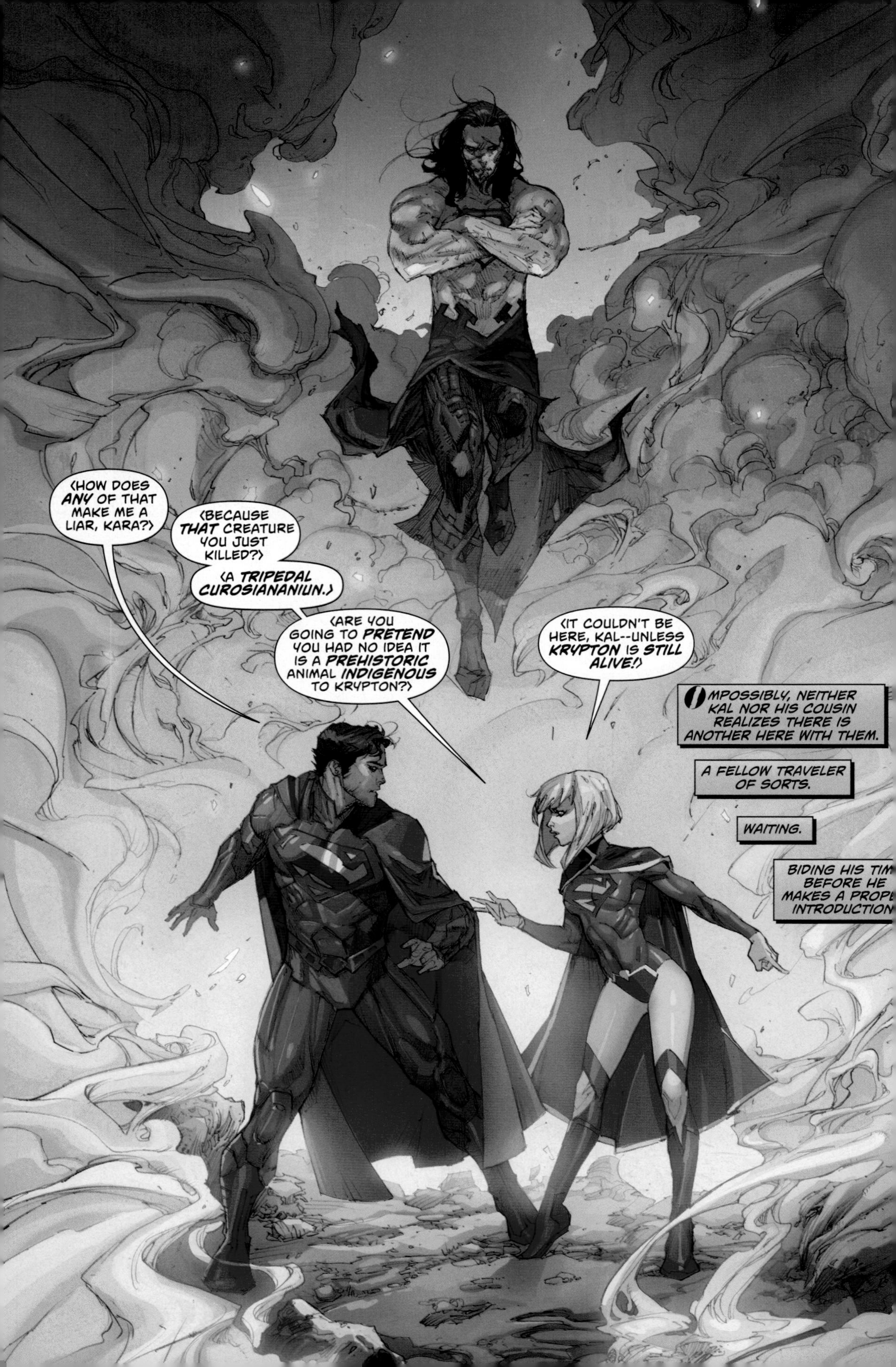
<HOW DOES ANY OF THAT MAKE ME A LIAR, KARA?>
<BECAUSE THAT CREATURE YOU JUST KILLED?>
<A TRIPEDAL CUROSIANANIUN.>
<ARE YOU GOING TO PRETEND YOU HAD NO IDEA IT IS A PREHISTORIC ANIMAL INDIGENOUS TO KRYPTON?>
<IT COULDN'T BE HERE, KAL--UNLESS KRYPTON IS STILL ALIVE!>
IMPOSSIBLY, NEITHER KAL NOR HIS COUSIN REALIZES THERE IS ANOTHER HERE WITH THEM.
A FELLOW TRAVELER OF SORTS.
WAITING.
BIDING HIS TIM BEFORE HE MAKES A PROPE INTRODUCTION

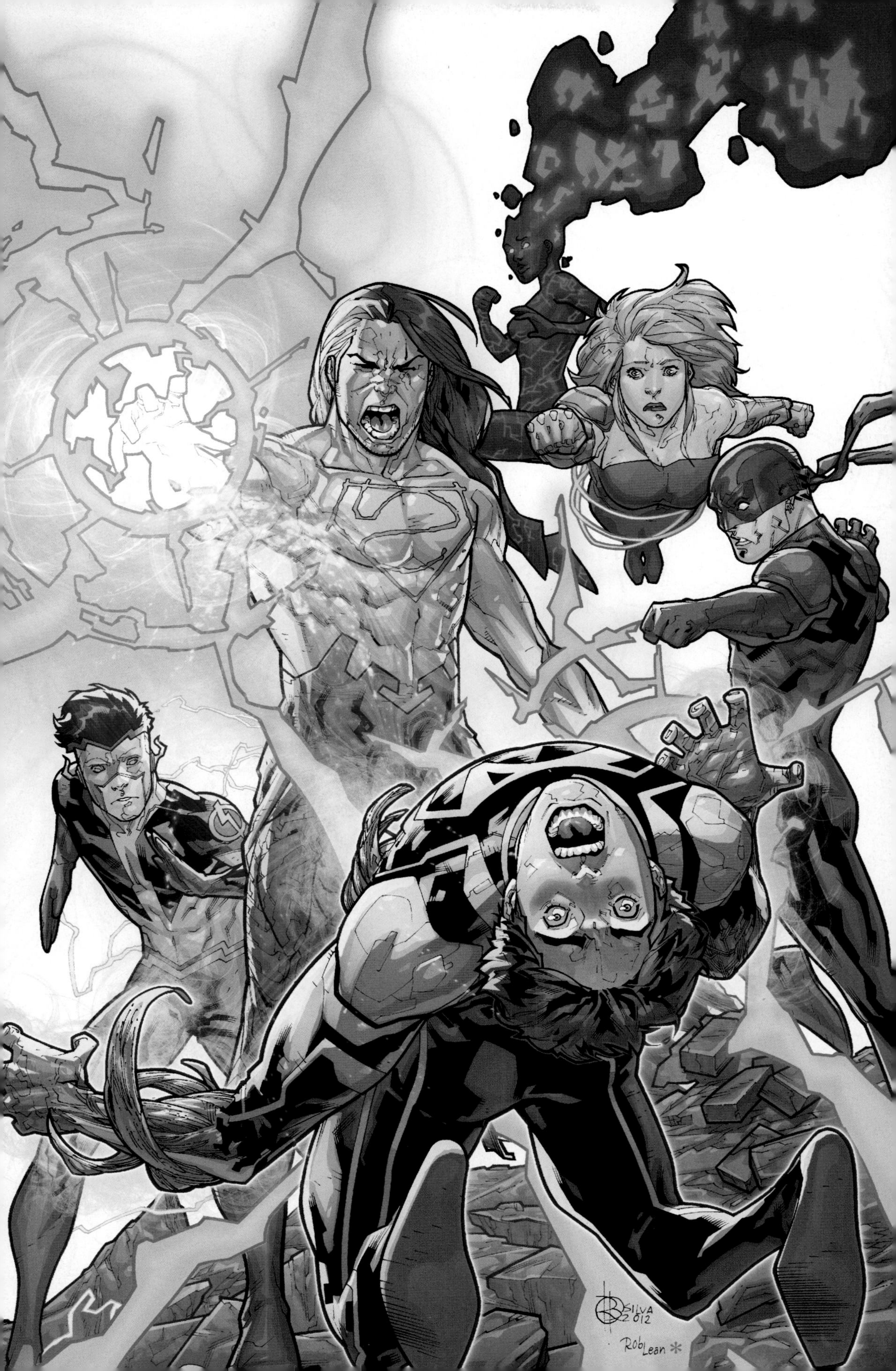
SILVA
2012
Rob Lean

THE FACE OF H'EL

TOM DEFALCO writer **R.B. SILVA** penciller **ROB LEAN** inker cover art by **R.B. SILVA & ROB LEAN WITH HI-FI**

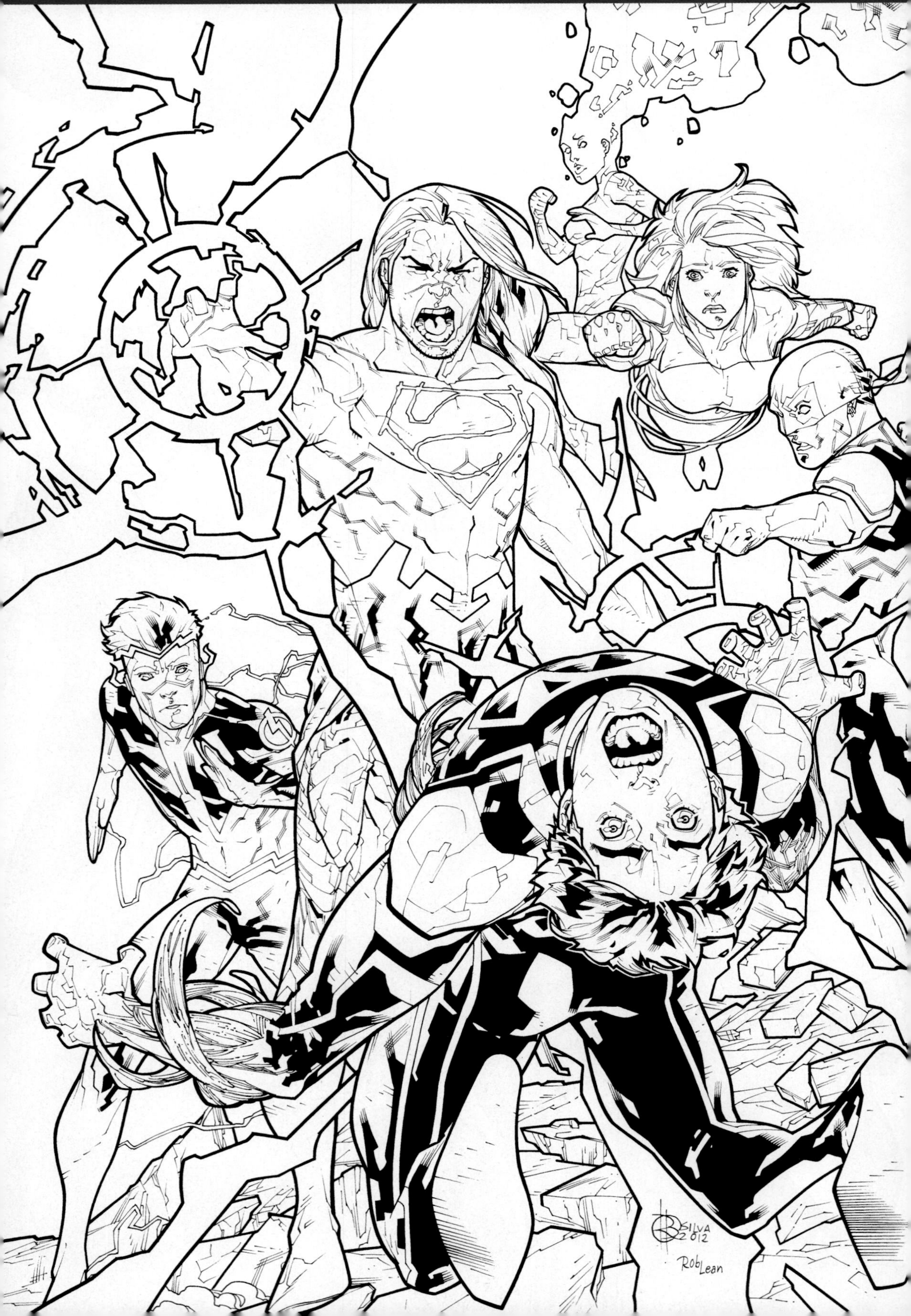

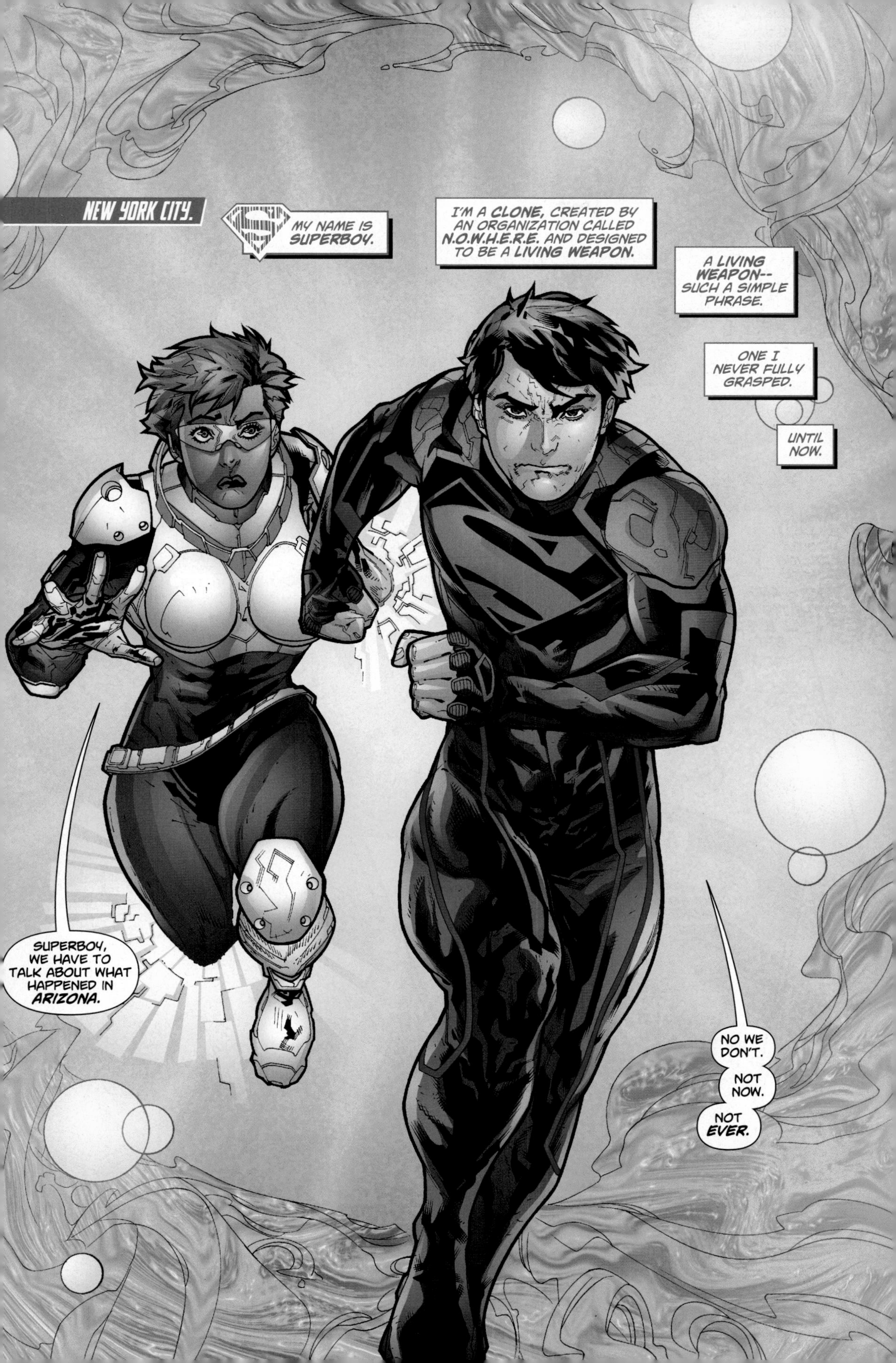
NEW YORK CITY.
MY NAME IS SUPERBOY.
I'M A CLONE, CREATED BY AN ORGANIZATION CALLED N.O.W.H.E.R.E. AND DESIGNED TO BE A LIVING WEAPON.
A LIVING WEAPON-- SUCH A SIMPLE PHRASE.
ONE I NEVER FULLY GRASPED.
UNTIL NOW.
SUPERBOY, WE HAVE TO TALK ABOUT WHAT HAPPENED IN ARIZONA.
NO WE DON'T.
NOT NOW.
NOT EVER.

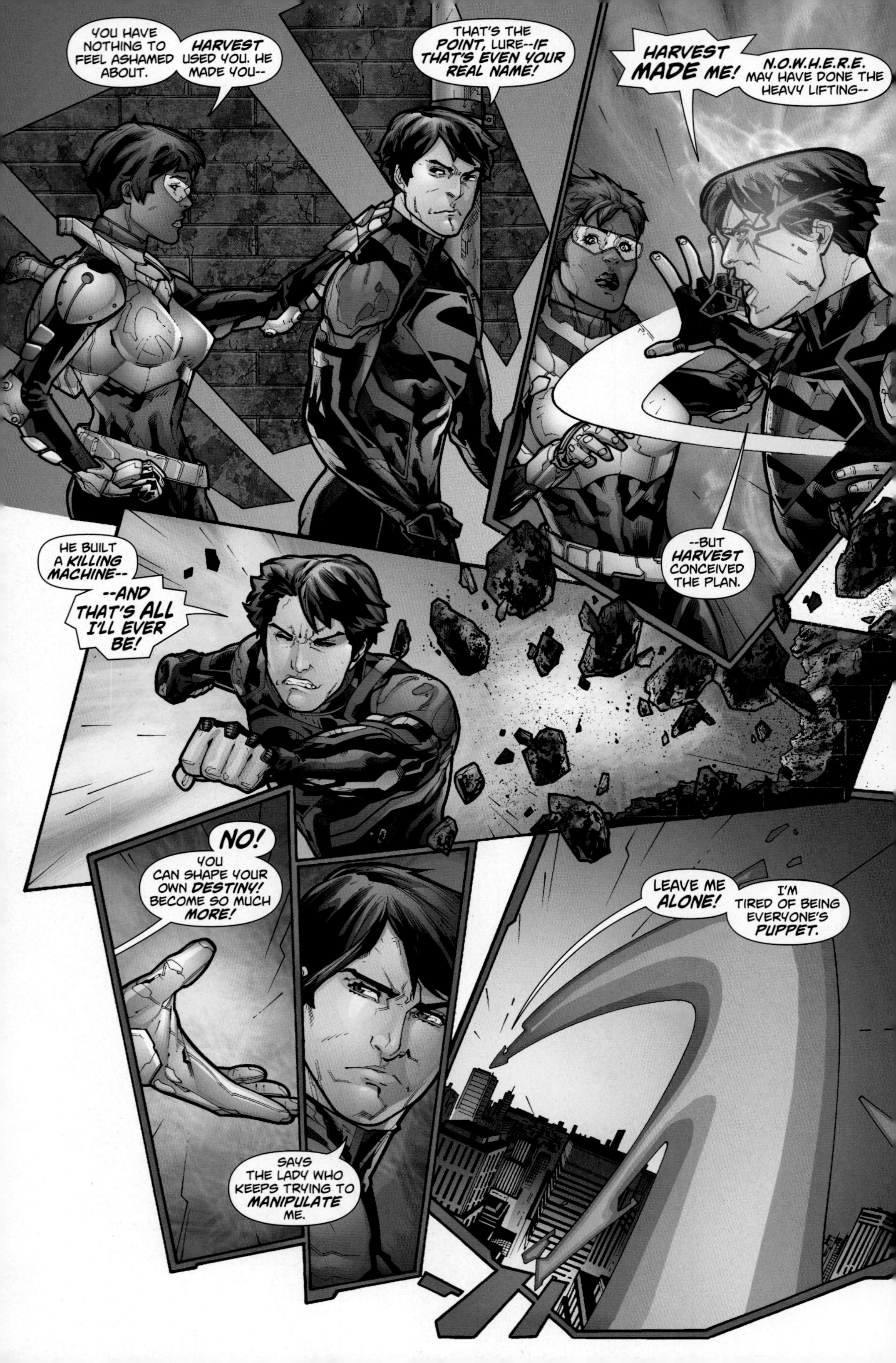
YOU HAVE NOTHING TO FEEL ASHAMED ABOUT.
HARVEST USED YOU. HE MADE YOU--
THAT'S THE POINT, LURE--IF THAT'S EVEN YOUR REAL NAME!
HARVEST MADE ME!
N.O.W.H.E.R.E. MAY HAVE DONE THE HEAVY LIFTING--
--BUT HARVEST CONCEIVED THE PLAN.
HE BUILT A KILLING MACHINE--
--AND THAT'S ALL I'LL EVER BE!
NO!
YOU CAN SHAPE YOUR OWN DESTINY! BECOME SO MUCH MORE!
SAYS THE LADY WHO KEEPS TRYING TO MANIPULATE ME.
LEAVE ME ALONE!
I'M TIRED OF BEING EVERYONE'S PUPPET.

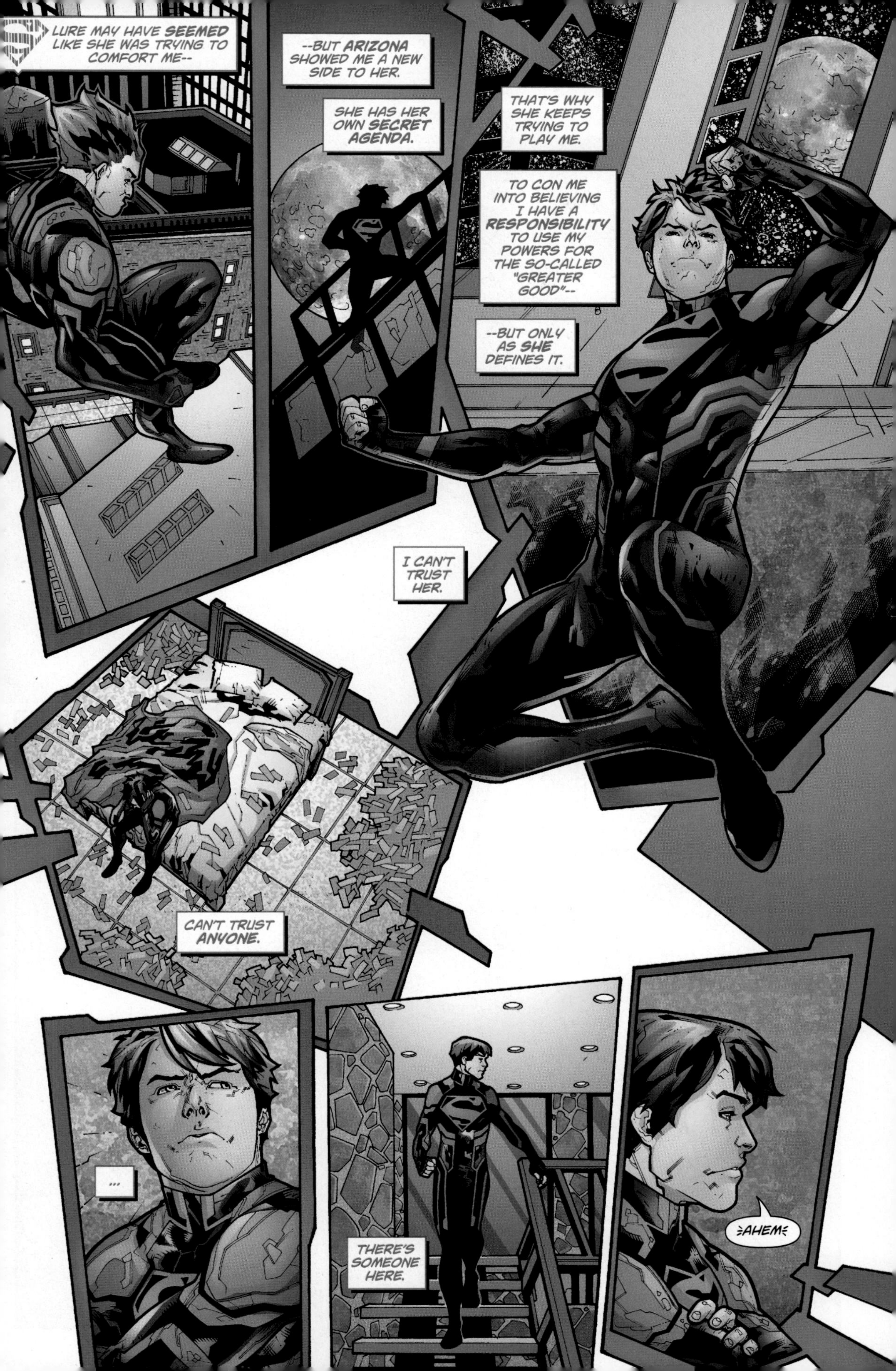
LURE MAY HAVE SEEMED LIKE SHE WAS TRYING TO COMFORT ME--
--BUT ARIZONA SHOWED ME A NEW SIDE TO HER.
SHE HAS HER OWN SECRET AGENDA.
THAT'S WHY SHE KEEPS TRYING TO PLAY ME.
TO CON ME INTO BELIEVING I HAVE A RESPONSIBILITY TO USE MY POWERS FOR THE SO-CALLED "GREATER GOOD"--
--BUT ONLY AS SHE DEFINES IT.
I CAN'T TRUST HER.
CAN'T TRUST ANYONE.
...
THERE'S SOMEONE HERE.
AHEM

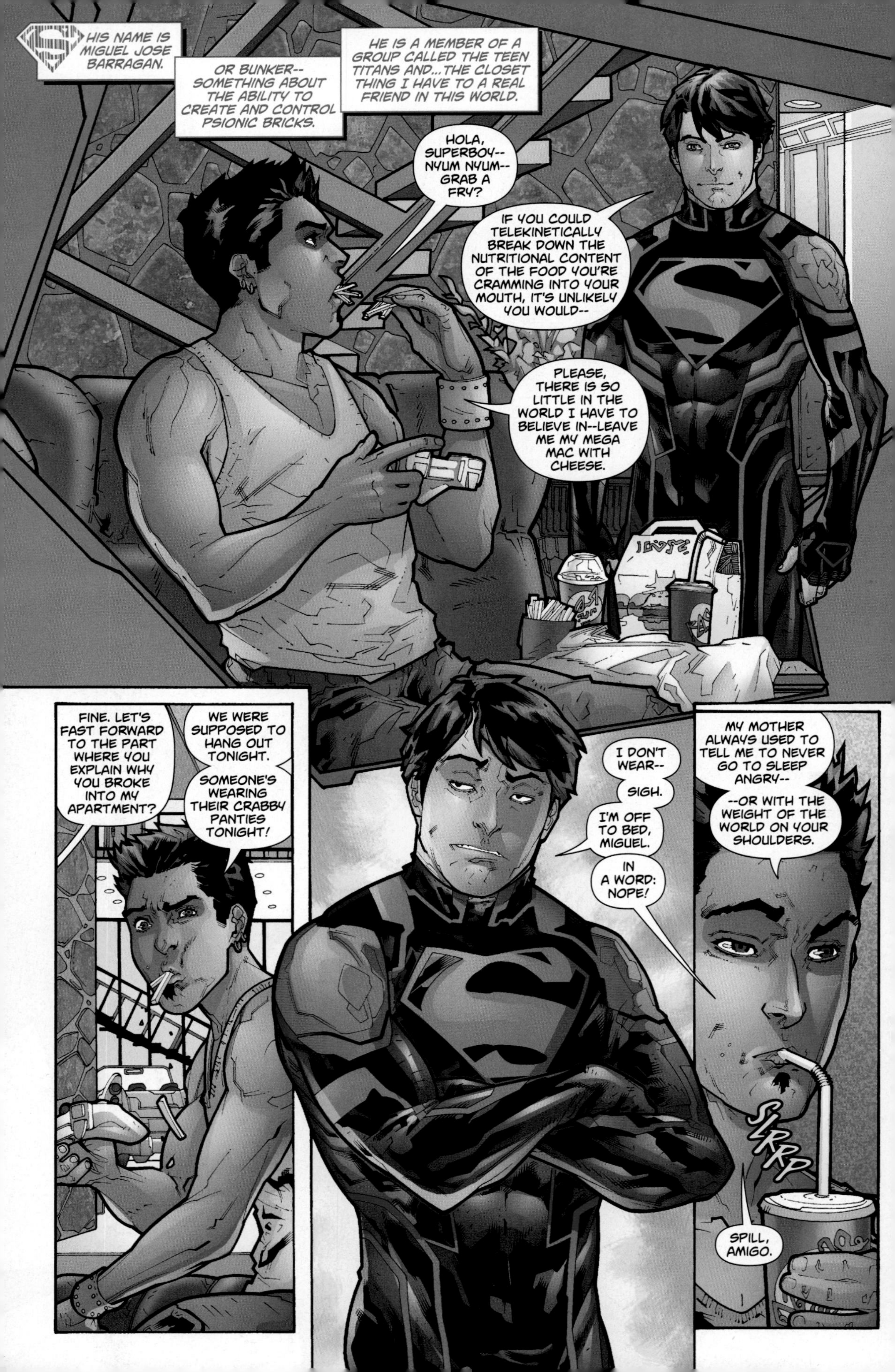
HIS NAME IS MIGUEL JOSE BARRAGAN.
OR BUNKER--SOMETHING ABOUT THE ABILITY TO CREATE AND CONTROL PSIONIC BRICKS.
HE IS A MEMBER OF A GROUP CALLED THE TEEN TITANS AND...THE CLOSET THING I HAVE TO A REAL FRIEND IN THIS WORLD.
HOLA, SUPERBOY--NYUM NYUM--GRAB A FRY?
IF YOU COULD TELEKINETICALLY BREAK DOWN THE NUTRITIONAL CONTENT OF THE FOOD YOU'RE CRAMMING INTO YOUR MOUTH, IT'S UNLIKELY YOU WOULD--
PLEASE, THERE IS SO LITTLE IN THE WORLD I HAVE TO BELIEVE IN--LEAVE ME MY MEGA MAC WITH CHEESE.
FINE. LET'S FAST FORWARD TO THE PART WHERE YOU EXPLAIN WHY YOU BROKE INTO MY APARTMENT?
WE WERE SUPPOSED TO HANG OUT TONIGHT.
SOMEONE'S WEARING THEIR CRABBY PANTIES TONIGHT!
I DON'T WEAR--
SIGH.
I'M OFF TO BED, MIGUEL.
IN A WORD: NOPE!
MY MOTHER ALWAYS USED TO TELL ME TO NEVER GO TO SLEEP ANGRY--
--OR WITH THE WEIGHT OF THE WORLD ON YOUR SHOULDERS.
SLRRP
SPILL, AMIGO.

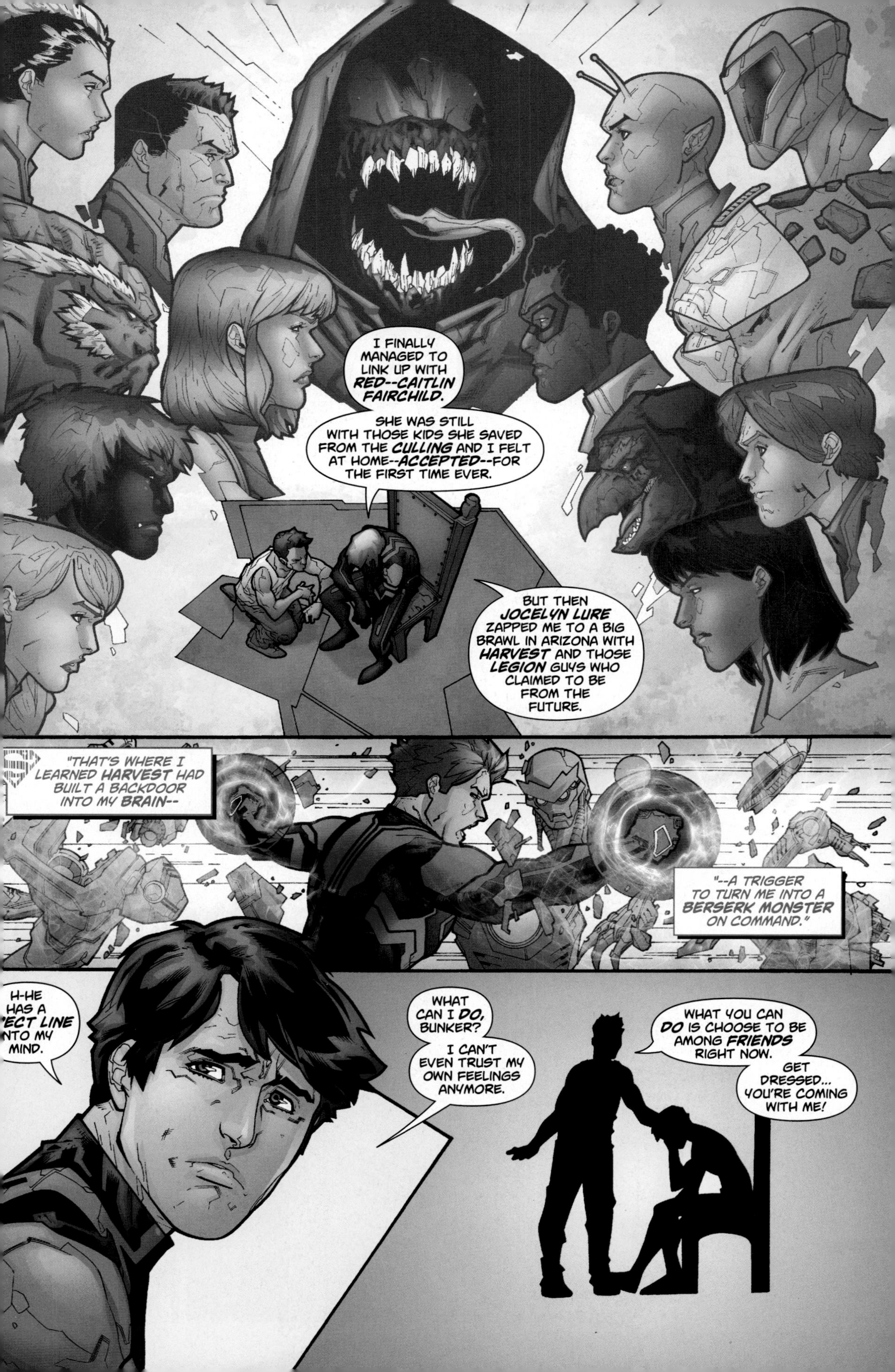
I FINALLY MANAGED TO LINK UP WITH RED--CAITLIN FAIRCHILD.
SHE WAS STILL WITH THOSE KIDS SHE SAVED FROM THE CULLING AND I FELT AT HOME--ACCEPTED--FOR THE FIRST TIME EVER.
BUT THEN JOCELYN LURE ZAPPED ME TO A BIG BRAWL IN ARIZONA WITH HARVEST AND THOSE LEGION GUYS WHO CLAIMED TO BE FROM THE FUTURE.
"THAT'S WHERE I LEARNED HARVEST HAD BUILT A BACKDOOR INTO MY BRAIN--
"--A TRIGGER TO TURN ME INTO A BERSERK MONSTER ON COMMAND."
H-HE HAS A ECT LINE NTO MY MIND.
WHAT CAN I DO, BUNKER?
I CAN'T EVEN TRUST MY OWN FEELINGS ANYMORE.
WHAT YOU CAN DO IS CHOOSE TO BE AMONG FRIENDS RIGHT NOW.
GET DRESSED... YOU'RE COMING WITH ME!

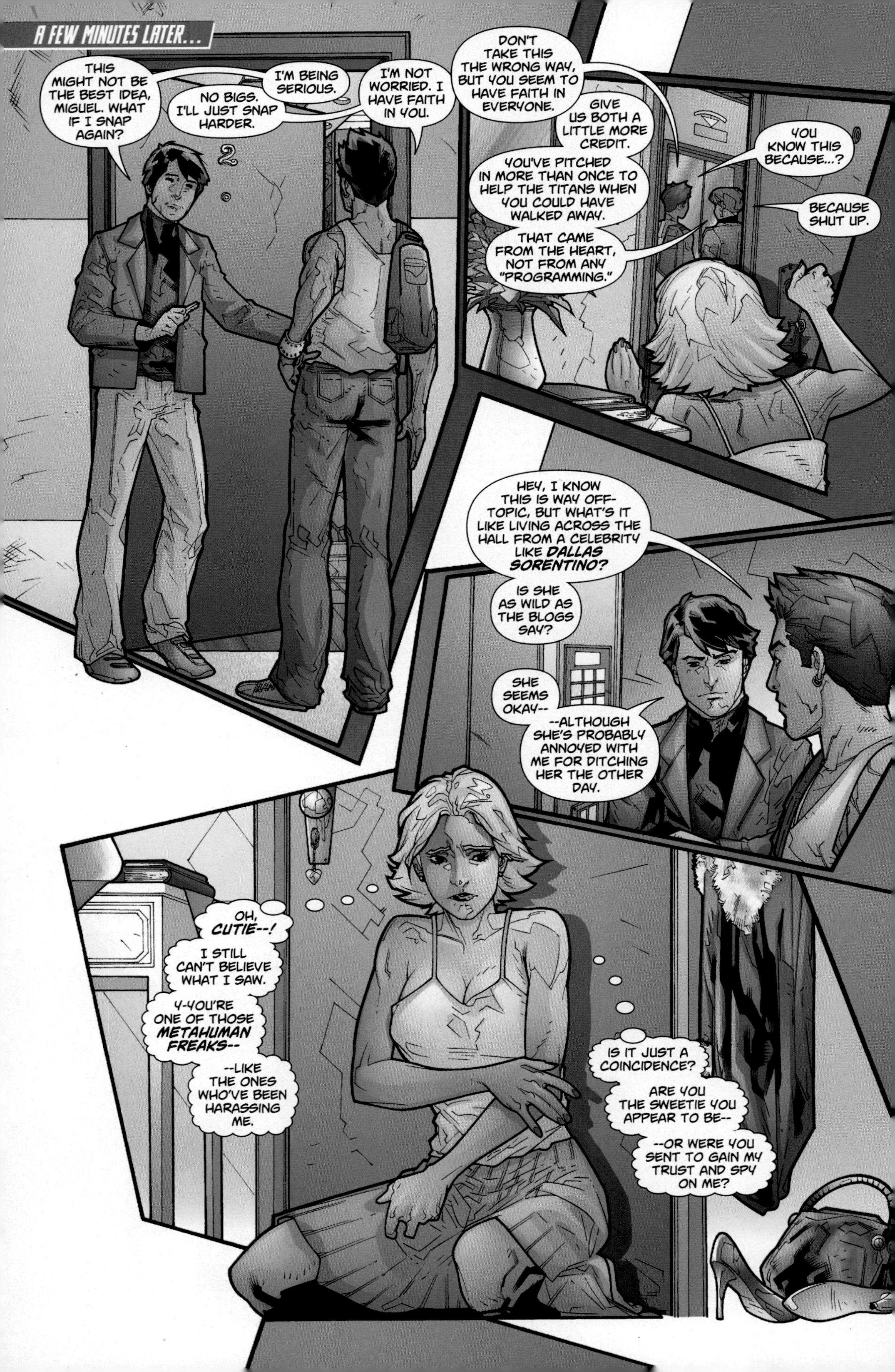
A FEW MINUTES LATER...
THIS MIGHT NOT BE THE BEST IDEA, MIGUEL. WHAT IF I SNAP AGAIN?
NO BIGS. I'LL JUST SNAP HARDER.
I'M BEING SERIOUS.
I'M NOT WORRIED. I HAVE FAITH IN YOU.
DON'T TAKE THIS THE WRONG WAY, BUT YOU SEEM TO HAVE FAITH IN EVERYONE.
GIVE US BOTH A LITTLE MORE CREDIT.
YOU'VE PITCHED IN MORE THAN ONCE TO HELP THE TITANS WHEN YOU COULD HAVE WALKED AWAY.
THAT CAME FROM THE HEART, NOT FROM ANY "PROGRAMMING."
YOU KNOW THIS BECAUSE...?
BECAUSE SHUT UP.
HEY, I KNOW THIS IS WAY OFF-TOPIC, BUT WHAT'S IT LIKE LIVING ACROSS THE HALL FROM A CELEBRITY LIKE DALLAS SORENTINO?
IS SHE AS WILD AS THE BLOGS SAY?
SHE SEEMS OKAY--
--ALTHOUGH SHE'S PROBABLY ANNOYED WITH ME FOR DITCHING HER THE OTHER DAY.
OH, CUTIE--!
I STILL CAN'T BELIEVE WHAT I SAW.
Y-YOU'RE ONE OF THOSE METAHUMAN FREAKS--
--LIKE THE ONES WHO'VE BEEN HARASSING ME.
IS IT JUST A COINCIDENCE?
ARE YOU THE SWEETIE YOU APPEAR TO BE--
--OR WERE YOU SENT TO GAIN MY TRUST AND SPY ON ME?

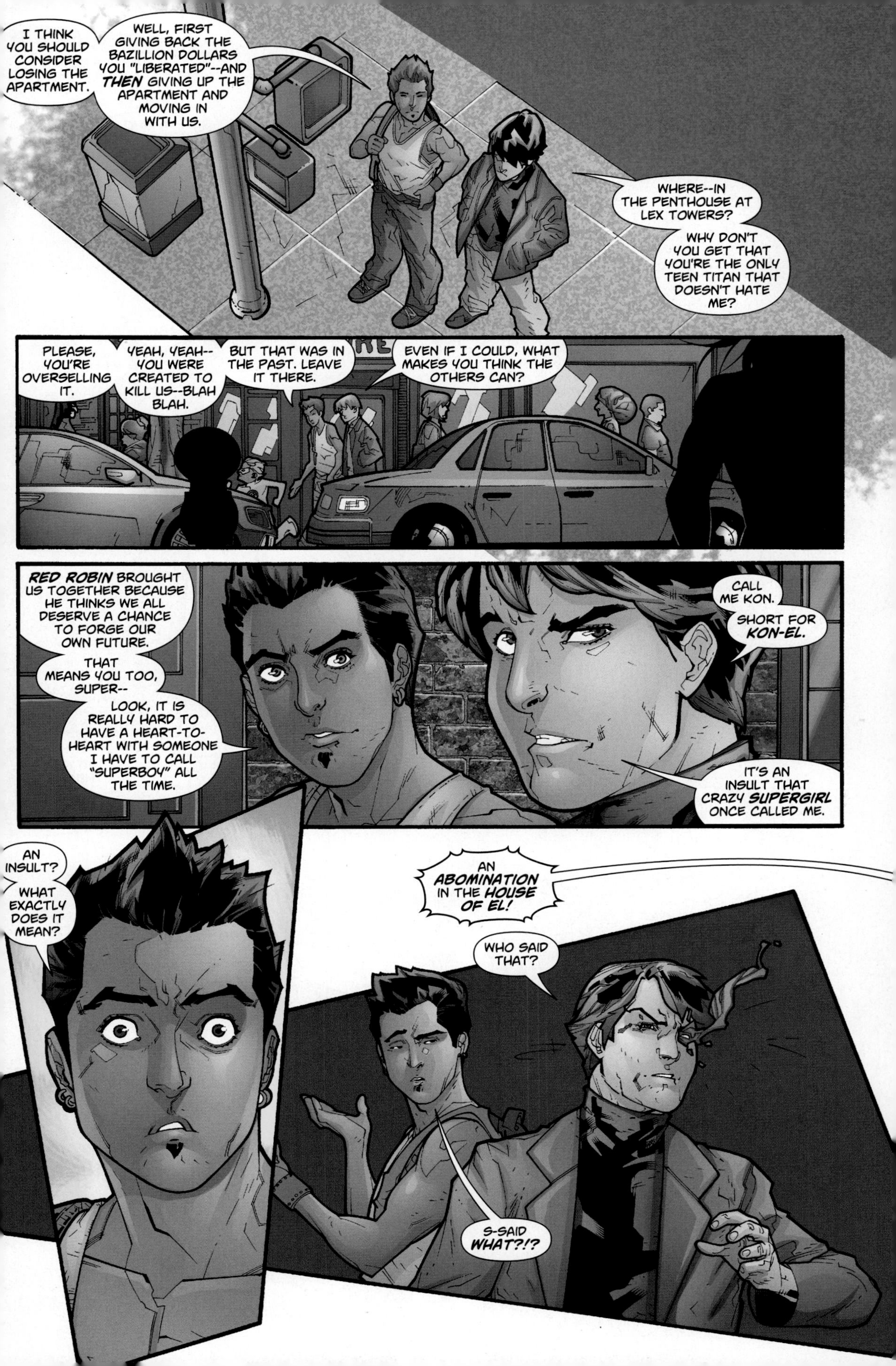
I THINK YOU SHOULD CONSIDER LOSING THE APARTMENT.
WELL, FIRST GIVING BACK THE BAZILLION DOLLARS YOU "LIBERATED"--AND THEN GIVING UP THE APARTMENT AND MOVING IN WITH US.
WHERE--IN THE PENTHOUSE AT LEX TOWERS?
WHY DON'T YOU GET THAT YOU'RE THE ONLY TEEN TITAN THAT DOESN'T HATE ME?
PLEASE, YOU'RE OVERSELLING IT.
YEAH, YEAH--YOU WERE CREATED TO KILL US--BLAH BLAH.
BUT THAT WAS IN THE PAST. LEAVE IT THERE.
EVEN IF I COULD, WHAT MAKES YOU THINK THE OTHERS CAN?
RED ROBIN BROUGHT US TOGETHER BECAUSE HE THINKS WE ALL DESERVE A CHANCE TO FORGE OUR OWN FUTURE.
THAT MEANS YOU TOO, SUPER--
LOOK, IT IS REALLY HARD TO HAVE A HEART-TO-HEART WITH SOMEONE I HAVE TO CALL "SUPERBOY" ALL THE TIME.
CALL ME KON.
SHORT FOR KON-EL.
IT'S AN INSULT THAT CRAZY SUPERGIRL ONCE CALLED ME.
AN INSULT?
WHAT EXACTLY DOES IT MEAN?
AN ABOMINATION IN THE HOUSE OF EL!
WHO SAID THAT?
S-SAID WHAT?!?

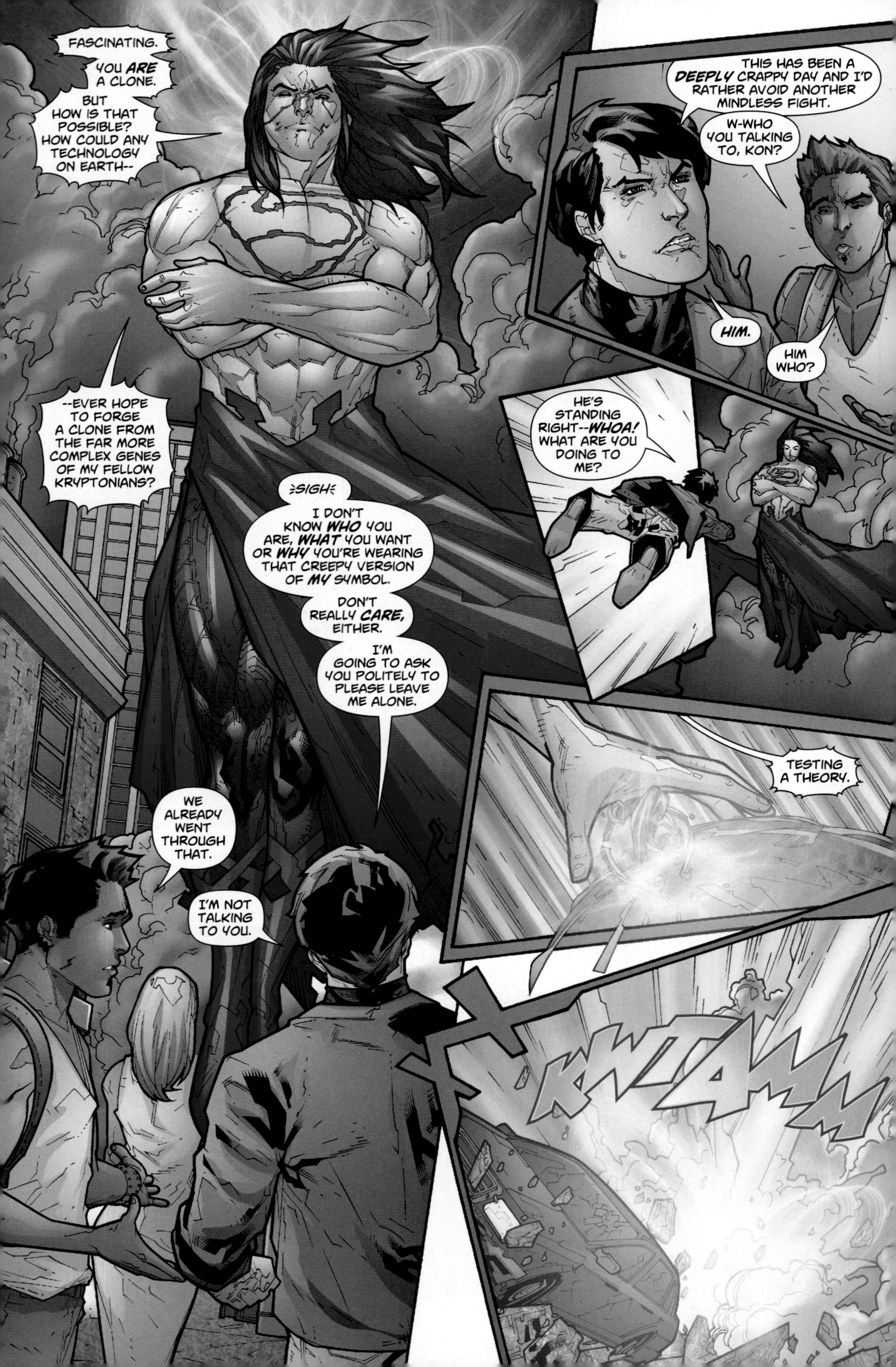
FASCINATING.
YOU ARE A CLONE.
BUT HOW IS THAT POSSIBLE? HOW COULD ANY TECHNOLOGY ON EARTH--
--EVER HOPE TO FORGE A CLONE FROM THE FAR MORE COMPLEX GENES OF MY FELLOW KRYPTONIANS?
THIS HAS BEEN A DEEPLY CRAPPY DAY AND I'D RATHER AVOID ANOTHER MINDLESS FIGHT.
W-WHO YOU TALKING TO, KON?
HIM.
HIM WHO?
HE'S STANDING RIGHT--WHOA! WHAT ARE YOU DOING TO ME?
SIGH
I DON'T KNOW WHO YOU ARE, WHAT YOU WANT OR WHY YOU'RE WEARING THAT CREEPY VERSION OF MY SYMBOL.
DON'T REALLY CARE, EITHER.
I'M GOING TO ASK YOU POLITELY TO PLEASE LEAVE ME ALONE.
WE ALREADY WENT THROUGH THAT.
I'M NOT TALKING TO YOU.
TESTING A THEORY.
KWTAMM

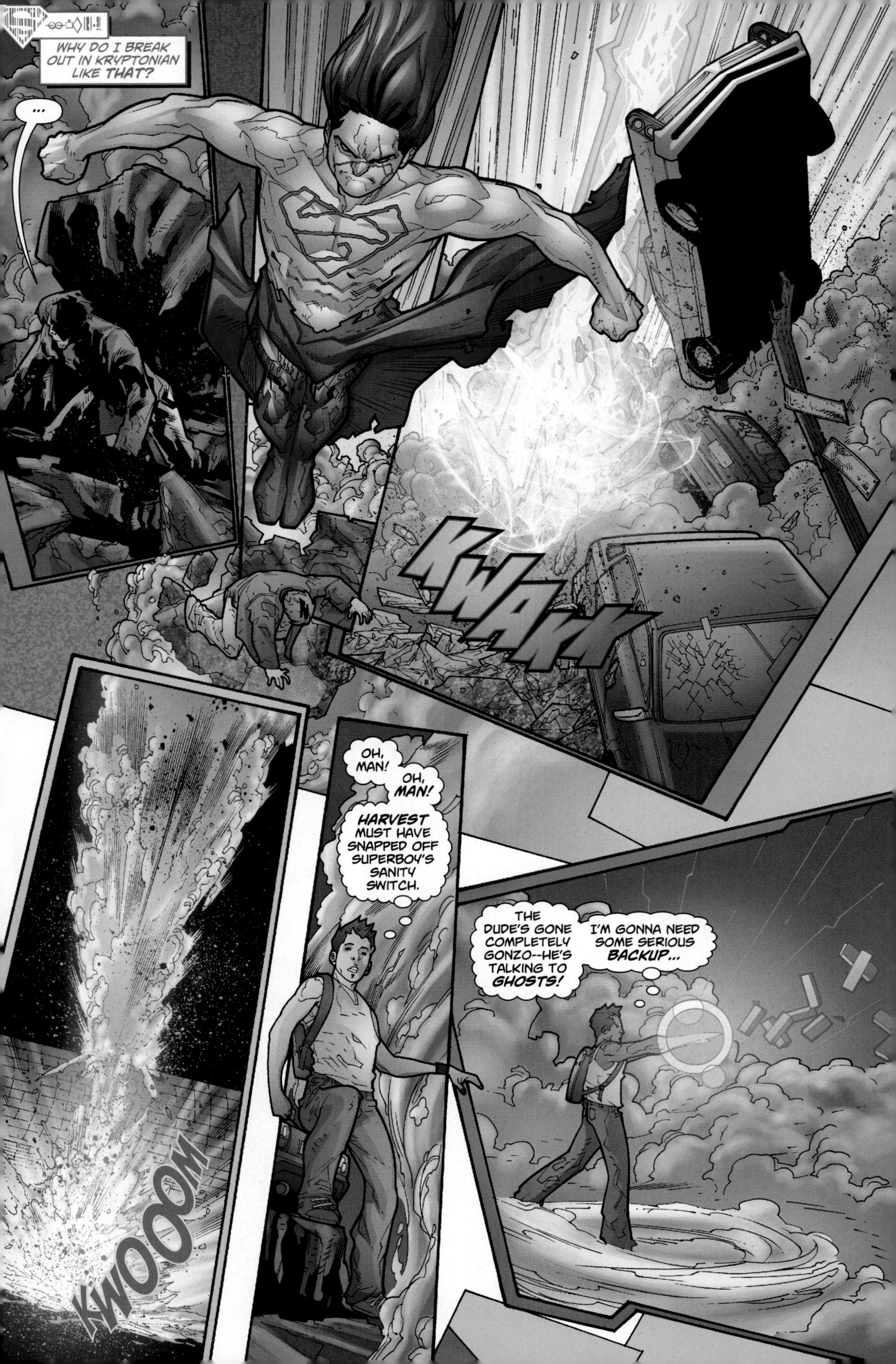
WHY DO I BREAK OUT IN KRYPTONIAN LIKE THAT?
...
KWAKK
KWOOOM
OH, MAN!
OH, MAN!
HARVEST MUST HAVE SNAPPED OFF SUPERBOY'S SANITY SWITCH.
THE DUDE'S GONE COMPLETELY GONZO--HE'S TALKING TO GHOSTS!
I'M GONNA NEED SOME SERIOUS BACKUP...

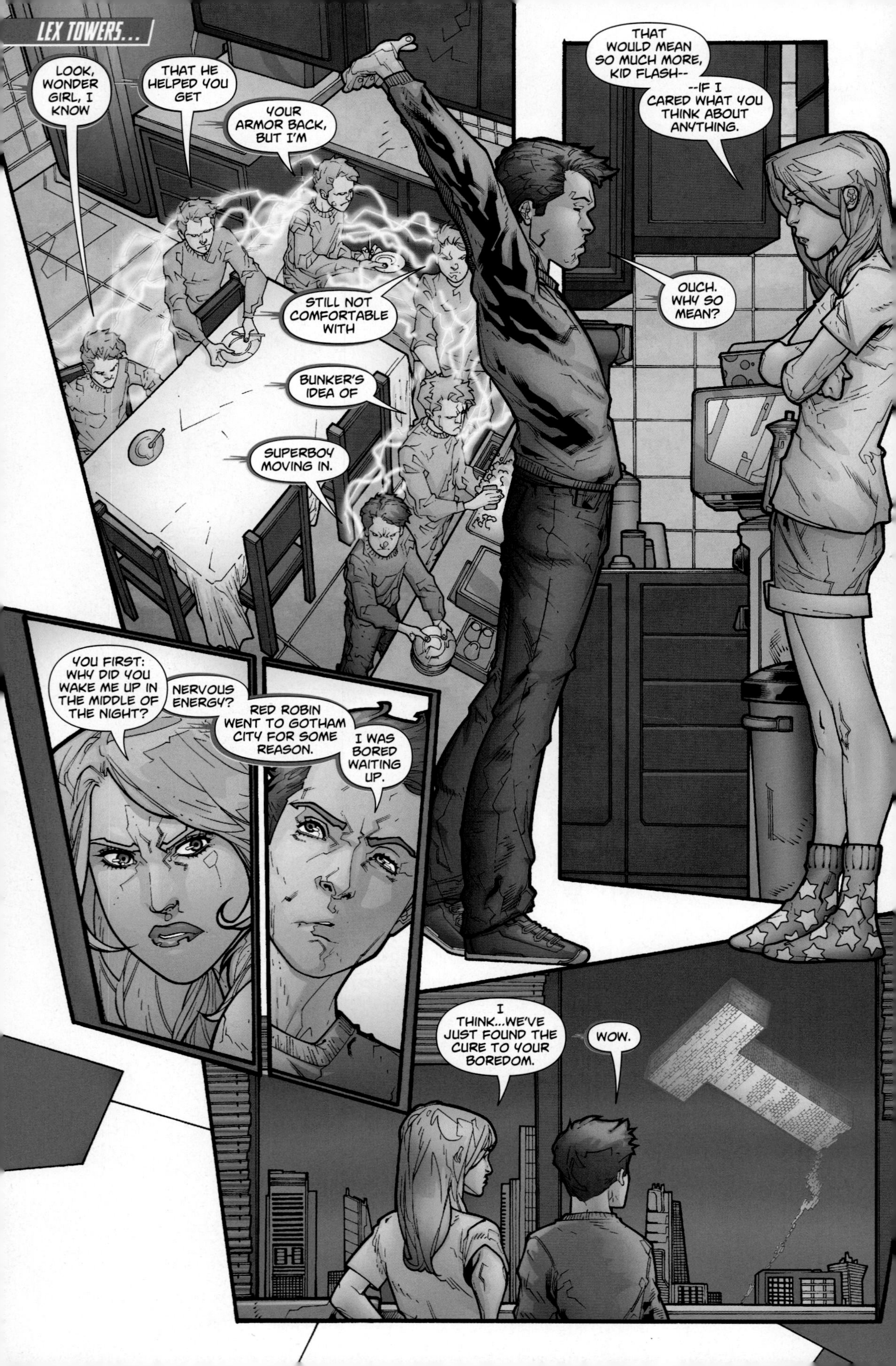
LEX TOWERS...
LOOK, WONDER GIRL, I KNOW
THAT HE HELPED YOU GET
YOUR ARMOR BACK, BUT I'M
STILL NOT COMFORTABLE WITH
BUNKER'S IDEA OF
SUPERBOY MOVING IN.
THAT WOULD MEAN SO MUCH MORE, KID FLASH--
--IF I CARED WHAT YOU THINK ABOUT ANYTHING.
OUCH. WHY SO MEAN?
YOU FIRST: WHY DID YOU WAKE ME UP IN THE MIDDLE OF THE NIGHT?
NERVOUS ENERGY?
RED ROBIN WENT TO GOTHAM CITY FOR SOME REASON.
I WAS BORED WAITING UP.
I THINK...WE'VE JUST FOUND THE CURE TO YOUR BOREDOM.
WOW.

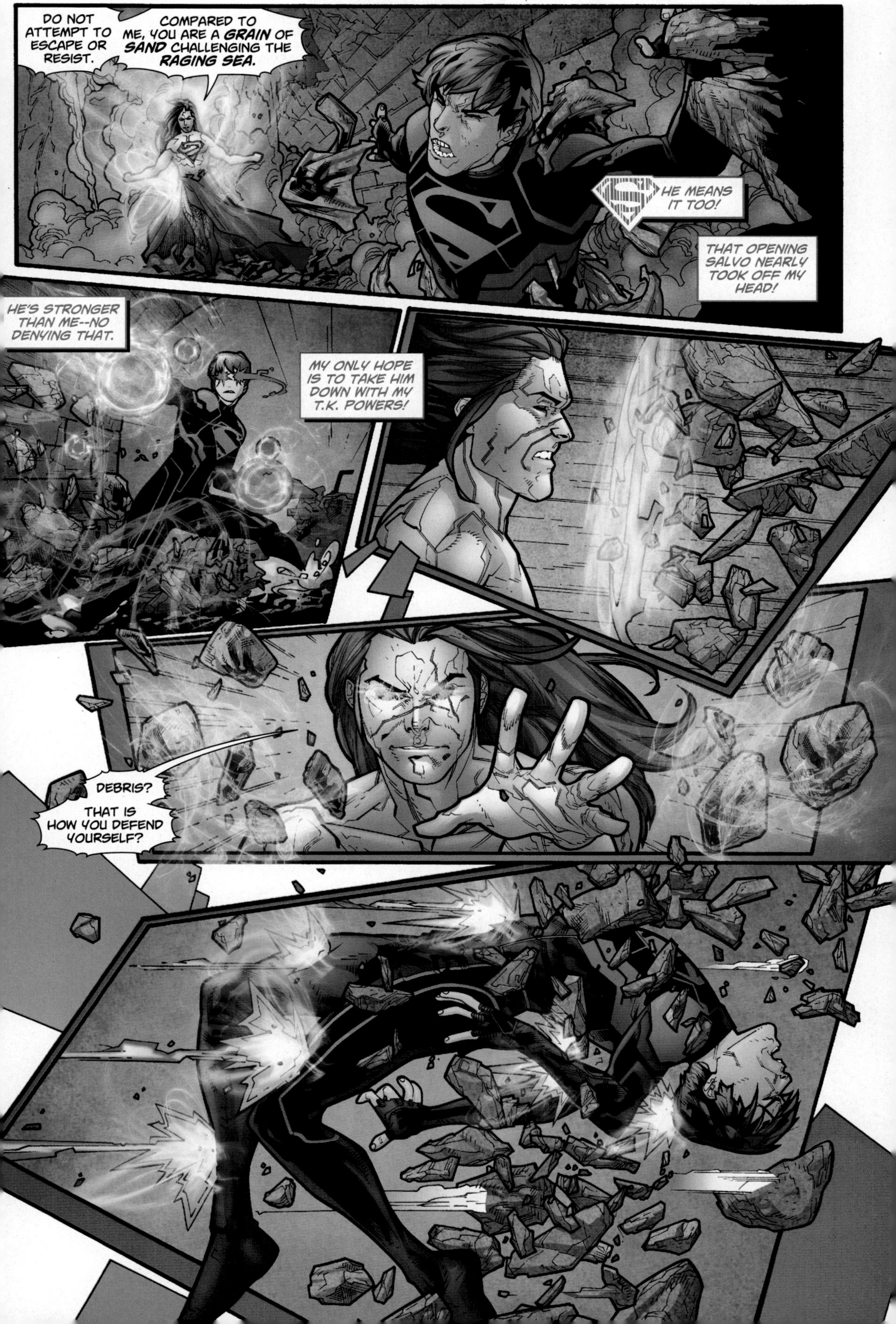
DO NOT ATTEMPT TO ESCAPE OR RESIST.
COMPARED TO ME, YOU ARE A GRAIN OF SAND CHALLENGING THE RAGING SEA.
HE MEANS IT TOO!
THAT OPENING SALVO NEARLY TOOK OFF MY HEAD!
HE'S STRONGER THAN ME--NO DENYING THAT.
MY ONLY HOPE IS TO TAKE HIM DOWN WITH MY T.K. POWERS!
DEBRIS?
THAT IS HOW YOU DEFEND YOURSELF?

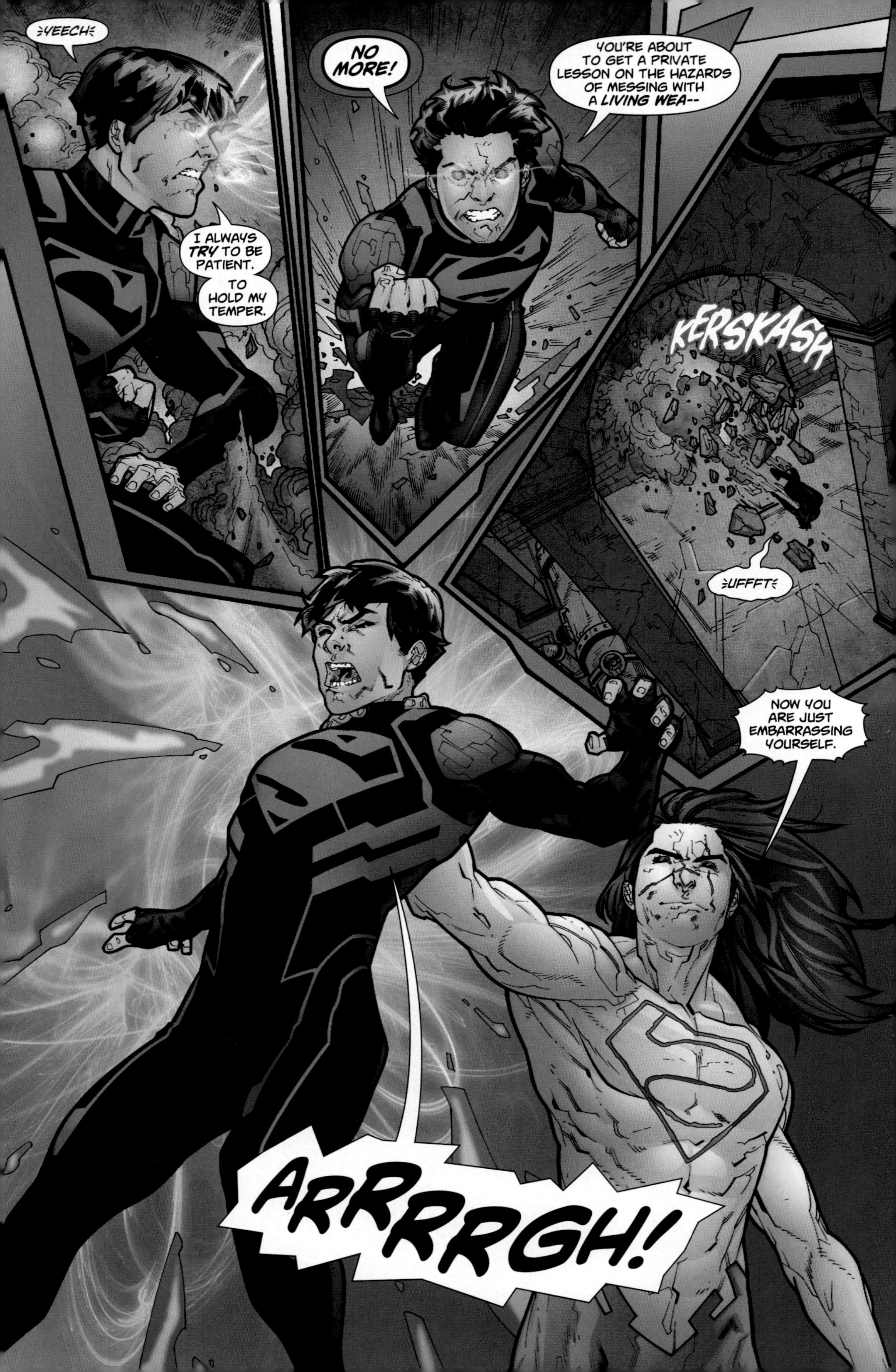
YEECH
I ALWAYS TRY TO BE PATIENT.
TO HOLD MY TEMPER.
NO MORE!
YOU'RE ABOUT TO GET A PRIVATE LESSON ON THE HAZARDS OF MESSING WITH A LIVING WEA--
KERSKASH
UFFFT
NOW YOU ARE JUST EMBARRASSING YOURSELF.
ARRRRRGH!

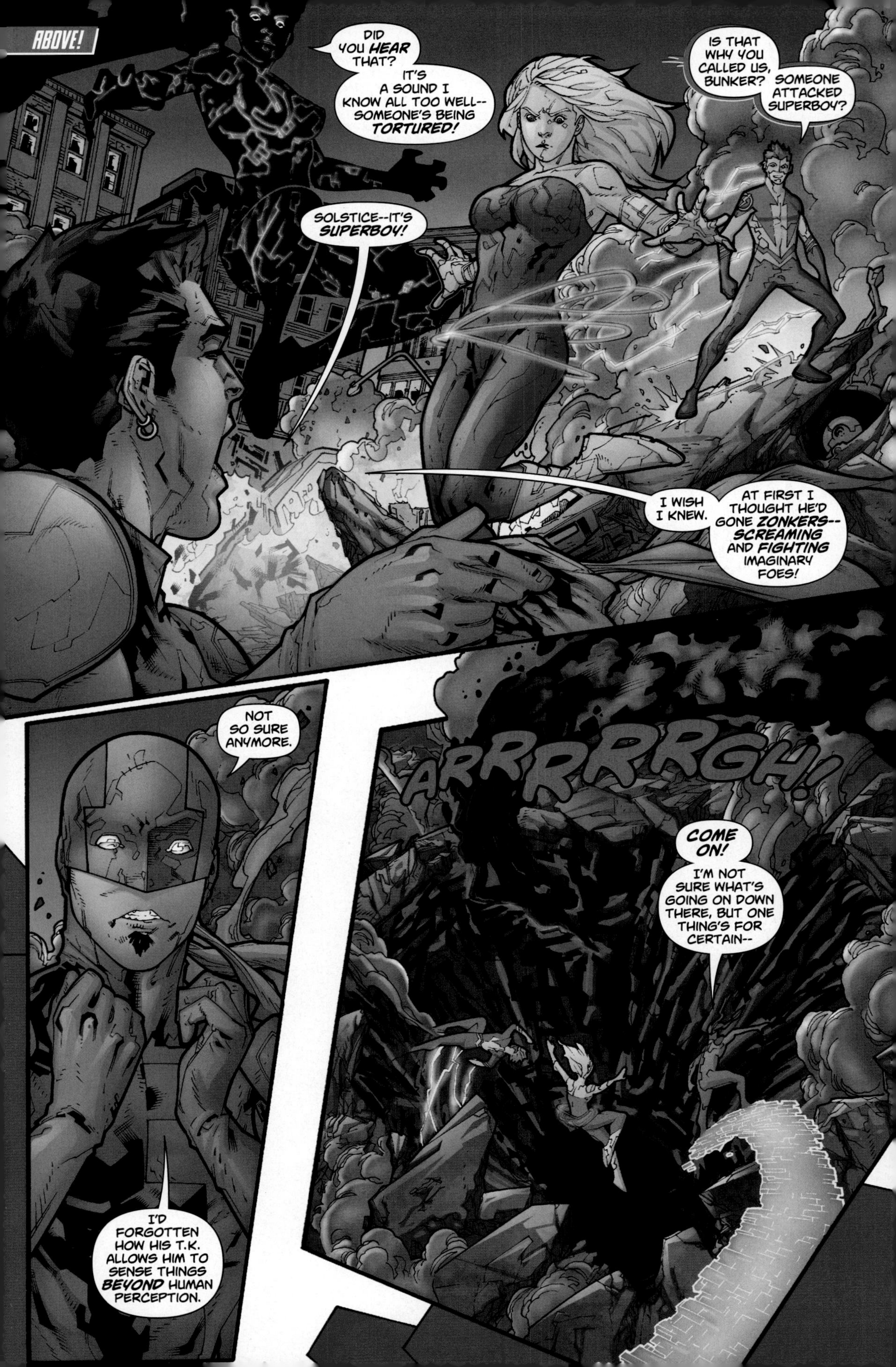
ABOVE!
DID YOU HEAR THAT?
IT'S A SOUND I KNOW ALL TOO WELL-- SOMEONE'S BEING TORTURED!
IS THAT WHY YOU CALLED US, BUNKER?
SOMEONE ATTACKED SUPERBOY?
SOLSTICE--IT'S SUPERBOY!
I WISH I KNEW.
AT FIRST I THOUGHT HE'D GONE ZONKERS-- SCREAMING AND FIGHTING IMAGINARY FOES!
NOT SO SURE ANYMORE.
I'D FORGOTTEN HOW HIS T.K. ALLOWS HIM TO SENSE THINGS BEYOND HUMAN PERCEPTION.
ARRRRRGH!
COME ON!
I'M NOT SURE WHAT'S GOING ON DOWN THERE, BUT ONE THING'S FOR CERTAIN--

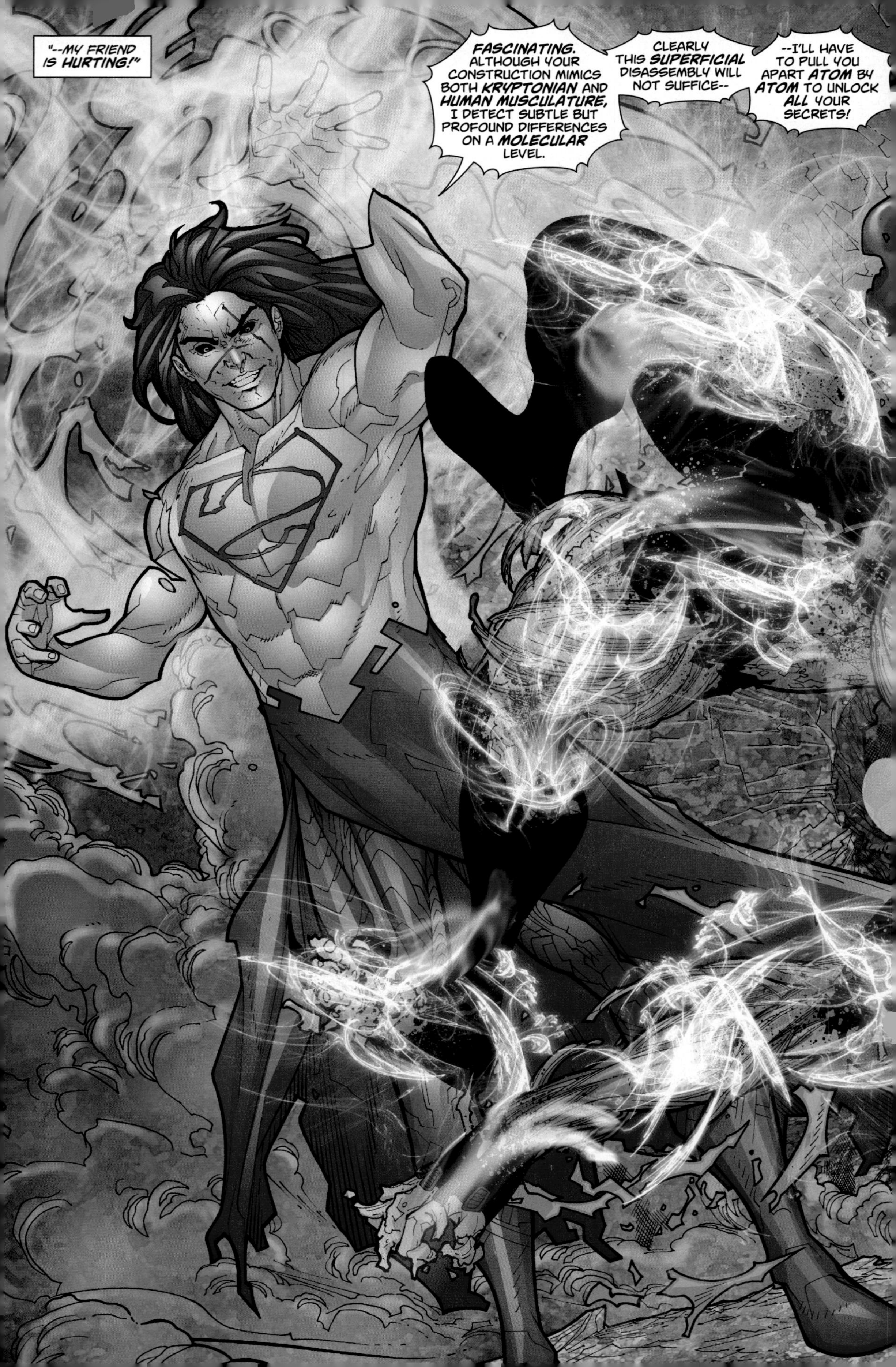
"--MY FRIEND IS HURTING!"
FASCINATING. ALTHOUGH YOUR CONSTRUCTION MIMICS BOTH KRYPTONIAN AND HUMAN MUSCULATURE, I DETECT SUBTLE BUT PROFOUND DIFFERENCES ON A MOLECULAR LEVEL.
CLEARLY THIS SUPERFICIAL DISASSEMBLY WILL NOT SUFFICE--
--I'LL HAVE TO PULL YOU APART ATOM BY ATOM TO UNLOCK ALL YOUR SECRETS!

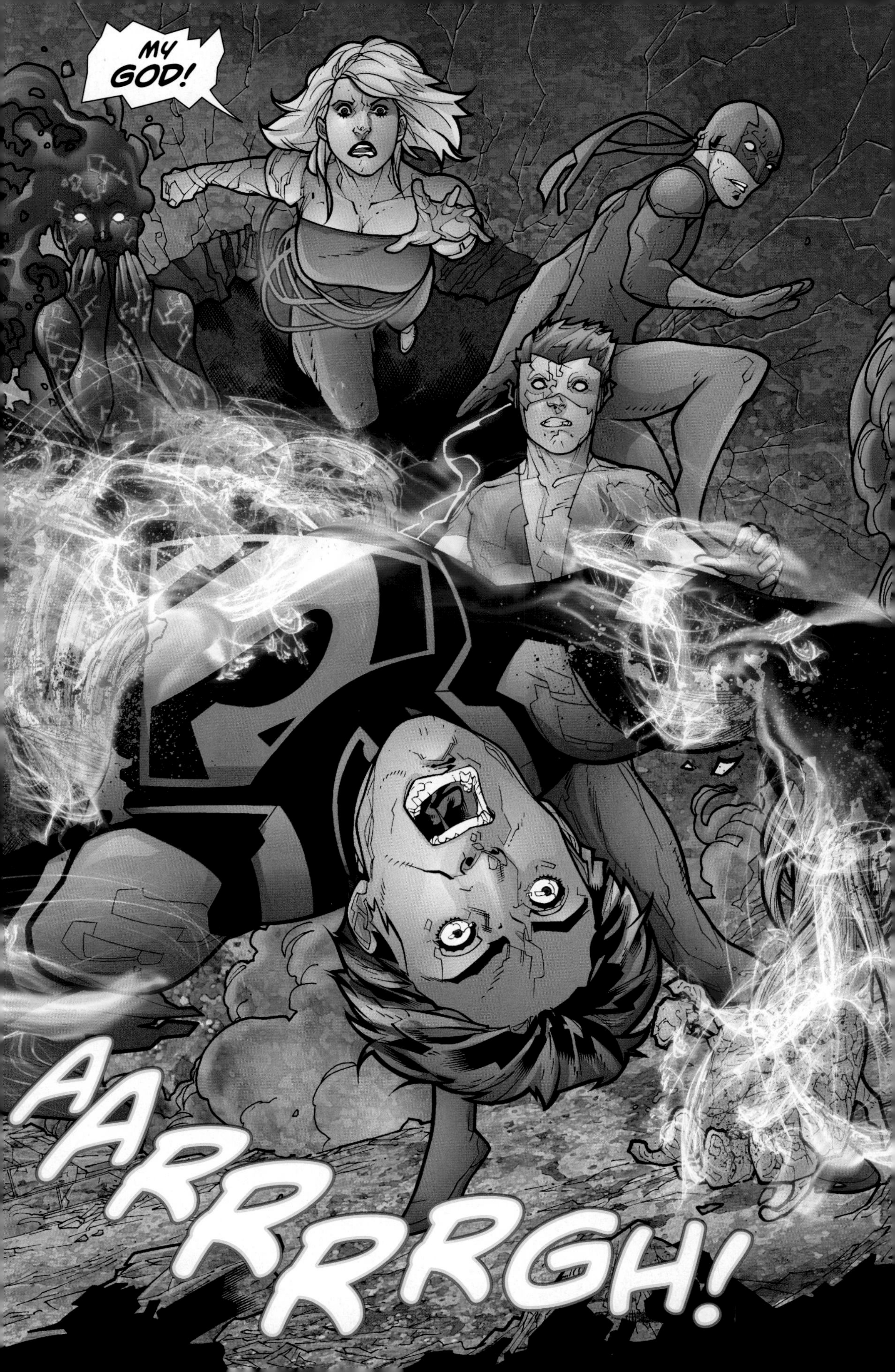
MY GOD!
AARRRRGH!

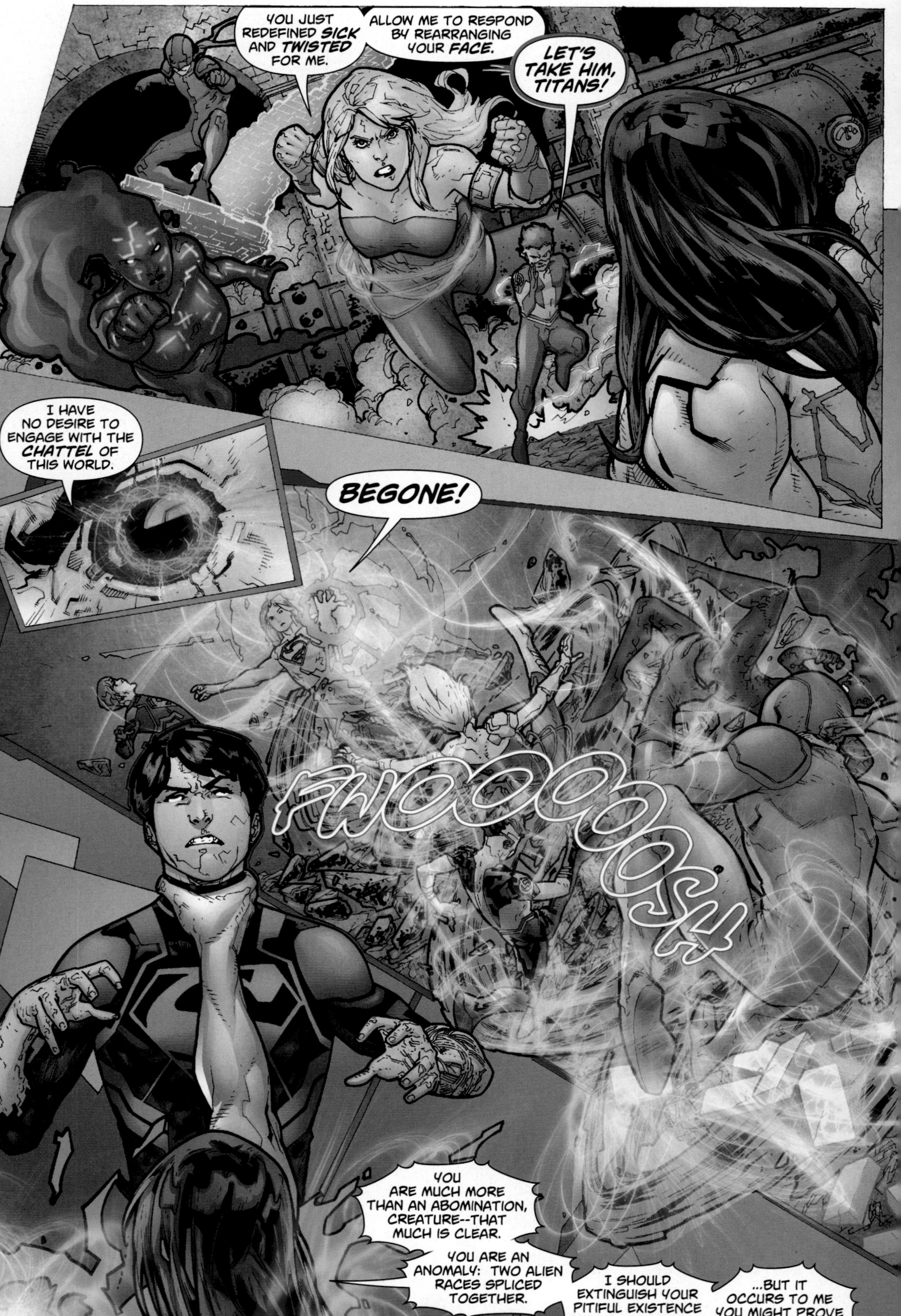
YOU JUST REDEFINED SICK AND TWISTED FOR ME.
ALLOW ME TO RESPOND BY REARRANGING YOUR FACE.
LET'S TAKE HIM, TITANS!
I HAVE NO DESIRE TO ENGAGE WITH THE CHATTEL OF THIS WORLD.
BEGONE!
FWOOOOOSH
YOU ARE MUCH MORE THAN AN ABOMINATION, CREATURE--THAT MUCH IS CLEAR.
YOU ARE AN ANOMALY: TWO ALIEN RACES SPLICED TOGETHER.
I SHOULD EXTINGUISH YOUR PITIFUL EXISTENCE WITH A GLANCE...
...BUT IT OCCURS TO ME YOU MIGHT PROVE USEFUL IN THE COMING DAYS.

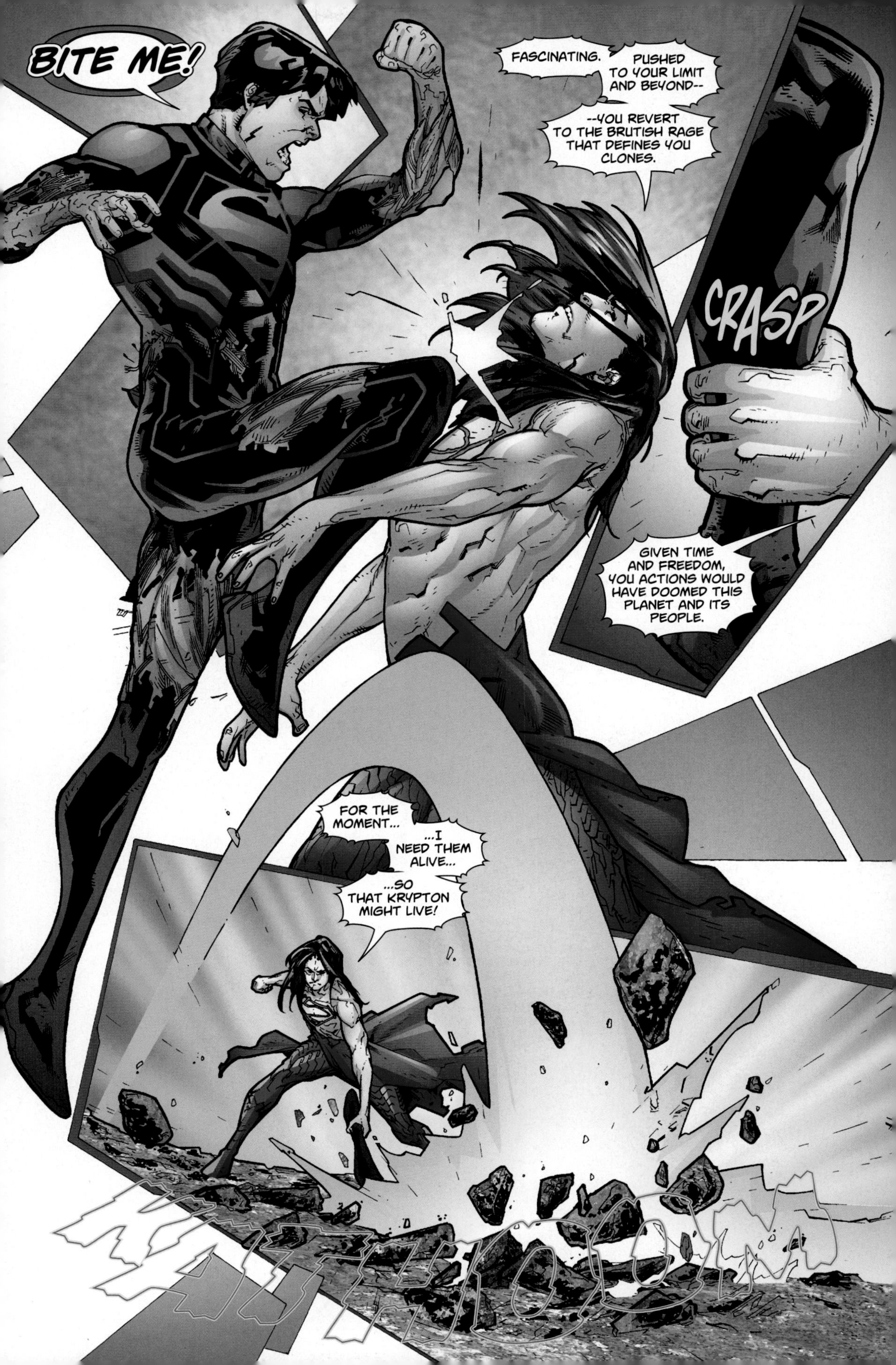
BITE ME!
FASCINATING.
PUSHED TO YOUR LIMIT AND BEYOND--
--YOU REVERT TO THE BRUTISH RAGE THAT DEFINES YOU CLONES.
CRASP
GIVEN TIME AND FREEDOM, YOU ACTIONS WOULD HAVE DOOMED THIS PLANET AND ITS PEOPLE.
FOR THE MOMENT...
...I NEED THEM ALIVE...
...SO THAT KRYPTON MIGHT LIVE!

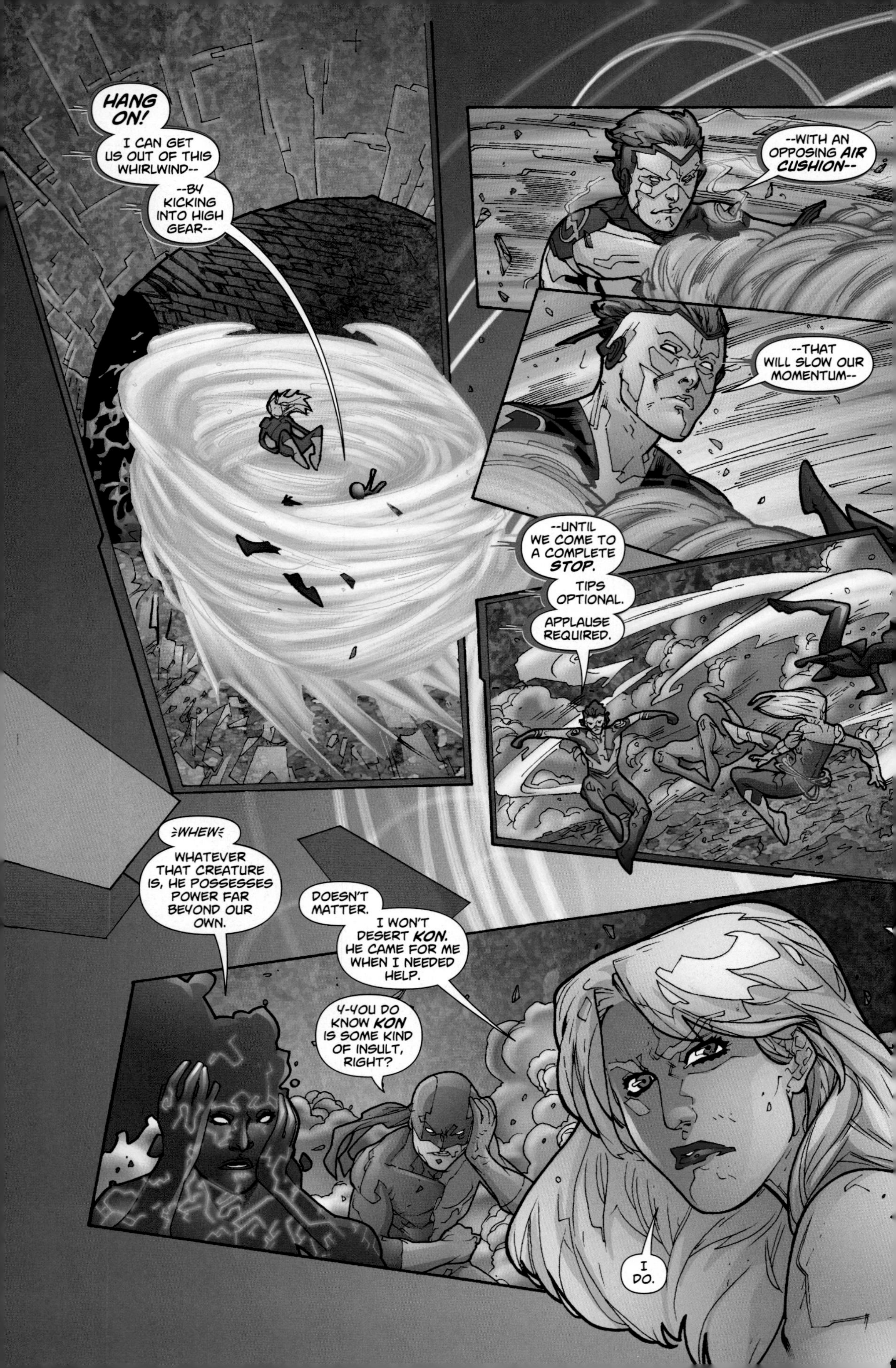
HANG ON!
I CAN GET US OUT OF THIS WHIRLWIND--
--BY KICKING INTO HIGH GEAR--
--WITH AN OPPOSING AIR CUSHION--
--THAT WILL SLOW OUR MOMENTUM--
--UNTIL WE COME TO A COMPLETE STOP.
TIPS OPTIONAL.
APPLAUSE REQUIRED.
WHEW
WHATEVER THAT CREATURE IS, HE POSSESSES POWER FAR BEYOND OUR OWN.
DOESN'T MATTER.
I WON'T DESERT KON. HE CAME FOR ME WHEN I NEEDED HELP.
Y-YOU DO KNOW KON IS SOME KIND OF INSULT, RIGHT?
I DO.

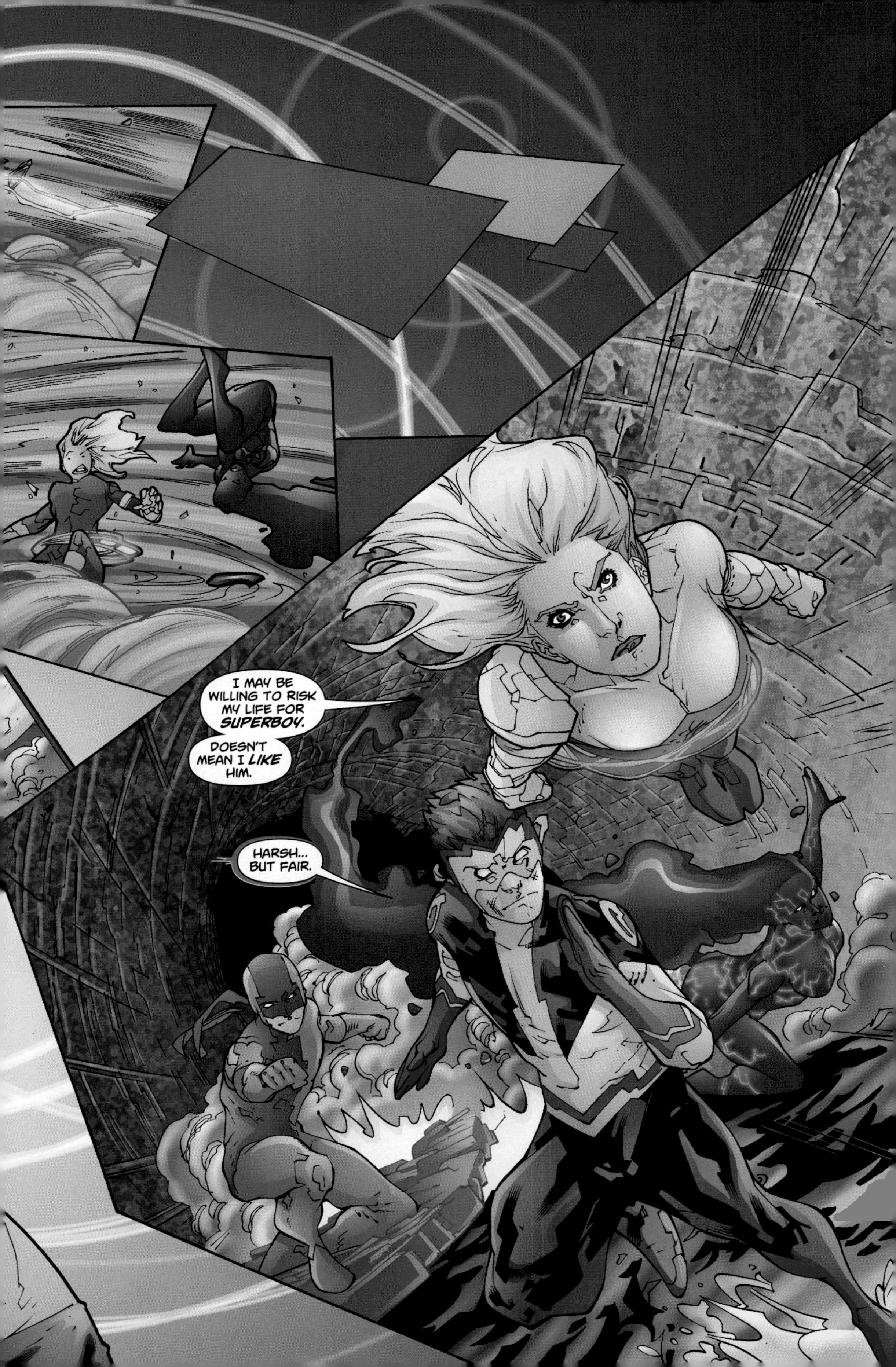

I MAY BE WILLING TO RISK MY LIFE FOR SUPERBOY.
DOESN'T MEAN I LIKE HIM.
HARSH... BUT FAIR.

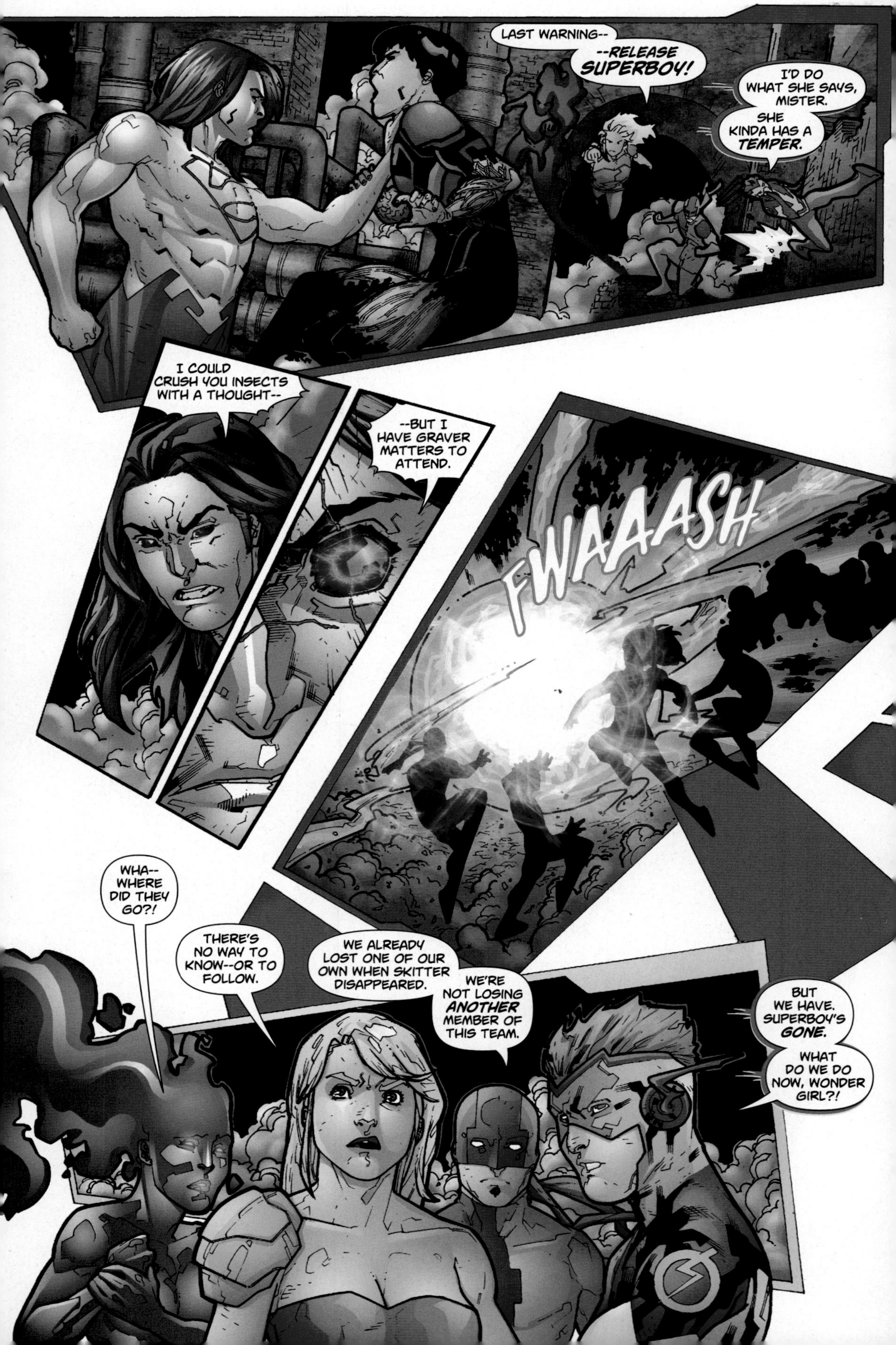
LAST WARNING--
--RELEASE SUPERBOY!
I'D DO WHAT SHE SAYS, MISTER.
SHE KINDA HAS A TEMPER.
I COULD CRUSH YOU INSECTS WITH A THOUGHT--
--BUT I HAVE GRAVER MATTERS TO ATTEND.
FWAAASH
WHA-- WHERE DID THEY GO?!
THERE'S NO WAY TO KNOW--OR TO FOLLOW.
WE ALREADY LOST ONE OF OUR OWN WHEN SKITTER DISAPPEARED.
WE'RE NOT LOSING ANOTHER MEMBER OF THIS TEAM.
BUT WE HAVE. SUPERBOY'S GONE.
WHAT DO WE DO NOW, WONDER GIRL?!

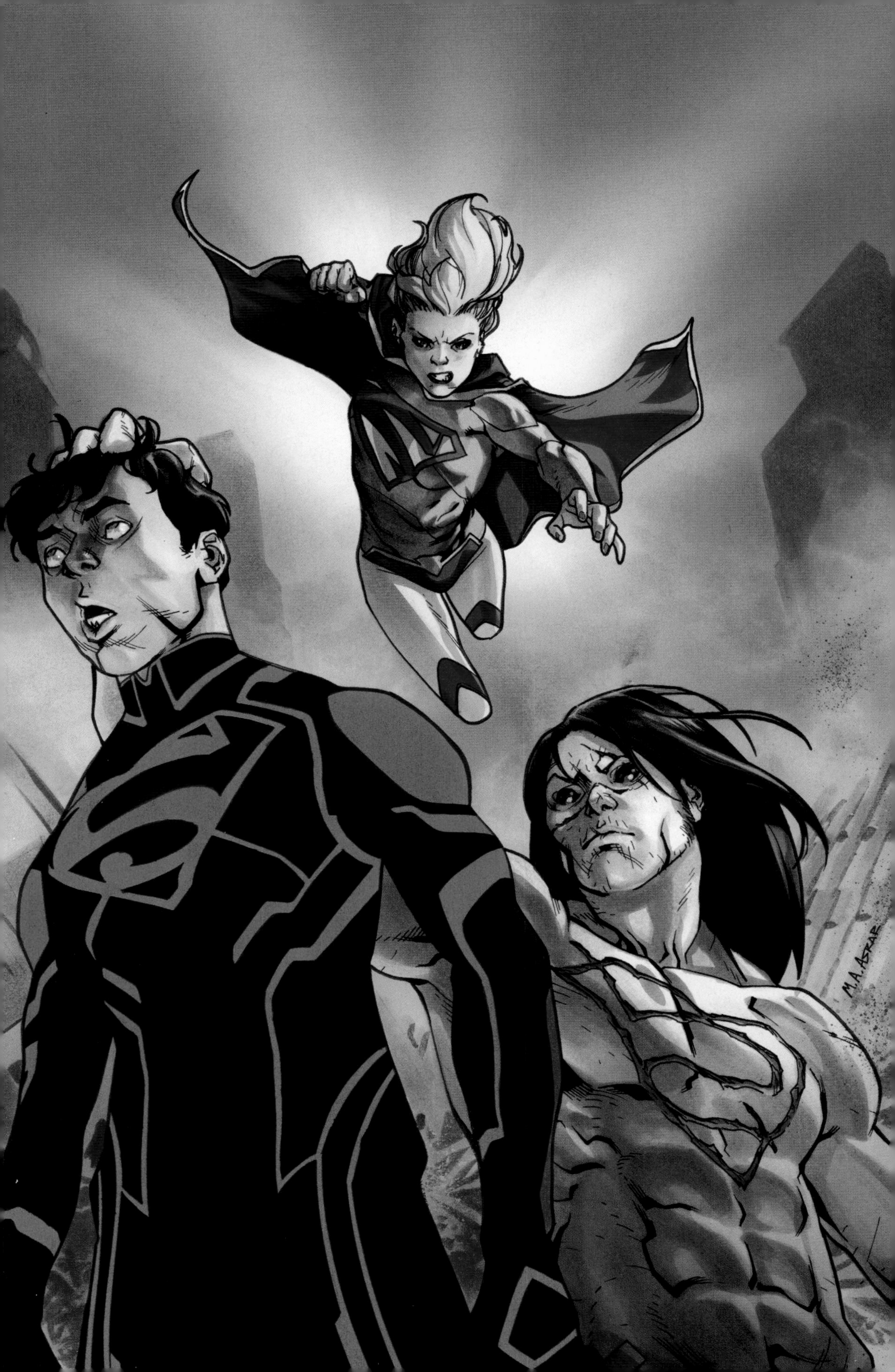
M.A. ASRAR

LAST SON OF KRYPTON

MIKE JOHNSON writer **MAHMUD ASRAR** artist cover art by **MAHMUD ASRAR & DAVE MCCAIG**

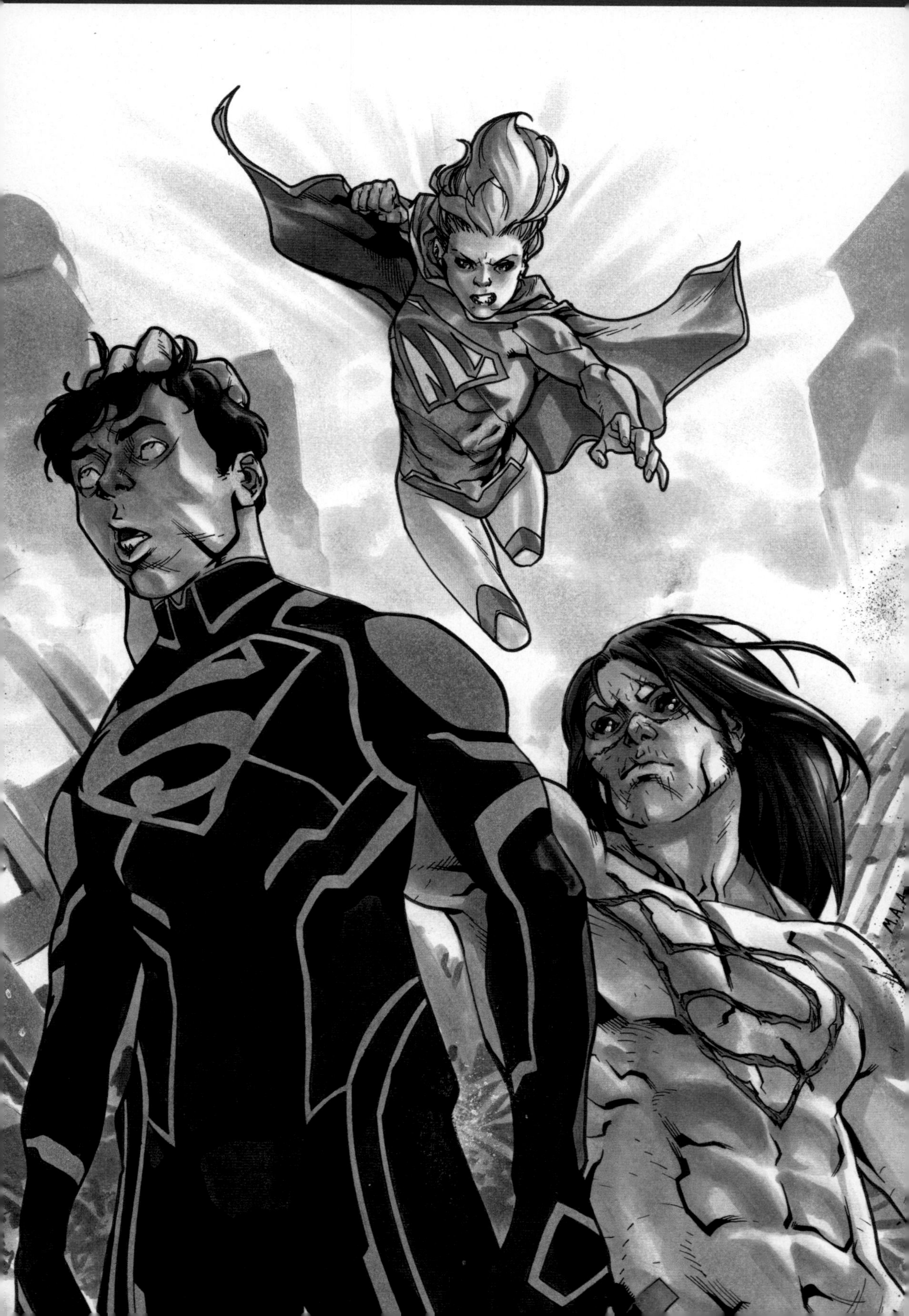
M.A.A

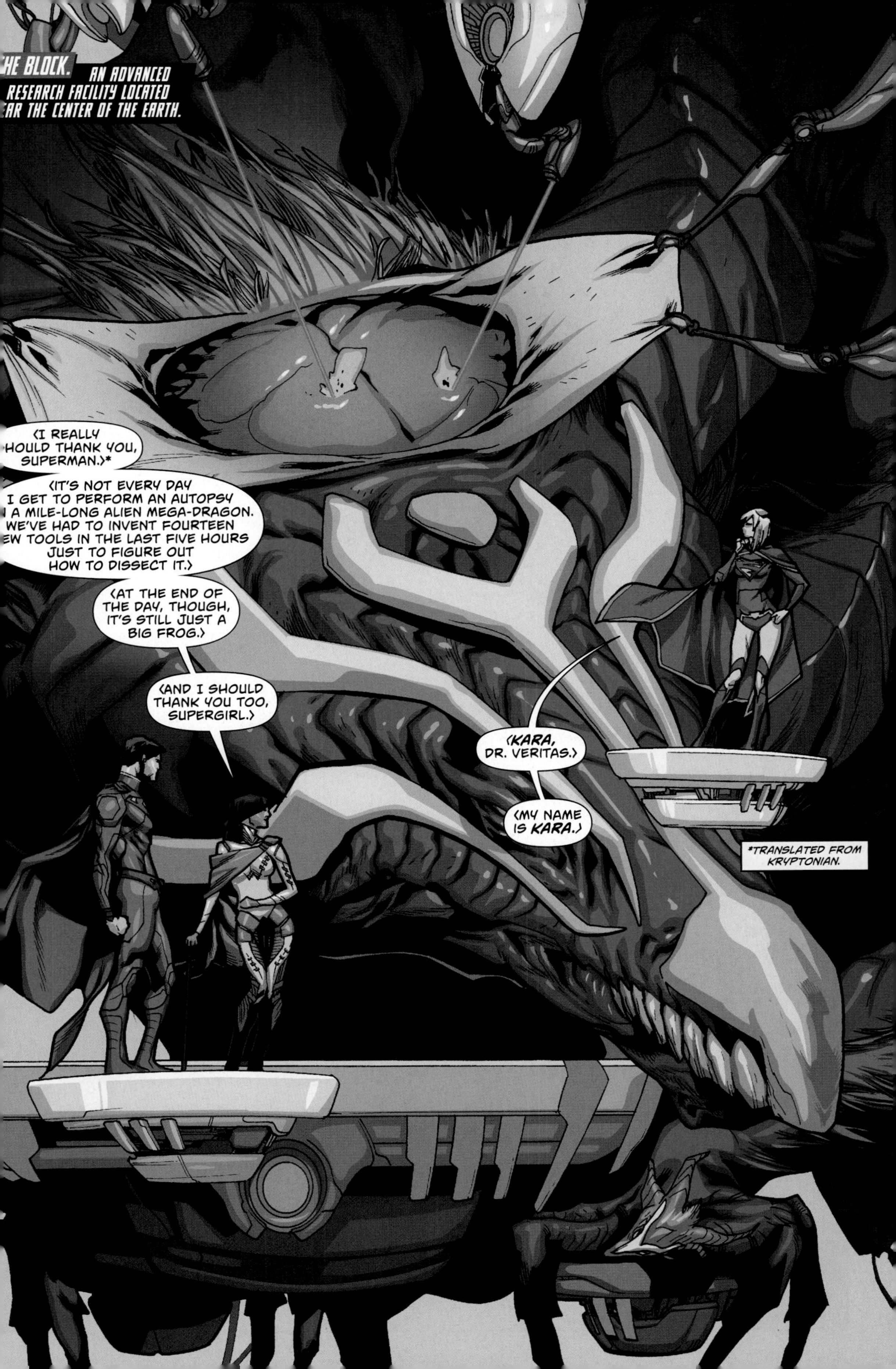
HE BLOCK. AN ADVANCED RESEARCH FACILITY LOCATED AR THE CENTER OF THE EARTH.
‹I REALLY HOULD THANK YOU, SUPERMAN.›*
‹IT'S NOT EVERY DAY I GET TO PERFORM AN AUTOPSY A MILE-LONG ALIEN MEGA-DRAGON. WE'VE HAD TO INVENT FOURTEEN EW TOOLS IN THE LAST FIVE HOURS JUST TO FIGURE OUT HOW TO DISSECT IT.›
‹AT THE END OF THE DAY, THOUGH, IT'S STILL JUST A BIG FROG.›
‹AND I SHOULD THANK YOU TOO, SUPERGIRL.›
‹KARA, DR. VERITAS.›
‹MY NAME IS KARA.›
*TRANSLATED FROM KRYPTONIAN.

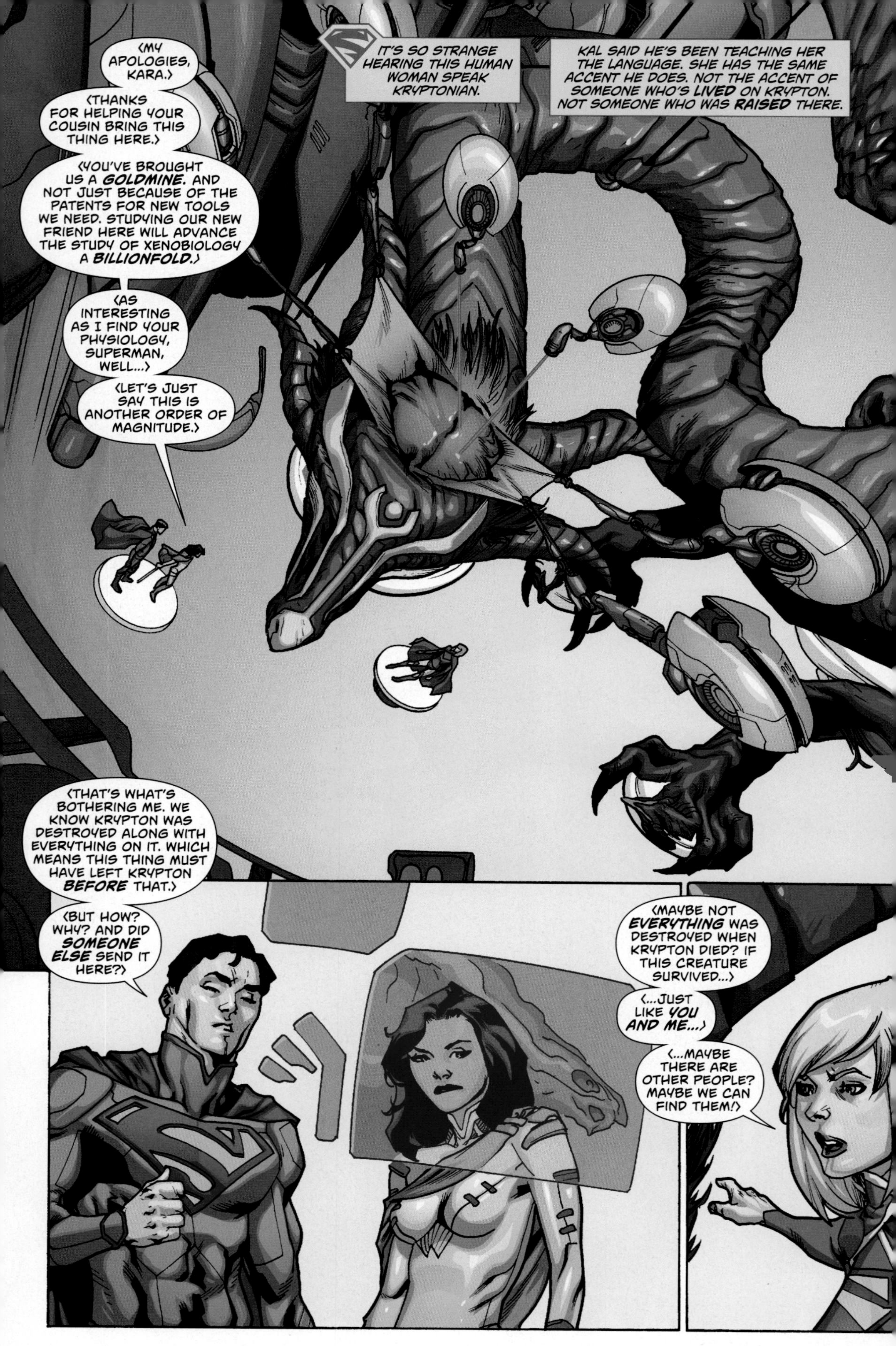
IT'S SO STRANGE HEARING THIS HUMAN WOMAN SPEAK KRYPTONIAN.
KAL SAID HE'S BEEN TEACHING HER THE LANGUAGE. SHE HAS THE SAME ACCENT HE DOES. NOT THE ACCENT OF SOMEONE WHO'S LIVED ON KRYPTON. NOT SOMEONE WHO WAS RAISED THERE.
‹MY APOLOGIES, KARA.›
‹THANKS FOR HELPING YOUR COUSIN BRING THIS THING HERE.›
‹YOU'VE BROUGHT US A GOLDMINE. AND NOT JUST BECAUSE OF THE PATENTS FOR NEW TOOLS WE NEED. STUDYING OUR NEW FRIEND HERE WILL ADVANCE THE STUDY OF XENOBIOLOGY A BILLIONFOLD.›
‹AS INTERESTING AS I FIND YOUR PHYSIOLOGY, SUPERMAN, WELL...›
‹LET'S JUST SAY THIS IS ANOTHER ORDER OF MAGNITUDE.›
‹THAT'S WHAT'S BOTHERING ME. WE KNOW KRYPTON WAS DESTROYED ALONG WITH EVERYTHING ON IT. WHICH MEANS THIS THING MUST HAVE LEFT KRYPTON BEFORE THAT.›
‹BUT HOW? WHY? AND DID SOMEONE ELSE SEND IT HERE?›
‹MAYBE NOT EVERYTHING WAS DESTROYED WHEN KRYPTON DIED? IF THIS CREATURE SURVIVED...›
‹...JUST LIKE YOU AND ME...›
‹...MAYBE THERE ARE OTHER PEOPLE? MAYBE WE CAN FIND THEM!›

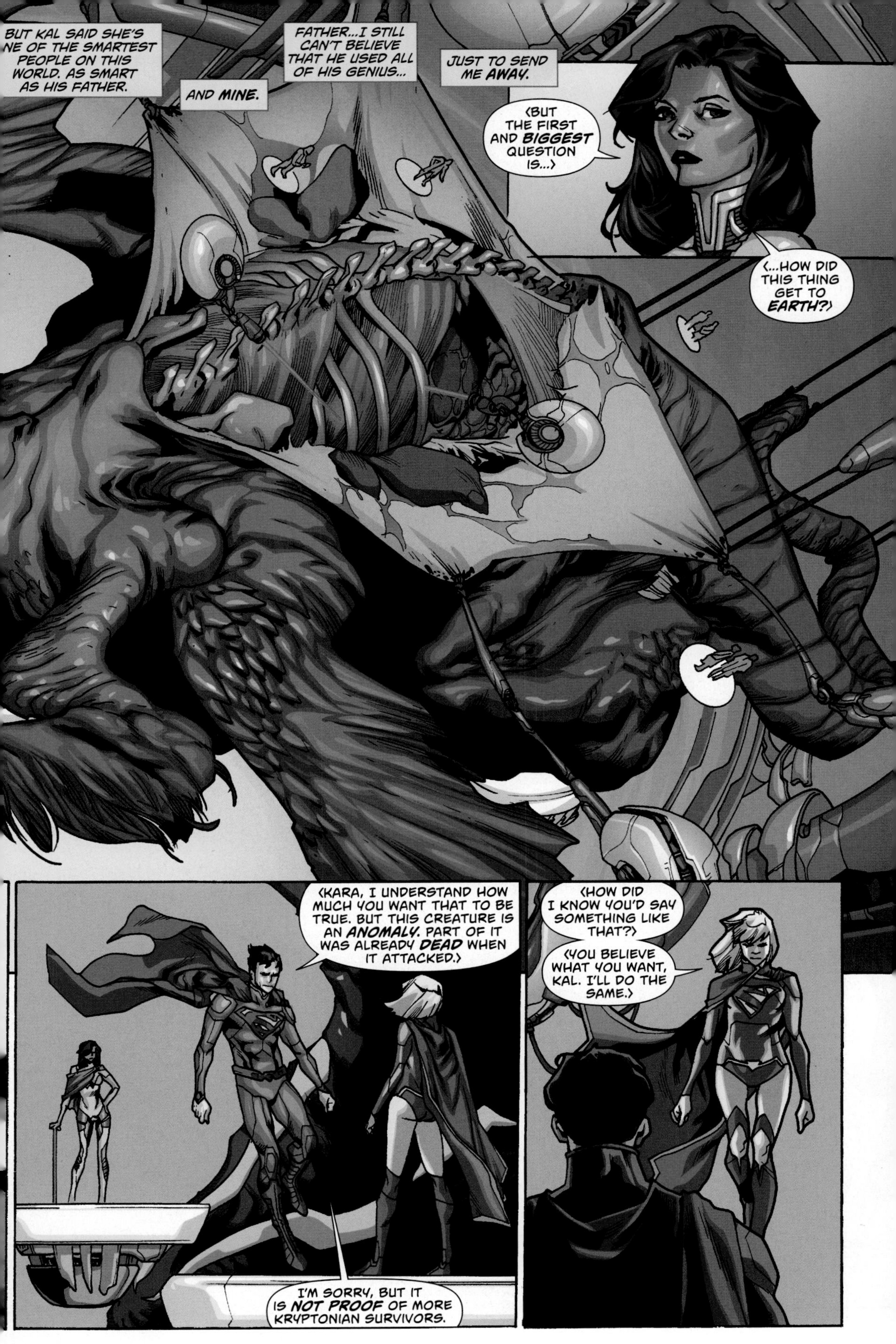
BUT KAL SAID SHE'S NE OF THE SMARTEST PEOPLE ON THIS WORLD. AS SMART AS HIS FATHER.
AND MINE.
FATHER...I STILL CAN'T BELIEVE THAT HE USED ALL OF HIS GENIUS...
JUST TO SEND ME AWAY.
‹BUT THE FIRST AND BIGGEST QUESTION IS...›
‹...HOW DID THIS THING GET TO EARTH?›
‹KARA, I UNDERSTAND HOW MUCH YOU WANT THAT TO BE TRUE. BUT THIS CREATURE IS AN ANOMALY. PART OF IT WAS ALREADY DEAD WHEN IT ATTACKED.›
I'M SORRY, BUT IT IS NOT PROOF OF MORE KRYPTONIAN SURVIVORS.
‹HOW DID I KNOW YOU'D SAY SOMETHING LIKE THAT?›
‹YOU BELIEVE WHAT YOU WANT, KAL. I'LL DO THE SAME.›

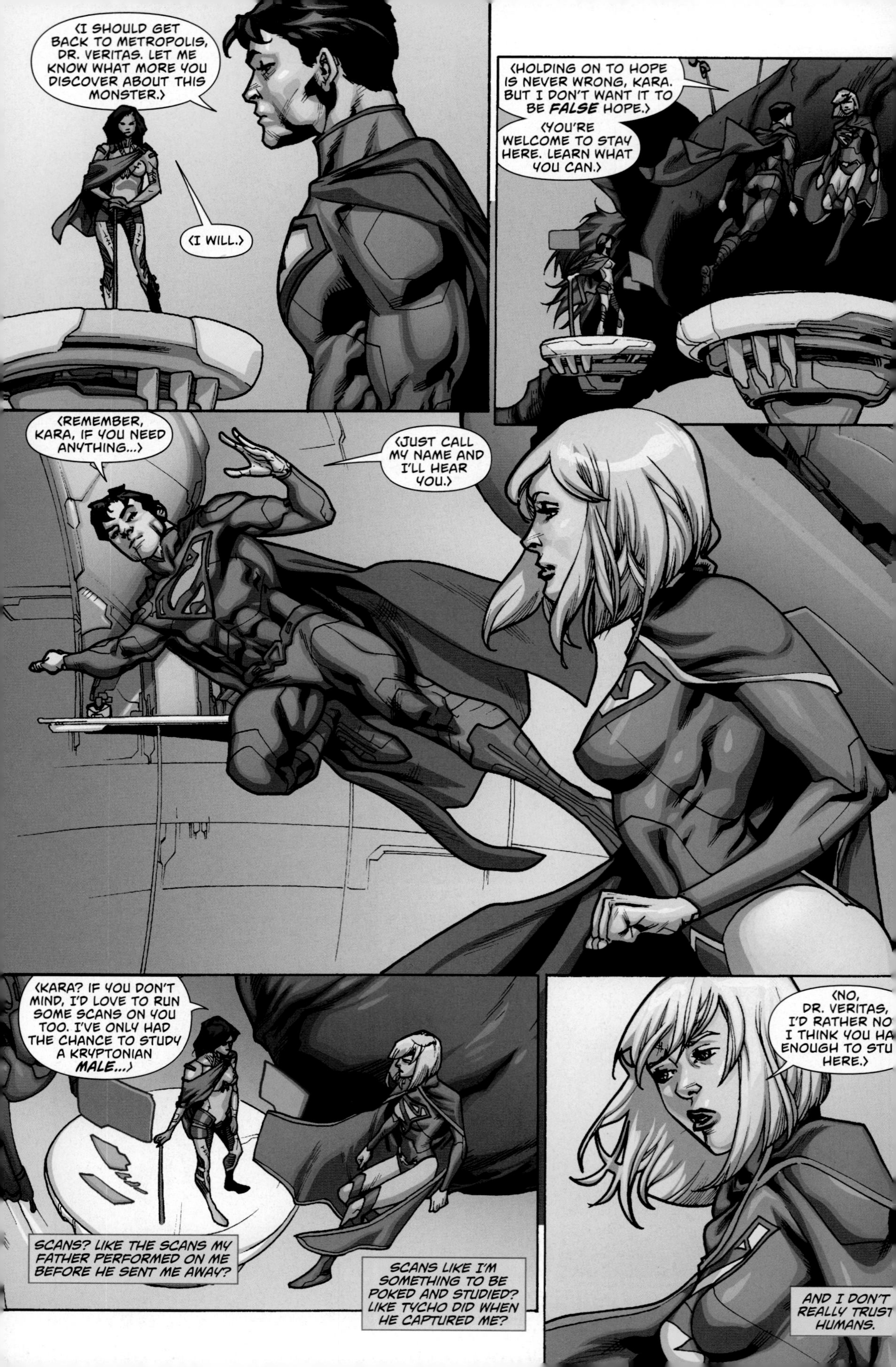

‹I SHOULD GET BACK TO METROPOLIS, DR. VERITAS. LET ME KNOW WHAT MORE YOU DISCOVER ABOUT THIS MONSTER.›
‹I WILL.›
‹HOLDING ON TO HOPE IS NEVER WRONG, KARA. BUT I DON'T WANT IT TO BE FALSE HOPE.›
‹YOU'RE WELCOME TO STAY HERE. LEARN WHAT YOU CAN.›
‹REMEMBER, KARA, IF YOU NEED ANYTHING...›
‹JUST CALL MY NAME AND I'LL HEAR YOU.›
‹KARA? IF YOU DON'T MIND, I'D LOVE TO RUN SOME SCANS ON YOU TOO. I'VE ONLY HAD THE CHANCE TO STUDY A KRYPTONIAN MALE...›
SCANS? LIKE THE SCANS MY FATHER PERFORMED ON ME BEFORE HE SENT ME AWAY?
SCANS LIKE I'M SOMETHING TO BE POKED AND STUDIED? LIKE TYCHO DID WHEN HE CAPTURED ME?
‹NO, DR. VERITAS, I'D RATHER NO I THINK YOU HA ENOUGH TO STU HERE.›
AND I DON'T REALLY TRUST HUMANS.

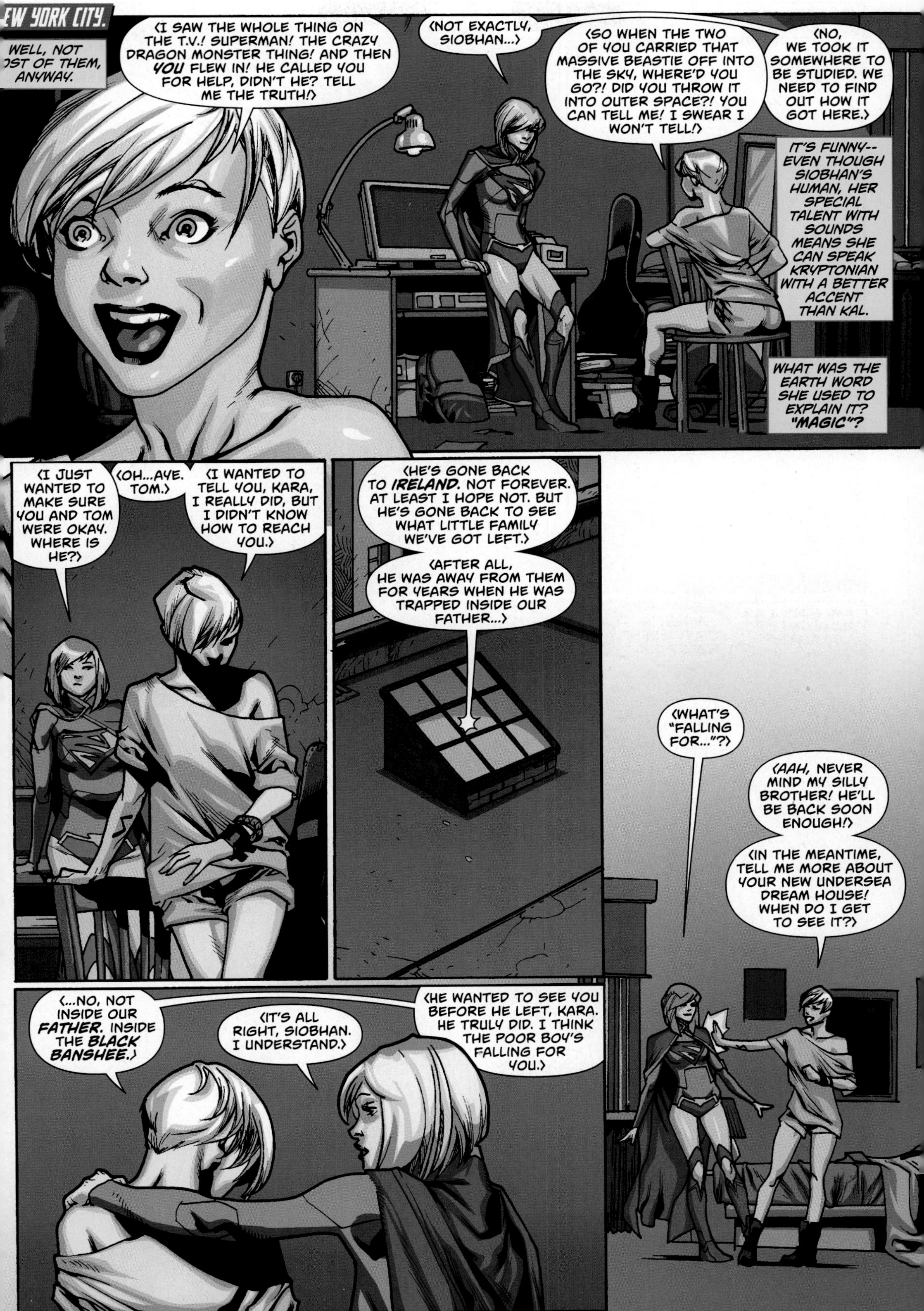

EW YORK CITY.
WELL, NOT
OST OF THEM,
ANYWAY.
‹I SAW THE WHOLE THING ON THE T.V.! SUPERMAN! THE CRAZY DRAGON MONSTER THING! AND THEN YOU FLEW IN! HE CALLED YOU FOR HELP, DIDN'T HE? TELL ME THE TRUTH!›
‹NOT EXACTLY, SIOBHAN...›
‹SO WHEN THE TWO OF YOU CARRIED THAT MASSIVE BEASTIE OFF INTO THE SKY, WHERE'D YOU GO?! DID YOU THROW IT INTO OUTER SPACE?! YOU CAN TELL ME! I SWEAR I WON'T TELL!›
‹NO, WE TOOK IT SOMEWHERE TO BE STUDIED. WE NEED TO FIND OUT HOW IT GOT HERE.›
IT'S FUNNY-- EVEN THOUGH SIOBHAN'S HUMAN, HER SPECIAL TALENT WITH SOUNDS MEANS SHE CAN SPEAK KRYPTONIAN WITH A BETTER ACCENT THAN KAL.
WHAT WAS THE EARTH WORD SHE USED TO EXPLAIN IT? "MAGIC"?
‹I JUST WANTED TO MAKE SURE YOU AND TOM WERE OKAY. WHERE IS HE?›
‹OH...AYE. TOM.›
‹I WANTED TO TELL YOU, KARA, I REALLY DID, BUT I DIDN'T KNOW HOW TO REACH YOU.›
‹HE'S GONE BACK TO IRELAND. NOT FOREVER. AT LEAST I HOPE NOT. BUT HE'S GONE BACK TO SEE WHAT LITTLE FAMILY WE'VE GOT LEFT.›
‹AFTER ALL, HE WAS AWAY FROM THEM FOR YEARS WHEN HE WAS TRAPPED INSIDE OUR FATHER...›
‹...NO, NOT INSIDE OUR FATHER. INSIDE THE BLACK BANSHEE.›
‹IT'S ALL RIGHT, SIOBHAN. I UNDERSTAND.›
‹HE WANTED TO SEE YOU BEFORE HE LEFT, KARA. HE TRULY DID. I THINK THE POOR BOY'S FALLING FOR YOU.›
‹WHAT'S "FALLING FOR..."?›
‹AAH, NEVER MIND MY SILLY BROTHER! HE'LL BE BACK SOON ENOUGH!›
‹IN THE MEANTIME, TELL ME MORE ABOUT YOUR NEW UNDERSEA DREAM HOUSE! WHEN DO I GET TO SEE IT?›

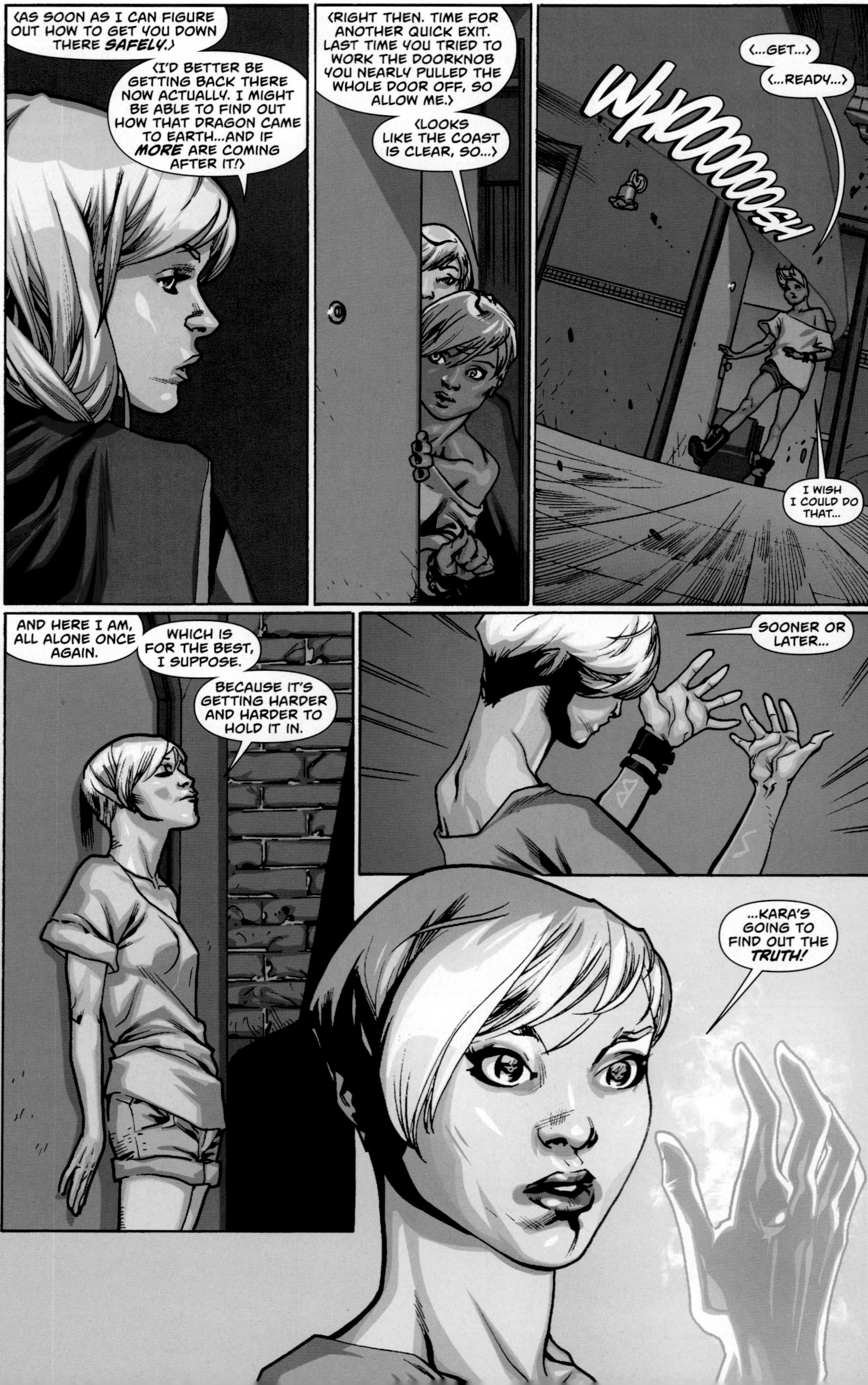
‹AS SOON AS I CAN FIGURE OUT HOW TO GET YOU DOWN THERE SAFELY.›
‹I'D BETTER BE GETTING BACK THERE NOW ACTUALLY. I MIGHT BE ABLE TO FIND OUT HOW THAT DRAGON CAME TO EARTH...AND IF MORE ARE COMING AFTER IT!›
‹RIGHT THEN. TIME FOR ANOTHER QUICK EXIT. LAST TIME YOU TRIED TO WORK THE DOORKNOB YOU NEARLY PULLED THE WHOLE DOOR OFF, SO ALLOW ME.›
‹LOOKS LIKE THE COAST IS CLEAR, SO...›
WHOOOOOOSH
‹...GET...›
‹...READY...›
I WISH I COULD DO THAT...
AND HERE I AM, ALL ALONE ONCE AGAIN.
WHICH IS FOR THE BEST, I SUPPOSE.
BECAUSE IT'S GETTING HARDER AND HARDER TO HOLD IT IN.
SOONER OR LATER...
...KARA'S GOING TO FIND OUT THE TRUTH!

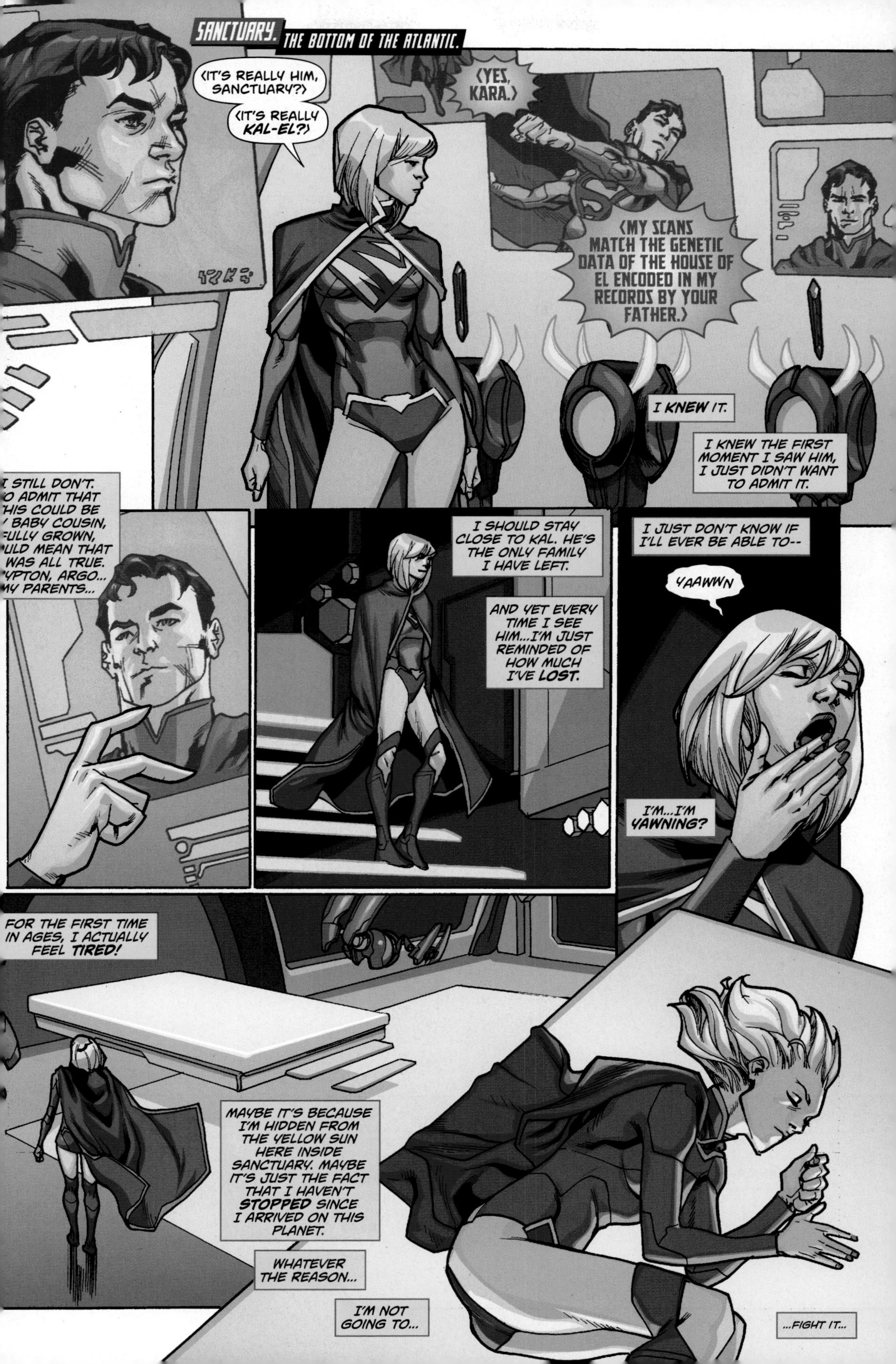
SANCTUARY. THE BOTTOM OF THE ATLANTIC.
‹IT'S REALLY HIM, SANCTUARY?›
‹IT'S REALLY KAL-EL?›
‹YES, KARA.›
‹MY SCANS MATCH THE GENETIC DATA OF THE HOUSE OF EL ENCODED IN MY RECORDS BY YOUR FATHER.›
I KNEW IT.
I KNEW THE FIRST MOMENT I SAW HIM, I JUST DIDN'T WANT TO ADMIT IT.
I STILL DON'T. O ADMIT THAT THIS COULD BE BABY COUSIN, FULLY GROWN, ULD MEAN THAT WAS ALL TRUE. YPTON, ARGO... MY PARENTS...
I SHOULD STAY CLOSE TO KAL. HE'S THE ONLY FAMILY I HAVE LEFT.
AND YET EVERY TIME I SEE HIM...I'M JUST REMINDED OF HOW MUCH I'VE LOST.
I JUST DON'T KNOW IF I'LL EVER BE ABLE TO--
YAAWWN
I'M...I'M YAWNING?
FOR THE FIRST TIME IN AGES, I ACTUALLY FEEL TIRED!
MAYBE IT'S BECAUSE I'M HIDDEN FROM THE YELLOW SUN HERE INSIDE SANCTUARY. MAYBE IT'S JUST THE FACT THAT I HAVEN'T STOPPED SINCE I ARRIVED ON THIS PLANET.
WHATEVER THE REASON...
I'M NOT GOING TO...
...FIGHT IT...

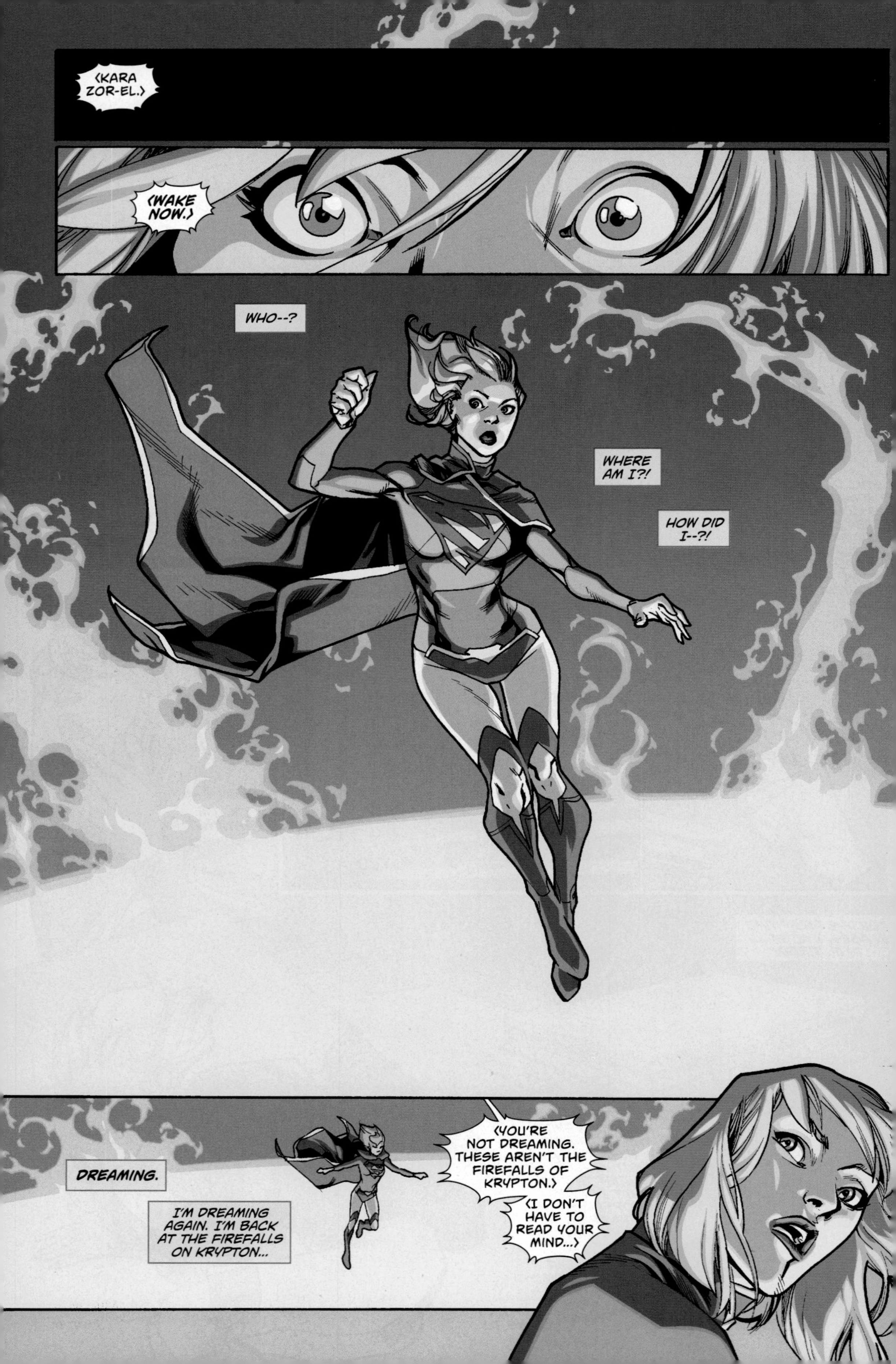

‹KARA ZOR-EL.›
‹WAKE NOW.›
WHO--?
WHERE AM I?!
HOW DID I--?!
DREAMING.
I'M DREAMING AGAIN. I'M BACK AT THE FIREFALLS ON KRYPTON...
‹YOU'RE NOT DREAMING. THESE AREN'T THE FIREFALLS OF KRYPTON.›
‹I DON'T HAVE TO READ YOUR MIND...›

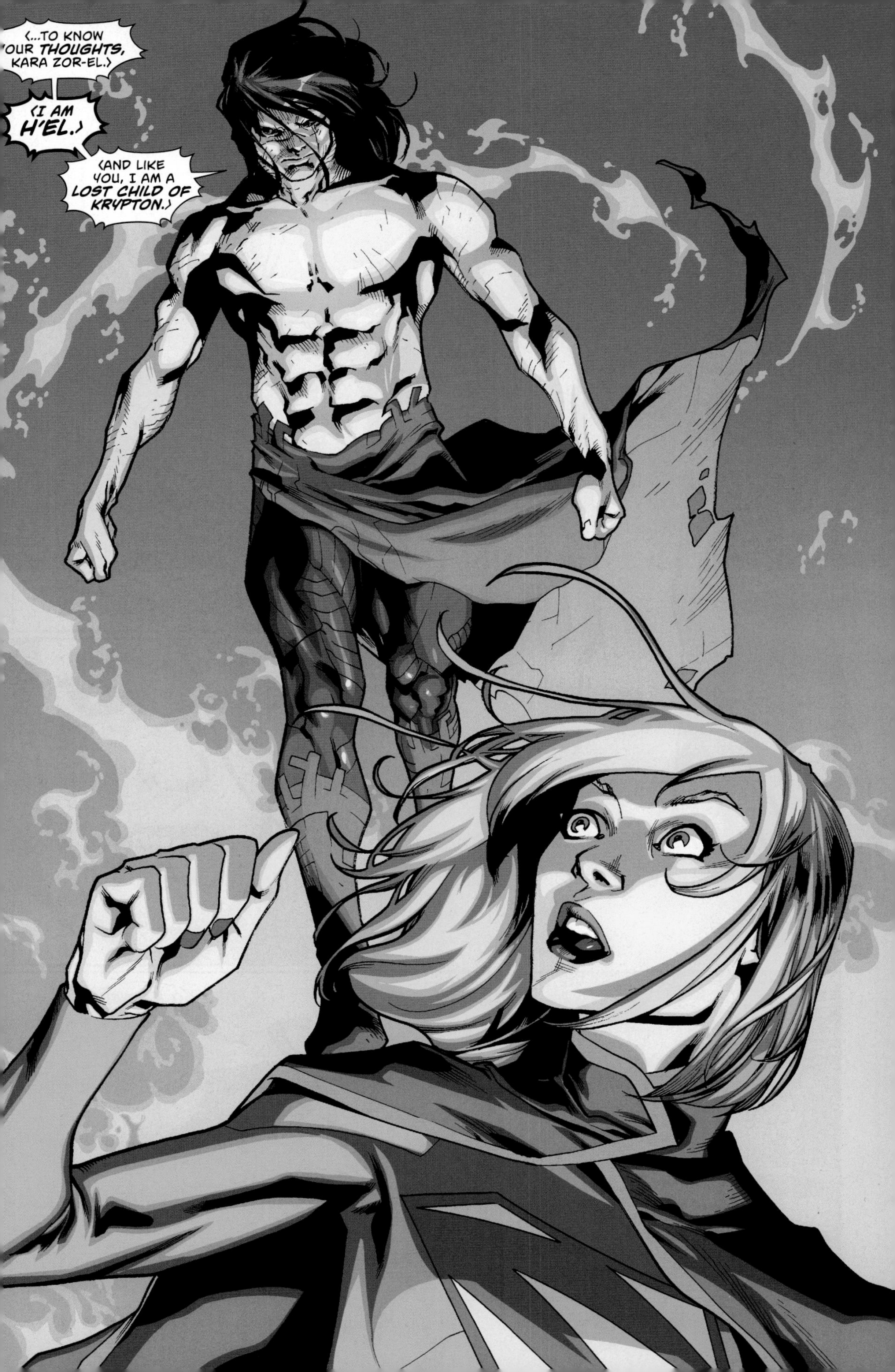
‹...TO KNOW YOUR THOUGHTS, KARA ZOR-EL.›
‹I AM H'EL.›
‹AND LIKE YOU, I AM A LOST CHILD OF KRYPTON.›

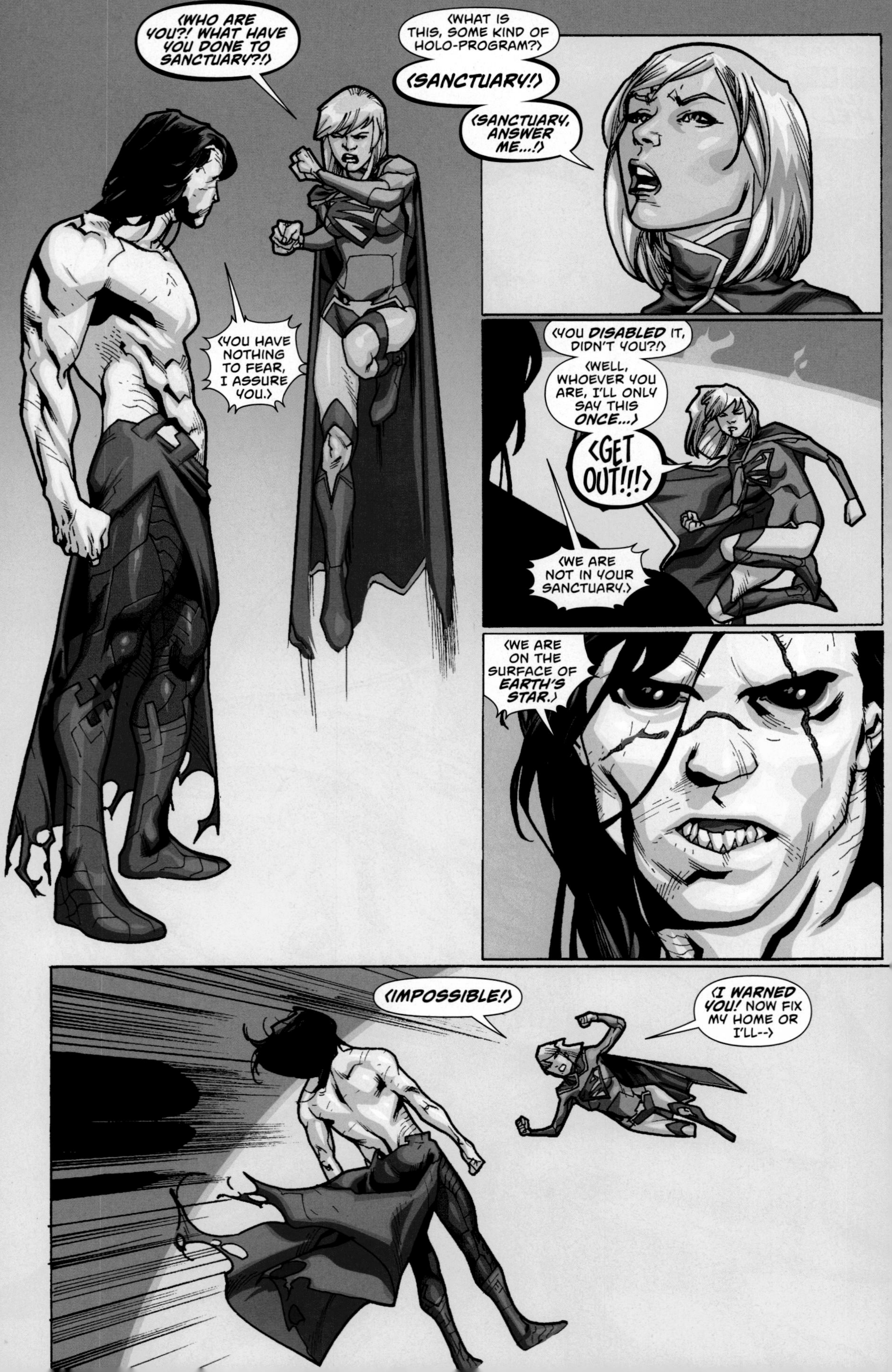
‹WHO ARE YOU?! WHAT HAVE YOU DONE TO SANCTUARY?!›
‹YOU HAVE NOTHING TO FEAR, I ASSURE YOU.›
‹WHAT IS THIS, SOME KIND OF HOLO-PROGRAM?›
‹SANCTUARY!›
‹SANCTUARY, ANSWER ME...!›
‹YOU DISABLED IT, DIDN'T YOU?!›
‹WELL, WHOEVER YOU ARE, I'LL ONLY SAY THIS ONCE...›
‹GET OUT!!!›
‹WE ARE NOT IN YOUR SANCTUARY.›
‹WE ARE ON THE SURFACE OF EARTH'S STAR.›
‹IMPOSSIBLE!›
‹I WARNED YOU! NOW FIX MY HOME OR I'LL--›

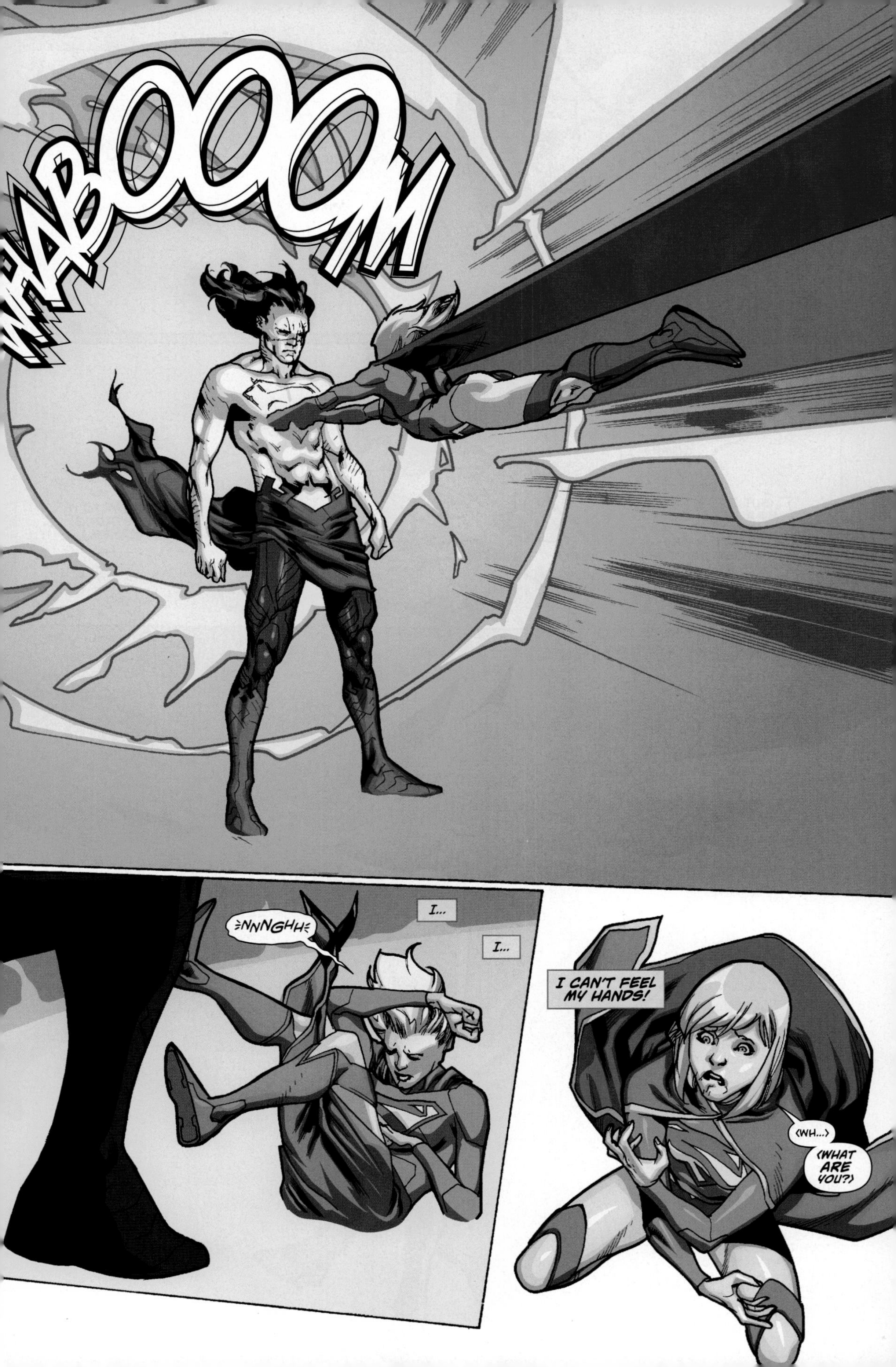
WHABOOOM
NNNGHH
I...
I...
I CAN'T FEEL MY HANDS!
‹WH...›
‹WHAT ARE YOU?›

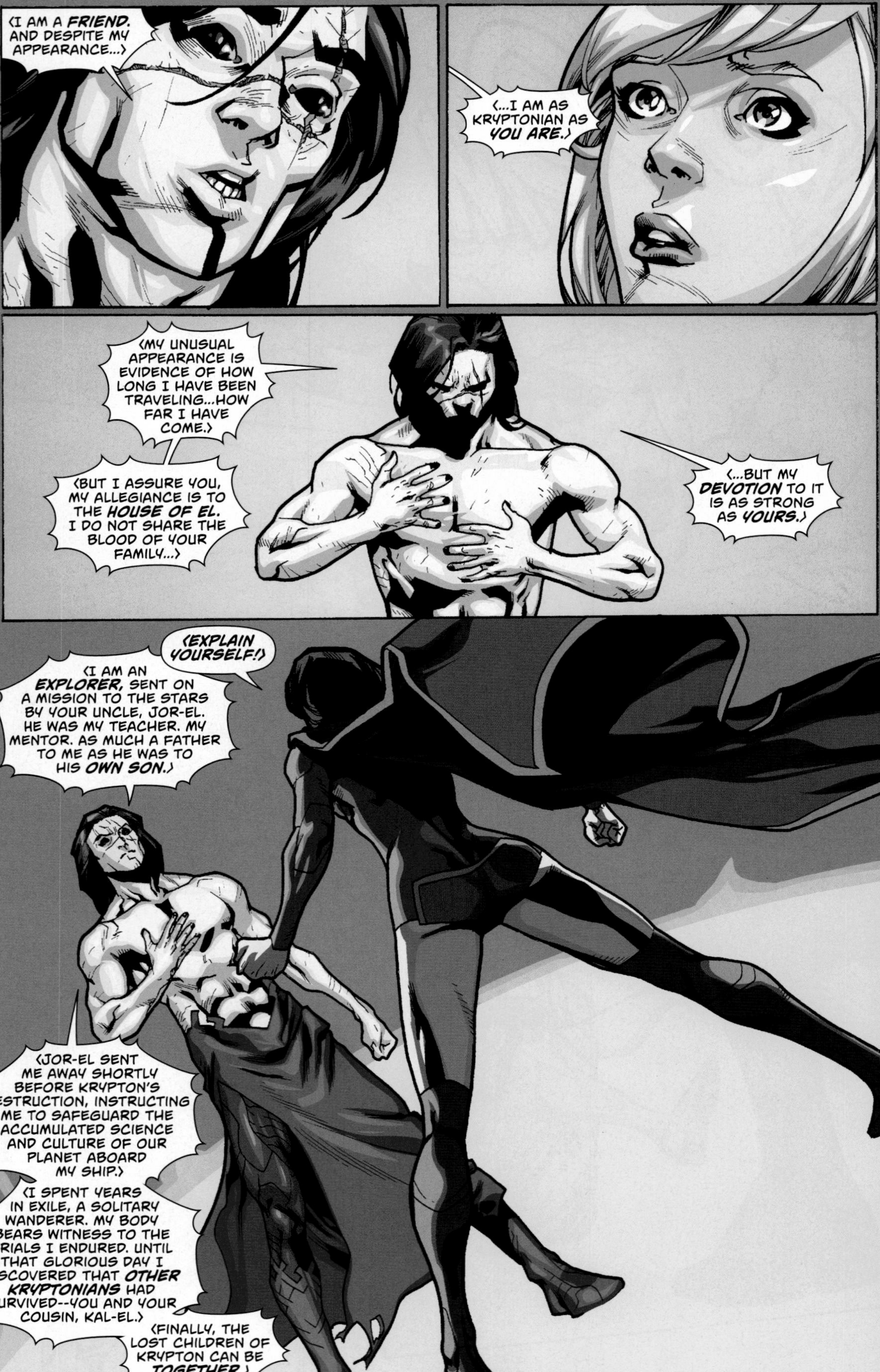
‹I AM A FRIEND. AND DESPITE MY APPEARANCE...›
‹...I AM AS KRYPTONIAN AS YOU ARE.›
‹MY UNUSUAL APPEARANCE IS EVIDENCE OF HOW LONG I HAVE BEEN TRAVELING...HOW FAR I HAVE COME.›
‹BUT I ASSURE YOU, MY ALLEGIANCE IS TO THE HOUSE OF EL. I DO NOT SHARE THE BLOOD OF YOUR FAMILY...›
‹...BUT MY DEVOTION TO IT IS AS STRONG AS YOURS.›
‹EXPLAIN YOURSELF!›
‹I AM AN EXPLORER, SENT ON A MISSION TO THE STARS BY YOUR UNCLE, JOR-EL. HE WAS MY TEACHER. MY MENTOR. AS MUCH A FATHER TO ME AS HE WAS TO HIS OWN SON.›
‹JOR-EL SENT ME AWAY SHORTLY BEFORE KRYPTON'S DESTRUCTION, INSTRUCTING ME TO SAFEGUARD THE ACCUMULATED SCIENCE AND CULTURE OF OUR PLANET ABOARD MY SHIP.›
‹I SPENT YEARS IN EXILE, A SOLITARY WANDERER. MY BODY BEARS WITNESS TO THE TRIALS I ENDURED. UNTIL THAT GLORIOUS DAY I DISCOVERED THAT OTHER KRYPTONIANS HAD SURVIVED--YOU AND YOUR COUSIN, KAL-EL.›
‹FINALLY, THE LOST CHILDREN OF KRYPTON CAN BE TOGETHER.›

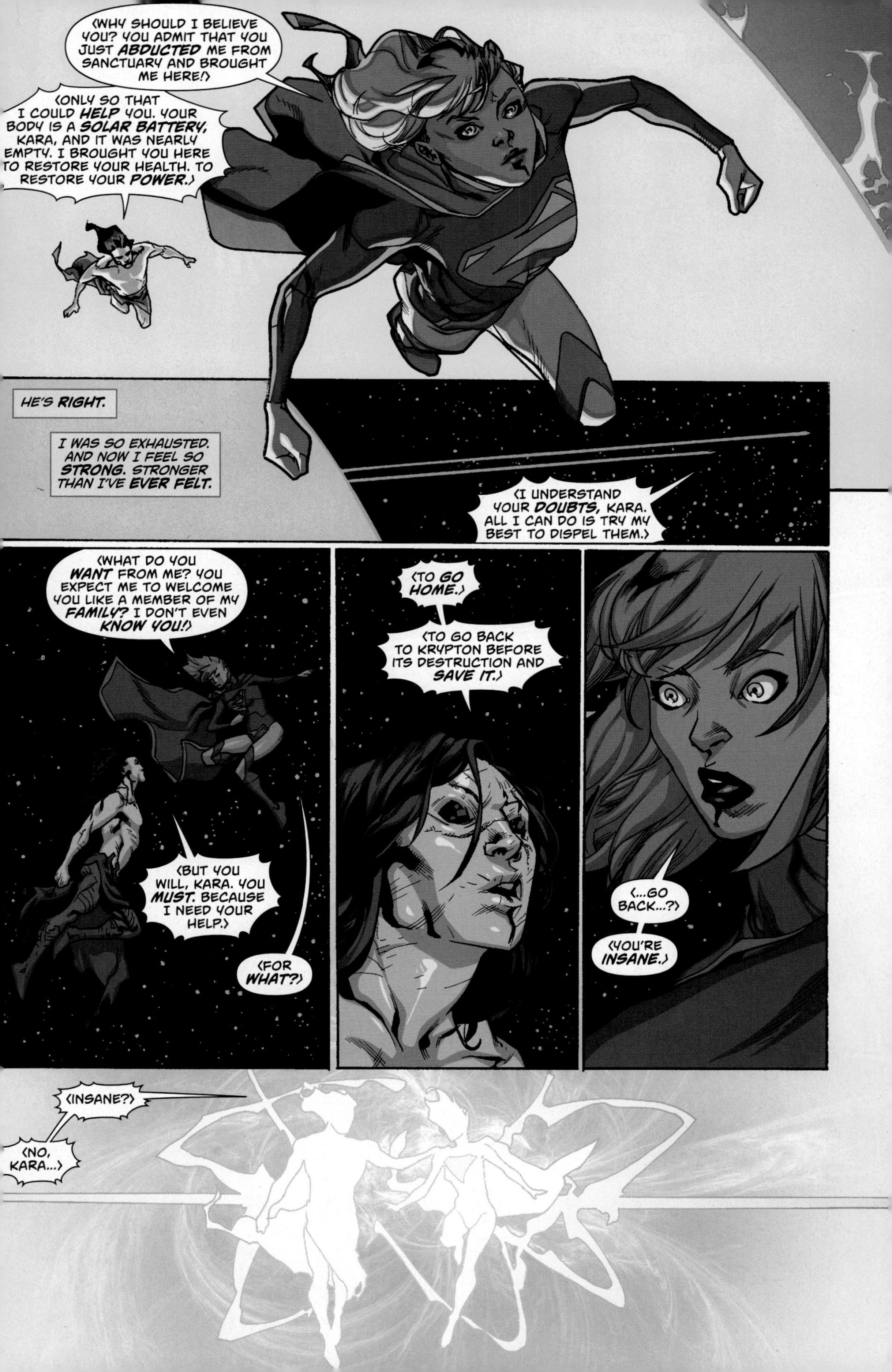
(WHY SHOULD I BELIEVE YOU? YOU ADMIT THAT YOU JUST ABDUCTED ME FROM SANCTUARY AND BROUGHT ME HERE!)
(ONLY SO THAT I COULD HELP YOU. YOUR BODY IS A SOLAR BATTERY, KARA, AND IT WAS NEARLY EMPTY. I BROUGHT YOU HERE TO RESTORE YOUR HEALTH. TO RESTORE YOUR POWER.)
HE'S RIGHT.
I WAS SO EXHAUSTED. AND NOW I FEEL SO STRONG. STRONGER THAN I'VE EVER FELT.
(I UNDERSTAND YOUR DOUBTS, KARA. ALL I CAN DO IS TRY MY BEST TO DISPEL THEM.)
(WHAT DO YOU WANT FROM ME? YOU EXPECT ME TO WELCOME YOU LIKE A MEMBER OF MY FAMILY? I DON'T EVEN KNOW YOU!)
(BUT YOU WILL, KARA. YOU MUST. BECAUSE I NEED YOUR HELP.)
(FOR WHAT?)
(TO GO HOME.)
(TO GO BACK TO KRYPTON BEFORE ITS DESTRUCTION AND SAVE IT.)
(...GO BACK...?)
(YOU'RE INSANE.)
(INSANE?)
(NO, KARA...)

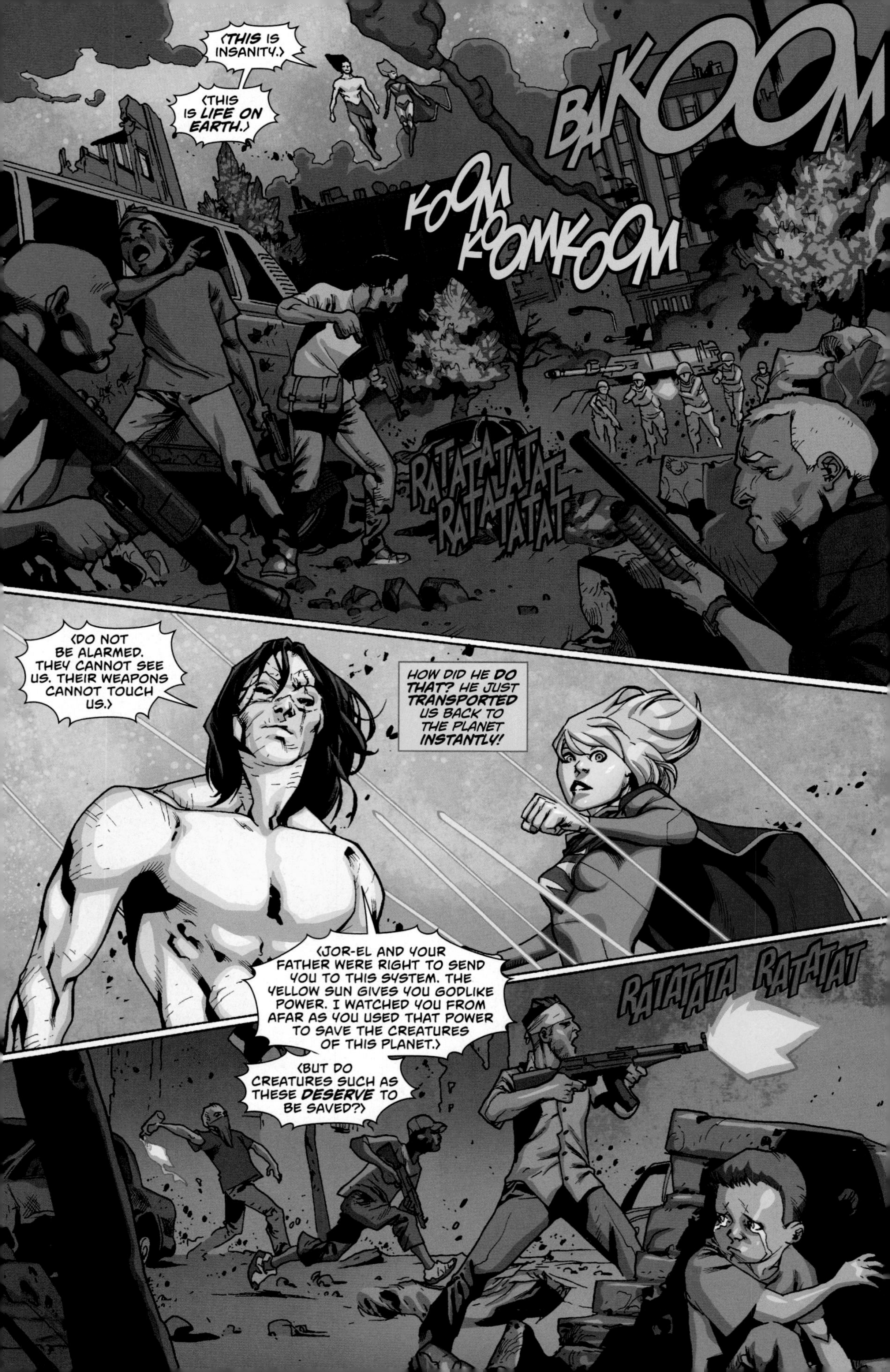

⟨THIS IS INSANITY.⟩
⟨THIS IS LIFE ON EARTH.⟩
BAKOOM
KOOM KOOMKOOM
RATATATATAT RATATATAT
⟨DO NOT BE ALARMED. THEY CANNOT SEE US. THEIR WEAPONS CANNOT TOUCH US.⟩
HOW DID HE DO THAT? HE JUST TRANSPORTED US BACK TO THE PLANET INSTANTLY!
⟨JOR-EL AND YOUR FATHER WERE RIGHT TO SEND YOU TO THIS SYSTEM. THE YELLOW SUN GIVES YOU GODLIKE POWER. I WATCHED YOU FROM AFAR AS YOU USED THAT POWER TO SAVE THE CREATURES OF THIS PLANET.⟩
RATATATA RATATAT
⟨BUT DO CREATURES SUCH AS THESE DESERVE TO BE SAVED?⟩

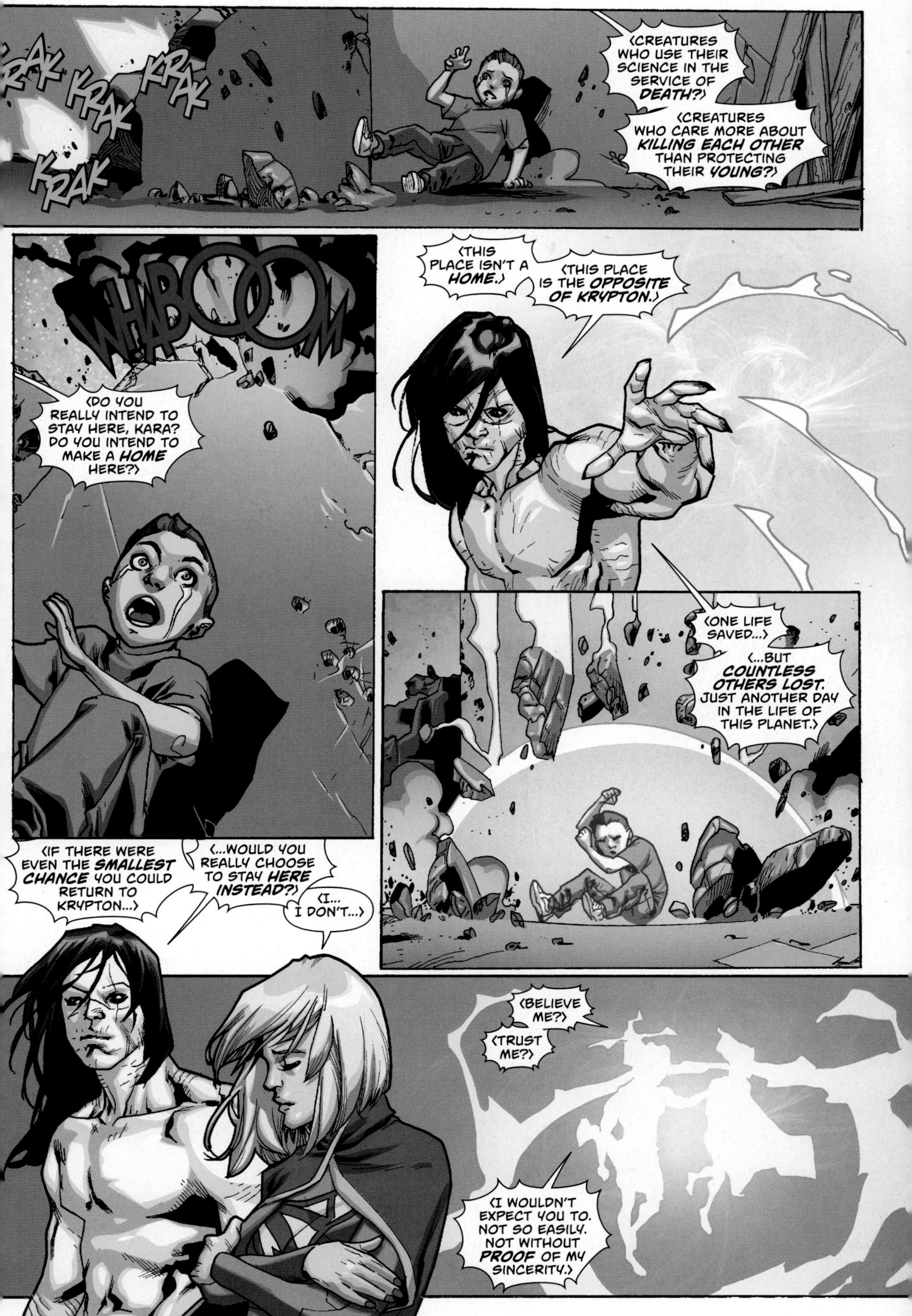
KRAK KRAK KRAK KRAK
‹CREATURES WHO USE THEIR SCIENCE IN THE SERVICE OF DEATH?›
‹CREATURES WHO CARE MORE ABOUT KILLING EACH OTHER THAN PROTECTING THEIR YOUNG?›
WHABOOOM
‹DO YOU REALLY INTEND TO STAY HERE, KARA? DO YOU INTEND TO MAKE A HOME HERE?›
‹THIS PLACE ISN'T A HOME.›
‹THIS PLACE IS THE OPPOSITE OF KRYPTON.›
‹ONE LIFE SAVED...›
‹...BUT COUNTLESS OTHERS LOST. JUST ANOTHER DAY IN THE LIFE OF THIS PLANET.›
‹IF THERE WERE EVEN THE SMALLEST CHANCE YOU COULD RETURN TO KRYPTON...›
‹...WOULD YOU REALLY CHOOSE TO STAY HERE INSTEAD?›
‹I... I DON'T...›
‹BELIEVE ME?›
‹TRUST ME?›
‹I WOULDN'T EXPECT YOU TO. NOT SO EASILY. NOT WITHOUT PROOF OF MY SINCERITY.›

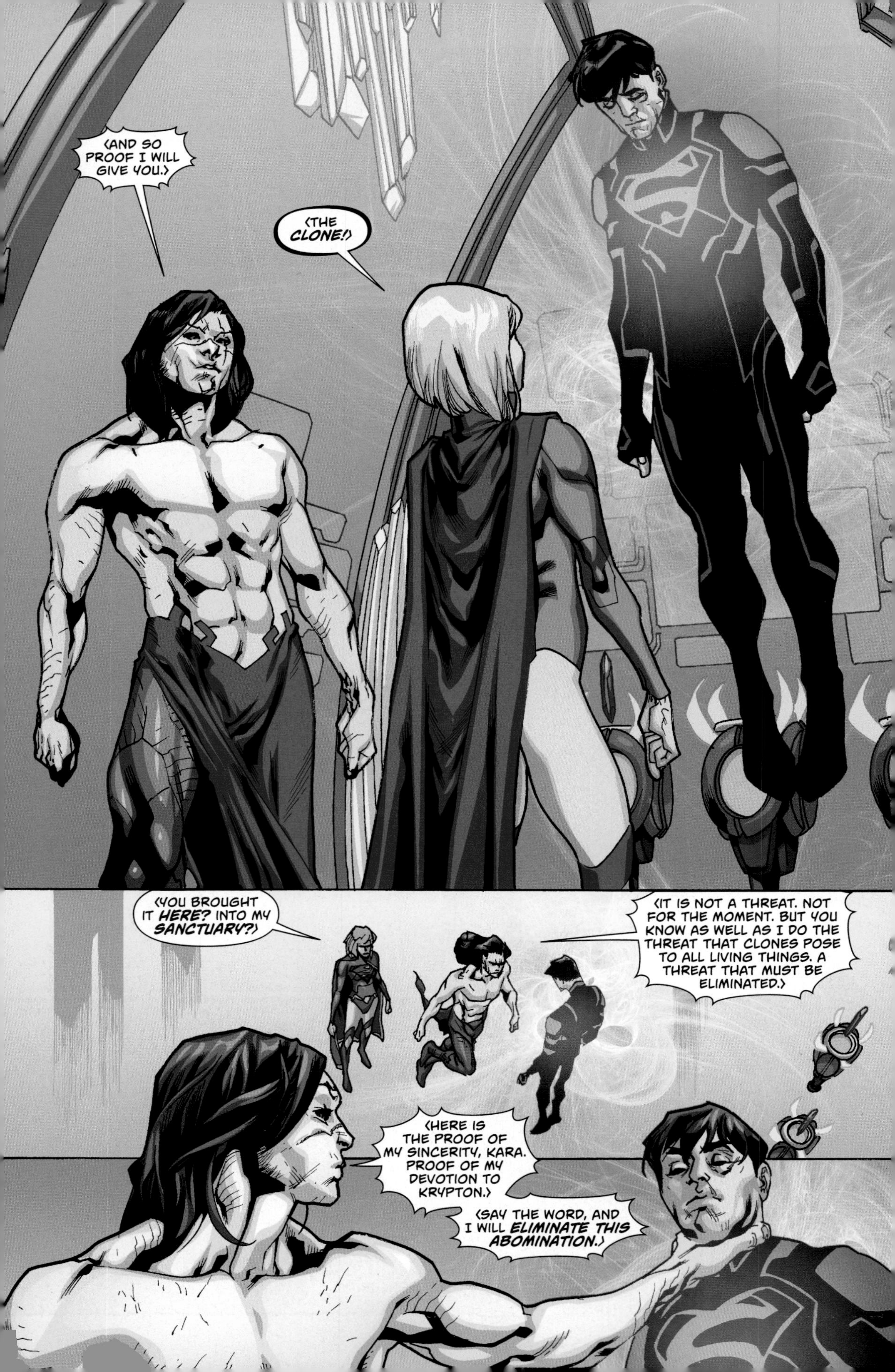
‹AND SO PROOF I WILL GIVE YOU.›
‹THE CLONE!›
‹YOU BROUGHT IT HERE? INTO MY SANCTUARY?›
‹IT IS NOT A THREAT. NOT FOR THE MOMENT. BUT YOU KNOW AS WELL AS I DO THE THREAT THAT CLONES POSE TO ALL LIVING THINGS. A THREAT THAT MUST BE ELIMINATED.›
‹HERE IS THE PROOF OF MY SINCERITY, KARA. PROOF OF MY DEVOTION TO KRYPTON.›
‹SAY THE WORD, AND I WILL ELIMINATE THIS ABOMINATION.›

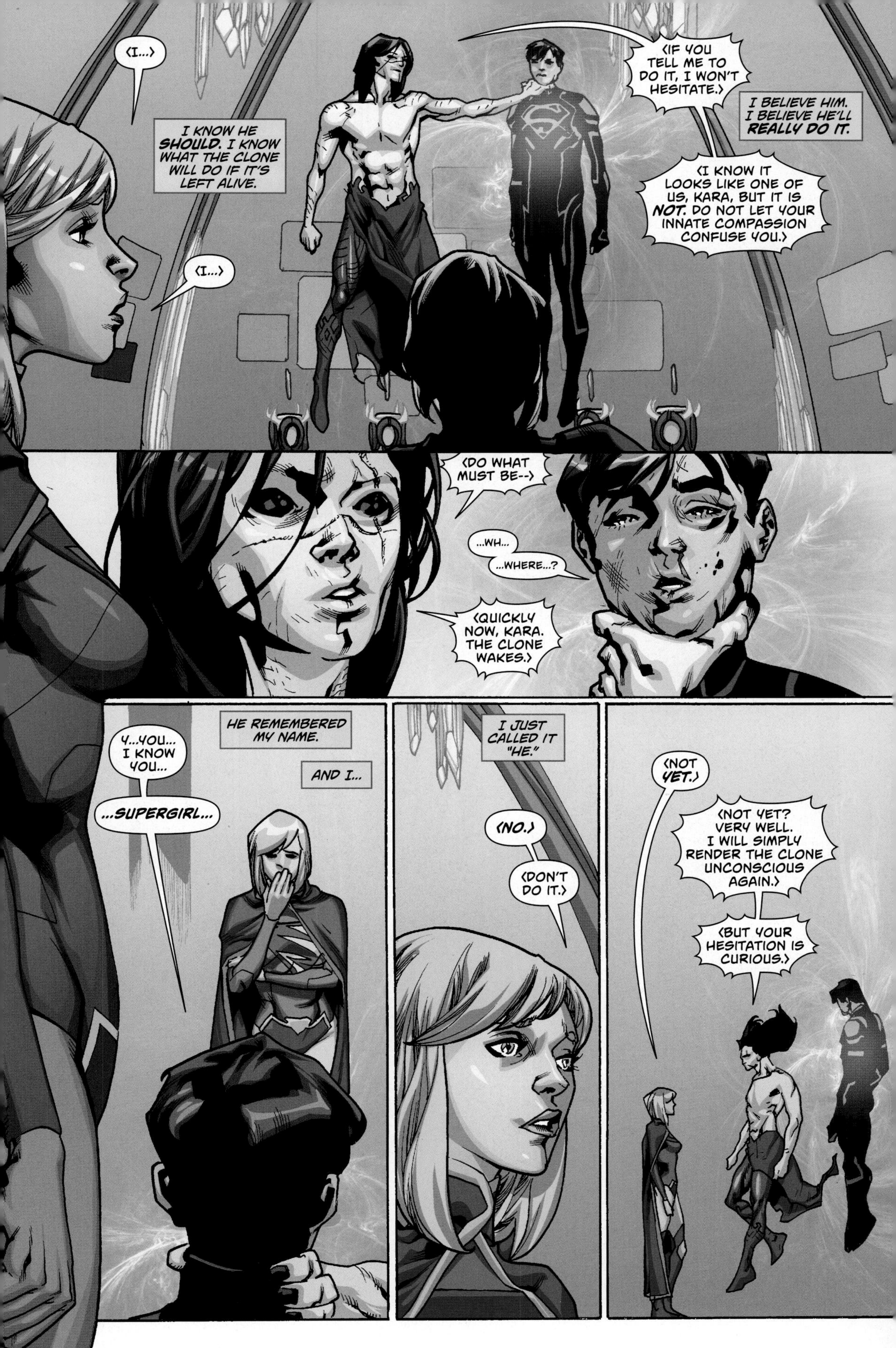

‹I...›
I KNOW HE SHOULD. I KNOW WHAT THE CLONE WILL DO IF IT'S LEFT ALIVE.
‹I...›
‹IF YOU TELL ME TO DO IT, I WON'T HESITATE.›
I BELIEVE HIM. I BELIEVE HE'LL REALLY DO IT.
‹I KNOW IT LOOKS LIKE ONE OF US, KARA, BUT IT IS NOT. DO NOT LET YOUR INNATE COMPASSION CONFUSE YOU.›
‹DO WHAT MUST BE--›
...WH...
...WHERE...?
‹QUICKLY NOW, KARA. THE CLONE WAKES.›
HE REMEMBERED MY NAME.
Y...YOU... I KNOW YOU...
AND I...
...SUPERGIRL...
I JUST CALLED IT "HE."
‹NO.›
‹DON'T DO IT.›
‹NOT YET.›
‹NOT YET? VERY WELL. I WILL SIMPLY RENDER THE CLONE UNCONSCIOUS AGAIN.›
‹BUT YOUR HESITATION IS CURIOUS.›

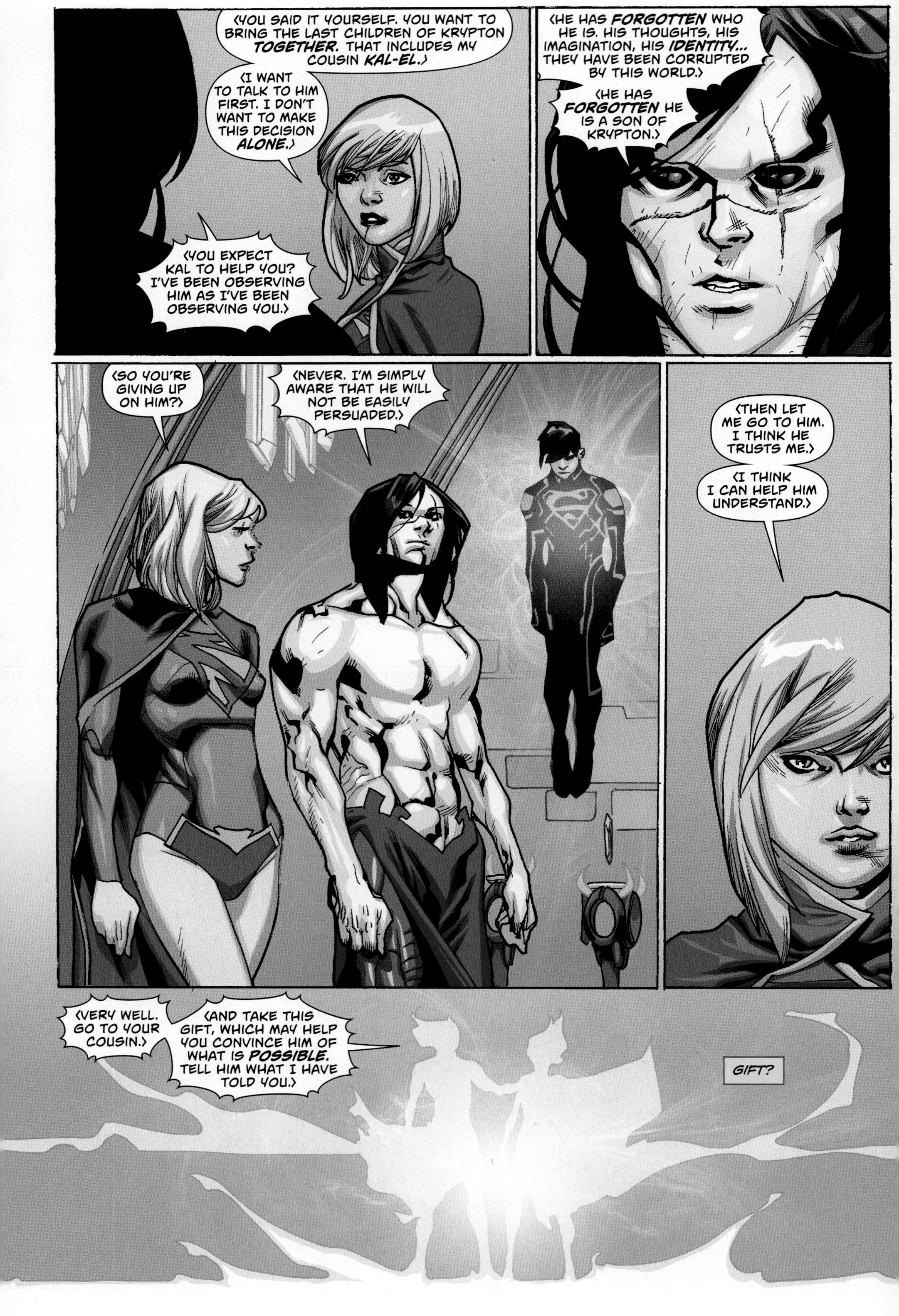
‹YOU SAID IT YOURSELF. YOU WANT TO BRING THE LAST CHILDREN OF KRYPTON TOGETHER. THAT INCLUDES MY COUSIN KAL-EL.›
‹I WANT TO TALK TO HIM FIRST. I DON'T WANT TO MAKE THIS DECISION ALONE.›
‹YOU EXPECT KAL TO HELP YOU? I'VE BEEN OBSERVING HIM AS I'VE BEEN OBSERVING YOU.›
‹HE HAS FORGOTTEN WHO HE IS. HIS THOUGHTS, HIS IMAGINATION, HIS IDENTITY... THEY HAVE BEEN CORRUPTED BY THIS WORLD.›
‹HE HAS FORGOTTEN HE IS A SON OF KRYPTON.›
‹SO YOU'RE GIVING UP ON HIM?›
‹NEVER. I'M SIMPLY AWARE THAT HE WILL NOT BE EASILY PERSUADED.›
‹THEN LET ME GO TO HIM. I THINK HE TRUSTS ME.›
‹I THINK I CAN HELP HIM UNDERSTAND.›
‹VERY WELL. GO TO YOUR COUSIN.›
‹AND TAKE THIS GIFT, WHICH MAY HELP YOU CONVINCE HIM OF WHAT IS POSSIBLE. TELL HIM WHAT I HAVE TOLD YOU.›
GIFT?

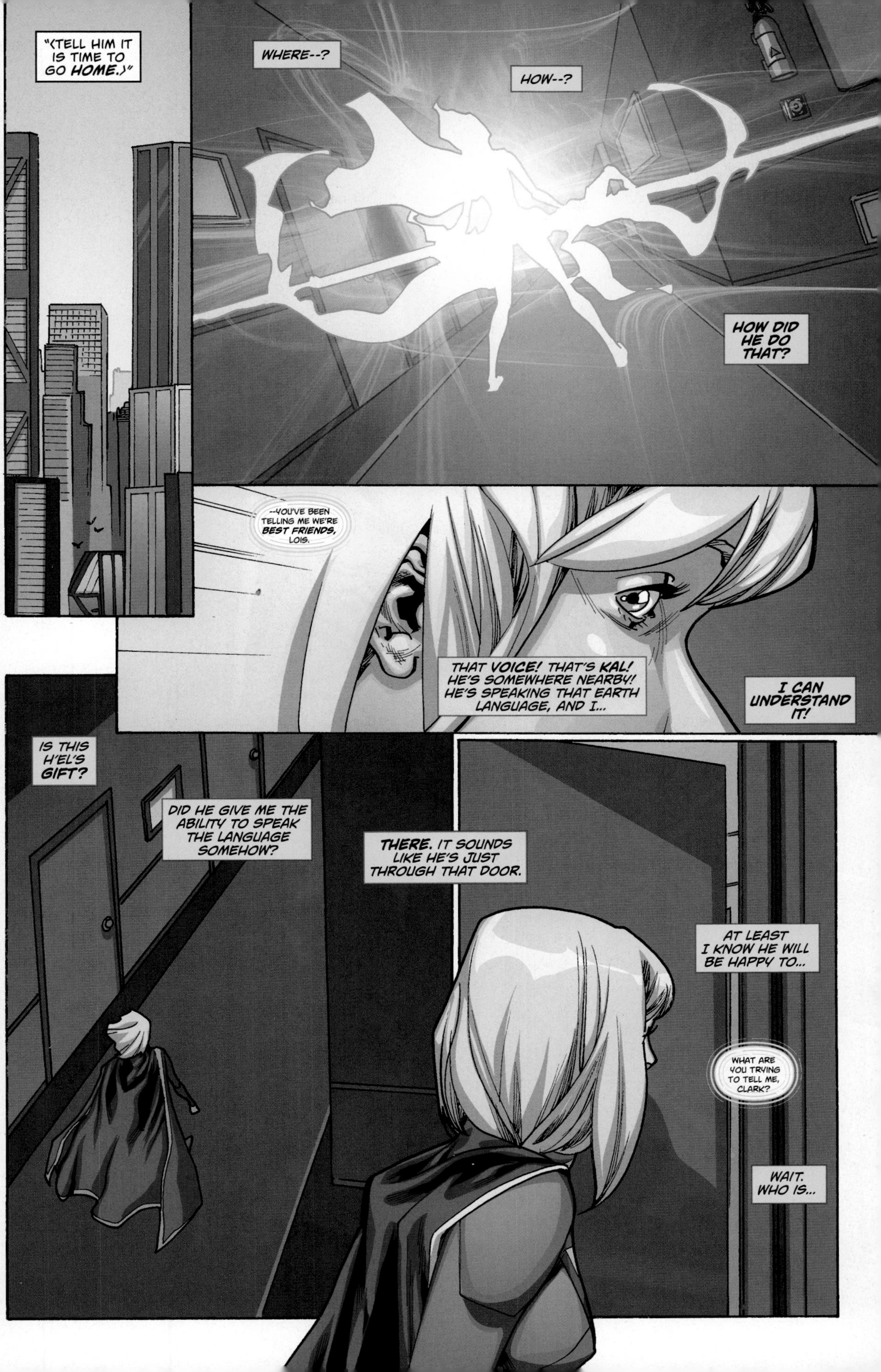
"⟨TELL HIM IT IS TIME TO GO HOME.⟩"
WHERE--?
HOW--?
HOW DID HE DO THAT?
--YOU'VE BEEN TELLING ME WE'RE BEST FRIENDS, LOIS.
THAT VOICE! THAT'S KAL! HE'S SOMEWHERE NEARBY! HE'S SPEAKING THAT EARTH LANGUAGE, AND I...
I CAN UNDERSTAND IT!
IS THIS H'EL'S GIFT?
DID HE GIVE ME THE ABILITY TO SPEAK THE LANGUAGE SOMEHOW?
THERE. IT SOUNDS LIKE HE'S JUST THROUGH THAT DOOR.
AT LEAST I KNOW HE WILL BE HAPPY TO...
WHAT ARE YOU TRYING TO TELL ME, CLARK?
WAIT. WHO IS...

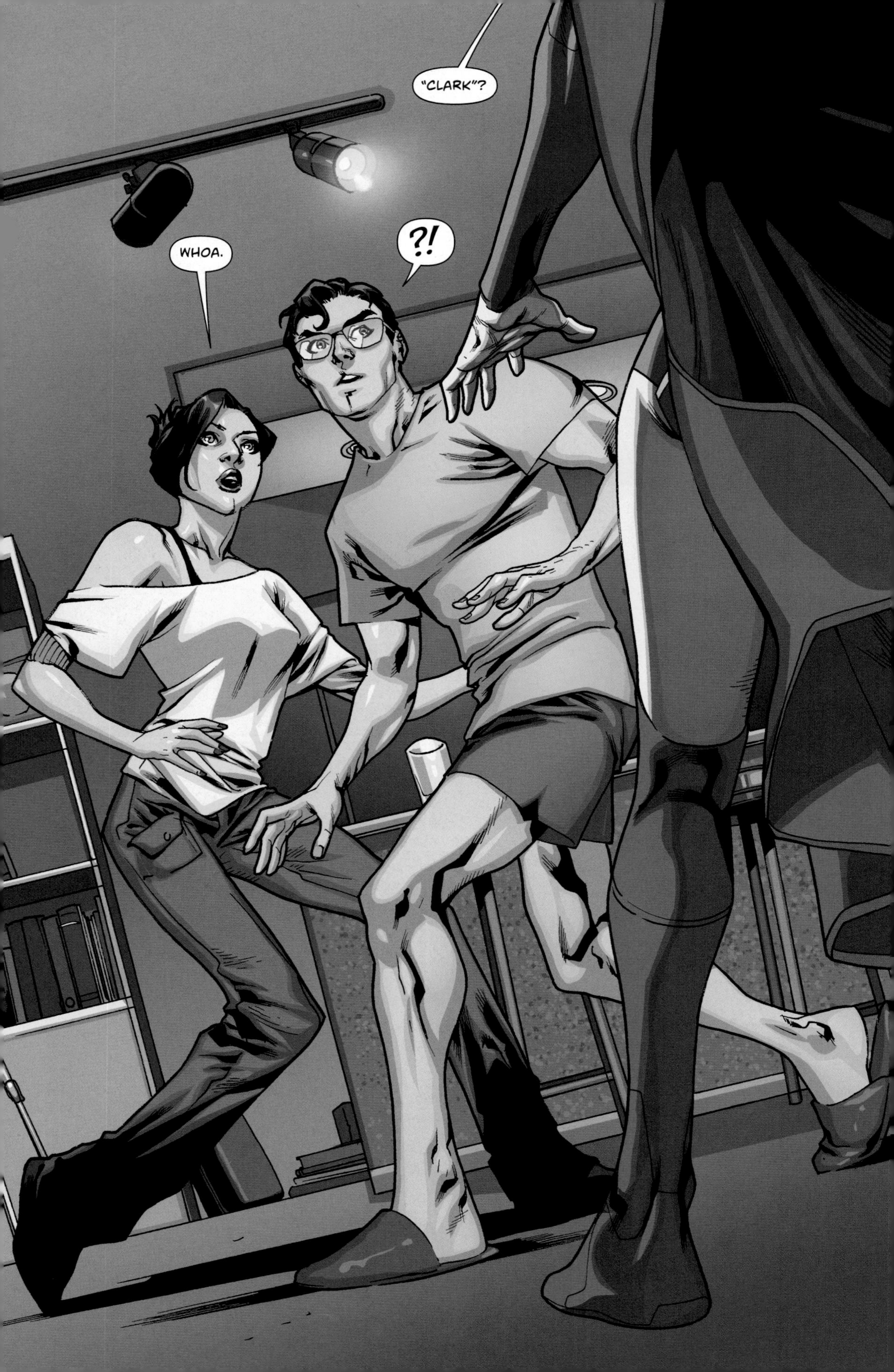
"CLARK"?
WHOA.
?!

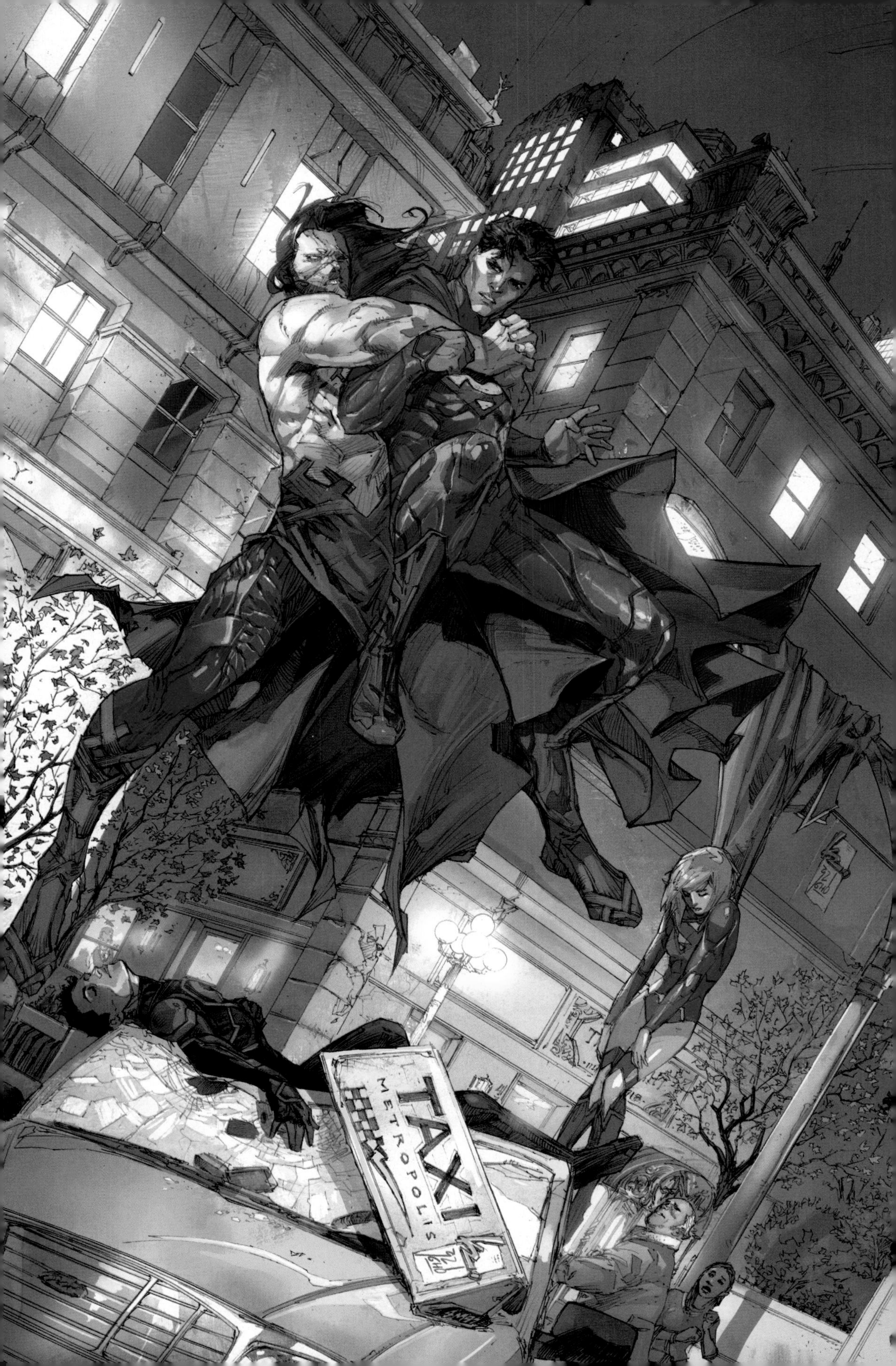
TAXI
METROPOLIS

BUILD A PARACHUTE ON YOUR WAY DOWN

SCOTT LOBDELL writer **KENNETH ROCAFORT** artist cover art by **KENNETH ROCAFORT & SUNNY GHO**

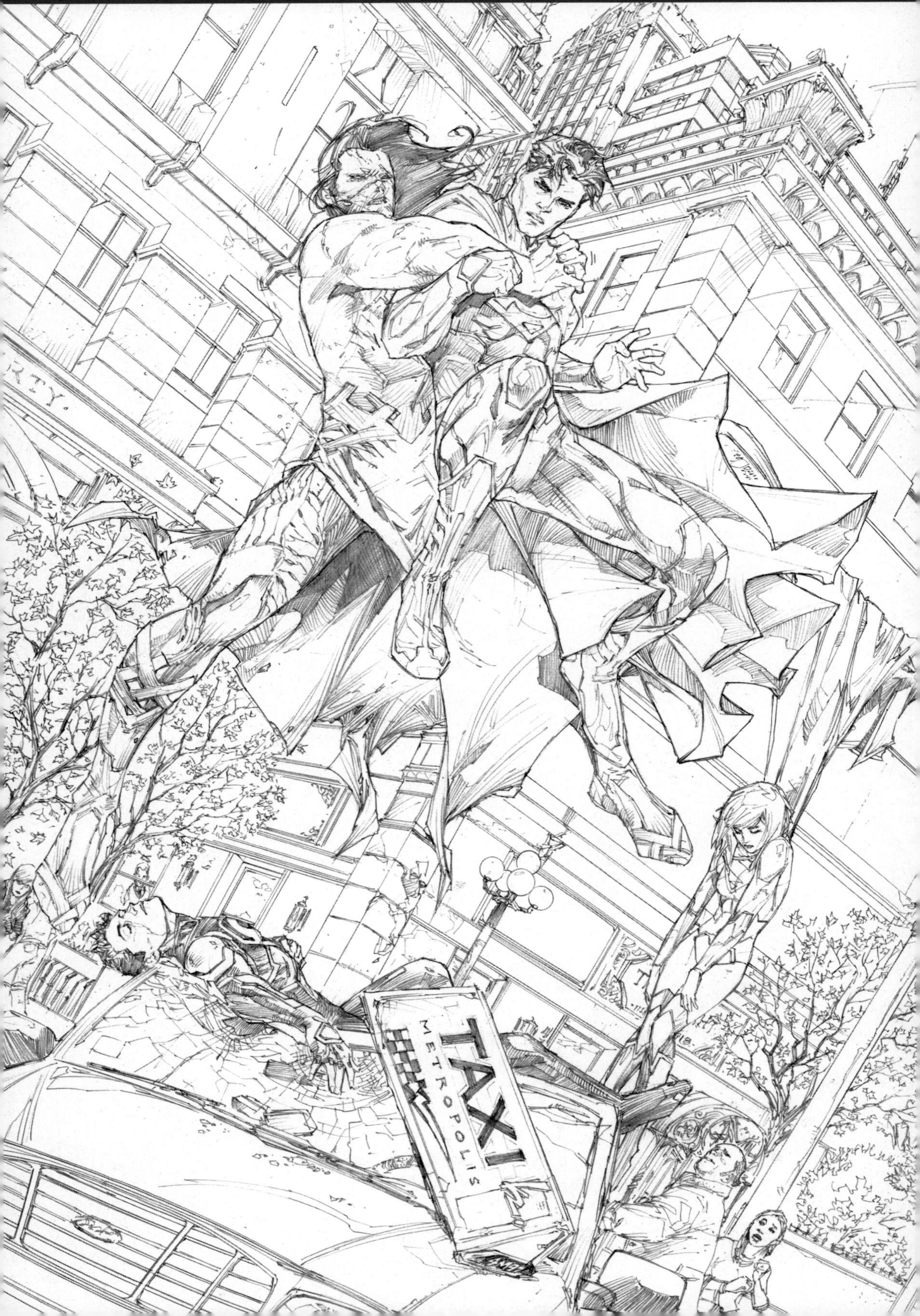
TAXI
METROPOLIS

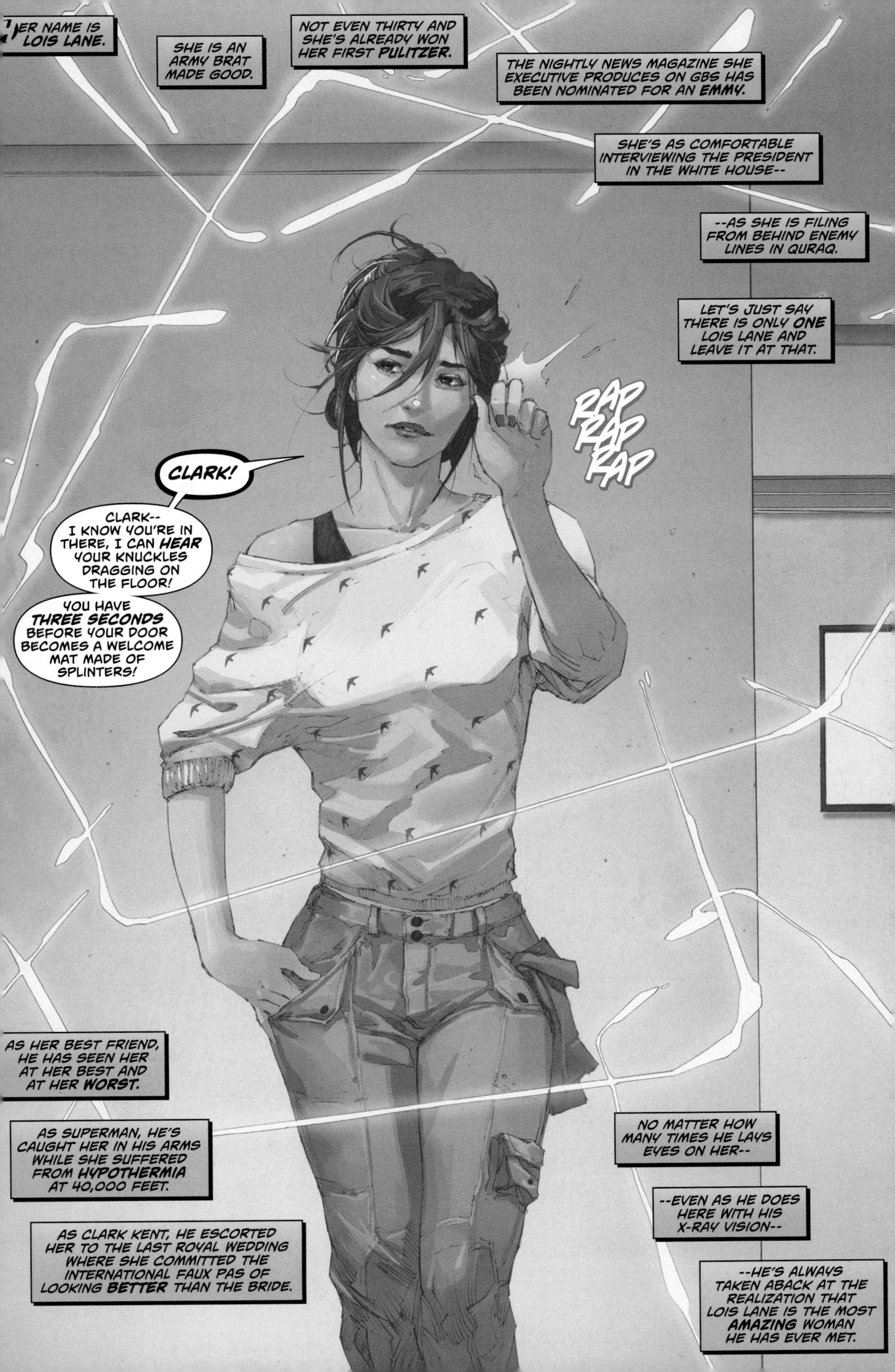
HER NAME IS LOIS LANE.
SHE IS AN ARMY BRAT MADE GOOD.
NOT EVEN THIRTY AND SHE'S ALREADY WON HER FIRST PULITZER.
THE NIGHTLY NEWS MAGAZINE SHE EXECUTIVE PRODUCES ON GBS HAS BEEN NOMINATED FOR AN EMMY.
SHE'S AS COMFORTABLE INTERVIEWING THE PRESIDENT IN THE WHITE HOUSE--
--AS SHE IS FILING FROM BEHIND ENEMY LINES IN QURAQ.
LET'S JUST SAY THERE IS ONLY ONE LOIS LANE AND LEAVE IT AT THAT.
RAP RAP RAP
CLARK!
CLARK-- I KNOW YOU'RE IN THERE, I CAN HEAR YOUR KNUCKLES DRAGGING ON THE FLOOR!
YOU HAVE THREE SECONDS BEFORE YOUR DOOR BECOMES A WELCOME MAT MADE OF SPLINTERS!
AS HER BEST FRIEND, HE HAS SEEN HER AT HER BEST AND AT HER WORST.
AS SUPERMAN, HE'S CAUGHT HER IN HIS ARMS WHILE SHE SUFFERED FROM HYPOTHERMIA AT 40,000 FEET.
AS CLARK KENT, HE ESCORTED HER TO THE LAST ROYAL WEDDING WHERE SHE COMMITTED THE INTERNATIONAL FAUX PAS OF LOOKING BETTER THAN THE BRIDE.
NO MATTER HOW MANY TIMES HE LAYS EYES ON HER--
--EVEN AS HE DOES HERE WITH HIS X-RAY VISION--
--HE'S ALWAYS TAKEN ABACK AT THE REALIZATION THAT LOIS LANE IS THE MOST AMAZING WOMAN HE HAS EVER MET.

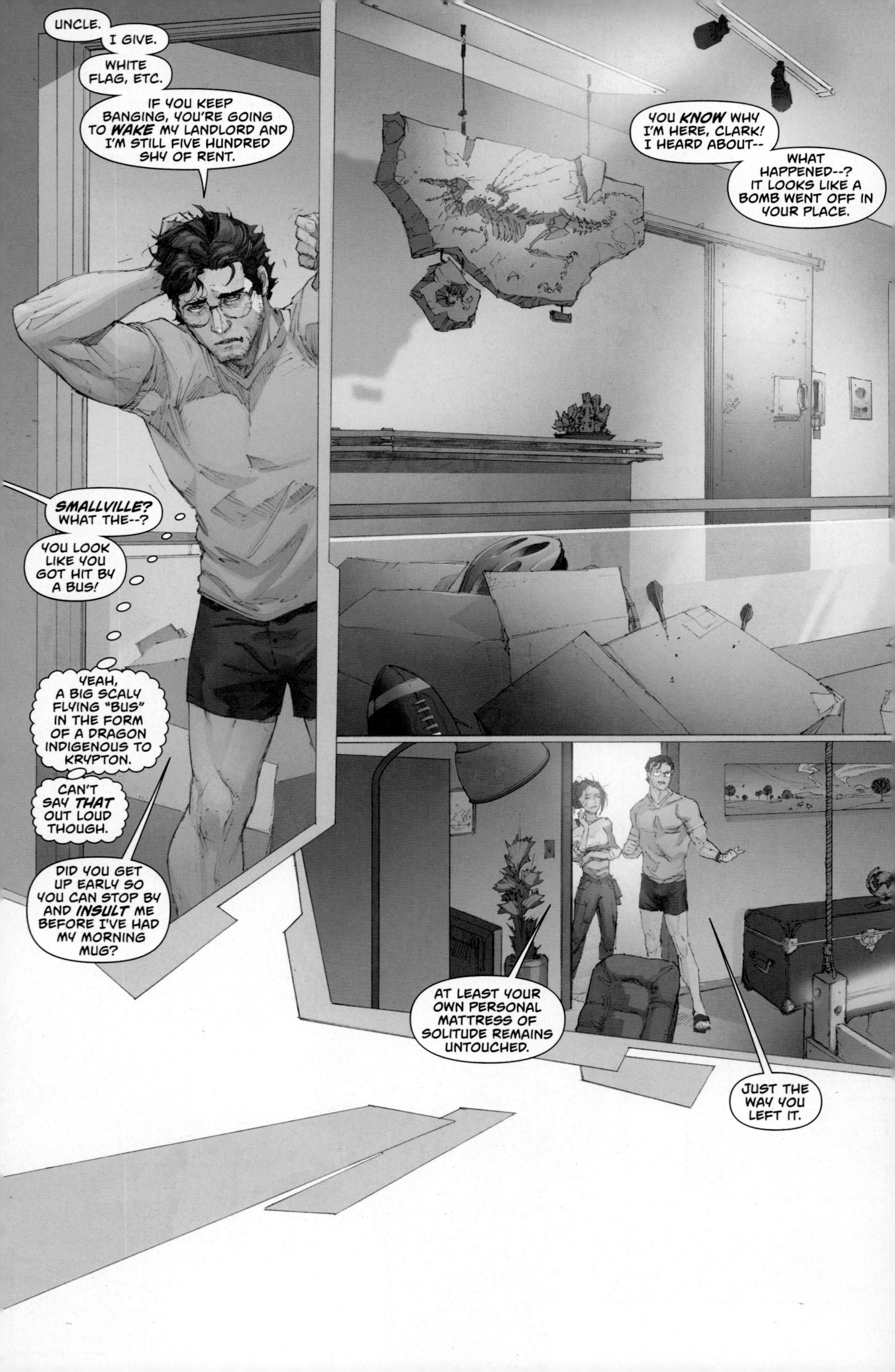
UNCLE.
I GIVE.
WHITE FLAG, ETC.
IF YOU KEEP BANGING, YOU'RE GOING TO *WAKE* MY LANDLORD AND I'M STILL FIVE HUNDRED SHY OF RENT.
YOU *KNOW* WHY I'M HERE, CLARK! I HEARD ABOUT--
WHAT HAPPENED--? IT LOOKS LIKE A BOMB WENT OFF IN YOUR PLACE.
SMALLVILLE? WHAT THE--?
YOU LOOK LIKE YOU GOT HIT BY A BUS!
YEAH, A BIG SCALY FLYING "BUS" IN THE FORM OF A DRAGON INDIGENOUS TO KRYPTON.
CAN'T SAY *THAT* OUT LOUD THOUGH.
DID YOU GET UP EARLY SO YOU CAN STOP BY AND *INSULT* ME BEFORE I'VE HAD MY MORNING MUG?
AT LEAST YOUR OWN PERSONAL MATTRESS OF SOLITUDE REMAINS UNTOUCHED.
JUST THE WAY YOU LEFT IT.

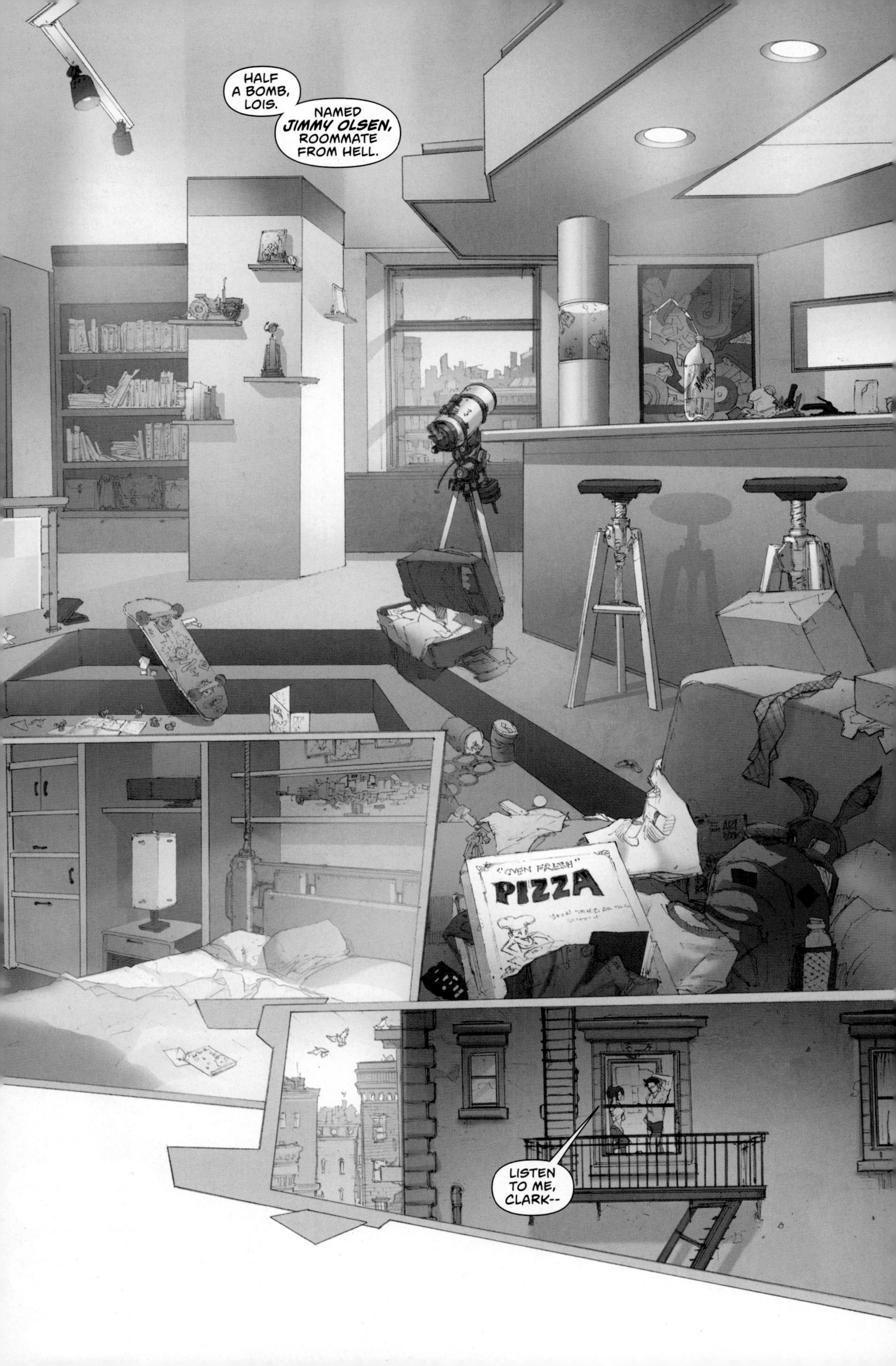
HALF A BOMB, LOIS.
NAMED *JIMMY OLSEN,* ROOMMATE FROM HELL.
"OVEN FRESH"
PIZZA
LISTEN TO ME, CLARK--

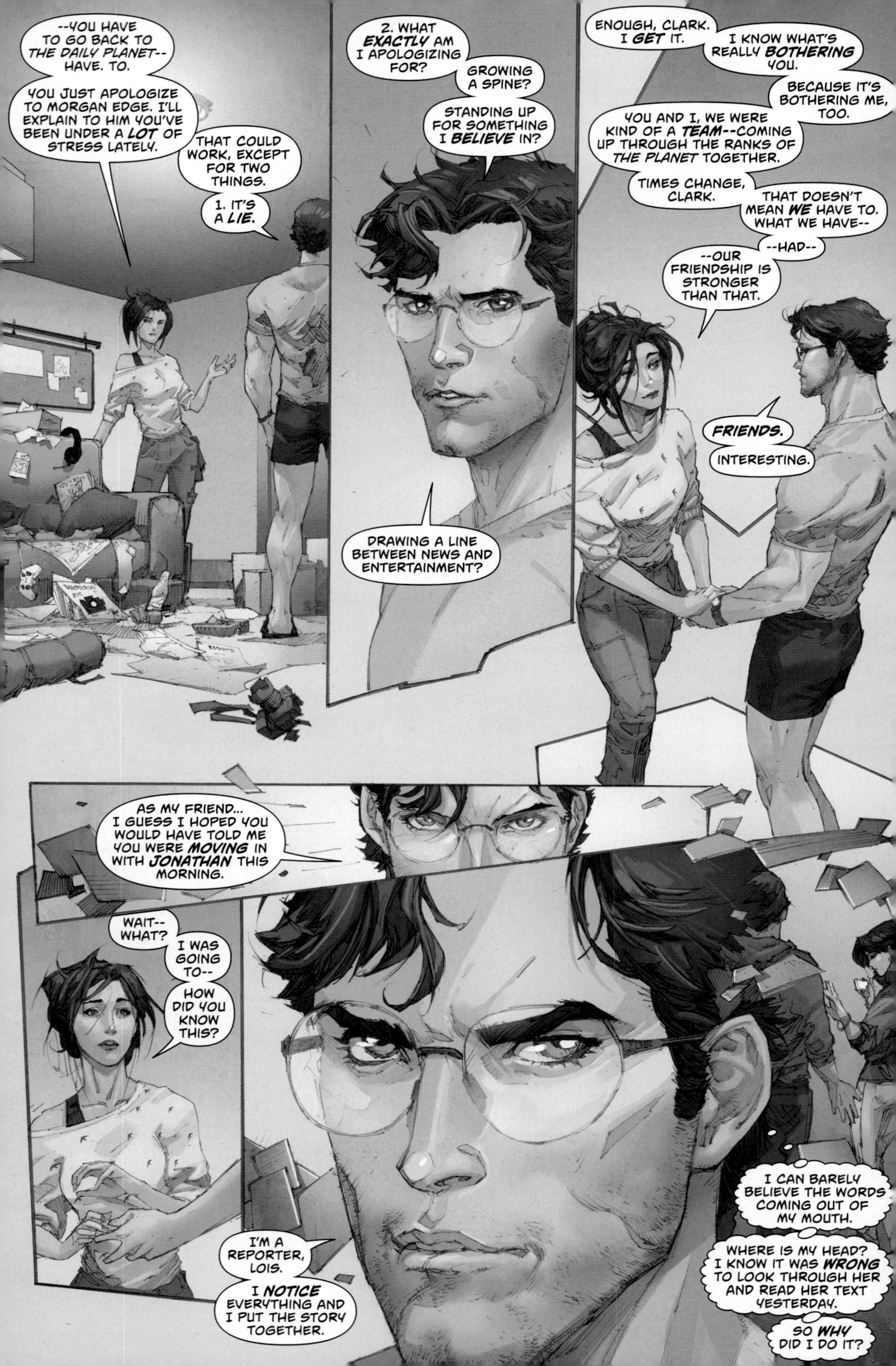

--YOU HAVE TO GO BACK TO *THE DAILY PLANET*--HAVE. TO.
YOU JUST APOLOGIZE TO MORGAN EDGE. I'LL EXPLAIN TO HIM YOU'VE BEEN UNDER A **LOT** OF STRESS LATELY.
THAT COULD WORK, EXCEPT FOR TWO THINGS.
1. IT'S A **LIE**.
2. WHAT **EXACTLY** AM I APOLOGIZING FOR?
GROWING A SPINE?
STANDING UP FOR SOMETHING I **BELIEVE** IN?
DRAWING A LINE BETWEEN NEWS AND ENTERTAINMENT?
ENOUGH, CLARK. I **GET** IT.
I KNOW WHAT'S REALLY **BOTHERING** YOU.
BECAUSE IT'S BOTHERING ME, TOO.
YOU AND I, WE WERE KIND OF A **TEAM**--COMING UP THROUGH THE RANKS OF *THE PLANET* TOGETHER.
TIMES CHANGE, CLARK.
THAT DOESN'T MEAN **WE** HAVE TO. WHAT WE HAVE--
--HAD--
--OUR FRIENDSHIP IS STRONGER THAN THAT.
FRIENDS.
INTERESTING.
AS MY FRIEND... I GUESS I HOPED YOU WOULD HAVE TOLD ME YOU WERE **MOVING** IN WITH **JONATHAN** THIS MORNING.
WAIT--WHAT?
I WAS GOING TO--
HOW DID YOU KNOW THIS?
I'M A REPORTER, LOIS.
I **NOTICE** EVERYTHING AND I PUT THE STORY TOGETHER.
I CAN BARELY BELIEVE THE WORDS COMING OUT OF MY MOUTH.
WHERE IS MY HEAD? I KNOW IT WAS **WRONG** TO LOOK THROUGH HER AND READ HER TEXT YESTERDAY.
SO **WHY** DID I DO IT?

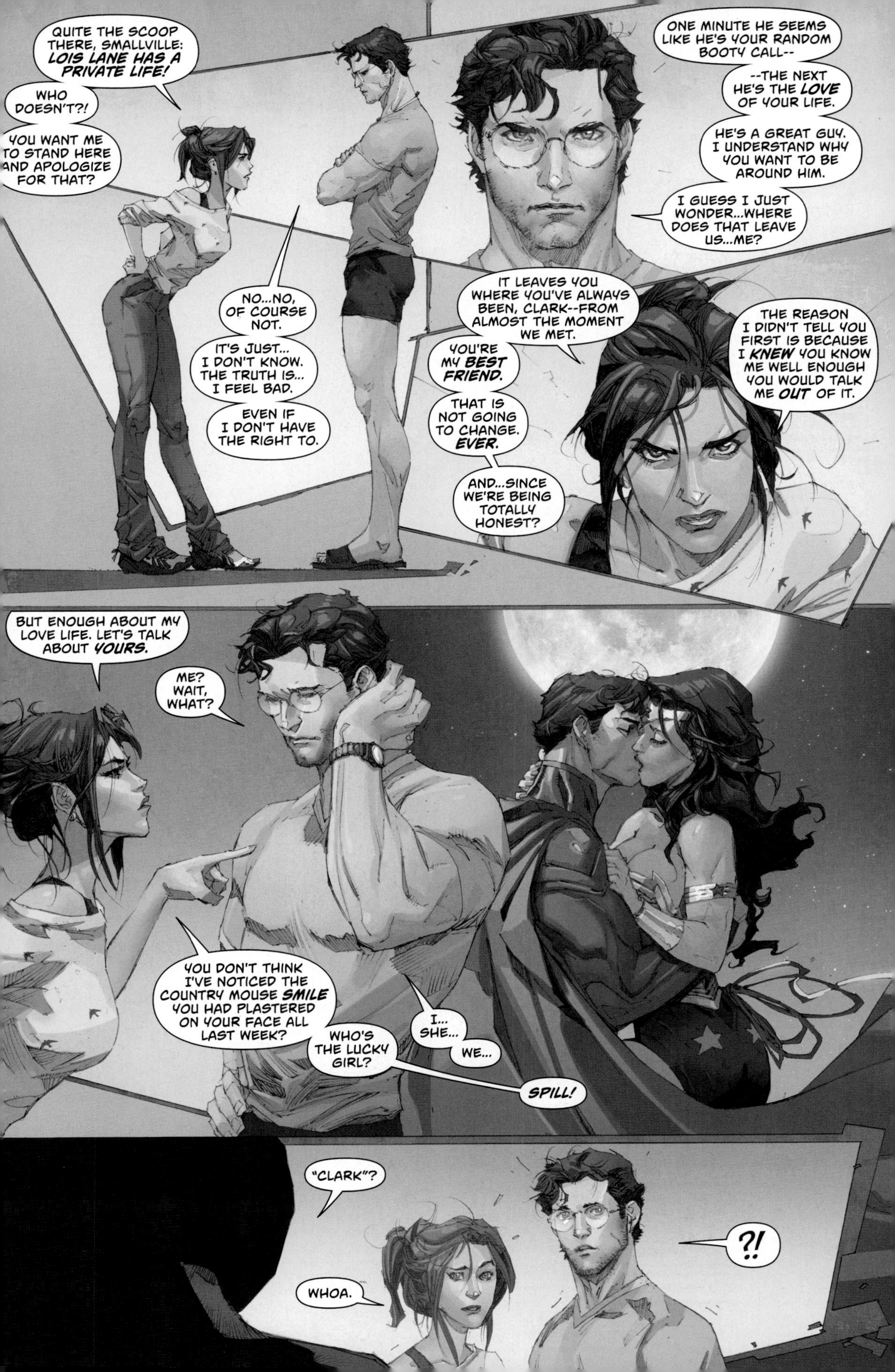

QUITE THE SCOOP THERE, SMALLVILLE: LOIS LANE HAS A PRIVATE LIFE!
WHO DOESN'T?!
YOU WANT ME TO STAND HERE AND APOLOGIZE FOR THAT?
NO...NO, OF COURSE NOT.
IT'S JUST... I DON'T KNOW. THE TRUTH IS... I FEEL BAD.
EVEN IF I DON'T HAVE THE RIGHT TO.
ONE MINUTE HE SEEMS LIKE HE'S YOUR RANDOM BOOTY CALL--
--THE NEXT HE'S THE LOVE OF YOUR LIFE.
HE'S A GREAT GUY. I UNDERSTAND WHY YOU WANT TO BE AROUND HIM.
I GUESS I JUST WONDER...WHERE DOES THAT LEAVE US...ME?
IT LEAVES YOU WHERE YOU'VE ALWAYS BEEN, CLARK--FROM ALMOST THE MOMENT WE MET.
YOU'RE MY BEST FRIEND.
THAT IS NOT GOING TO CHANGE. EVER.
AND...SINCE WE'RE BEING TOTALLY HONEST?
THE REASON I DIDN'T TELL YOU FIRST IS BECAUSE I KNEW YOU KNOW ME WELL ENOUGH YOU WOULD TALK ME OUT OF IT.
BUT ENOUGH ABOUT MY LOVE LIFE. LET'S TALK ABOUT YOURS.
ME? WAIT, WHAT?
YOU DON'T THINK I'VE NOTICED THE COUNTRY MOUSE SMILE YOU HAD PLASTERED ON YOUR FACE ALL LAST WEEK?
WHO'S THE LUCKY GIRL?
I... SHE...
WE...
SPILL!
"CLARK"?
?!
WHOA.

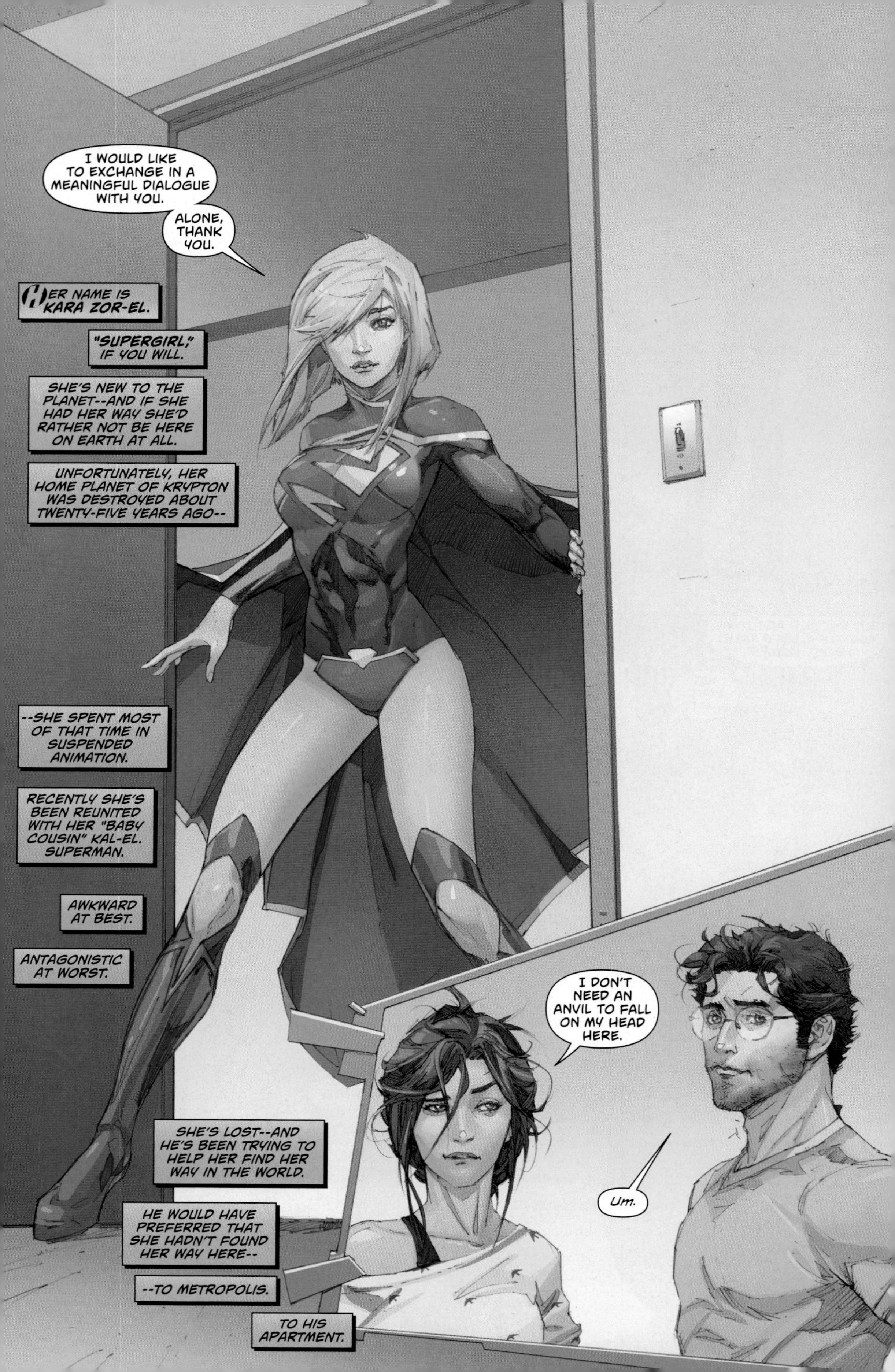
I WOULD LIKE TO EXCHANGE IN A MEANINGFUL DIALOGUE WITH YOU.
ALONE, THANK YOU.
HER NAME IS KARA ZOR-EL.
"SUPERGIRL," IF YOU WILL.
SHE'S NEW TO THE PLANET--AND IF SHE HAD HER WAY SHE'D RATHER NOT BE HERE ON EARTH AT ALL.
UNFORTUNATELY, HER HOME PLANET OF KRYPTON WAS DESTROYED ABOUT TWENTY-FIVE YEARS AGO--
--SHE SPENT MOST OF THAT TIME IN SUSPENDED ANIMATION.
RECENTLY SHE'S BEEN REUNITED WITH HER "BABY COUSIN" KAL-EL. SUPERMAN.
AWKWARD AT BEST.
ANTAGONISTIC AT WORST.
SHE'S LOST--AND HE'S BEEN TRYING TO HELP HER FIND HER WAY IN THE WORLD.
HE WOULD HAVE PREFERRED THAT SHE HADN'T FOUND HER WAY HERE--
--TO METROPOLIS.
TO HIS APARTMENT.
I DON'T NEED AN ANVIL TO FALL ON MY HEAD HERE.
Um.

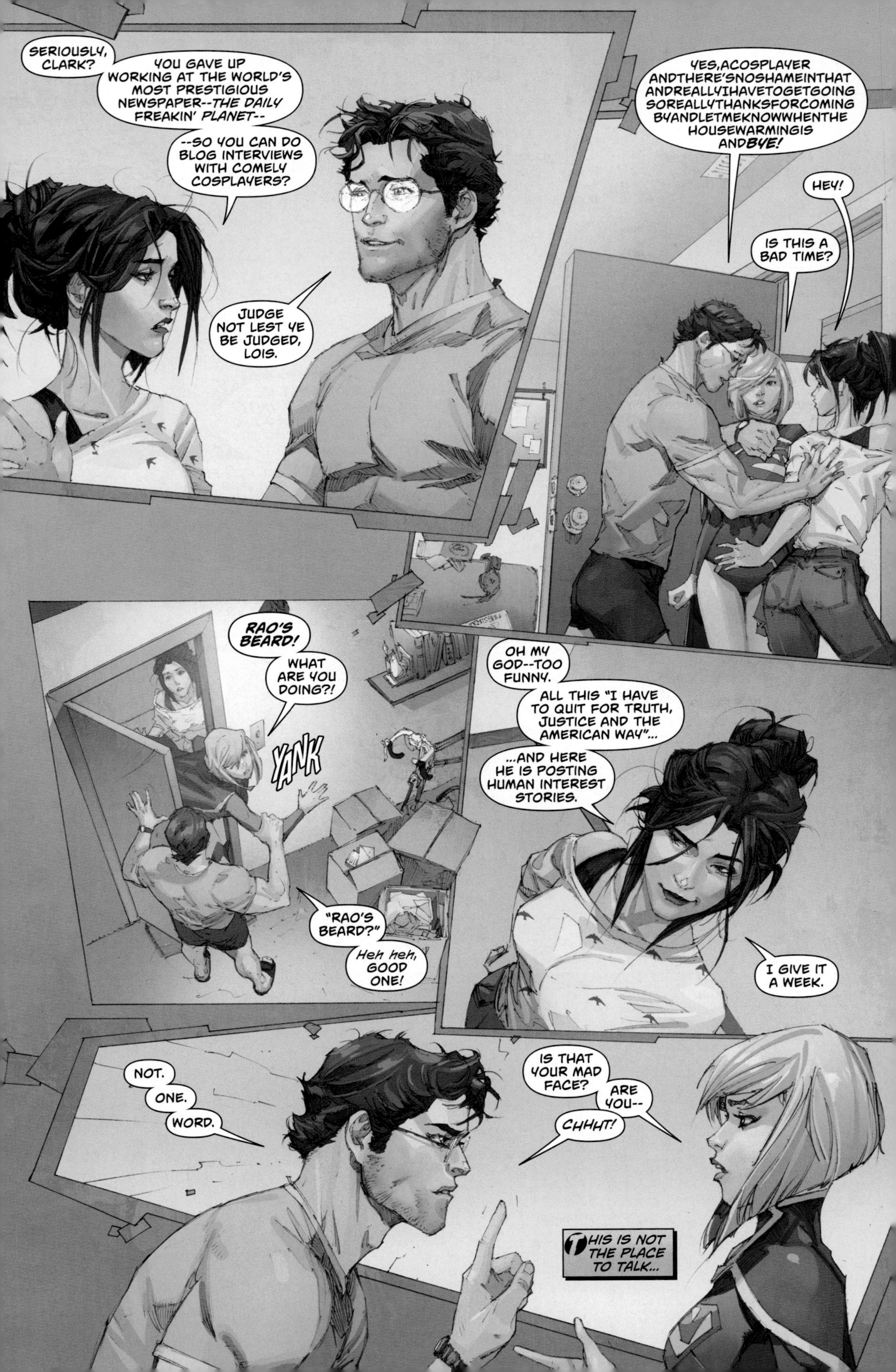
SERIOUSLY, CLARK?
YOU GAVE UP WORKING AT THE WORLD'S MOST PRESTIGIOUS NEWSPAPER--*THE DAILY FREAKIN' PLANET*--
--SO YOU CAN DO BLOG INTERVIEWS WITH COMELY COSPLAYERS?
JUDGE NOT LEST YE BE JUDGED, LOIS.
YES,ACOSPLAYER ANDTHERE'SNOSHAMEINTHAT ANDREALLYIHAVETOGETGOING SOREALLYTHANKSFORCOMING BYANDLETMEKNOWWHENTHE HOUSEWARMINGIS AND**BYE!**
HEY!
IS THIS A BAD TIME?
RAO'S BEARD!
WHAT ARE YOU DOING?!
YANK
"RAO'S BEARD?"
Heh heh, GOOD ONE!
OH MY GOD--TOO FUNNY.
ALL THIS "I HAVE TO QUIT FOR TRUTH, JUSTICE AND THE AMERICAN WAY"...
...AND HERE HE IS POSTING HUMAN INTEREST STORIES.
I GIVE IT A WEEK.
NOT.
ONE.
WORD.
IS THAT YOUR MAD FACE?
ARE YOU--
CHHHT!
THIS IS NOT THE PLACE TO TALK...

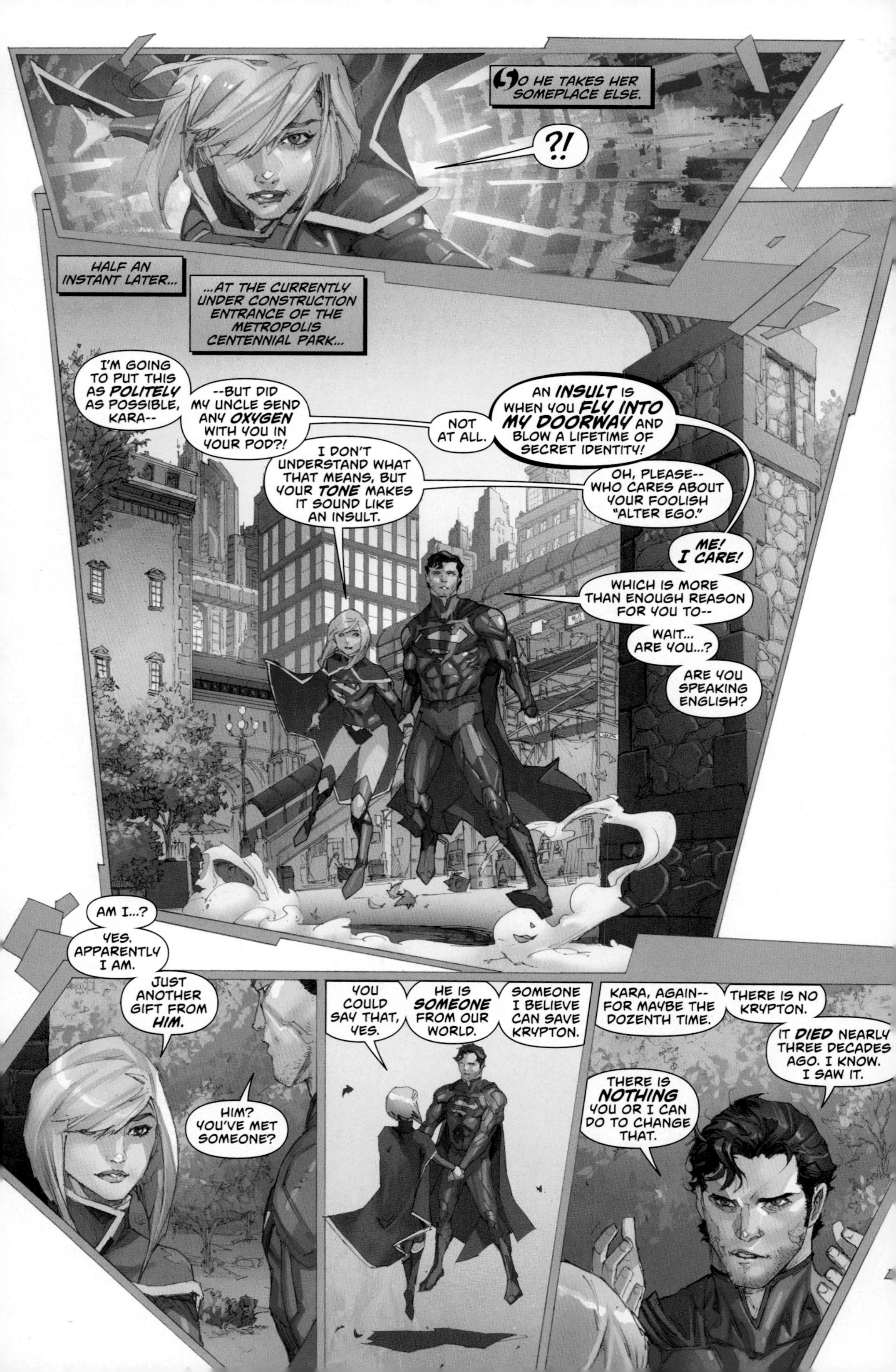
SO HE TAKES HER SOMEPLACE ELSE.
?!
HALF AN INSTANT LATER...
...AT THE CURRENTLY UNDER CONSTRUCTION ENTRANCE OF THE METROPOLIS CENTENNIAL PARK...
I'M GOING TO PUT THIS AS POLITELY AS POSSIBLE, KARA--
--BUT DID MY UNCLE SEND ANY OXYGEN WITH YOU IN YOUR POD?!
I DON'T UNDERSTAND WHAT THAT MEANS, BUT YOUR TONE MAKES IT SOUND LIKE AN INSULT.
NOT AT ALL.
AN INSULT IS WHEN YOU FLY INTO MY DOORWAY AND BLOW A LIFETIME OF SECRET IDENTITY!
OH, PLEASE-- WHO CARES ABOUT YOUR FOOLISH "ALTER EGO."
ME! I CARE!
WHICH IS MORE THAN ENOUGH REASON FOR YOU TO--
WAIT... ARE YOU...?
ARE YOU SPEAKING ENGLISH?
AM I...?
YES. APPARENTLY I AM.
JUST ANOTHER GIFT FROM HIM.
HIM? YOU'VE MET SOMEONE?
YOU COULD SAY THAT, YES.
HE IS SOMEONE FROM OUR WORLD.
SOMEONE I BELIEVE CAN SAVE KRYPTON.
KARA, AGAIN-- FOR MAYBE THE DOZENTH TIME.
THERE IS NO KRYPTON.
IT DIED NEARLY THREE DECADES AGO. I KNOW. I SAW IT.
THERE IS NOTHING YOU OR I CAN DO TO CHANGE THAT.

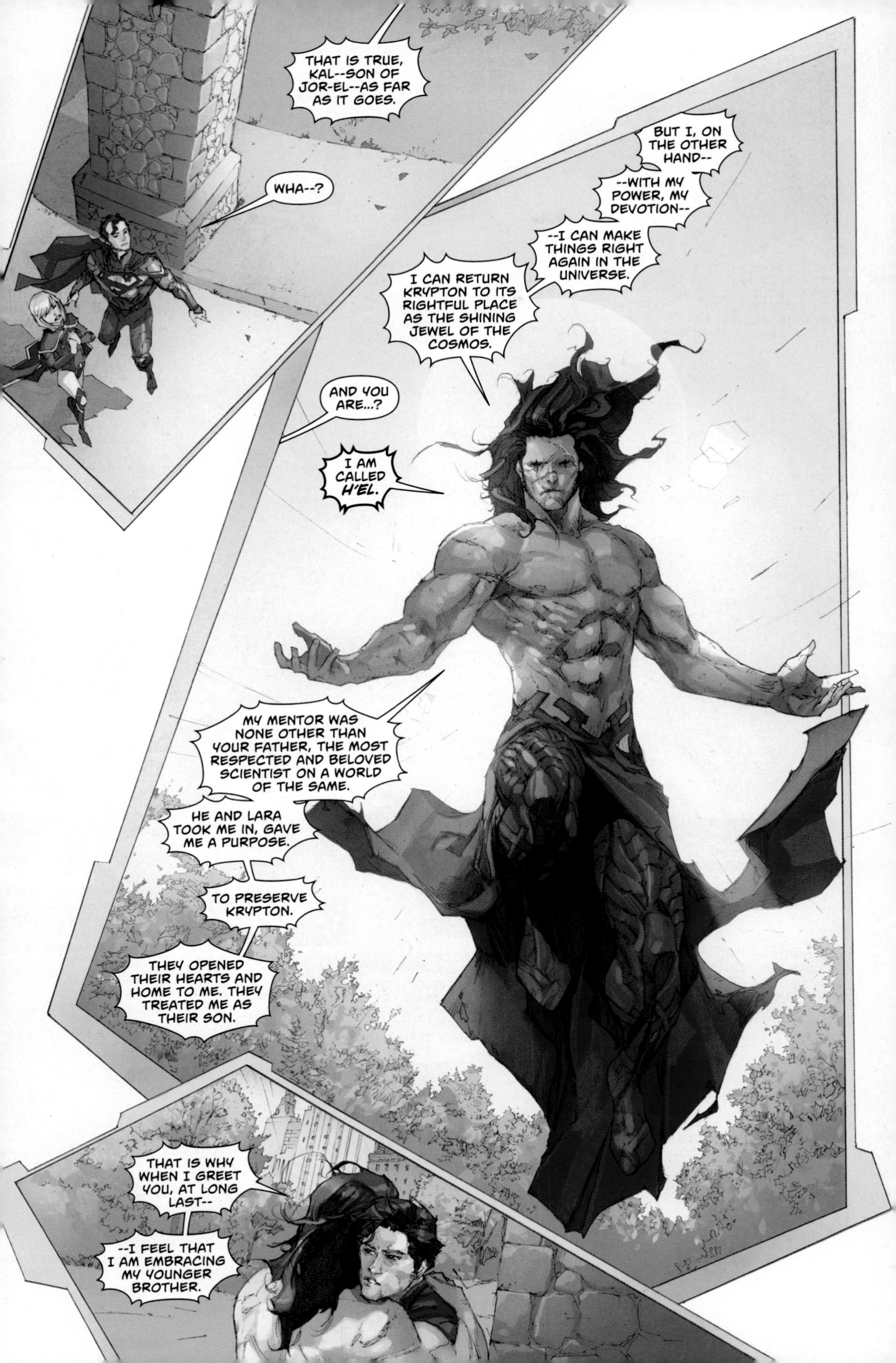
THAT IS TRUE, KAL--SON OF JOR-EL--AS FAR AS IT GOES.
WHA--?
BUT I, ON THE OTHER HAND--
--WITH MY POWER, MY DEVOTION--
--I CAN MAKE THINGS RIGHT AGAIN IN THE UNIVERSE.
I CAN RETURN KRYPTON TO ITS RIGHTFUL PLACE AS THE SHINING JEWEL OF THE COSMOS.
AND YOU ARE...?
I AM CALLED *H'EL.*
MY MENTOR WAS NONE OTHER THAN YOUR FATHER, THE MOST RESPECTED AND BELOVED SCIENTIST ON A WORLD OF THE SAME.
HE AND LARA TOOK ME IN, GAVE ME A PURPOSE.
TO PRESERVE KRYPTON.
THEY OPENED THEIR HEARTS AND HOME TO ME. THEY TREATED ME AS THEIR SON.
THAT IS WHY WHEN I GREET YOU, AT LONG LAST--
--I FEEL THAT I AM EMBRACING MY YOUNGER BROTHER.

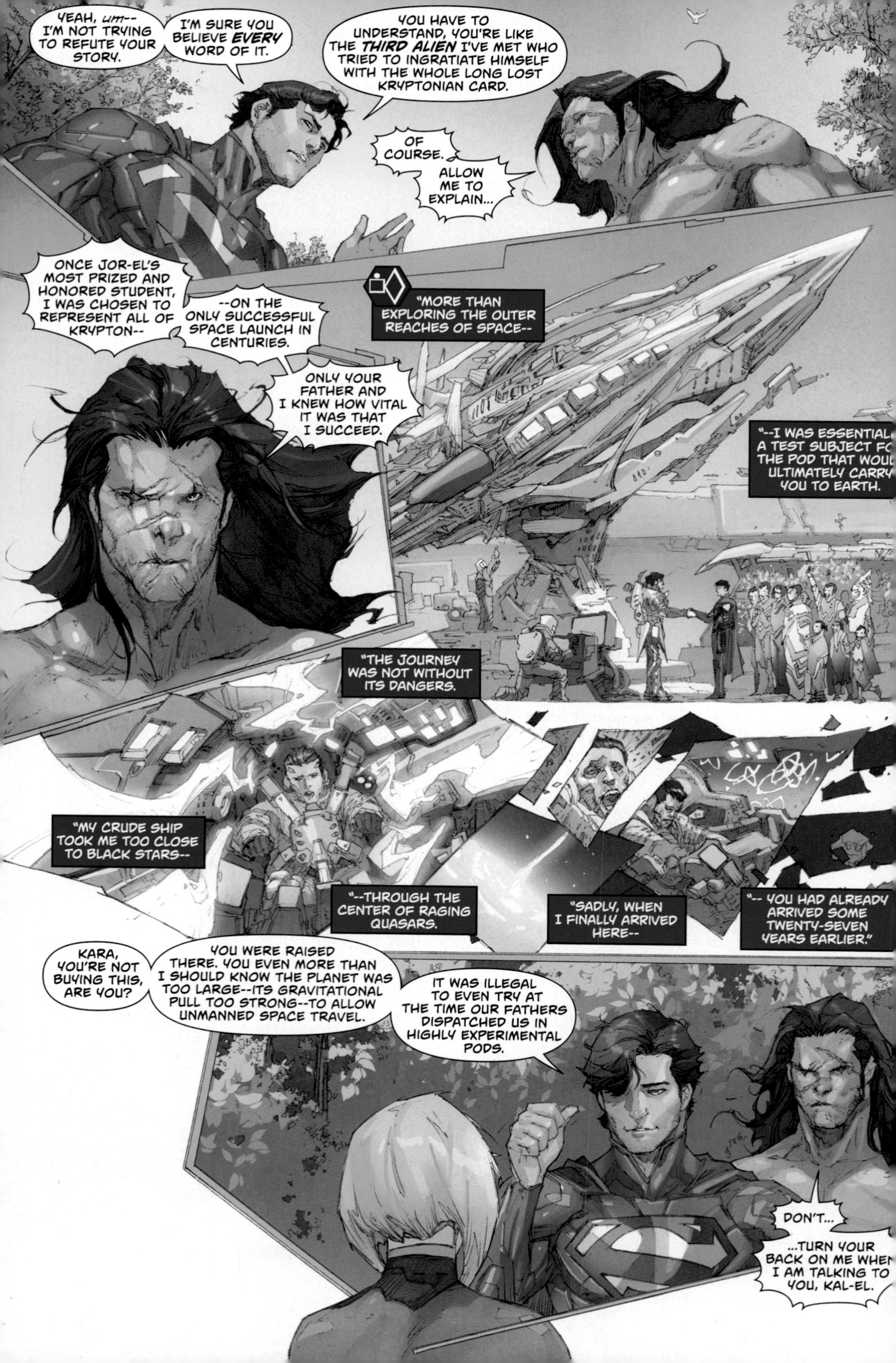
YEAH, *UM*--
I'M NOT TRYING TO REFUTE YOUR STORY.
I'M SURE YOU BELIEVE **EVERY** WORD OF IT.
YOU HAVE TO UNDERSTAND, YOU'RE LIKE THE **THIRD ALIEN** I'VE MET WHO TRIED TO INGRATIATE HIMSELF WITH THE WHOLE LONG LOST KRYPTONIAN CARD.
OF COURSE.
ALLOW ME TO EXPLAIN...
ONCE JOR-EL'S MOST PRIZED AND HONORED STUDENT, I WAS CHOSEN TO REPRESENT ALL OF KRYPTON--
--ON THE ONLY SUCCESSFUL SPACE LAUNCH IN CENTURIES.
ONLY YOUR FATHER AND I KNEW HOW VITAL IT WAS THAT I SUCCEED.
"MORE THAN EXPLORING THE OUTER REACHES OF SPACE--
"--I WAS ESSENTIAL A TEST SUBJECT FO THE POD THAT WOUL ULTIMATELY CARRY YOU TO EARTH.
"THE JOURNEY WAS NOT WITHOUT ITS DANGERS.
"MY CRUDE SHIP TOOK ME TOO CLOSE TO BLACK STARS--
"--THROUGH THE CENTER OF RAGING QUASARS.
"SADLY, WHEN I FINALLY ARRIVED HERE--
"-- YOU HAD ALREADY ARRIVED SOME TWENTY-SEVEN YEARS EARLIER."
KARA, YOU'RE NOT BUYING THIS, ARE YOU?
YOU WERE RAISED THERE. YOU EVEN MORE THAN I SHOULD KNOW THE PLANET WAS TOO LARGE--ITS GRAVITATIONAL PULL TOO STRONG--TO ALLOW UNMANNED SPACE TRAVEL.
IT WAS ILLEGAL TO EVEN TRY AT THE TIME OUR FATHERS DISPATCHED US IN HIGHLY EXPERIMENTAL PODS.
DON'T...
...TURN YOUR BACK ON ME WHEN I AM TALKING TO YOU, KAL-EL.

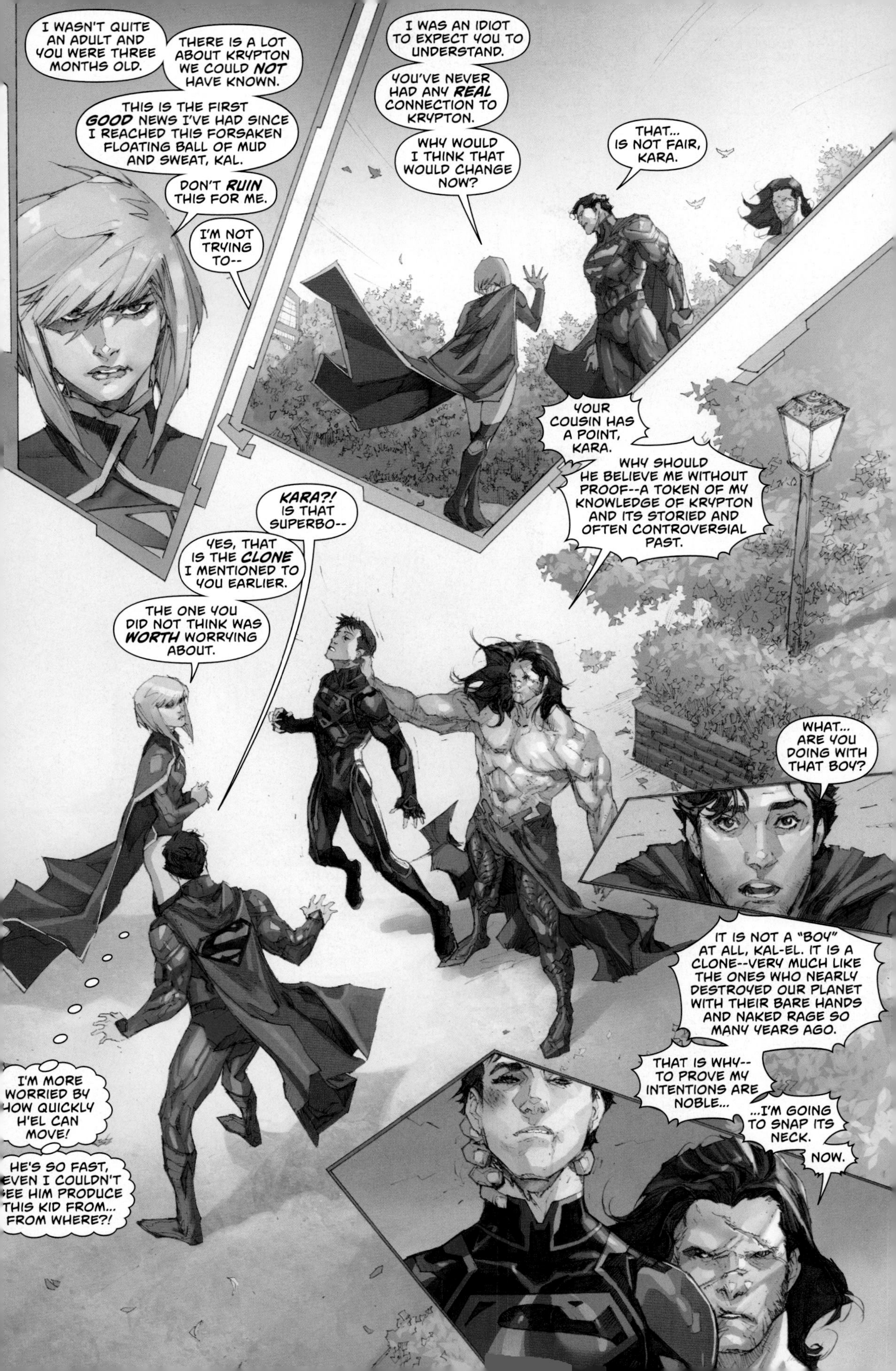
I WASN'T QUITE AN ADULT AND YOU WERE THREE MONTHS OLD.
THERE IS A LOT ABOUT KRYPTON WE COULD **NOT** HAVE KNOWN.
THIS IS THE FIRST **GOOD** NEWS I'VE HAD SINCE I REACHED THIS FORSAKEN FLOATING BALL OF MUD AND SWEAT, KAL.
DON'T **RUIN** THIS FOR ME.
I'M NOT TRYING TO--
I WAS AN IDIOT TO EXPECT YOU TO UNDERSTAND.
YOU'VE NEVER HAD ANY **REAL** CONNECTION TO KRYPTON.
WHY WOULD I THINK THAT WOULD CHANGE NOW?
THAT... IS NOT FAIR, KARA.
YOUR COUSIN HAS A POINT, KARA.
WHY SHOULD HE BELIEVE ME WITHOUT PROOF--A TOKEN OF MY KNOWLEDGE OF KRYPTON AND ITS STORIED AND OFTEN CONTROVERSIAL PAST.
KARA?! IS THAT SUPERBO--
YES, THAT IS THE **CLONE** I MENTIONED TO YOU EARLIER.
THE ONE YOU DID NOT THINK WAS **WORTH** WORRYING ABOUT.
WHAT... ARE YOU DOING WITH THAT BOY?
IT IS NOT A "BOY" AT ALL, KAL-EL. IT IS A CLONE--VERY MUCH LIKE THE ONES WHO NEARLY DESTROYED OUR PLANET WITH THEIR BARE HANDS AND NAKED RAGE SO MANY YEARS AGO.
THAT IS WHY--TO PROVE MY INTENTIONS ARE NOBLE...
...I'M GOING TO SNAP ITS NECK.
NOW.
I'M MORE WORRIED BY HOW QUICKLY H'EL CAN MOVE!
HE'S SO FAST, EVEN I COULDN'T SEE HIM PRODUCE THIS KID FROM... FROM WHERE?!

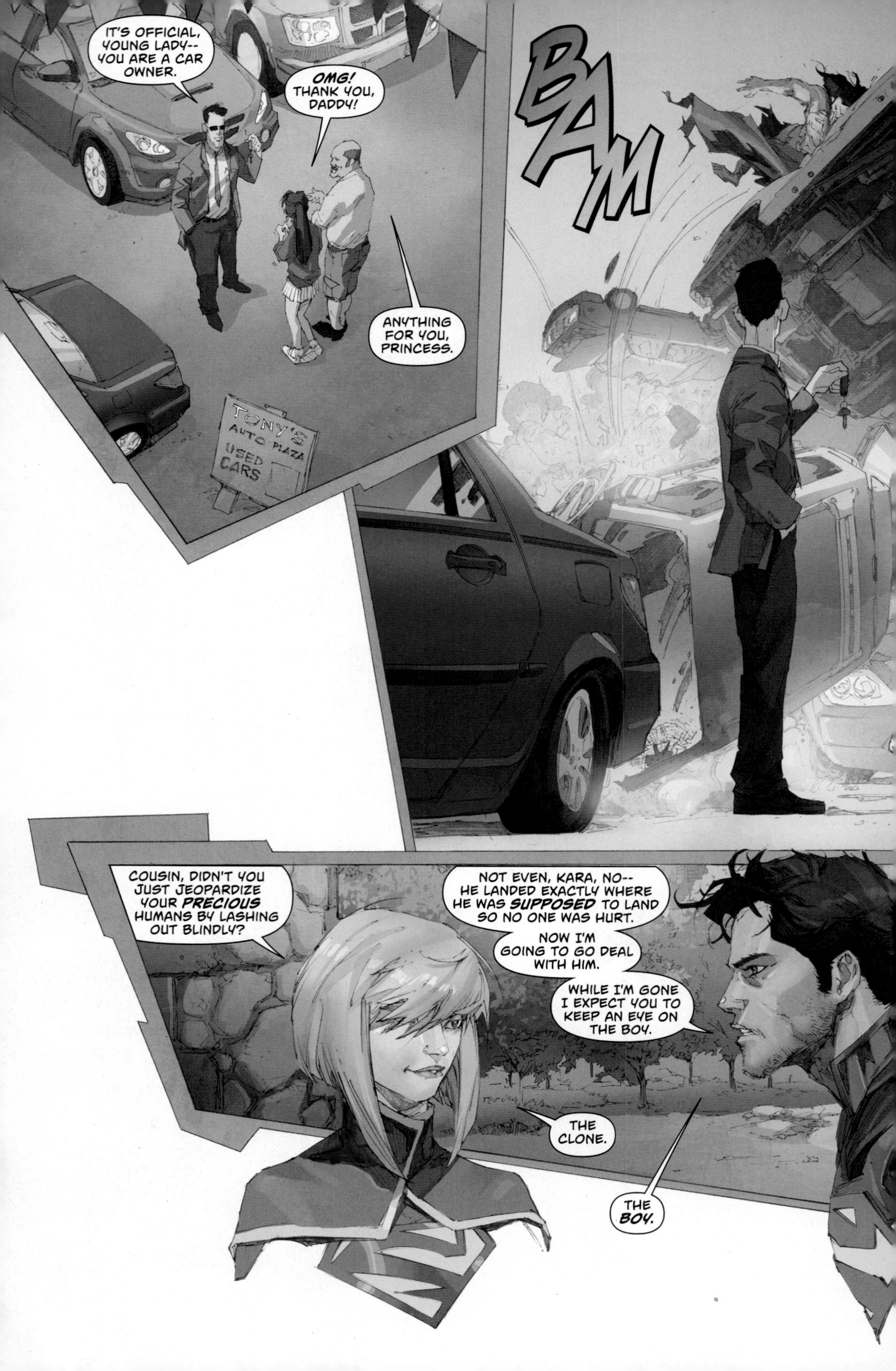
IT'S OFFICIAL, YOUNG LADY-- YOU ARE A CAR OWNER.
OMG! THANK YOU, DADDY!
ANYTHING FOR YOU, PRINCESS.
TONY'S AUTO PLAZA USED CARS
BAM
COUSIN, DIDN'T YOU JUST JEOPARDIZE YOUR PRECIOUS HUMANS BY LASHING OUT BLINDLY?
NOT EVEN, KARA, NO-- HE LANDED EXACTLY WHERE HE WAS SUPPOSED TO LAND SO NO ONE WAS HURT.
NOW I'M GOING TO GO DEAL WITH HIM.
WHILE I'M GONE I EXPECT YOU TO KEEP AN EYE ON THE BOY.
THE CLONE.
THE BOY.

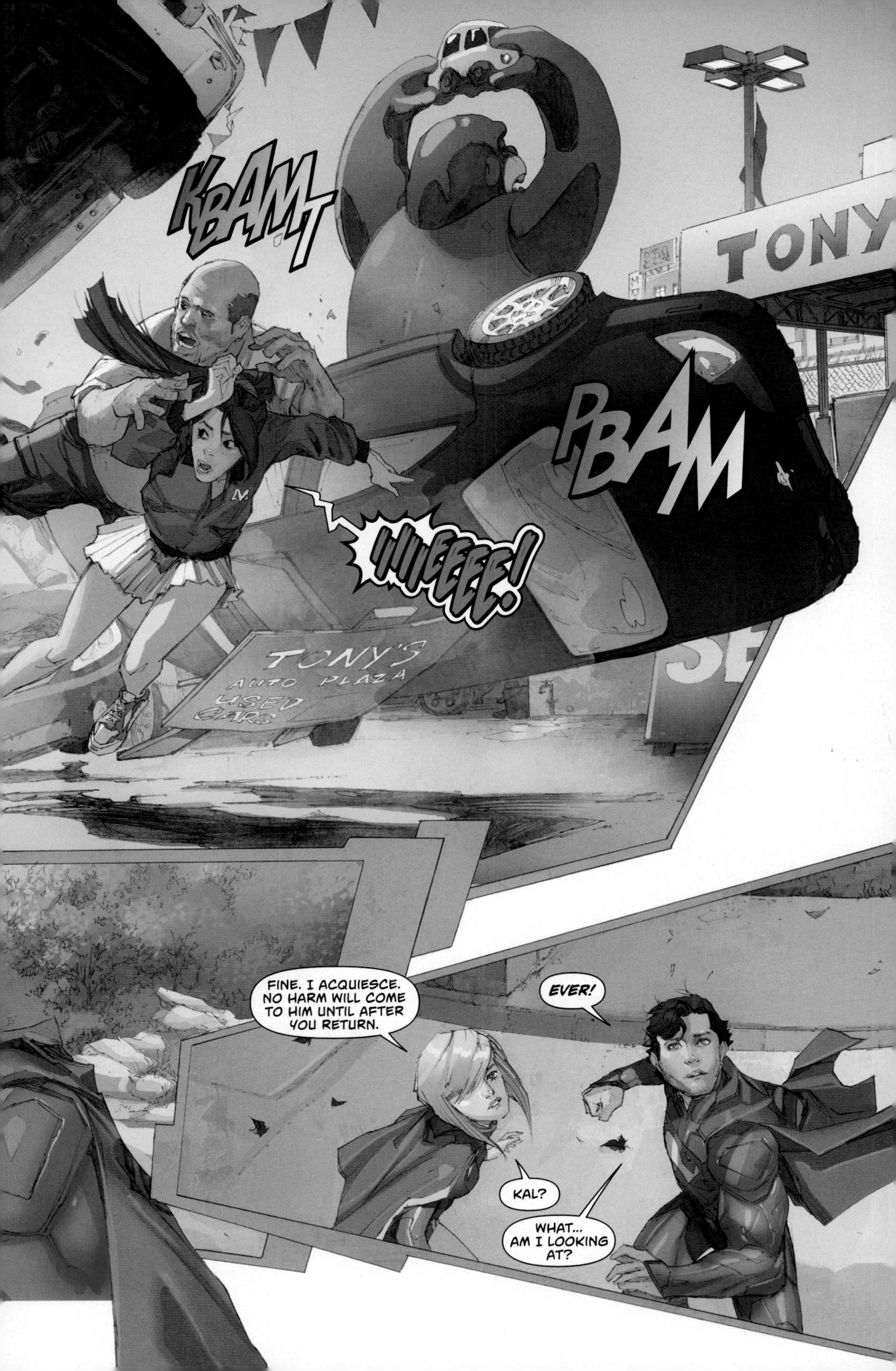
KBAMT
PBAM
IIIIIIEEEE!
TONY
TONY'S
AUTO PLAZA
USED
CARS
FINE. I ACQUIESCE. NO HARM WILL COME TO HIM UNTIL AFTER YOU RETURN.
EVER!
KAL?
WHAT... AM I LOOKING AT?

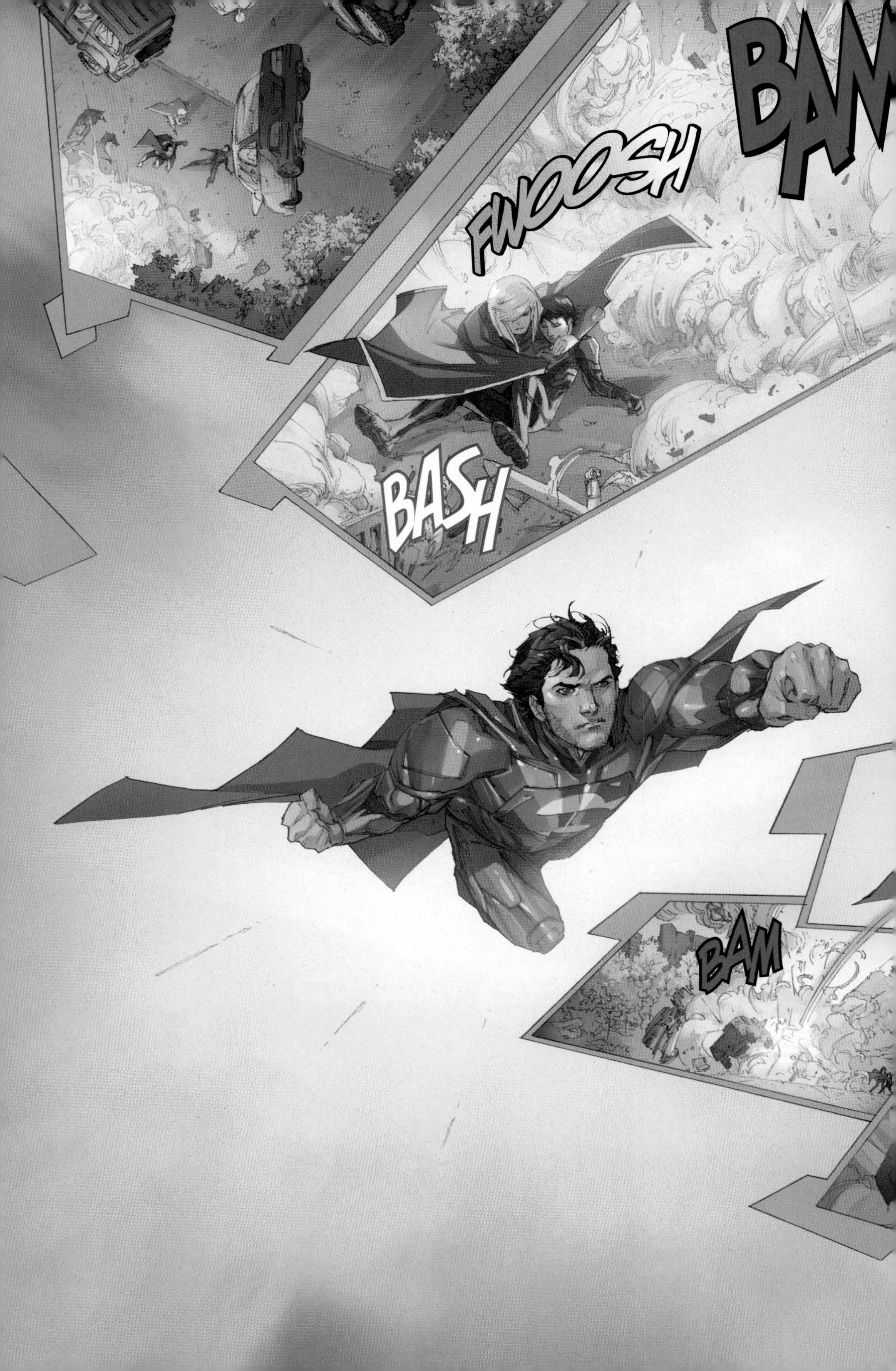
BAM
FWOOSH
BASH
BAM

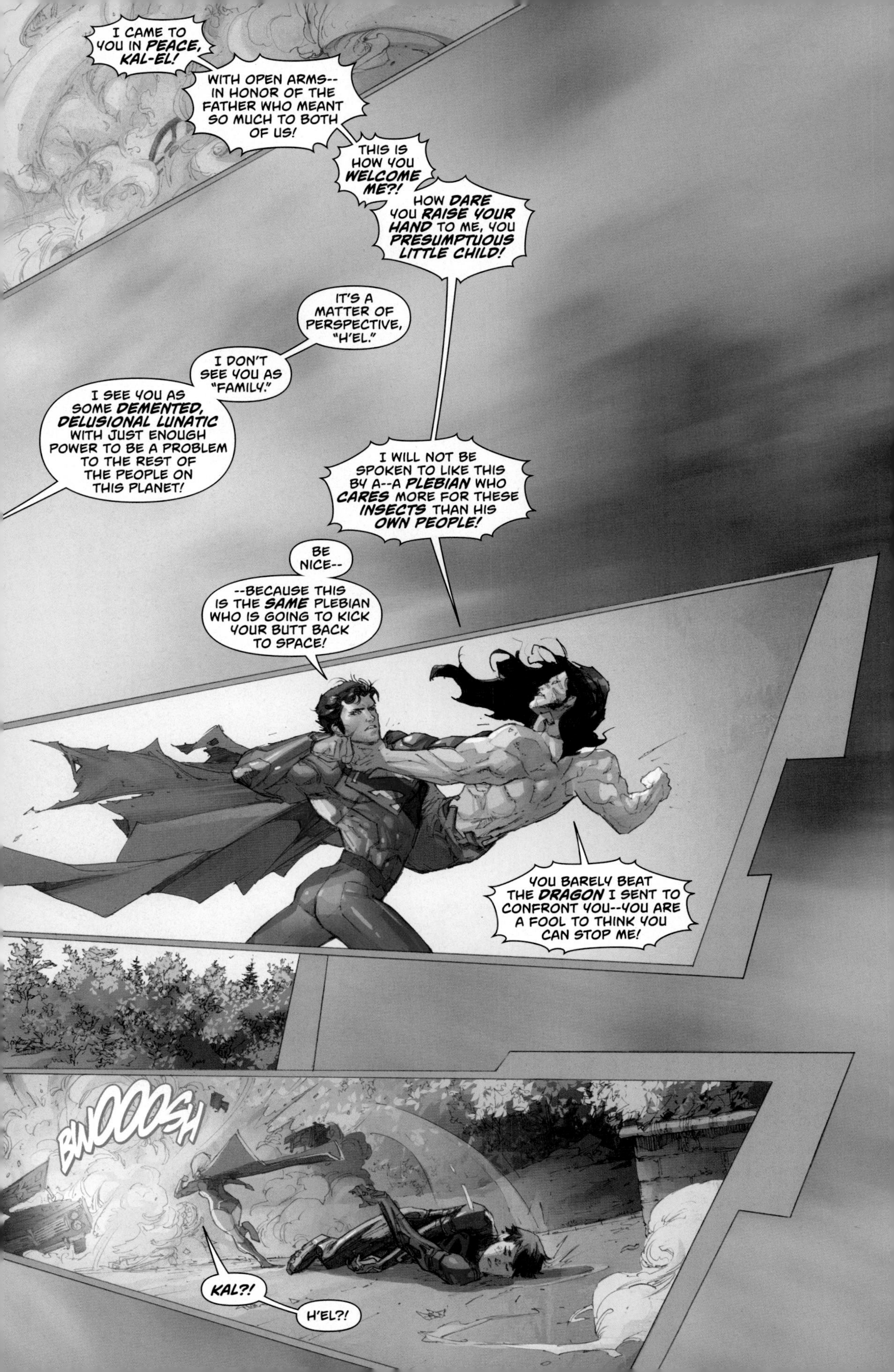
I CAME TO YOU IN PEACE, KAL-EL!
WITH OPEN ARMS-- IN HONOR OF THE FATHER WHO MEANT SO MUCH TO BOTH OF US!
THIS IS HOW YOU WELCOME ME?!
HOW DARE YOU RAISE YOUR HAND TO ME, YOU PRESUMPTUOUS LITTLE CHILD!
IT'S A MATTER OF PERSPECTIVE, "H'EL."
I DON'T SEE YOU AS "FAMILY."
I SEE YOU AS SOME DEMENTED, DELUSIONAL LUNATIC WITH JUST ENOUGH POWER TO BE A PROBLEM TO THE REST OF THE PEOPLE ON THIS PLANET!
I WILL NOT BE SPOKEN TO LIKE THIS BY A--A PLEBIAN WHO CARES MORE FOR THESE INSECTS THAN HIS OWN PEOPLE!
BE NICE--
--BECAUSE THIS IS THE SAME PLEBIAN WHO IS GOING TO KICK YOUR BUTT BACK TO SPACE!
YOU BARELY BEAT THE DRAGON I SENT TO CONFRONT YOU--YOU ARE A FOOL TO THINK YOU CAN STOP ME!
BWOOOSH
KAL?!
H'EL?!

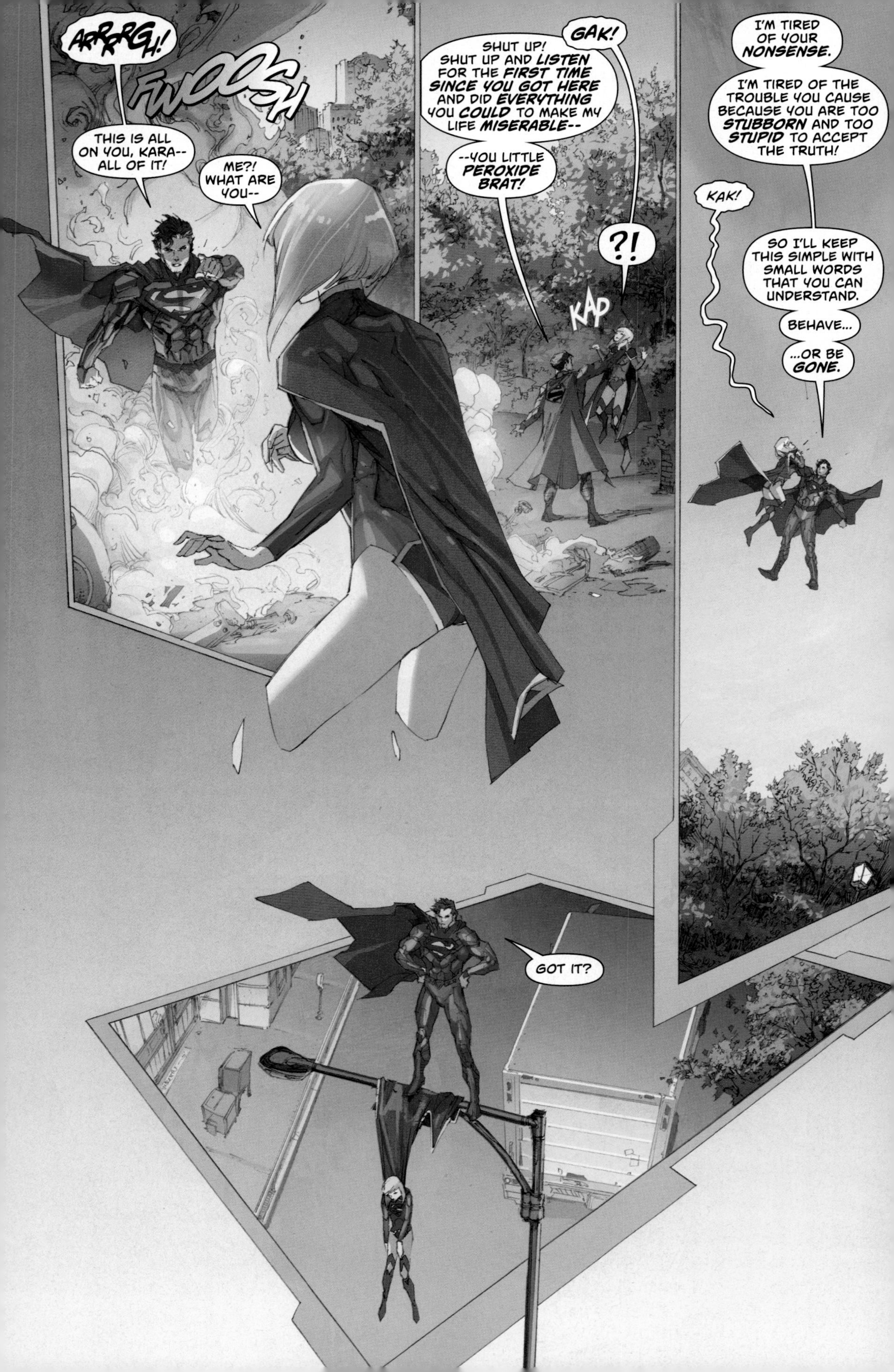
ARRRRGH!
FWOOSH
THIS IS ALL ON YOU, KARA-- ALL OF IT!
ME?! WHAT ARE YOU--
SHUT UP! SHUT UP AND LISTEN FOR THE FIRST TIME SINCE YOU GOT HERE AND DID EVERYTHING YOU COULD TO MAKE MY LIFE MISERABLE--
GAK!
--YOU LITTLE PEROXIDE BRAT!
?!
KAP
I'M TIRED OF YOUR NONSENSE.
I'M TIRED OF THE TROUBLE YOU CAUSE BECAUSE YOU ARE TOO STUBBORN AND TOO STUPID TO ACCEPT THE TRUTH!
KAK!
SO I'LL KEEP THIS SIMPLE WITH SMALL WORDS THAT YOU CAN UNDERSTAND.
BEHAVE...
...OR BE GONE.
GOT IT?

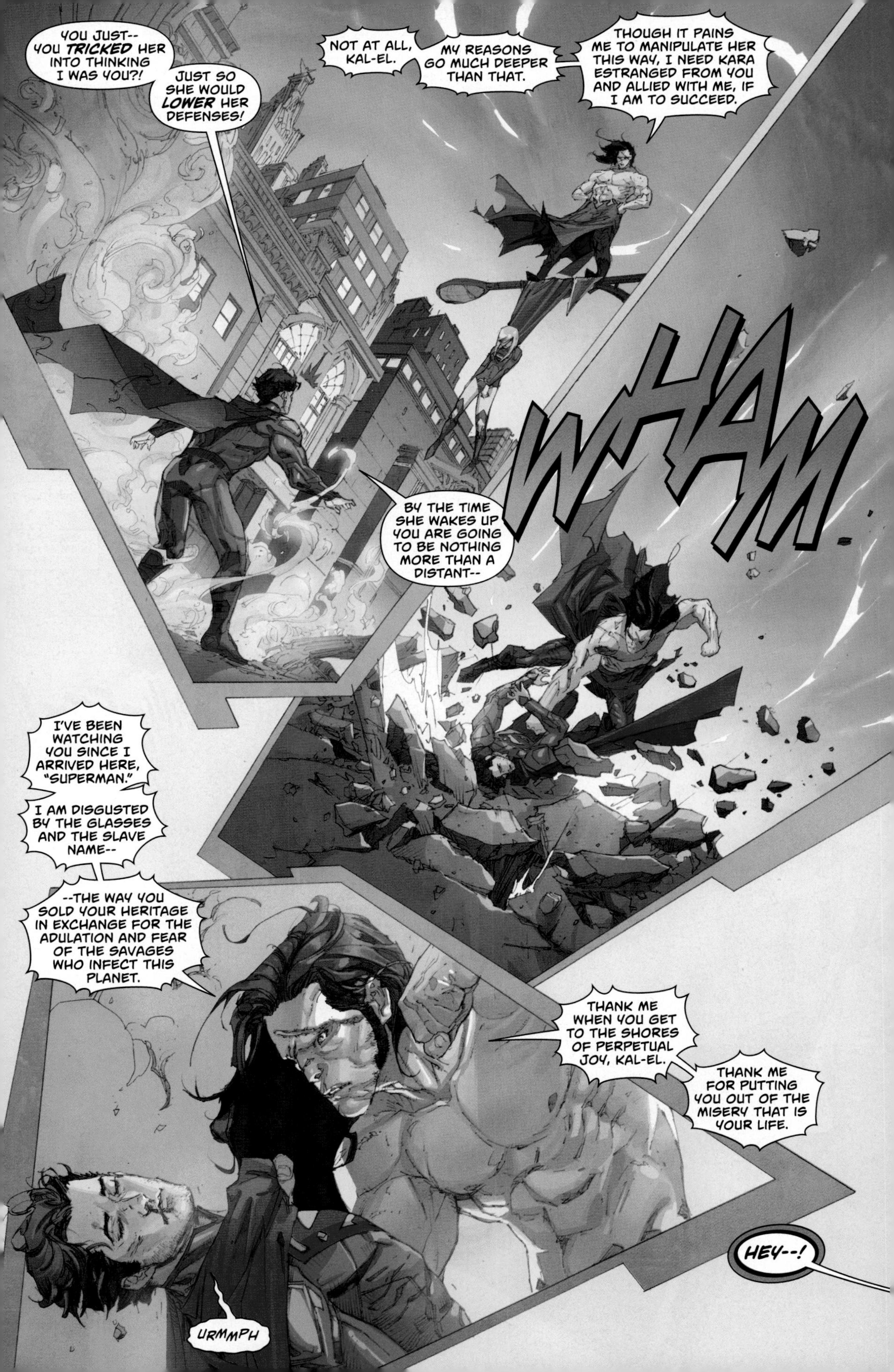
YOU JUST-- YOU TRICKED HER INTO THINKING I WAS YOU?!
JUST SO SHE WOULD LOWER HER DEFENSES!
NOT AT ALL, KAL-EL.
MY REASONS GO MUCH DEEPER THAN THAT.
THOUGH IT PAINS ME TO MANIPULATE HER THIS WAY, I NEED KARA ESTRANGED FROM YOU AND ALLIED WITH ME, IF I AM TO SUCCEED.
BY THE TIME SHE WAKES UP YOU ARE GOING TO BE NOTHING MORE THAN A DISTANT--
WHAM
I'VE BEEN WATCHING YOU SINCE I ARRIVED HERE, "SUPERMAN."
I AM DISGUSTED BY THE GLASSES AND THE SLAVE NAME--
--THE WAY YOU SOLD YOUR HERITAGE IN EXCHANGE FOR THE ADULATION AND FEAR OF THE SAVAGES WHO INFECT THIS PLANET.
THANK ME WHEN YOU GET TO THE SHORES OF PERPETUAL JOY, KAL-EL.
THANK ME FOR PUTTING YOU OUT OF THE MISERY THAT IS YOUR LIFE.
HEY--!
URMMPH

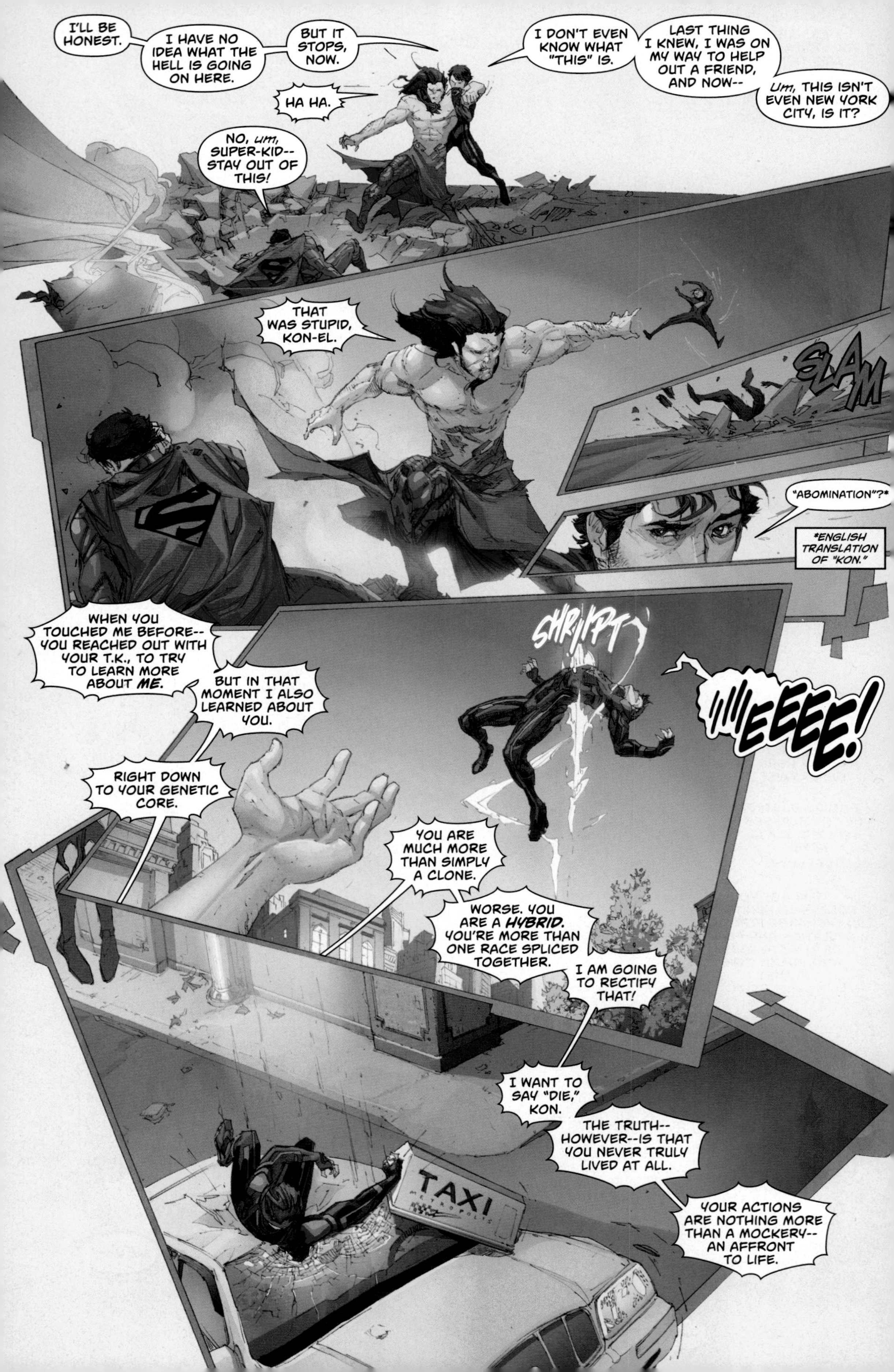
I'LL BE HONEST.
I HAVE NO IDEA WHAT THE HELL IS GOING ON HERE.
BUT IT STOPS, NOW.
HA HA.
I DON'T EVEN KNOW WHAT "THIS" IS.
LAST THING I KNEW, I WAS ON MY WAY TO HELP OUT A FRIEND, AND NOW--
Um, THIS ISN'T EVEN NEW YORK CITY, IS IT?
NO, um, SUPER-KID-- STAY OUT OF THIS!
THAT WAS STUPID, KON-EL.
SLAM
"ABOMINATION"?*
*ENGLISH TRANSLATION OF "KON."
WHEN YOU TOUCHED ME BEFORE-- YOU REACHED OUT WITH YOUR T.K., TO TRY TO LEARN MORE ABOUT ME.
BUT IN THAT MOMENT I ALSO LEARNED ABOUT YOU.
SHRIPT
EEEE!
RIGHT DOWN TO YOUR GENETIC CORE.
YOU ARE MUCH MORE THAN SIMPLY A CLONE.
WORSE. YOU ARE A HYBRID. YOU'RE MORE THAN ONE RACE SPLICED TOGETHER.
I AM GOING TO RECTIFY THAT!
I WANT TO SAY "DIE," KON.
THE TRUTH-- HOWEVER--IS THAT YOU NEVER TRULY LIVED AT ALL.
TAXI
METROPOLIS
YOUR ACTIONS ARE NOTHING MORE THAN A MOCKERY-- AN AFFRONT TO LIFE.

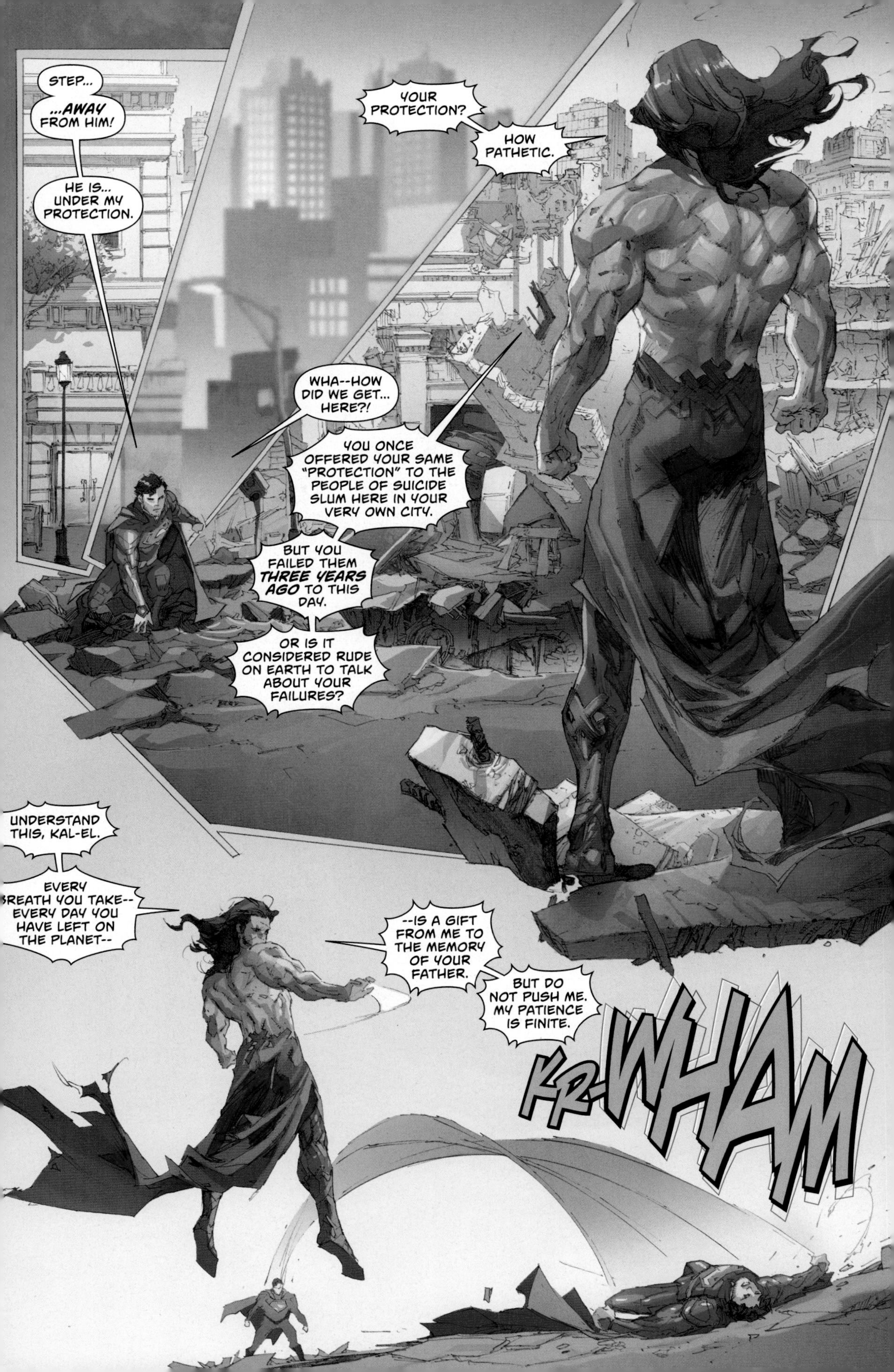
STEP...
...AWAY FROM HIM!
HE IS... UNDER MY PROTECTION.
YOUR PROTECTION?
HOW PATHETIC.
WHA--HOW DID WE GET... HERE?!
YOU ONCE OFFERED YOUR SAME "PROTECTION" TO THE PEOPLE OF SUICIDE SLUM HERE IN YOUR VERY OWN CITY.
BUT YOU FAILED THEM THREE YEARS AGO TO THIS DAY.
OR IS IT CONSIDERED RUDE ON EARTH TO TALK ABOUT YOUR FAILURES?
UNDERSTAND THIS, KAL-EL.
EVERY BREATH YOU TAKE-- EVERY DAY YOU HAVE LEFT ON THE PLANET--
--IS A GIFT FROM ME TO THE MEMORY OF YOUR FATHER.
BUT DO NOT PUSH ME. MY PATIENCE IS FINITE.
KR-WHAM

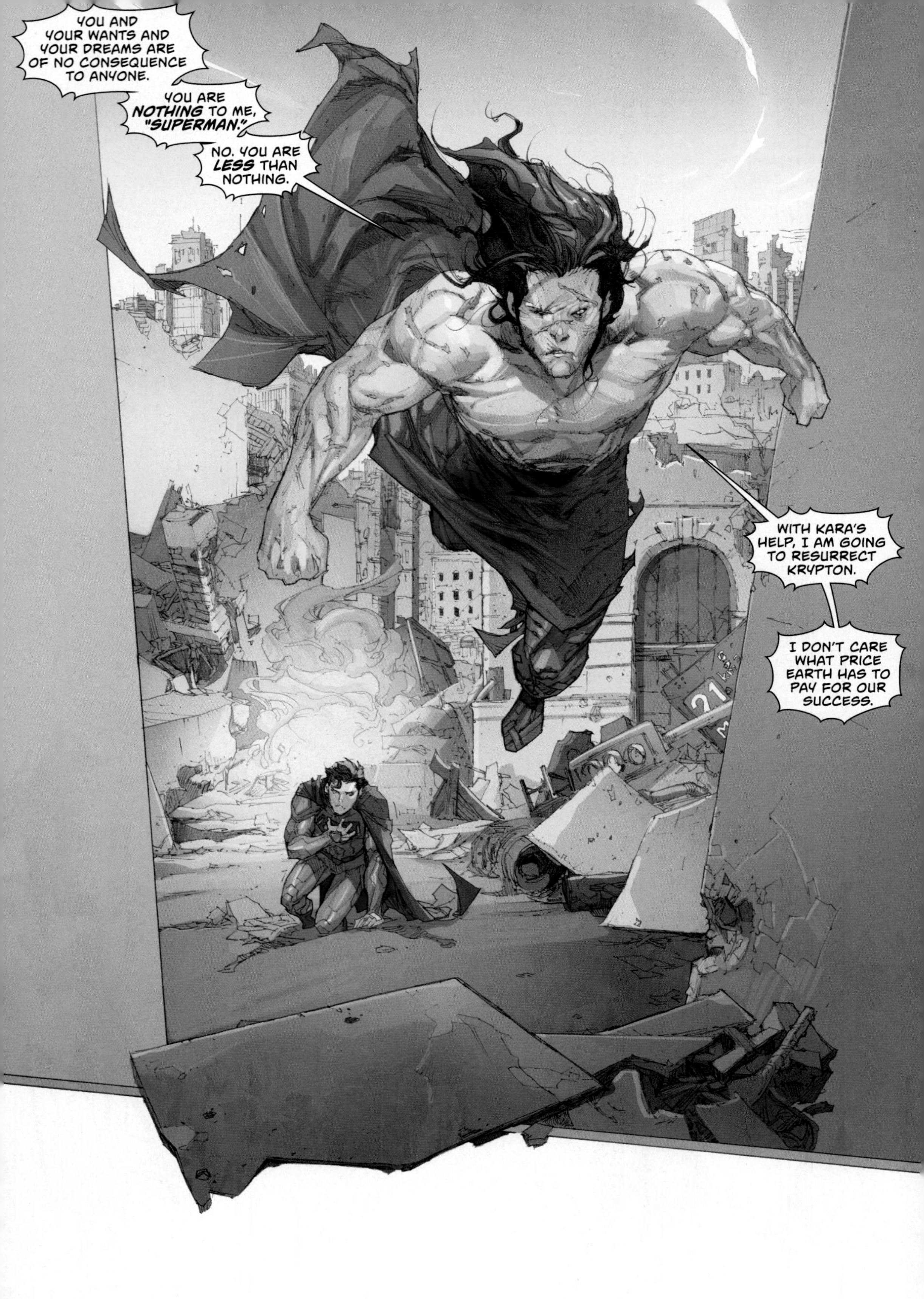
YOU AND YOUR WANTS AND YOUR DREAMS ARE OF NO CONSEQUENCE TO ANYONE.
YOU ARE *NOTHING* TO ME, *"SUPERMAN."*
NO. YOU ARE *LESS* THAN NOTHING.
WITH KARA'S HELP, I AM GOING TO RESURRECT KRYPTON.
I DON'T CARE WHAT PRICE EARTH HAS TO PAY FOR OUR SUCCESS.

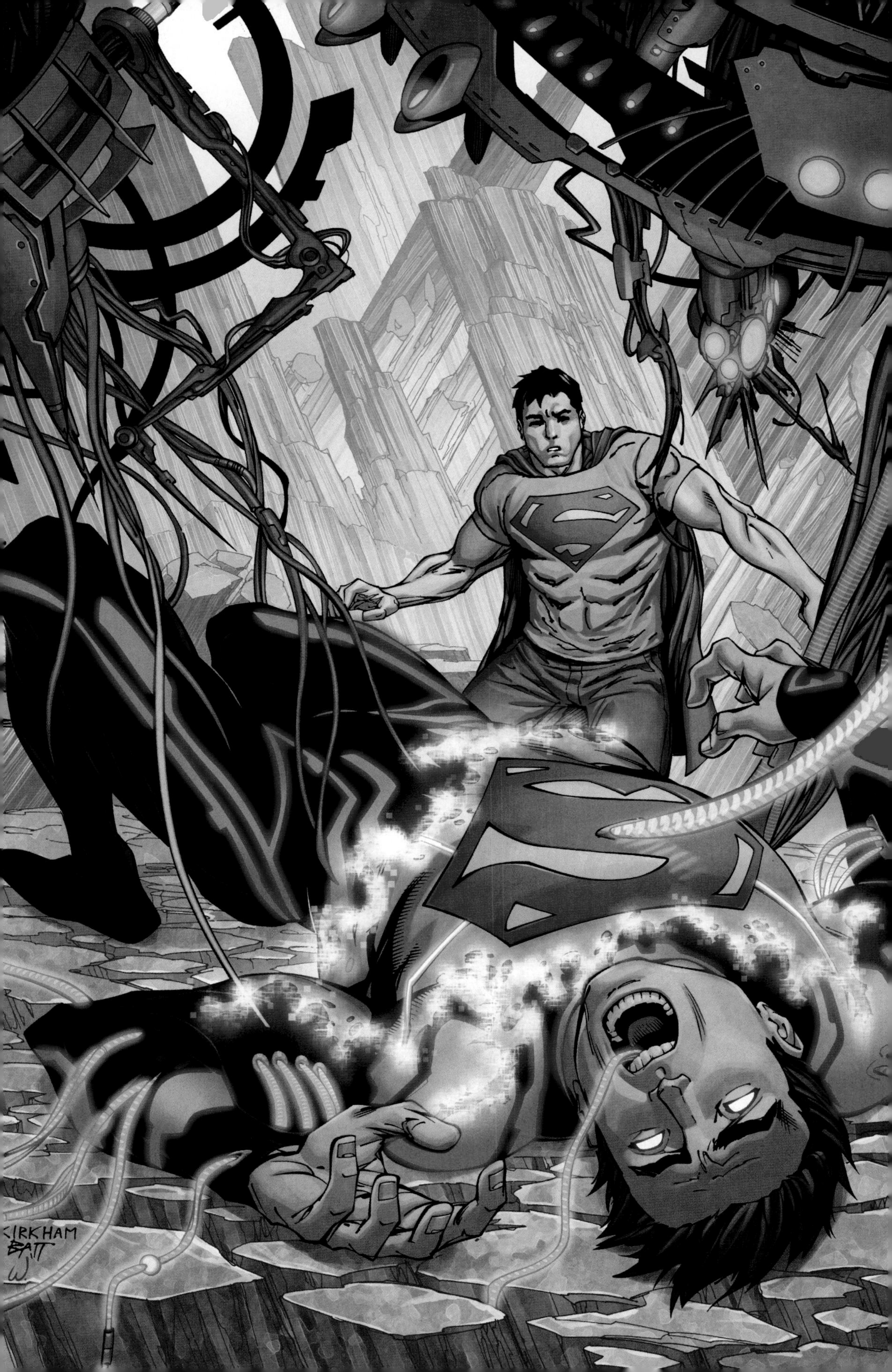
KIRKHAM
BATT

SHATTERED STEEL

TOM DEFALCO writer **RON FRENZ** breakdowns **ROGER ROBINSON, IBAN COELLO, AND AMILCAR PINNA** artists
cover art by **TYLER KIRKHAM, BATT, AND JASON WRIGHT**

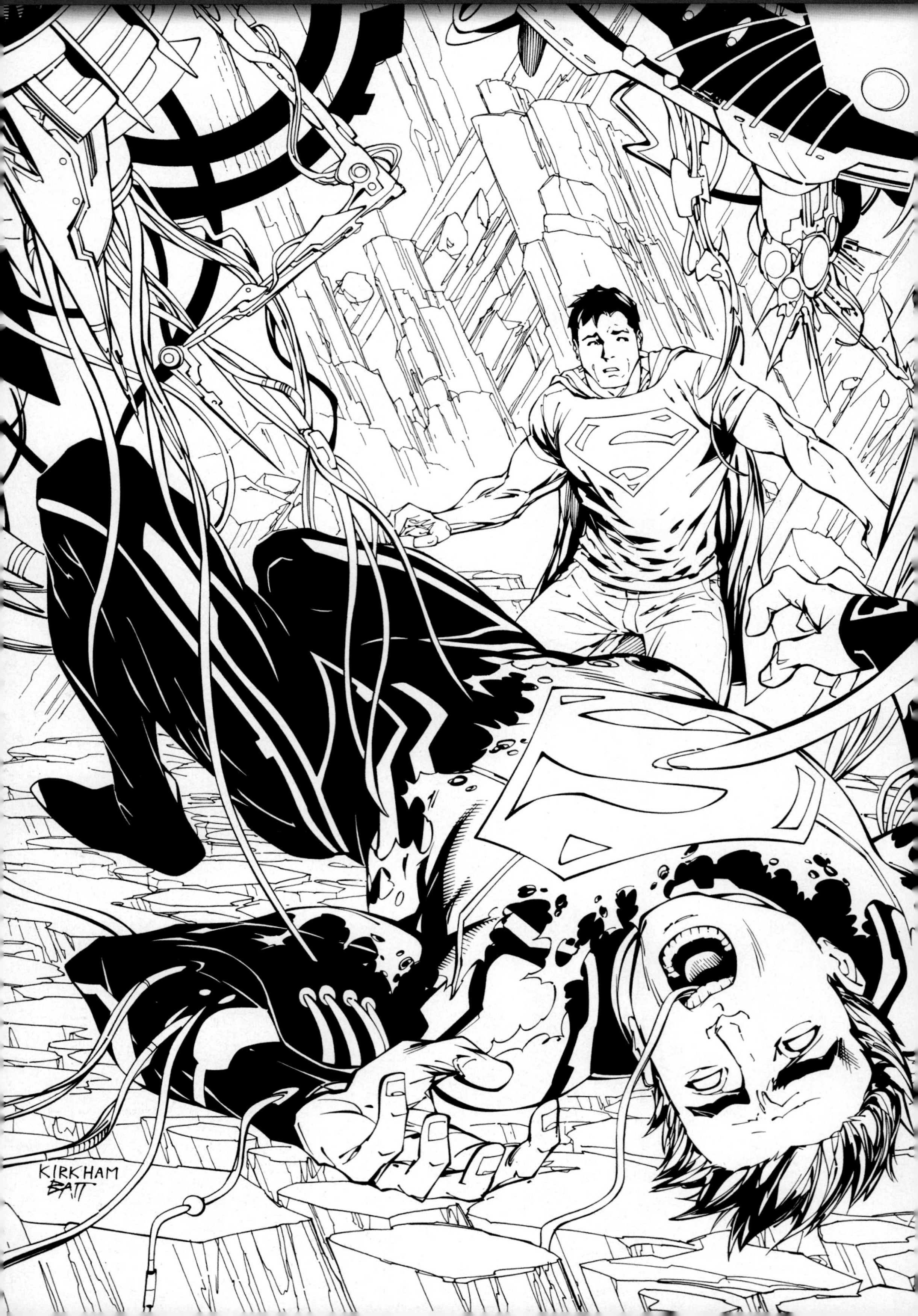
KIRKHAM
BATT

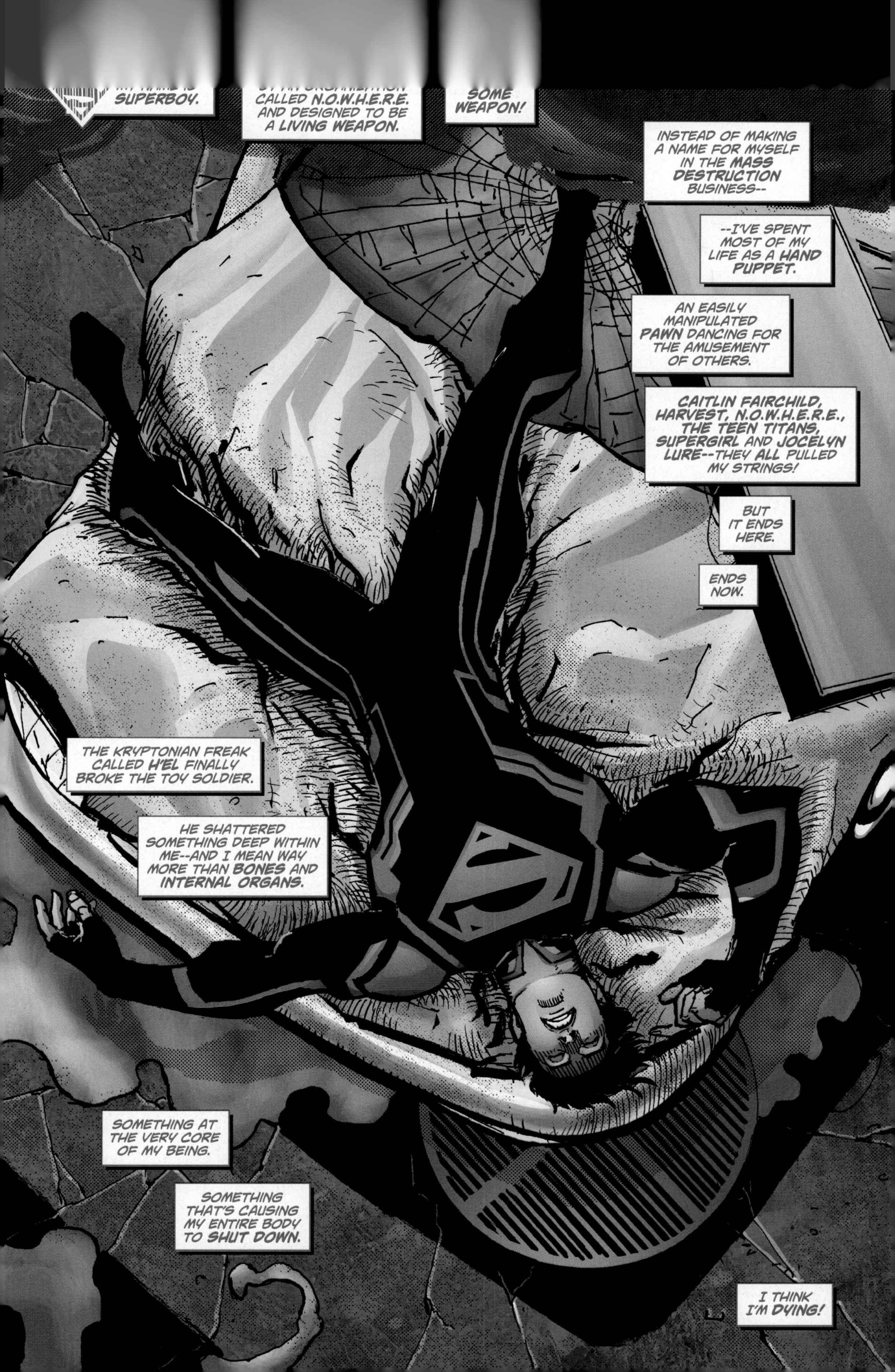
SUPERBOY.
CALLED N.O.W.H.E.R.E. AND DESIGNED TO BE A LIVING WEAPON.
SOME WEAPON!
INSTEAD OF MAKING A NAME FOR MYSELF IN THE MASS DESTRUCTION BUSINESS--
--I'VE SPENT MOST OF MY LIFE AS A HAND PUPPET.
AN EASILY MANIPULATED PAWN DANCING FOR THE AMUSEMENT OF OTHERS.
CAITLIN FAIRCHILD, HARVEST, N.O.W.H.E.R.E., THE TEEN TITANS, SUPERGIRL AND JOCELYN LURE--THEY ALL PULLED MY STRINGS!
BUT IT ENDS HERE.
ENDS NOW.
THE KRYPTONIAN FREAK CALLED H'EL FINALLY BROKE THE TOY SOLDIER.
HE SHATTERED SOMETHING DEEP WITHIN ME--AND I MEAN WAY MORE THAN BONES AND INTERNAL ORGANS.
SOMETHING AT THE VERY CORE OF MY BEING.
SOMETHING THAT'S CAUSING MY ENTIRE BODY TO SHUT DOWN.
I THINK I'M DYING!

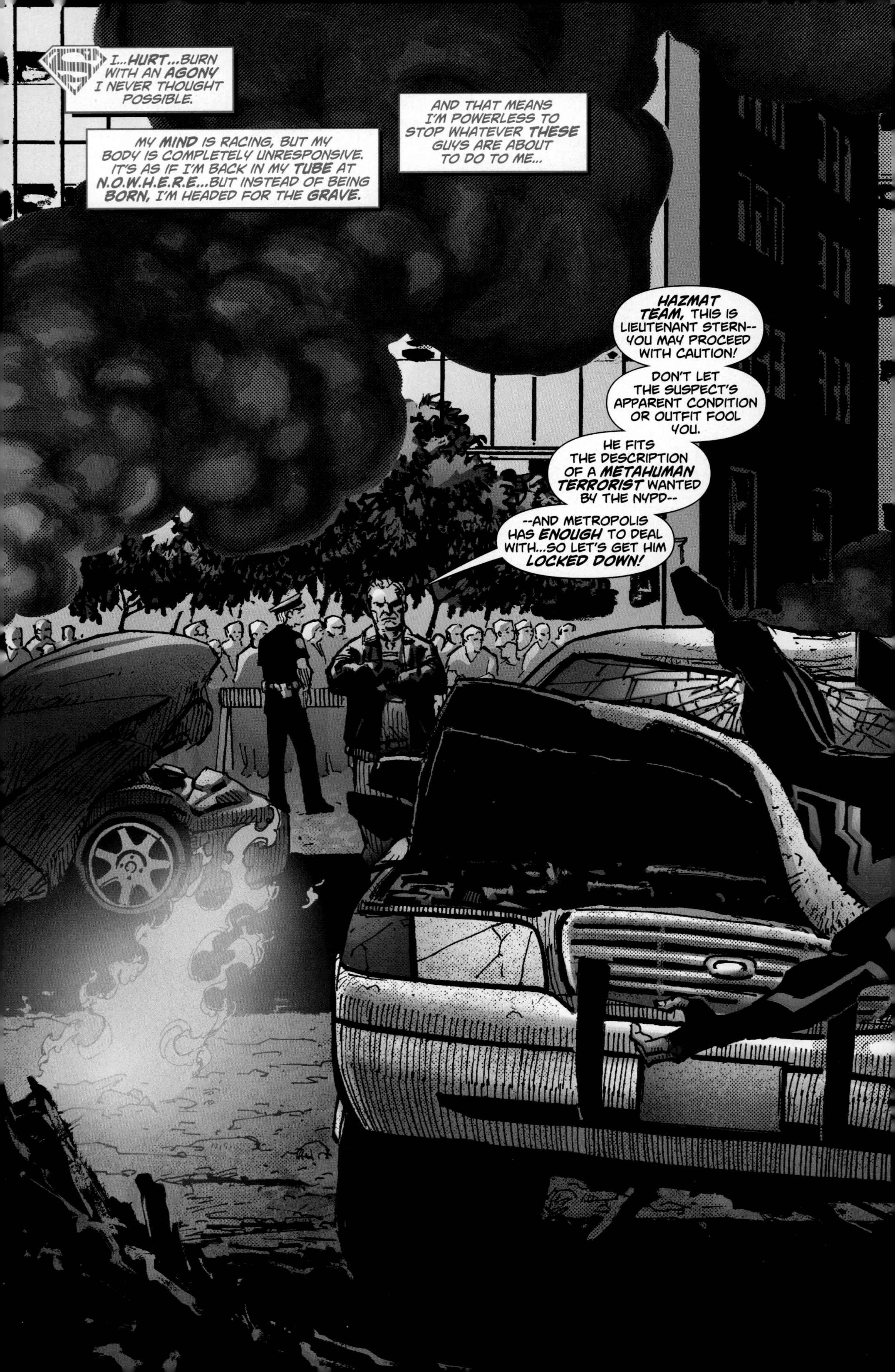
I...HURT...BURN WITH AN AGONY I NEVER THOUGHT POSSIBLE.
MY MIND IS RACING, BUT MY BODY IS COMPLETELY UNRESPONSIVE. IT'S AS IF I'M BACK IN MY TUBE AT N.O.W.H.E.R.E...BUT INSTEAD OF BEING BORN, I'M HEADED FOR THE GRAVE.
AND THAT MEANS I'M POWERLESS TO STOP WHATEVER THESE GUYS ARE ABOUT TO DO TO ME...
HAZMAT TEAM, THIS IS LIEUTENANT STERN--YOU MAY PROCEED WITH CAUTION!
DON'T LET THE SUSPECT'S APPARENT CONDITION OR OUTFIT FOOL YOU.
HE FITS THE DESCRIPTION OF A METAHUMAN TERRORIST WANTED BY THE NYPD--
--AND METROPOLIS HAS ENOUGH TO DEAL WITH...SO LET'S GET HIM LOCKED DOWN!

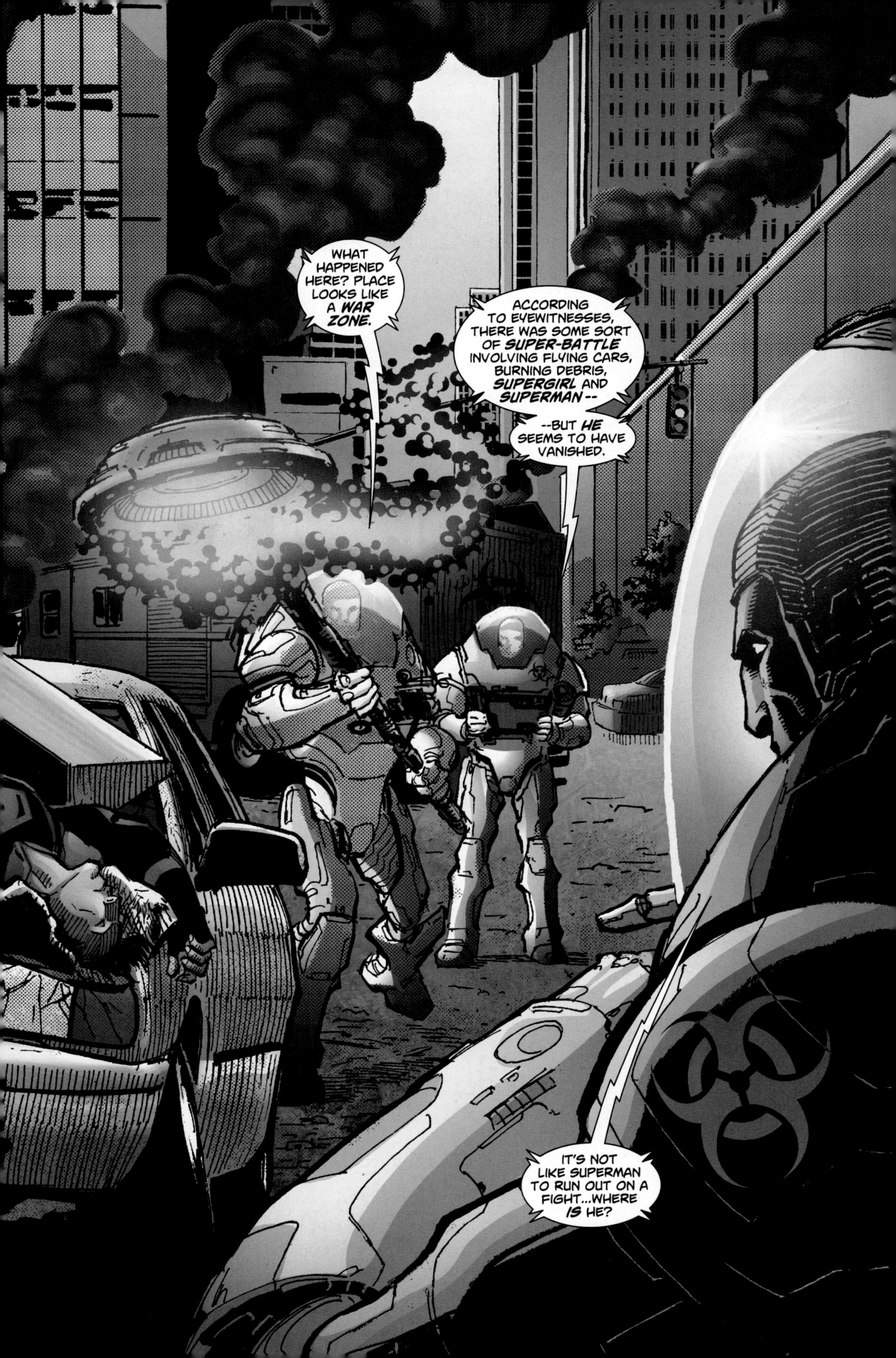
WHAT HAPPENED HERE? PLACE LOOKS LIKE A WAR ZONE.
ACCORDING TO EYEWITNESSES, THERE WAS SOME SORT OF SUPER-BATTLE INVOLVING FLYING CARS, BURNING DEBRIS, SUPERGIRL AND SUPERMAN--
--BUT HE SEEMS TO HAVE VANISHED.
IT'S NOT LIKE SUPERMAN TO RUN OUT ON A FIGHT...WHERE IS HE?

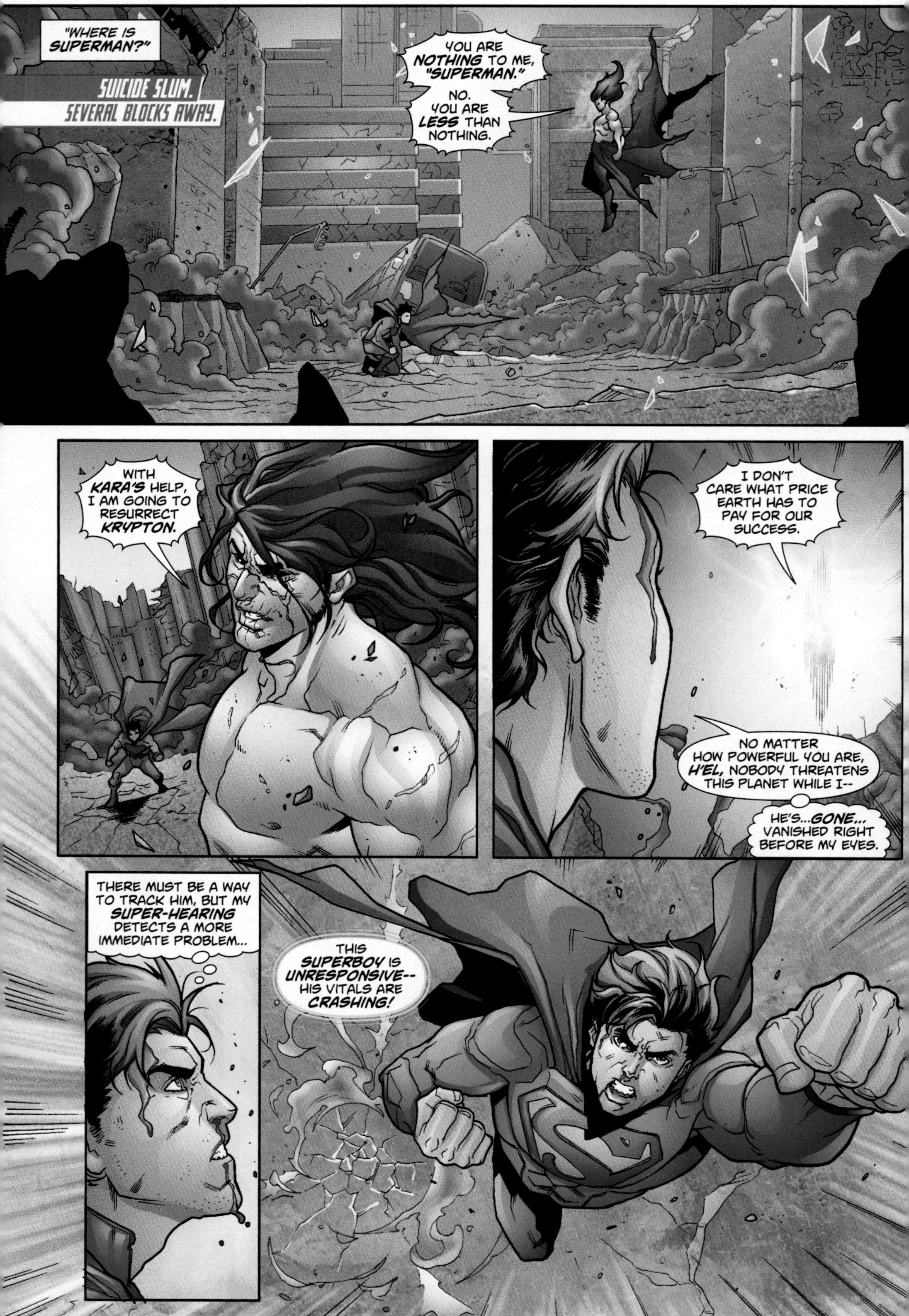
"WHERE IS SUPERMAN?"
SUICIDE SLUM. SEVERAL BLOCKS AWAY.
YOU ARE NOTHING TO ME, "SUPERMAN."
NO. YOU ARE LESS THAN NOTHING.
WITH KARA'S HELP, I AM GOING TO RESURRECT KRYPTON.
I DON'T CARE WHAT PRICE EARTH HAS TO PAY FOR OUR SUCCESS.
NO MATTER HOW POWERFUL YOU ARE, H'EL, NOBODY THREATENS THIS PLANET WHILE I--
HE'S...GONE... VANISHED RIGHT BEFORE MY EYES.
THERE MUST BE A WAY TO TRACK HIM, BUT MY SUPER-HEARING DETECTS A MORE IMMEDIATE PROBLEM...
THIS SUPERBOY IS UNRESPONSIVE-- HIS VITALS ARE CRASHING!

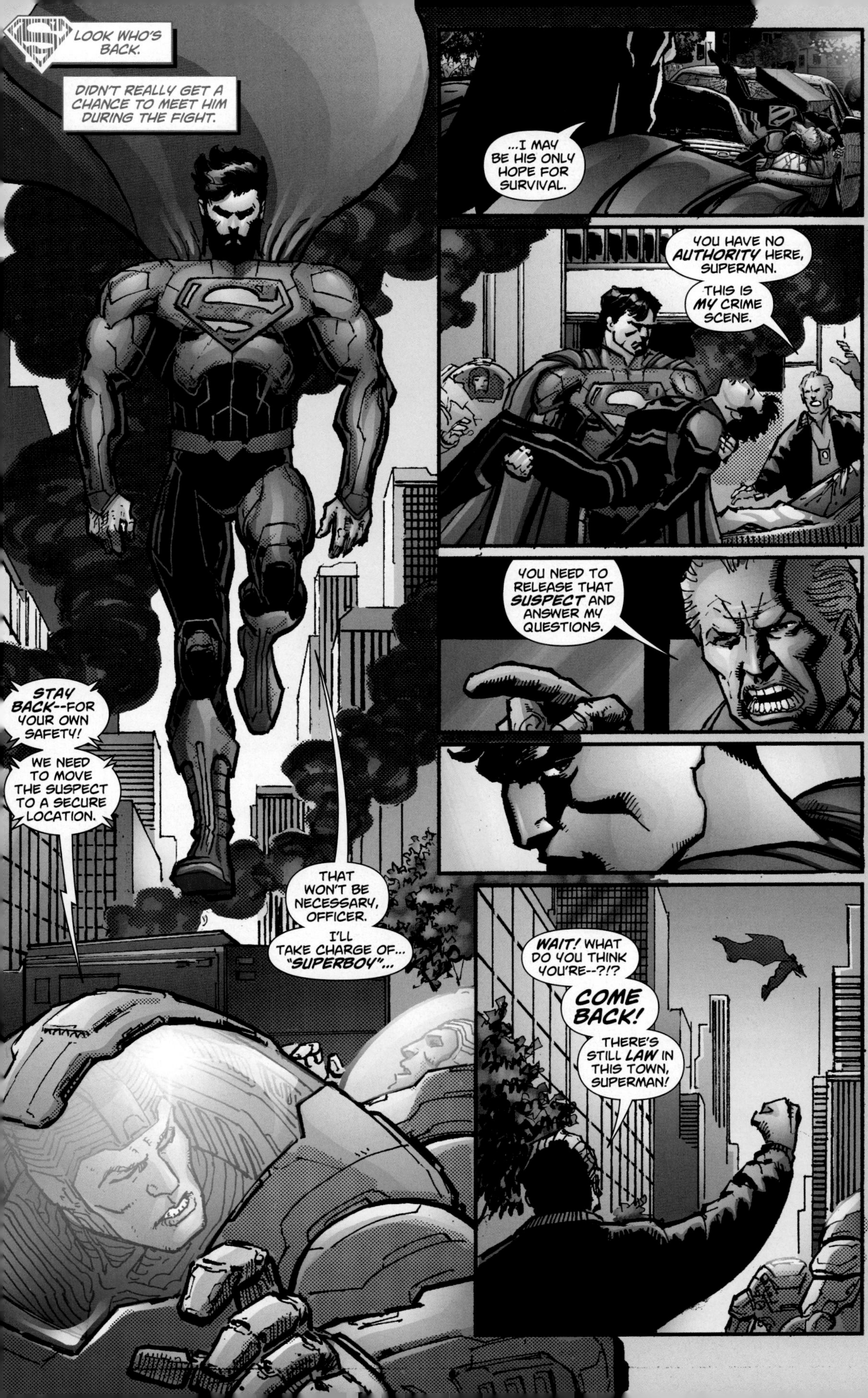
LOOK WHO'S BACK.
DIDN'T REALLY GET A CHANCE TO MEET HIM DURING THE FIGHT.
STAY BACK--FOR YOUR OWN SAFETY!
WE NEED TO MOVE THE SUSPECT TO A SECURE LOCATION.
THAT WON'T BE NECESSARY, OFFICER.
I'LL TAKE CHARGE OF... "SUPERBOY"...
...I MAY BE HIS ONLY HOPE FOR SURVIVAL.
YOU HAVE NO AUTHORITY HERE, SUPERMAN.
THIS IS MY CRIME SCENE.
YOU NEED TO RELEASE THAT SUSPECT AND ANSWER MY QUESTIONS.
WAIT! WHAT DO YOU THINK YOU'RE--?!?
COME BACK!
THERE'S STILL LAW IN THIS TOWN, SUPERMAN!

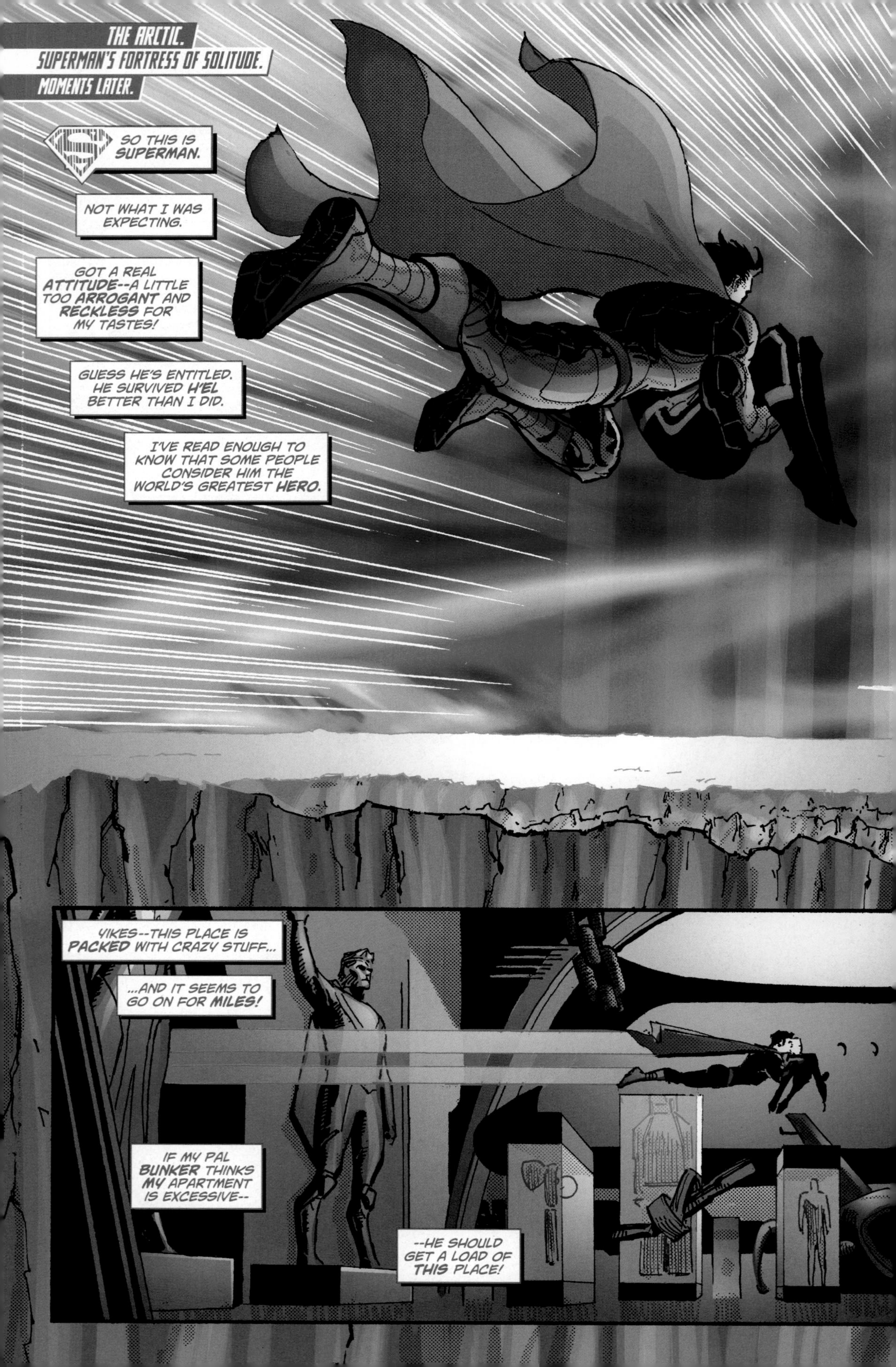

THE ARCTIC.
SUPERMAN'S FORTRESS OF SOLITUDE.
MOMENTS LATER.
SO THIS IS SUPERMAN.
NOT WHAT I WAS EXPECTING.
GOT A REAL ATTITUDE--A LITTLE TOO ARROGANT AND RECKLESS FOR MY TASTES!
GUESS HE'S ENTITLED. HE SURVIVED H'EL BETTER THAN I DID.
I'VE READ ENOUGH TO KNOW THAT SOME PEOPLE CONSIDER HIM THE WORLD'S GREATEST HERO.
YIKES--THIS PLACE IS PACKED WITH CRAZY STUFF...
...AND IT SEEMS TO GO ON FOR MILES!
IF MY PAL BUNKER THINKS MY APARTMENT IS EXCESSIVE--
--HE SHOULD GET A LOAD OF THIS PLACE!

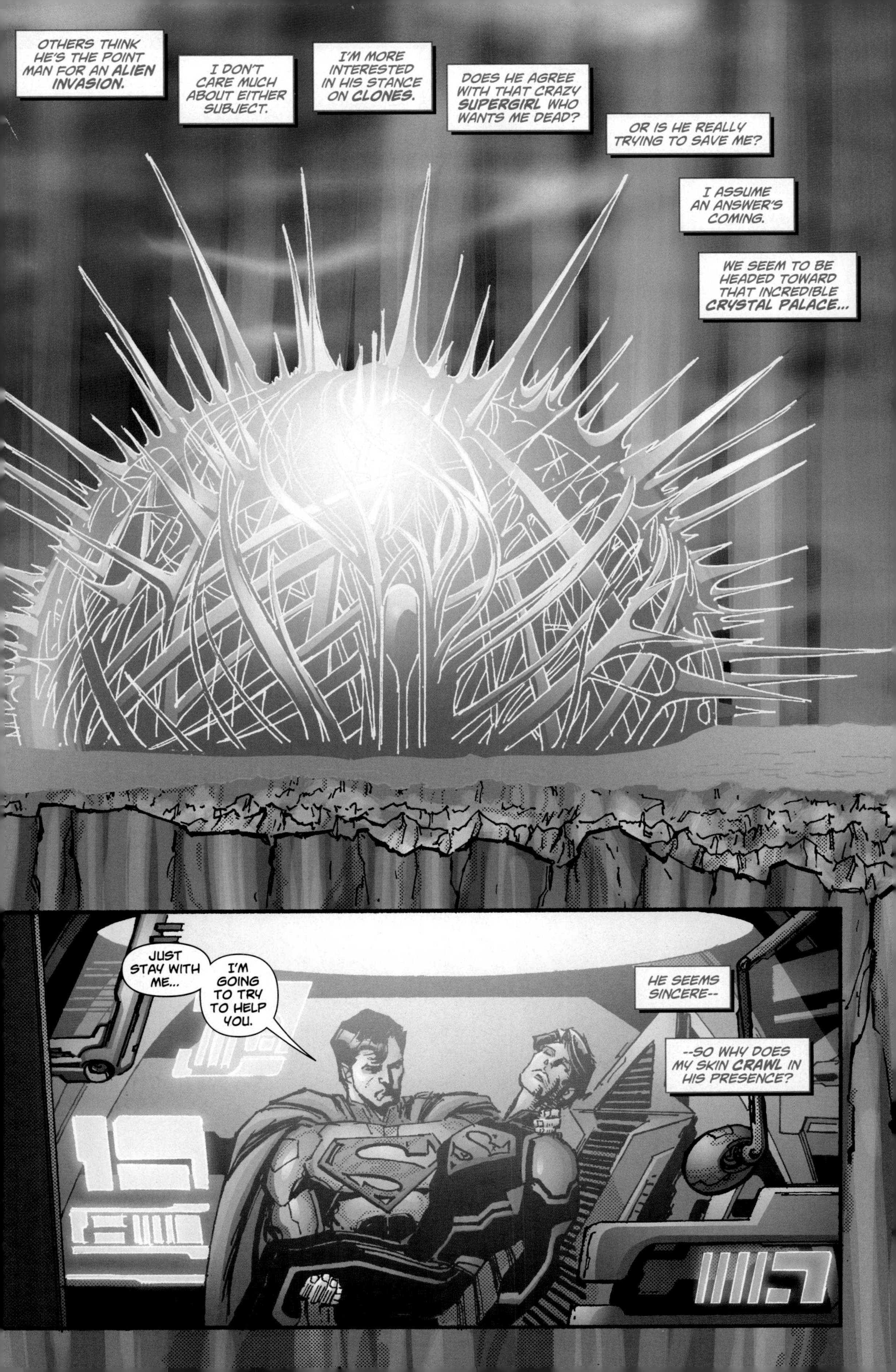
OTHERS THINK HE'S THE POINT MAN FOR AN ALIEN INVASION.
I DON'T CARE MUCH ABOUT EITHER SUBJECT.
I'M MORE INTERESTED IN HIS STANCE ON CLONES.
DOES HE AGREE WITH THAT CRAZY SUPERGIRL WHO WANTS ME DEAD?
OR IS HE REALLY TRYING TO SAVE ME?
I ASSUME AN ANSWER'S COMING.
WE SEEM TO BE HEADED TOWARD THAT INCREDIBLE CRYSTAL PALACE...
JUST STAY WITH ME...
I'M GOING TO TRY TO HELP YOU.
HE SEEMS SINCERE--
--SO WHY DOES MY SKIN CRAWL IN HIS PRESENCE?

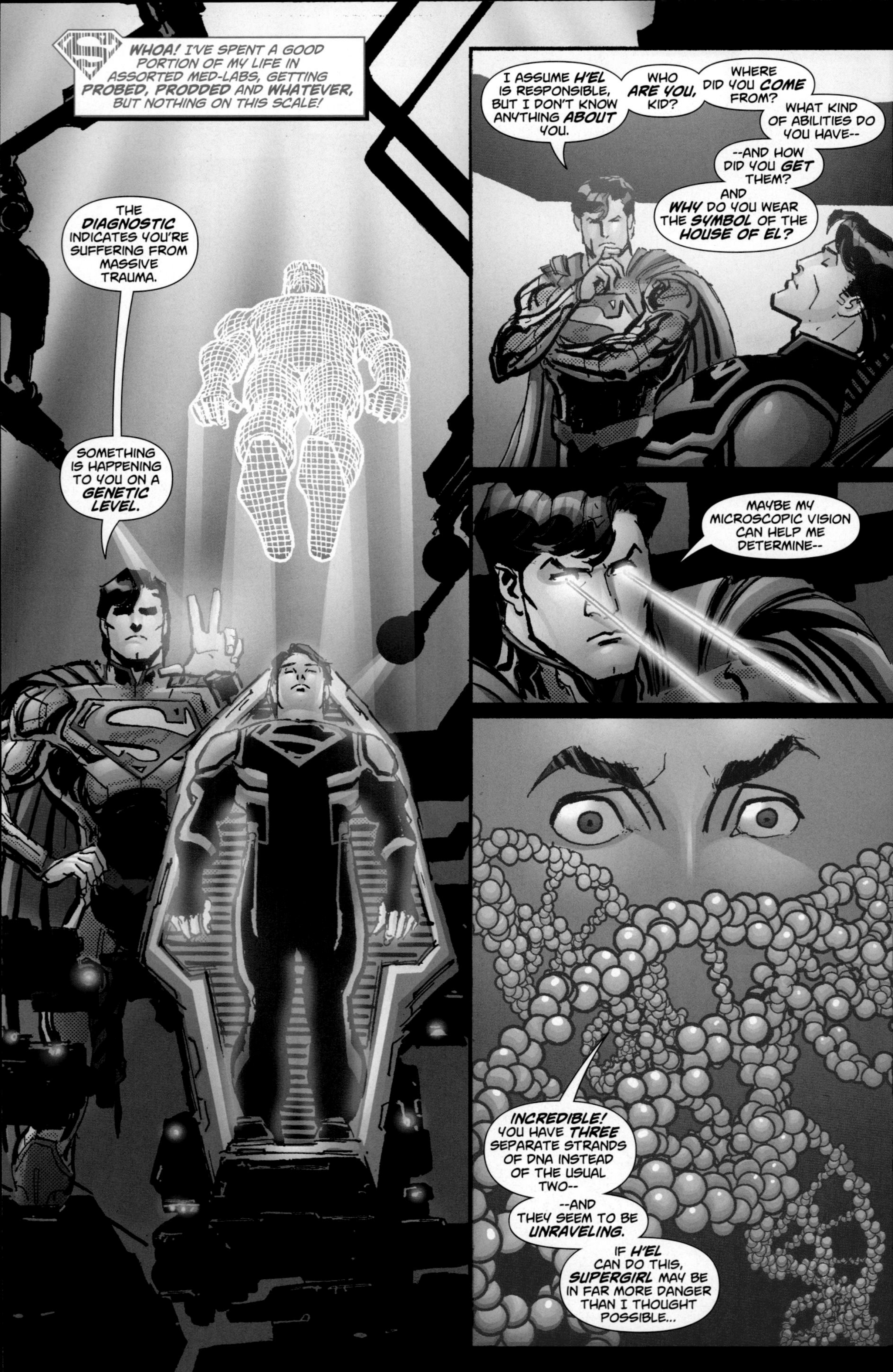
WHOA! I'VE SPENT A GOOD PORTION OF MY LIFE IN ASSORTED MED-LABS, GETTING PROBED, PRODDED AND WHATEVER, BUT NOTHING ON THIS SCALE!
THE DIAGNOSTIC INDICATES YOU'RE SUFFERING FROM MASSIVE TRAUMA.
SOMETHING IS HAPPENING TO YOU ON A GENETIC LEVEL.
I ASSUME H'EL IS RESPONSIBLE, BUT I DON'T KNOW ANYTHING ABOUT YOU.
WHO ARE YOU, KID?
WHERE DID YOU COME FROM?
WHAT KIND OF ABILITIES DO YOU HAVE--
--AND HOW DID YOU GET THEM?
AND WHY DO YOU WEAR THE SYMBOL OF THE HOUSE OF EL?
MAYBE MY MICROSCOPIC VISION CAN HELP ME DETERMINE--
INCREDIBLE! YOU HAVE THREE SEPARATE STRANDS OF DNA INSTEAD OF THE USUAL TWO--
--AND THEY SEEM TO BE UNRAVELING.
IF H'EL CAN DO THIS, SUPERGIRL MAY BE IN FAR MORE DANGER THAN I THOUGHT POSSIBLE...

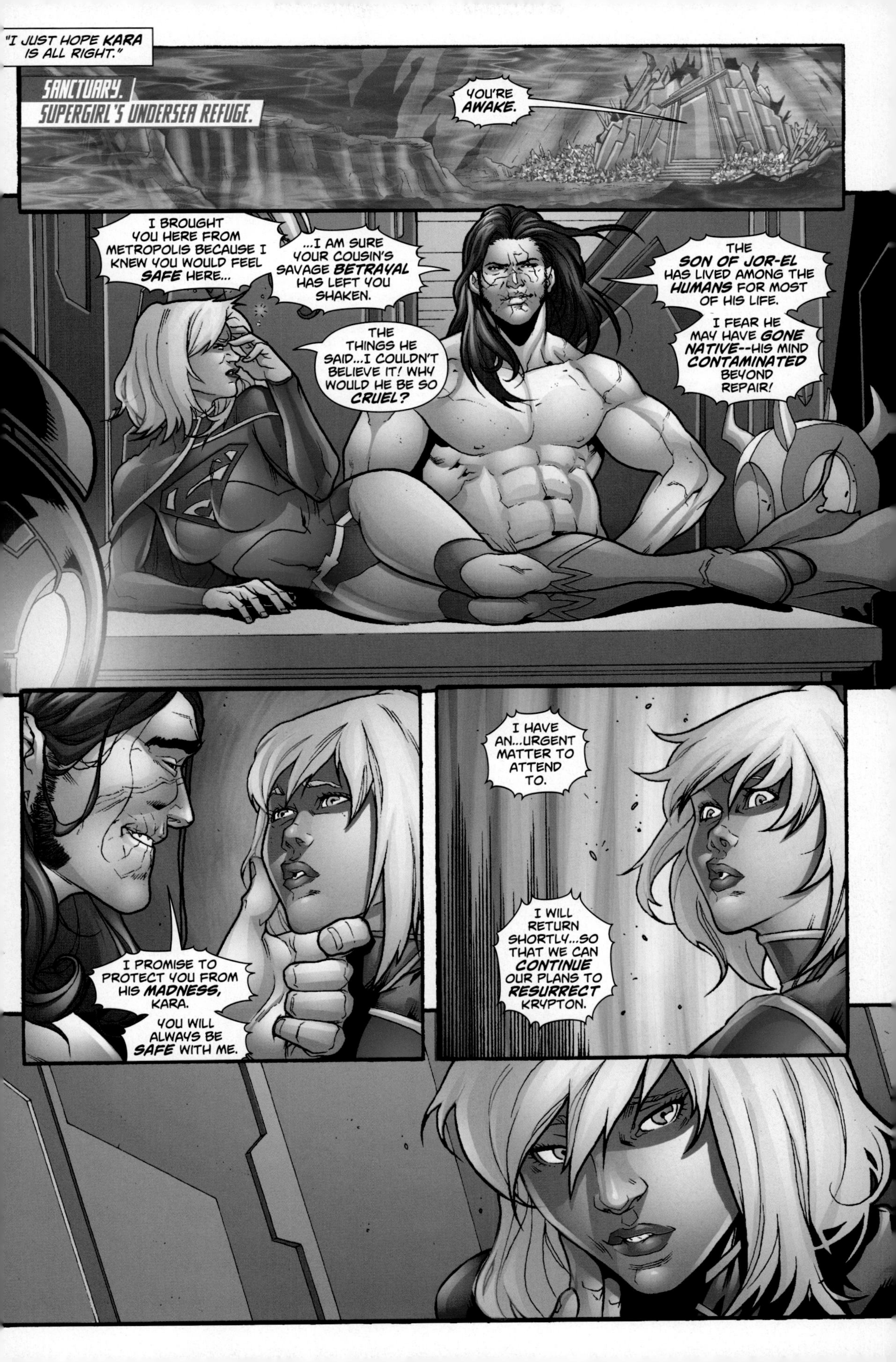
"I JUST HOPE KARA IS ALL RIGHT."
SANCTUARY. SUPERGIRL'S UNDERSEA REFUGE.
YOU'RE AWAKE.
I BROUGHT YOU HERE FROM METROPOLIS BECAUSE I KNEW YOU WOULD FEEL SAFE HERE...
...I AM SURE YOUR COUSIN'S SAVAGE BETRAYAL HAS LEFT YOU SHAKEN.
THE THINGS HE SAID...I COULDN'T BELIEVE IT! WHY WOULD HE BE SO CRUEL?
THE SON OF JOR-EL HAS LIVED AMONG THE HUMANS FOR MOST OF HIS LIFE.
I FEAR HE MAY HAVE GONE NATIVE--HIS MIND CONTAMINATED BEYOND REPAIR!
I PROMISE TO PROTECT YOU FROM HIS MADNESS, KARA.
YOU WILL ALWAYS BE SAFE WITH ME.
I HAVE AN...URGENT MATTER TO ATTEND TO.
I WILL RETURN SHORTLY...SO THAT WE CAN CONTINUE OUR PLANS TO RESURRECT KRYPTON.

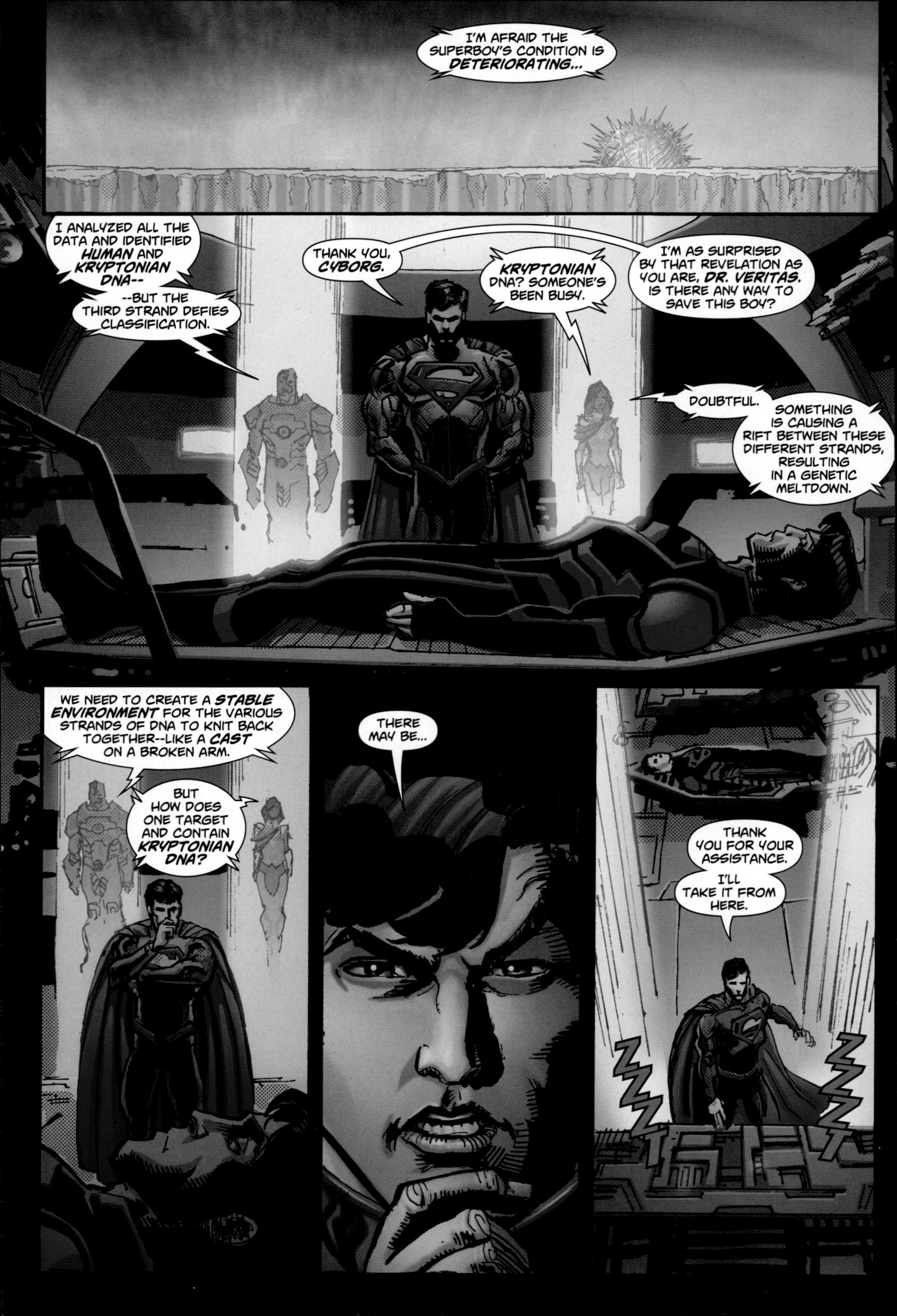
I'M AFRAID THE SUPERBOY'S CONDITION IS DETERIORATING...
I ANALYZED ALL THE DATA AND IDENTIFIED HUMAN AND KRYPTONIAN DNA--
--BUT THE THIRD STRAND DEFIES CLASSIFICATION.
THANK YOU, CYBORG.
KRYPTONIAN DNA? SOMEONE'S BEEN BUSY.
I'M AS SURPRISED BY THAT REVELATION AS YOU ARE, DR. VERITAS. IS THERE ANY WAY TO SAVE THIS BOY?
DOUBTFUL.
SOMETHING IS CAUSING A RIFT BETWEEN THESE DIFFERENT STRANDS, RESULTING IN A GENETIC MELTDOWN.
WE NEED TO CREATE A STABLE ENVIRONMENT FOR THE VARIOUS STRANDS OF DNA TO KNIT BACK TOGETHER--LIKE A CAST ON A BROKEN ARM.
BUT HOW DOES ONE TARGET AND CONTAIN KRYPTONIAN DNA?
THERE MAY BE...
THANK YOU FOR YOUR ASSISTANCE.
I'LL TAKE IT FROM HERE.
ZZZ
ZZZ

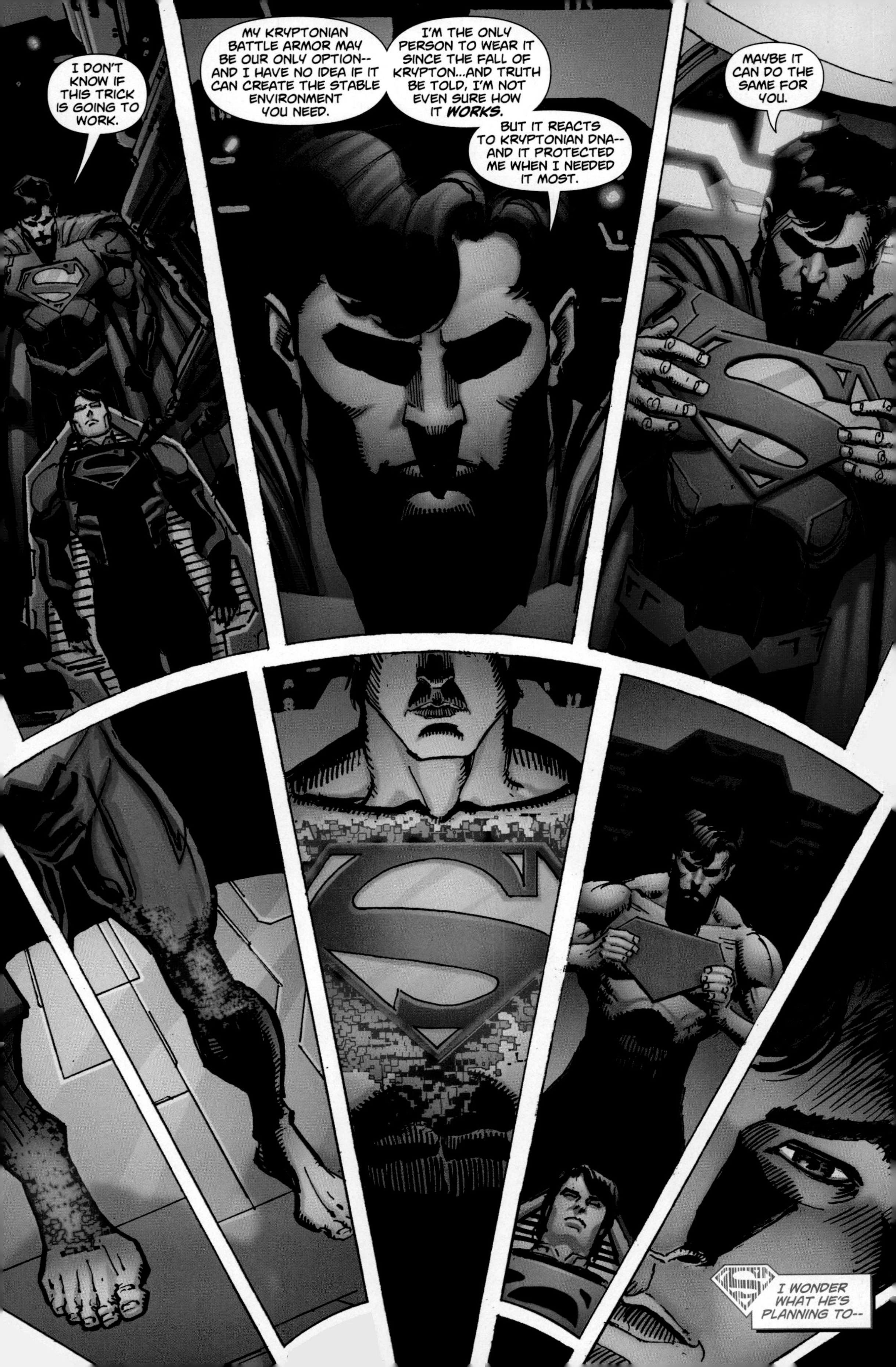
I DON'T KNOW IF THIS TRICK IS GOING TO WORK.
MY KRYPTONIAN BATTLE ARMOR MAY BE OUR ONLY OPTION--AND I HAVE NO IDEA IF IT CAN CREATE THE STABLE ENVIRONMENT YOU NEED.
I'M THE ONLY PERSON TO WEAR IT SINCE THE FALL OF KRYPTON...AND TRUTH BE TOLD, I'M NOT EVEN SURE HOW IT ***WORKS.***
BUT IT REACTS TO KRYPTONIAN DNA--AND IT PROTECTED ME WHEN I NEEDED IT MOST.
MAYBE IT CAN DO THE SAME FOR YOU.
I WONDER WHAT HE'S PLANNING TO--

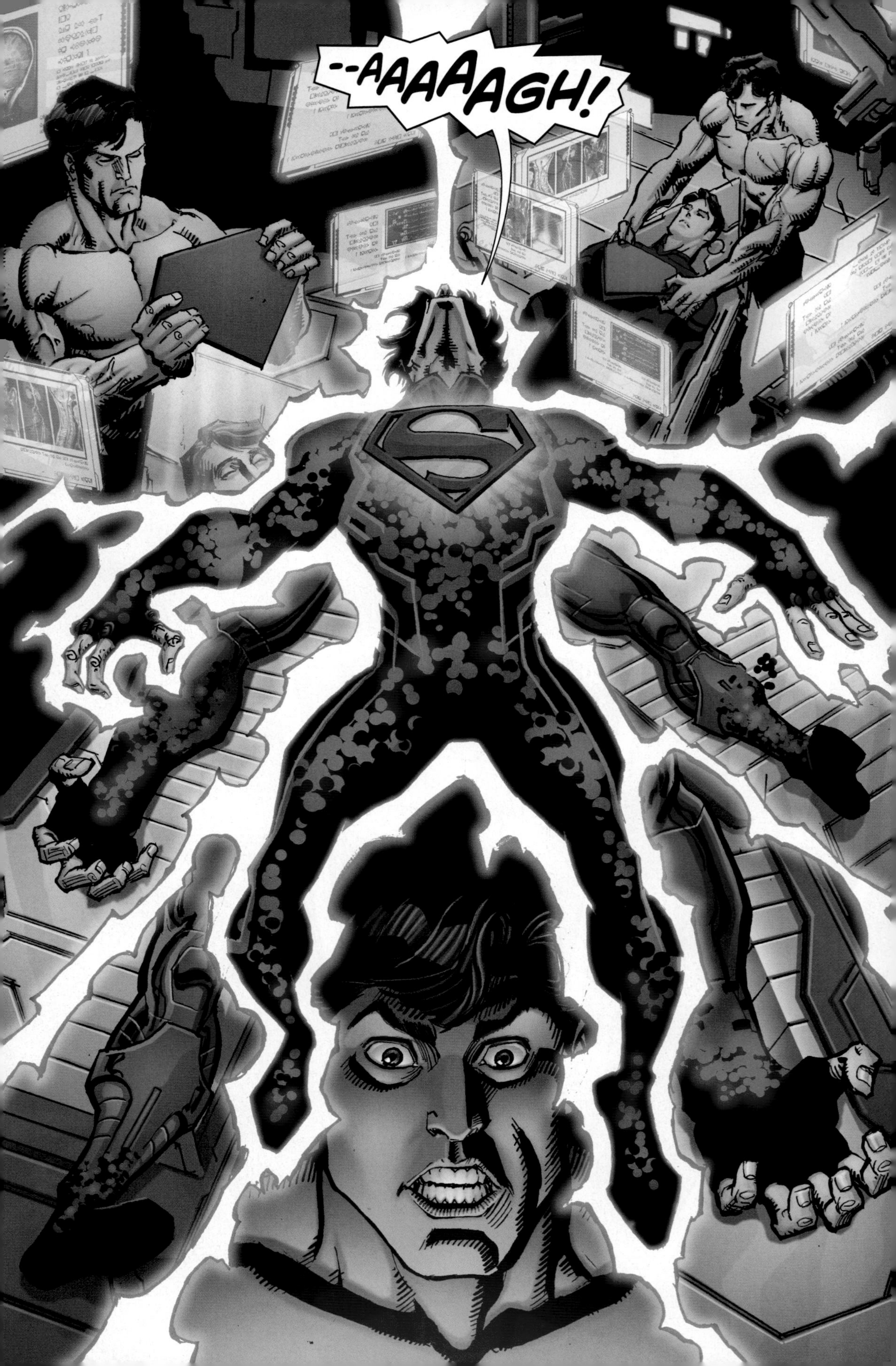
--AAAAAGH!

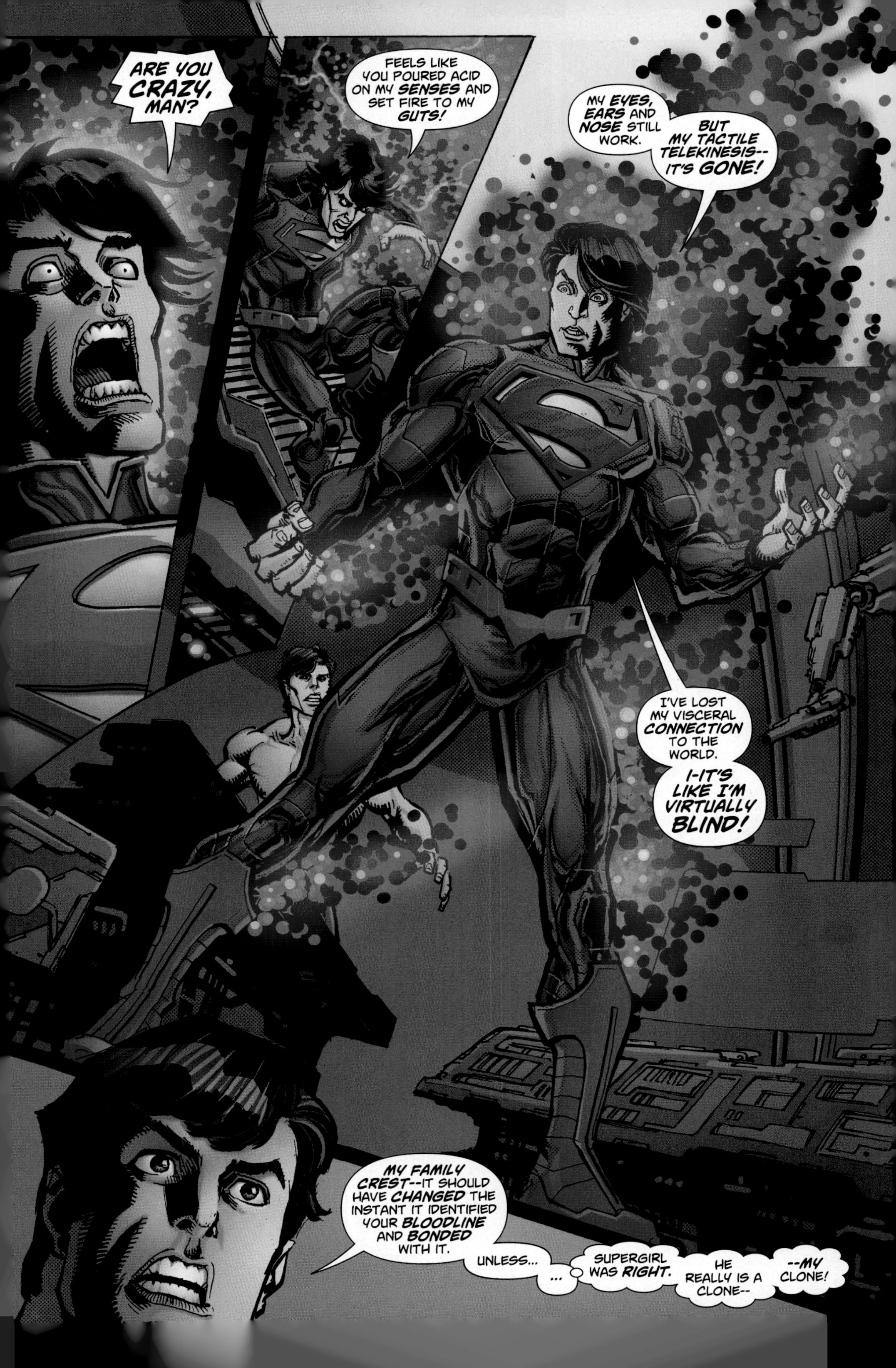
ARE YOU CRAZY, MAN?
FEELS LIKE YOU POURED ACID ON MY SENSES AND SET FIRE TO MY GUTS!
MY EYES, EARS AND NOSE STILL WORK.
BUT MY TACTILE TELEKINESIS-- IT'S GONE!
I'VE LOST MY VISCERAL CONNECTION TO THE WORLD.
I-IT'S LIKE I'M VIRTUALLY BLIND!
MY FAMILY CREST--IT SHOULD HAVE CHANGED THE INSTANT IT IDENTIFIED YOUR BLOODLINE AND BONDED WITH IT.
UNLESS...
...
SUPERGIRL WAS RIGHT.
HE REALLY IS A CLONE--
--MY CLONE!

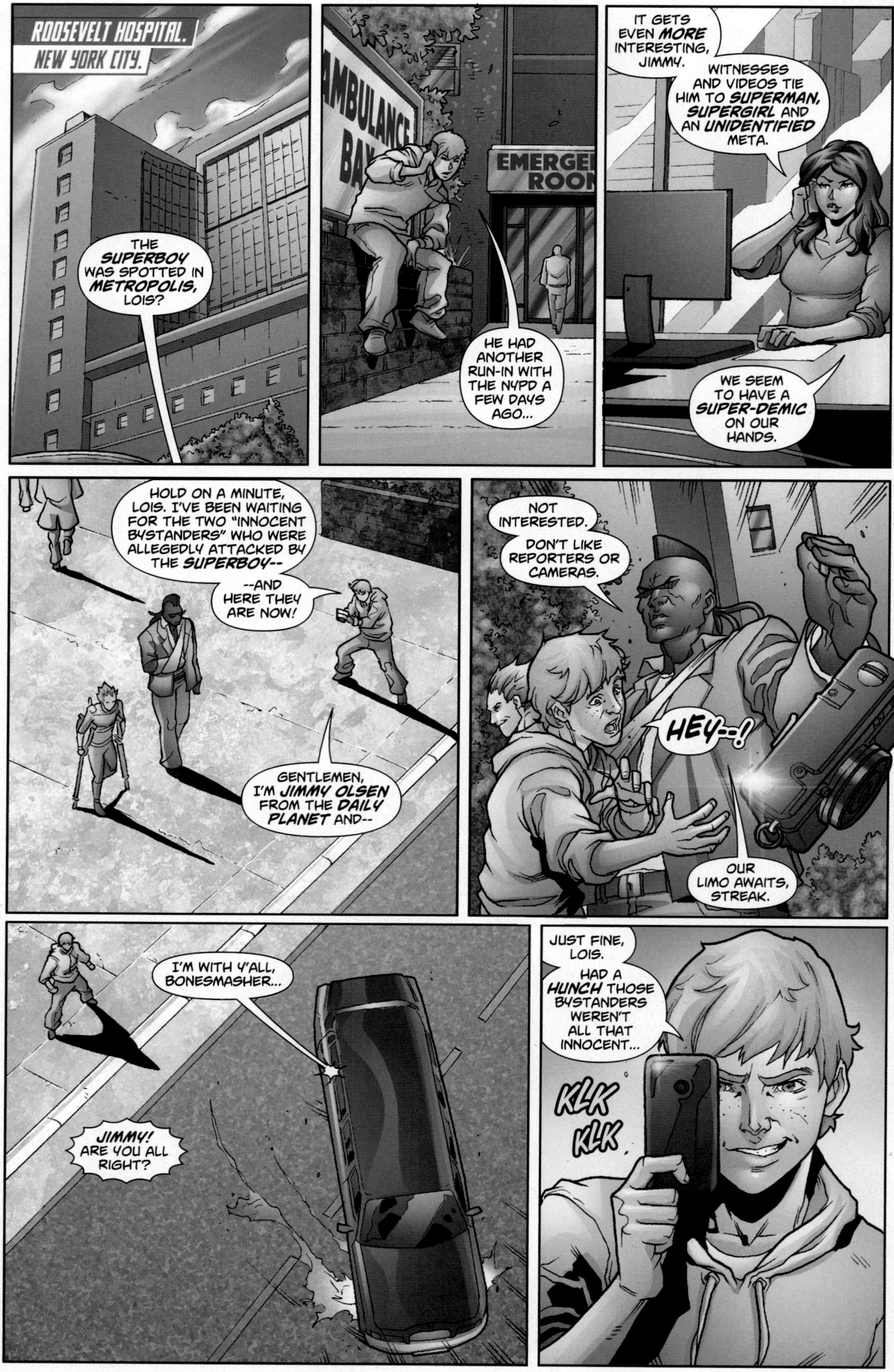

ROOSEVELT HOSPITAL. NEW YORK CITY.
THE SUPERBOY WAS SPOTTED IN METROPOLIS, LOIS?
AMBULANCE BAY
EMERGE ROOM
HE HAD ANOTHER RUN-IN WITH THE NYPD A FEW DAYS AGO...
IT GETS EVEN MORE INTERESTING, JIMMY.
WITNESSES AND VIDEOS TIE HIM TO SUPERMAN, SUPERGIRL AND AN UNIDENTIFIED META.
WE SEEM TO HAVE A SUPER-DEMIC ON OUR HANDS.
HOLD ON A MINUTE, LOIS. I'VE BEEN WAITING FOR THE TWO "INNOCENT BYSTANDERS" WHO WERE ALLEGEDLY ATTACKED BY THE SUPERBOY--
--AND HERE THEY ARE NOW!
GENTLEMEN, I'M JIMMY OLSEN FROM THE DAILY PLANET AND--
NOT INTERESTED.
DON'T LIKE REPORTERS OR CAMERAS.
HEY--!
OUR LIMO AWAITS, STREAK.
I'M WITH Y'ALL, BONESMASHER...
JIMMY! ARE YOU ALL RIGHT?
JUST FINE, LOIS.
HAD A HUNCH THOSE BYSTANDERS WEREN'T ALL THAT INNOCENT...
KLK KLK

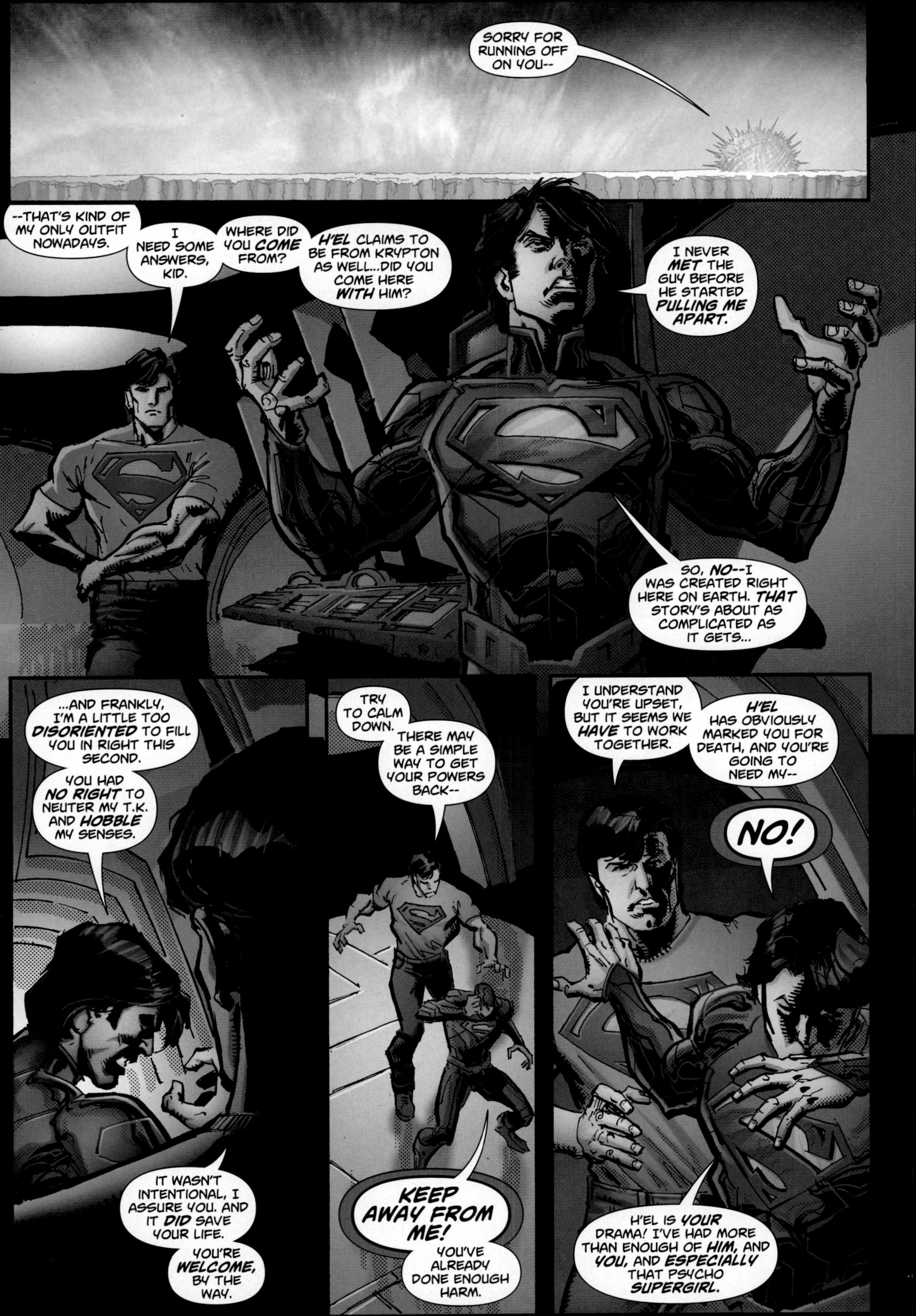
SORRY FOR RUNNING OFF ON YOU--
--THAT'S KIND OF MY ONLY OUTFIT NOWADAYS.
I NEED SOME ANSWERS, KID.
WHERE DID YOU COME FROM?
H'EL CLAIMS TO BE FROM KRYPTON AS WELL...DID YOU COME HERE WITH HIM?
I NEVER MET THE GUY BEFORE HE STARTED PULLING ME APART.
SO, NO--I WAS CREATED RIGHT HERE ON EARTH. THAT STORY'S ABOUT AS COMPLICATED AS IT GETS...
...AND FRANKLY, I'M A LITTLE TOO DISORIENTED TO FILL YOU IN RIGHT THIS SECOND.
YOU HAD NO RIGHT TO NEUTER MY T.K. AND HOBBLE MY SENSES.
IT WASN'T INTENTIONAL, I ASSURE YOU. AND IT DID SAVE YOUR LIFE.
YOU'RE WELCOME, BY THE WAY.
TRY TO CALM DOWN.
THERE MAY BE A SIMPLE WAY TO GET YOUR POWERS BACK--
KEEP AWAY FROM ME!
YOU'VE ALREADY DONE ENOUGH HARM.
I UNDERSTAND YOU'RE UPSET, BUT IT SEEMS WE HAVE TO WORK TOGETHER.
H'EL HAS OBVIOUSLY MARKED YOU FOR DEATH, AND YOU'RE GOING TO NEED MY--
NO!
H'EL IS YOUR DRAMA! I'VE HAD MORE THAN ENOUGH OF HIM, AND YOU, AND ESPECIALLY THAT PSYCHO SUPERGIRL.

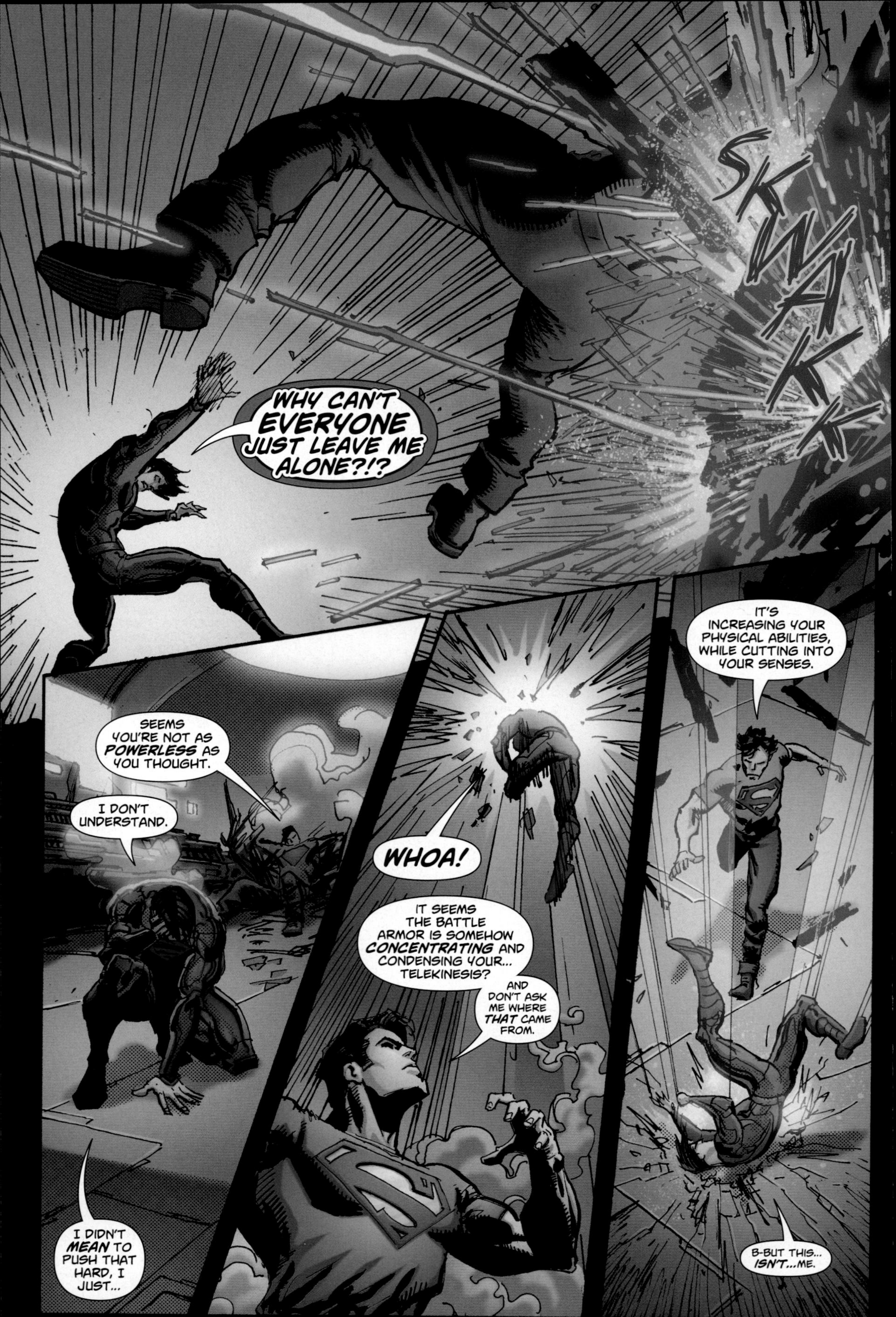
SKWAKKK
WHY CAN'T EVERYONE JUST LEAVE ME ALONE?!?
SEEMS YOU'RE NOT AS POWERLESS AS YOU THOUGHT.
I DON'T UNDERSTAND.
I DIDN'T MEAN TO PUSH THAT HARD, I JUST...
WHOA!
IT SEEMS THE BATTLE ARMOR IS SOMEHOW CONCENTRATING AND CONDENSING YOUR... TELEKINESIS?
AND DON'T ASK ME WHERE THAT CAME FROM.
IT'S INCREASING YOUR PHYSICAL ABILITIES, WHILE CUTTING INTO YOUR SENSES.
B-BUT THIS... ISN'T... ME.

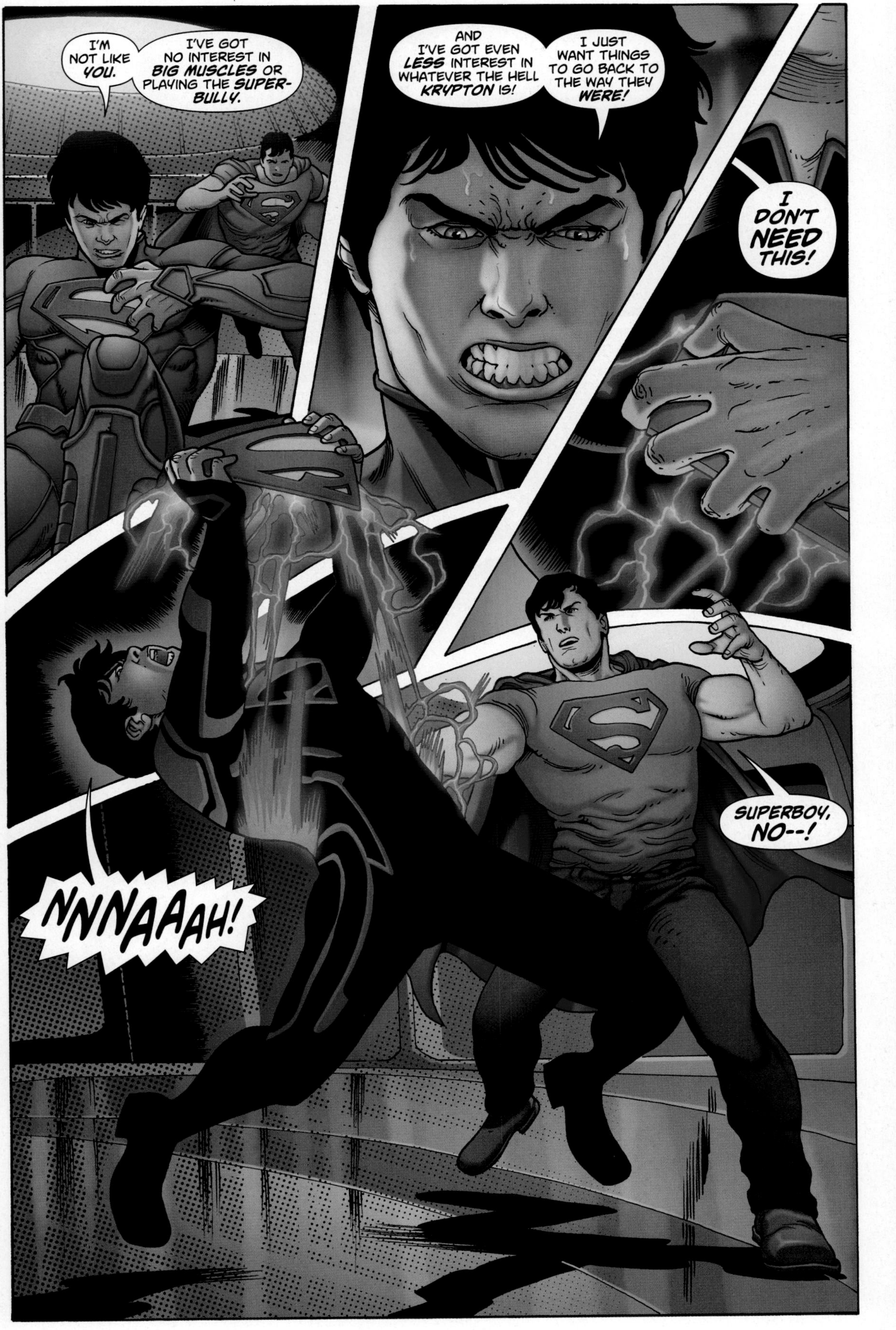
I'M NOT LIKE YOU.
I'VE GOT NO INTEREST IN BIG MUSCLES OR PLAYING THE SUPER-BULLY.
AND I'VE GOT EVEN LESS INTEREST IN WHATEVER THE HELL KRYPTON IS!
I JUST WANT THINGS TO GO BACK TO THE WAY THEY WERE!
I DON'T NEED THIS!
SUPERBOY, NO--!
NNNAAAAH!

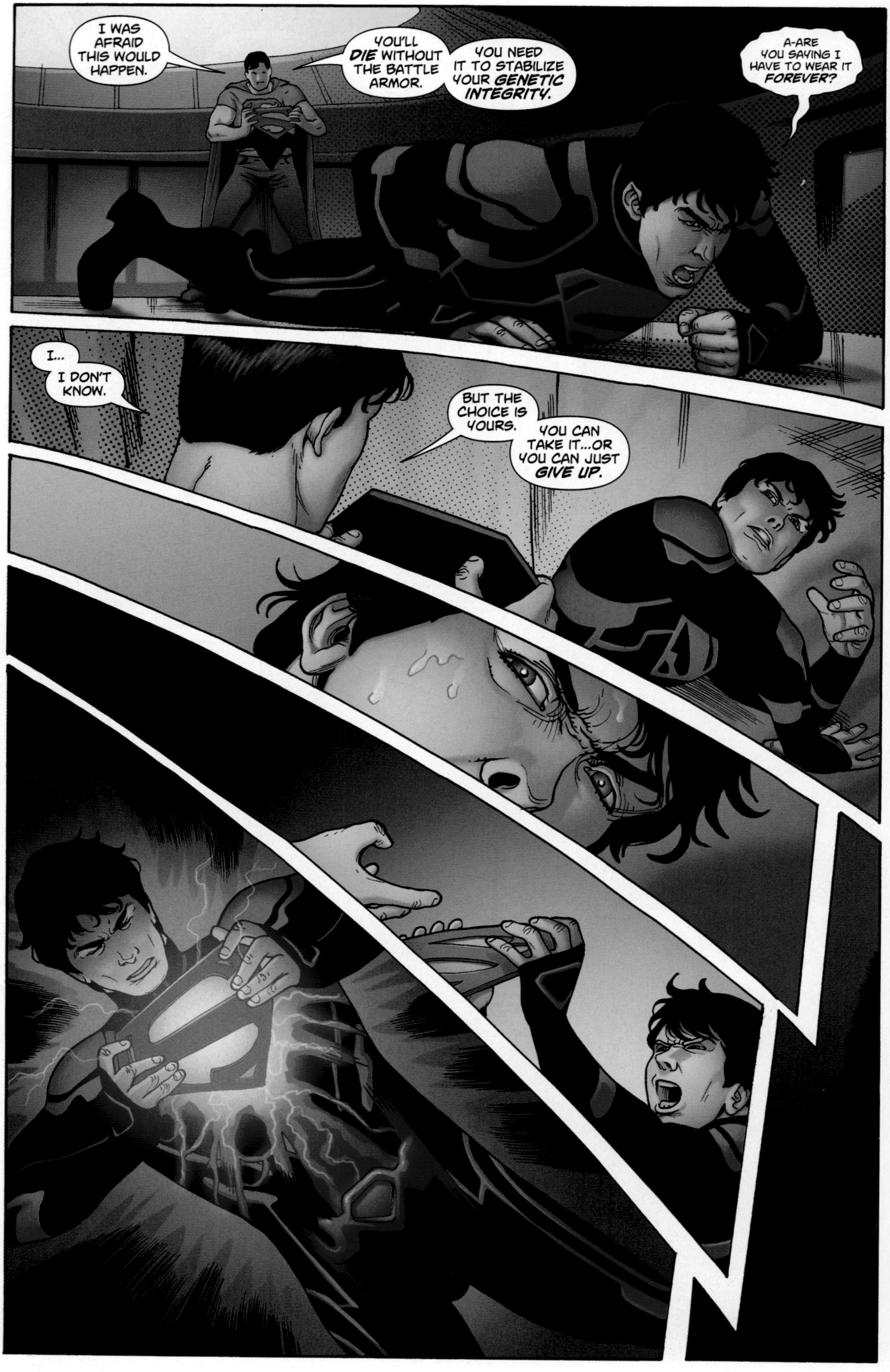

I WAS AFRAID THIS WOULD HAPPEN.
YOU'LL DIE WITHOUT THE BATTLE ARMOR.
YOU NEED IT TO STABILIZE YOUR GENETIC INTEGRITY.
A-ARE YOU SAYING I HAVE TO WEAR IT FOREVER?
I... I DON'T KNOW.
BUT THE CHOICE IS YOURS.
YOU CAN TAKE IT...OR YOU CAN JUST GIVE UP.

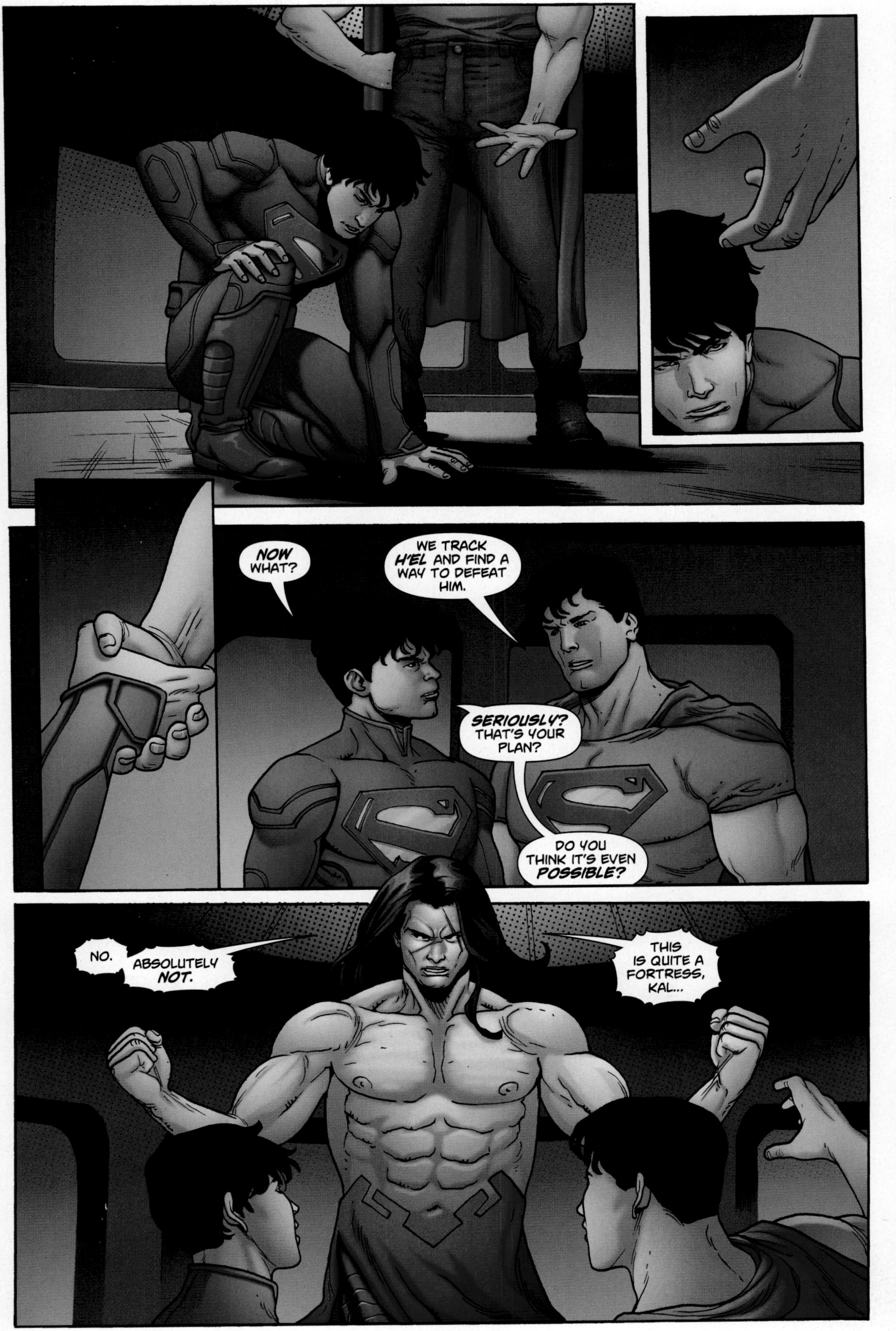
NOW WHAT?
WE TRACK H'EL AND FIND A WAY TO DEFEAT HIM.
SERIOUSLY? THAT'S YOUR PLAN?
DO YOU THINK IT'S EVEN POSSIBLE?
NO.
ABSOLUTELY NOT.
THIS IS QUITE A FORTRESS, KAL...

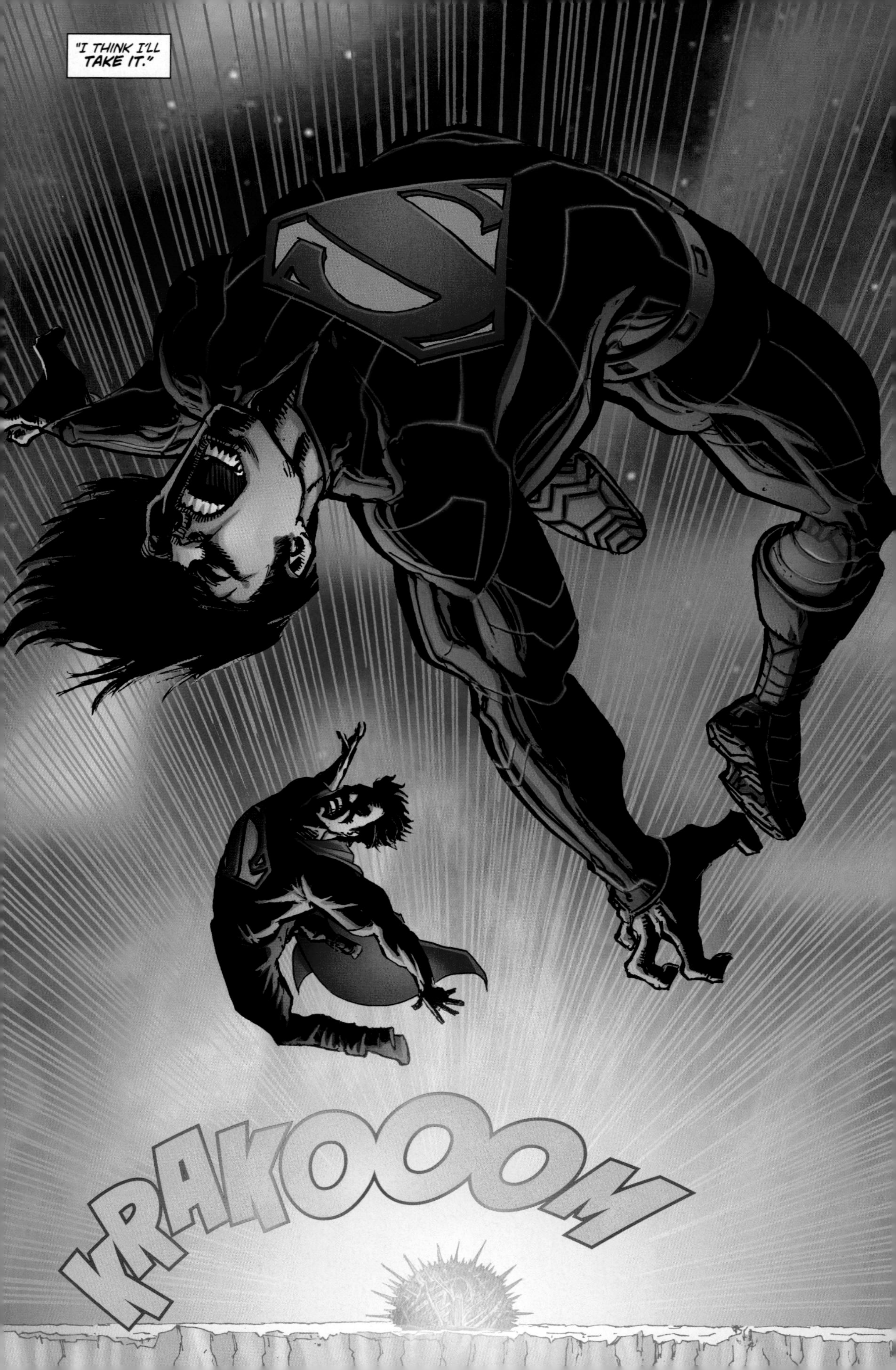
"I THINK I'LL TAKE IT."
KRAKOOOM

INTO KANDOR

MIKE JOHNSON writer **MAHMUD ASRAR** penciller **MAHMUD ASRAR, SCOTT HANNA, AND MARC DEERING** inkers
cover art by **MAHMUD ASRAR & DAVE MCCAIG**

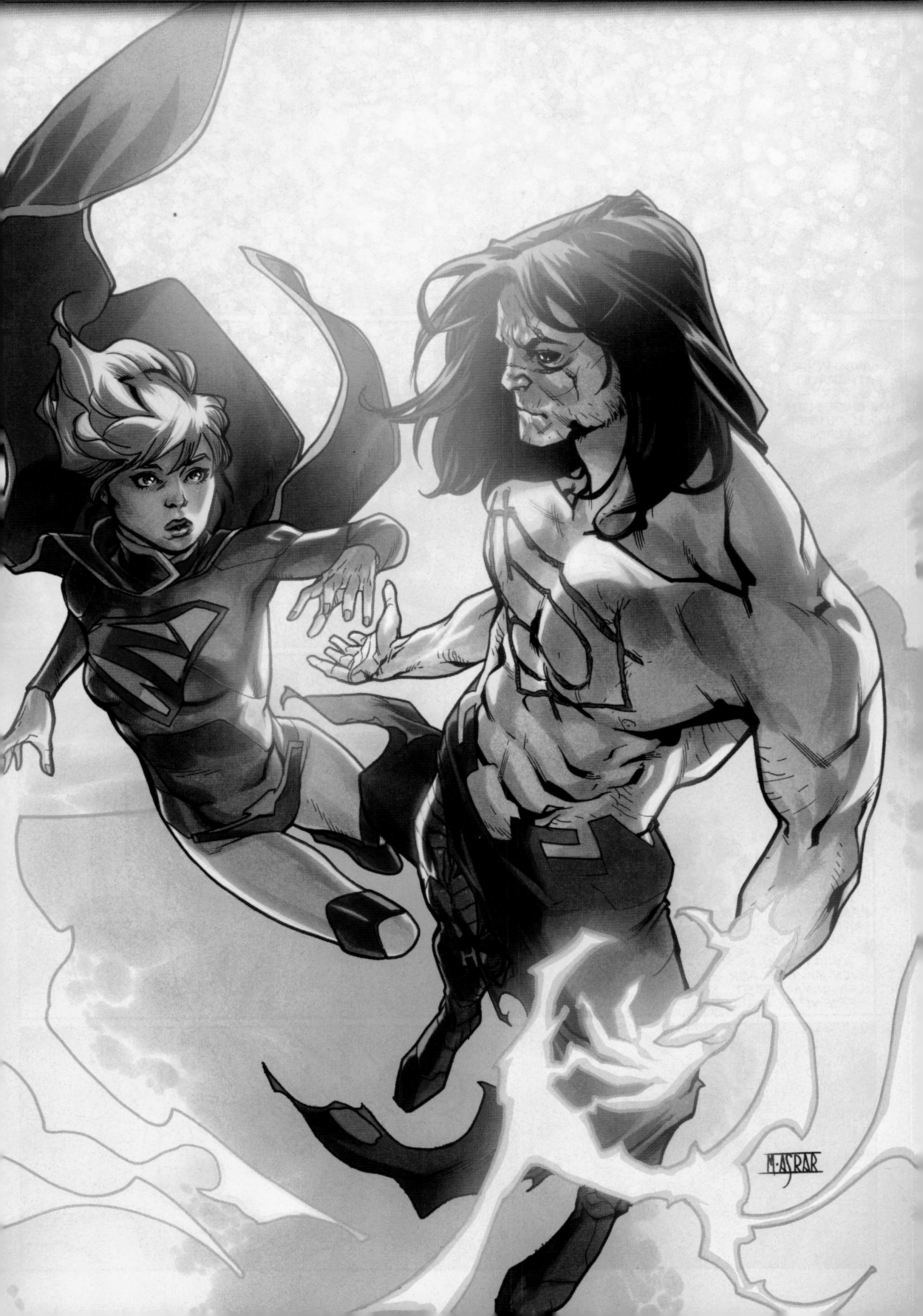
M. ASRAR

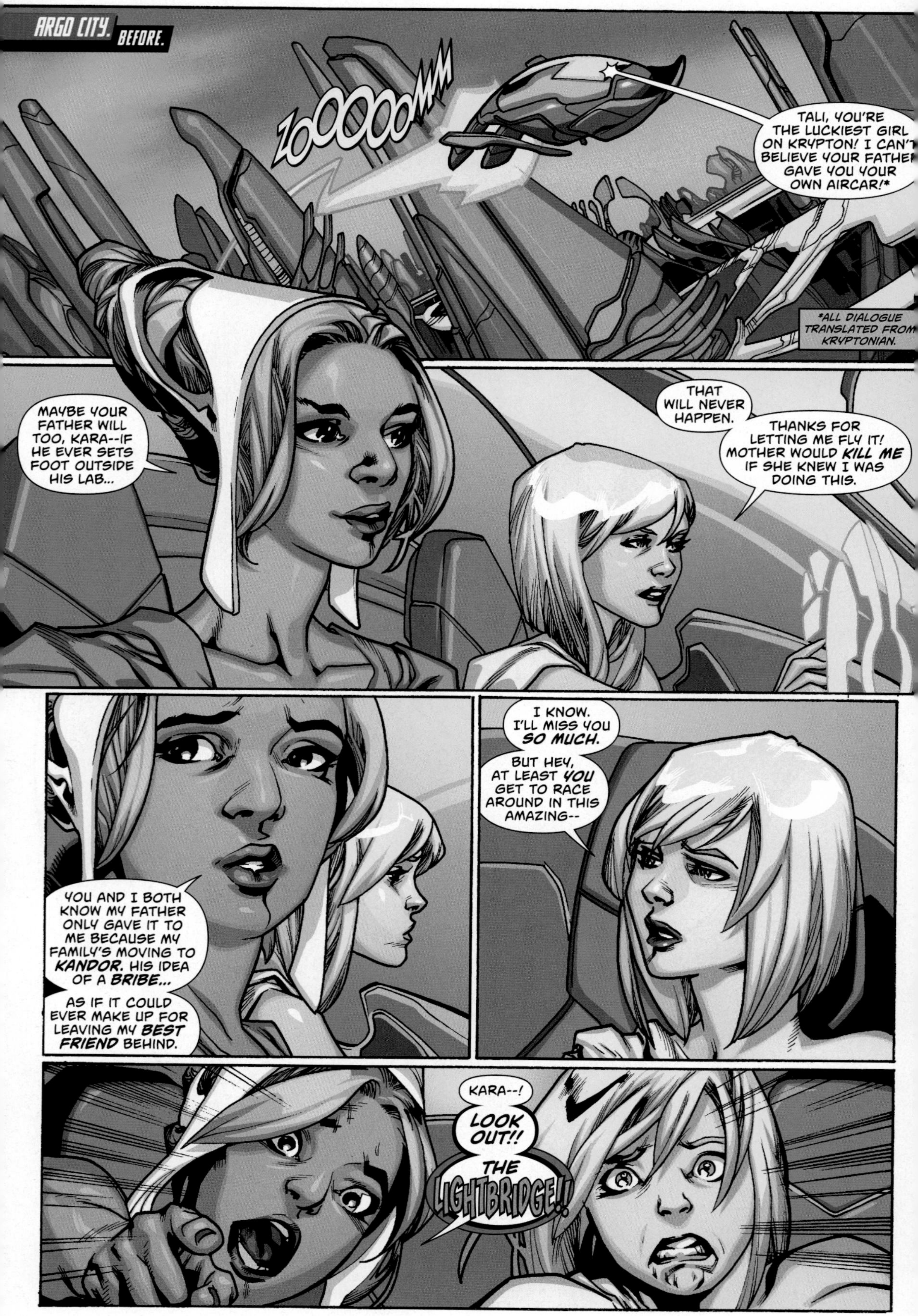
ARGO CITY. BEFORE.
ZOOOOOMMM
TALI, YOU'RE THE LUCKIEST GIRL ON KRYPTON! I CAN'T BELIEVE YOUR FATHER GAVE YOU YOUR OWN AIRCAR!*
*ALL DIALOGUE TRANSLATED FROM KRYPTONIAN.
MAYBE YOUR FATHER WILL TOO, KARA--IF HE EVER SETS FOOT OUTSIDE HIS LAB...
THAT WILL NEVER HAPPEN.
THANKS FOR LETTING ME FLY IT! MOTHER WOULD KILL ME IF SHE KNEW I WAS DOING THIS.
YOU AND I BOTH KNOW MY FATHER ONLY GAVE IT TO ME BECAUSE MY FAMILY'S MOVING TO KANDOR. HIS IDEA OF A BRIBE...
AS IF IT COULD EVER MAKE UP FOR LEAVING MY BEST FRIEND BEHIND.
I KNOW. I'LL MISS YOU SO MUCH.
BUT HEY, AT LEAST YOU GET TO RACE AROUND IN THIS AMAZING--
KARA--!
LOOK OUT!!
THE LIGHTBRIDGE!!

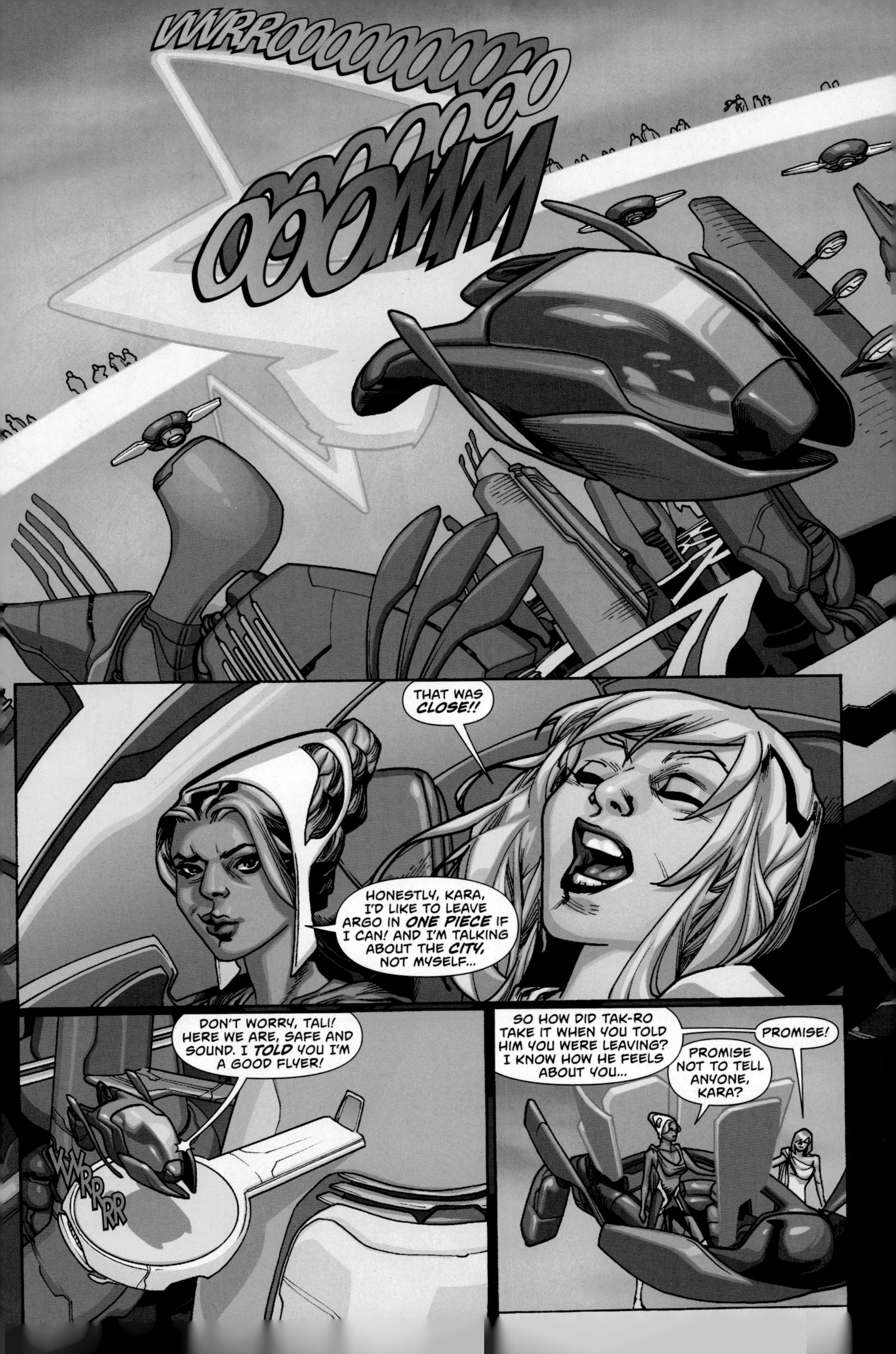
VWROOOOOOOOOOOOOOOOMM
THAT WAS CLOSE!!
HONESTLY, KARA, I'D LIKE TO LEAVE ARGO IN ONE PIECE IF I CAN! AND I'M TALKING ABOUT THE CITY, NOT MYSELF...
DON'T WORRY, TALI! HERE WE ARE, SAFE AND SOUND. I TOLD YOU I'M A GOOD FLYER!
VWRRRR
SO HOW DID TAK-RO TAKE IT WHEN YOU TOLD HIM YOU WERE LEAVING? I KNOW HOW HE FEELS ABOUT YOU...
PROMISE NOT TO TELL ANYONE, KARA?
PROMISE!

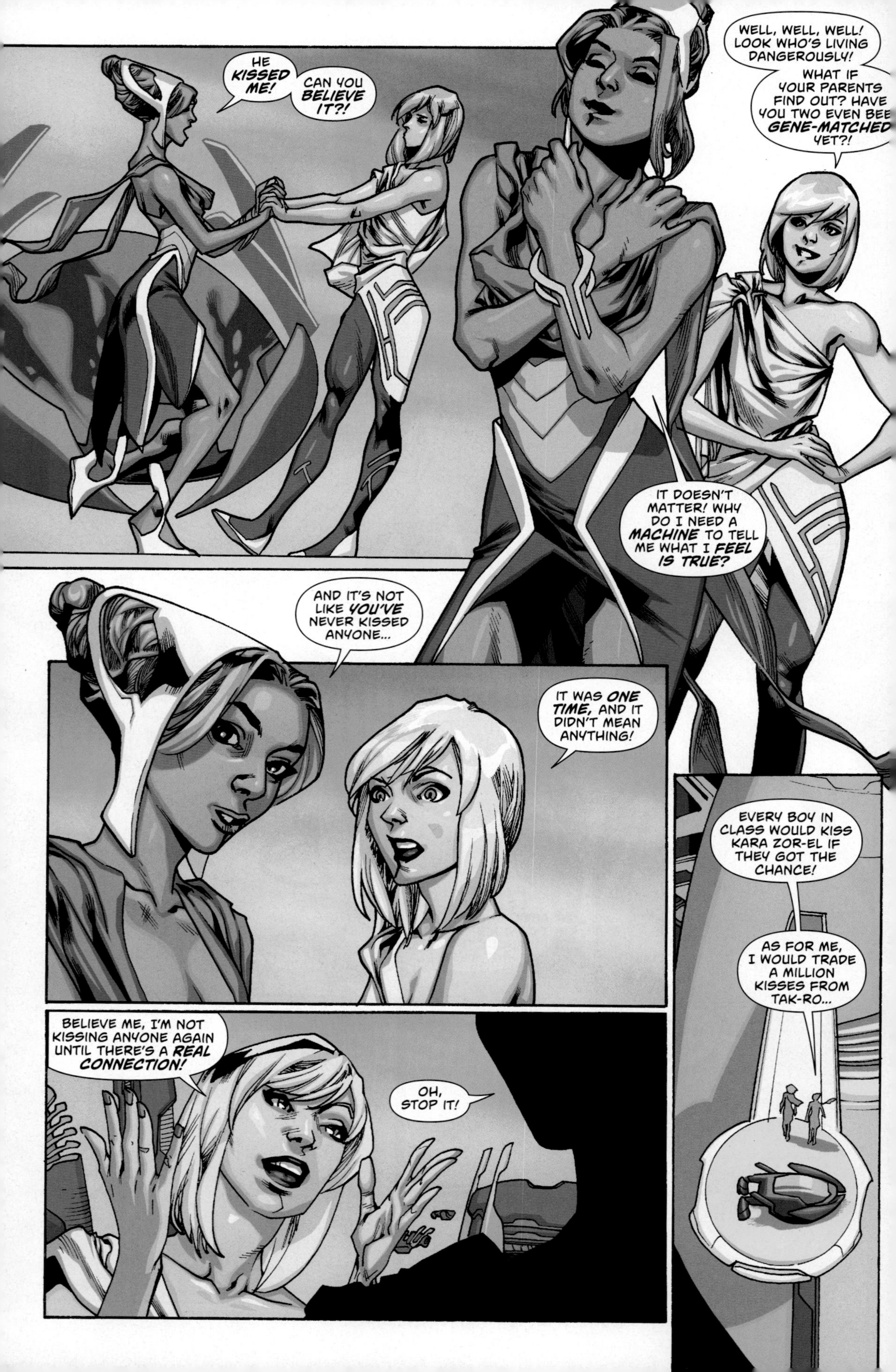
HE KISSED ME!
CAN YOU BELIEVE IT?!
WELL, WELL, WELL! LOOK WHO'S LIVING DANGEROUSLY!
WHAT IF YOUR PARENTS FIND OUT? HAVE YOU TWO EVEN BEE GENE-MATCHED YET?!
IT DOESN'T MATTER! WHY DO I NEED A MACHINE TO TELL ME WHAT I FEEL IS TRUE?
AND IT'S NOT LIKE YOU'VE NEVER KISSED ANYONE...
IT WAS ONE TIME, AND IT DIDN'T MEAN ANYTHING!
EVERY BOY IN CLASS WOULD KISS KARA ZOR-EL IF THEY GOT THE CHANCE!
AS FOR ME, I WOULD TRADE A MILLION KISSES FROM TAK-RO...
BELIEVE ME, I'M NOT KISSING ANYONE AGAIN UNTIL THERE'S A REAL CONNECTION!
OH, STOP IT!

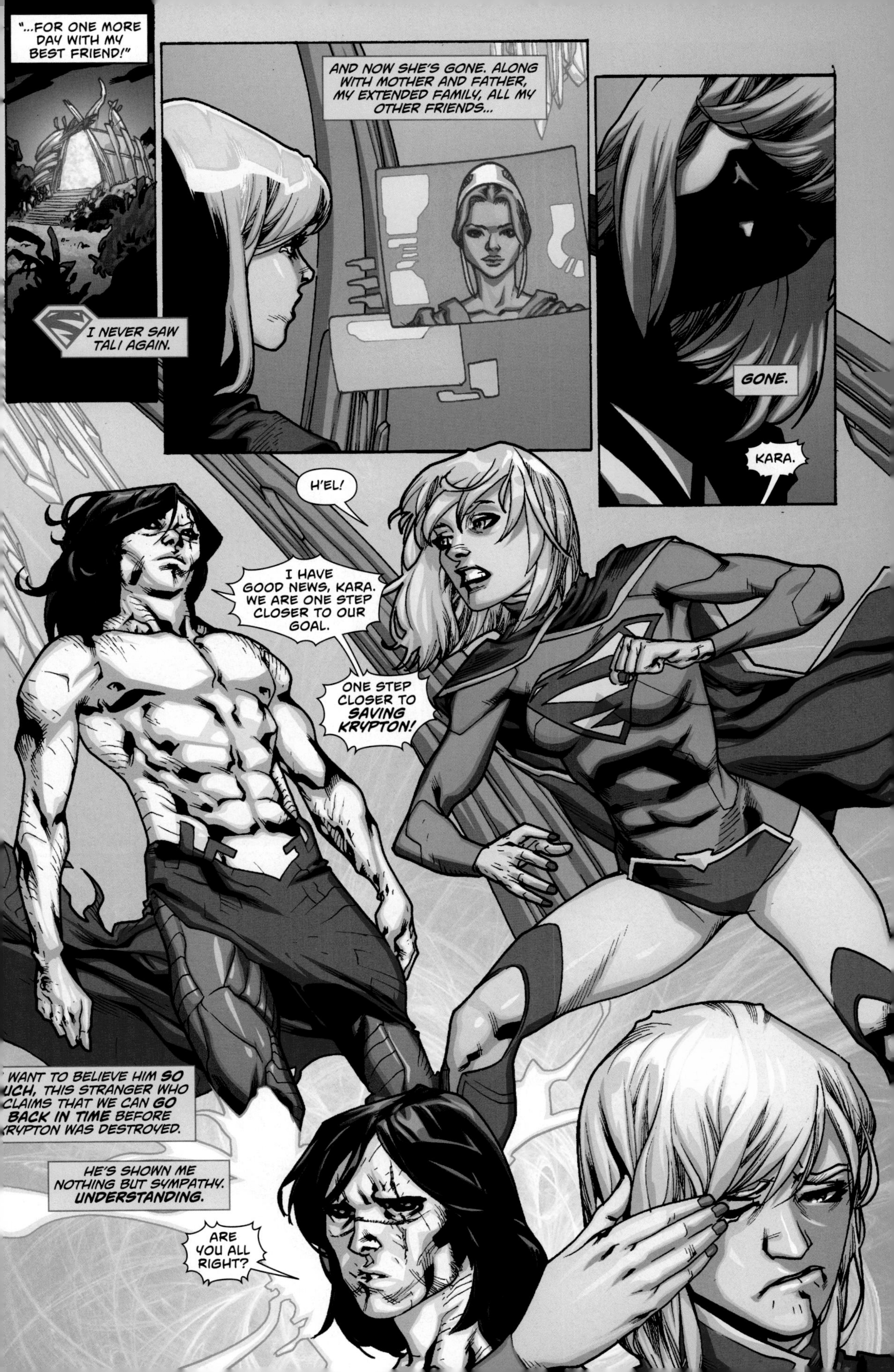
"...FOR ONE MORE DAY WITH MY BEST FRIEND!"
I NEVER SAW TALI AGAIN.
AND NOW SHE'S GONE. ALONG WITH MOTHER AND FATHER, MY EXTENDED FAMILY, ALL MY OTHER FRIENDS...
GONE.
KARA.
H'EL!
I HAVE GOOD NEWS, KARA. WE ARE ONE STEP CLOSER TO OUR GOAL.
ONE STEP CLOSER TO SAVING KRYPTON!
WANT TO BELIEVE HIM SO UCH, THIS STRANGER WHO CLAIMS THAT WE CAN GO BACK IN TIME BEFORE RYPTON WAS DESTROYED.
HE'S SHOWN ME NOTHING BUT SYMPATHY. UNDERSTANDING.
ARE YOU ALL RIGHT?

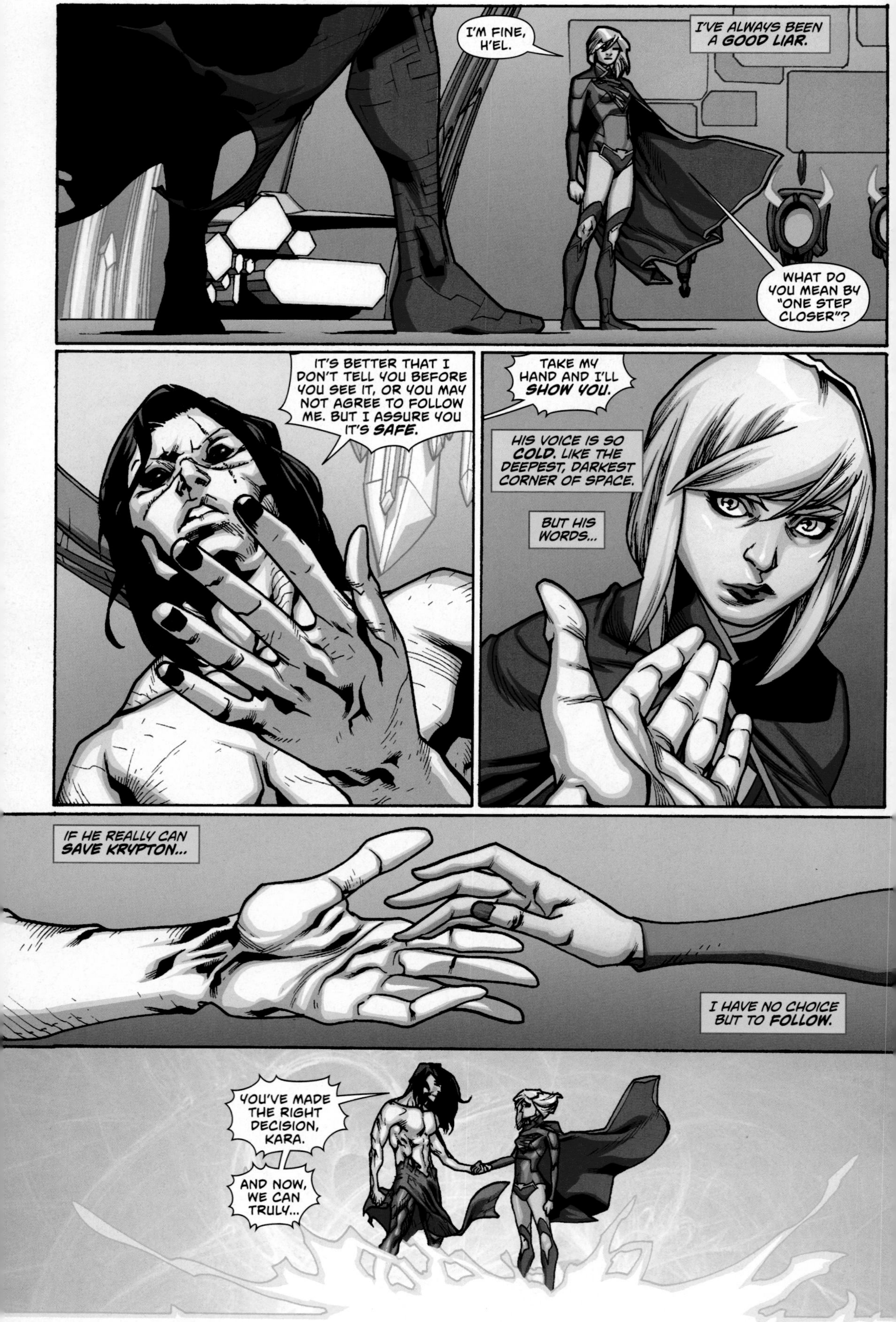
I'M FINE, H'EL.
I'VE ALWAYS BEEN A GOOD LIAR.
WHAT DO YOU MEAN BY "ONE STEP CLOSER"?
IT'S BETTER THAT I DON'T TELL YOU BEFORE YOU SEE IT, OR YOU MAY NOT AGREE TO FOLLOW ME. BUT I ASSURE YOU IT'S SAFE.
TAKE MY HAND AND I'LL SHOW YOU.
HIS VOICE IS SO COLD. LIKE THE DEEPEST, DARKEST CORNER OF SPACE.
BUT HIS WORDS...
IF HE REALLY CAN SAVE KRYPTON...
I HAVE NO CHOICE BUT TO FOLLOW.
YOU'VE MADE THE RIGHT DECISION, KARA.
AND NOW, WE CAN TRULY...

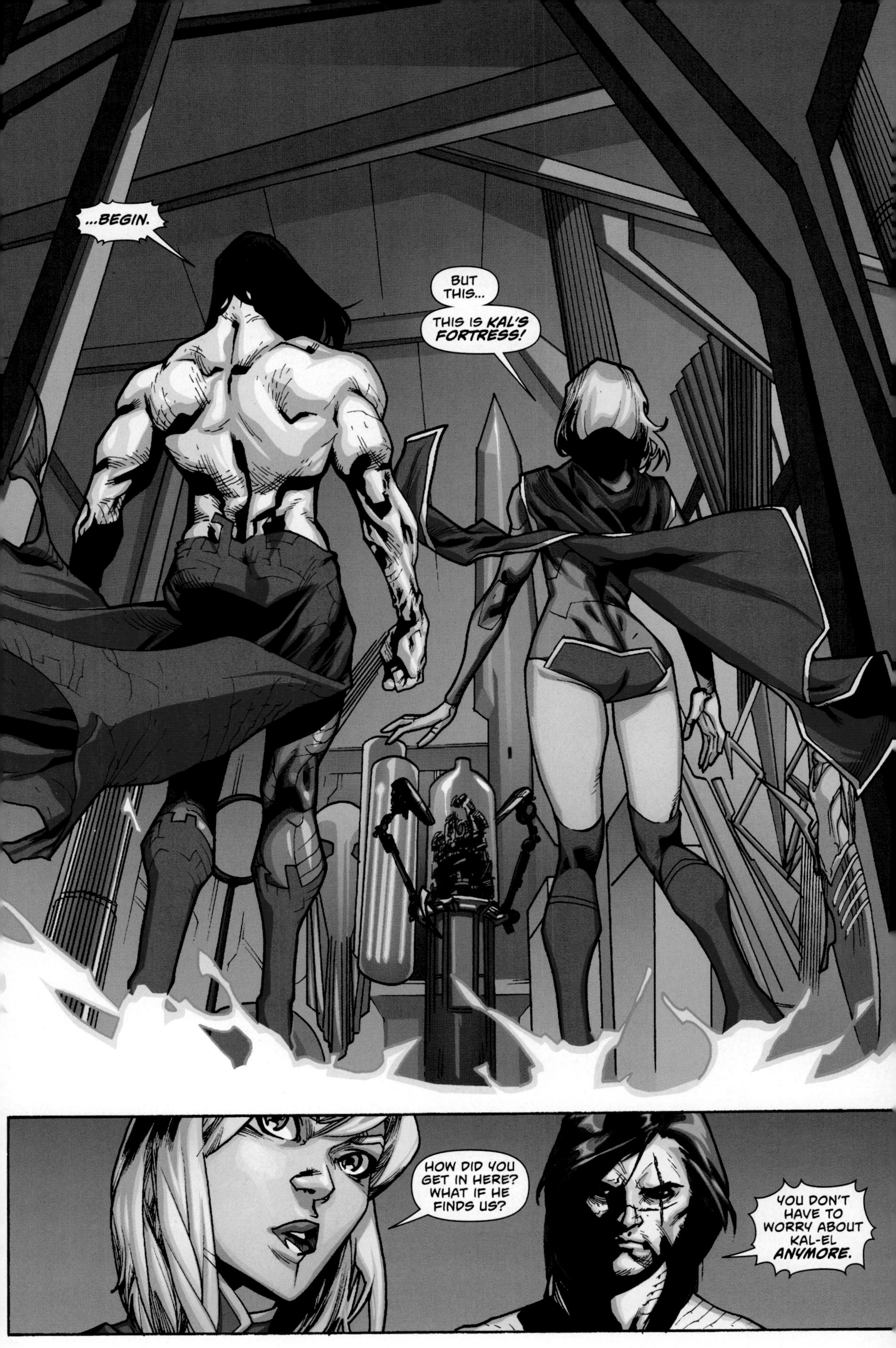

...BEGIN.
BUT THIS...
THIS IS KAL'S FORTRESS!
HOW DID YOU GET IN HERE? WHAT IF HE FINDS US?
YOU DON'T HAVE TO WORRY ABOUT KAL-EL ANYMORE.

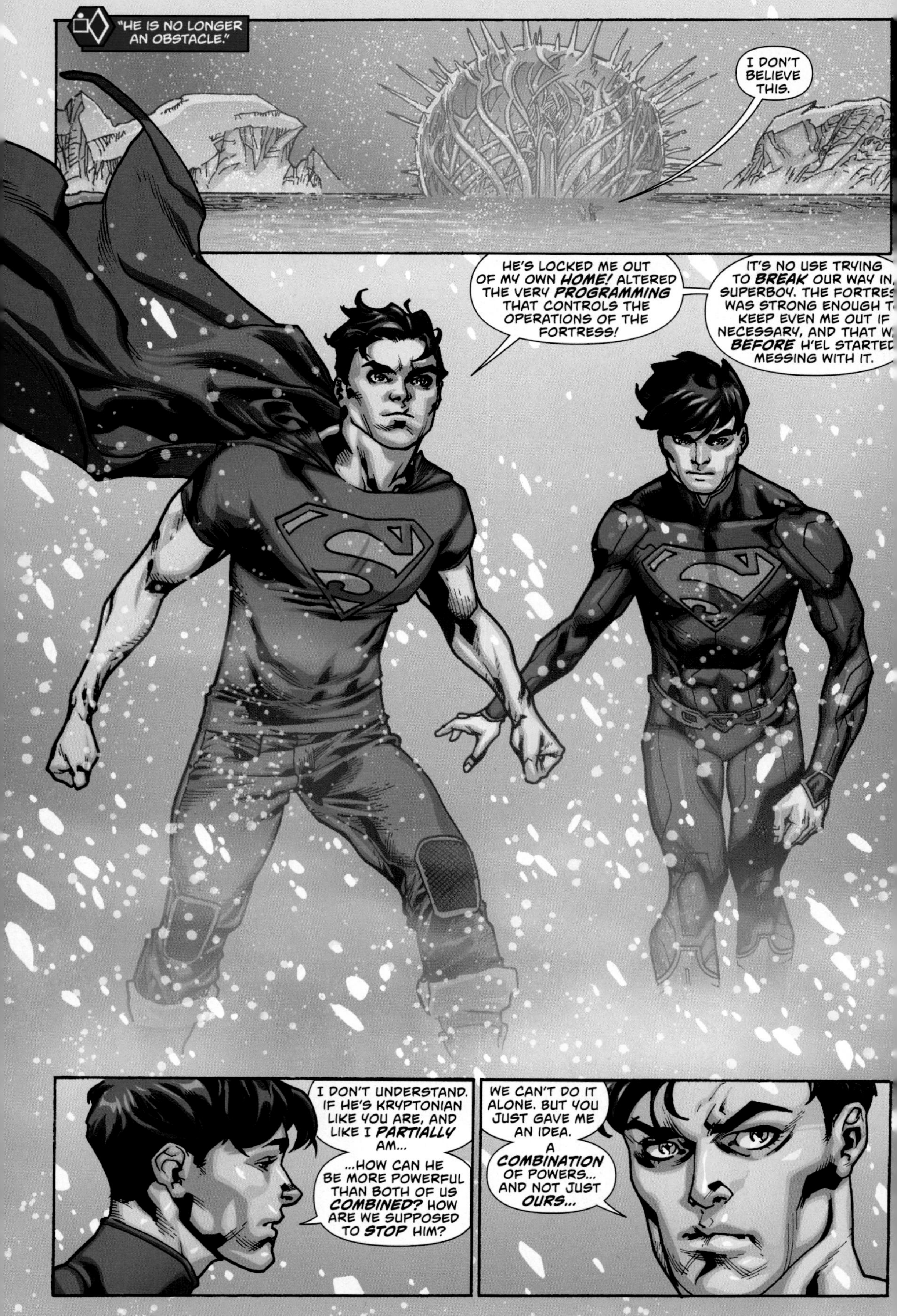
"HE IS NO LONGER AN OBSTACLE."
I DON'T BELIEVE THIS.
HE'S LOCKED ME OUT OF MY OWN HOME! ALTERED THE VERY PROGRAMMING THAT CONTROLS THE OPERATIONS OF THE FORTRESS!
IT'S NO USE TRYING TO BREAK OUR WAY IN, SUPERBOY. THE FORTRES WAS STRONG ENOUGH T KEEP EVEN ME OUT IF NECESSARY, AND THAT W BEFORE H'EL STARTED MESSING WITH IT.
I DON'T UNDERSTAND. IF HE'S KRYPTONIAN LIKE YOU ARE, AND LIKE I PARTIALLY AM...
...HOW CAN HE BE MORE POWERFUL THAN BOTH OF US COMBINED? HOW ARE WE SUPPOSED TO STOP HIM?
WE CAN'T DO IT ALONE. BUT YOU JUST GAVE ME AN IDEA.
A COMBINATION OF POWERS... AND NOT JUST OURS...

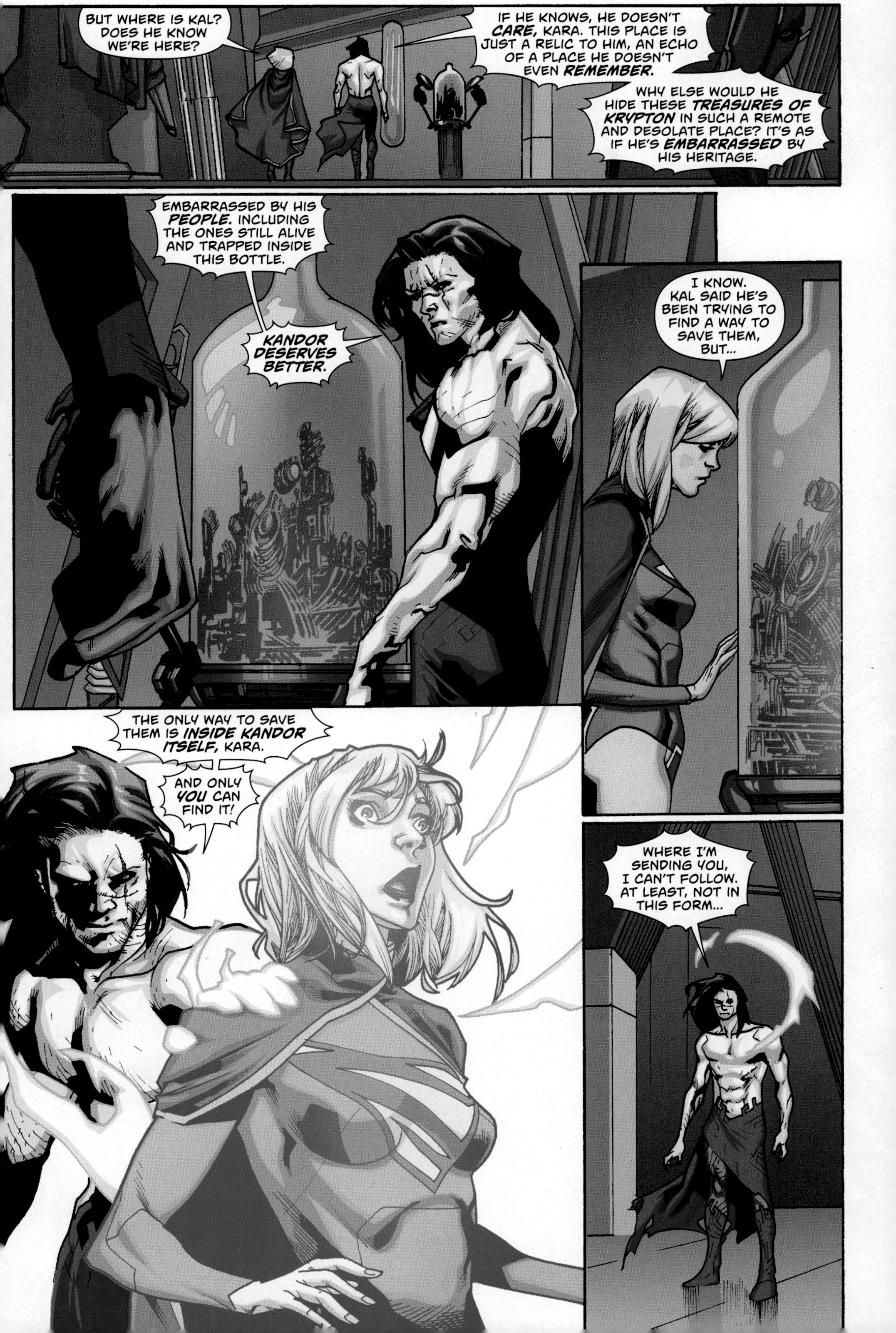
BUT WHERE IS KAL? DOES HE KNOW WE'RE HERE?
IF HE KNOWS, HE DOESN'T CARE, KARA. THIS PLACE IS JUST A RELIC TO HIM, AN ECHO OF A PLACE HE DOESN'T EVEN REMEMBER.
WHY ELSE WOULD HE HIDE THESE TREASURES OF KRYPTON IN SUCH A REMOTE AND DESOLATE PLACE? IT'S AS IF HE'S EMBARRASSED BY HIS HERITAGE.
EMBARRASSED BY HIS PEOPLE. INCLUDING THE ONES STILL ALIVE AND TRAPPED INSIDE THIS BOTTLE.
KANDOR DESERVES BETTER.
I KNOW. KAL SAID HE'S BEEN TRYING TO FIND A WAY TO SAVE THEM, BUT...
THE ONLY WAY TO SAVE THEM IS INSIDE KANDOR ITSELF, KARA.
AND ONLY YOU CAN FIND IT!
WHERE I'M SENDING YOU, I CAN'T FOLLOW. AT LEAST, NOT IN THIS FORM...

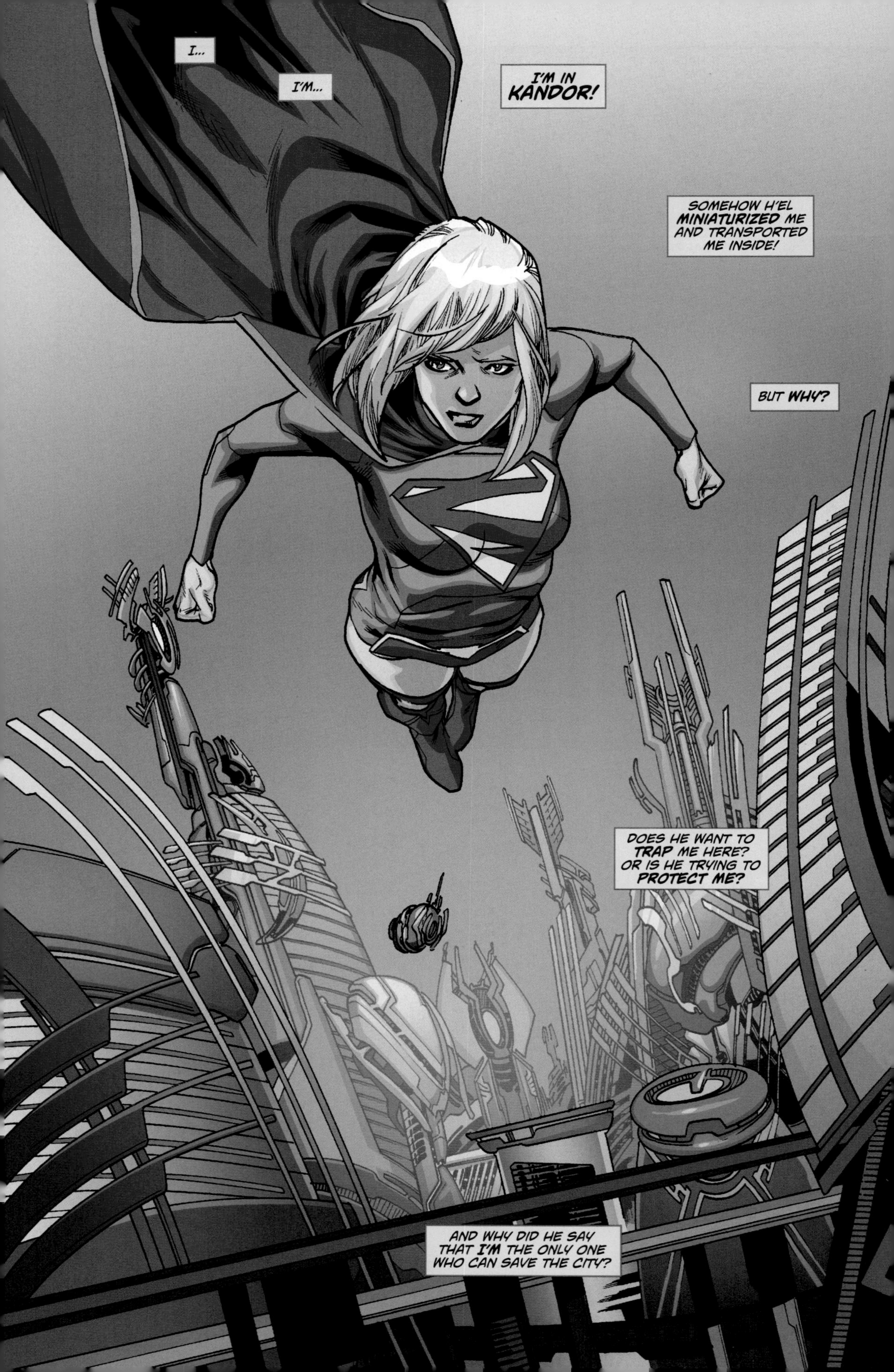
I...
I'M...
I'M IN KANDOR!
SOMEHOW H'EL MINIATURIZED ME AND TRANSPORTED ME INSIDE!
BUT WHY?
DOES HE WANT TO TRAP ME HERE? OR IS HE TRYING TO PROTECT ME?
AND WHY DID HE SAY THAT I'M THE ONLY ONE WHO CAN SAVE THE CITY?

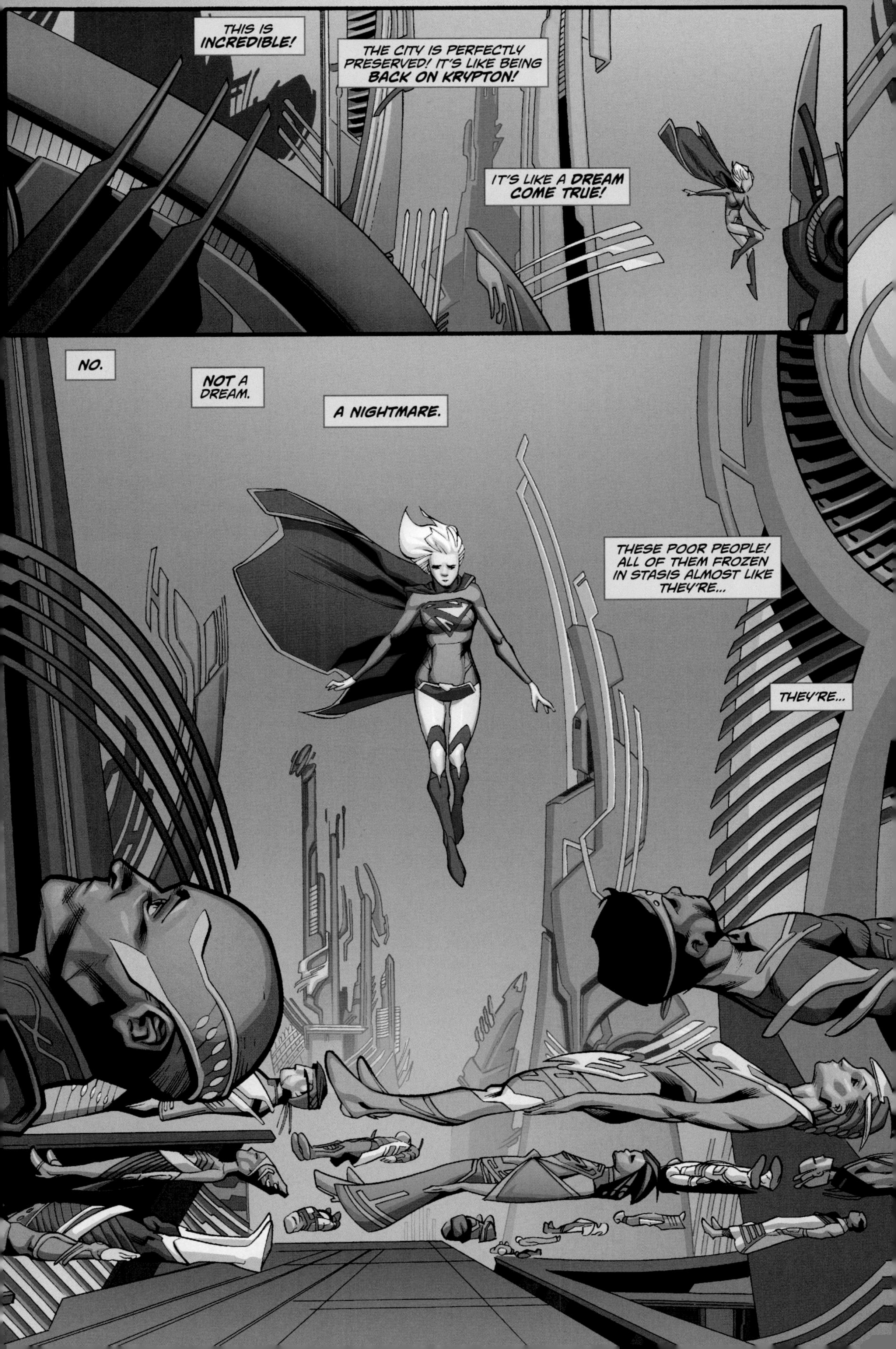
THIS IS INCREDIBLE!
THE CITY IS PERFECTLY PRESERVED! IT'S LIKE BEING BACK ON KRYPTON!
IT'S LIKE A DREAM COME TRUE!
NO.
NOT A DREAM.
A NIGHTMARE.
THESE POOR PEOPLE! ALL OF THEM FROZEN IN STASIS ALMOST LIKE THEY'RE...
THEY'RE...

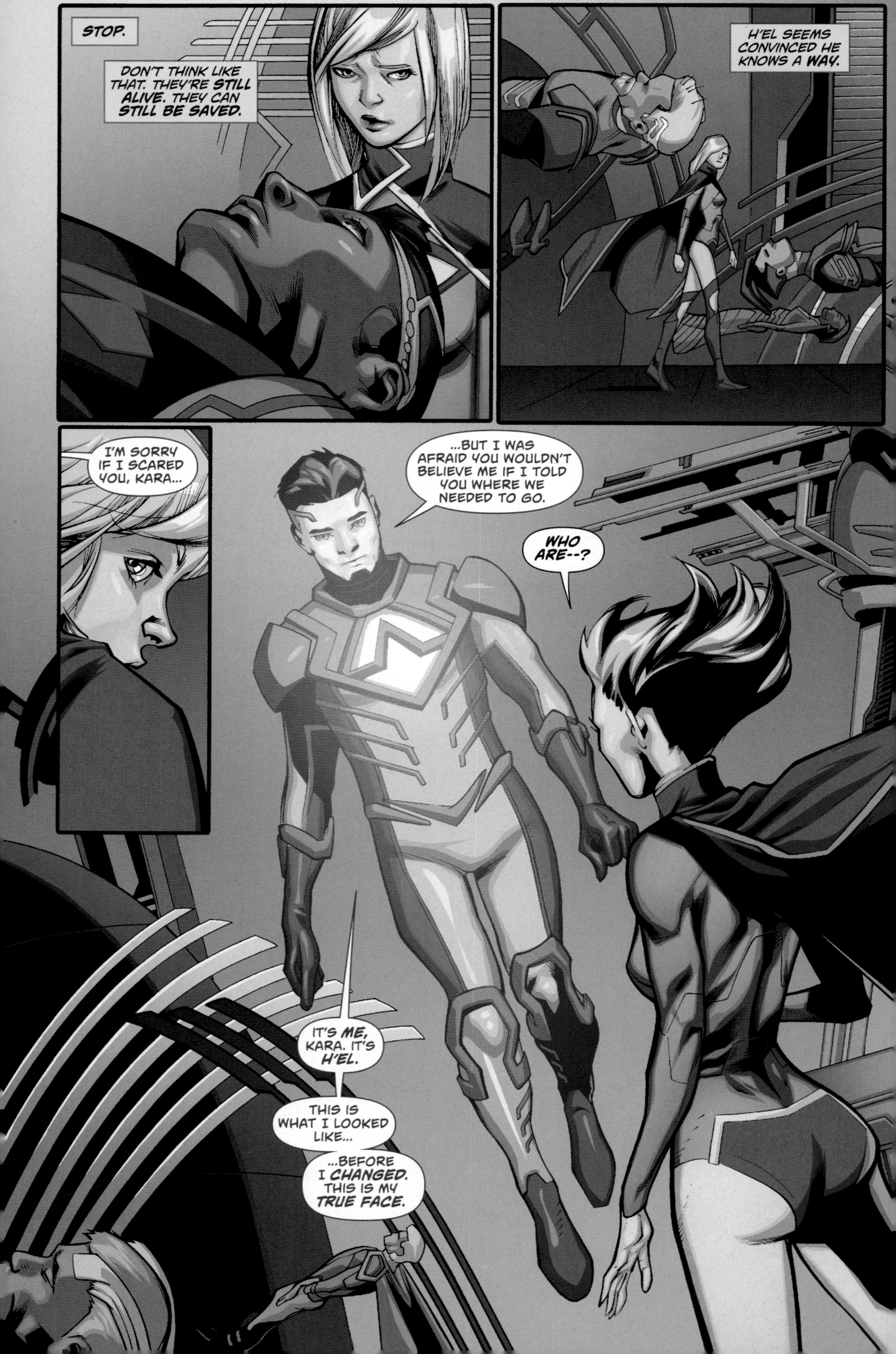
STOP.
DON'T THINK LIKE THAT. THEY'RE STILL ALIVE. THEY CAN STILL BE SAVED.
H'EL SEEMS CONVINCED HE KNOWS A WAY.
I'M SORRY IF I SCARED YOU, KARA...
...BUT I WAS AFRAID YOU WOULDN'T BELIEVE ME IF I TOLD YOU WHERE WE NEEDED TO GO.
WHO ARE--?
IT'S ME, KARA. IT'S H'EL.
THIS IS WHAT I LOOKED LIKE...
...BEFORE I CHANGED. THIS IS MY TRUE FACE.

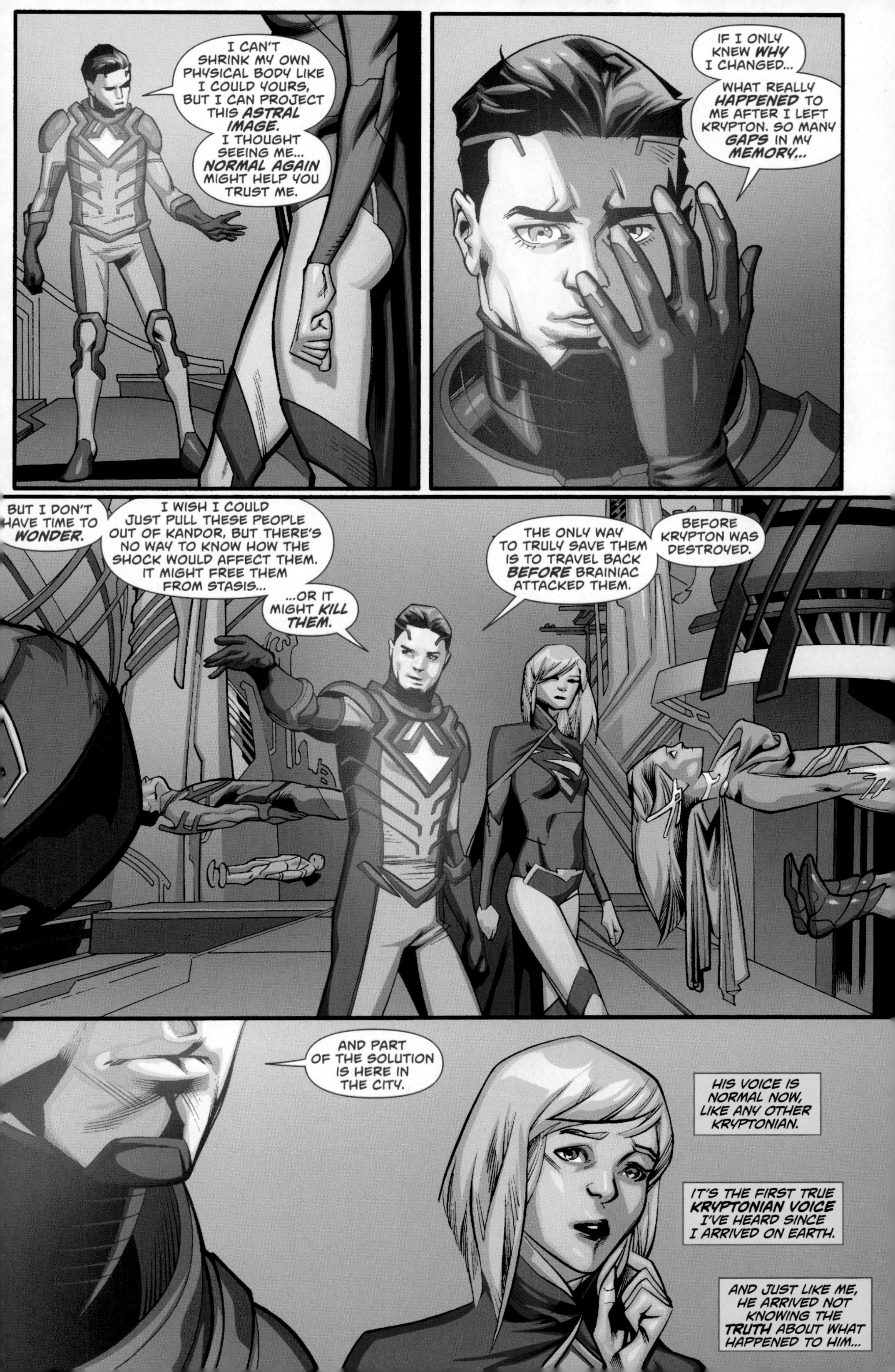

I CAN'T SHRINK MY OWN PHYSICAL BODY LIKE I COULD YOURS, BUT I CAN PROJECT THIS ASTRAL IMAGE.
I THOUGHT SEEING ME... NORMAL AGAIN MIGHT HELP YOU TRUST ME.
IF I ONLY KNEW WHY I CHANGED...
WHAT REALLY HAPPENED TO ME AFTER I LEFT KRYPTON. SO MANY GAPS IN MY MEMORY...
BUT I DON'T HAVE TIME TO WONDER.
I WISH I COULD JUST PULL THESE PEOPLE OUT OF KANDOR, BUT THERE'S NO WAY TO KNOW HOW THE SHOCK WOULD AFFECT THEM. IT MIGHT FREE THEM FROM STASIS...
...OR IT MIGHT KILL THEM.
THE ONLY WAY TO TRULY SAVE THEM IS TO TRAVEL BACK BEFORE BRAINIAC ATTACKED THEM.
BEFORE KRYPTON WAS DESTROYED.
AND PART OF THE SOLUTION IS HERE IN THE CITY.
HIS VOICE IS NORMAL NOW, LIKE ANY OTHER KRYPTONIAN.
IT'S THE FIRST TRUE KRYPTONIAN VOICE I'VE HEARD SINCE I ARRIVED ON EARTH.
AND JUST LIKE ME, HE ARRIVED NOT KNOWING THE TRUTH ABOUT WHAT HAPPENED TO HIM...

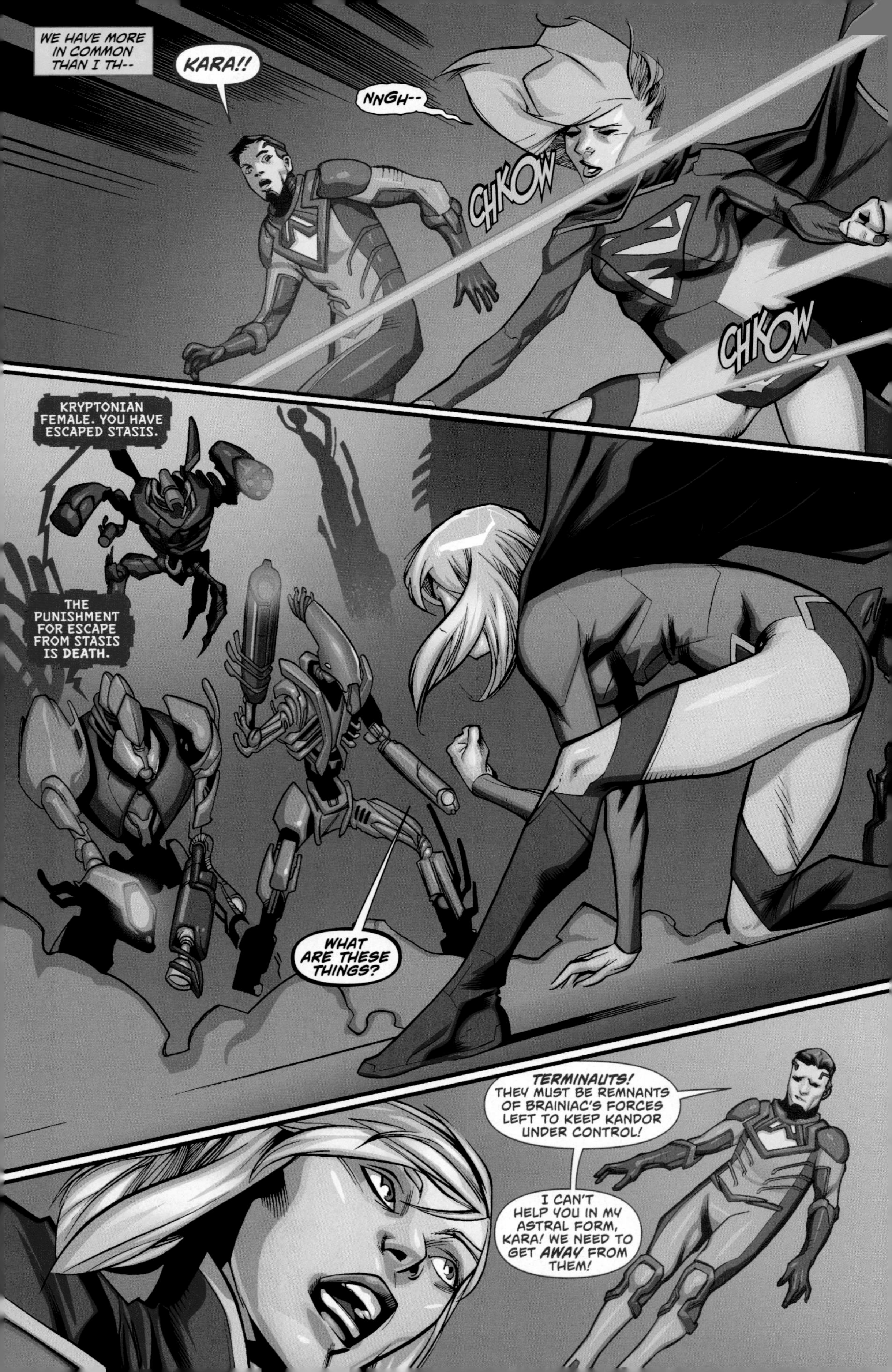
WE HAVE MORE IN COMMON THAN I TH--
KARA!!
NNGH--
CHKOW
CHKOW
KRYPTONIAN FEMALE. YOU HAVE ESCAPED STASIS.
THE PUNISHMENT FOR ESCAPE FROM STASIS IS DEATH.
WHAT ARE THESE THINGS?
TERMINAUTS! THEY MUST BE REMNANTS OF BRAINIAC'S FORCES LEFT TO KEEP KANDOR UNDER CONTROL!
I CAN'T HELP YOU IN MY ASTRAL FORM, KARA! WE NEED TO GET AWAY FROM THEM!

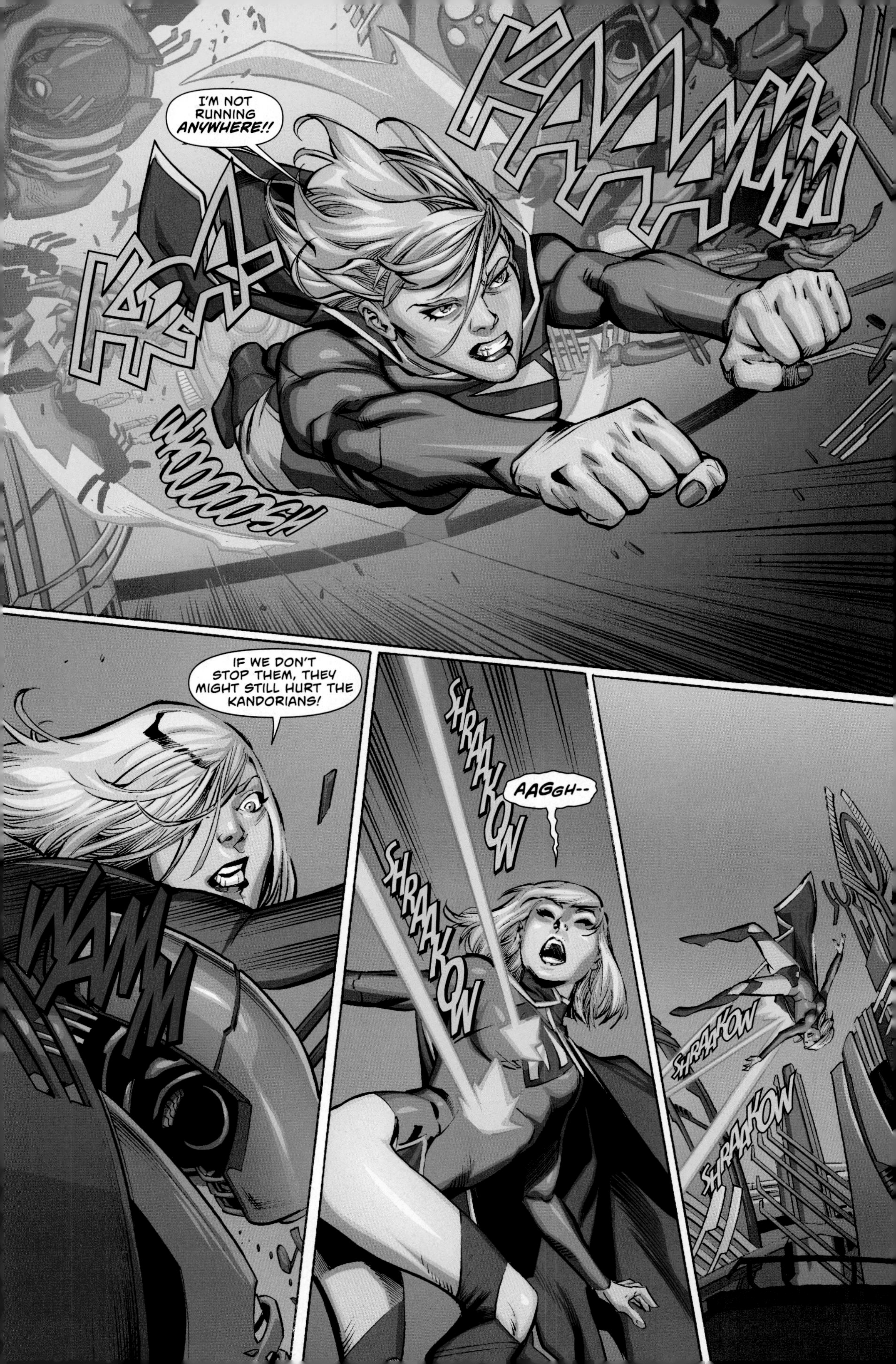
I'M NOT RUNNING ANYWHERE!!
KAAAMM
KRSSH
WHOOOOSH
IF WE DON'T STOP THEM, THEY MIGHT STILL HURT THE KANDORIANS!
WAMM
SHRAAKOW
AAGGH--
SHRAAKOW
SHRAAKOW
SHRAAKOW

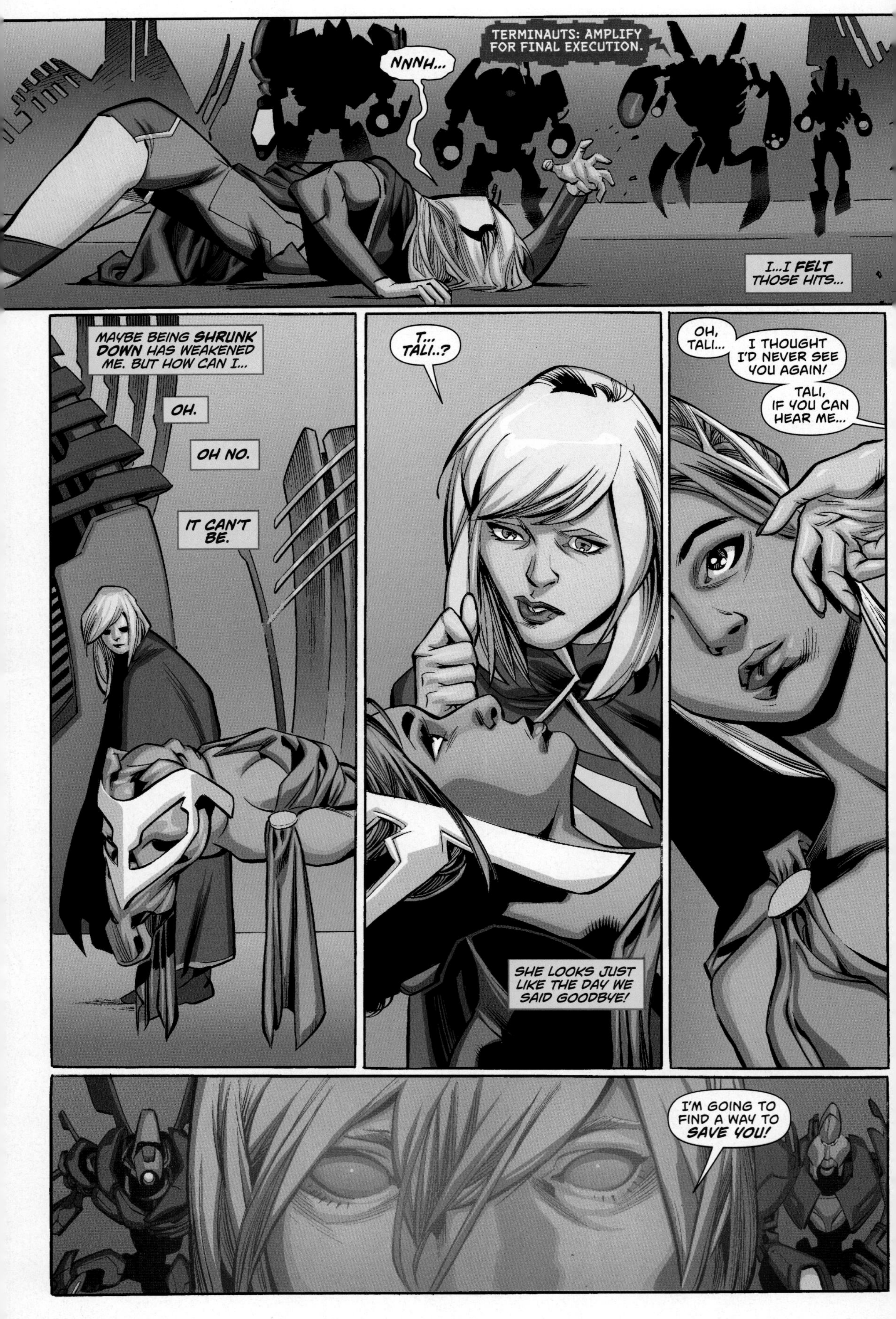
TERMINAUTS: AMPLIFY FOR FINAL EXECUTION.
NNNH...
I...I FELT THOSE HITS...
MAYBE BEING SHRUNK DOWN HAS WEAKENED ME. BUT HOW CAN I...
OH.
OH NO.
IT CAN'T BE.
T... TALI..?
SHE LOOKS JUST LIKE THE DAY WE SAID GOODBYE!
OH, TALI...
I THOUGHT I'D NEVER SEE YOU AGAIN!
TALI, IF YOU CAN HEAR ME...
I'M GOING TO FIND A WAY TO SAVE YOU!

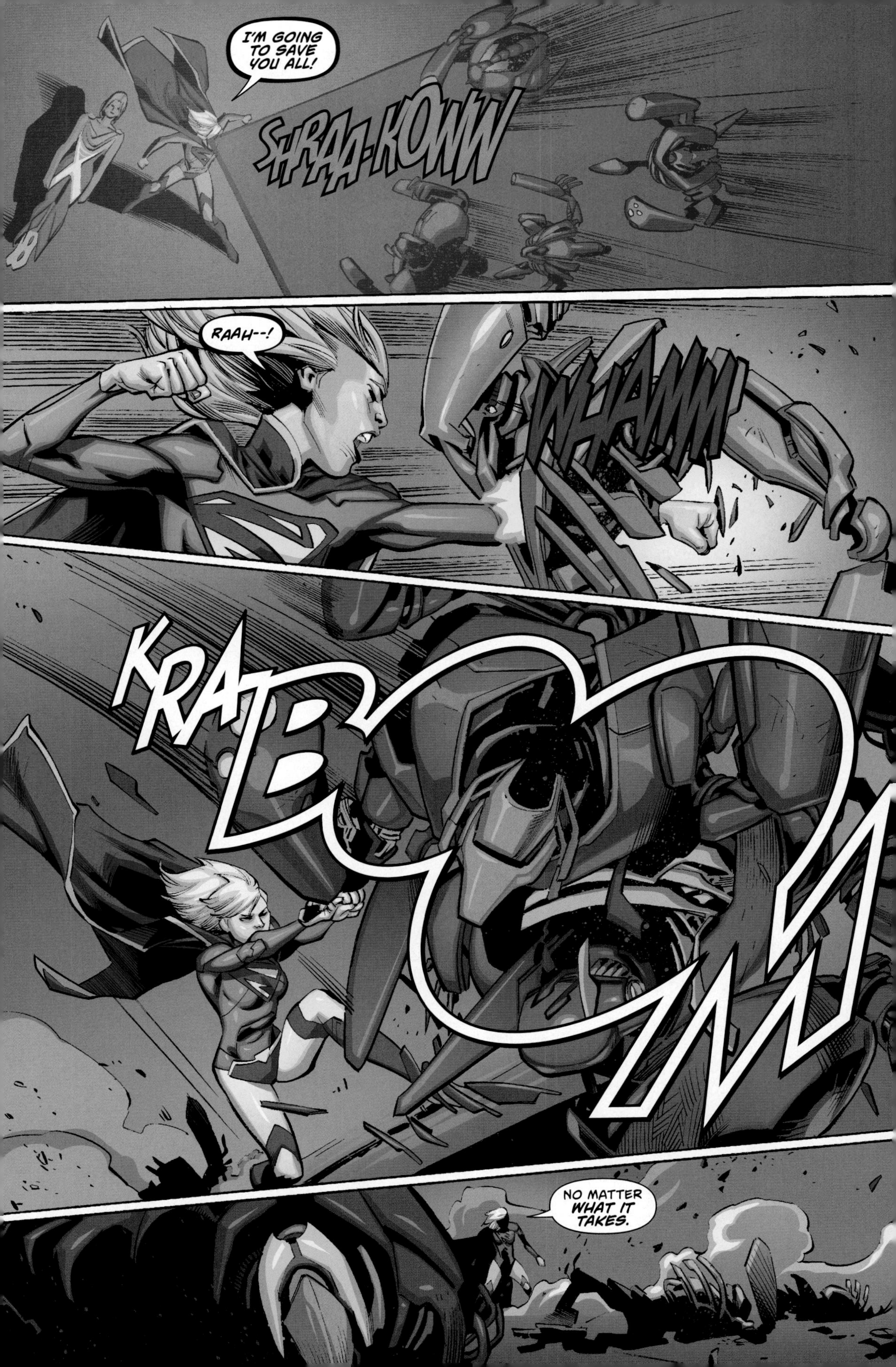
I'M GOING TO SAVE YOU ALL!
SHRAA-KOWW
RAAH--!
WHAMM
KRAT-BOOM
NO MATTER WHAT IT TAKES.

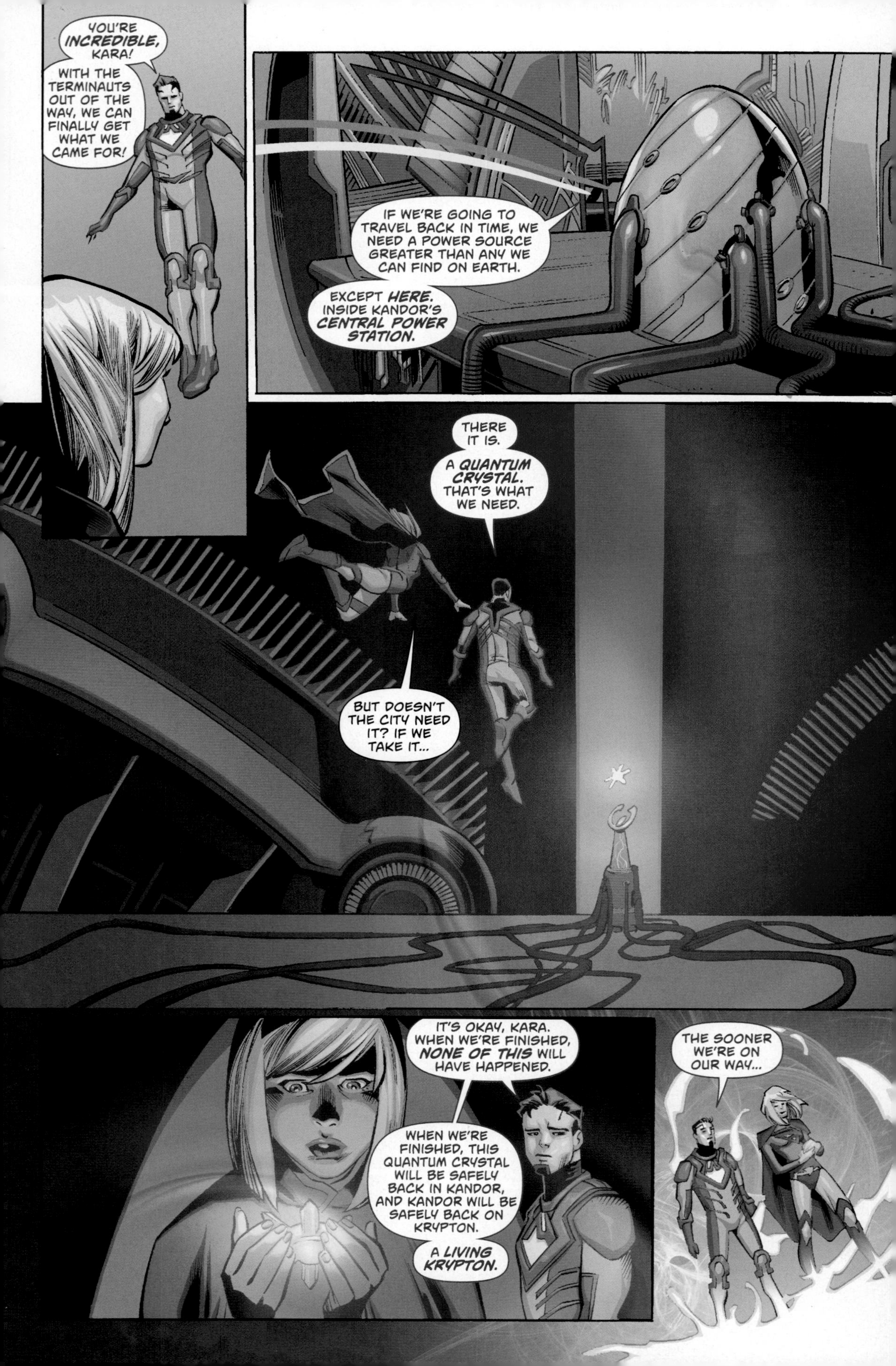
YOU'RE INCREDIBLE, KARA!
WITH THE TERMINAUTS OUT OF THE WAY, WE CAN FINALLY GET WHAT WE CAME FOR!
IF WE'RE GOING TO TRAVEL BACK IN TIME, WE NEED A POWER SOURCE GREATER THAN ANY WE CAN FIND ON EARTH.
EXCEPT HERE. INSIDE KANDOR'S CENTRAL POWER STATION.
THERE IT IS.
A QUANTUM CRYSTAL. THAT'S WHAT WE NEED.
BUT DOESN'T THE CITY NEED IT? IF WE TAKE IT...
IT'S OKAY, KARA. WHEN WE'RE FINISHED, NONE OF THIS WILL HAVE HAPPENED.
WHEN WE'RE FINISHED, THIS QUANTUM CRYSTAL WILL BE SAFELY BACK IN KANDOR, AND KANDOR WILL BE SAFELY BACK ON KRYPTON.
A LIVING KRYPTON.
THE SOONER WE'RE ON OUR WAY...

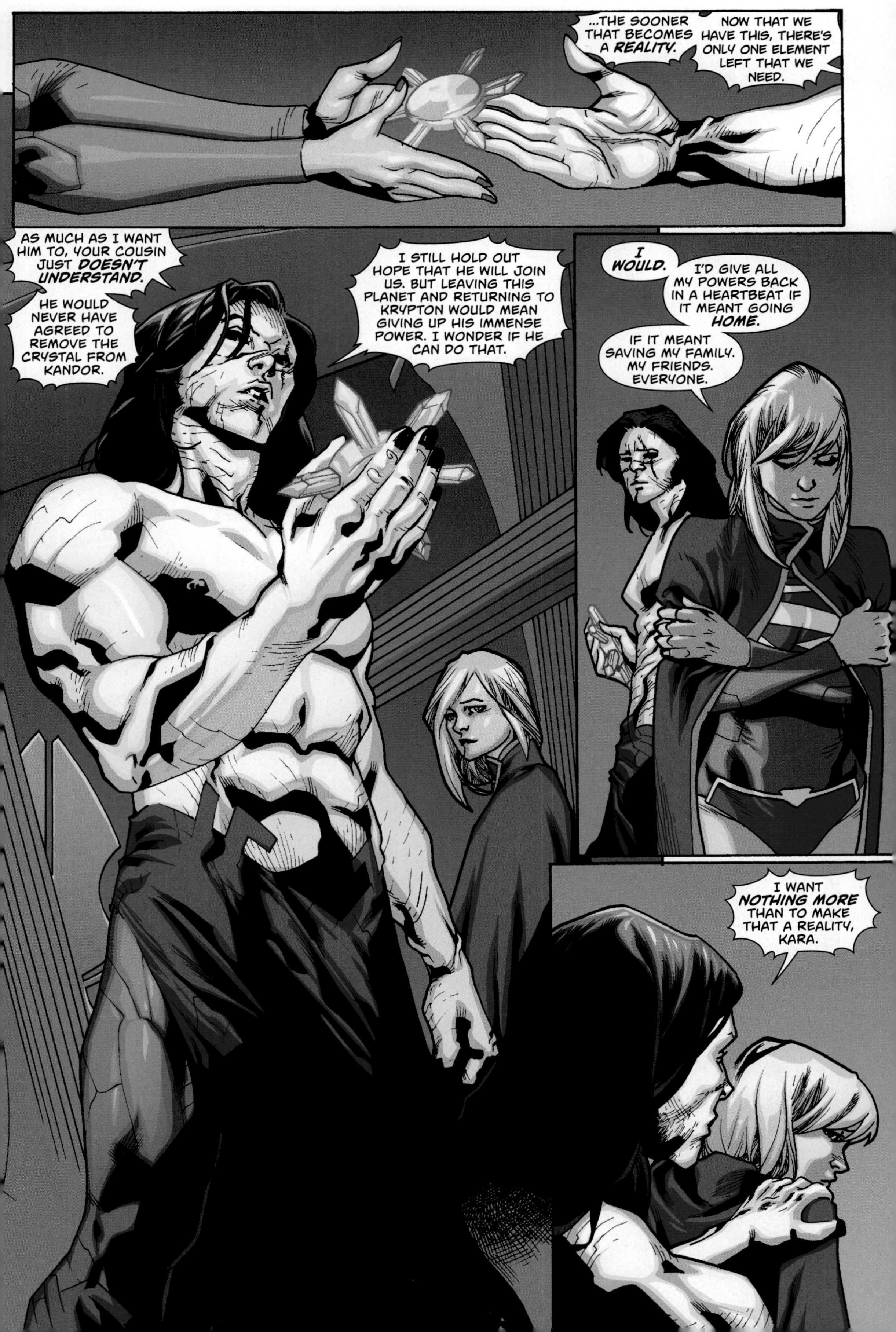
...THE SOONER THAT BECOMES A REALITY.
NOW THAT WE HAVE THIS, THERE'S ONLY ONE ELEMENT LEFT THAT WE NEED.
AS MUCH AS I WANT HIM TO, YOUR COUSIN JUST DOESN'T UNDERSTAND.
HE WOULD NEVER HAVE AGREED TO REMOVE THE CRYSTAL FROM KANDOR.
I STILL HOLD OUT HOPE THAT HE WILL JOIN US. BUT LEAVING THIS PLANET AND RETURNING TO KRYPTON WOULD MEAN GIVING UP HIS IMMENSE POWER. I WONDER IF HE CAN DO THAT.
I WOULD.
I'D GIVE ALL MY POWERS BACK IN A HEARTBEAT IF IT MEANT GOING HOME.
IF IT MEANT SAVING MY FAMILY. MY FRIENDS. EVERYONE.
I WANT NOTHING MORE THAN TO MAKE THAT A REALITY, KARA.

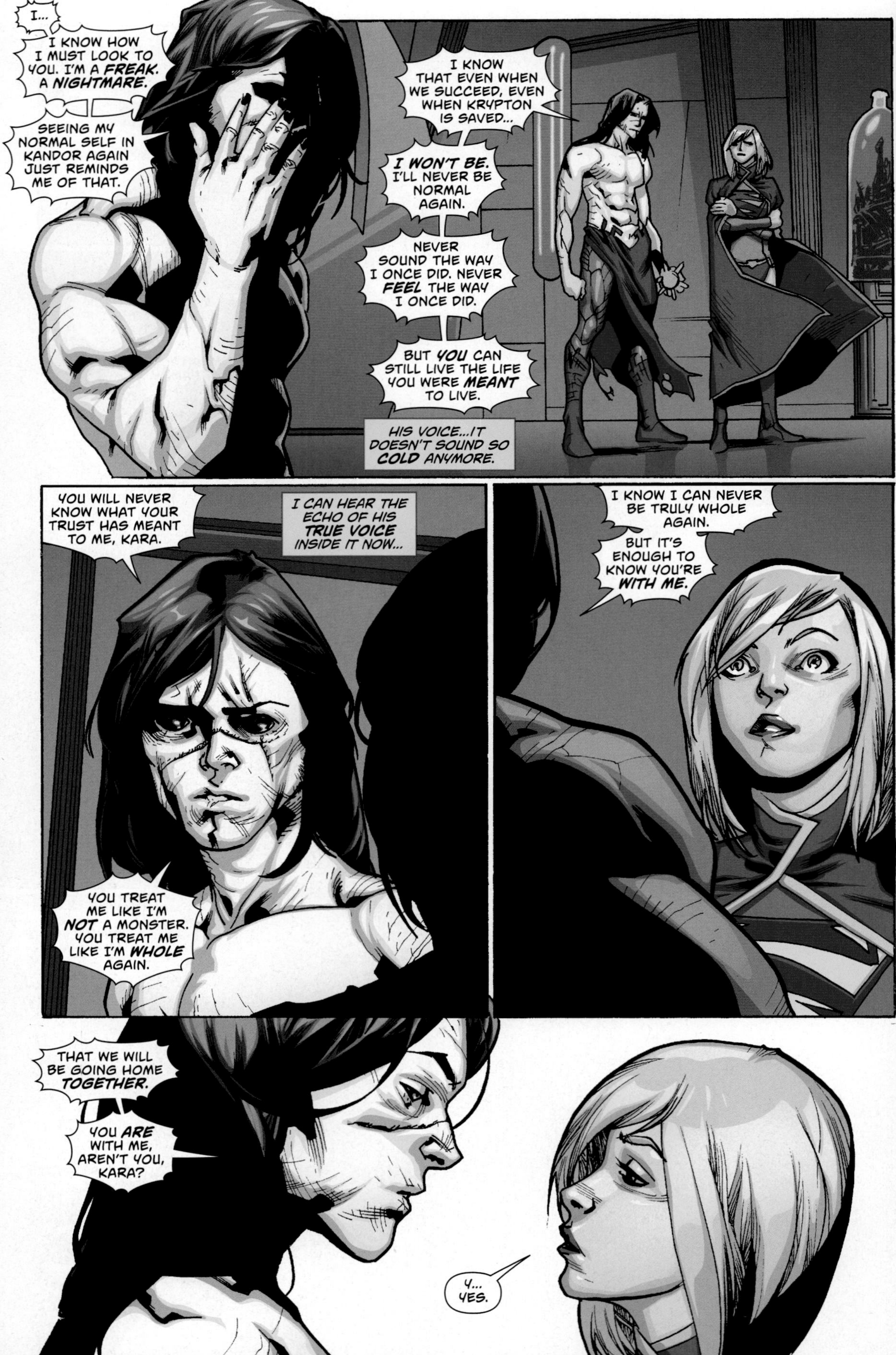
I...
I KNOW HOW I MUST LOOK TO YOU. I'M A FREAK. A NIGHTMARE.
SEEING MY NORMAL SELF IN KANDOR AGAIN JUST REMINDS ME OF THAT.
I KNOW THAT EVEN WHEN WE SUCCEED, EVEN WHEN KRYPTON IS SAVED...
I WON'T BE. I'LL NEVER BE NORMAL AGAIN.
NEVER SOUND THE WAY I ONCE DID. NEVER FEEL THE WAY I ONCE DID.
BUT YOU CAN STILL LIVE THE LIFE YOU WERE MEANT TO LIVE.
HIS VOICE...IT DOESN'T SOUND SO COLD ANYMORE.
YOU WILL NEVER KNOW WHAT YOUR TRUST HAS MEANT TO ME, KARA.
I CAN HEAR THE ECHO OF HIS TRUE VOICE INSIDE IT NOW...
YOU TREAT ME LIKE I'M NOT A MONSTER. YOU TREAT ME LIKE I'M WHOLE AGAIN.
I KNOW I CAN NEVER BE TRULY WHOLE AGAIN.
BUT IT'S ENOUGH TO KNOW YOU'RE WITH ME.
THAT WE WILL BE GOING HOME TOGETHER.
YOU ARE WITH ME, AREN'T YOU, KARA?
Y... YES.

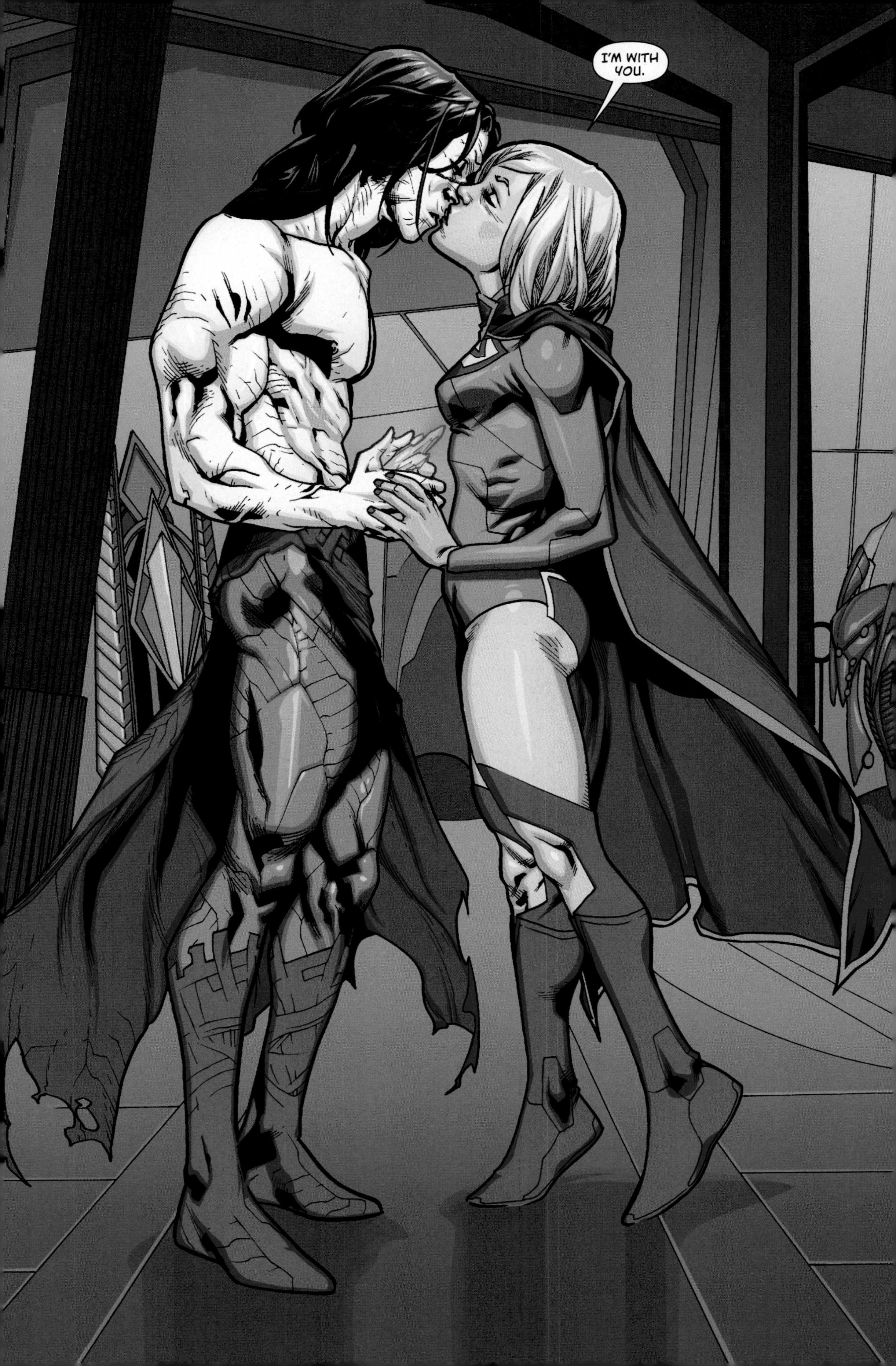
I'M WITH YOU.

BECAUSE I'M A SCORPION

SCOTT LOBDELL writer **KENNETH ROCAFORT** artist cover art by **KENNETH ROCAFORT & SUNNY GHO**

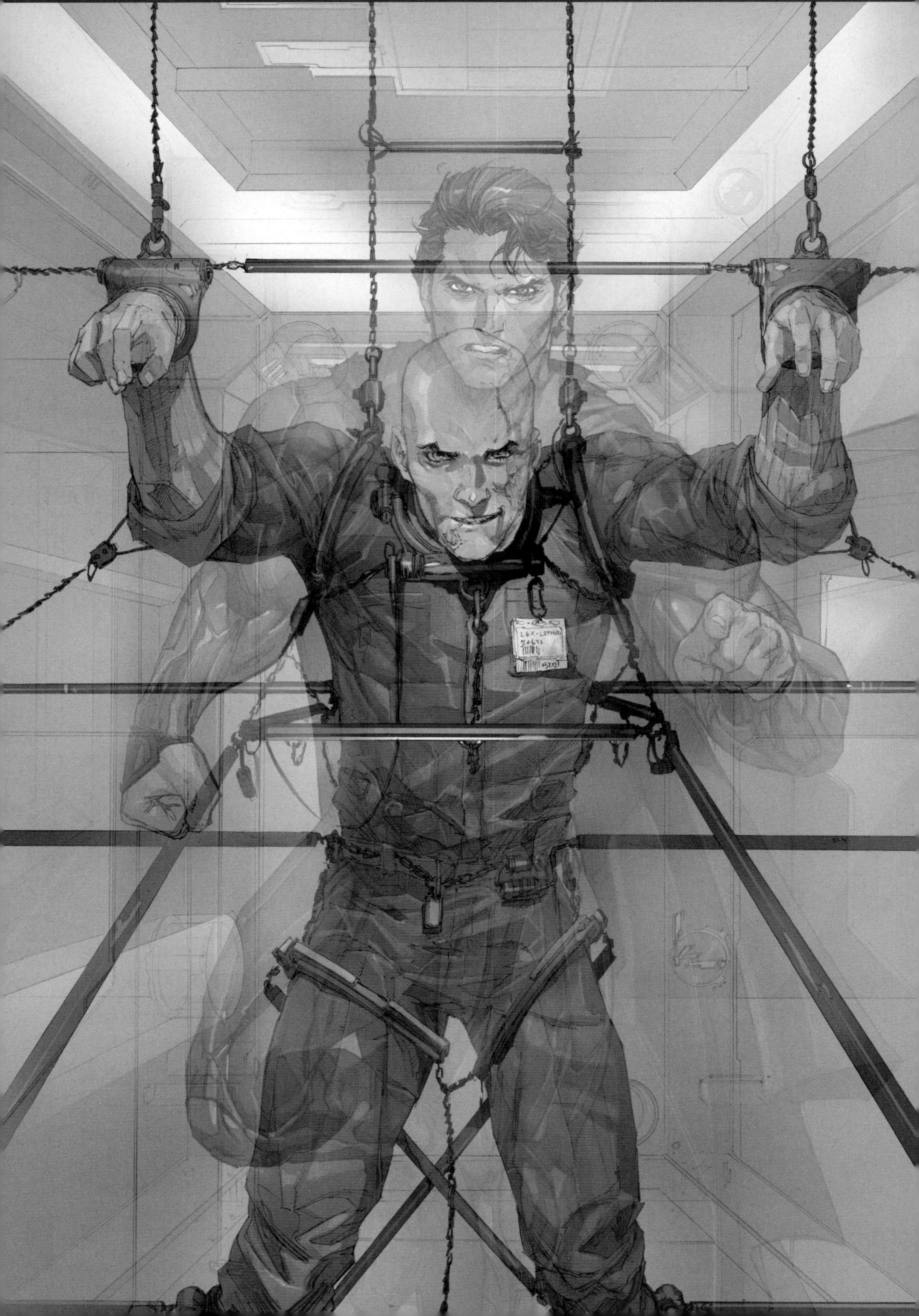

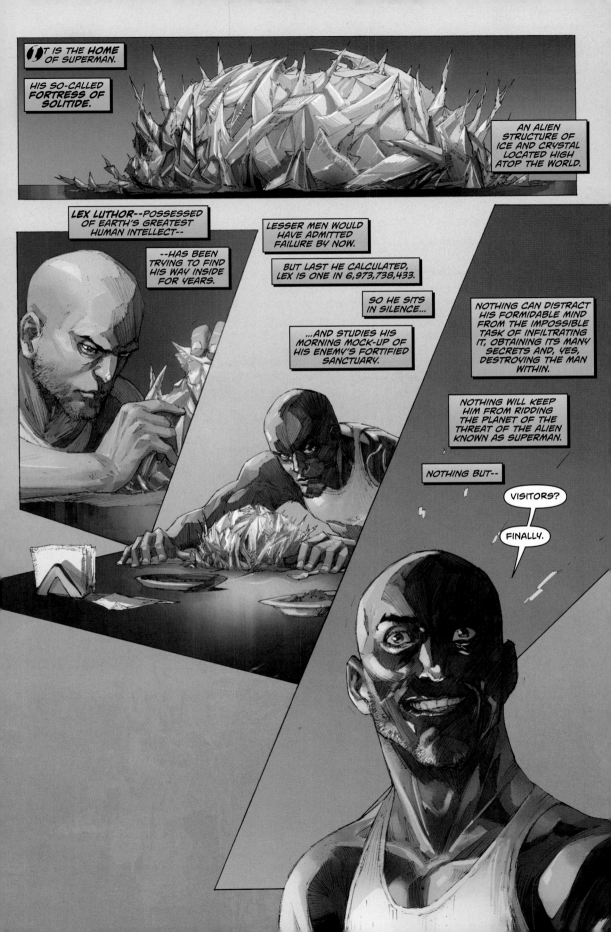

IT IS THE HOME OF SUPERMAN.

HIS SO-CALLED FORTRESS OF SOLITIDE.

AN ALIEN STRUCTURE OF ICE AND CRYSTAL LOCATED HIGH ATOP THE WORLD.

LEX LUTHOR--POSSESSED OF EARTH'S GREATEST HUMAN INTELLECT--

--HAS BEEN TRYING TO FIND HIS WAY INSIDE FOR YEARS.

LESSER MEN WOULD HAVE ADMITTED FAILURE BY NOW.

BUT LAST HE CALCULATED, LEX IS ONE IN 6,973,738,433.

SO HE SITS IN SILENCE...

...AND STUDIES HIS MORNING MOCK-UP OF HIS ENEMY'S FORTIFIED SANCTUARY.

NOTHING CAN DISTRACT HIS FORMIDABLE MIND FROM THE IMPOSSIBLE TASK OF INFILTRATING IT, OBTAINING ITS MANY SECRETS AND, YES, DESTROYING THE MAN WITHIN.

NOTHING WILL KEEP HIM FROM RIDDING THE PLANET OF THE THREAT OF THE ALIEN KNOWN AS SUPERMAN.

NOTHING BUT--

VISITORS?

FINALLY.

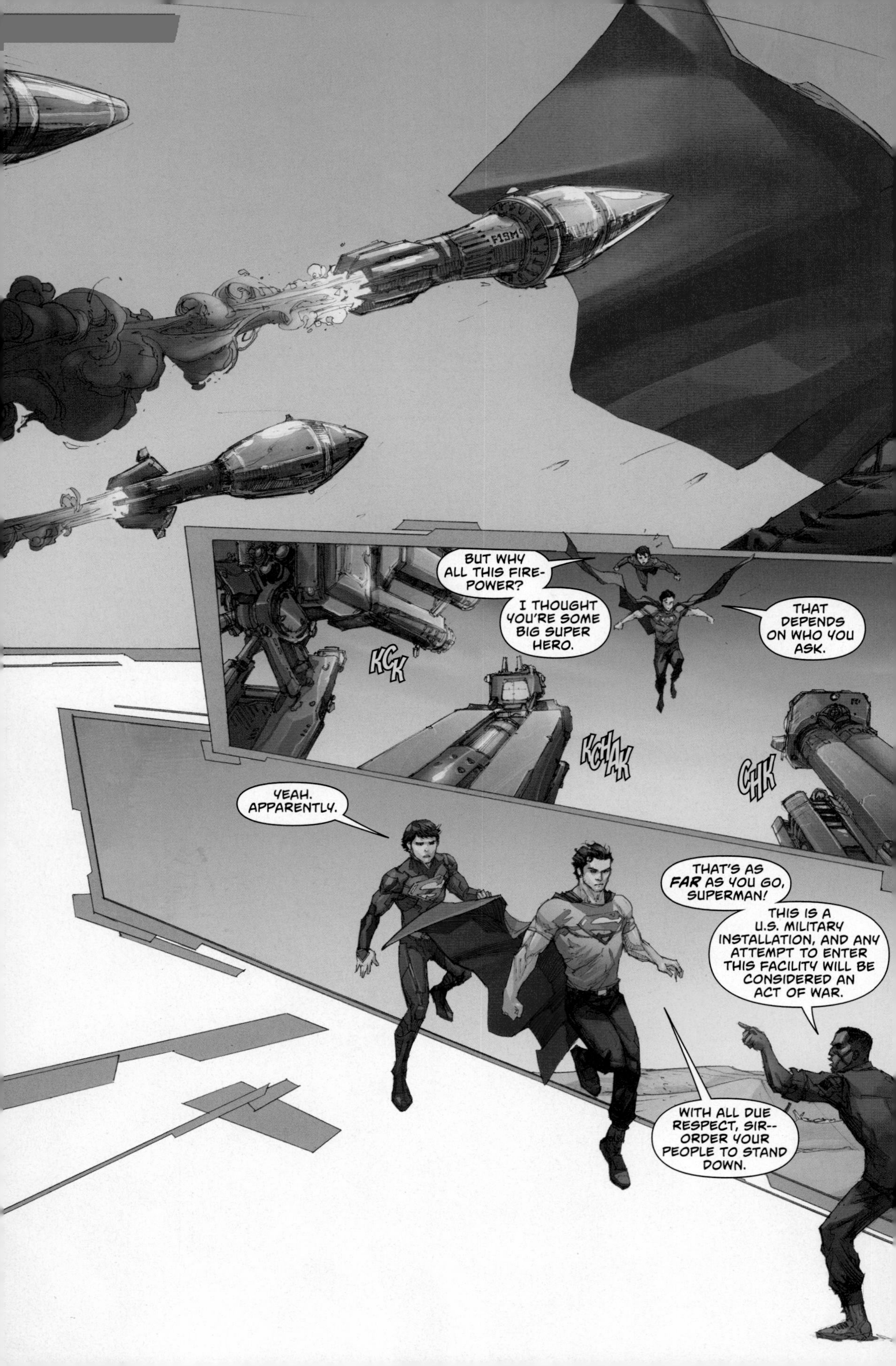

BUT WHY ALL THIS FIRE-POWER?
I THOUGHT YOU'RE SOME BIG SUPER HERO.
THAT DEPENDS ON WHO YOU ASK.
KCK
KCHAK
CHK
YEAH. APPARENTLY.
THAT'S AS **FAR** AS YOU GO, SUPERMAN!
THIS IS A U.S. MILITARY INSTALLATION, AND ANY ATTEMPT TO ENTER THIS FACILITY WILL BE CONSIDERED AN ACT OF WAR.
WITH ALL DUE RESPECT, SIR-- ORDER YOUR PEOPLE TO STAND DOWN.

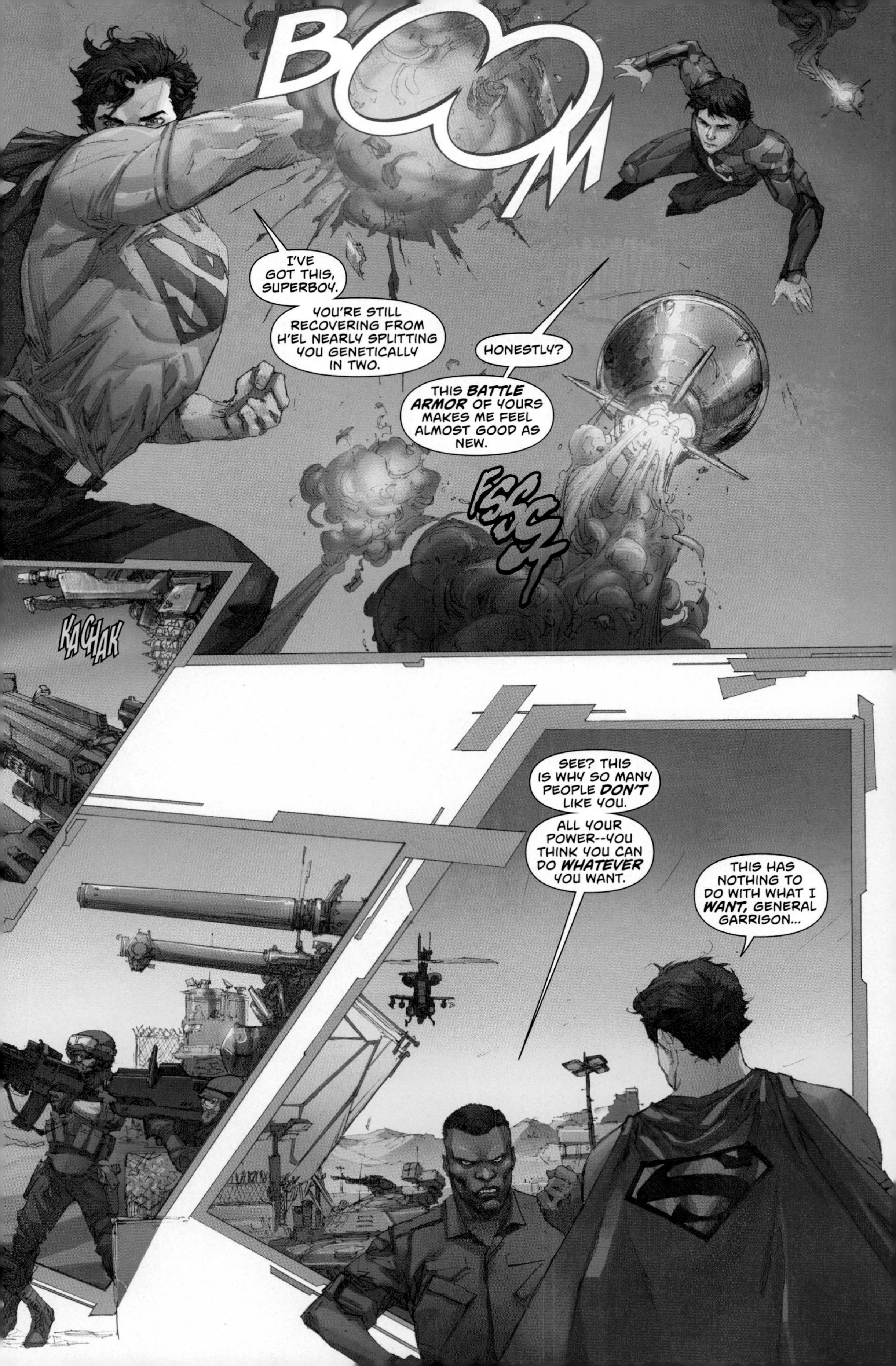
BOOM
I'VE GOT THIS, SUPERBOY.
YOU'RE STILL RECOVERING FROM H'EL NEARLY SPLITTING YOU GENETICALLY IN TWO.
HONESTLY?
THIS **BATTLE ARMOR** OF YOURS MAKES ME FEEL ALMOST GOOD AS NEW.
FSSG
KACHAK
SEE? THIS IS WHY SO MANY PEOPLE **DON'T** LIKE YOU.
ALL YOUR POWER--YOU THINK YOU CAN DO **WHATEVER** YOU WANT.
THIS HAS NOTHING TO DO WITH WHAT I **WANT,** GENERAL GARRISON...

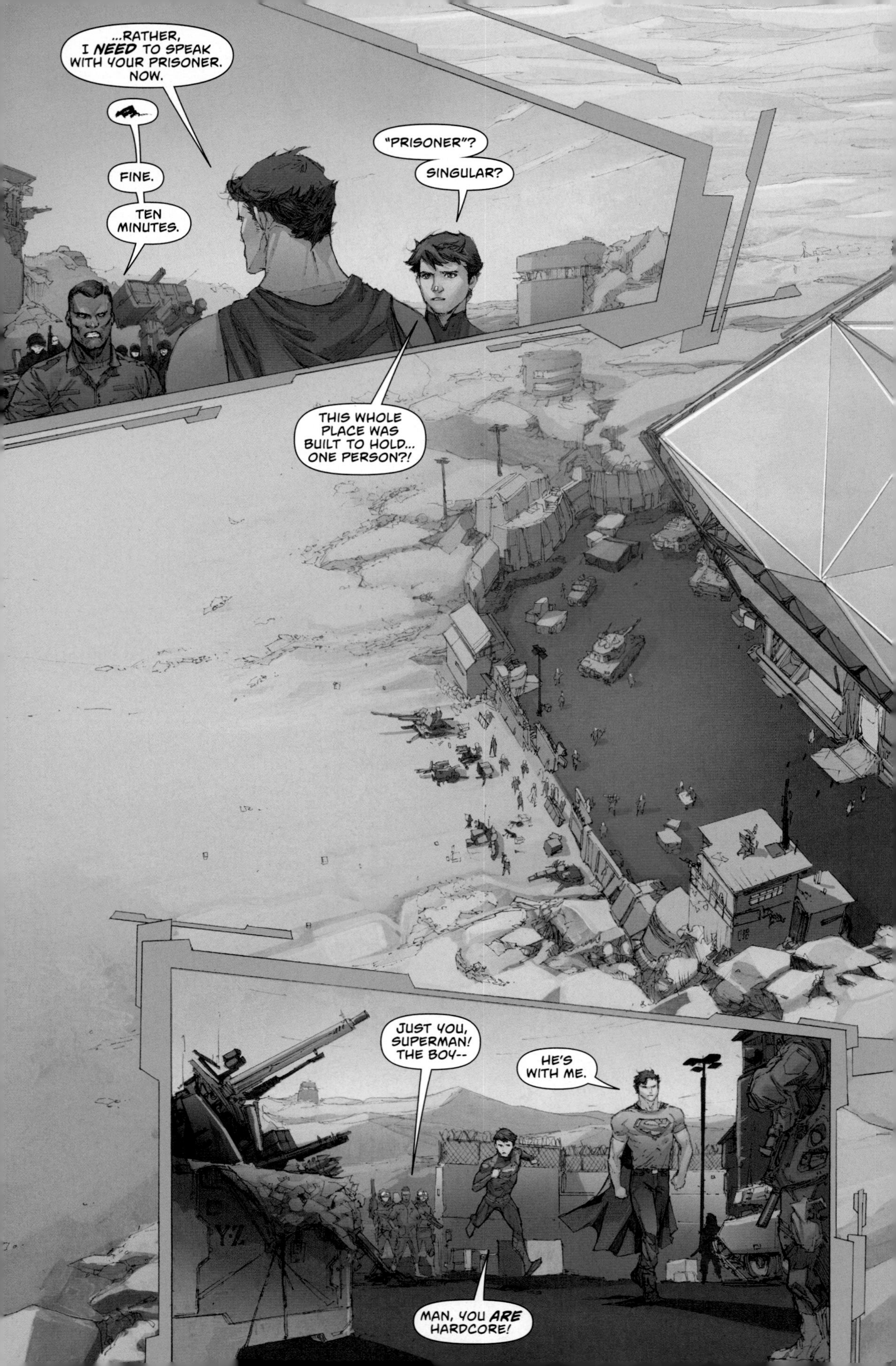
...RATHER, I NEED TO SPEAK WITH YOUR PRISONER. NOW.
FINE.
TEN MINUTES.
"PRISONER"?
SINGULAR?
THIS WHOLE PLACE WAS BUILT TO HOLD... ONE PERSON?!
JUST YOU, SUPERMAN! THE BOY--
HE'S WITH ME.
MAN, YOU ARE HARDCORE!

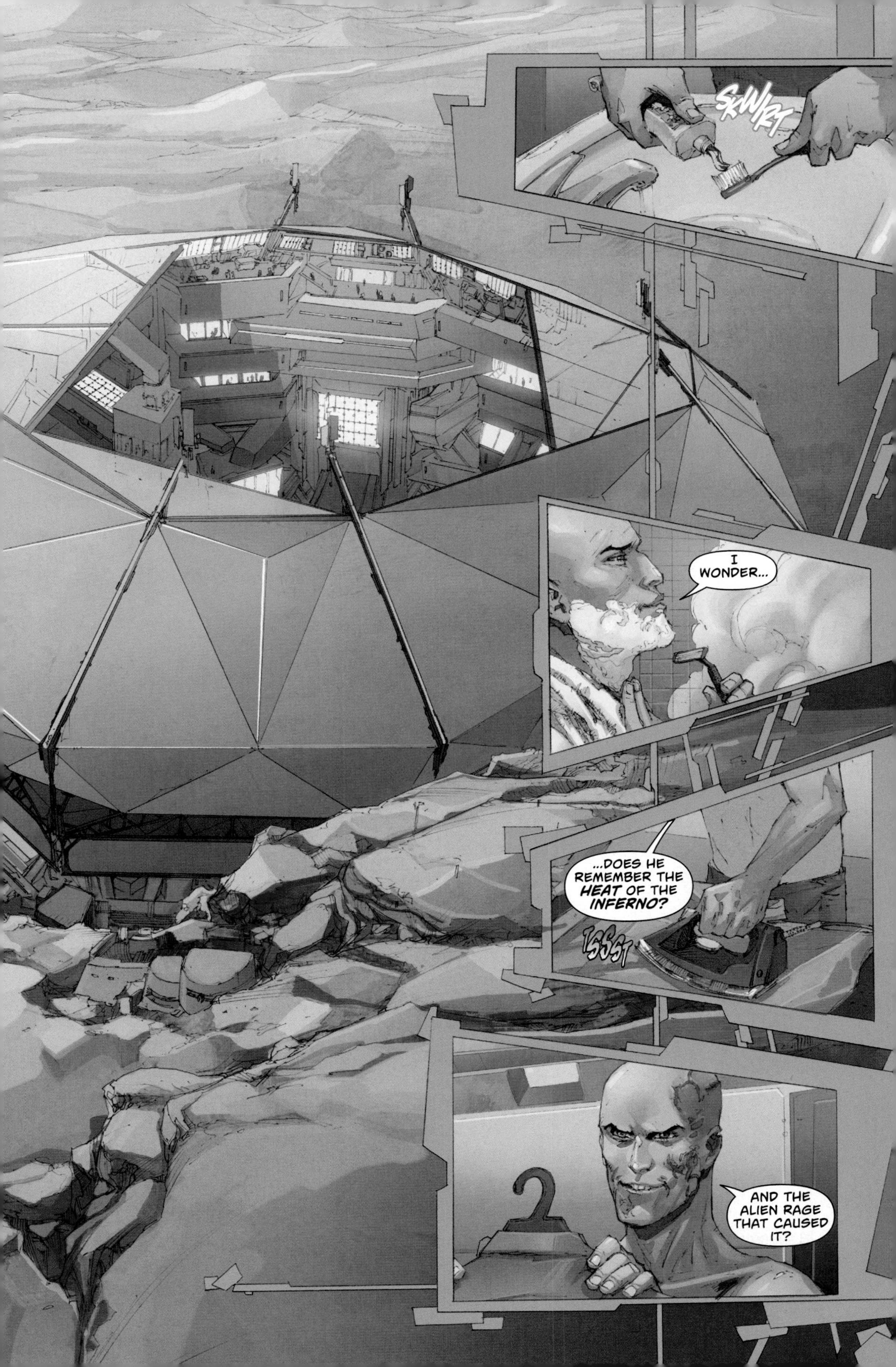
SKWIRT
I WONDER...
...DOES HE REMEMBER THE *HEAT* OF THE *INFERNO?*
TSSST
AND THE ALIEN RAGE THAT CAUSED IT?

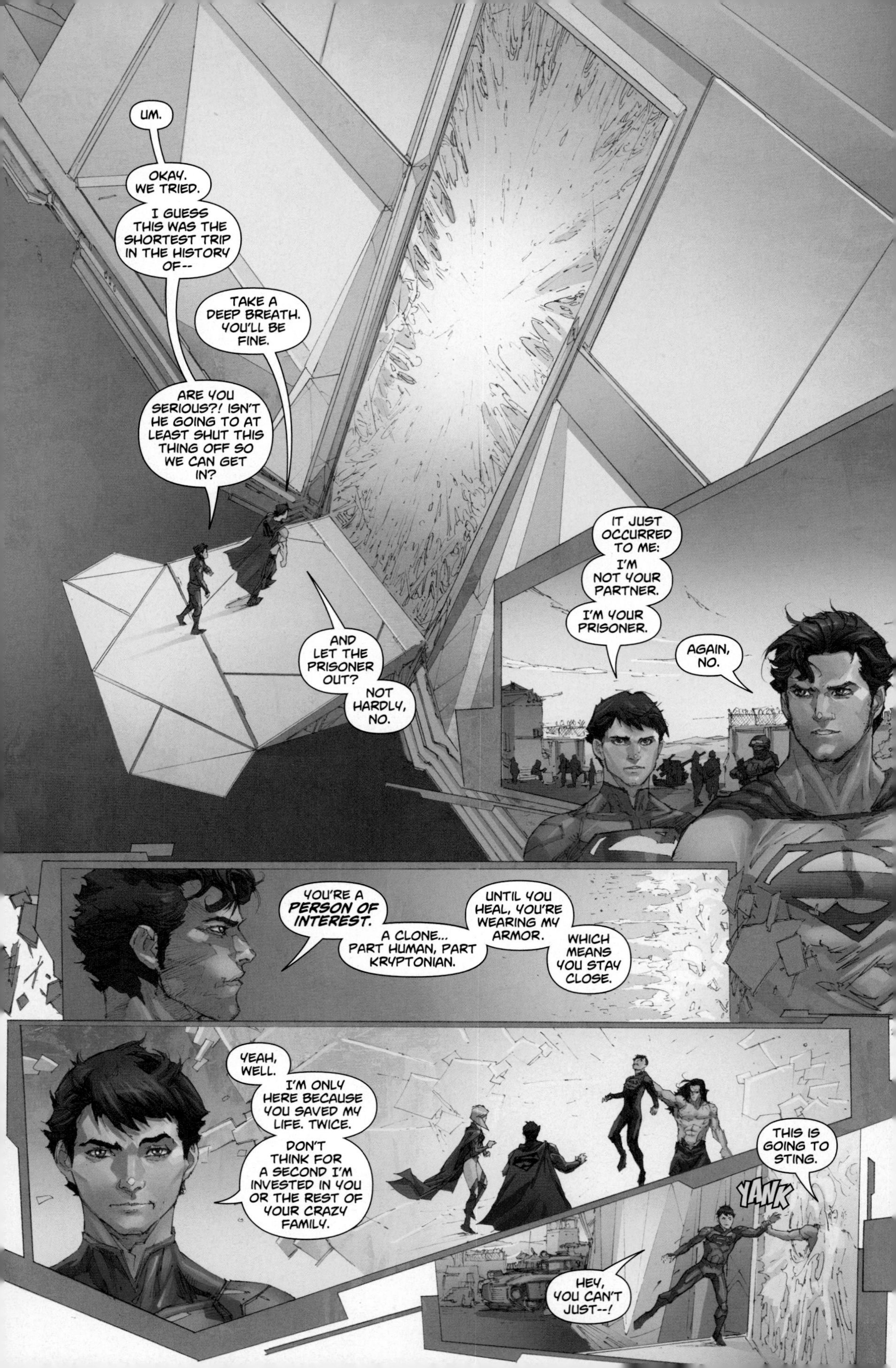
UM.
OKAY. WE TRIED.
I GUESS THIS WAS THE SHORTEST TRIP IN THE HISTORY OF--
TAKE A DEEP BREATH. YOU'LL BE FINE.
ARE YOU SERIOUS?! ISN'T HE GOING TO AT LEAST SHUT THIS THING OFF SO WE CAN GET IN?
AND LET THE PRISONER OUT?
NOT HARDLY, NO.
IT JUST OCCURRED TO ME: I'M NOT YOUR PARTNER.
I'M YOUR PRISONER.
AGAIN, NO.
YOU'RE A **PERSON OF INTEREST**.
A CLONE... PART HUMAN, PART KRYPTONIAN.
UNTIL YOU HEAL, YOU'RE WEARING MY ARMOR.
WHICH MEANS YOU STAY CLOSE.
YEAH, WELL.
I'M ONLY HERE BECAUSE YOU SAVED MY LIFE. TWICE.
DON'T THINK FOR A SECOND I'M INVESTED IN YOU OR THE REST OF YOUR CRAZY FAMILY.
THIS IS GOING TO STING.
YANK
HEY, YOU CAN'T JUST--!

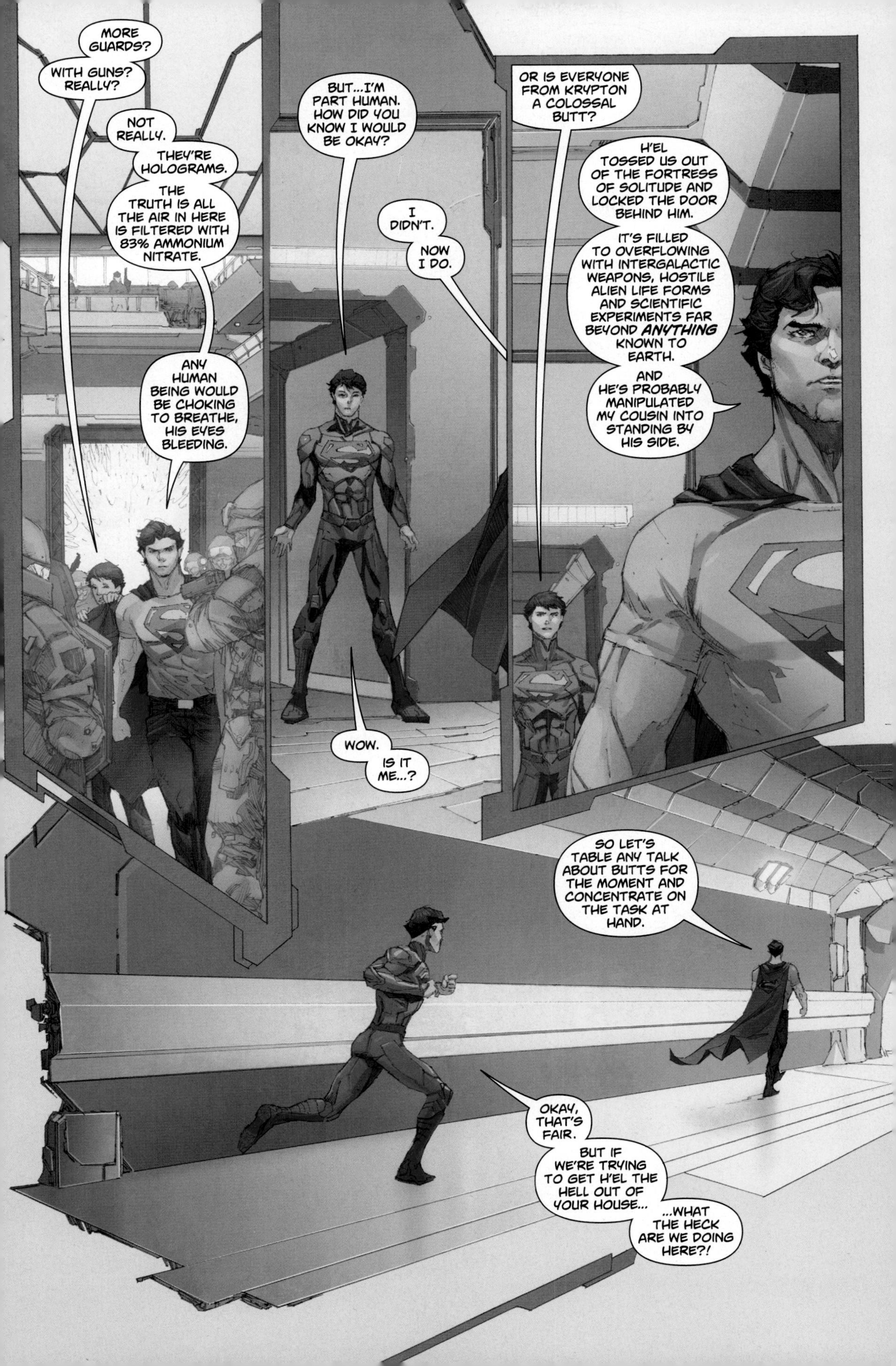

MORE GUARDS?
WITH GUNS? REALLY?
NOT REALLY.
THEY'RE HOLOGRAMS.
THE TRUTH IS ALL THE AIR IN HERE IS FILTERED WITH 83% AMMONIUM NITRATE.
ANY HUMAN BEING WOULD BE CHOKING TO BREATHE, HIS EYES BLEEDING.
BUT...I'M PART HUMAN. HOW DID YOU KNOW I WOULD BE OKAY?
I DIDN'T.
NOW I DO.
WOW.
IS IT ME...?
OR IS EVERYONE FROM KRYPTON A COLOSSAL BUTT?
H'EL TOSSED US OUT OF THE FORTRESS OF SOLITUDE AND LOCKED THE DOOR BEHIND HIM.
IT'S FILLED TO OVERFLOWING WITH INTERGALACTIC WEAPONS, HOSTILE ALIEN LIFE FORMS AND SCIENTIFIC EXPERIMENTS FAR BEYOND *ANYTHING* KNOWN TO EARTH.
AND HE'S PROBABLY MANIPULATED MY COUSIN INTO STANDING BY HIS SIDE.
SO LET'S TABLE ANY TALK ABOUT BUTTS FOR THE MOMENT AND CONCENTRATE ON THE TASK AT HAND.
OKAY, THAT'S FAIR.
BUT IF WE'RE TRYING TO GET H'EL THE HELL OUT OF YOUR HOUSE...
...WHAT THE HECK ARE WE DOING HERE?!

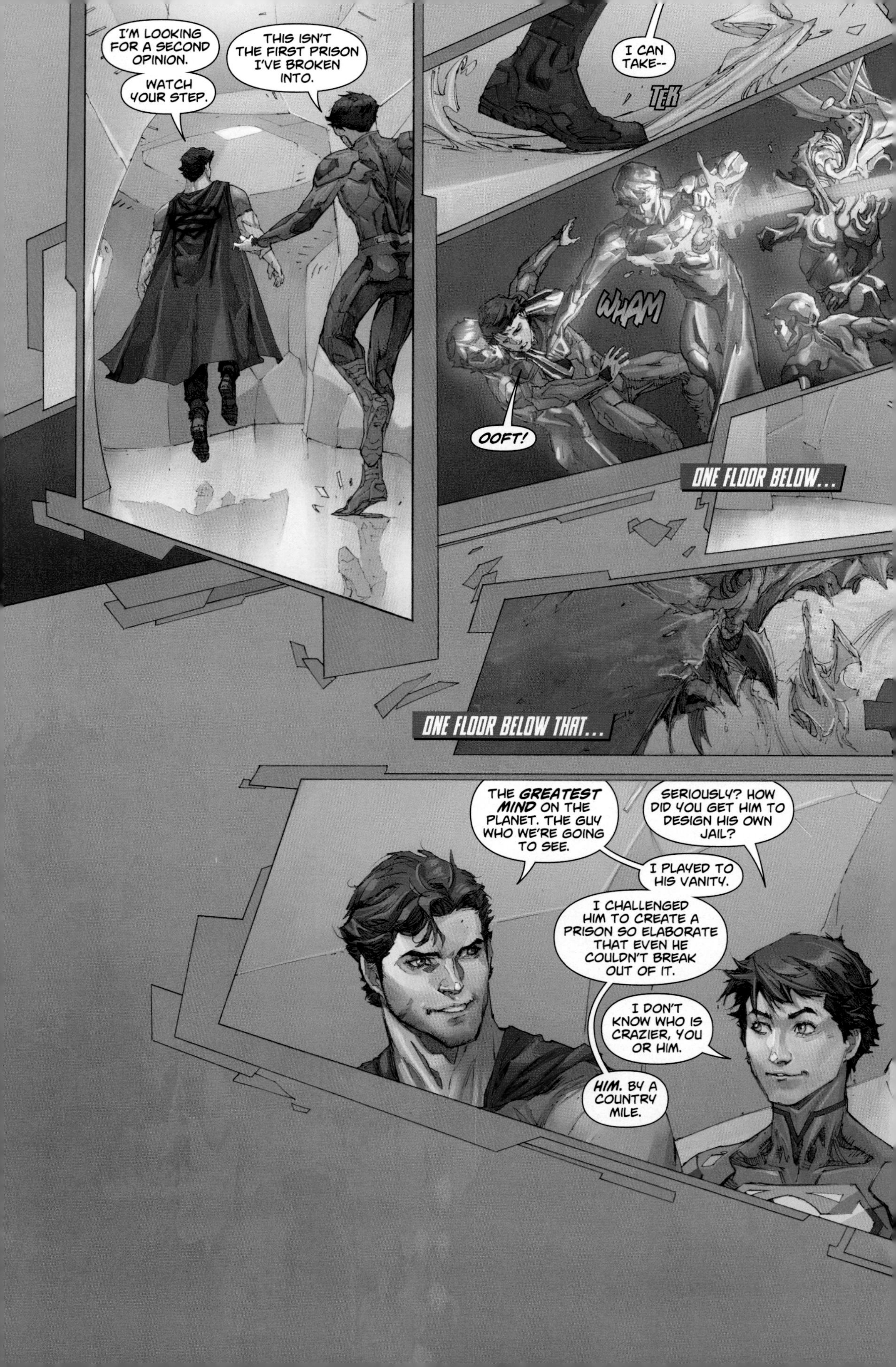
I'M LOOKING FOR A SECOND OPINION.
WATCH YOUR STEP.
THIS ISN'T THE FIRST PRISON I'VE BROKEN INTO.
I CAN TAKE--
TEK
WHAM
OOFT!
ONE FLOOR BELOW...
ONE FLOOR BELOW THAT...
THE GREATEST MIND ON THE PLANET. THE GUY WHO WE'RE GOING TO SEE.
SERIOUSLY? HOW DID YOU GET HIM TO DESIGN HIS OWN JAIL?
I PLAYED TO HIS VANITY.
I CHALLENGED HIM TO CREATE A PRISON SO ELABORATE THAT EVEN HE COULDN'T BREAK OUT OF IT.
I DON'T KNOW WHO IS CRAZIER, YOU OR HIM.
HIM. BY A COUNTRY MILE.

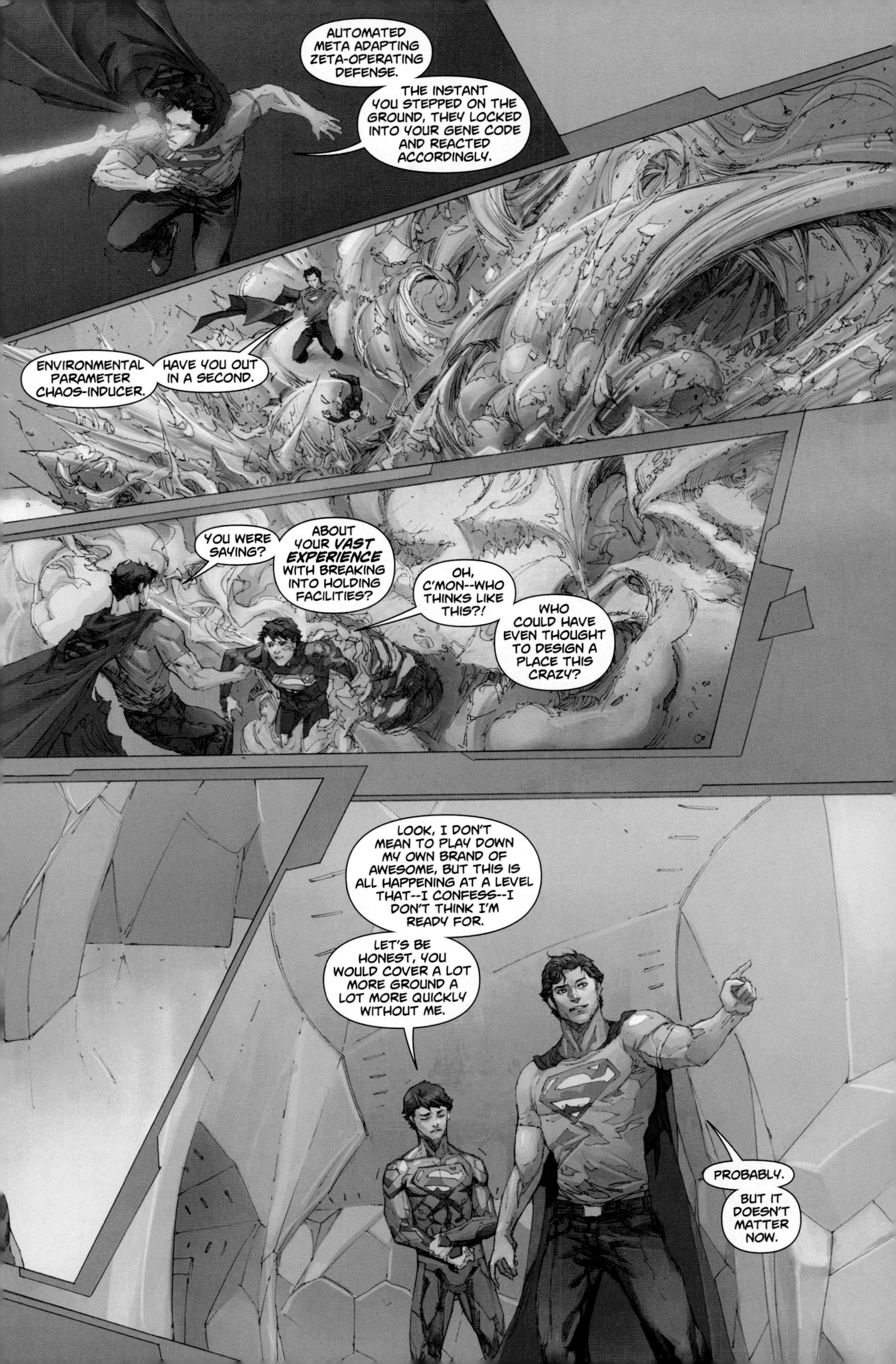
AUTOMATED META ADAPTING ZETA-OPERATING DEFENSE.
THE INSTANT YOU STEPPED ON THE GROUND, THEY LOCKED INTO YOUR GENE CODE AND REACTED ACCORDINGLY.
ENVIRONMENTAL PARAMETER CHAOS-INDUCER.
HAVE YOU OUT IN A SECOND.
YOU WERE SAYING?
ABOUT YOUR VAST EXPERIENCE WITH BREAKING INTO HOLDING FACILITIES?
OH, C'MON--WHO THINKS LIKE THIS?!
WHO COULD HAVE EVEN THOUGHT TO DESIGN A PLACE THIS CRAZY?
LOOK, I DON'T MEAN TO PLAY DOWN MY OWN BRAND OF AWESOME, BUT THIS IS ALL HAPPENING AT A LEVEL THAT--I CONFESS--I DON'T THINK I'M READY FOR.
LET'S BE HONEST, YOU WOULD COVER A LOT MORE GROUND A LOT MORE QUICKLY WITHOUT ME.
PROBABLY.
BUT IT DOESN'T MATTER NOW.

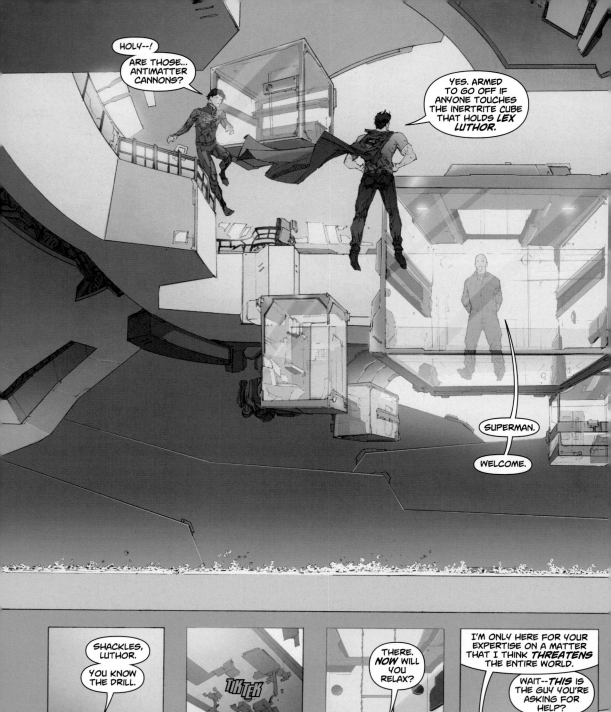

HOLY--! ARE THOSE... ANTIMATTER CANNONS?

YES. ARMED TO GO OFF IF ANYONE TOUCHES THE INERTRITE CUBE THAT HOLDS *LEX LUTHOR.*

SUPERMAN. WELCOME.

SHACKLES, LUTHOR. YOU KNOW THE DRILL.

TIK TEK

YOU WOUND ME. VERY WELL. "SHACKLES."

THERE. *NOW* WILL YOU RELAX?

NEVER.

I'M ONLY HERE FOR YOUR EXPERTISE ON A MATTER THAT I THINK *THREATENS* THE ENTIRE WORLD.

WAIT--*THIS IS* THE GUY YOU'RE ASKING FOR HELP?

EVEN WITH MY T.K. DAMPED DOWN BY THIS SUIT I CAN TELL YOU THIS GUY IS ALL KINDS OF EVIL.

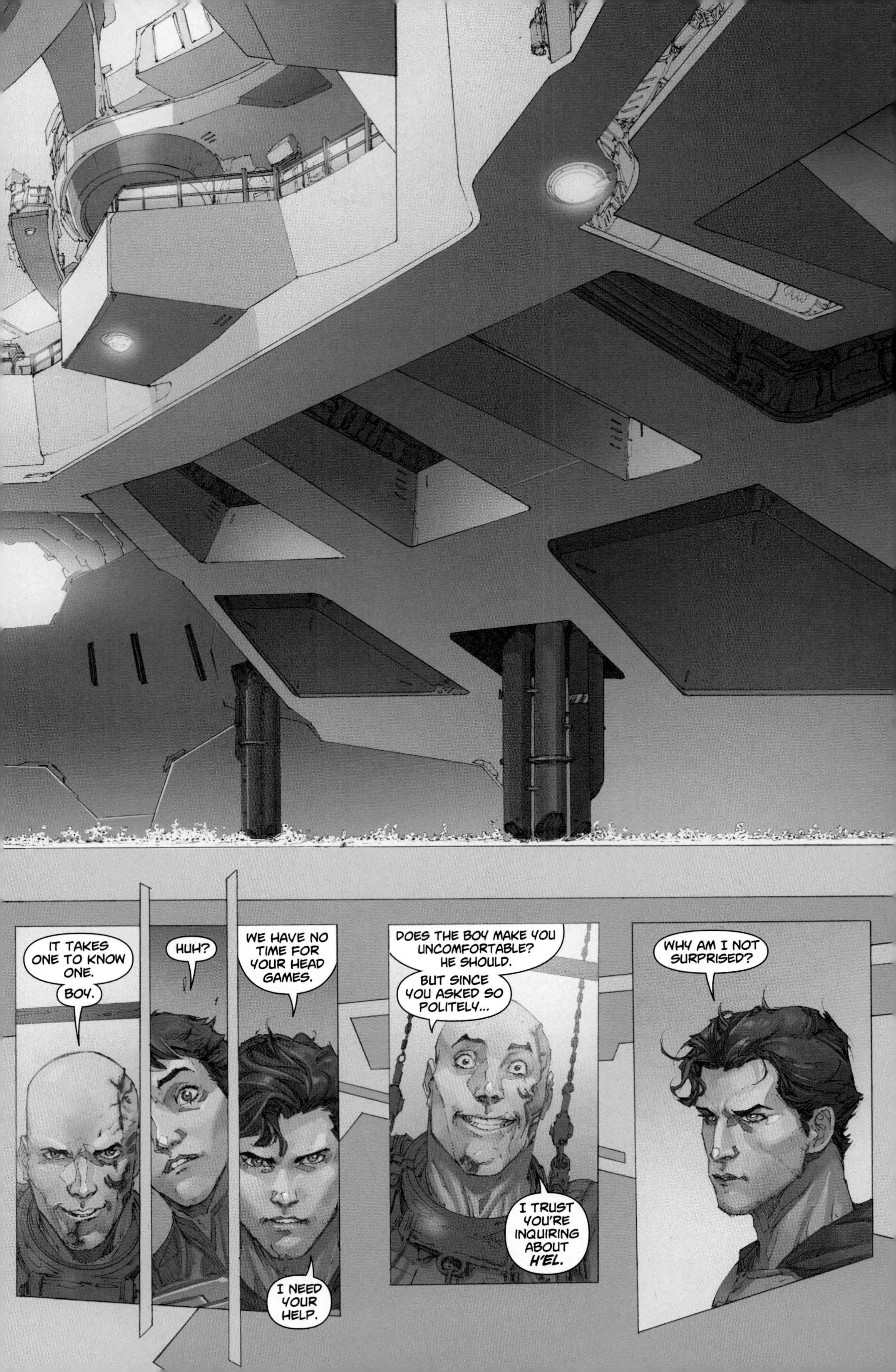
IT TAKES ONE TO KNOW ONE.
BOY.
HUH?
WE HAVE NO TIME FOR YOUR HEAD GAMES.
I NEED YOUR HELP.
DOES THE BOY MAKE YOU UNCOMFORTABLE? HE SHOULD.
BUT SINCE YOU ASKED SO POLITELY...
I TRUST YOU'RE INQUIRING ABOUT H'EL.
WHY AM I NOT SURPRISED?

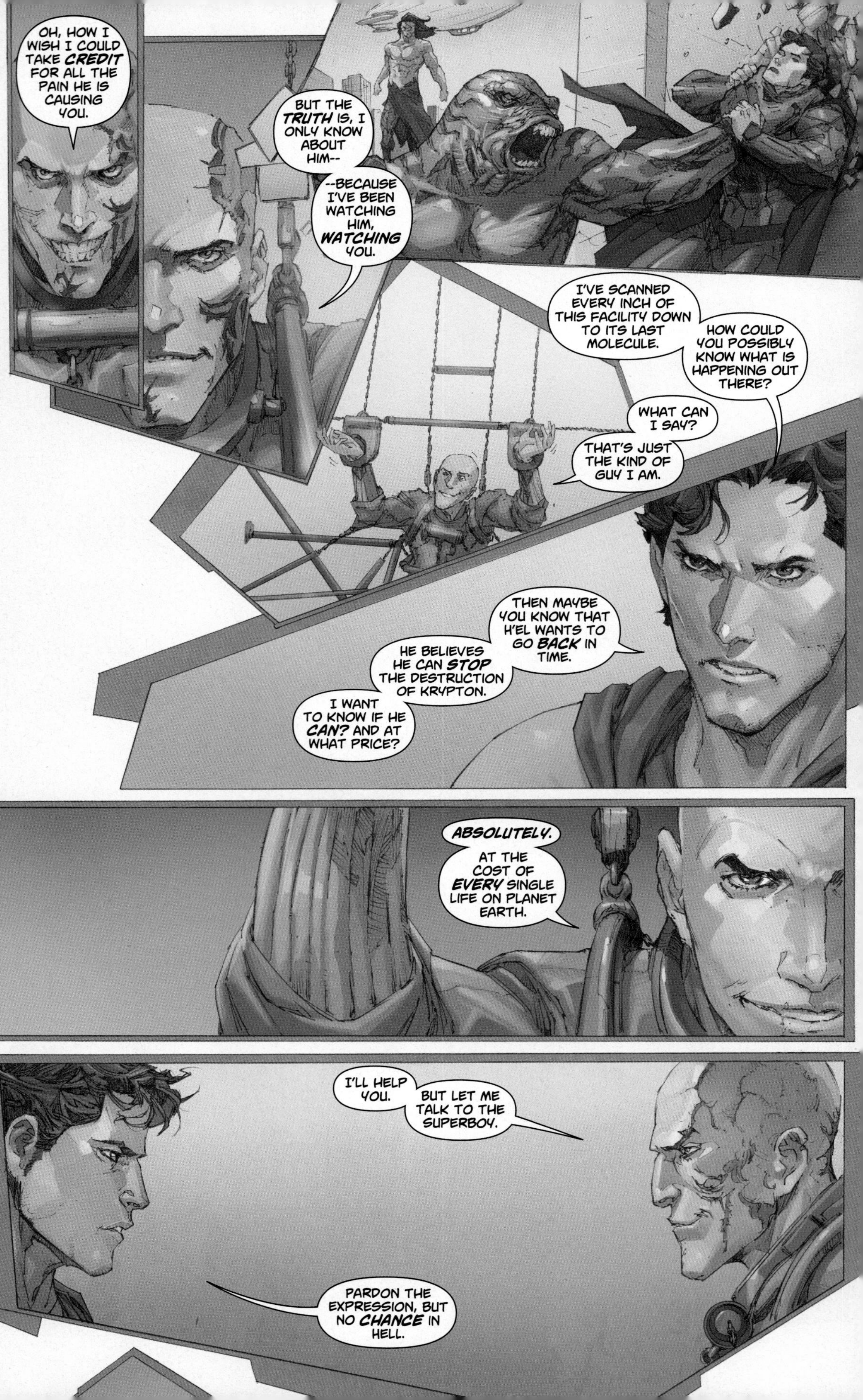

OH, HOW I WISH I COULD TAKE CREDIT FOR ALL THE PAIN HE IS CAUSING YOU.
BUT THE TRUTH IS, I ONLY KNOW ABOUT HIM--
--BECAUSE I'VE BEEN WATCHING HIM, WATCHING YOU.
I'VE SCANNED EVERY INCH OF THIS FACILITY DOWN TO ITS LAST MOLECULE.
HOW COULD YOU POSSIBLY KNOW WHAT IS HAPPENING OUT THERE?
WHAT CAN I SAY?
THAT'S JUST THE KIND OF GUY I AM.
THEN MAYBE YOU KNOW THAT H'EL WANTS TO GO BACK IN TIME.
HE BELIEVES HE CAN STOP THE DESTRUCTION OF KRYPTON.
I WANT TO KNOW IF HE CAN? AND AT WHAT PRICE?
ABSOLUTELY.
AT THE COST OF EVERY SINGLE LIFE ON PLANET EARTH.
I'LL HELP YOU.
BUT LET ME TALK TO THE SUPERBOY.
PARDON THE EXPRESSION, BUT NO CHANCE IN HELL.

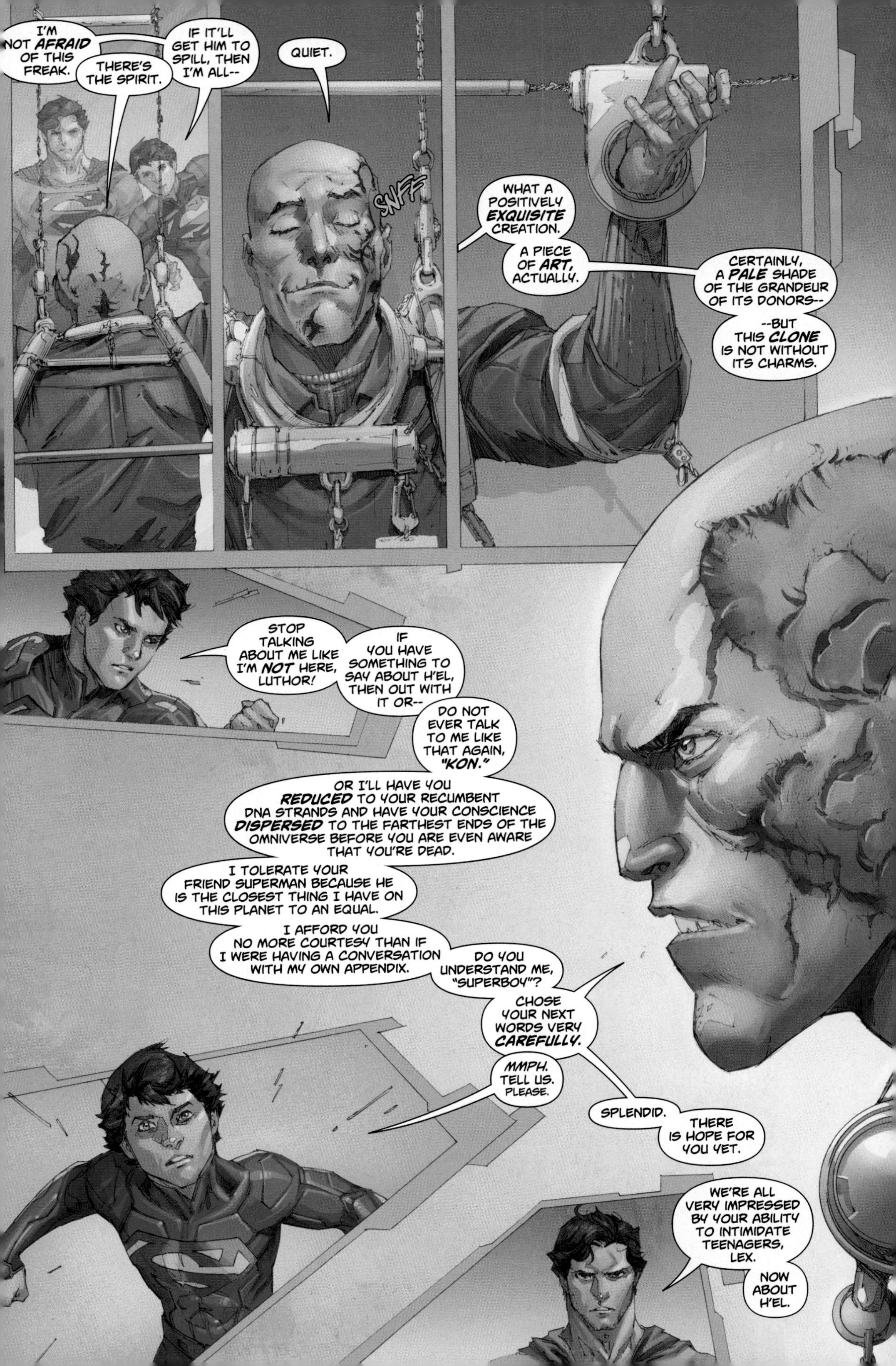
I'M NOT AFRAID OF THIS FREAK.
IF IT'LL GET HIM TO SPILL, THEN I'M ALL--
THERE'S THE SPIRIT.
QUIET.
SNIFF
WHAT A POSITIVELY EXQUISITE CREATION.
A PIECE OF ART, ACTUALLY.
CERTAINLY, A PALE SHADE OF THE GRANDEUR OF ITS DONORS--
--BUT THIS CLONE IS NOT WITHOUT ITS CHARMS.
STOP TALKING ABOUT ME LIKE I'M NOT HERE, LUTHOR!
IF YOU HAVE SOMETHING TO SAY ABOUT H'EL, THEN OUT WITH IT OR--
DO NOT EVER TALK TO ME LIKE THAT AGAIN, "KON."
OR I'LL HAVE YOU REDUCED TO YOUR RECUMBENT DNA STRANDS AND HAVE YOUR CONSCIENCE DISPERSED TO THE FARTHEST ENDS OF THE OMNIVERSE BEFORE YOU ARE EVEN AWARE THAT YOU'RE DEAD.
I TOLERATE YOUR FRIEND SUPERMAN BECAUSE HE IS THE CLOSEST THING I HAVE ON THIS PLANET TO AN EQUAL.
I AFFORD YOU NO MORE COURTESY THAN IF I WERE HAVING A CONVERSATION WITH MY OWN APPENDIX.
DO YOU UNDERSTAND ME, "SUPERBOY"?
CHOSE YOUR NEXT WORDS VERY CAREFULLY.
MMPH. TELL US. PLEASE.
SPLENDID.
THERE IS HOPE FOR YOU YET.
WE'RE ALL VERY IMPRESSED BY YOUR ABILITY TO INTIMIDATE TEENAGERS, LEX.
NOW ABOUT H'EL.

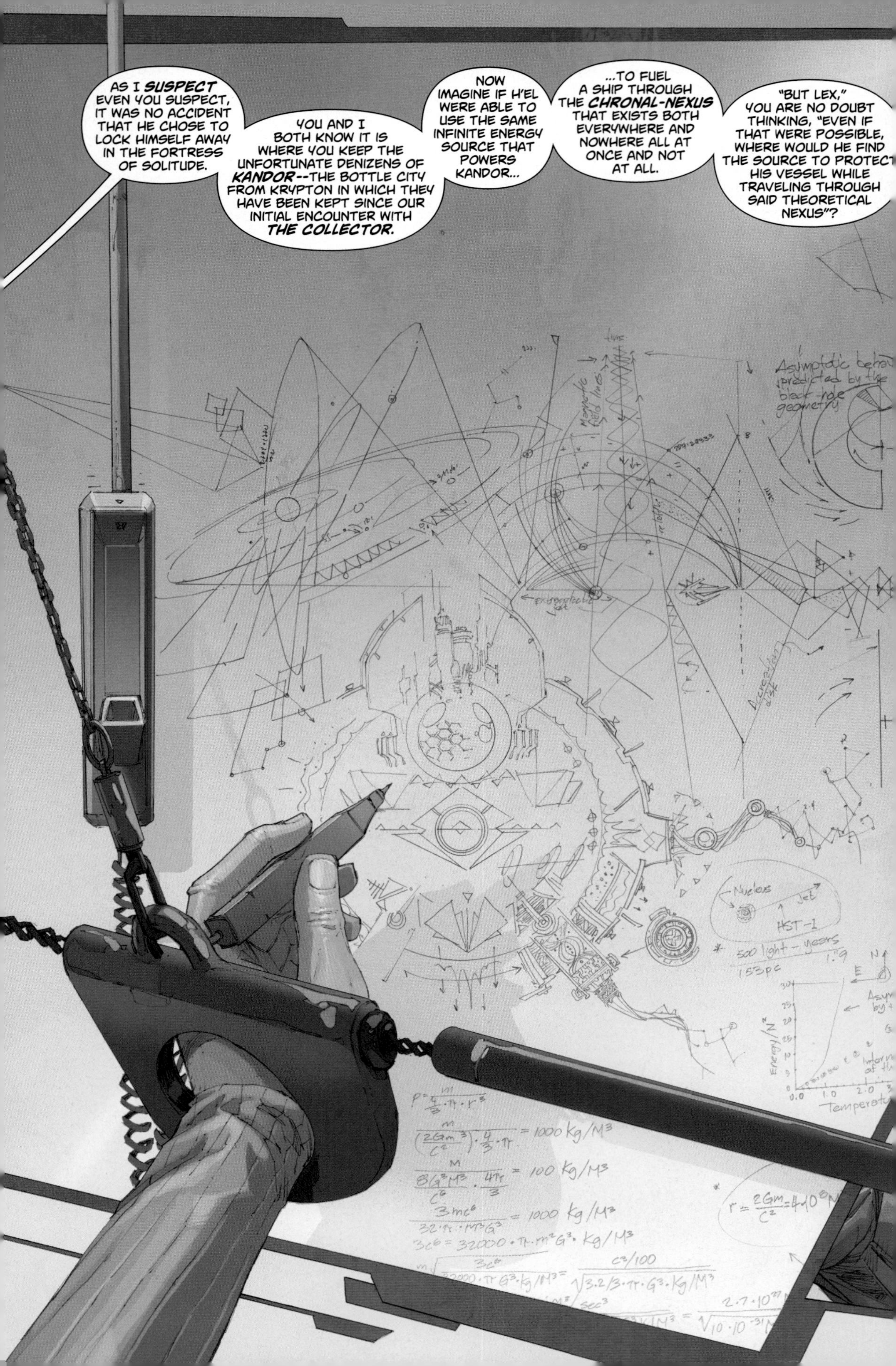
AS I *SUSPECT* EVEN YOU SUSPECT, IT WAS NO ACCIDENT THAT HE CHOSE TO LOCK HIMSELF AWAY IN THE FORTRESS OF SOLITUDE.
YOU AND I BOTH KNOW IT IS WHERE YOU KEEP THE UNFORTUNATE DENIZENS OF *KANDOR*--THE BOTTLE CITY FROM KRYPTON IN WHICH THEY HAVE BEEN KEPT SINCE OUR INITIAL ENCOUNTER WITH ***THE COLLECTOR***.
NOW IMAGINE IF H'EL WERE ABLE TO USE THE SAME INFINITE ENERGY SOURCE THAT POWERS KANDOR...
...TO FUEL A SHIP THROUGH THE ***CHRONAL-NEXUS*** THAT EXISTS BOTH EVERYWHERE AND NOWHERE ALL AT ONCE AND NOT AT ALL.
"BUT LEX," YOU ARE NO DOUBT THINKING, "EVEN IF THAT WERE POSSIBLE, WHERE WOULD HE FIND THE SOURCE TO PROTECT HIS VESSEL WHILE TRAVELING THROUGH SAID THEORETICAL NEXUS"?

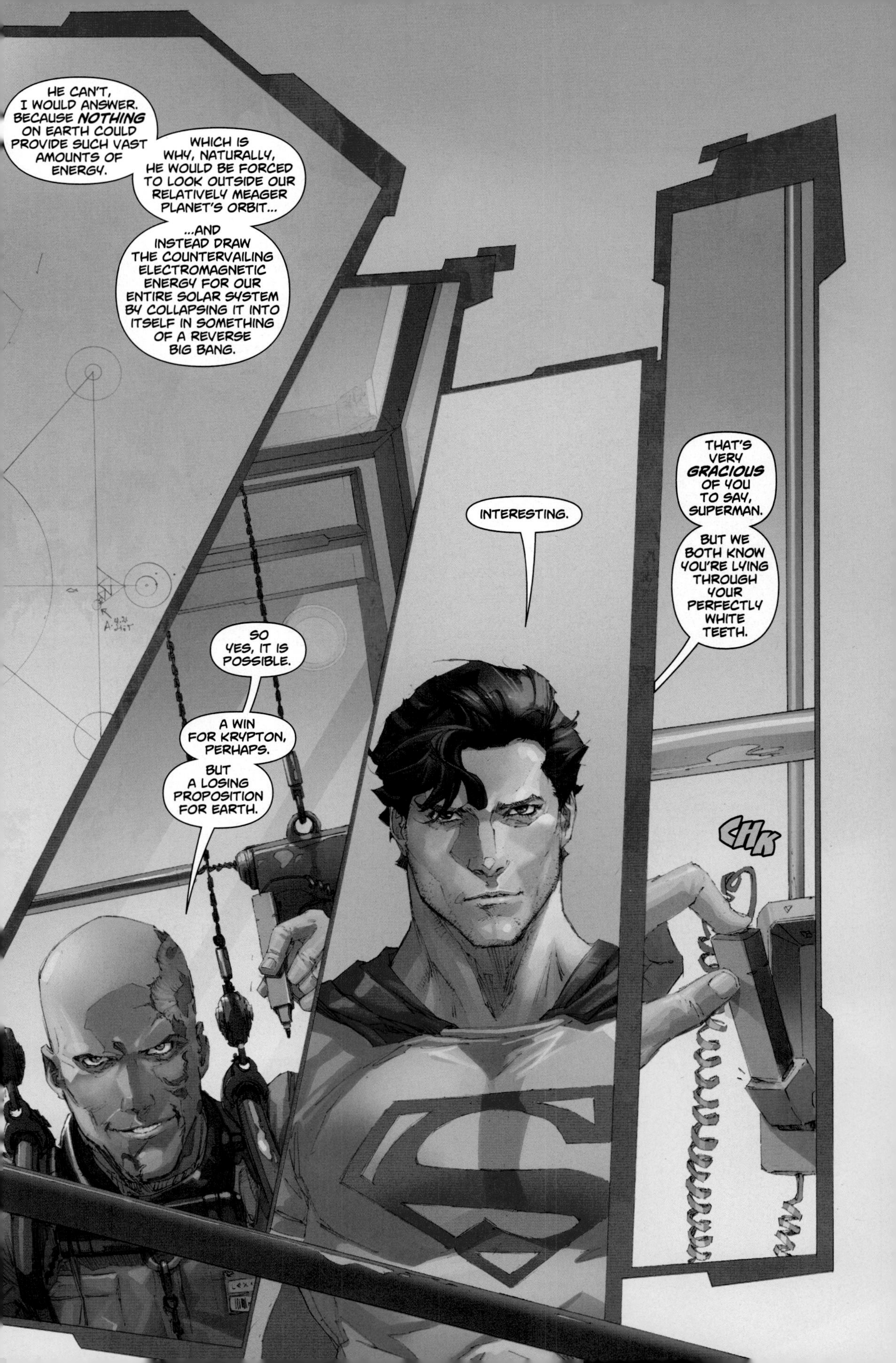
HE CAN'T, I WOULD ANSWER. BECAUSE NOTHING ON EARTH COULD PROVIDE SUCH VAST AMOUNTS OF ENERGY.
WHICH IS WHY, NATURALLY, HE WOULD BE FORCED TO LOOK OUTSIDE OUR RELATIVELY MEAGER PLANET'S ORBIT...
...AND INSTEAD DRAW THE COUNTERVAILING ELECTROMAGNETIC ENERGY FOR OUR ENTIRE SOLAR SYSTEM BY COLLAPSING IT INTO ITSELF IN SOMETHING OF A REVERSE BIG BANG.
SO YES, IT IS POSSIBLE.
A WIN FOR KRYPTON, PERHAPS.
BUT A LOSING PROPOSITION FOR EARTH.
INTERESTING.
THAT'S VERY GRACIOUS OF YOU TO SAY, SUPERMAN.
BUT WE BOTH KNOW YOU'RE LYING THROUGH YOUR PERFECTLY WHITE TEETH.
CHK

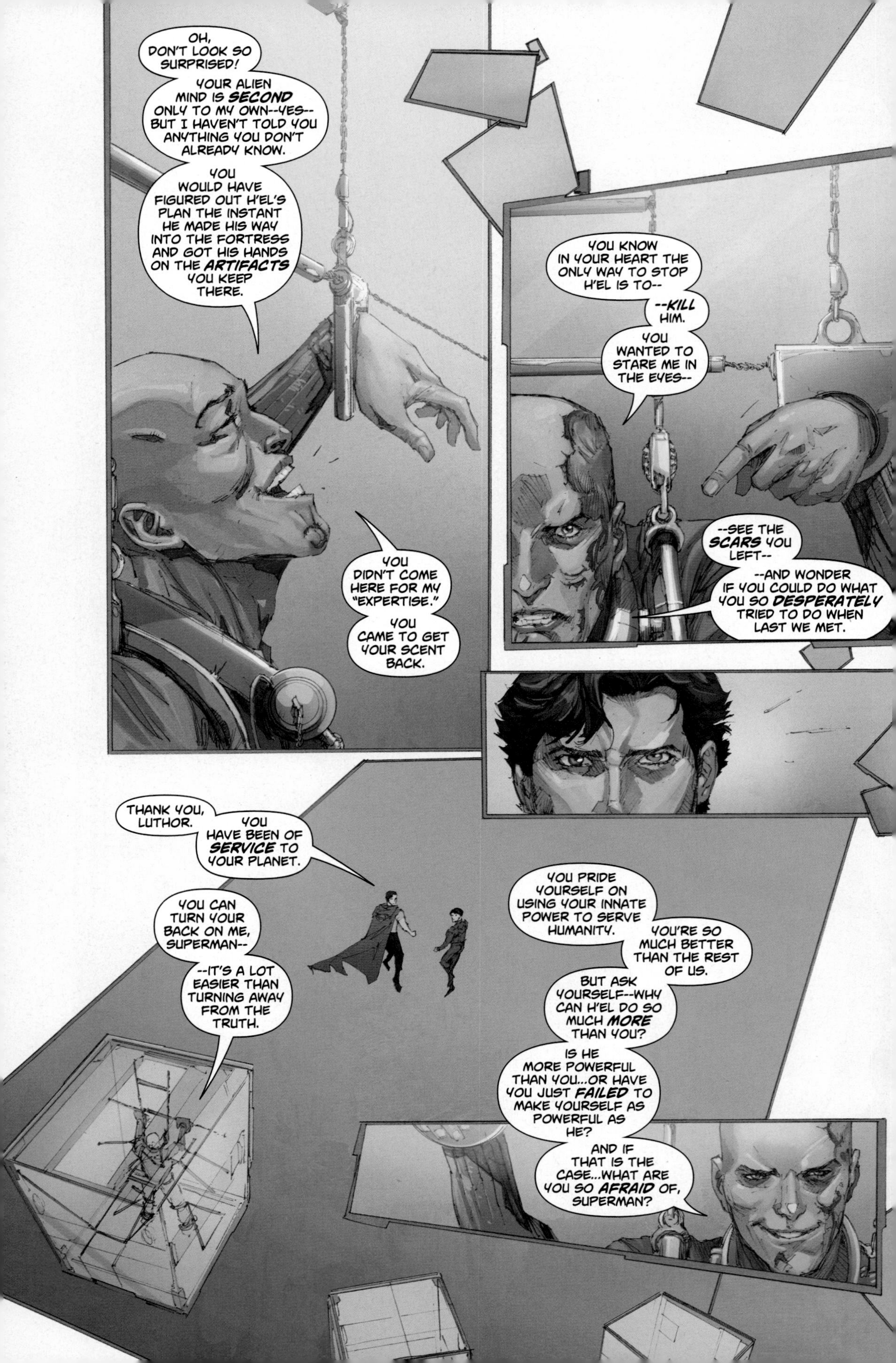
OH, DON'T LOOK SO SURPRISED!
YOUR ALIEN MIND IS SECOND ONLY TO MY OWN--YES-- BUT I HAVEN'T TOLD YOU ANYTHING YOU DON'T ALREADY KNOW.
YOU WOULD HAVE FIGURED OUT H'EL'S PLAN THE INSTANT HE MADE HIS WAY INTO THE FORTRESS AND GOT HIS HANDS ON THE ARTIFACTS YOU KEEP THERE.
YOU DIDN'T COME HERE FOR MY "EXPERTISE."
YOU CAME TO GET YOUR SCENT BACK.
YOU KNOW IN YOUR HEART THE ONLY WAY TO STOP H'EL IS TO--
--KILL HIM.
YOU WANTED TO STARE ME IN THE EYES--
--SEE THE SCARS YOU LEFT--
--AND WONDER IF YOU COULD DO WHAT YOU SO DESPERATELY TRIED TO DO WHEN LAST WE MET.
THANK YOU, LUTHOR.
YOU HAVE BEEN OF SERVICE TO YOUR PLANET.
YOU CAN TURN YOUR BACK ON ME, SUPERMAN--
--IT'S A LOT EASIER THAN TURNING AWAY FROM THE TRUTH.
YOU PRIDE YOURSELF ON USING YOUR INNATE POWER TO SERVE HUMANITY.
YOU'RE SO MUCH BETTER THAN THE REST OF US.
BUT ASK YOURSELF--WHY CAN H'EL DO SO MUCH MORE THAN YOU?
IS HE MORE POWERFUL THAN YOU...OR HAVE YOU JUST FAILED TO MAKE YOURSELF AS POWERFUL AS HE?
AND IF THAT IS THE CASE...WHAT ARE YOU SO AFRAID OF, SUPERMAN?

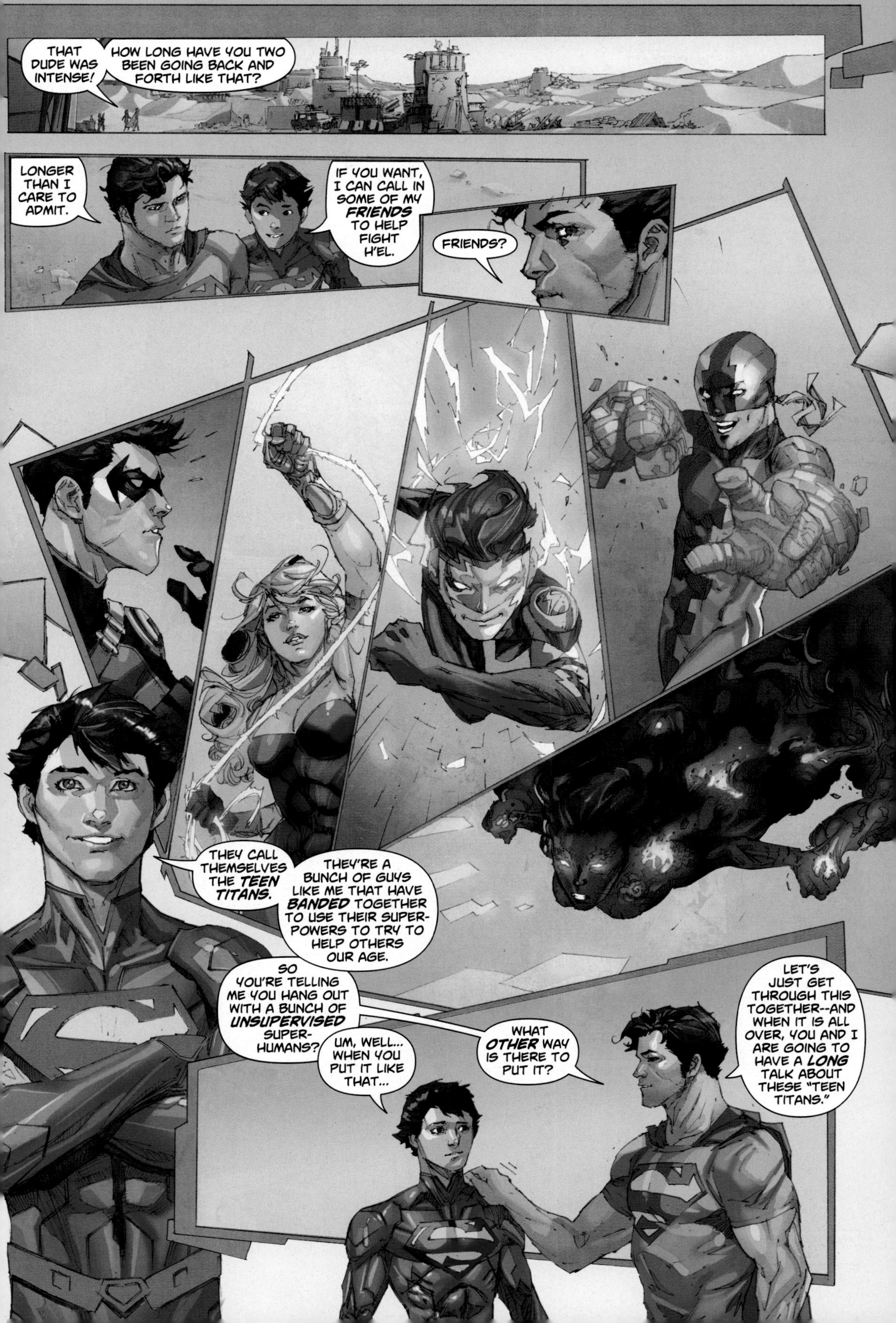
THAT DUDE WAS INTENSE!
HOW LONG HAVE YOU TWO BEEN GOING BACK AND FORTH LIKE THAT?
LONGER THAN I CARE TO ADMIT.
IF YOU WANT, I CAN CALL IN SOME OF MY FRIENDS TO HELP FIGHT H'EL.
FRIENDS?
THEY CALL THEMSELVES THE TEEN TITANS.
THEY'RE A BUNCH OF GUYS LIKE ME THAT HAVE BANDED TOGETHER TO USE THEIR SUPER-POWERS TO TRY TO HELP OTHERS OUR AGE.
SO YOU'RE TELLING ME YOU HANG OUT WITH A BUNCH OF UNSUPERVISED SUPER-HUMANS?
UM, WELL... WHEN YOU PUT IT LIKE THAT...
WHAT OTHER WAY IS THERE TO PUT IT?
LET'S JUST GET THROUGH THIS TOGETHER--AND WHEN IT IS ALL OVER, YOU AND I ARE GOING TO HAVE A LONG TALK ABOUT THESE "TEEN TITANS."

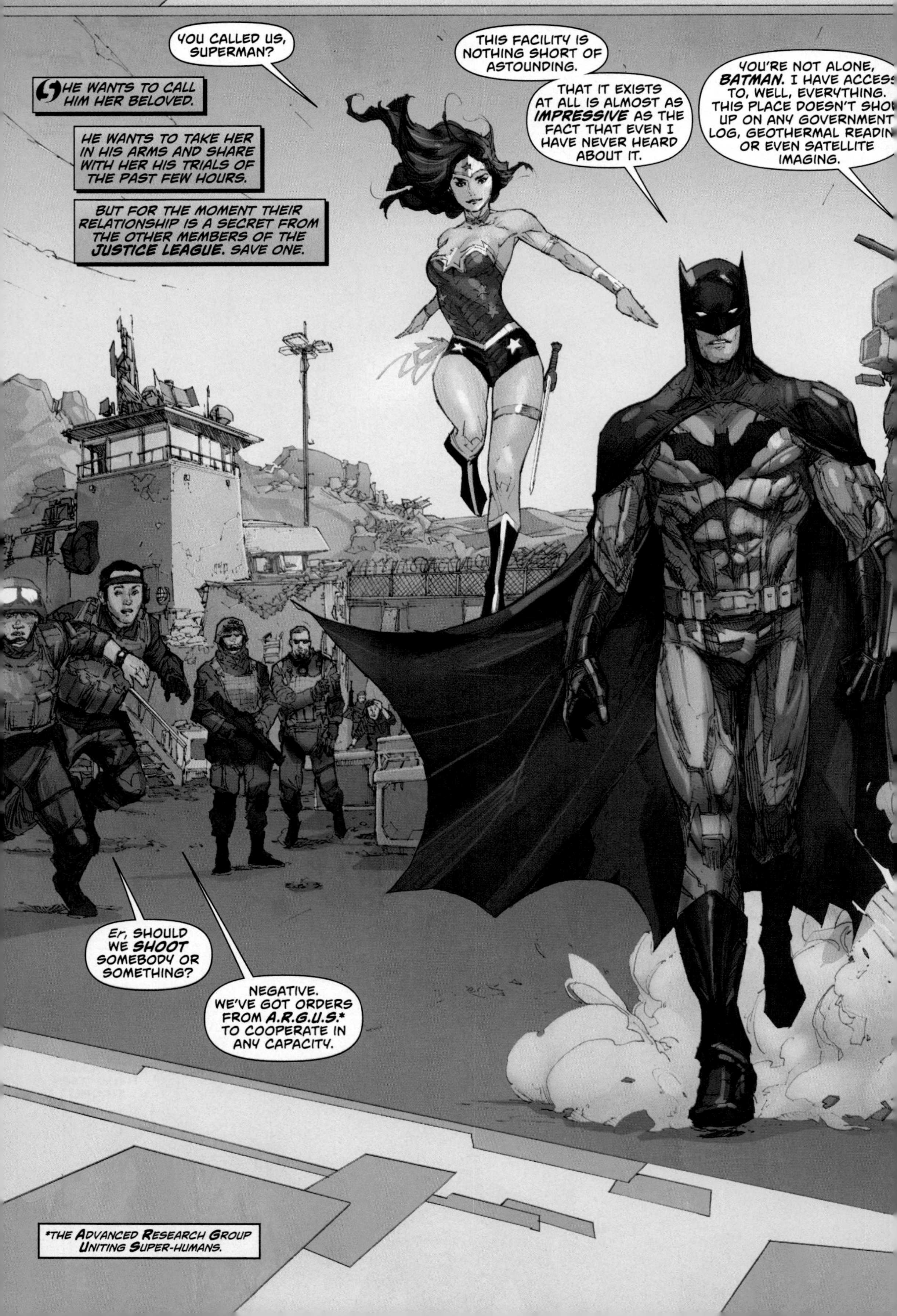
SHE WANTS TO CALL HIM HER BELOVED.
HE WANTS TO TAKE HER IN HIS ARMS AND SHARE WITH HER HIS TRIALS OF THE PAST FEW HOURS.
BUT FOR THE MOMENT THEIR RELATIONSHIP IS A SECRET FROM THE OTHER MEMBERS OF THE JUSTICE LEAGUE. SAVE ONE.
YOU CALLED US, SUPERMAN?
THIS FACILITY IS NOTHING SHORT OF ASTOUNDING.
THAT IT EXISTS AT ALL IS ALMOST AS IMPRESSIVE AS THE FACT THAT EVEN I HAVE NEVER HEARD ABOUT IT.
YOU'RE NOT ALONE, BATMAN. I HAVE ACCESS TO, WELL, EVERYTHING. THIS PLACE DOESN'T SHOW UP ON ANY GOVERNMENT LOG, GEOTHERMAL READING OR EVEN SATELLITE IMAGING.
Er, SHOULD WE SHOOT SOMEBODY OR SOMETHING?
NEGATIVE. WE'VE GOT ORDERS FROM A.R.G.U.S.* TO COOPERATE IN ANY CAPACITY.
*THE ADVANCED RESEARCH GROUP UNITING SUPER-HUMANS.

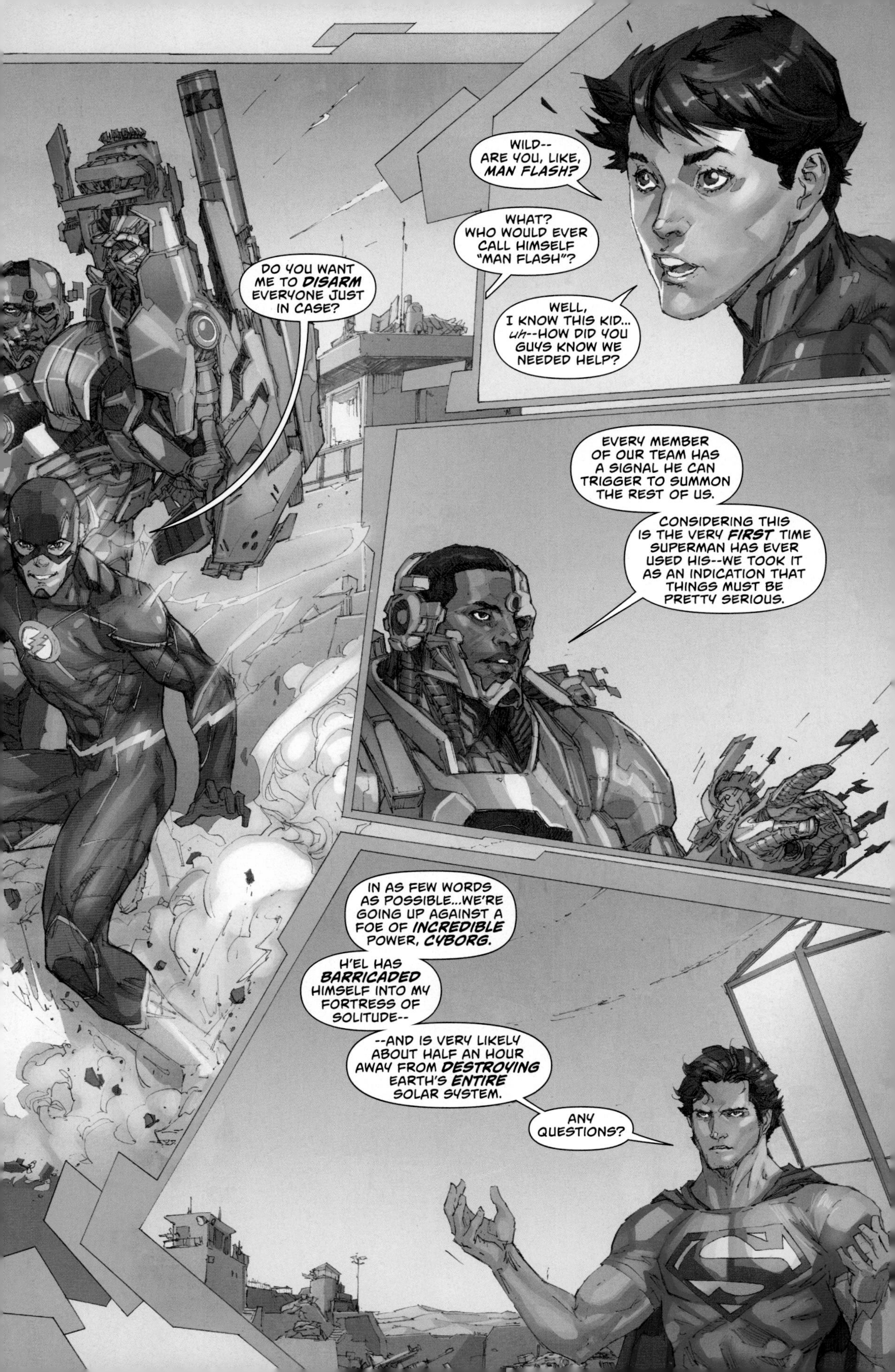
WILD-- ARE YOU, LIKE, MAN FLASH?
WHAT? WHO WOULD EVER CALL HIMSELF "MAN FLASH"?
WELL, I KNOW THIS KID... uh--HOW DID YOU GUYS KNOW WE NEEDED HELP?
DO YOU WANT ME TO DISARM EVERYONE JUST IN CASE?
EVERY MEMBER OF OUR TEAM HAS A SIGNAL HE CAN TRIGGER TO SUMMON THE REST OF US.
CONSIDERING THIS IS THE VERY FIRST TIME SUPERMAN HAS EVER USED HIS--WE TOOK IT AS AN INDICATION THAT THINGS MUST BE PRETTY SERIOUS.
IN AS FEW WORDS AS POSSIBLE...WE'RE GOING UP AGAINST A FOE OF INCREDIBLE POWER, CYBORG.
H'EL HAS BARRICADED HIMSELF INTO MY FORTRESS OF SOLITUDE--
--AND IS VERY LIKELY ABOUT HALF AN HOUR AWAY FROM DESTROYING EARTH'S ENTIRE SOLAR SYSTEM.
ANY QUESTIONS?

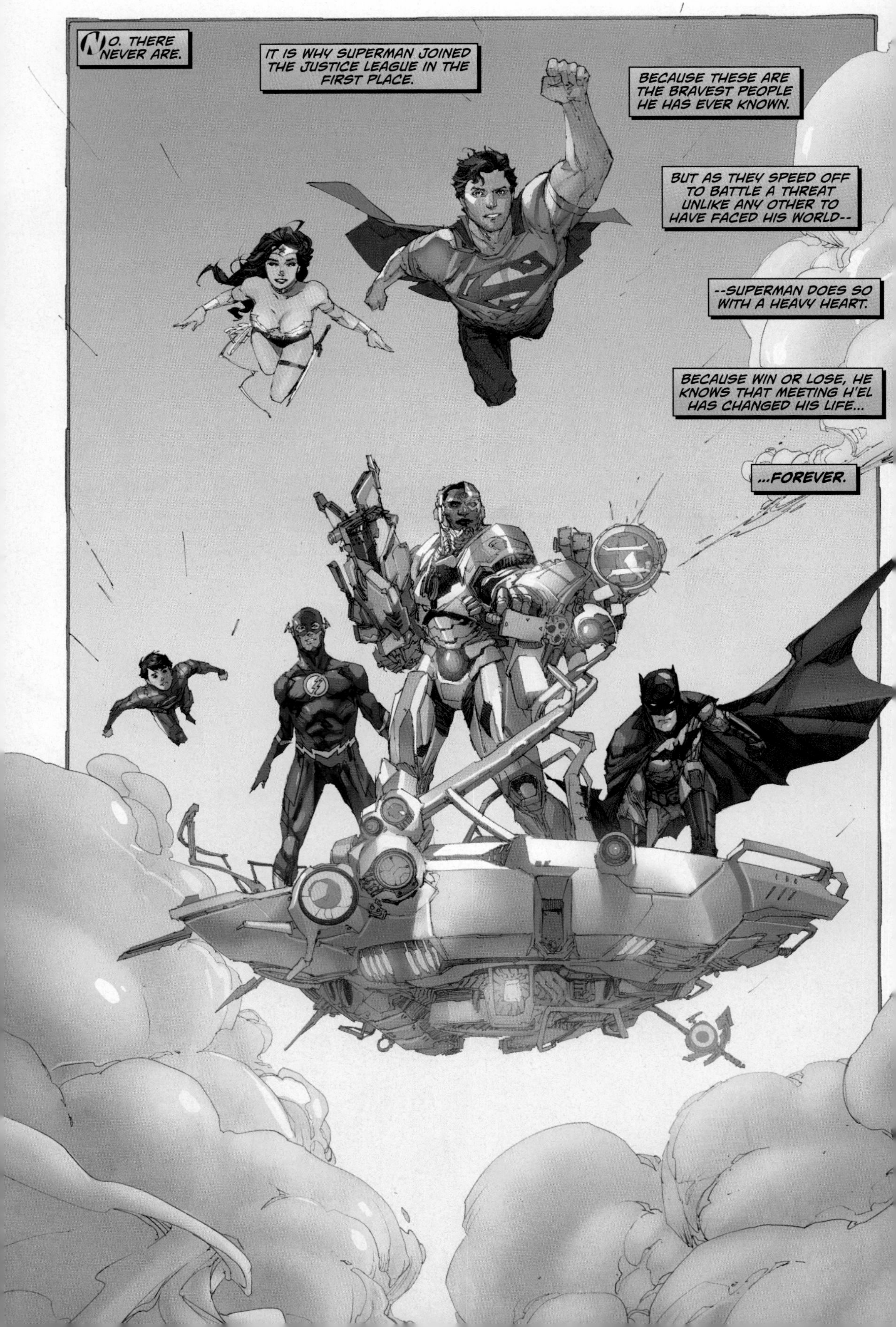
NO. THERE NEVER ARE.
IT IS WHY SUPERMAN JOINED THE JUSTICE LEAGUE IN THE FIRST PLACE.
BECAUSE THESE ARE THE BRAVEST PEOPLE HE HAS EVER KNOWN.
BUT AS THEY SPEED OFF TO BATTLE A THREAT UNLIKE ANY OTHER TO HAVE FACED HIS WORLD--
--SUPERMAN DOES SO WITH A HEAVY HEART.
BECAUSE WIN OR LOSE, HE KNOWS THAT MEETING H'EL HAS CHANGED HIS LIFE...
...FOREVER.

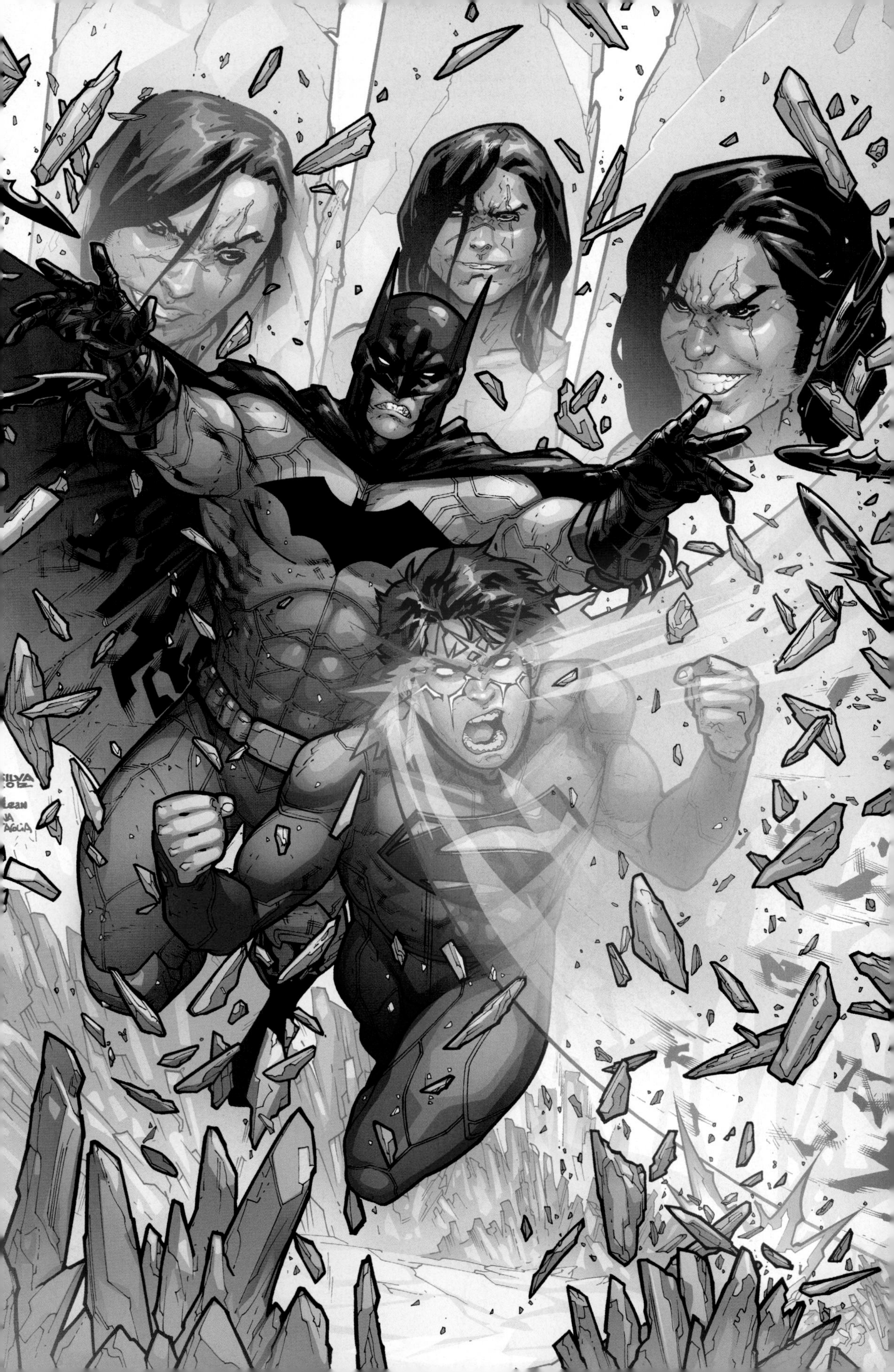

TRIGGERS!

TOM DEFALCO writer RON FRENZ thumbnails IBAN COELLO & AMILCAR PINNA pencillers ROB LEAN & AMILCAR PINNA inkers
cover art by R.B. SILVA & ROB LEAN WITH JAVA TARTAGLIA

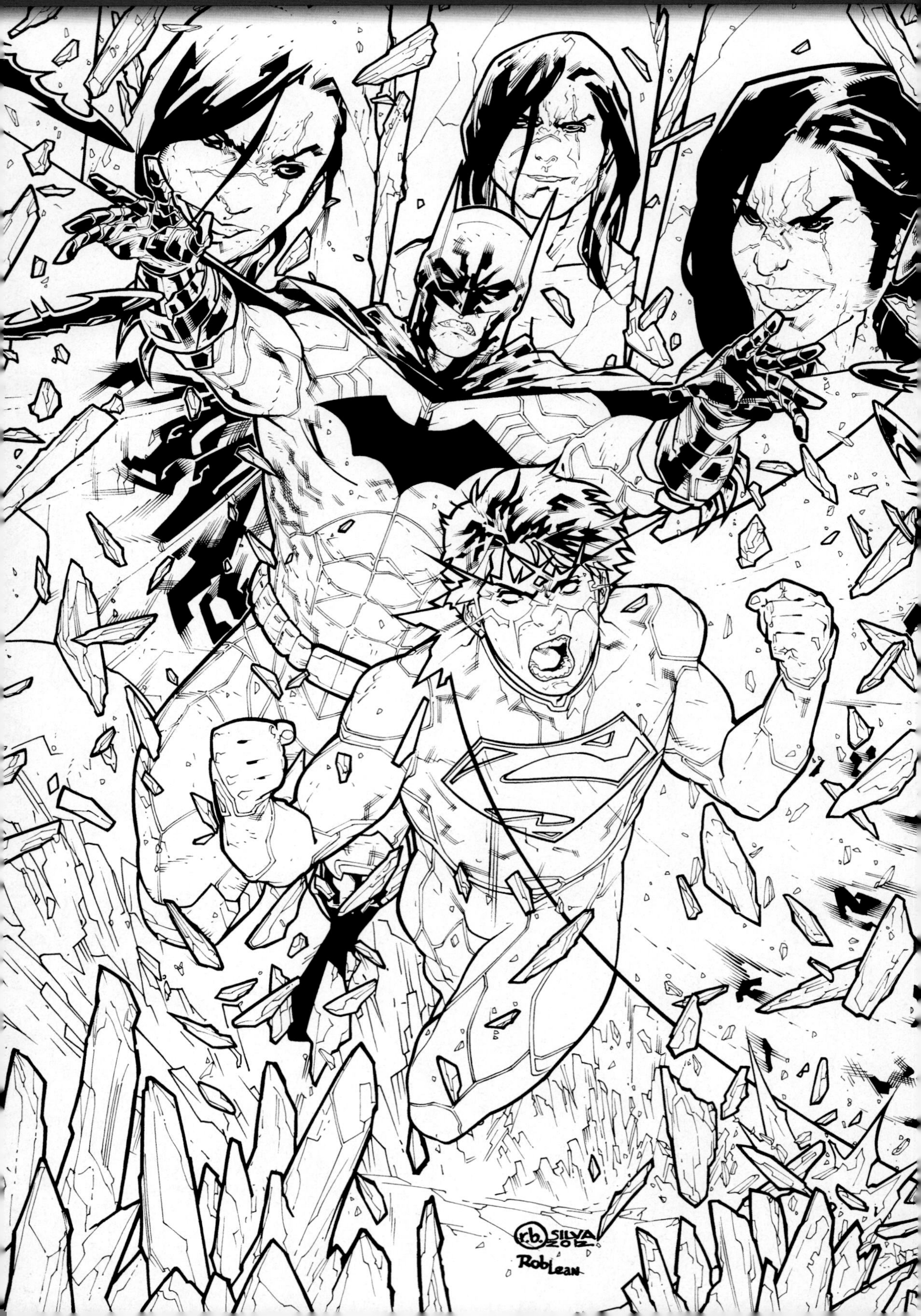

r.b. SILVA 2012
Rob Lean

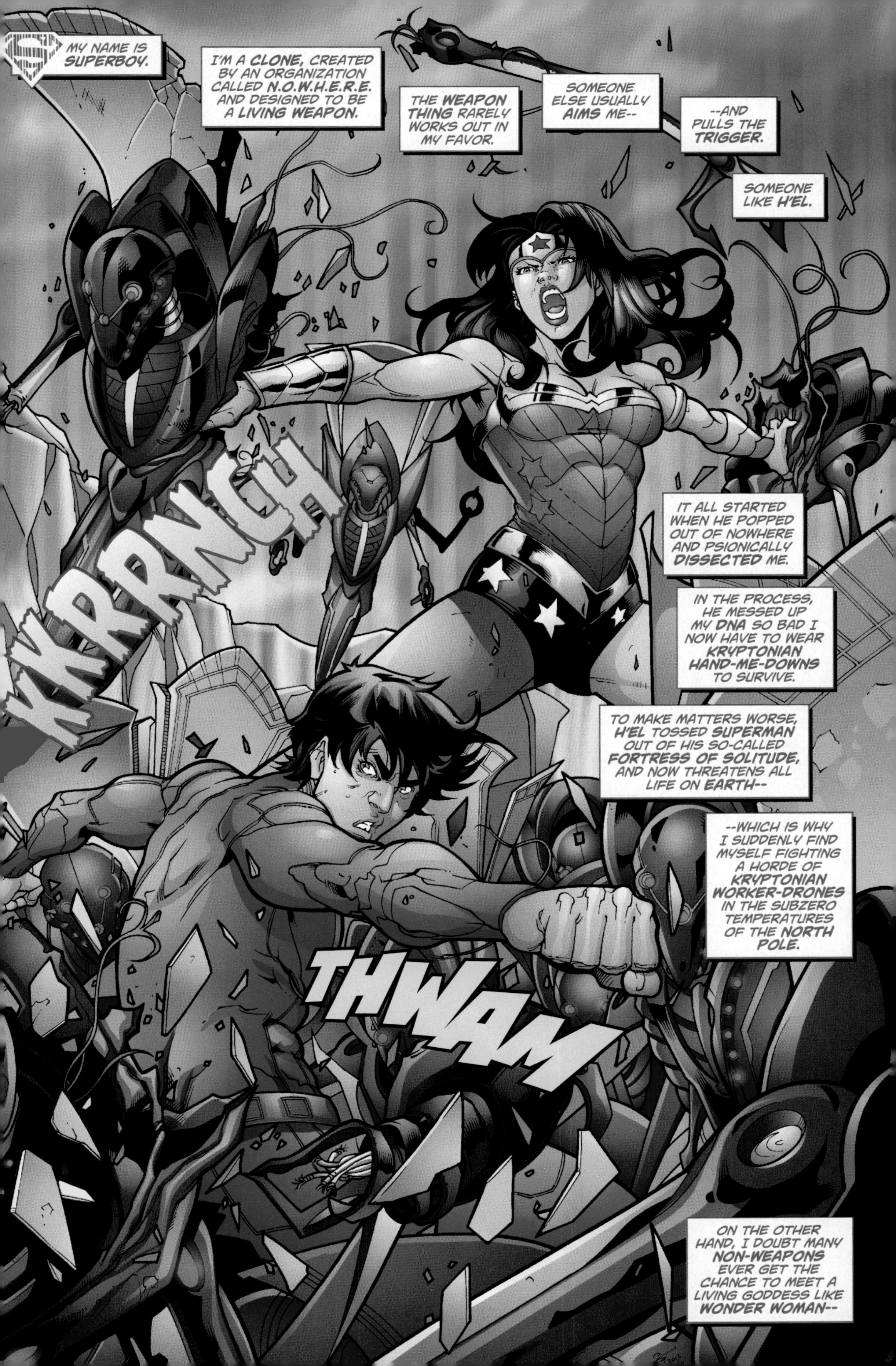
MY NAME IS SUPERBOY.
I'M A CLONE, CREATED BY AN ORGANIZATION CALLED N.O.W.H.E.R.E. AND DESIGNED TO BE A LIVING WEAPON.
THE WEAPON THING RARELY WORKS OUT IN MY FAVOR.
SOMEONE ELSE USUALLY AIMS ME--
--AND PULLS THE TRIGGER.
SOMEONE LIKE H'EL.
KKRRNCH
IT ALL STARTED WHEN HE POPPED OUT OF NOWHERE AND PSIONICALLY DISSECTED ME.
IN THE PROCESS, HE MESSED UP MY DNA SO BAD I NOW HAVE TO WEAR KRYPTONIAN HAND-ME-DOWNS TO SURVIVE.
TO MAKE MATTERS WORSE, H'EL TOSSED SUPERMAN OUT OF HIS SO-CALLED FORTRESS OF SOLITUDE, AND NOW THREATENS ALL LIFE ON EARTH--
--WHICH IS WHY I SUDDENLY FIND MYSELF FIGHTING A HORDE OF KRYPTONIAN WORKER-DRONES IN THE SUBZERO TEMPERATURES OF THE NORTH POLE.
THWAM
ON THE OTHER HAND, I DOUBT MANY NON-WEAPONS EVER GET THE CHANCE TO MEET A LIVING GODDESS LIKE WONDER WOMAN--

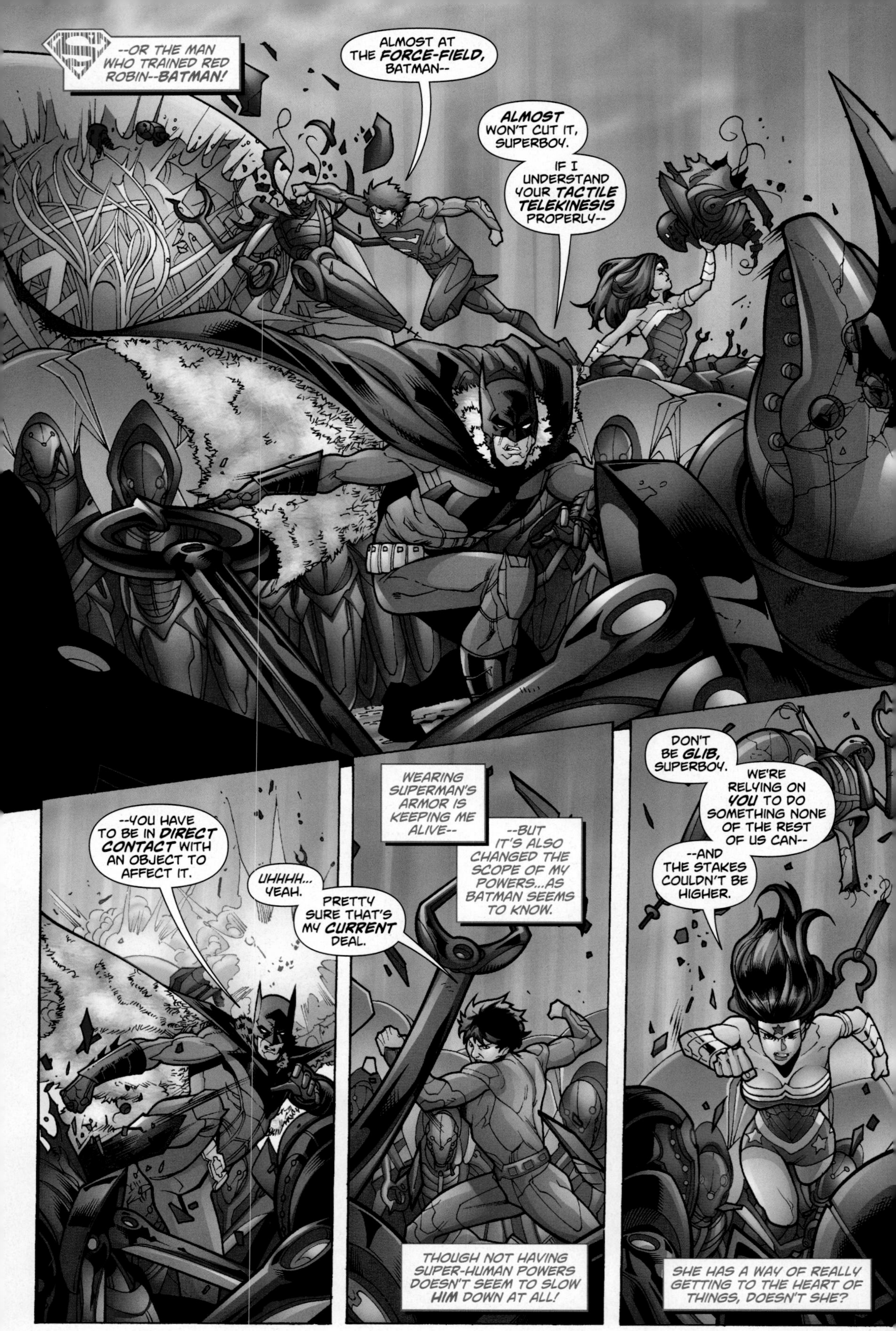
--OR THE MAN WHO TRAINED RED ROBIN--BATMAN!
ALMOST AT THE FORCE-FIELD, BATMAN--
ALMOST WON'T CUT IT, SUPERBOY.
IF I UNDERSTAND YOUR TACTILE TELEKINESIS PROPERLY--
--YOU HAVE TO BE IN DIRECT CONTACT WITH AN OBJECT TO AFFECT IT.
UHHHH... YEAH.
PRETTY SURE THAT'S MY CURRENT DEAL.
WEARING SUPERMAN'S ARMOR IS KEEPING ME ALIVE--
--BUT IT'S ALSO CHANGED THE SCOPE OF MY POWERS...AS BATMAN SEEMS TO KNOW.
THOUGH NOT HAVING SUPER-HUMAN POWERS DOESN'T SEEM TO SLOW HIM DOWN AT ALL!
DON'T BE GLIB, SUPERBOY.
WE'RE RELYING ON YOU TO DO SOMETHING NONE OF THE REST OF US CAN--
--AND THE STAKES COULDN'T BE HIGHER.
SHE HAS A WAY OF REALLY GETTING TO THE HEART OF THINGS, DOESN'T SHE?

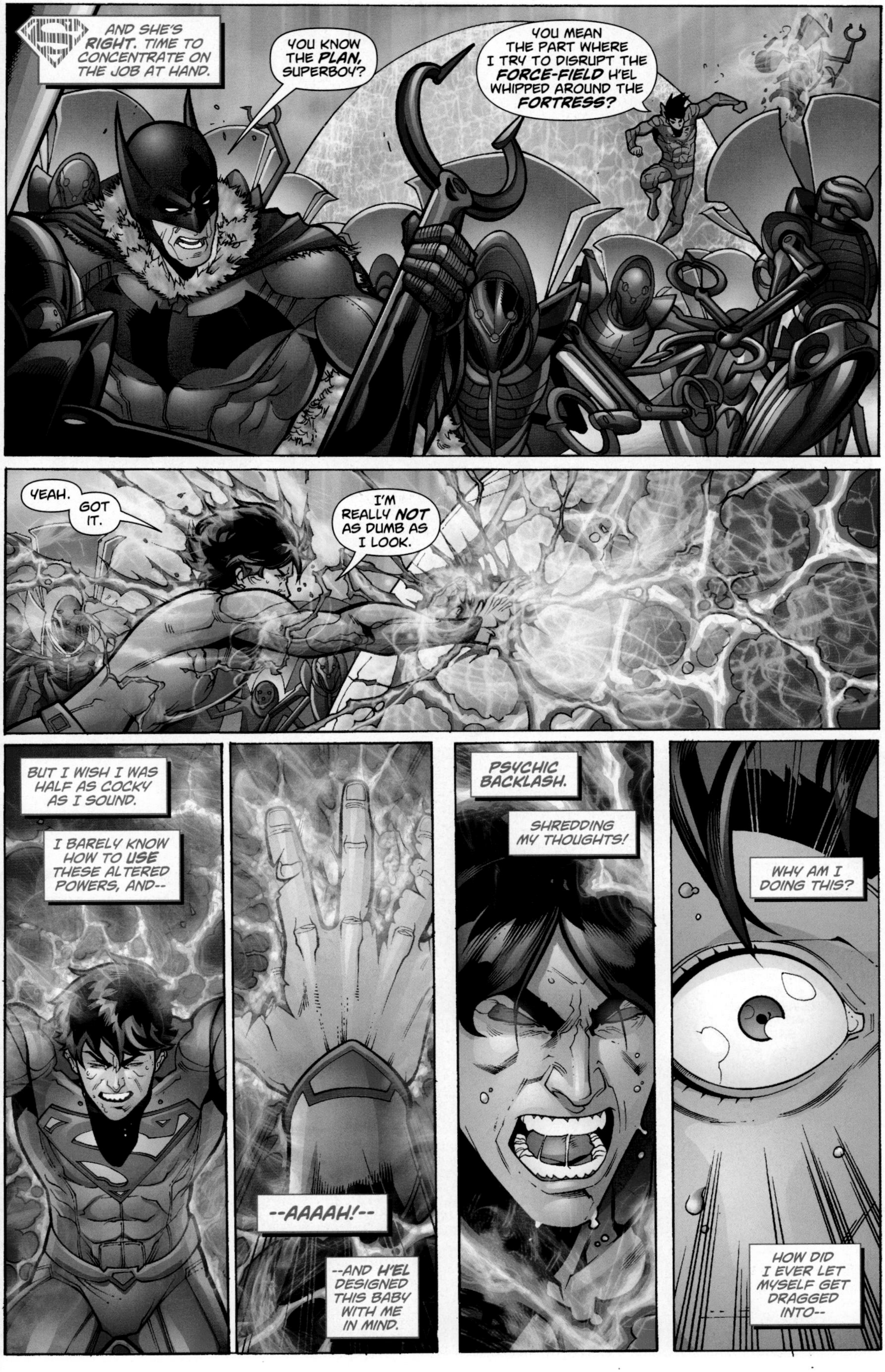
AND SHE'S RIGHT. TIME TO CONCENTRATE ON THE JOB AT HAND.
YOU KNOW THE PLAN, SUPERBOY?
YOU MEAN THE PART WHERE I TRY TO DISRUPT THE FORCE-FIELD H'EL WHIPPED AROUND THE FORTRESS?
YEAH. GOT IT.
I'M REALLY NOT AS DUMB AS I LOOK.
BUT I WISH I WAS HALF AS COCKY AS I SOUND.
I BARELY KNOW HOW TO USE THESE ALTERED POWERS, AND--
--AAAAH!--
--AND H'EL DESIGNED THIS BABY WITH ME IN MIND.
PSYCHIC BACKLASH.
SHREDDING MY THOUGHTS!
WHY AM I DOING THIS?
HOW DID I EVER LET MYSELF GET DRAGGED INTO--

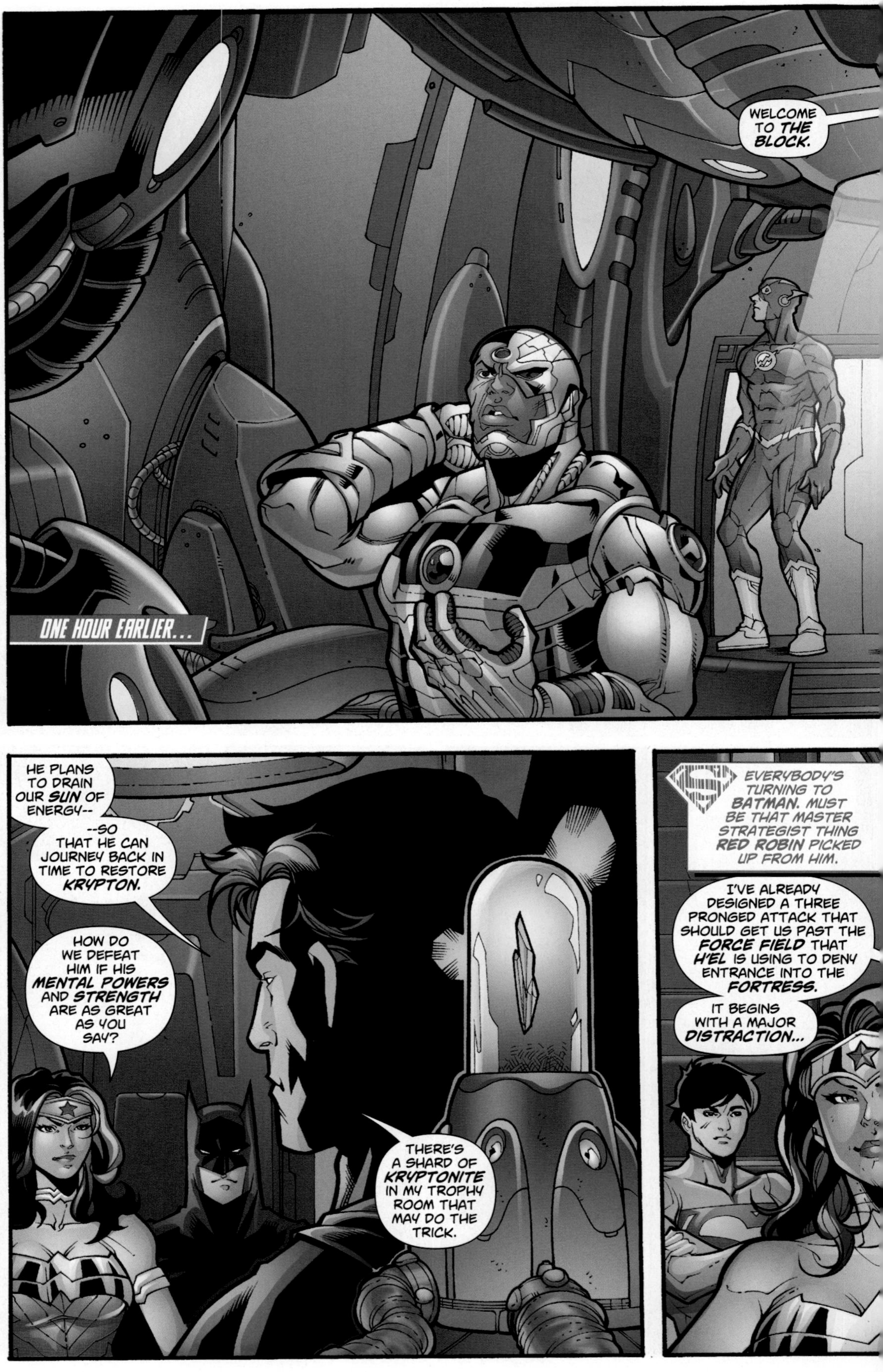

WELCOME TO THE BLOCK.
ONE HOUR EARLIER...
HE PLANS TO DRAIN OUR SUN OF ENERGY--
--SO THAT HE CAN JOURNEY BACK IN TIME TO RESTORE KRYPTON.
HOW DO WE DEFEAT HIM IF HIS MENTAL POWERS AND STRENGTH ARE AS GREAT AS YOU SAY?
THERE'S A SHARD OF KRYPTONITE IN MY TROPHY ROOM THAT MAY DO THE TRICK.
EVERYBODY'S TURNING TO BATMAN. MUST BE THAT MASTER STRATEGIST THING RED ROBIN PICKED UP FROM HIM.
I'VE ALREADY DESIGNED A THREE PRONGED ATTACK THAT SHOULD GET US PAST THE FORCE FIELD THAT H'EL IS USING TO DENY ENTRANCE INTO THE FORTRESS.
IT BEGINS WITH A MAJOR DISTRACTION...

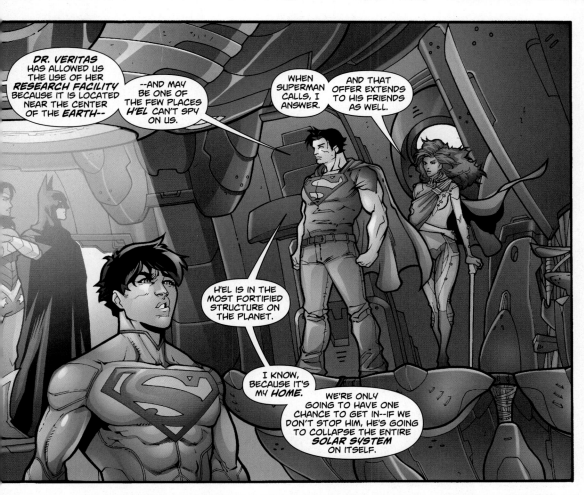

DR. VERITAS HAS ALLOWED US THE USE OF HER *RESEARCH FACILITY* BECAUSE IT IS LOCATED NEAR THE CENTER OF THE *EARTH*--

--AND MAY BE ONE OF THE FEW PLACES H'EL CAN'T SPY ON US.

WHEN SUPERMAN CALLS, I ANSWER.

AND THAT OFFER EXTENDS TO HIS FRIENDS AS WELL.

H'EL IS IN THE MOST FORTIFIED STRUCTURE ON THE PLANET.

I KNOW, BECAUSE IT'S MY *HOME*.

WE'RE ONLY GOING TO HAVE ONE CHANCE TO GET IN--IF WE DON'T STOP HIM, HE'S GOING TO COLLAPSE THE ENTIRE *SOLAR SYSTEM* ON ITSELF.

THAT *DISTRACTION* IS OUR FRONTAL ASSAULT--MEANT AS *COVER* TO GET ME UP CLOSE WITH THIS FORCE FIELD.

I CAN EITHER KILL MYSELF PULLING IT DOWN--

--OR GET WIPED OUT OF *EXISTENCE* WHEN H'EL DESTROYS THE EARTH.

I MAY NOT CARE WHAT HAPPENS TO SOME *DEAD* PLANET...

...BUT I KNOW I CAN'T AFFORD TO LOSE *THIS* ONE!

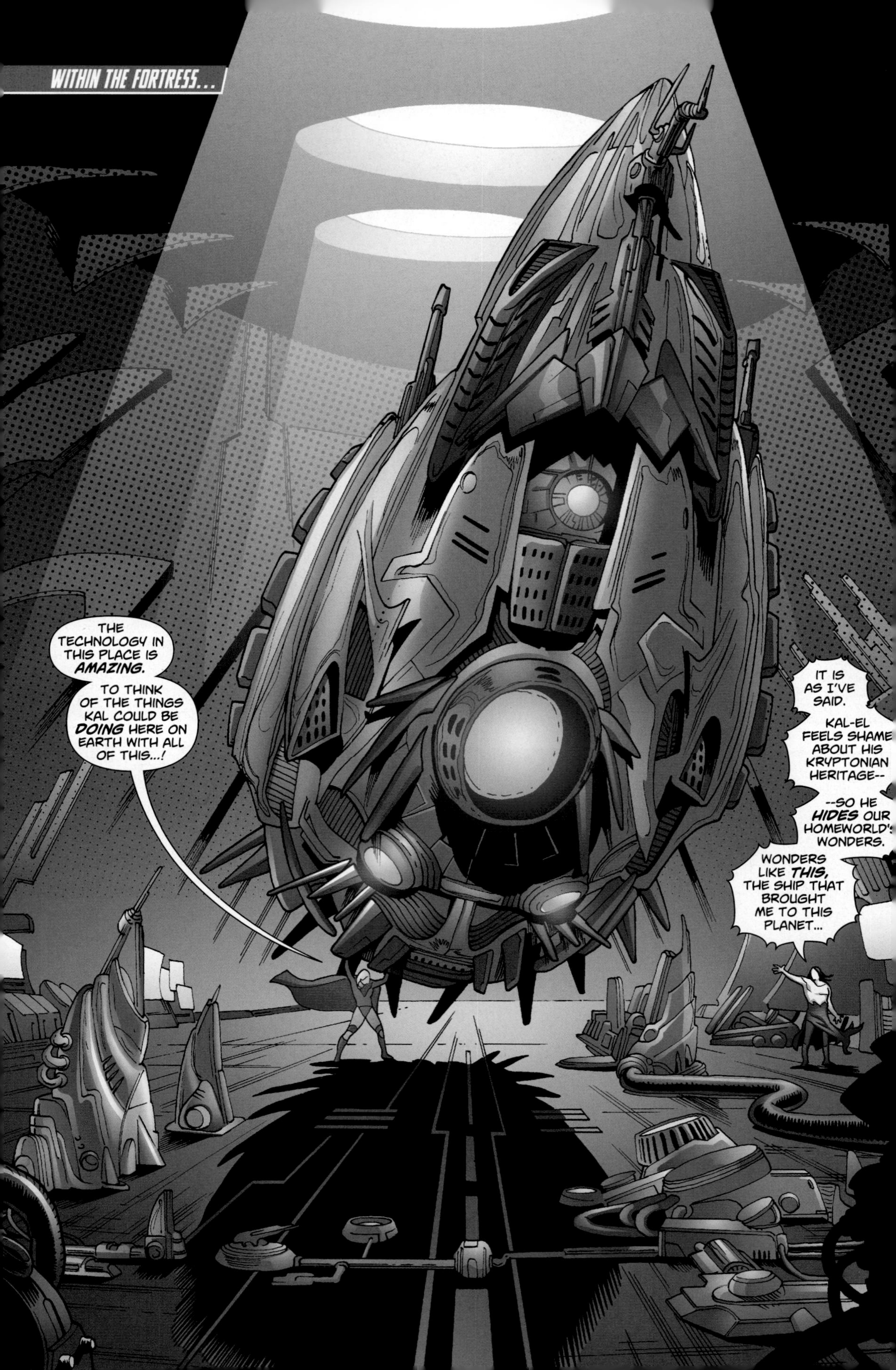
WITHIN THE FORTRESS...
THE TECHNOLOGY IN THIS PLACE IS AMAZING.
TO THINK OF THE THINGS KAL COULD BE DOING HERE ON EARTH WITH ALL OF THIS...!
IT IS AS I'VE SAID.
KAL-EL FEELS SHAME ABOUT HIS KRYPTONIAN HERITAGE--
--SO HE HIDES OUR HOMEWORLD'S WONDERS.
WONDERS LIKE THIS, THE SHIP THAT BROUGHT ME TO THIS PLANET...

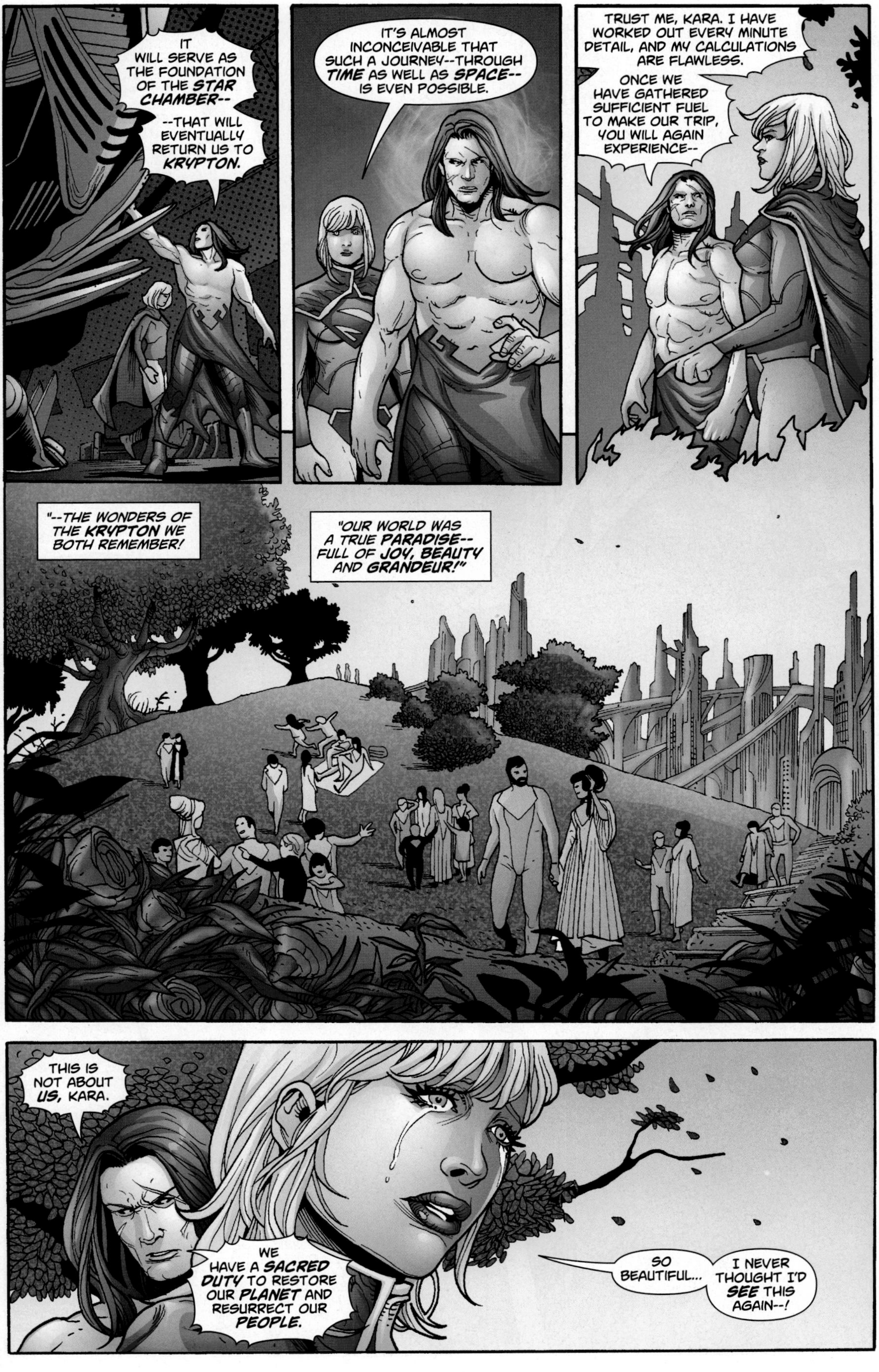
IT WILL SERVE AS THE FOUNDATION OF THE STAR CHAMBER--
--THAT WILL EVENTUALLY RETURN US TO KRYPTON.
IT'S ALMOST INCONCEIVABLE THAT SUCH A JOURNEY--THROUGH TIME AS WELL AS SPACE--IS EVEN POSSIBLE.
TRUST ME, KARA. I HAVE WORKED OUT EVERY MINUTE DETAIL, AND MY CALCULATIONS ARE FLAWLESS.
ONCE WE HAVE GATHERED SUFFICIENT FUEL TO MAKE OUR TRIP, YOU WILL AGAIN EXPERIENCE--
"--THE WONDERS OF THE KRYPTON WE BOTH REMEMBER!
"OUR WORLD WAS A TRUE PARADISE--FULL OF JOY, BEAUTY AND GRANDEUR!"
THIS IS NOT ABOUT US, KARA.
WE HAVE A SACRED DUTY TO RESTORE OUR PLANET AND RESURRECT OUR PEOPLE.
SO BEAUTIFUL...
I NEVER THOUGHT I'D SEE THIS AGAIN--!

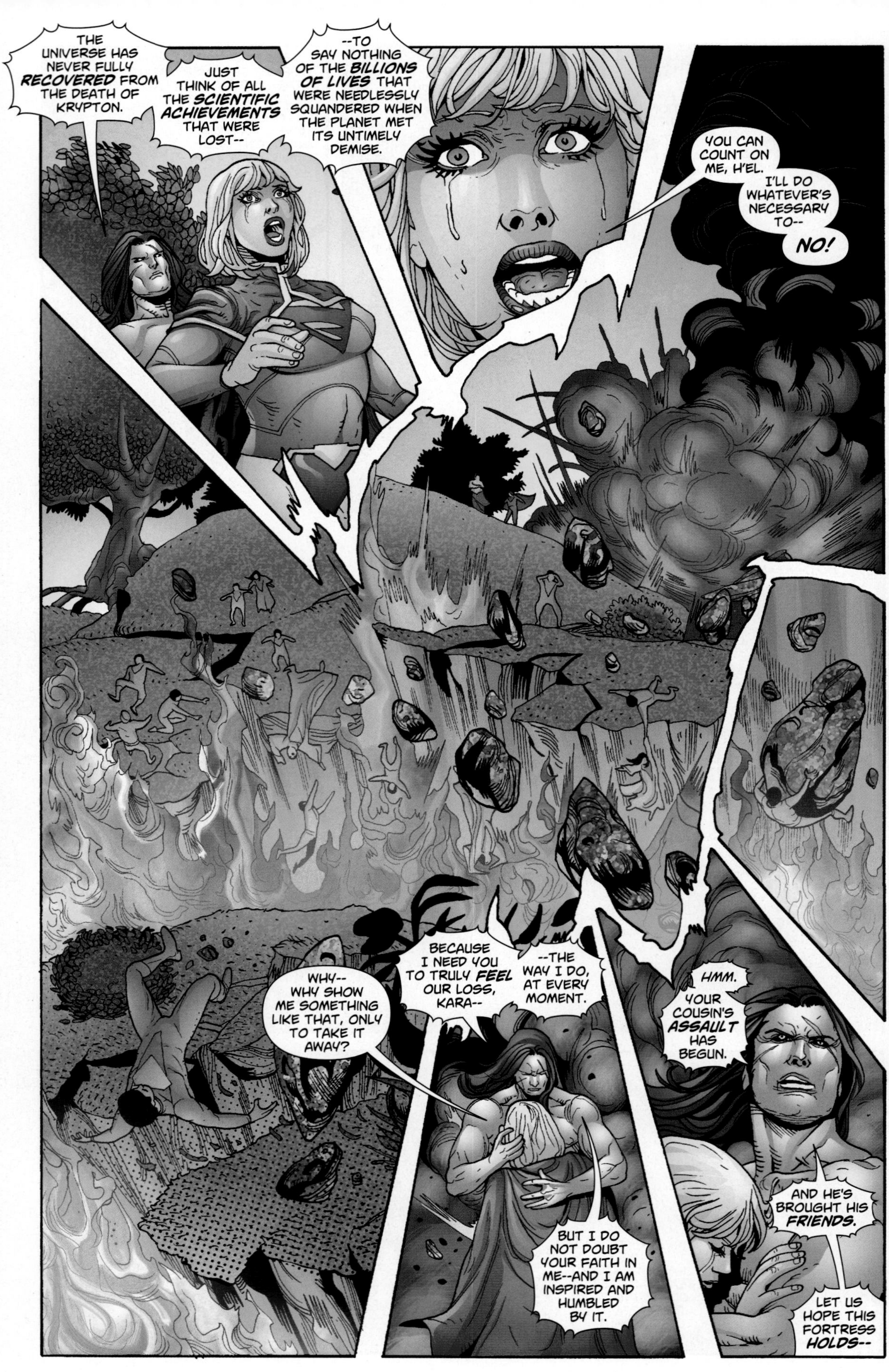

THE UNIVERSE HAS NEVER FULLY RECOVERED FROM THE DEATH OF KRYPTON.
JUST THINK OF ALL THE SCIENTIFIC ACHIEVEMENTS THAT WERE LOST--
--TO SAY NOTHING OF THE BILLIONS OF LIVES THAT WERE NEEDLESSLY SQUANDERED WHEN THE PLANET MET ITS UNTIMELY DEMISE.
YOU CAN COUNT ON ME, H'EL.
I'LL DO WHATEVER'S NECESSARY TO--
NO!
WHY-- WHY SHOW ME SOMETHING LIKE THAT, ONLY TO TAKE IT AWAY?
BECAUSE I NEED YOU TO TRULY FEEL OUR LOSS, KARA--
--THE WAY I DO, AT EVERY MOMENT.
BUT I DO NOT DOUBT YOUR FAITH IN ME--AND I AM INSPIRED AND HUMBLED BY IT.
HMM.
YOUR COUSIN'S ASSAULT HAS BEGUN.
AND HE'S BROUGHT HIS FRIENDS.
LET US HOPE THIS FORTRESS HOLDS--

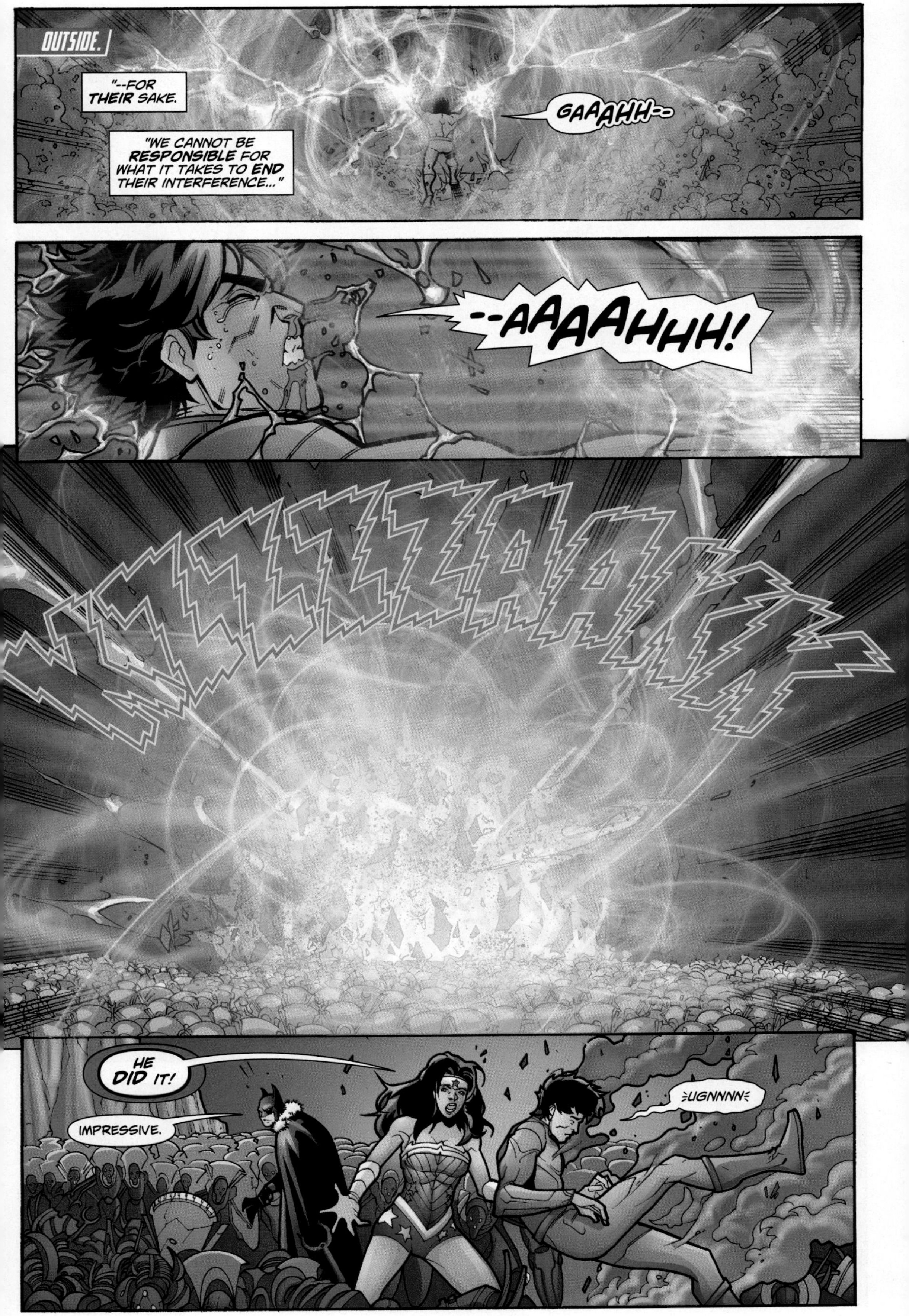
OUTSIDE.
"--FOR THEIR SAKE.
"WE CANNOT BE RESPONSIBLE FOR WHAT IT TAKES TO END THEIR INTERFERENCE..."
GAAAHH--
--AAAAHHH!
HE DID IT!
IMPRESSIVE.
UGNNNN

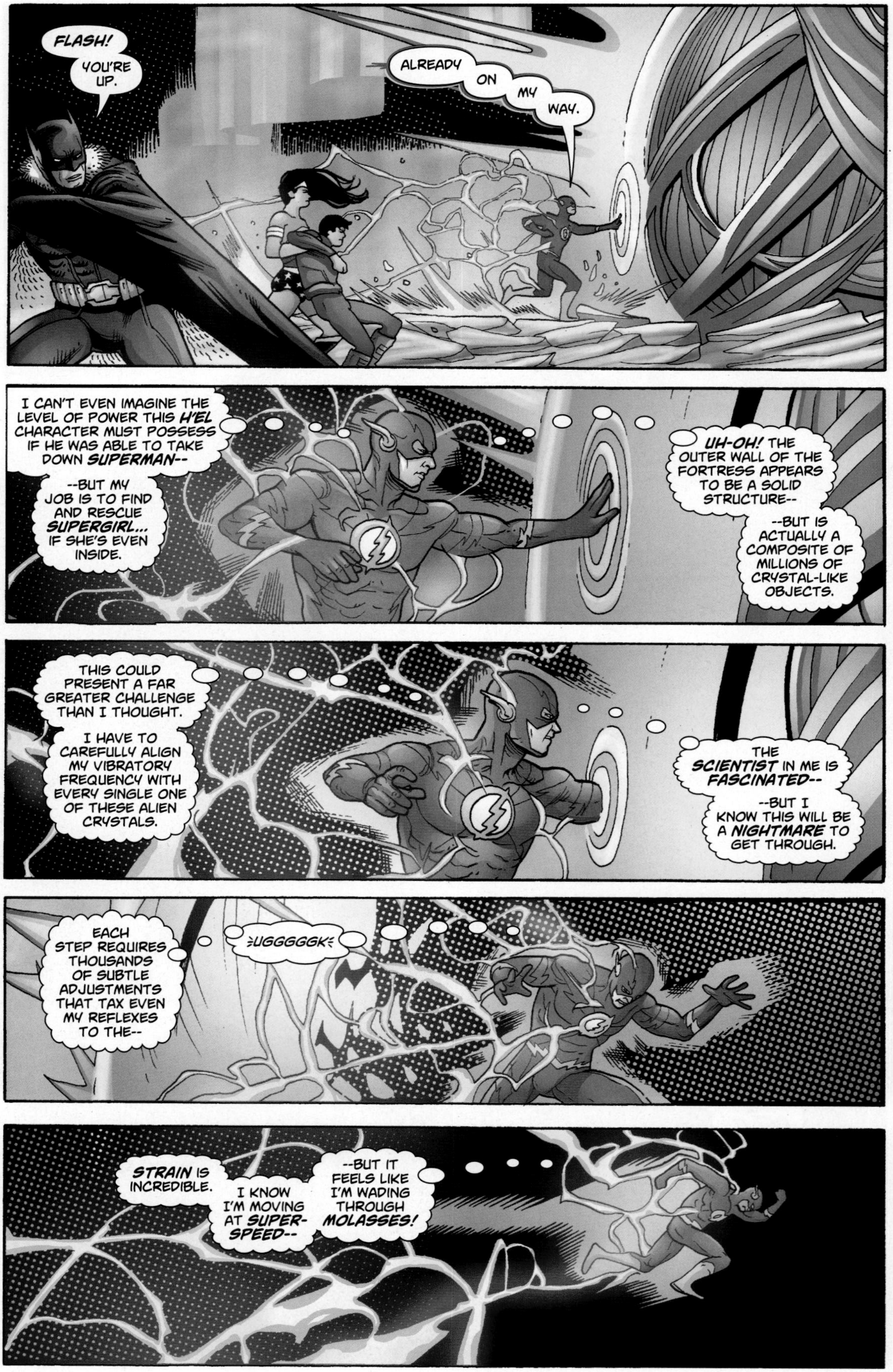
FLASH! YOU'RE UP.
ALREADY ON MY WAY.
I CAN'T EVEN IMAGINE THE LEVEL OF POWER THIS H'EL CHARACTER MUST POSSESS IF HE WAS ABLE TO TAKE DOWN SUPERMAN--
--BUT MY JOB IS TO FIND AND RESCUE SUPERGIRL... IF SHE'S EVEN INSIDE.
UH-OH! THE OUTER WALL OF THE FORTRESS APPEARS TO BE A SOLID STRUCTURE--
--BUT IS ACTUALLY A COMPOSITE OF MILLIONS OF CRYSTAL-LIKE OBJECTS.
THIS COULD PRESENT A FAR GREATER CHALLENGE THAN I THOUGHT.
I HAVE TO CAREFULLY ALIGN MY VIBRATORY FREQUENCY WITH EVERY SINGLE ONE OF THESE ALIEN CRYSTALS.
THE SCIENTIST IN ME IS FASCINATED--
--BUT I KNOW THIS WILL BE A NIGHTMARE TO GET THROUGH.
EACH STEP REQUIRES THOUSANDS OF SUBTLE ADJUSTMENTS THAT TAX EVEN MY REFLEXES TO THE--
UGGGGGK
STRAIN IS INCREDIBLE.
I KNOW I'M MOVING AT SUPER-SPEED--
--BUT IT FEELS LIKE I'M WADING THROUGH MOLASSES!

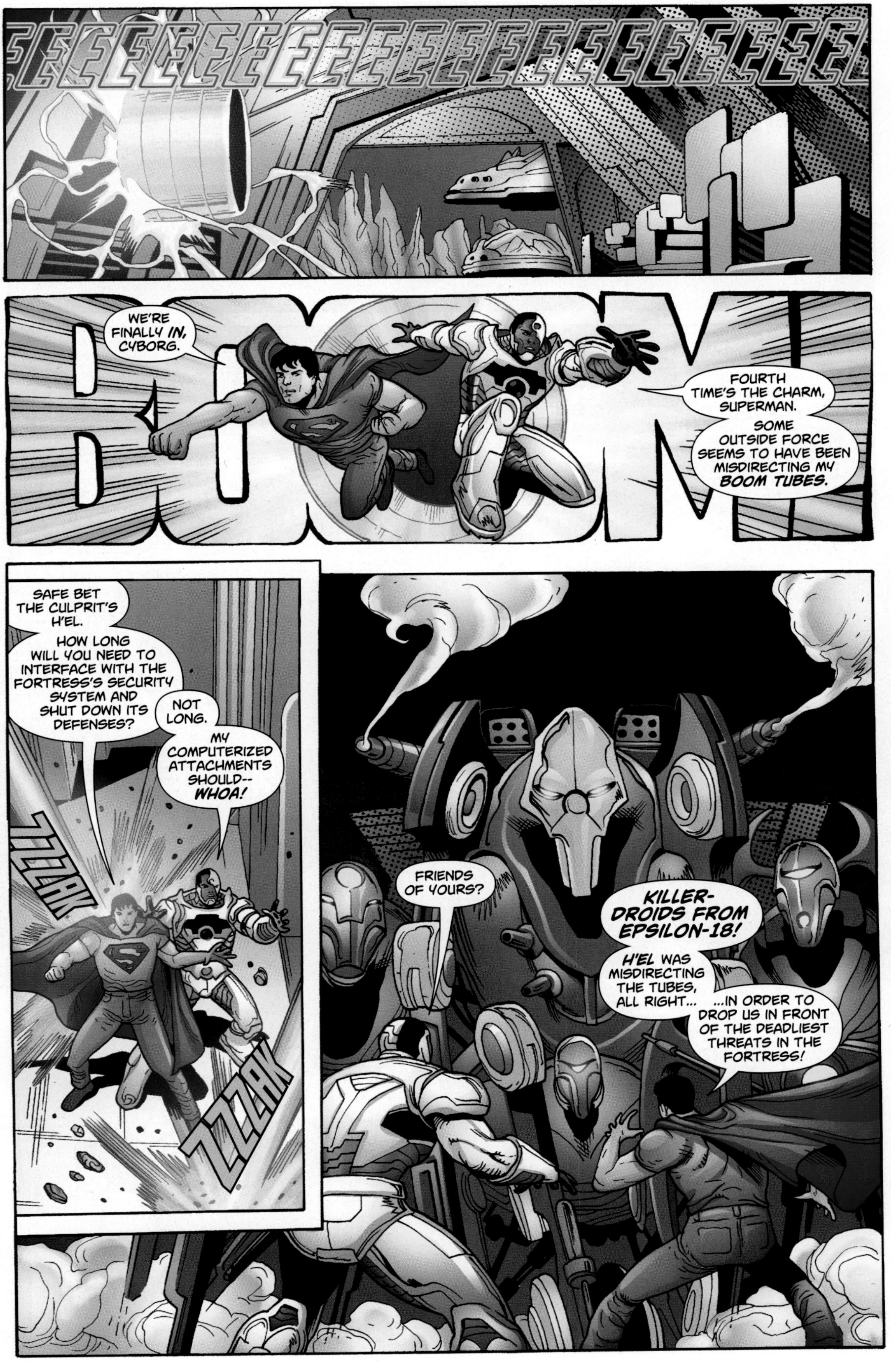
BOOM!
WE'RE FINALLY IN, CYBORG.
FOURTH TIME'S THE CHARM, SUPERMAN.
SOME OUTSIDE FORCE SEEMS TO HAVE BEEN MISDIRECTING MY BOOM TUBES.
SAFE BET THE CULPRIT'S H'EL.
HOW LONG WILL YOU NEED TO INTERFACE WITH THE FORTRESS'S SECURITY SYSTEM AND SHUT DOWN ITS DEFENSES?
NOT LONG.
MY COMPUTERIZED ATTACHMENTS SHOULD-- WHOA!
ZZZAK
ZZZAK
FRIENDS OF YOURS?
KILLER-DROIDS FROM EPSILON-18!
H'EL WAS MISDIRECTING THE TUBES, ALL RIGHT...
...IN ORDER TO DROP US IN FRONT OF THE DEADLIEST THREATS IN THE FORTRESS!

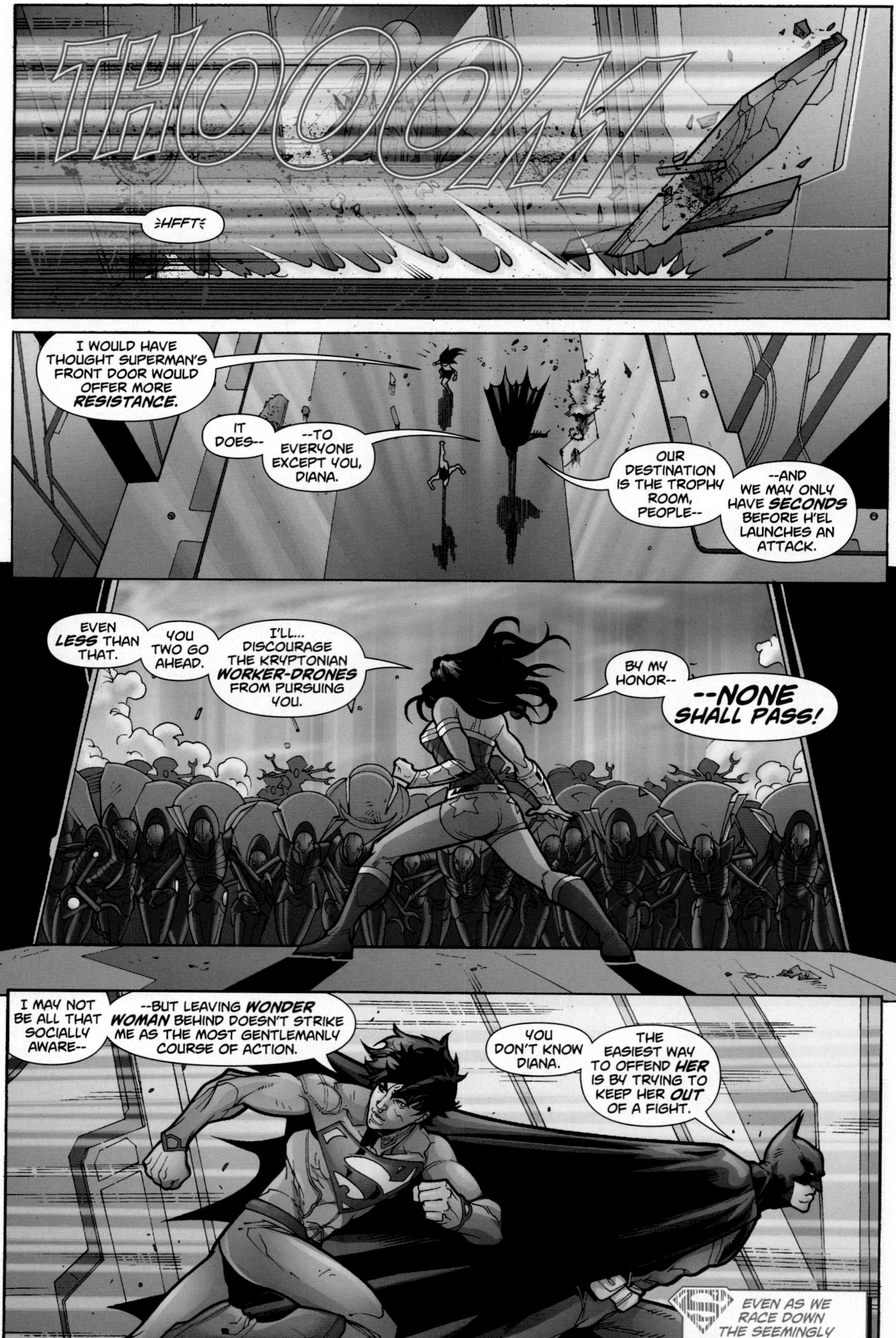
THOOOM!
HFFT
I WOULD HAVE THOUGHT SUPERMAN'S FRONT DOOR WOULD OFFER MORE RESISTANCE.
IT DOES--
--TO EVERYONE EXCEPT YOU, DIANA.
OUR DESTINATION IS THE TROPHY ROOM, PEOPLE--
--AND WE MAY ONLY HAVE SECONDS BEFORE H'EL LAUNCHES AN ATTACK.
EVEN LESS THAN THAT.
YOU TWO GO AHEAD.
I'LL... DISCOURAGE THE KRYPTONIAN WORKER-DRONES FROM PURSUING YOU.
BY MY HONOR--
--NONE SHALL PASS!
I MAY NOT BE ALL THAT SOCIALLY AWARE--
--BUT LEAVING WONDER WOMAN BEHIND DOESN'T STRIKE ME AS THE MOST GENTLEMANLY COURSE OF ACTION.
YOU DON'T KNOW DIANA.
THE EASIEST WAY TO OFFEND HER IS BY TRYING TO KEEP HER OUT OF A FIGHT.
EVEN AS WE RACE DOWN THE SEEMINGLY ENDLESS CORRIDORS--

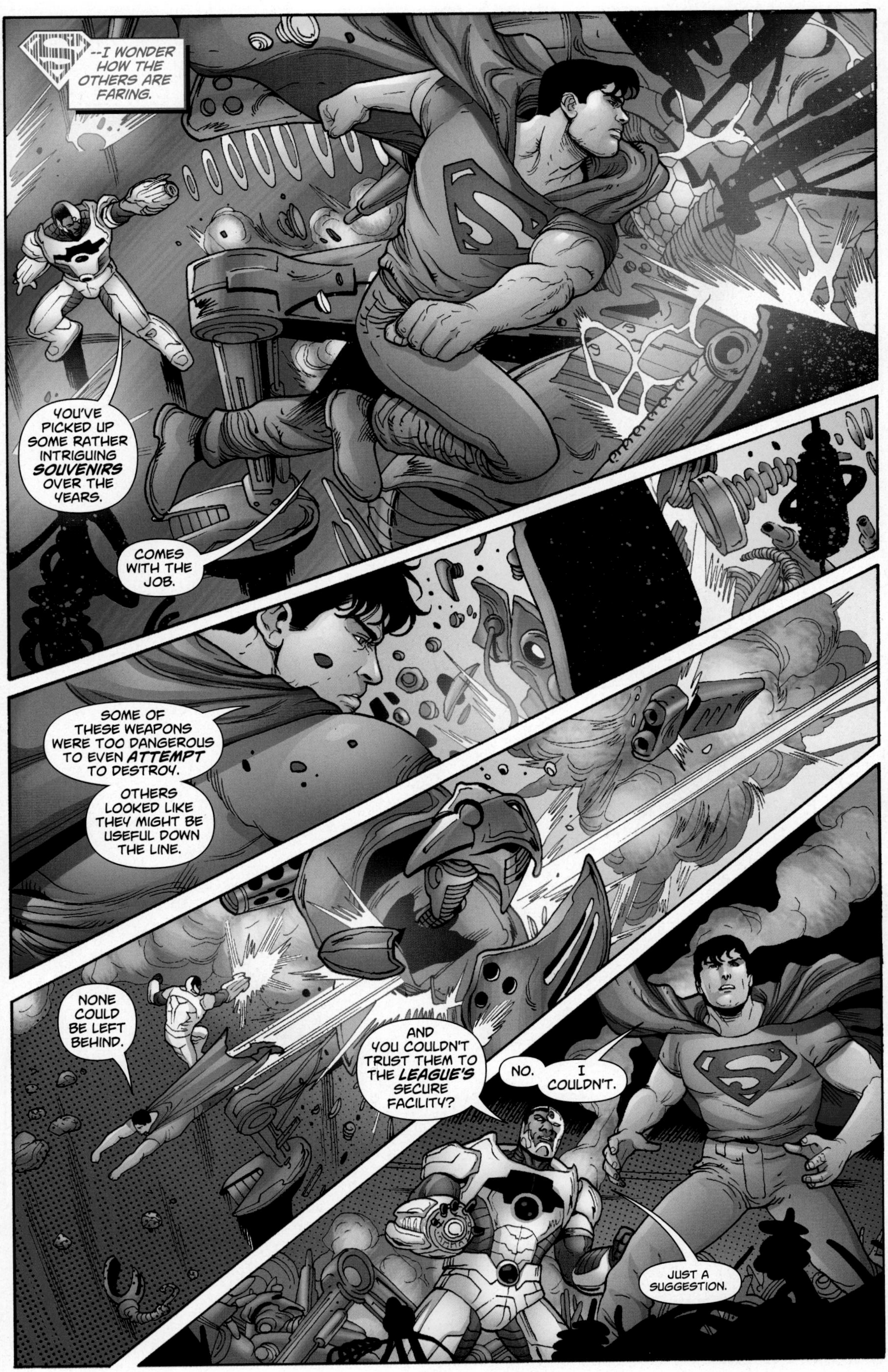
--I WONDER HOW THE OTHERS ARE FARING.
YOU'VE PICKED UP SOME RATHER INTRIGUING SOUVENIRS OVER THE YEARS.
COMES WITH THE JOB.
SOME OF THESE WEAPONS WERE TOO DANGEROUS TO EVEN ATTEMPT TO DESTROY.
OTHERS LOOKED LIKE THEY MIGHT BE USEFUL DOWN THE LINE.
NONE COULD BE LEFT BEHIND.
AND YOU COULDN'T TRUST THEM TO THE LEAGUE'S SECURE FACILITY?
NO.
I COULDN'T.
JUST A SUGGESTION.

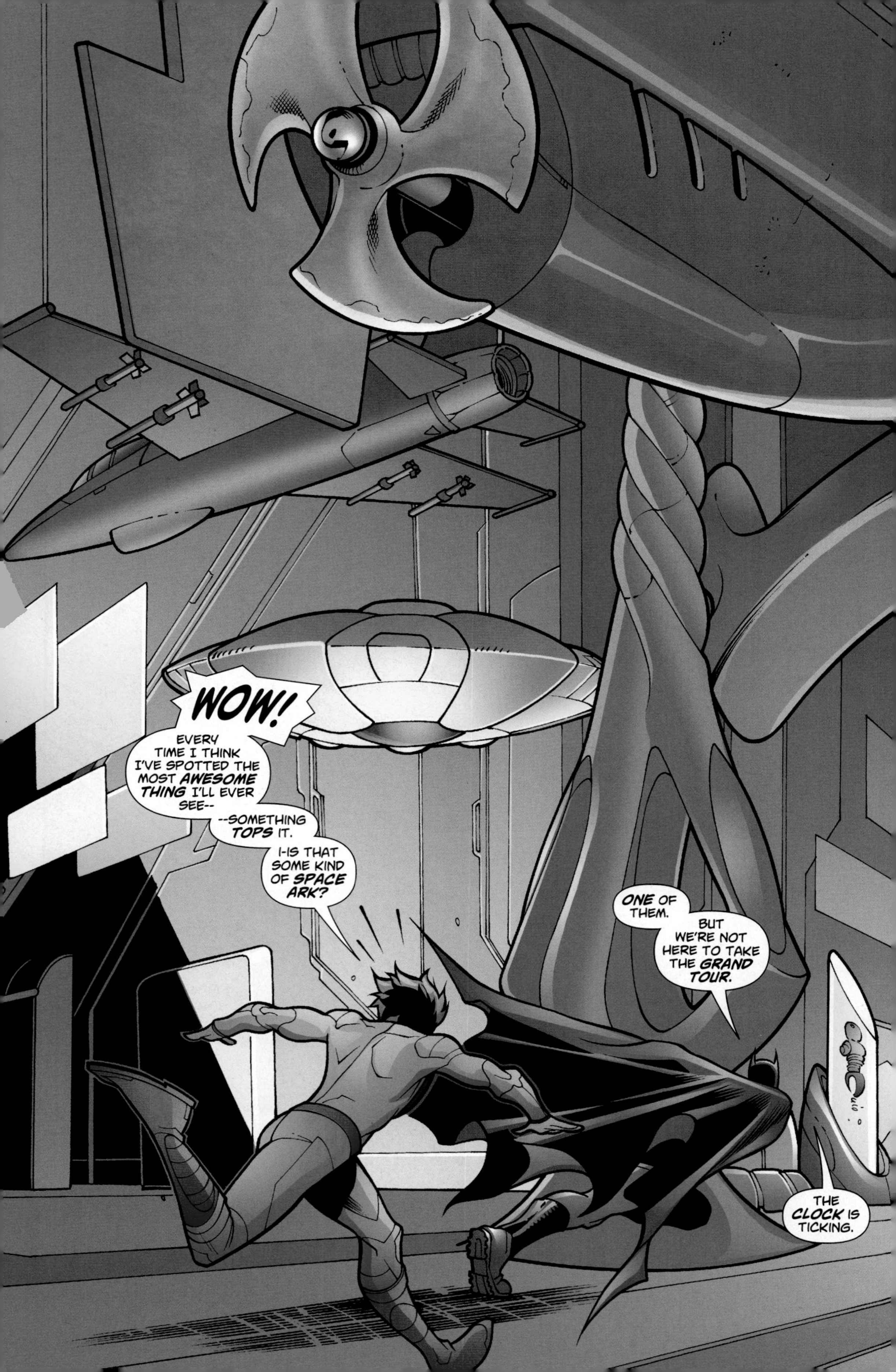
WOW!
EVERY TIME I THINK I'VE SPOTTED THE MOST **AWESOME THING** I'LL EVER SEE--
--SOMETHING **TOPS** IT.
I-IS THAT SOME KIND OF **SPACE ARK?**
ONE OF THEM.
BUT WE'RE NOT HERE TO TAKE THE **GRAND TOUR**.
THE **CLOCK** IS TICKING.

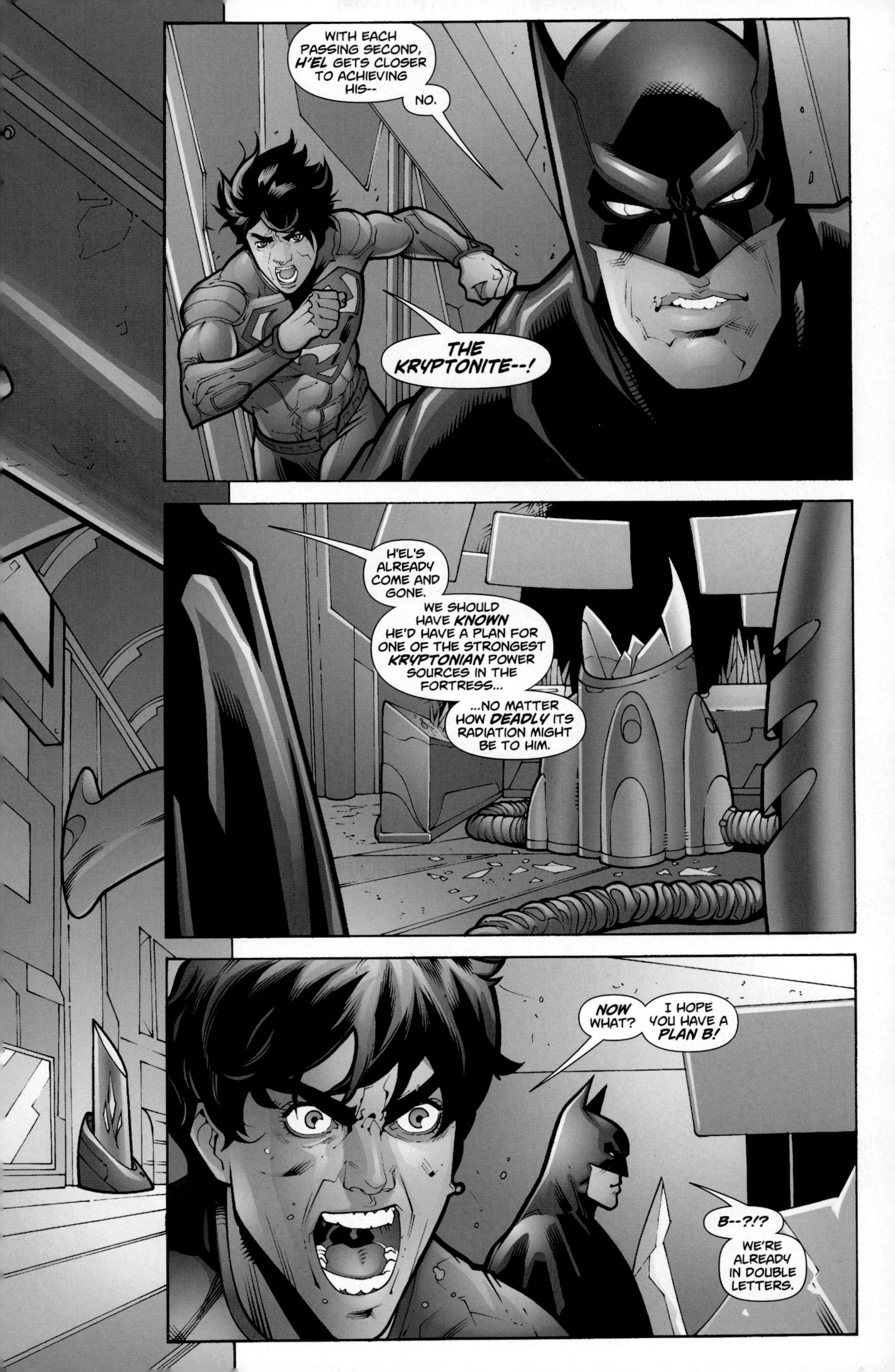
WITH EACH PASSING SECOND, H'EL GETS CLOSER TO ACHIEVING HIS--
NO.
THE KRYPTONITE--!
H'EL'S ALREADY COME AND GONE.
WE SHOULD HAVE KNOWN HE'D HAVE A PLAN FOR ONE OF THE STRONGEST KRYPTONIAN POWER SOURCES IN THE FORTRESS...
...NO MATTER HOW DEADLY ITS RADIATION MIGHT BE TO HIM.
NOW WHAT?
I HOPE YOU HAVE A PLAN B!
B--?!?
WE'RE ALREADY IN DOUBLE LETTERS.

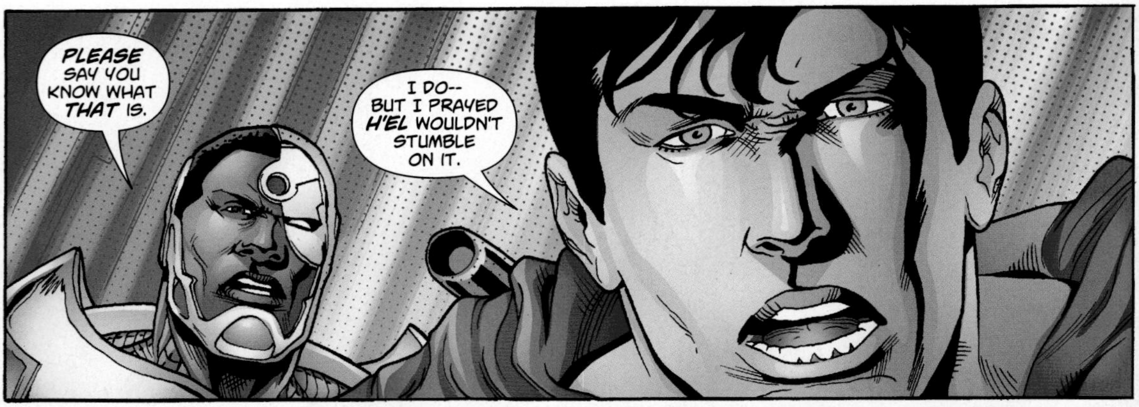
PLEASE SAY YOU KNOW WHAT THAT IS.
I DO-- BUT I PRAYED H'EL WOULDN'T STUMBLE ON IT.

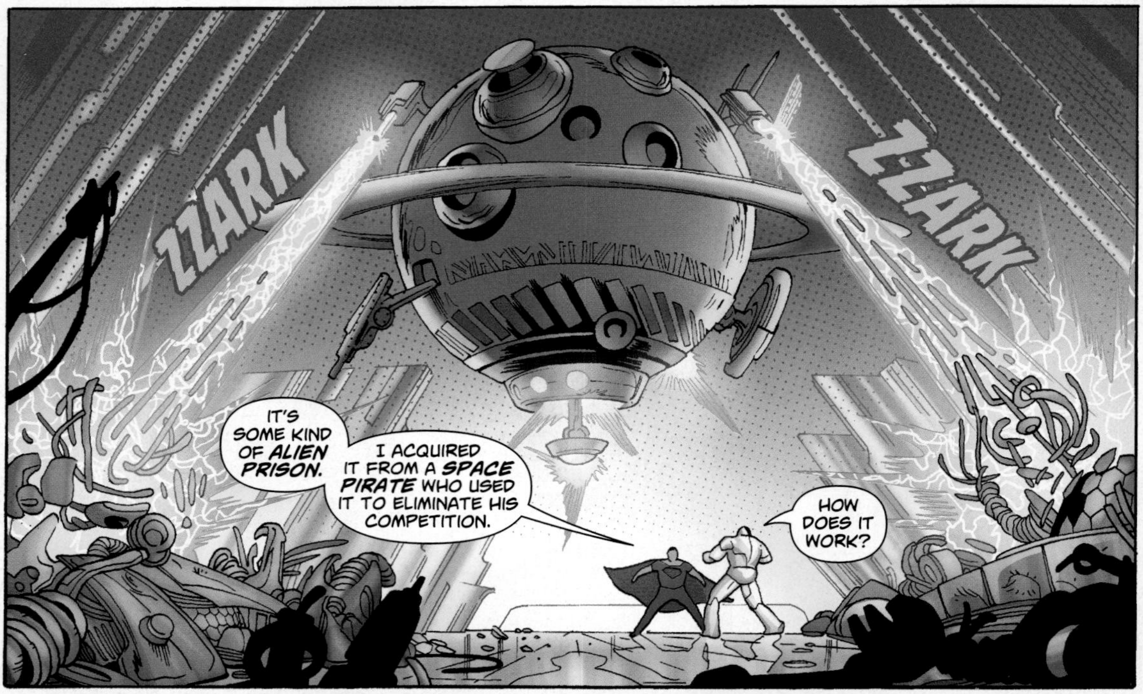
ZZARK
ZZARK
IT'S SOME KIND OF ALIEN PRISON.
I ACQUIRED IT FROM A SPACE PIRATE WHO USED IT TO ELIMINATE HIS COMPETITION.
HOW DOES IT WORK?

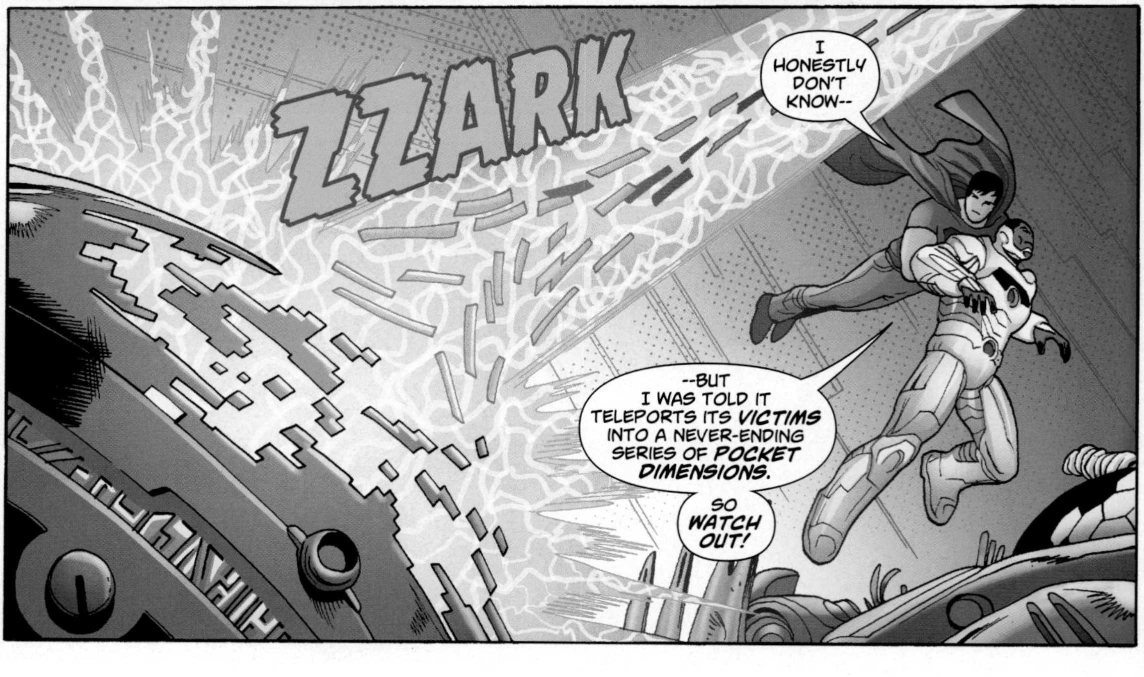
ZZARK
I HONESTLY DON'T KNOW--
--BUT I WAS TOLD IT TELEPORTS ITS VICTIMS INTO A NEVER-ENDING SERIES OF POCKET DIMENSIONS.
SO WATCH OUT!

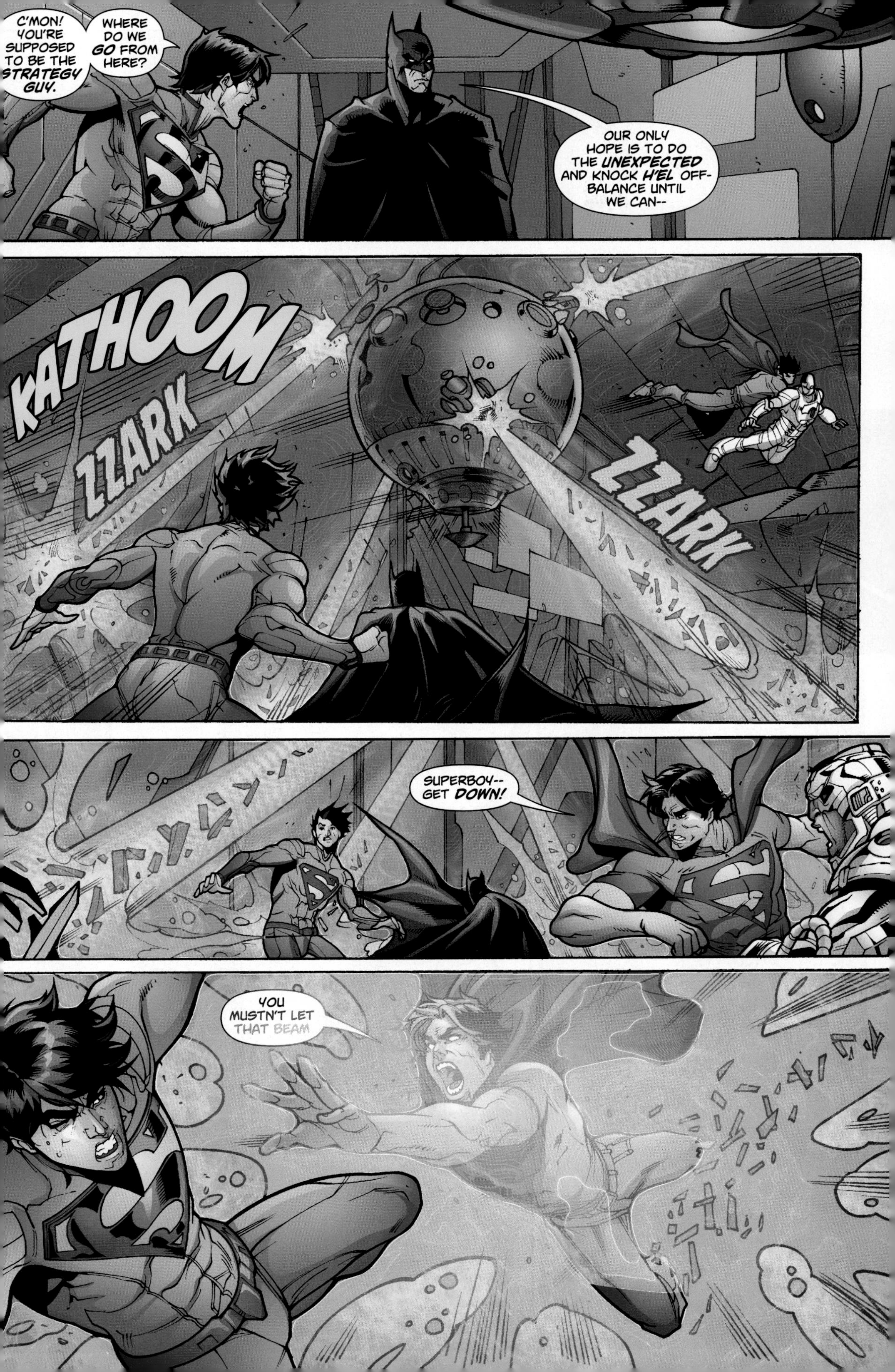
C'MON! YOU'RE SUPPOSED TO BE THE STRATEGY GUY.
WHERE DO WE GO FROM HERE?
OUR ONLY HOPE IS TO DO THE UNEXPECTED AND KNOCK H'EL OFF-BALANCE UNTIL WE CAN--
KATHOOM
ZZARK
ZZARK
SUPERBOY-- GET DOWN!
YOU MUSTN'T LET THAT BEAM

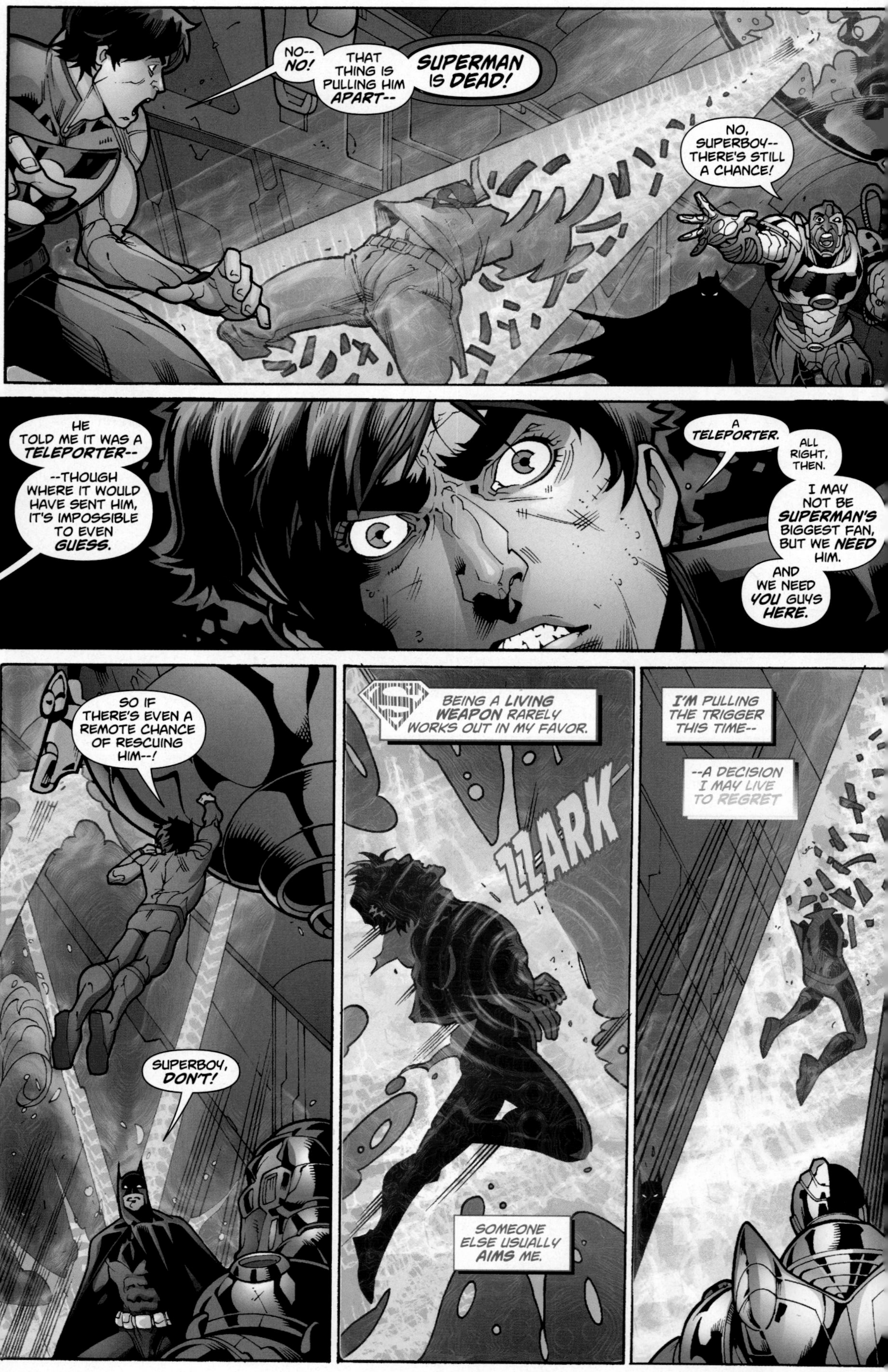

NO-- NO!
THAT THING IS PULLING HIM APART--
SUPERMAN IS DEAD!
NO, SUPERBOY-- THERE'S STILL A CHANCE!
HE TOLD ME IT WAS A TELEPORTER--
--THOUGH WHERE IT WOULD HAVE SENT HIM, IT'S IMPOSSIBLE TO EVEN GUESS.
A TELEPORTER.
ALL RIGHT, THEN.
I MAY NOT BE SUPERMAN'S BIGGEST FAN, BUT WE NEED HIM.
AND WE NEED YOU GUYS HERE.
SO IF THERE'S EVEN A REMOTE CHANCE OF RESCUING HIM--!
SUPERBOY, DON'T!
BEING A LIVING WEAPON RARELY WORKS OUT IN MY FAVOR.
ZZARK
SOMEONE ELSE USUALLY AIMS ME.
I'M PULLING THE TRIGGER THIS TIME--
--A DECISION I MAY LIVE TO REGRET

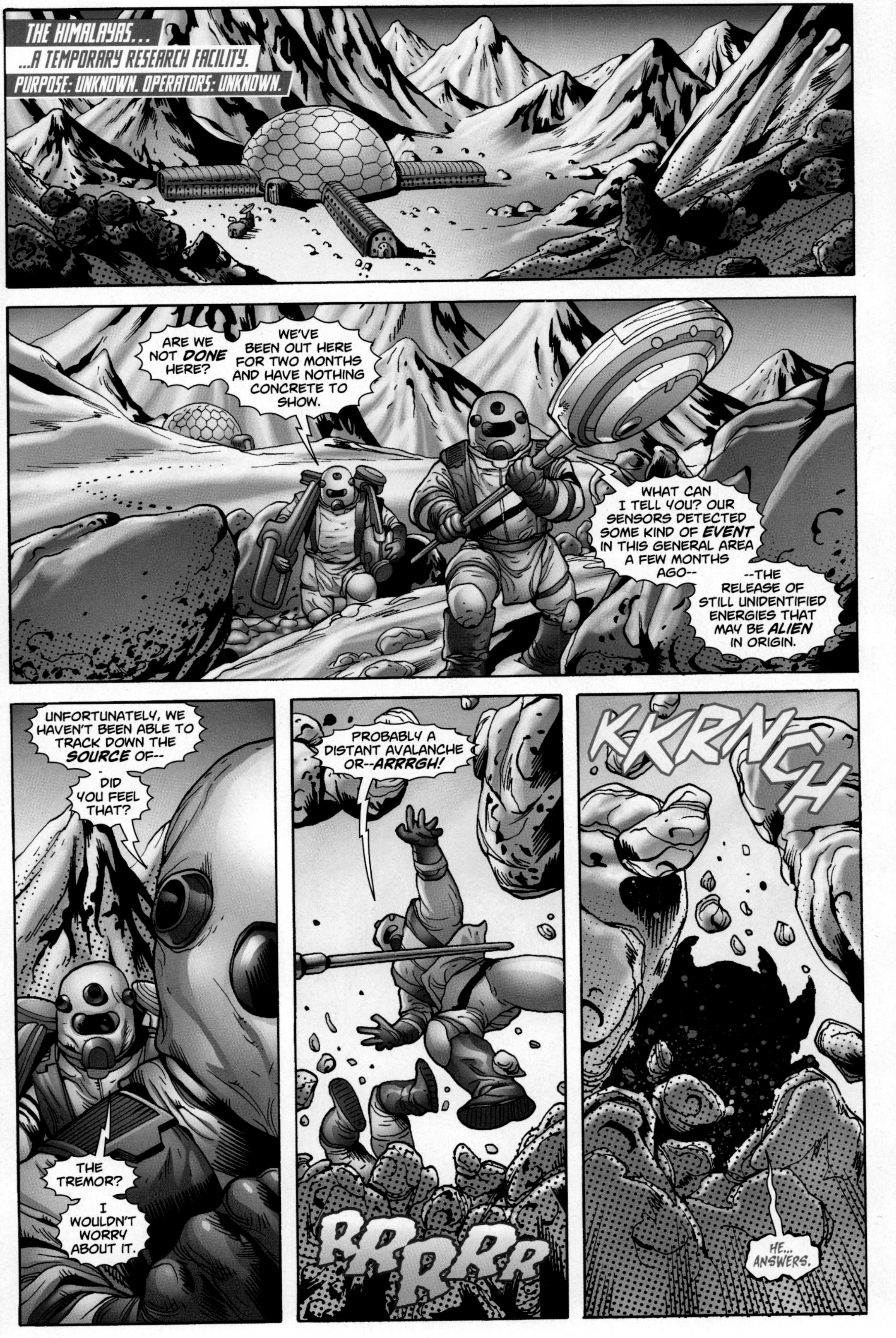
THE HIMALAYAS...
...A TEMPORARY RESEARCH FACILITY.
PURPOSE: UNKNOWN. OPERATORS: UNKNOWN.
ARE WE NOT DONE HERE?
WE'VE BEEN OUT HERE FOR TWO MONTHS AND HAVE NOTHING CONCRETE TO SHOW.
WHAT CAN I TELL YOU? OUR SENSORS DETECTED SOME KIND OF EVENT IN THIS GENERAL AREA A FEW MONTHS AGO--
--THE RELEASE OF STILL UNIDENTIFIED ENERGIES THAT MAY BE ALIEN IN ORIGIN.
UNFORTUNATELY, WE HAVEN'T BEEN ABLE TO TRACK DOWN THE SOURCE OF--
DID YOU FEEL THAT?
THE TREMOR?
I WOULDN'T WORRY ABOUT IT.
PROBABLY A DISTANT AVALANCHE OR--ARRRGH!
RRRRR
KKRNCH
HE... ANSWERS.

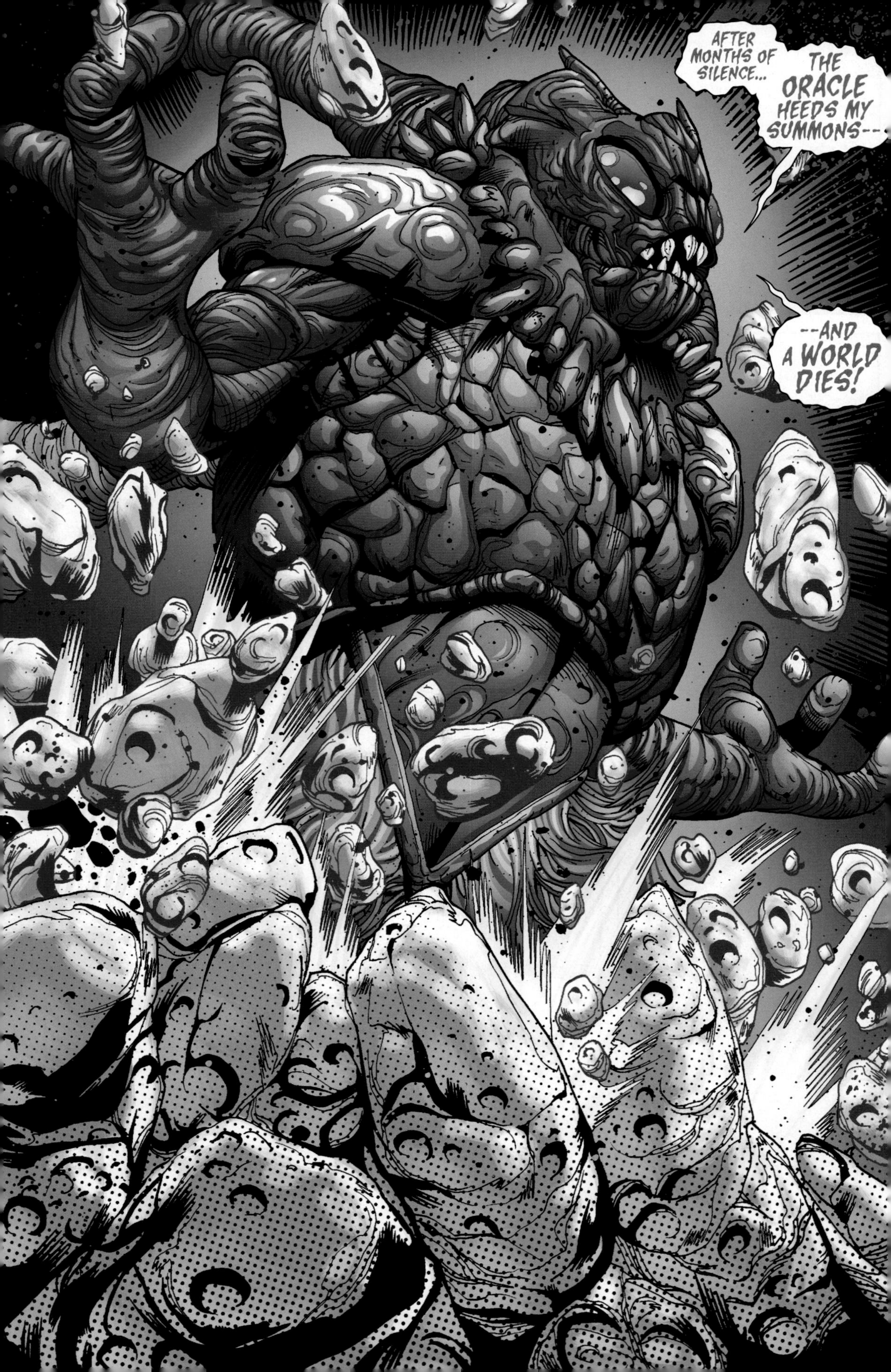

AFTER MONTHS OF SILENCE...
THE ORACLE HEEDS MY SUMMONS---
--AND A WORLD DIES!

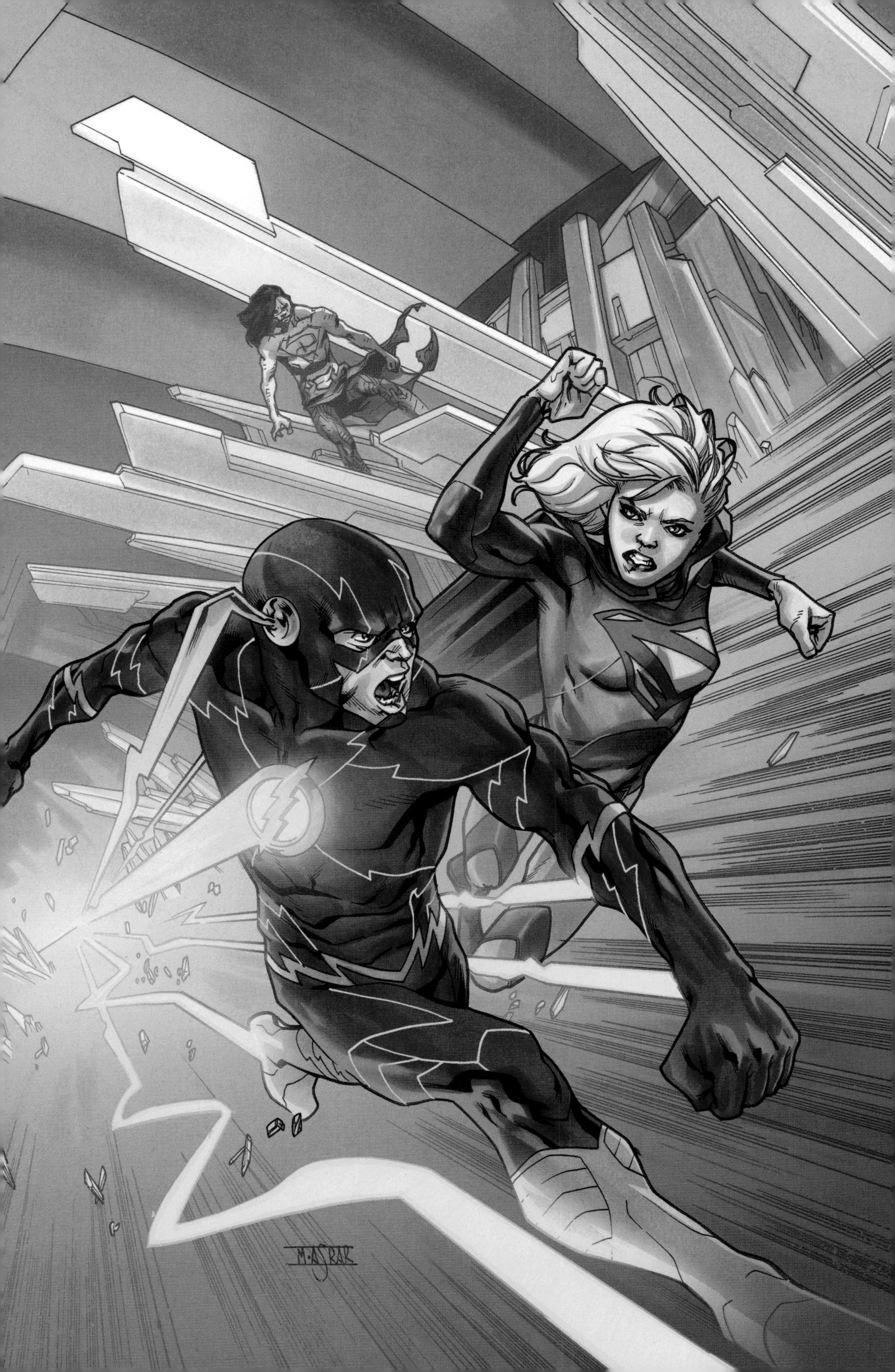
M·ASRAK

FAST & FASTER

MIKE JOHNSON writer MAHMUD ASRAR artist cover art by MAHMUD ASRAR & DAVE MCCAIG

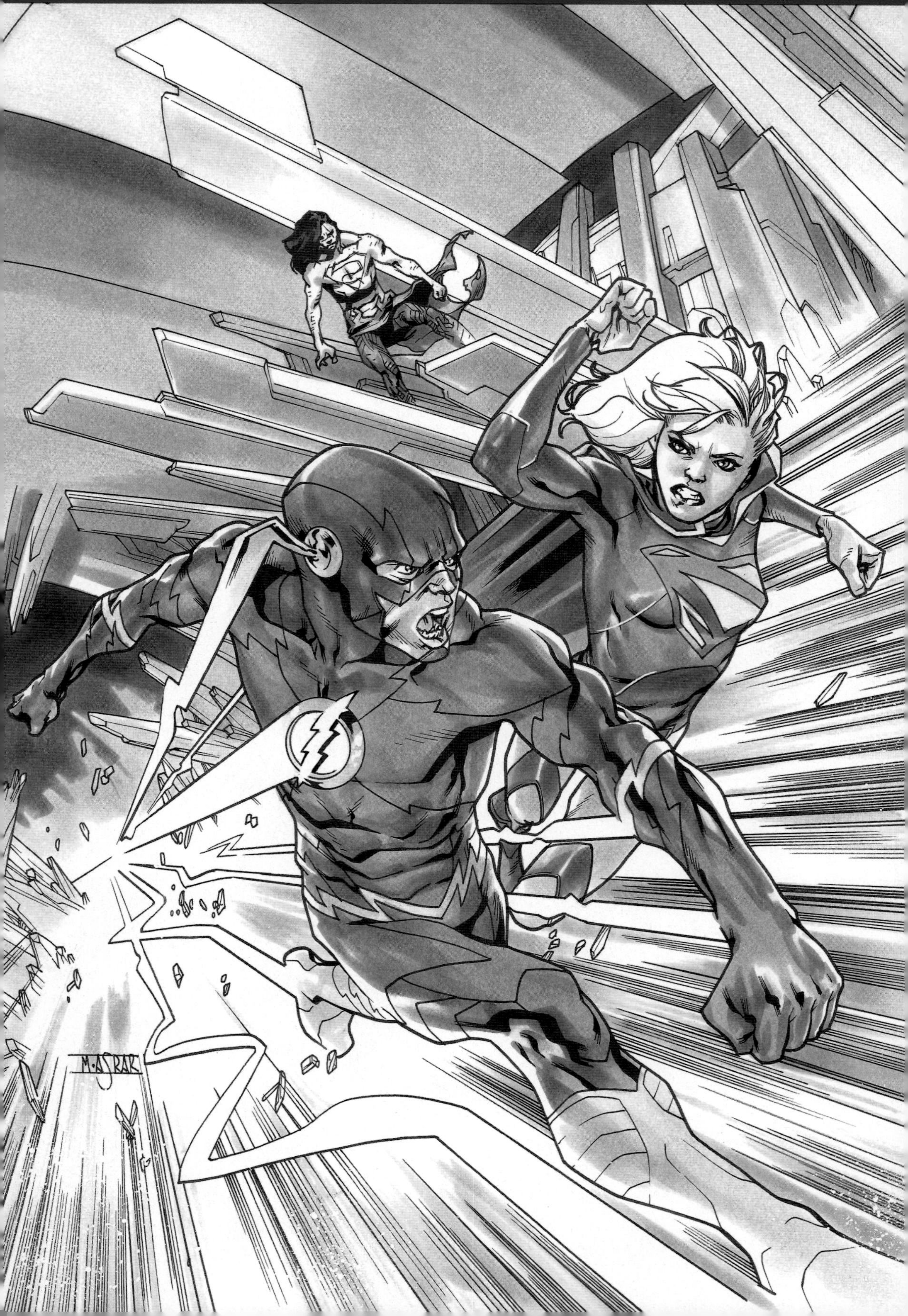
M.ASRAR

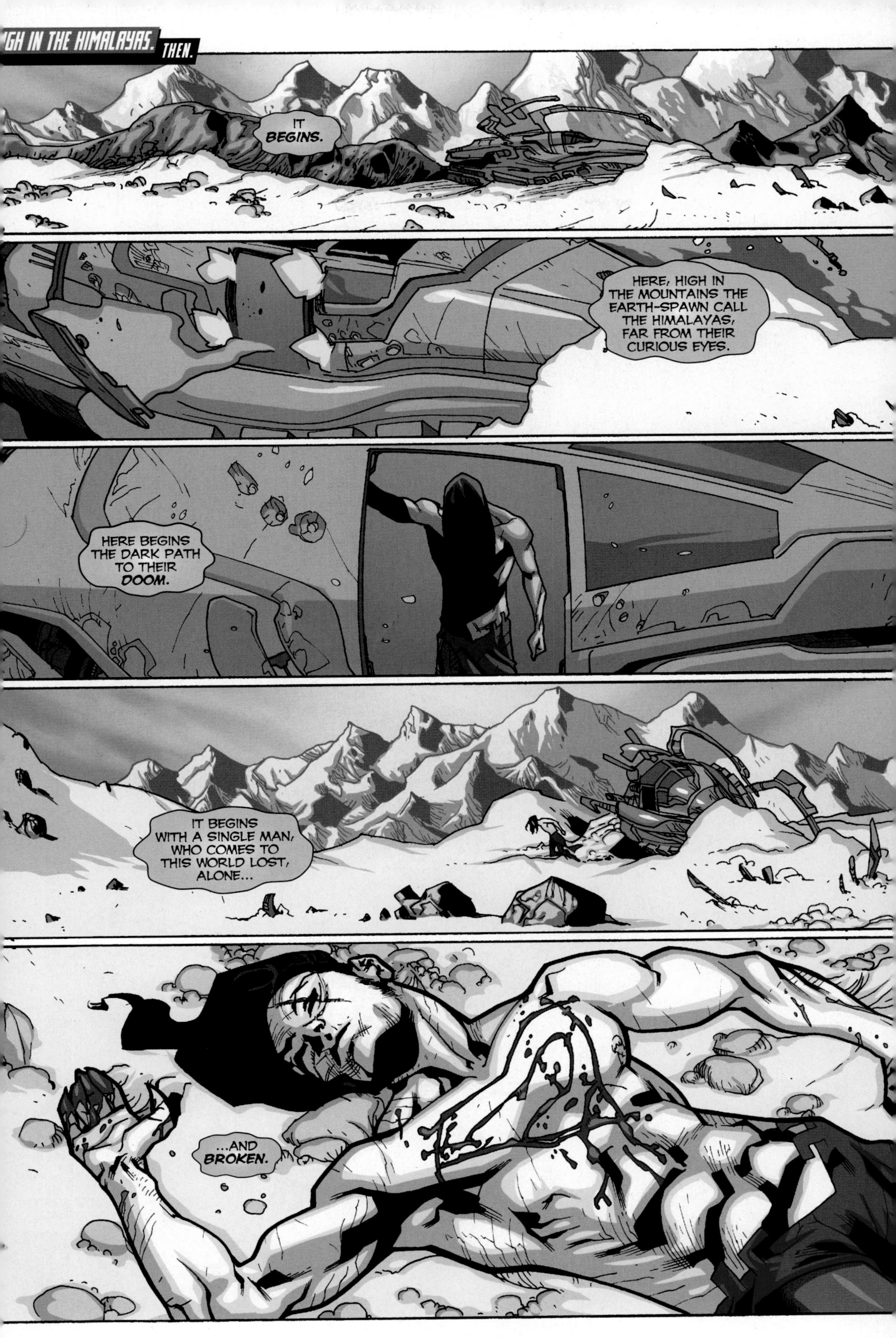
GH IN THE HIMALAYAS.
THEN.
IT BEGINS.
HERE, HIGH IN THE MOUNTAINS THE EARTH-SPAWN CALL THE HIMALAYAS, FAR FROM THEIR CURIOUS EYES.
HERE BEGINS THE DARK PATH TO THEIR DOOM.
IT BEGINS WITH A SINGLE MAN, WHO COMES TO THIS WORLD LOST, ALONE...
...AND BROKEN.

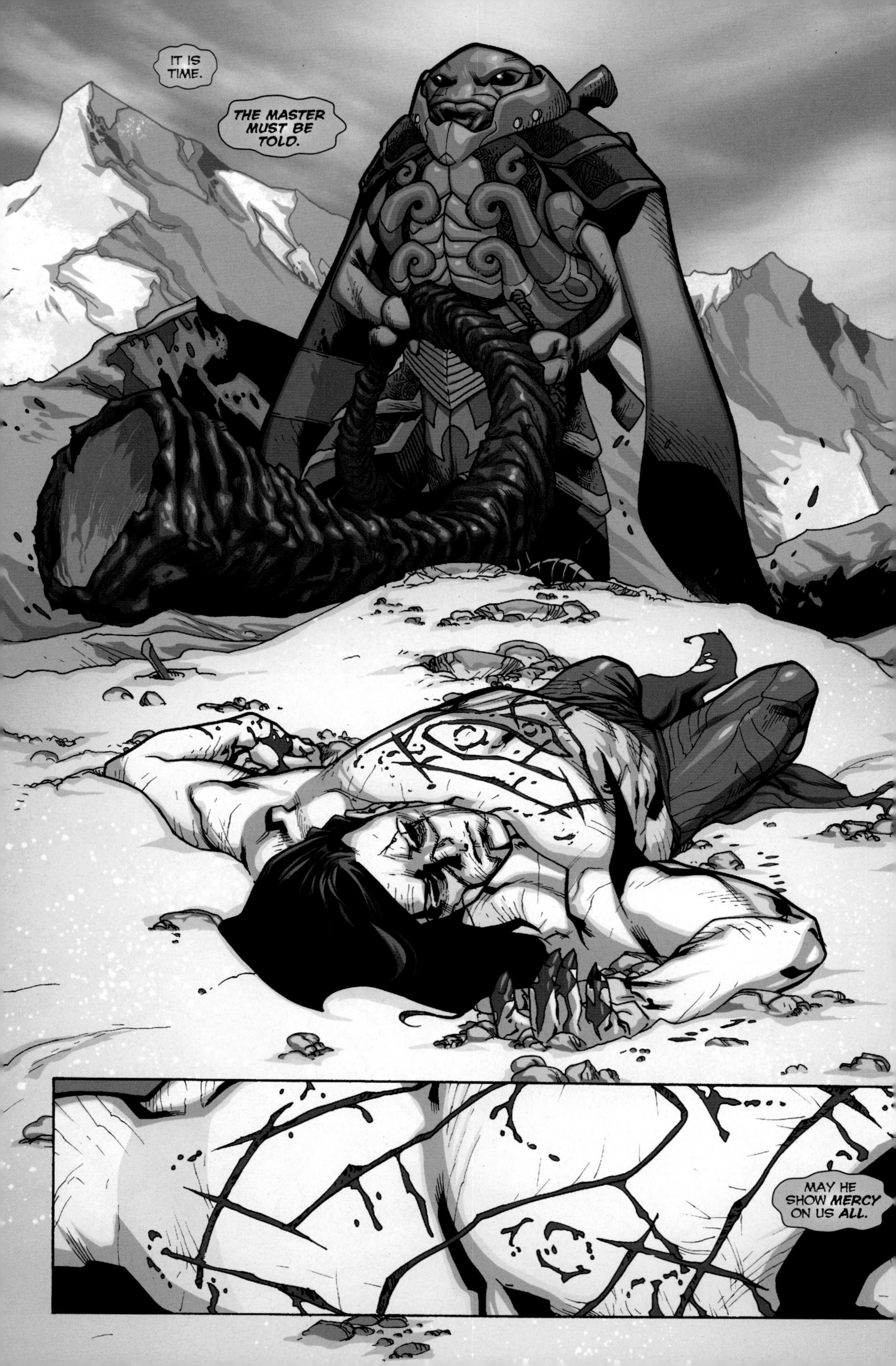
IT IS TIME.
THE MASTER MUST BE TOLD.
MAY HE SHOW MERCY ON US ALL.

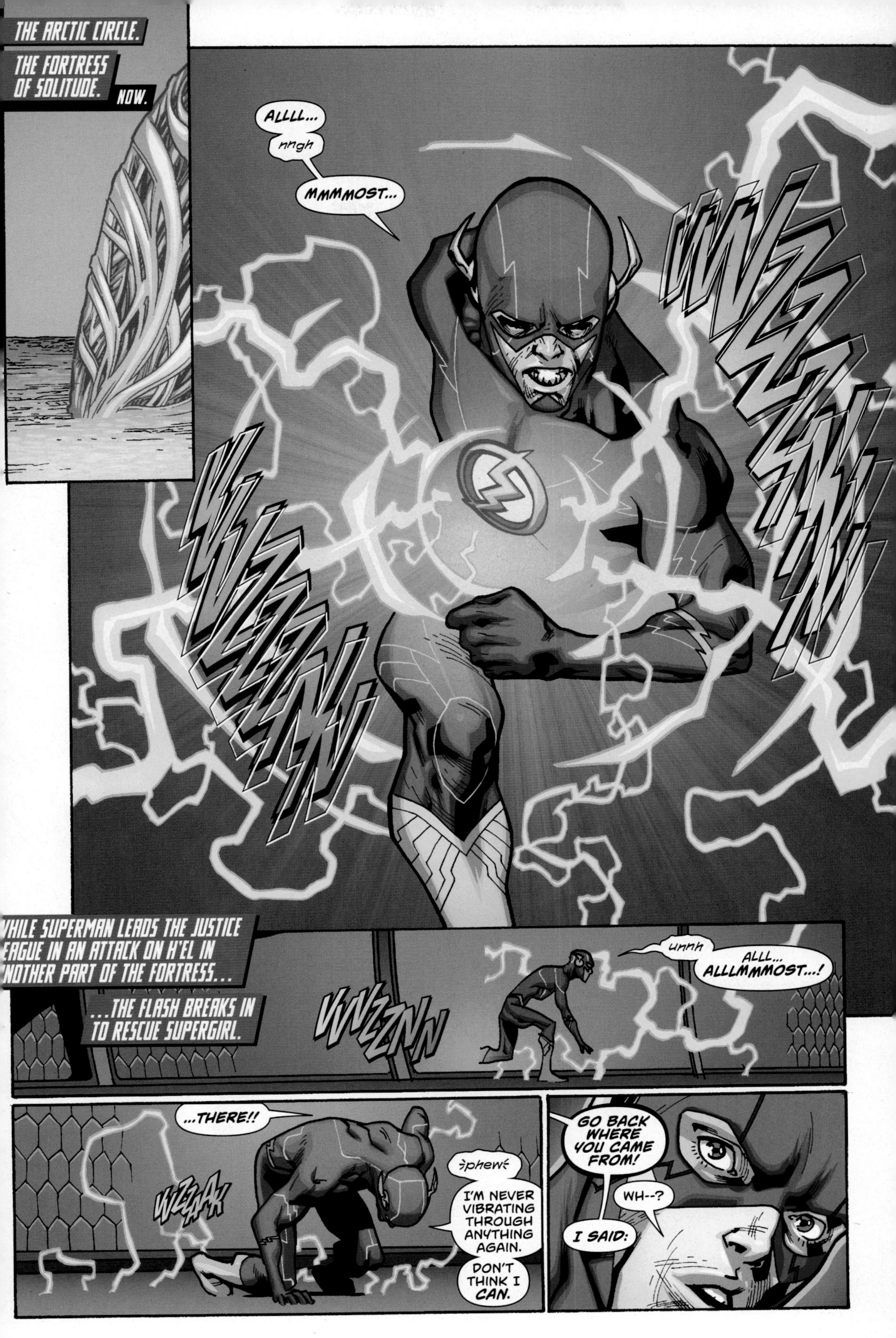
THE ARCTIC CIRCLE.
THE FORTRESS OF SOLITUDE.
NOW.
ALLLL...
nngh
MMMMOST...
VVVZZNN
VVVZZNN
WHILE SUPERMAN LEADS THE JUSTICE LEAGUE IN AN ATTACK ON H'EL IN ANOTHER PART OF THE FORTRESS...
...THE FLASH BREAKS IN TO RESCUE SUPERGIRL.
VVVZZNN
unnh
ALLL... ALLLMMMOST...!
...THERE!!
WZZAK
phew
I'M NEVER VIBRATING THROUGH ANYTHING AGAIN.
DON'T THINK I CAN.
GO BACK WHERE YOU CAME FROM!
WH--?
I SAID:

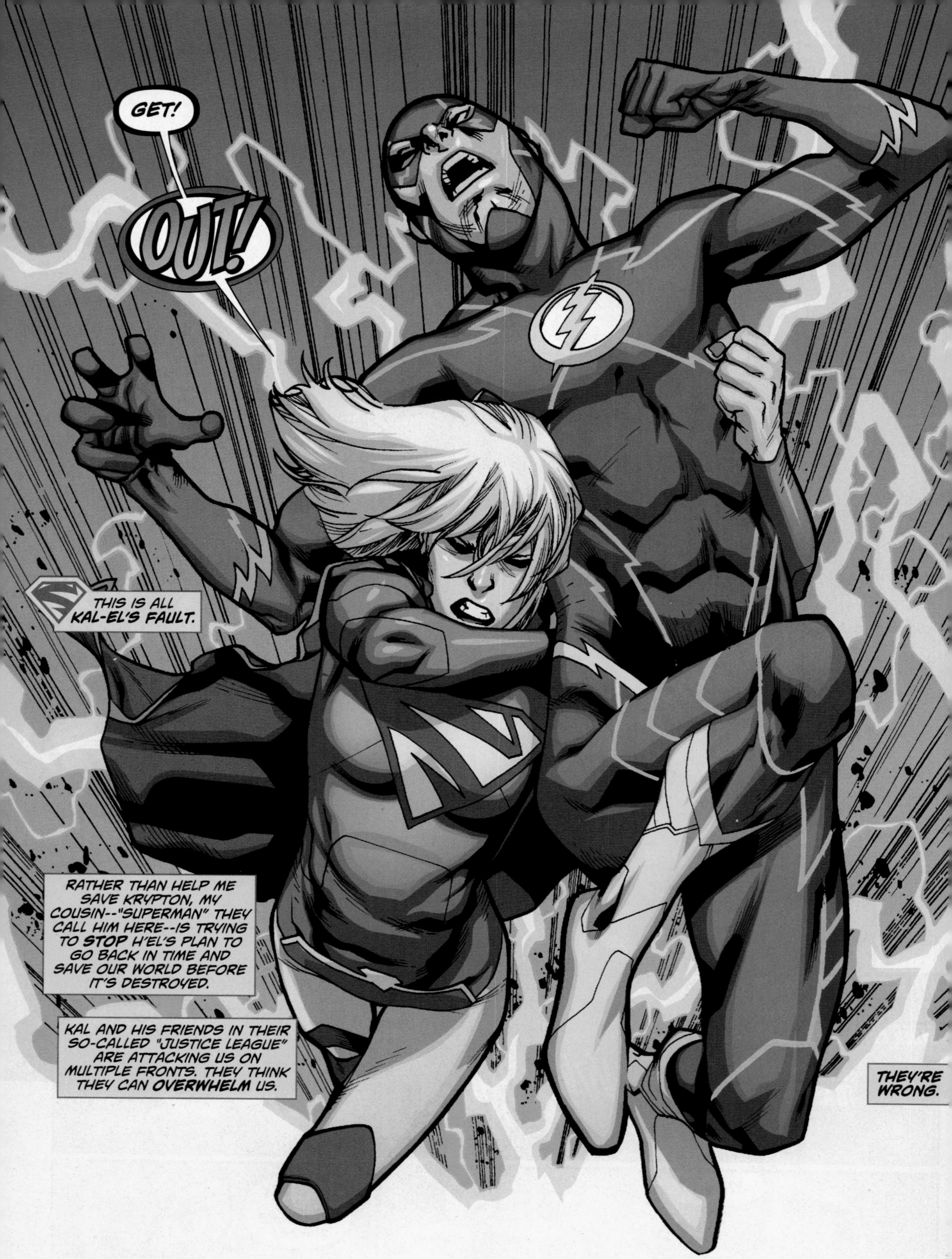
GET!
OUT!
THIS IS ALL KAL-EL'S FAULT.
RATHER THAN HELP ME SAVE KRYPTON, MY COUSIN--"SUPERMAN" THEY CALL HIM HERE--IS TRYING TO STOP H'EL'S PLAN TO GO BACK IN TIME AND SAVE OUR WORLD BEFORE IT'S DESTROYED.
KAL AND HIS FRIENDS IN THEIR SO-CALLED "JUSTICE LEAGUE" ARE ATTACKING US ON MULTIPLE FRONTS. THEY THINK THEY CAN OVERWHELM US.
THEY'RE WRONG.

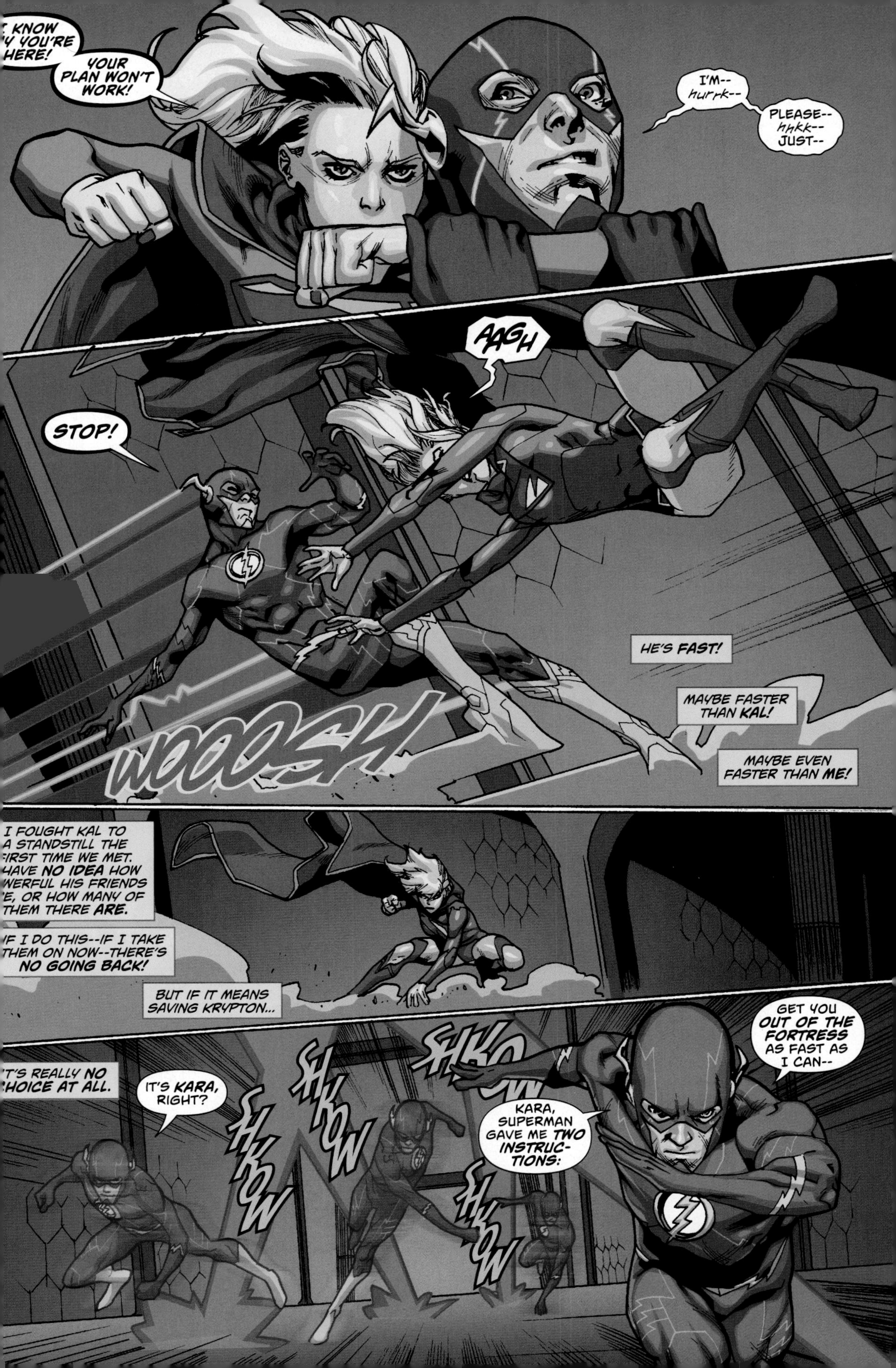

I KNOW
YOU'RE
HERE!
YOUR PLAN WON'T WORK!
I'M-- hurrk--
PLEASE-- hhkk-- JUST--
AAGH
STOP!
HE'S FAST!
MAYBE FASTER THAN KAL!
MAYBE EVEN FASTER THAN ME!
WOOOSH
I FOUGHT KAL TO A STANDSTILL THE FIRST TIME WE MET.
HAVE NO IDEA HOW
WERFUL HIS FRIENDS
E, OR HOW MANY OF THEM THERE ARE.
IF I DO THIS--IF I TAKE THEM ON NOW--THERE'S NO GOING BACK!
BUT IF IT MEANS SAVING KRYPTON...
IT'S REALLY NO CHOICE AT ALL.
IT'S KARA, RIGHT?
KARA, SUPERMAN GAVE ME TWO INSTRUCTIONS:
GET YOU OUT OF THE FORTRESS AS FAST AS I CAN--
SHKOW
SHKOW
SHKOW
SHKOW

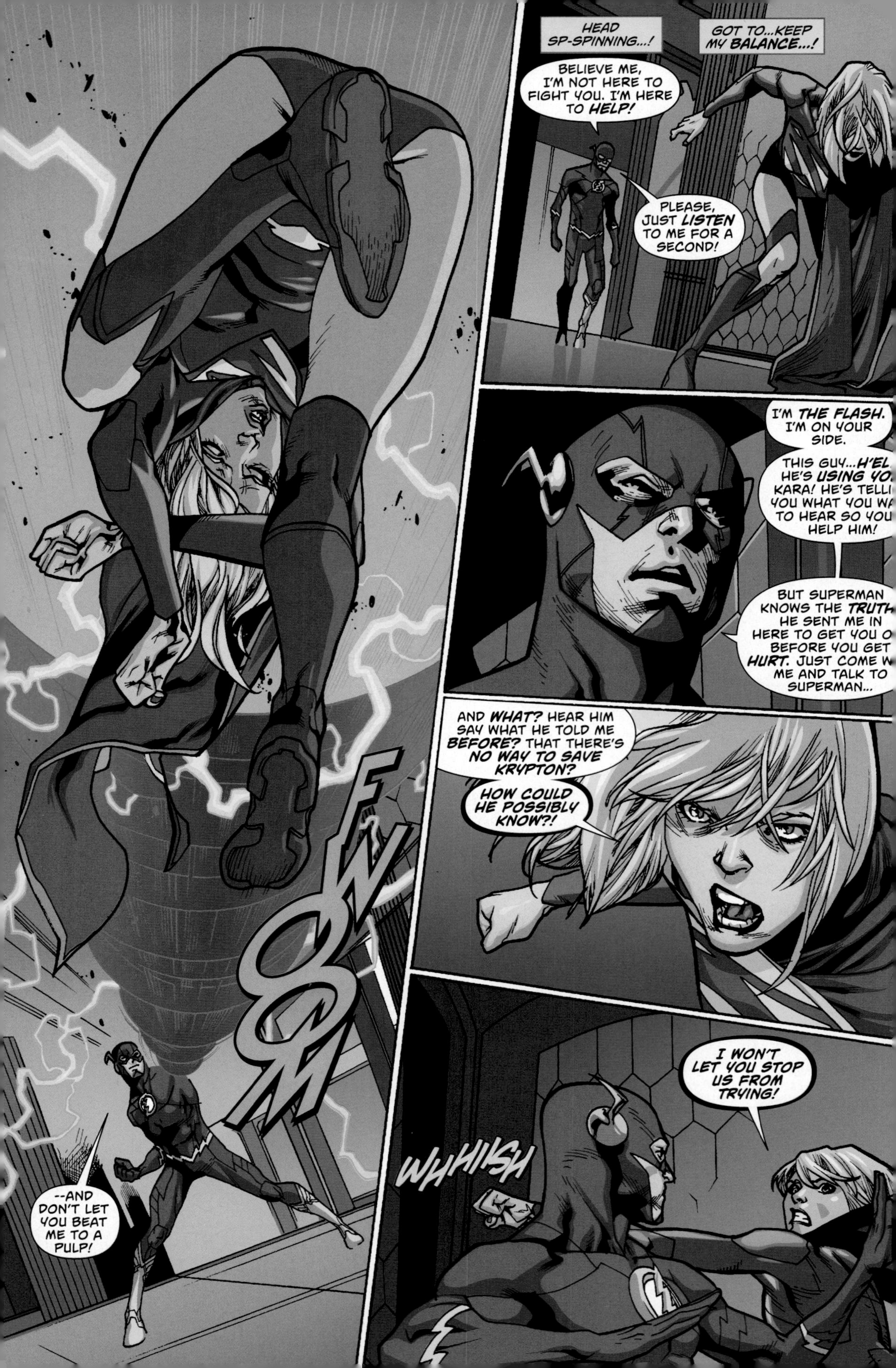
FWOOM
--AND DON'T LET YOU BEAT ME TO A PULP!
HEAD SP-SPINNING...!
GOT TO...KEEP MY BALANCE...!
BELIEVE ME, I'M NOT HERE TO FIGHT YOU. I'M HERE TO HELP!
PLEASE, JUST LISTEN TO ME FOR A SECOND!
I'M THE FLASH. I'M ON YOUR SIDE.
THIS GUY...H'EL HE'S USING YO KARA! HE'S TELLI YOU WHAT YOU WA TO HEAR SO YOU HELP HIM!
BUT SUPERMAN KNOWS THE TRUTH HE SENT ME IN HERE TO GET YOU O BEFORE YOU GET HURT. JUST COME W ME AND TALK TO SUPERMAN...
AND WHAT? HEAR HIM SAY WHAT HE TOLD ME BEFORE? THAT THERE'S NO WAY TO SAVE KRYPTON?
HOW COULD HE POSSIBLY KNOW?!
WHHISH
I WON'T LET YOU STOP US FROM TRYING!

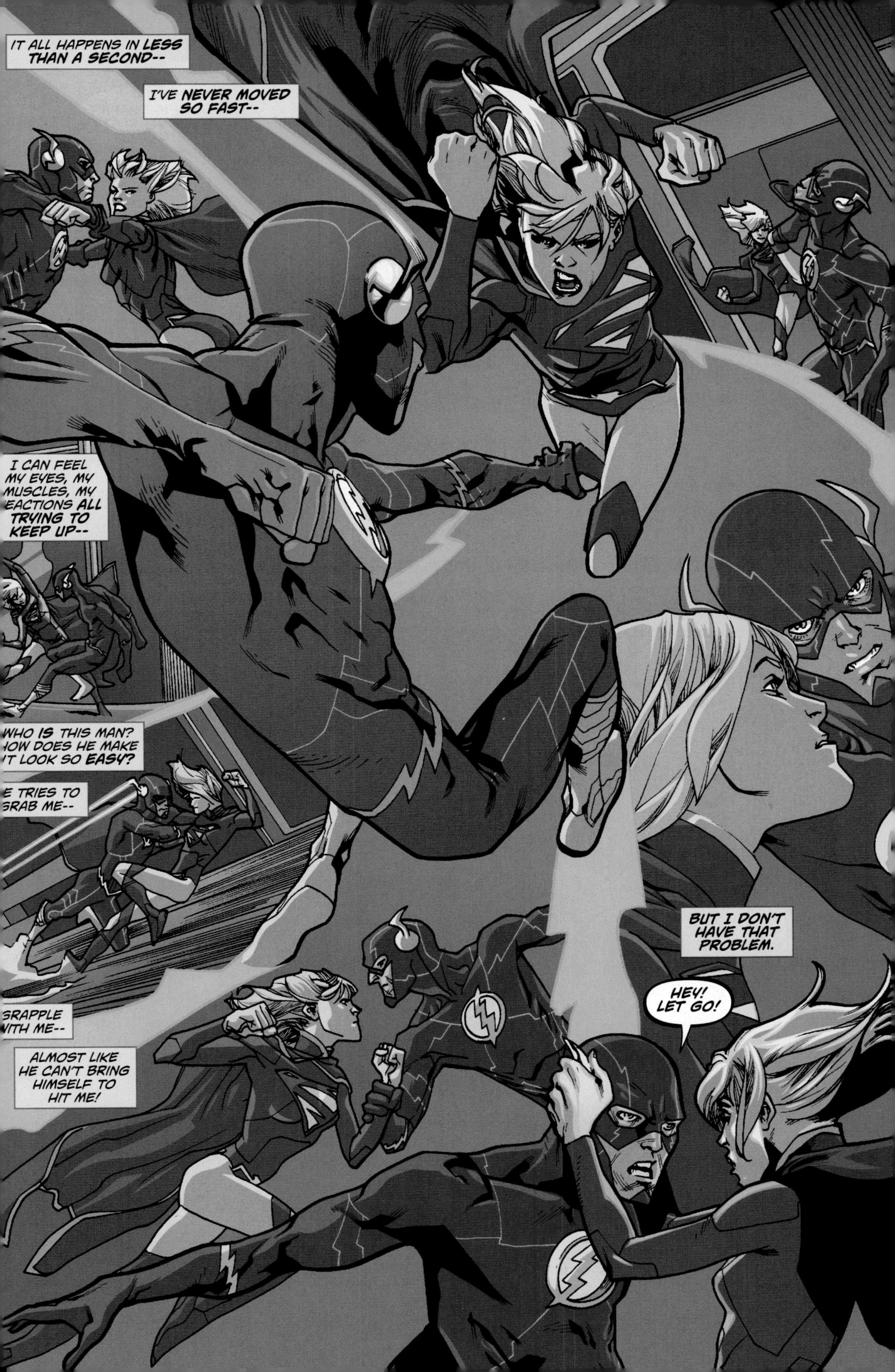
IT ALL HAPPENS IN LESS THAN A SECOND--
I'VE NEVER MOVED SO FAST--
I CAN FEEL MY EYES, MY MUSCLES, MY EACTIONS ALL TRYING TO KEEP UP--
WHO IS THIS MAN? OW DOES HE MAKE T LOOK SO EASY?
E TRIES TO GRAB ME--
GRAPPLE WITH ME--
ALMOST LIKE HE CAN'T BRING HIMSELF TO HIT ME!
BUT I DON'T HAVE THAT PROBLEM.
HEY! LET GO!

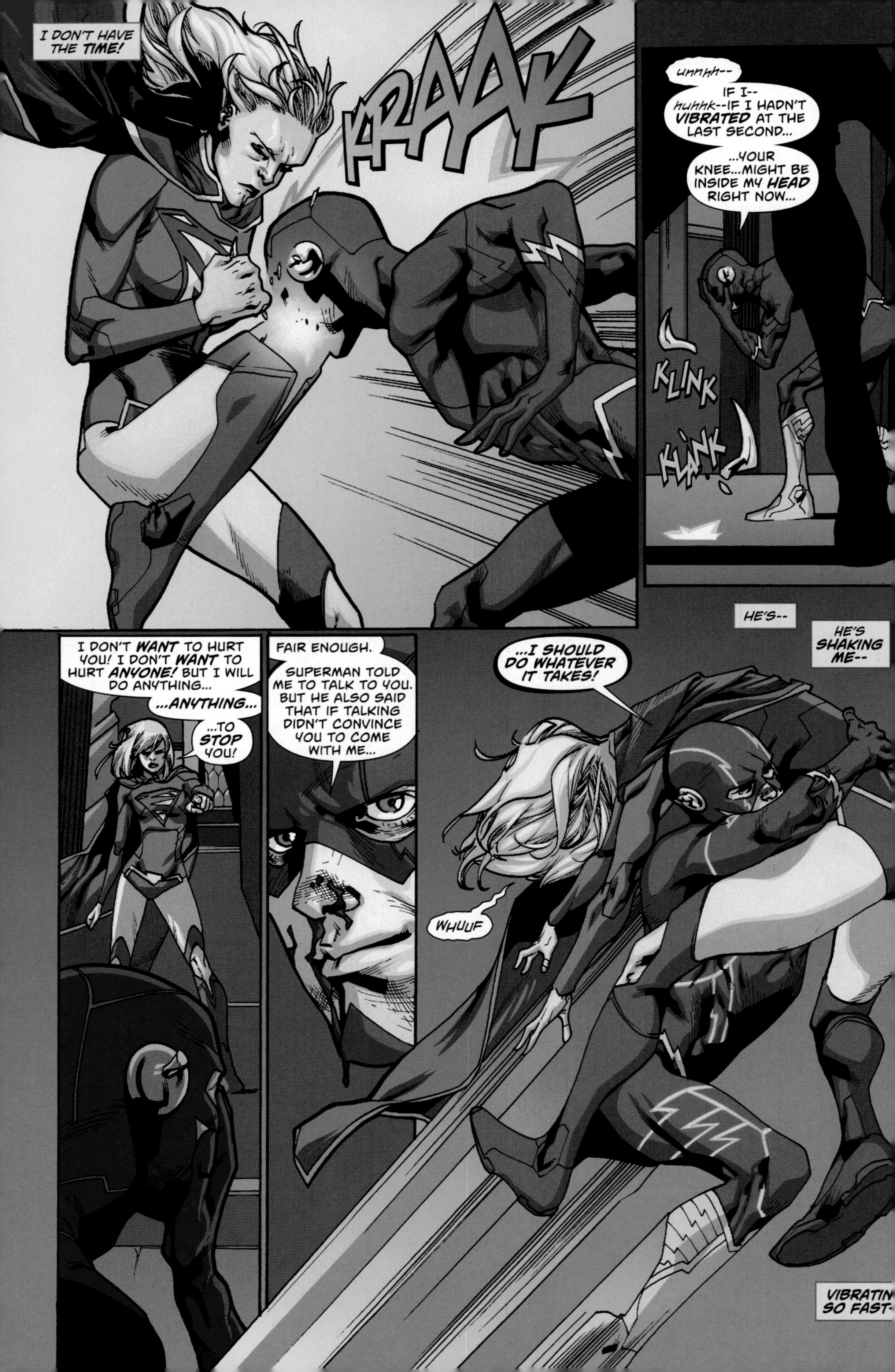
I DON'T HAVE THE TIME!
KRAAK
unnhh--
IF I-- huhhk--IF I HADN'T VIBRATED AT THE LAST SECOND...
...YOUR KNEE...MIGHT BE INSIDE MY HEAD RIGHT NOW...
KLINK
KLANK
I DON'T WANT TO HURT YOU! I DON'T WANT TO HURT ANYONE! BUT I WILL DO ANYTHING...
...ANYTHING...
...TO STOP YOU!
FAIR ENOUGH.
SUPERMAN TOLD ME TO TALK TO YOU. BUT HE ALSO SAID THAT IF TALKING DIDN'T CONVINCE YOU TO COME WITH ME...
...I SHOULD DO WHATEVER IT TAKES!
HE'S--
HE'S SHAKING ME--
WHUUF
VIBRATIN SO FAST-

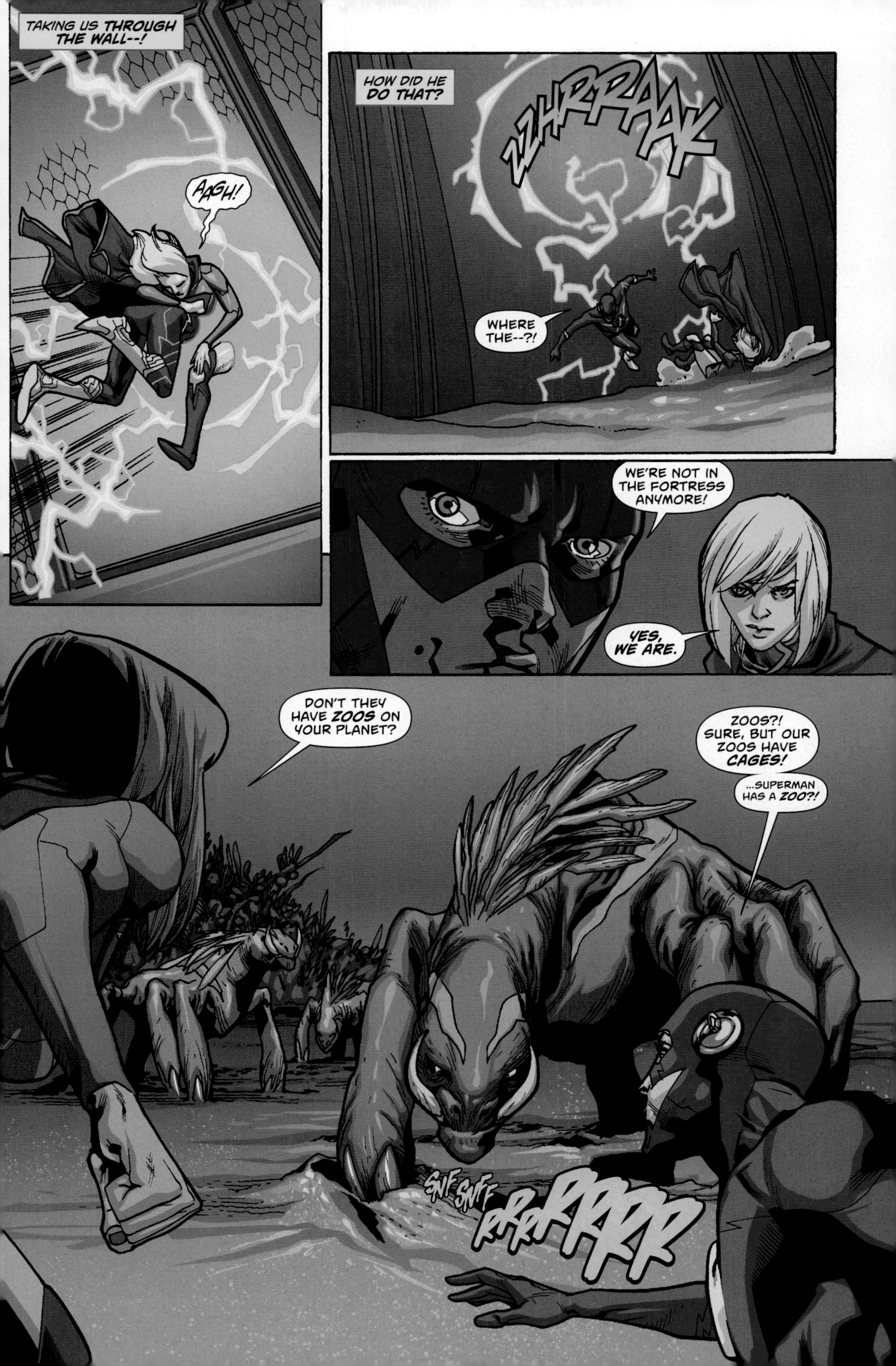
TAKING US THROUGH THE WALL--!
AAGH!
HOW DID HE DO THAT?
ZZHRRAAK
WHERE THE--?!
WE'RE NOT IN THE FORTRESS ANYMORE!
YES, WE ARE.
DON'T THEY HAVE ZOOS ON YOUR PLANET?
ZOOS?! SURE, BUT OUR ZOOS HAVE CAGES!
...SUPERMAN HAS A ZOO?!
SNF SNFF
RRRRRRRR

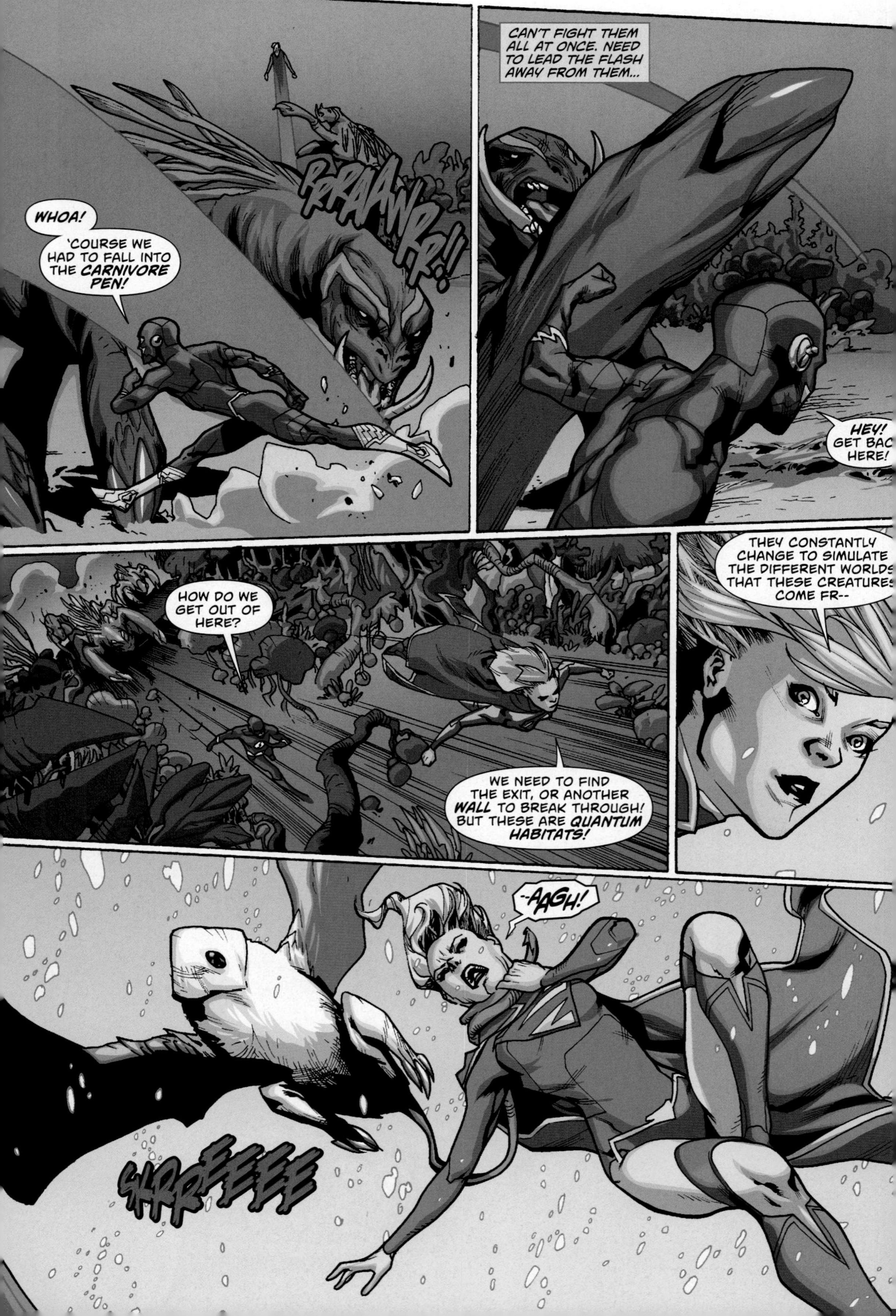
BRRAAWRR!!
WHOA!
'COURSE WE HAD TO FALL INTO THE CARNIVORE PEN!
CAN'T FIGHT THEM ALL AT ONCE. NEED TO LEAD THE FLASH AWAY FROM THEM...
HEY! GET BAC HERE!
HOW DO WE GET OUT OF HERE?
WE NEED TO FIND THE EXIT, OR ANOTHER WALL TO BREAK THROUGH! BUT THESE ARE QUANTUM HABITATS!
THEY CONSTANTLY CHANGE TO SIMULATE THE DIFFERENT WORLDS THAT THESE CREATURES COME FR--
--AAGH!
SKREEEEE

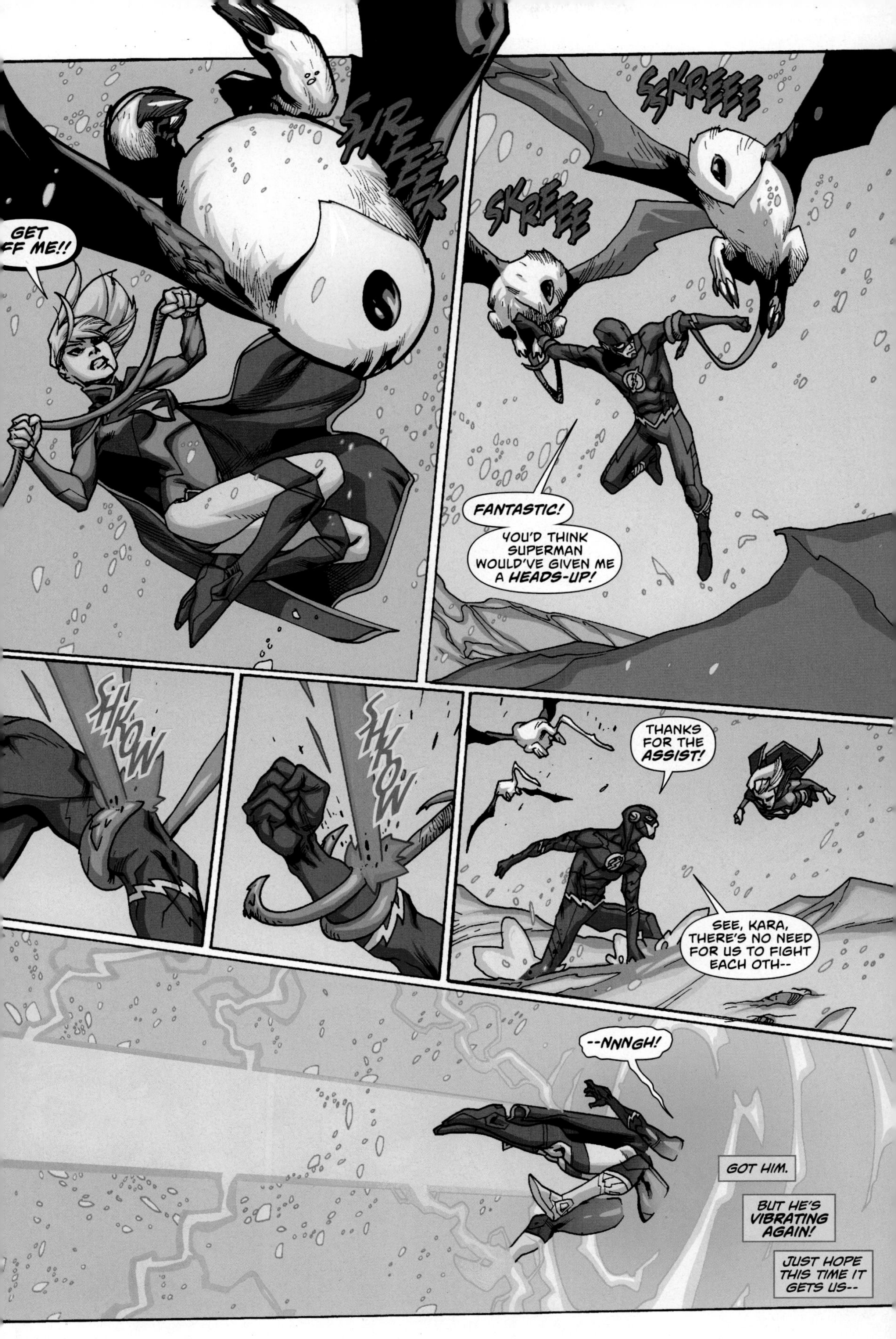
SHREEEK
GET
FF ME!!
SKREEE
SKREEE
FANTASTIC!
YOU'D THINK SUPERMAN WOULD'VE GIVEN ME A HEADS-UP!
SHKOW
SHKOW
THANKS FOR THE ASSIST!
SEE, KARA, THERE'S NO NEED FOR US TO FIGHT EACH OTH--
--NNNGH!
GOT HIM.
BUT HE'S VIBRATING AGAIN!
JUST HOPE THIS TIME IT GETS US--

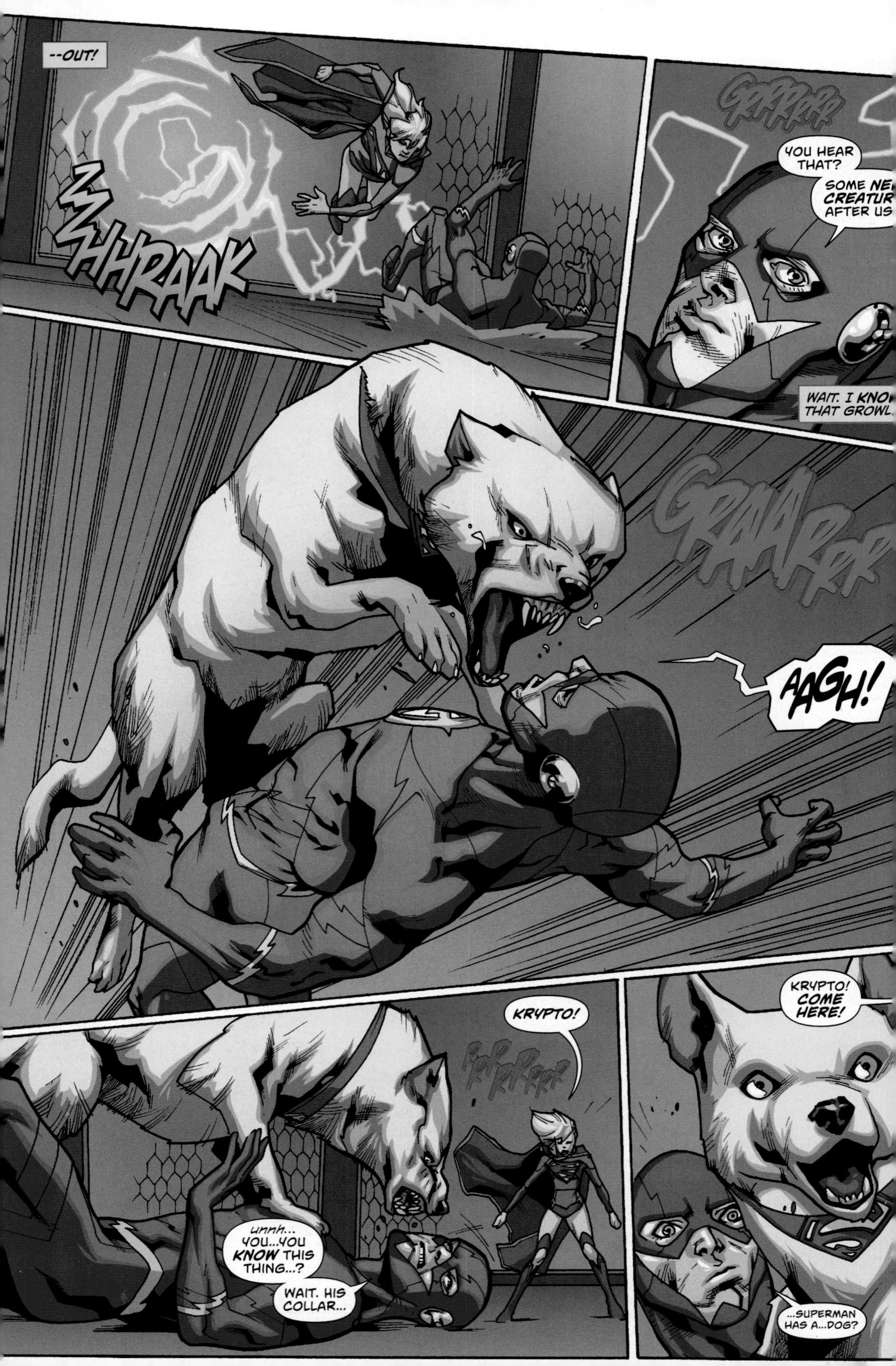
--OUT!
ZZZHHRAAK
GRRRRR
YOU HEAR THAT?
SOME NE
CREATUR
AFTER US
WAIT. I KNO
THAT GROWL.
GRAARRR
AAGH!
RRRRRRR
KRYPTO!
unnh... YOU...YOU KNOW THIS THING...?
WAIT. HIS COLLAR...
KRYPTO! COME HERE!
...SUPERMAN HAS A...DOG?

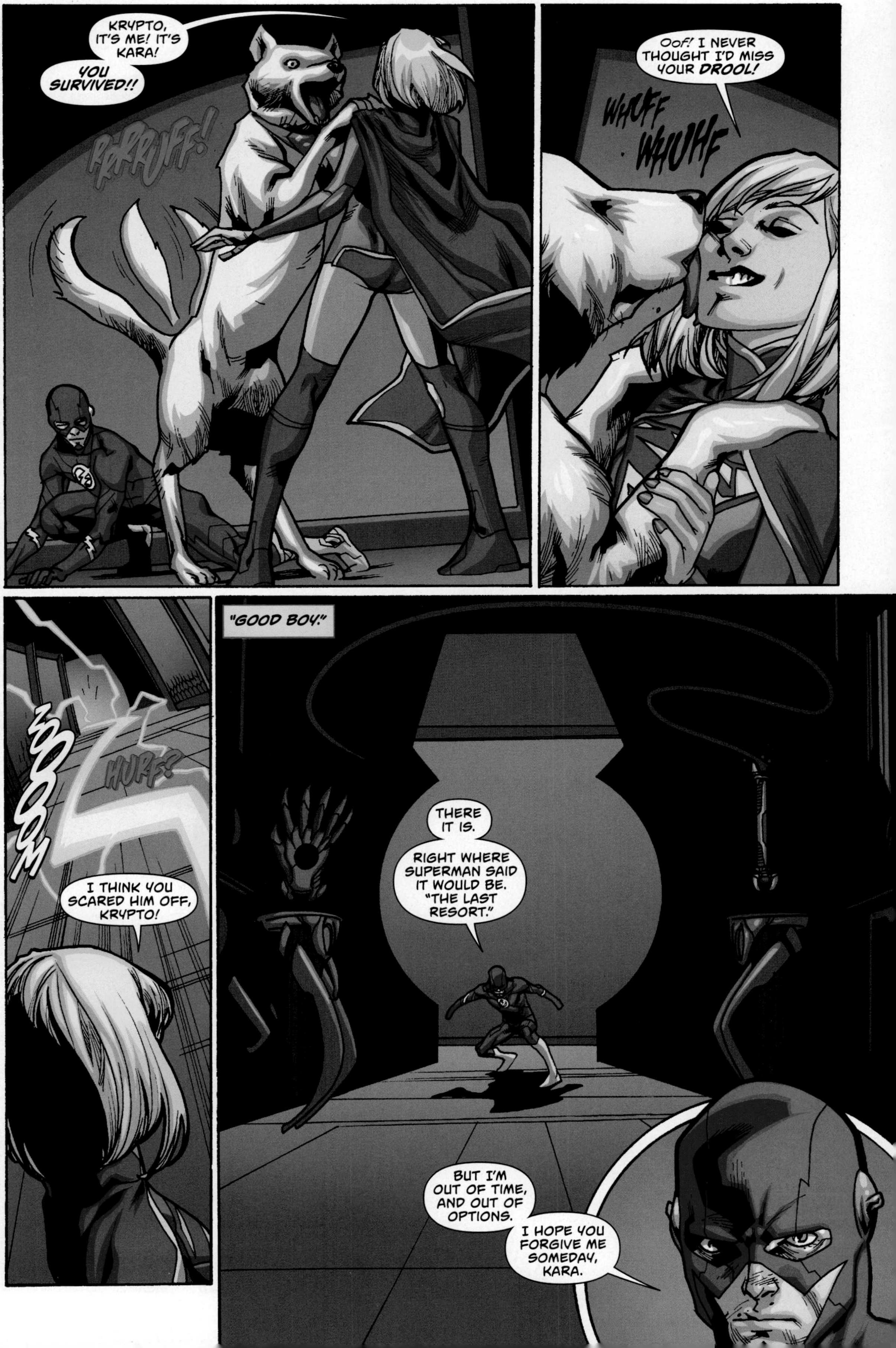
KRYPTO, IT'S ME! IT'S KARA!
YOU SURVIVED!!
RRRROWFF!
Oof! I NEVER THOUGHT I'D MISS YOUR DROOL!
WHUFF WHUHF
ZOOOOM
HURF?
I THINK YOU SCARED HIM OFF, KRYPTO!
"GOOD BOY."
THERE IT IS.
RIGHT WHERE SUPERMAN SAID IT WOULD BE. "THE LAST RESORT."
BUT I'M OUT OF TIME, AND OUT OF OPTIONS.
I HOPE YOU FORGIVE ME SOMEDAY, KARA.

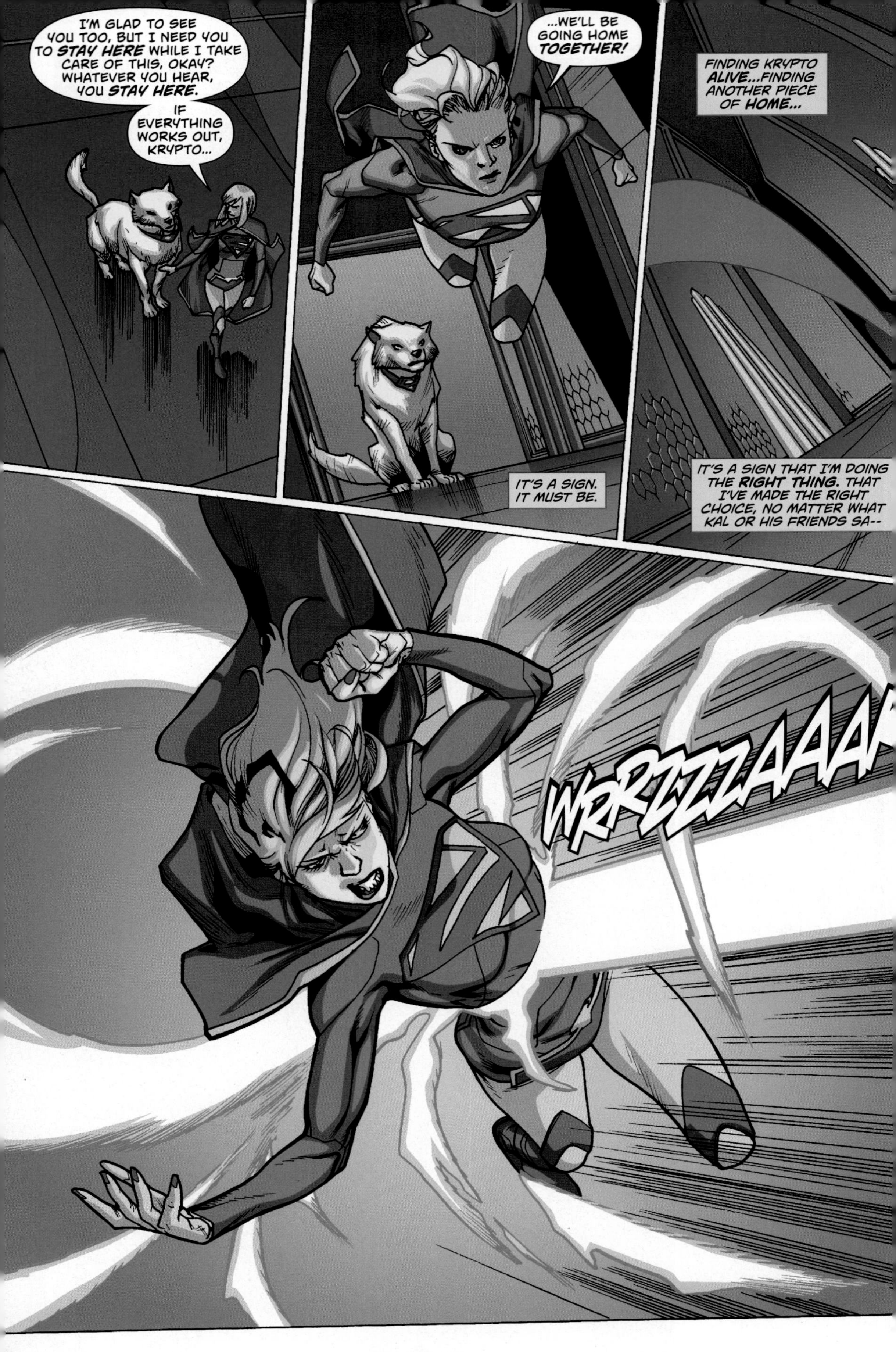
I'M GLAD TO SEE YOU TOO, BUT I NEED YOU TO STAY HERE WHILE I TAKE CARE OF THIS, OKAY? WHATEVER YOU HEAR, YOU STAY HERE.
IF EVERYTHING WORKS OUT, KRYPTO...
...WE'LL BE GOING HOME TOGETHER!
FINDING KRYPTO ALIVE...FINDING ANOTHER PIECE OF HOME...
IT'S A SIGN. IT MUST BE.
IT'S A SIGN THAT I'M DOING THE RIGHT THING. THAT I'VE MADE THE RIGHT CHOICE, NO MATTER WHAT KAL OR HIS FRIENDS SA--
WRRZZZAAA

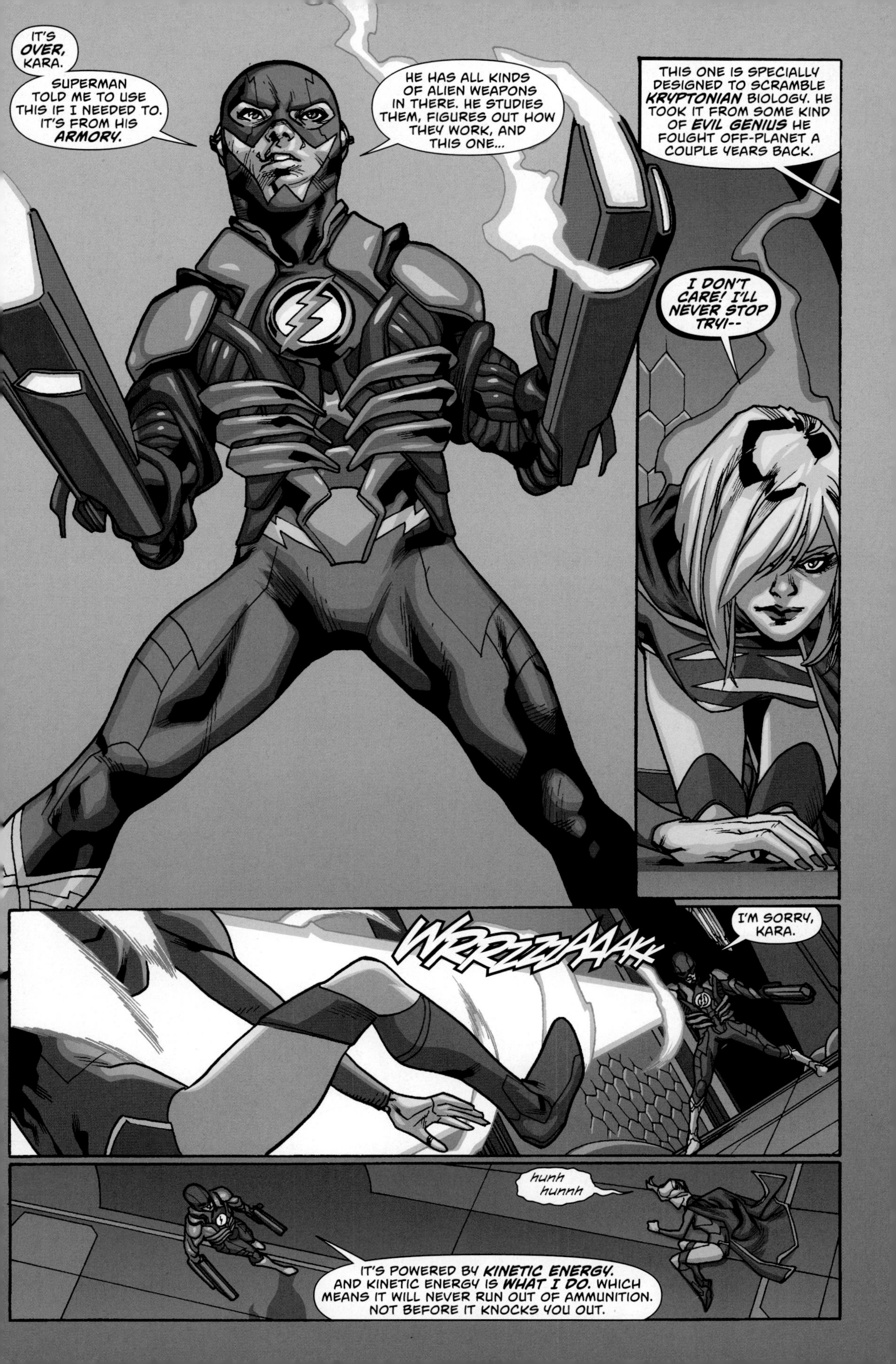

IT'S OVER, KARA.
SUPERMAN TOLD ME TO USE THIS IF I NEEDED TO. IT'S FROM HIS ARMORY.
HE HAS ALL KINDS OF ALIEN WEAPONS IN THERE. HE STUDIES THEM, FIGURES OUT HOW THEY WORK, AND THIS ONE...
THIS ONE IS SPECIALLY DESIGNED TO SCRAMBLE KRYPTONIAN BIOLOGY. HE TOOK IT FROM SOME KIND OF EVIL GENIUS HE FOUGHT OFF-PLANET A COUPLE YEARS BACK.
I DON'T CARE! I'LL NEVER STOP TRYI--
WRRZZZAAAKK
I'M SORRY, KARA.
hunh hunnh
IT'S POWERED BY KINETIC ENERGY. AND KINETIC ENERGY IS WHAT I DO. WHICH MEANS IT WILL NEVER RUN OUT OF AMMUNITION. NOT BEFORE IT KNOCKS YOU OUT.

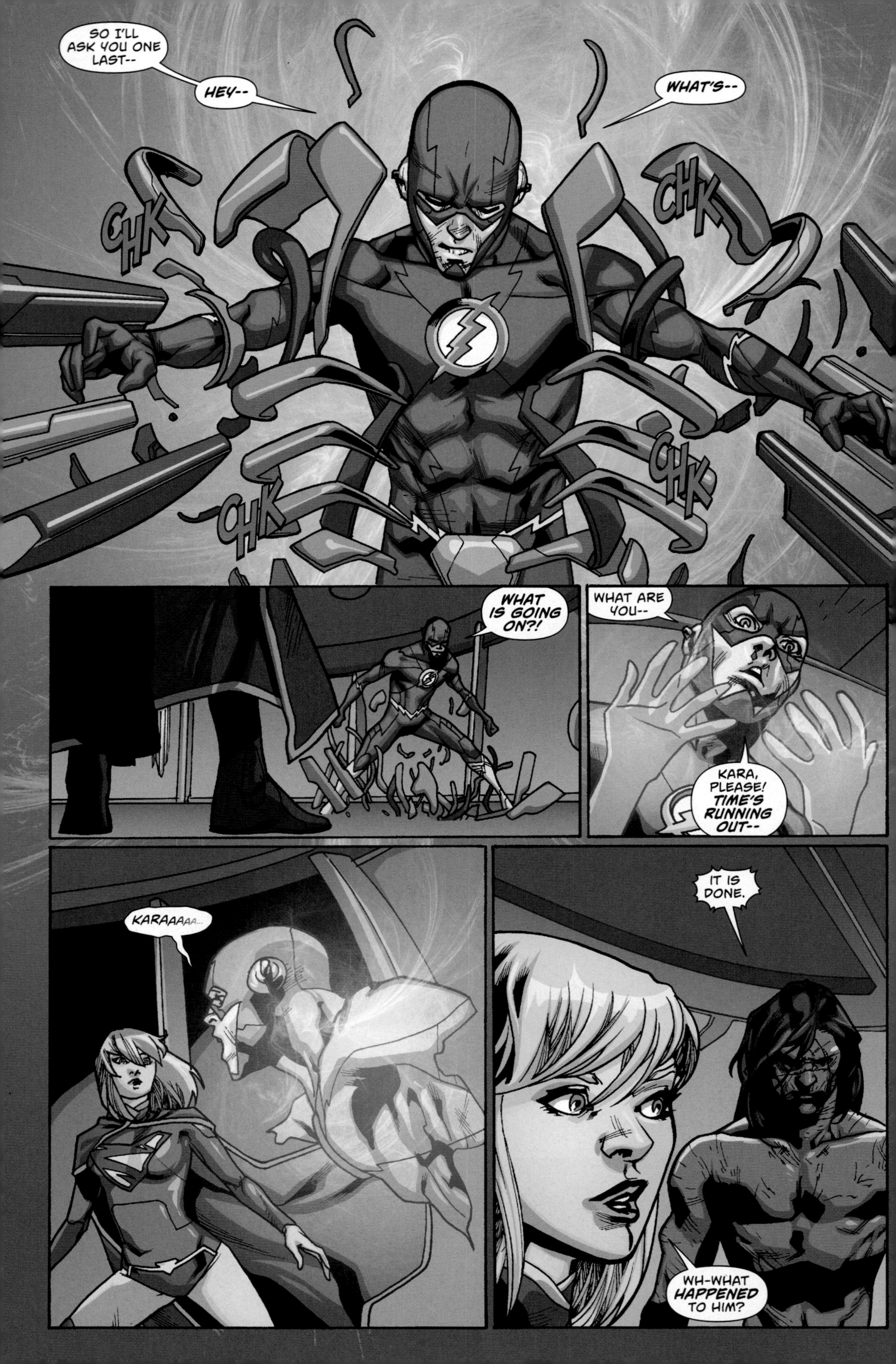
SO I'LL ASK YOU ONE LAST--
HEY--
WHAT'S--
CHK
CHK
CHK
CHK
WHAT IS GOING ON?!
WHAT ARE YOU--
KARA, PLEASE! TIME'S RUNNING OUT--
KARAAAAA...
IT IS DONE.
WH-WHAT HAPPENED TO HIM?

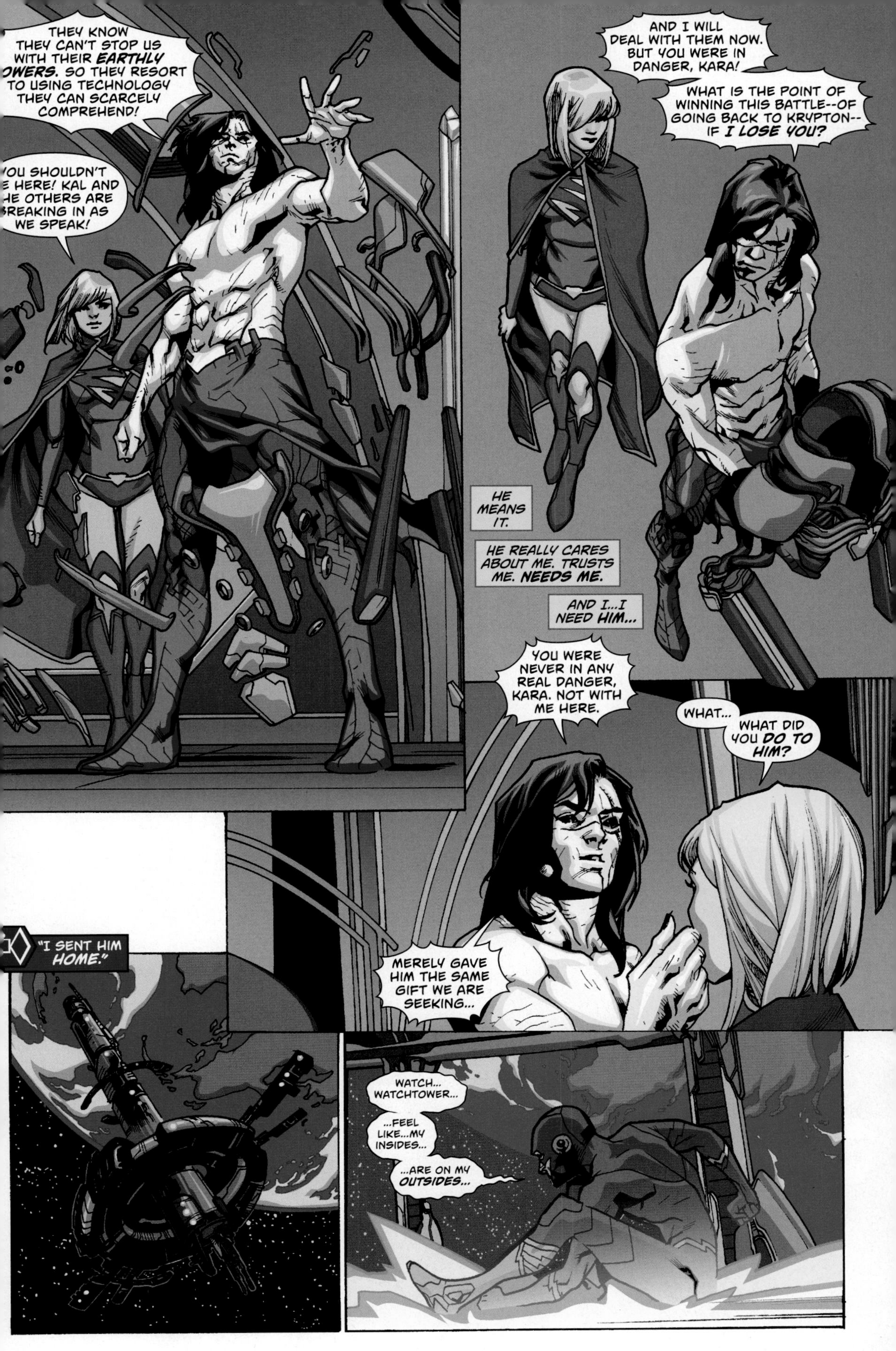
THEY KNOW THEY CAN'T STOP US WITH THEIR EARTHLY OWERS. SO THEY RESORT TO USING TECHNOLOGY THEY CAN SCARCELY COMPREHEND!
OU SHOULDN'T E HERE! KAL AND HE OTHERS ARE REAKING IN AS WE SPEAK!
AND I WILL DEAL WITH THEM NOW. BUT YOU WERE IN DANGER, KARA!
WHAT IS THE POINT OF WINNING THIS BATTLE--OF GOING BACK TO KRYPTON--IF I LOSE YOU?
HE MEANS IT.
HE REALLY CARES ABOUT ME. TRUSTS ME. NEEDS ME.
AND I...I NEED HIM...
YOU WERE NEVER IN ANY REAL DANGER, KARA. NOT WITH ME HERE.
WHAT...
WHAT DID YOU DO TO HIM?
"I SENT HIM HOME."
MERELY GAVE HIM THE SAME GIFT WE ARE SEEKING...
WATCH... WATCHTOWER...
...FEEL LIKE...MY INSIDES...
...ARE ON MY OUTSIDES...

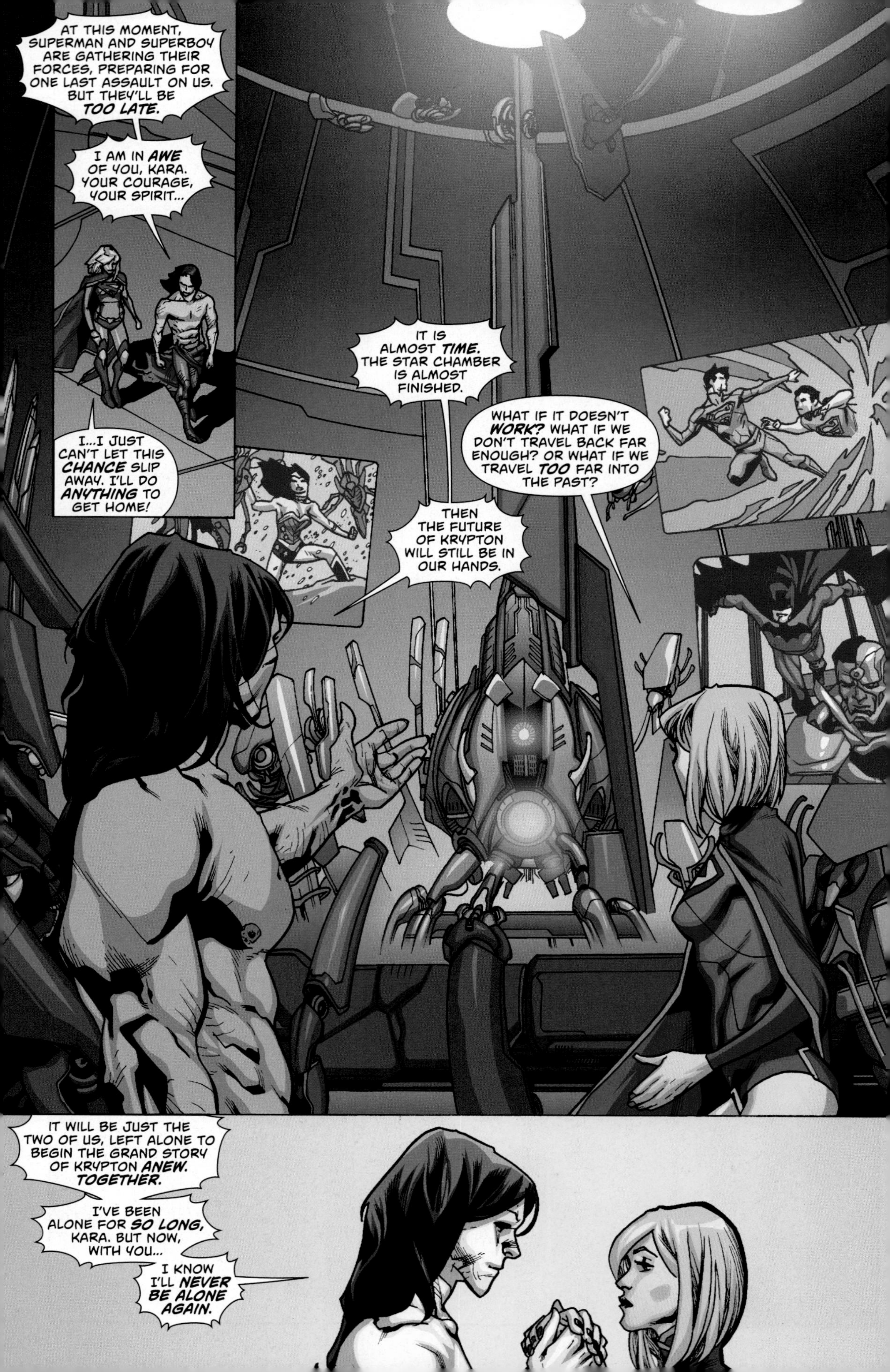

AT THIS MOMENT, SUPERMAN AND SUPERBOY ARE GATHERING THEIR FORCES, PREPARING FOR ONE LAST ASSAULT ON US. BUT THEY'LL BE TOO LATE.
I AM IN AWE OF YOU, KARA. YOUR COURAGE, YOUR SPIRIT...
I...I JUST CAN'T LET THIS CHANCE SLIP AWAY. I'LL DO ANYTHING TO GET HOME!
IT IS ALMOST TIME. THE STAR CHAMBER IS ALMOST FINISHED.
WHAT IF IT DOESN'T WORK? WHAT IF WE DON'T TRAVEL BACK FAR ENOUGH? OR WHAT IF WE TRAVEL TOO FAR INTO THE PAST?
THEN THE FUTURE OF KRYPTON WILL STILL BE IN OUR HANDS.
IT WILL BE JUST THE TWO OF US, LEFT ALONE TO BEGIN THE GRAND STORY OF KRYPTON ANEW. TOGETHER.
I'VE BEEN ALONE FOR SO LONG, KARA. BUT NOW, WITH YOU...
I KNOW I'LL NEVER BE ALONE AGAIN.

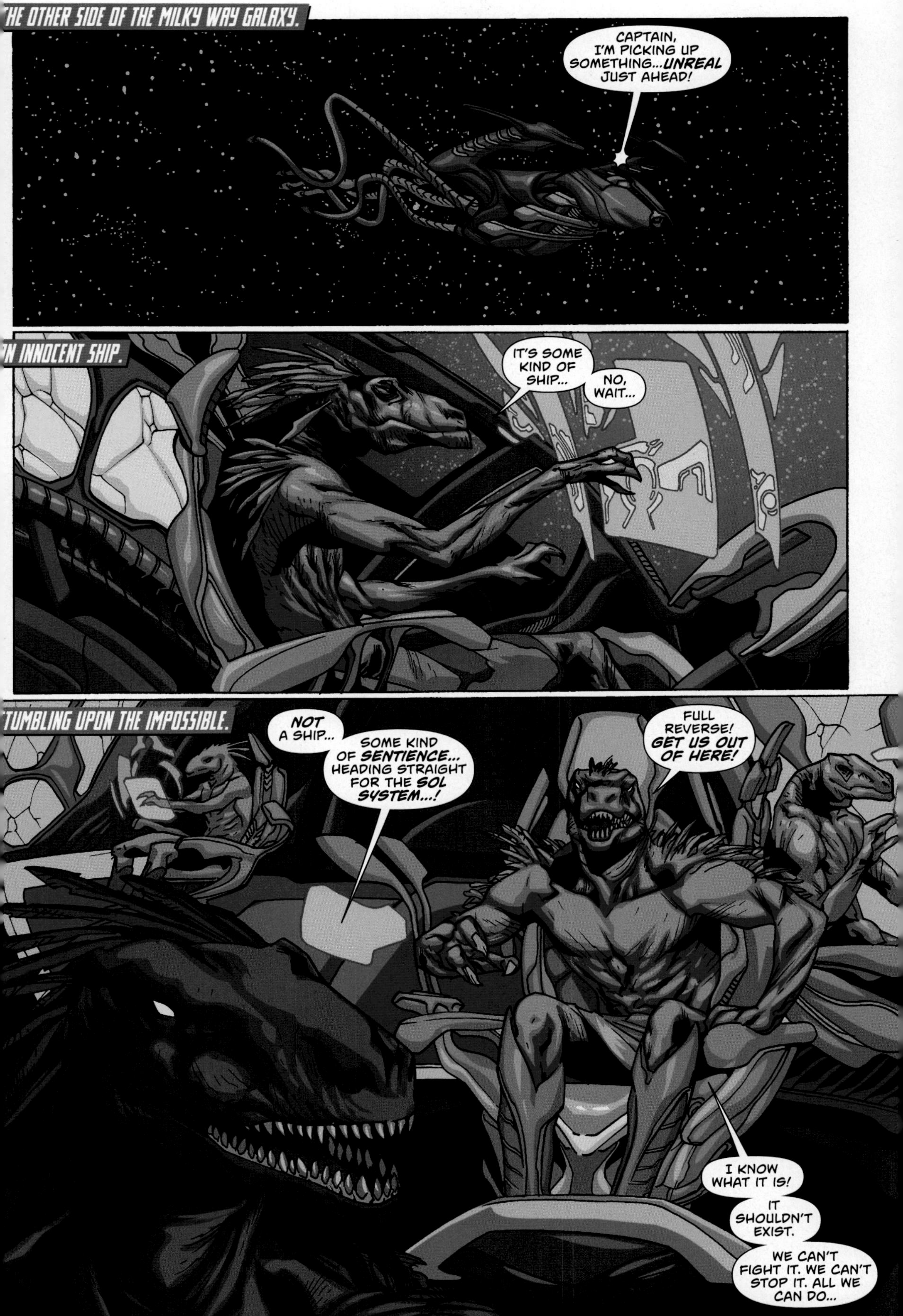
HE OTHER SIDE OF THE MILKY WAY GALAXY.
CAPTAIN, I'M PICKING UP SOMETHING...UNREAL JUST AHEAD!
N INNOCENT SHIP.
IT'S SOME KIND OF SHIP...
NO, WAIT...
TUMBLING UPON THE IMPOSSIBLE.
NOT A SHIP...
SOME KIND OF SENTIENCE... HEADING STRAIGHT FOR THE SOL SYSTEM...!
FULL REVERSE! GET US OUT OF HERE!
I KNOW WHAT IT IS!
IT SHOULDN'T EXIST.
WE CAN'T FIGHT IT. WE CAN'T STOP IT. ALL WE CAN DO...

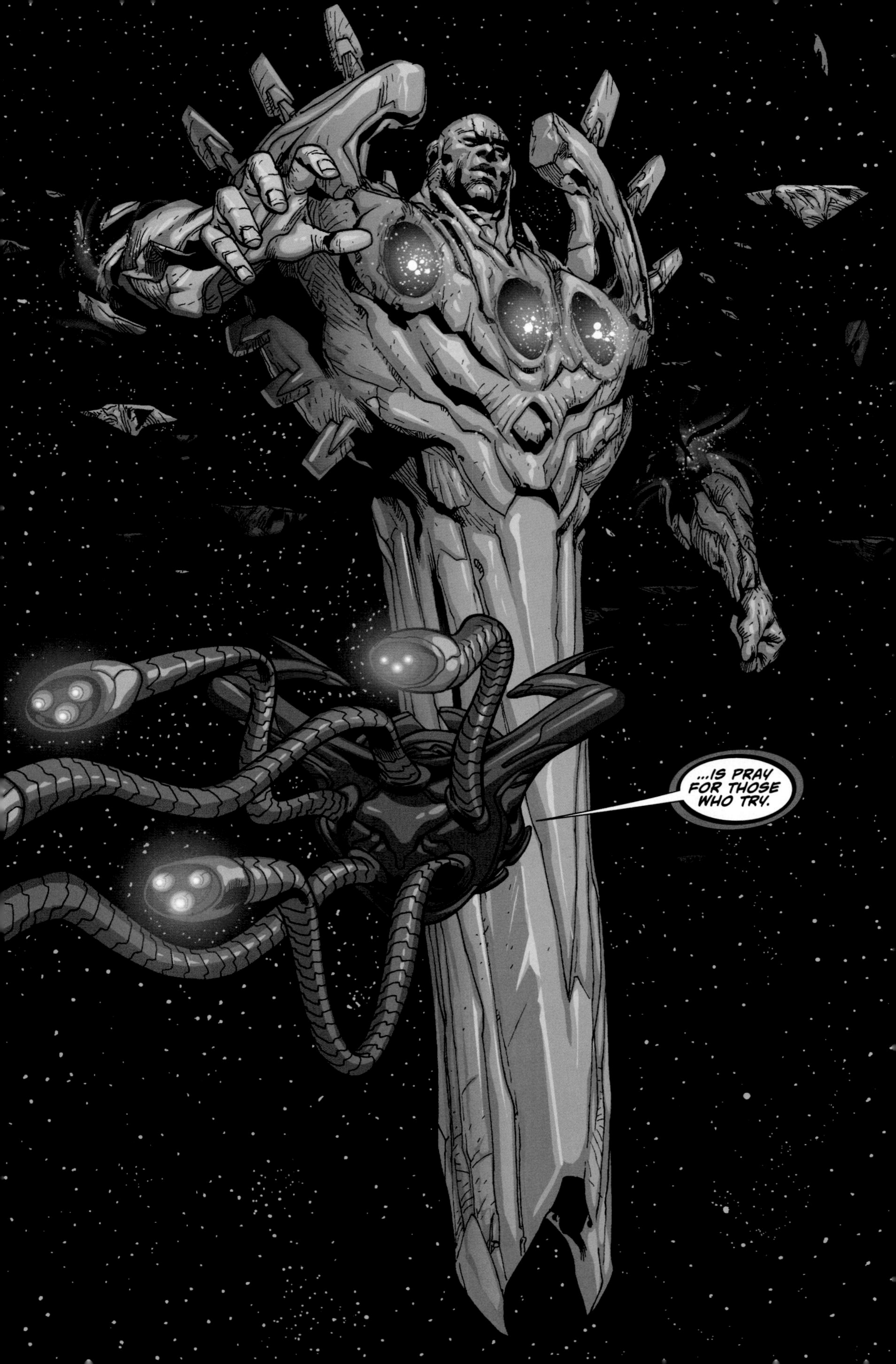
...IS PRAY FOR THOSE WHO TRY.

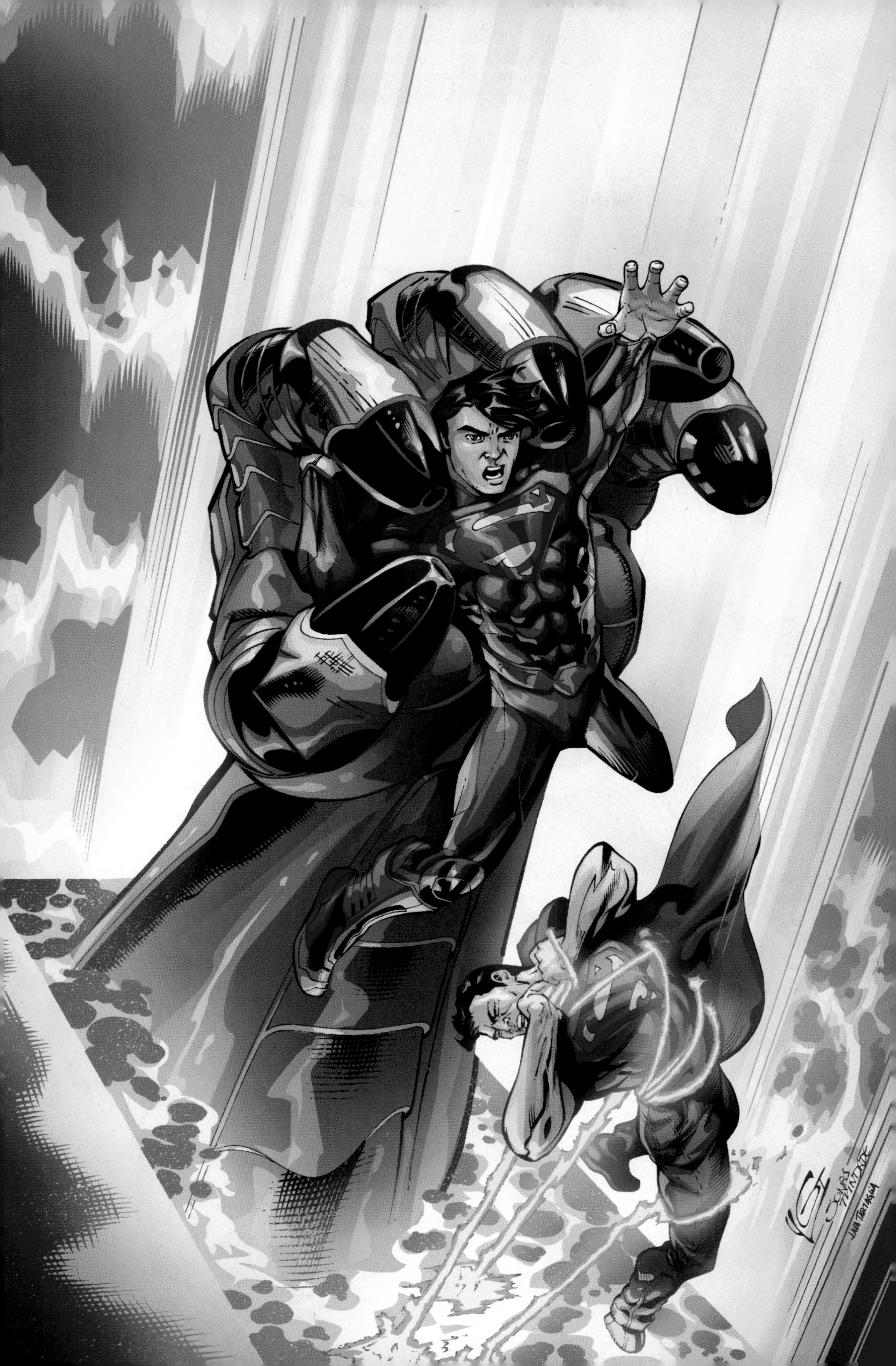

LOST HORIZONS

TOM DEFALCO writer YVEL GUICHET, IBAN COELLO, TOM DERENICK AND JULIUS GOPEZ pencillers
JONAS TRINDADE, ROB LEAN, TOM DERENICK, AND JULIUS GOPEZ Inkers cover art by YVEL GUICHET, JONAS TRINDADE & JAVA TARTAGLIA

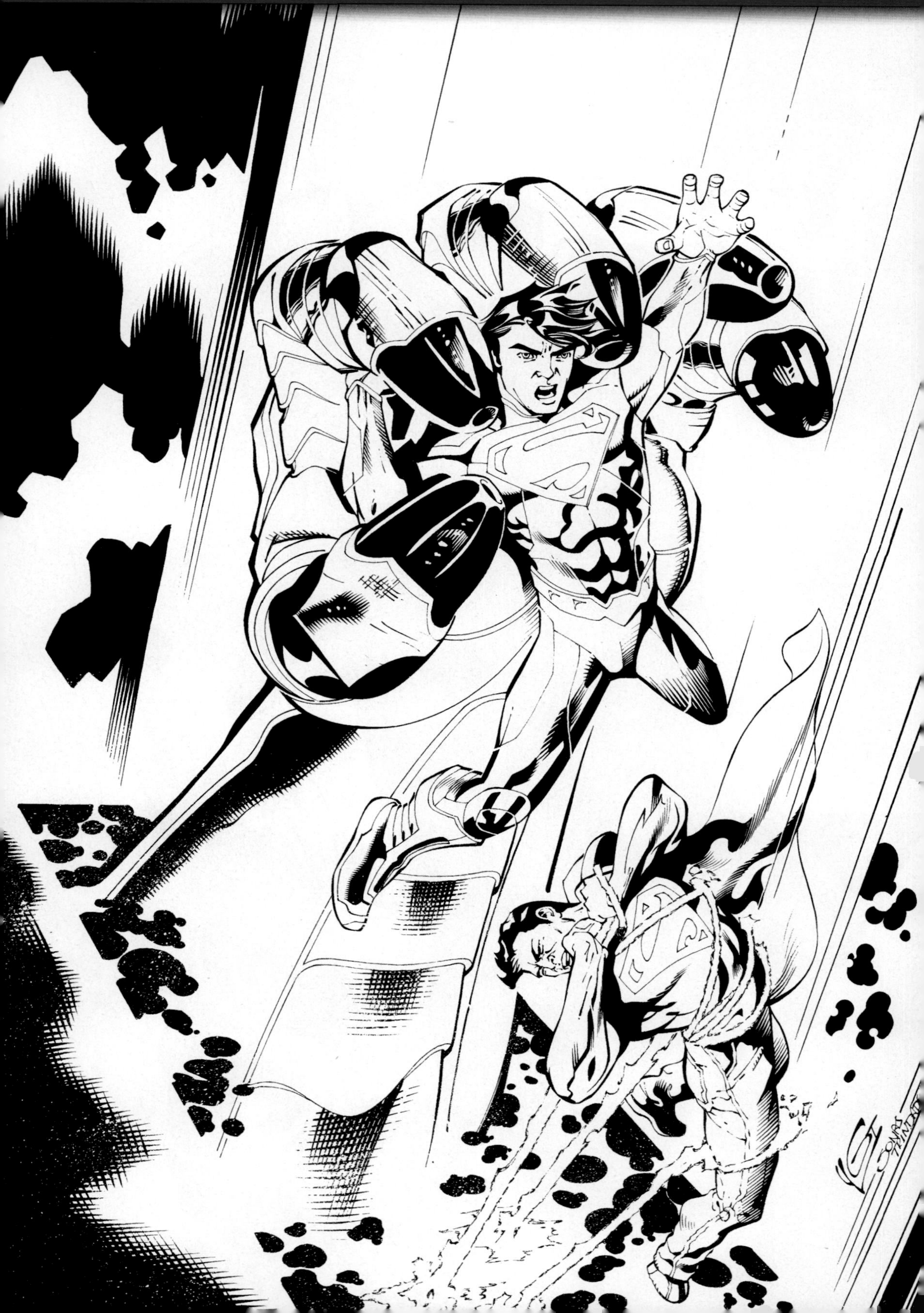

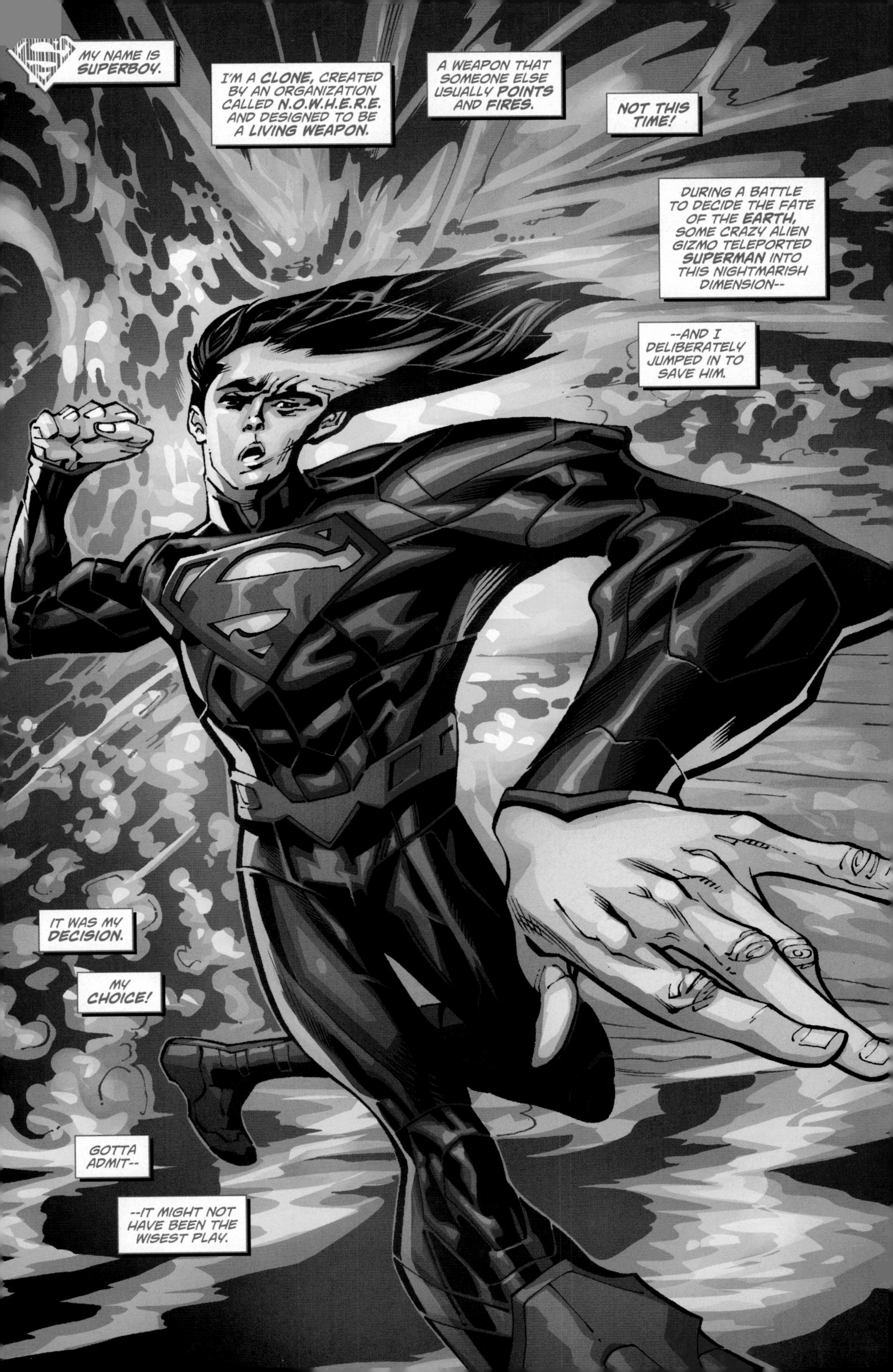
MY NAME IS SUPERBOY.
I'M A CLONE, CREATED BY AN ORGANIZATION CALLED N.O.W.H.E.R.E. AND DESIGNED TO BE A LIVING WEAPON.
A WEAPON THAT SOMEONE ELSE USUALLY POINTS AND FIRES.
NOT THIS TIME!
DURING A BATTLE TO DECIDE THE FATE OF THE EARTH, SOME CRAZY ALIEN GIZMO TELEPORTED SUPERMAN INTO THIS NIGHTMARISH DIMENSION--
--AND I DELIBERATELY JUMPED IN TO SAVE HIM.
IT WAS MY DECISION.
MY CHOICE!
GOTTA ADMIT--
--IT MIGHT NOT HAVE BEEN THE WISEST PLAY.

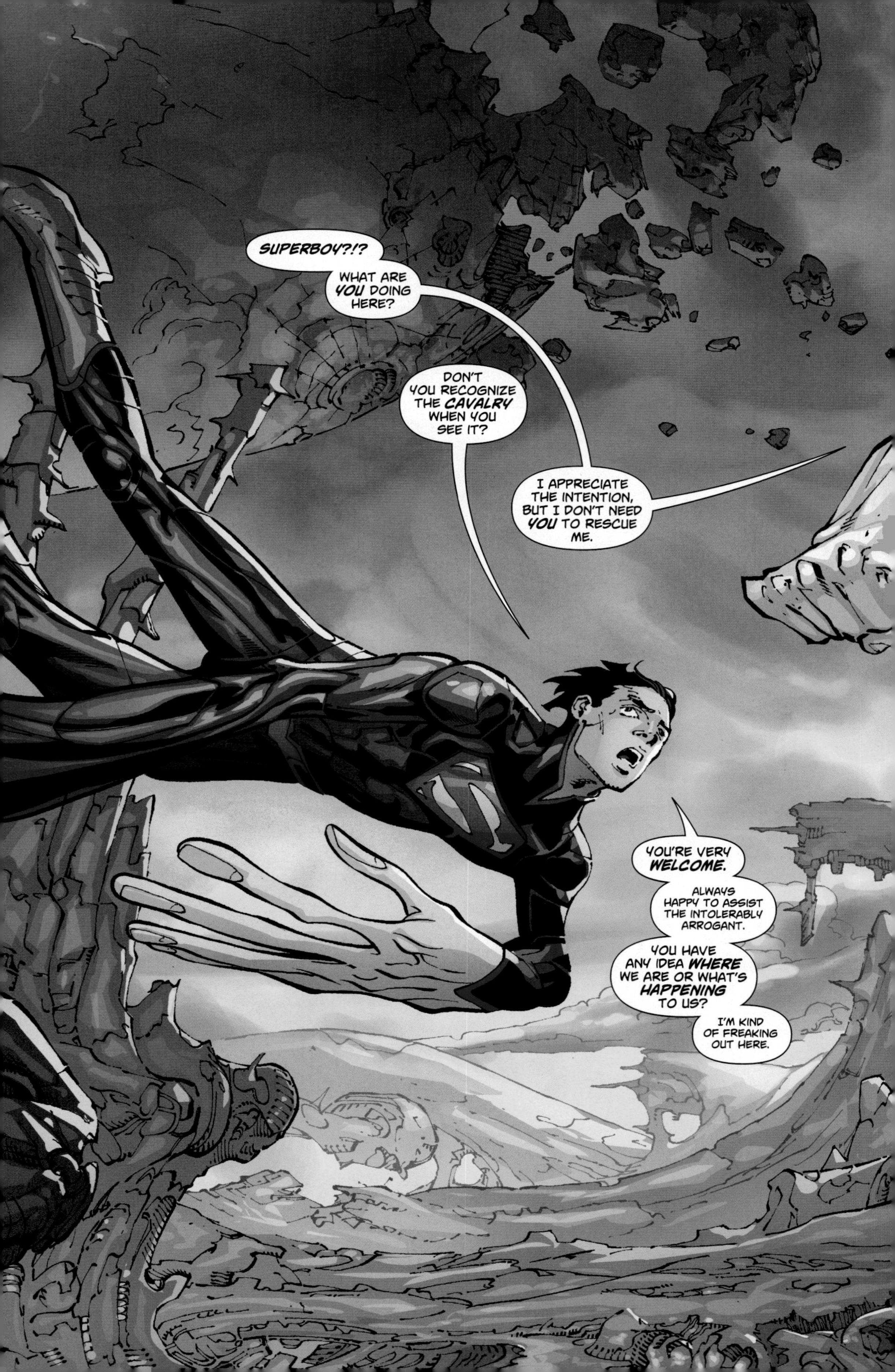
SUPERBOY?!?
WHAT ARE YOU DOING HERE?
DON'T YOU RECOGNIZE THE CAVALRY WHEN YOU SEE IT?
I APPRECIATE THE INTENTION, BUT I DON'T NEED YOU TO RESCUE ME.
YOU'RE VERY WELCOME.
ALWAYS HAPPY TO ASSIST THE INTOLERABLY ARROGANT.
YOU HAVE ANY IDEA WHERE WE ARE OR WHAT'S HAPPENING TO US?
I'M KIND OF FREAKING OUT HERE.

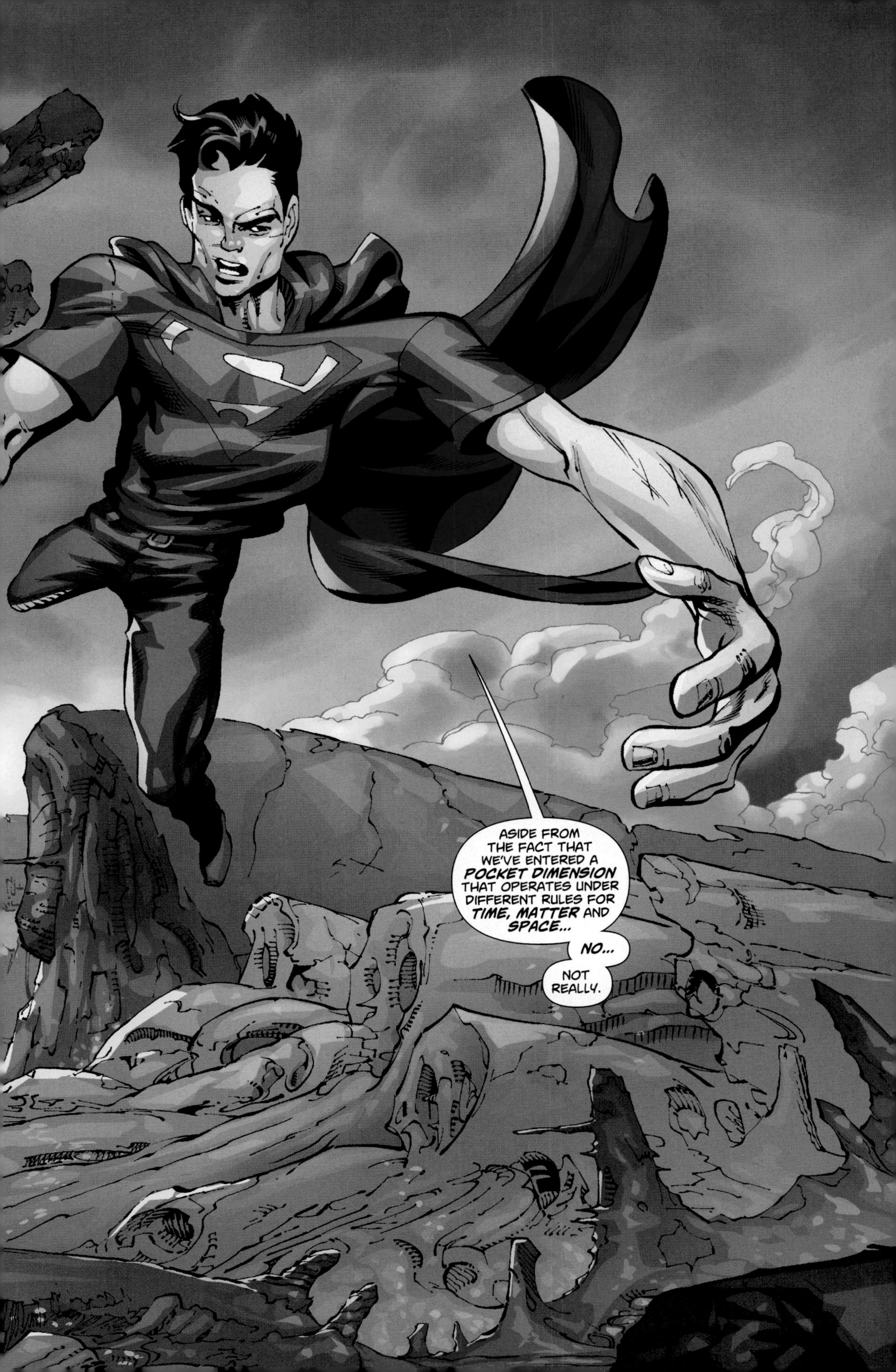
ASIDE FROM THE FACT THAT WE'VE ENTERED A *POCKET DIMENSION* THAT OPERATES UNDER DIFFERENT RULES FOR *TIME, MATTER* AND *SPACE...*
NO...
NOT REALLY.

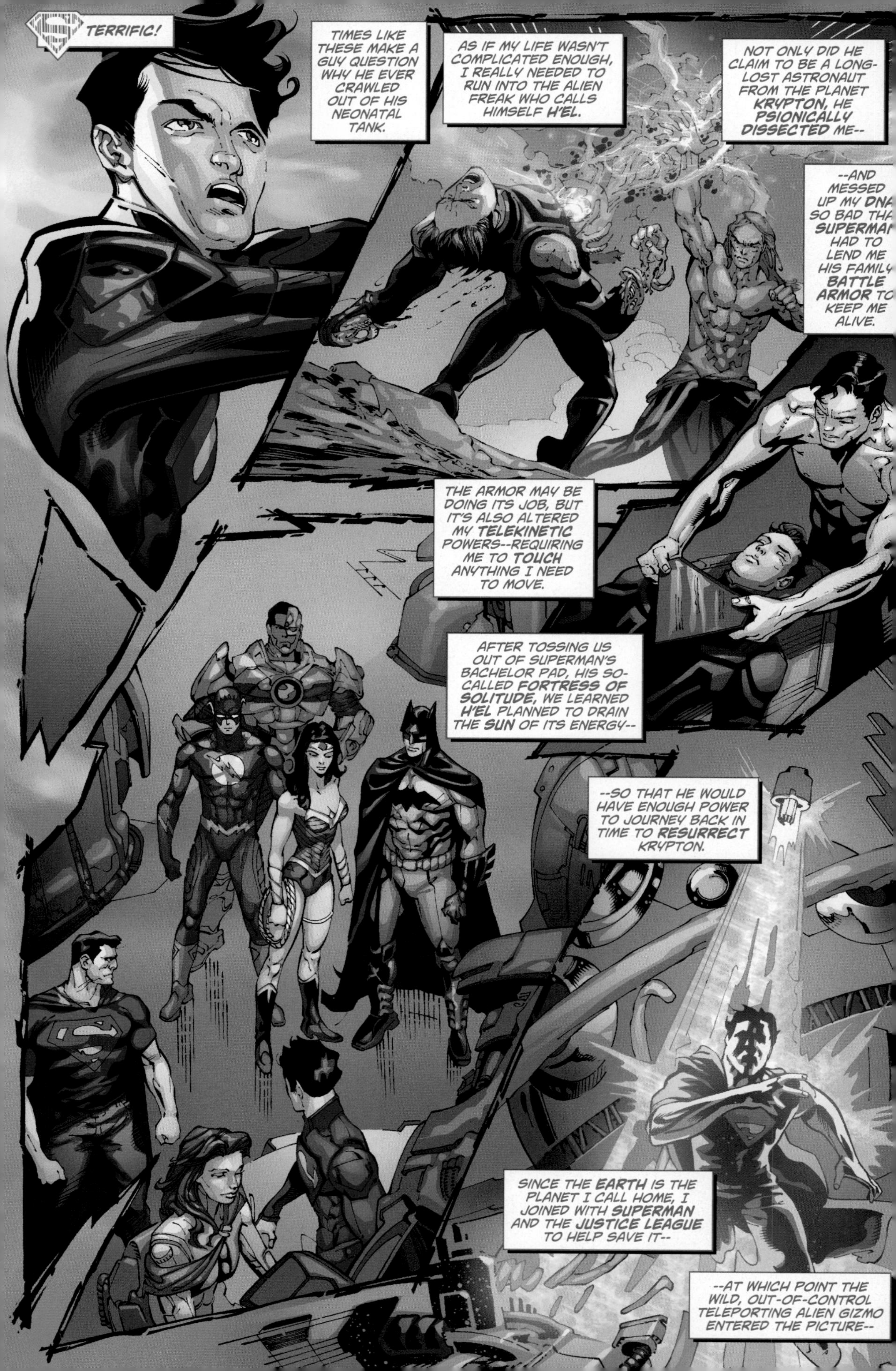
TERRIFIC!
TIMES LIKE THESE MAKE A GUY QUESTION WHY HE EVER CRAWLED OUT OF HIS NEONATAL TANK.
AS IF MY LIFE WASN'T COMPLICATED ENOUGH, I REALLY NEEDED TO RUN INTO THE ALIEN FREAK WHO CALLS HIMSELF H'EL.
NOT ONLY DID HE CLAIM TO BE A LONG-LOST ASTRONAUT FROM THE PLANET KRYPTON, HE PSIONICALLY DISSECTED ME--
--AND MESSED UP MY DNA SO BAD THAT SUPERMAN HAD TO LEND ME HIS FAMILY BATTLE ARMOR TO KEEP ME ALIVE.
THE ARMOR MAY BE DOING ITS JOB, BUT IT'S ALSO ALTERED MY TELEKINETIC POWERS--REQUIRING ME TO TOUCH ANYTHING I NEED TO MOVE.
AFTER TOSSING US OUT OF SUPERMAN'S BACHELOR PAD, HIS SO-CALLED FORTRESS OF SOLITUDE, WE LEARNED H'EL PLANNED TO DRAIN THE SUN OF ITS ENERGY--
--SO THAT HE WOULD HAVE ENOUGH POWER TO JOURNEY BACK IN TIME TO RESURRECT KRYPTON.
SINCE THE EARTH IS THE PLANET I CALL HOME, I JOINED WITH SUPERMAN AND THE JUSTICE LEAGUE TO HELP SAVE IT--
--AT WHICH POINT THE WILD, OUT-OF-CONTROL TELEPORTING ALIEN GIZMO ENTERED THE PICTURE--

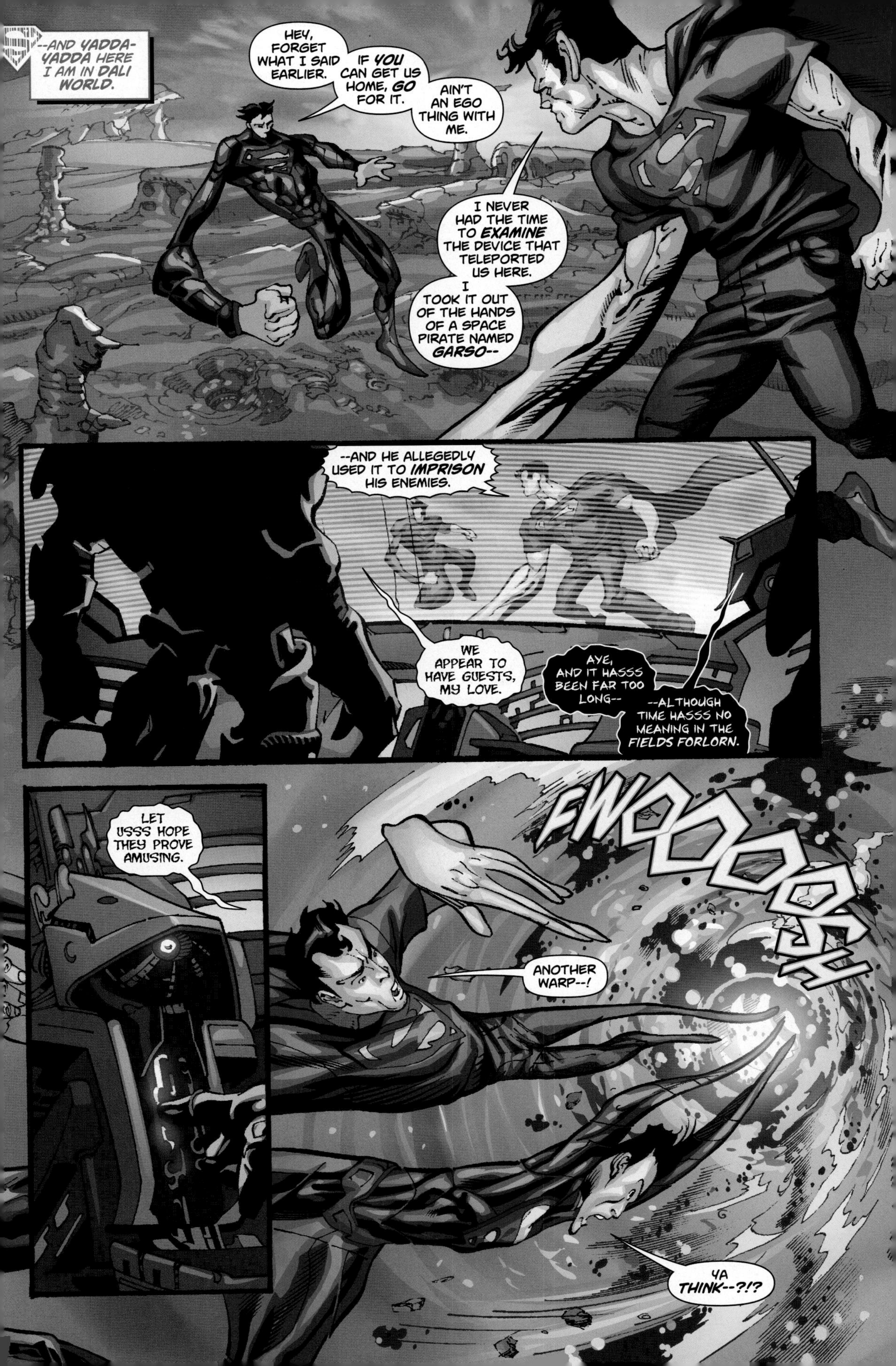

--AND YADDA-YADDA HERE I AM IN DALI WORLD.
HEY, FORGET WHAT I SAID EARLIER.
IF YOU CAN GET US HOME, GO FOR IT.
AIN'T AN EGO THING WITH ME.
I NEVER HAD THE TIME TO EXAMINE THE DEVICE THAT TELEPORTED US HERE.
I TOOK IT OUT OF THE HANDS OF A SPACE PIRATE NAMED GARSO--
--AND HE ALLEGEDLY USED IT TO IMPRISON HIS ENEMIES.
WE APPEAR TO HAVE GUESTS, MY LOVE.
AYE, AND IT HASSS BEEN FAR TOO LONG--
--ALTHOUGH TIME HASSS NO MEANING IN THE FIELDS FORLORN.
LET USSS HOPE THEY PROVE AMUSING.
FWOOOOOSH
ANOTHER WARP--!
YA THINK--?!?

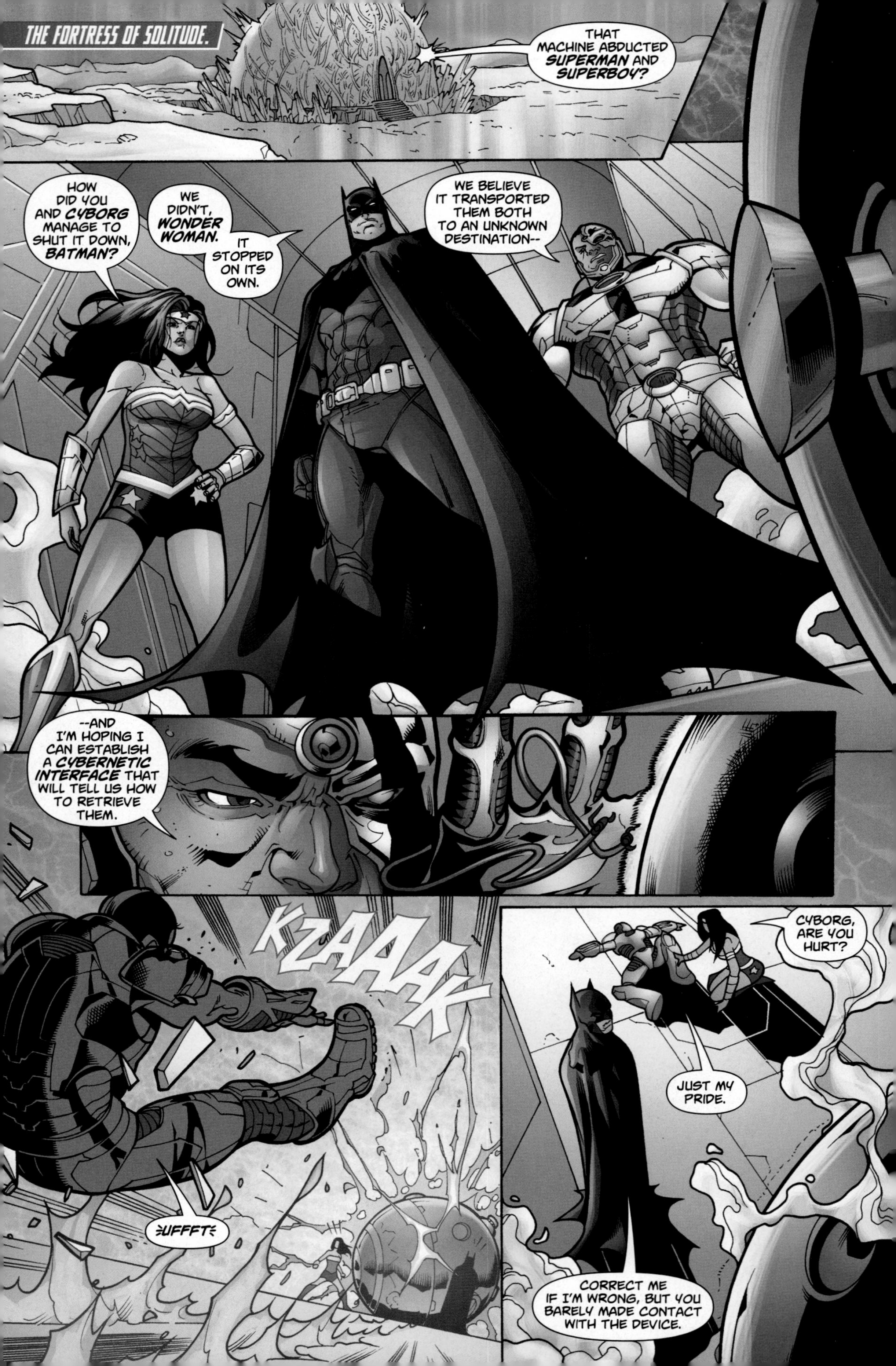
THE FORTRESS OF SOLITUDE.
THAT MACHINE ABDUCTED SUPERMAN AND SUPERBOY?
HOW DID YOU AND CYBORG MANAGE TO SHUT IT DOWN, BATMAN?
WE DIDN'T, WONDER WOMAN.
IT STOPPED ON ITS OWN.
WE BELIEVE IT TRANSPORTED THEM BOTH TO AN UNKNOWN DESTINATION--
--AND I'M HOPING I CAN ESTABLISH A CYBERNETIC INTERFACE THAT WILL TELL US HOW TO RETRIEVE THEM.
KZAAAK
UFFFT
CYBORG, ARE YOU HURT?
JUST MY PRIDE.
CORRECT ME IF I'M WRONG, BUT YOU BARELY MADE CONTACT WITH THE DEVICE.

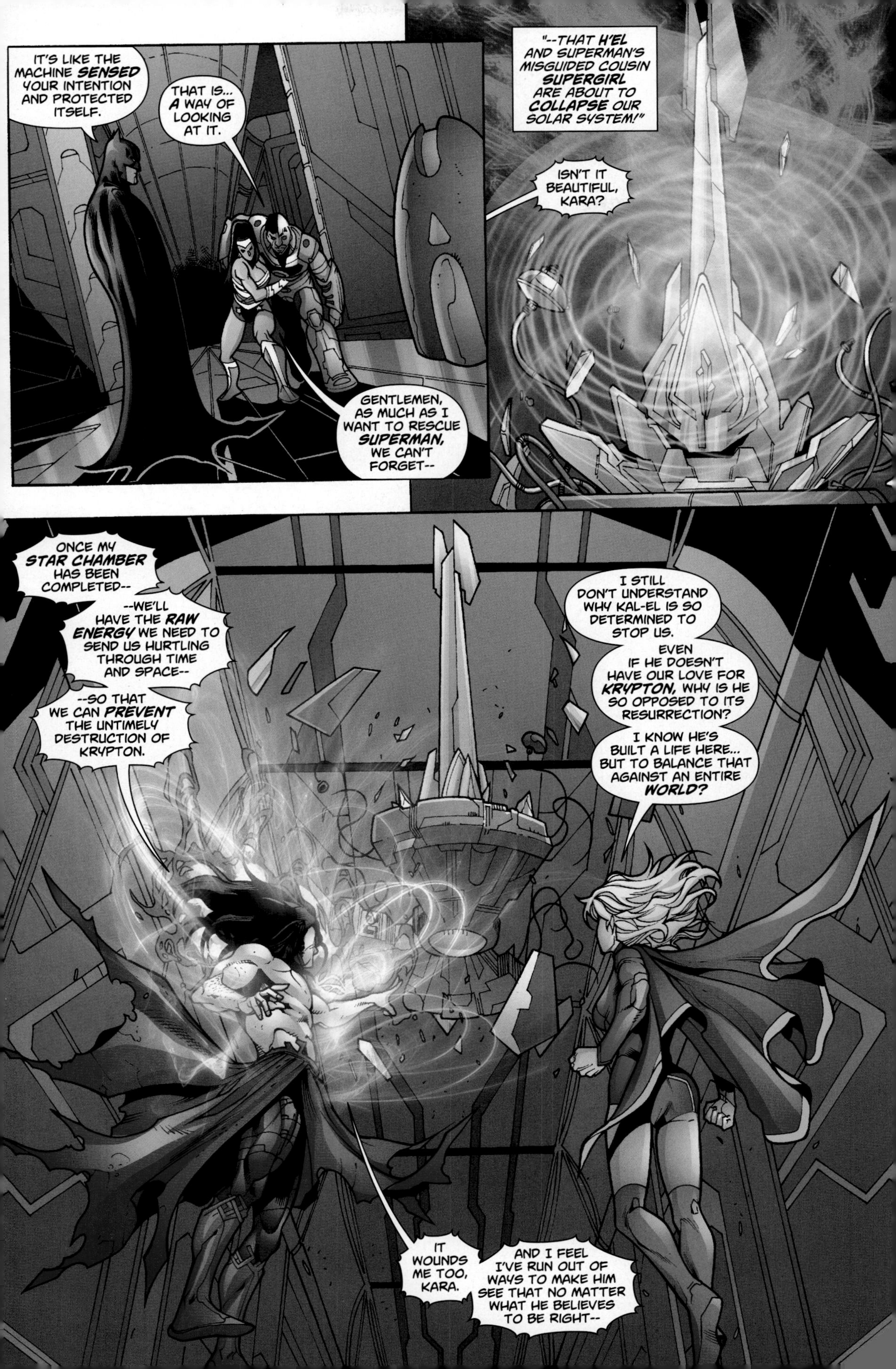
IT'S LIKE THE MACHINE SENSED YOUR INTENTION AND PROTECTED ITSELF.
THAT IS... A WAY OF LOOKING AT IT.
GENTLEMEN, AS MUCH AS I WANT TO RESCUE SUPERMAN, WE CAN'T FORGET--
"--THAT H'EL AND SUPERMAN'S MISGUIDED COUSIN SUPERGIRL ARE ABOUT TO COLLAPSE OUR SOLAR SYSTEM!"
ISN'T IT BEAUTIFUL, KARA?
ONCE MY STAR CHAMBER HAS BEEN COMPLETED--
--WE'LL HAVE THE RAW ENERGY WE NEED TO SEND US HURTLING THROUGH TIME AND SPACE--
--SO THAT WE CAN PREVENT THE UNTIMELY DESTRUCTION OF KRYPTON.
I STILL DON'T UNDERSTAND WHY KAL-EL IS SO DETERMINED TO STOP US.
EVEN IF HE DOESN'T HAVE OUR LOVE FOR KRYPTON, WHY IS HE SO OPPOSED TO ITS RESURRECTION?
I KNOW HE'S BUILT A LIFE HERE... BUT TO BALANCE THAT AGAINST AN ENTIRE WORLD?
IT WOUNDS ME TOO, KARA.
AND I FEEL I'VE RUN OUT OF WAYS TO MAKE HIM SEE THAT NO MATTER WHAT HE BELIEVES TO BE RIGHT--

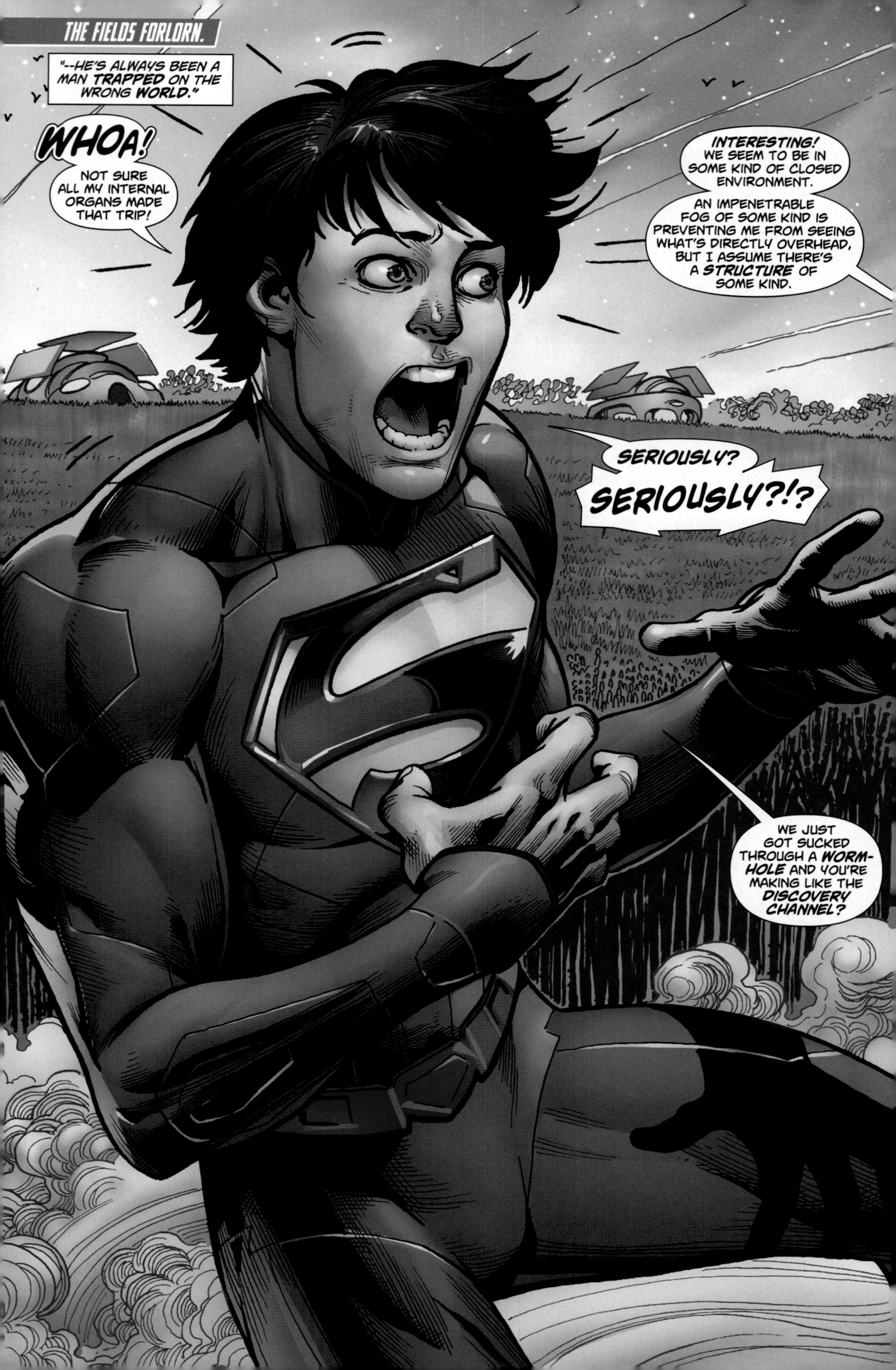
THE FIELDS FORLORN.
"--HE'S ALWAYS BEEN A MAN TRAPPED ON THE WRONG WORLD."
WHOA! NOT SURE ALL MY INTERNAL ORGANS MADE THAT TRIP!
INTERESTING! WE SEEM TO BE IN SOME KIND OF CLOSED ENVIRONMENT.
AN IMPENETRABLE FOG OF SOME KIND IS PREVENTING ME FROM SEEING WHAT'S DIRECTLY OVERHEAD, BUT I ASSUME THERE'S A STRUCTURE OF SOME KIND.
SERIOUSLY? SERIOUSLY?!?
WE JUST GOT SUCKED THROUGH A WORM-HOLE AND YOU'RE MAKING LIKE THE DISCOVERY CHANNEL?

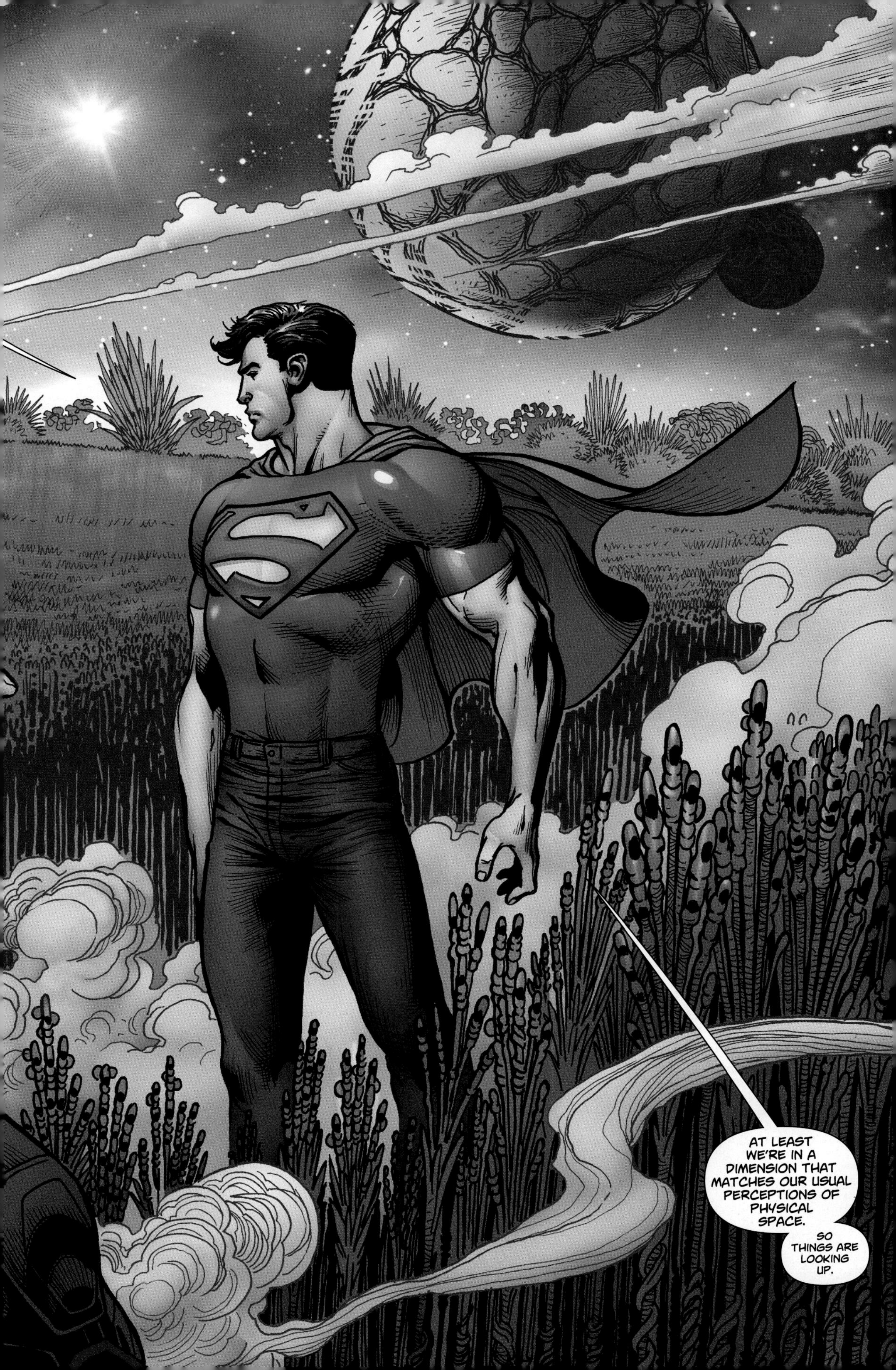
AT LEAST WE'RE IN A DIMENSION THAT MATCHES OUR USUAL PERCEPTIONS OF PHYSICAL SPACE.
SO THINGS ARE LOOKING UP.

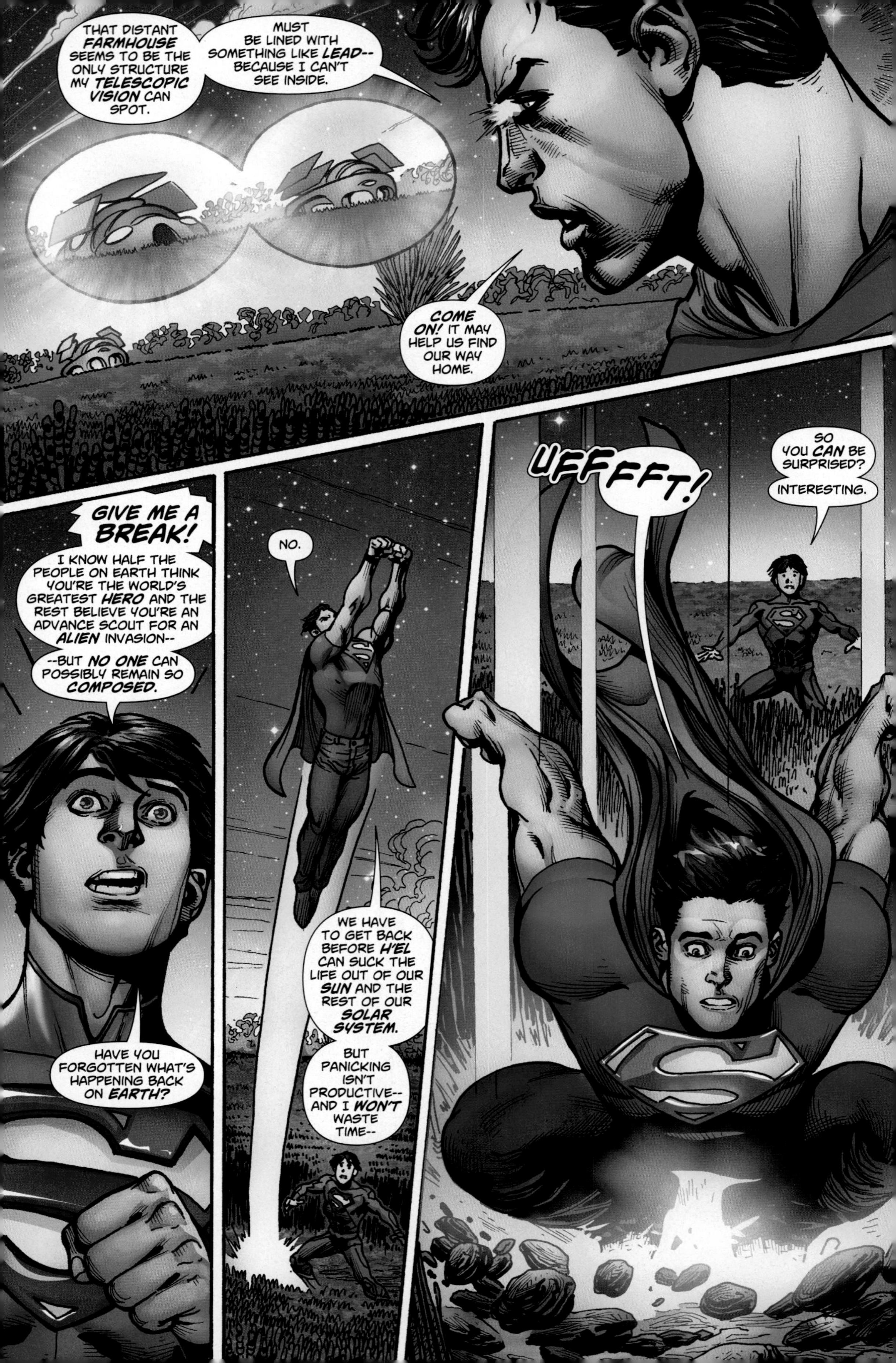
THAT DISTANT FARMHOUSE SEEMS TO BE THE ONLY STRUCTURE MY TELESCOPIC VISION CAN SPOT.
MUST BE LINED WITH SOMETHING LIKE LEAD-- BECAUSE I CAN'T SEE INSIDE.
COME ON! IT MAY HELP US FIND OUR WAY HOME.
GIVE ME A BREAK!
I KNOW HALF THE PEOPLE ON EARTH THINK YOU'RE THE WORLD'S GREATEST HERO AND THE REST BELIEVE YOU'RE AN ADVANCE SCOUT FOR AN ALIEN INVASION--
--BUT NO ONE CAN POSSIBLY REMAIN SO COMPOSED.
HAVE YOU FORGOTTEN WHAT'S HAPPENING BACK ON EARTH?
NO.
WE HAVE TO GET BACK BEFORE H'EL CAN SUCK THE LIFE OUT OF OUR SUN AND THE REST OF OUR SOLAR SYSTEM.
BUT PANICKING ISN'T PRODUCTIVE-- AND I WON'T WASTE TIME--
UFFFFT!
SO YOU CAN BE SURPRISED?
INTERESTING.

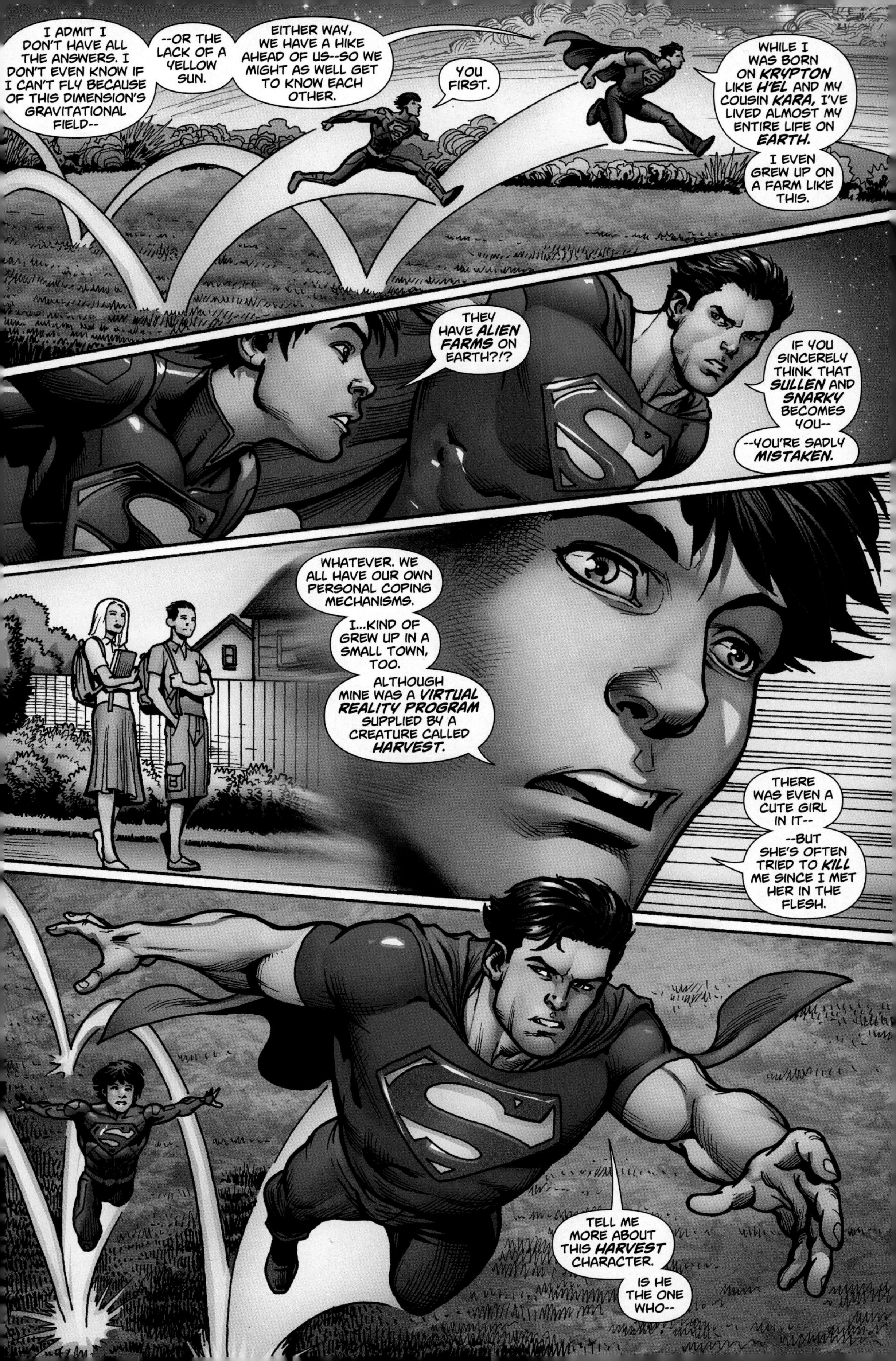
I ADMIT I DON'T HAVE ALL THE ANSWERS. I DON'T EVEN KNOW IF I CAN'T FLY BECAUSE OF THIS DIMENSION'S GRAVITATIONAL FIELD--
--OR THE LACK OF A YELLOW SUN.
EITHER WAY, WE HAVE A HIKE AHEAD OF US--SO WE MIGHT AS WELL GET TO KNOW EACH OTHER.
YOU FIRST.
WHILE I WAS BORN ON KRYPTON LIKE H'EL AND MY COUSIN KARA, I'VE LIVED ALMOST MY ENTIRE LIFE ON EARTH.
I EVEN GREW UP ON A FARM LIKE THIS.
THEY HAVE ALIEN FARMS ON EARTH?!?
IF YOU SINCERELY THINK THAT SULLEN AND SNARKY BECOMES YOU--
--YOU'RE SADLY MISTAKEN.
WHATEVER. WE ALL HAVE OUR OWN PERSONAL COPING MECHANISMS.
I...KIND OF GREW UP IN A SMALL TOWN, TOO.
ALTHOUGH MINE WAS A VIRTUAL REALITY PROGRAM SUPPLIED BY A CREATURE CALLED HARVEST.
THERE WAS EVEN A CUTE GIRL IN IT--
--BUT SHE'S OFTEN TRIED TO KILL ME SINCE I MET HER IN THE FLESH.
TELL ME MORE ABOUT THIS HARVEST CHARACTER.
IS HE THE ONE WHO--

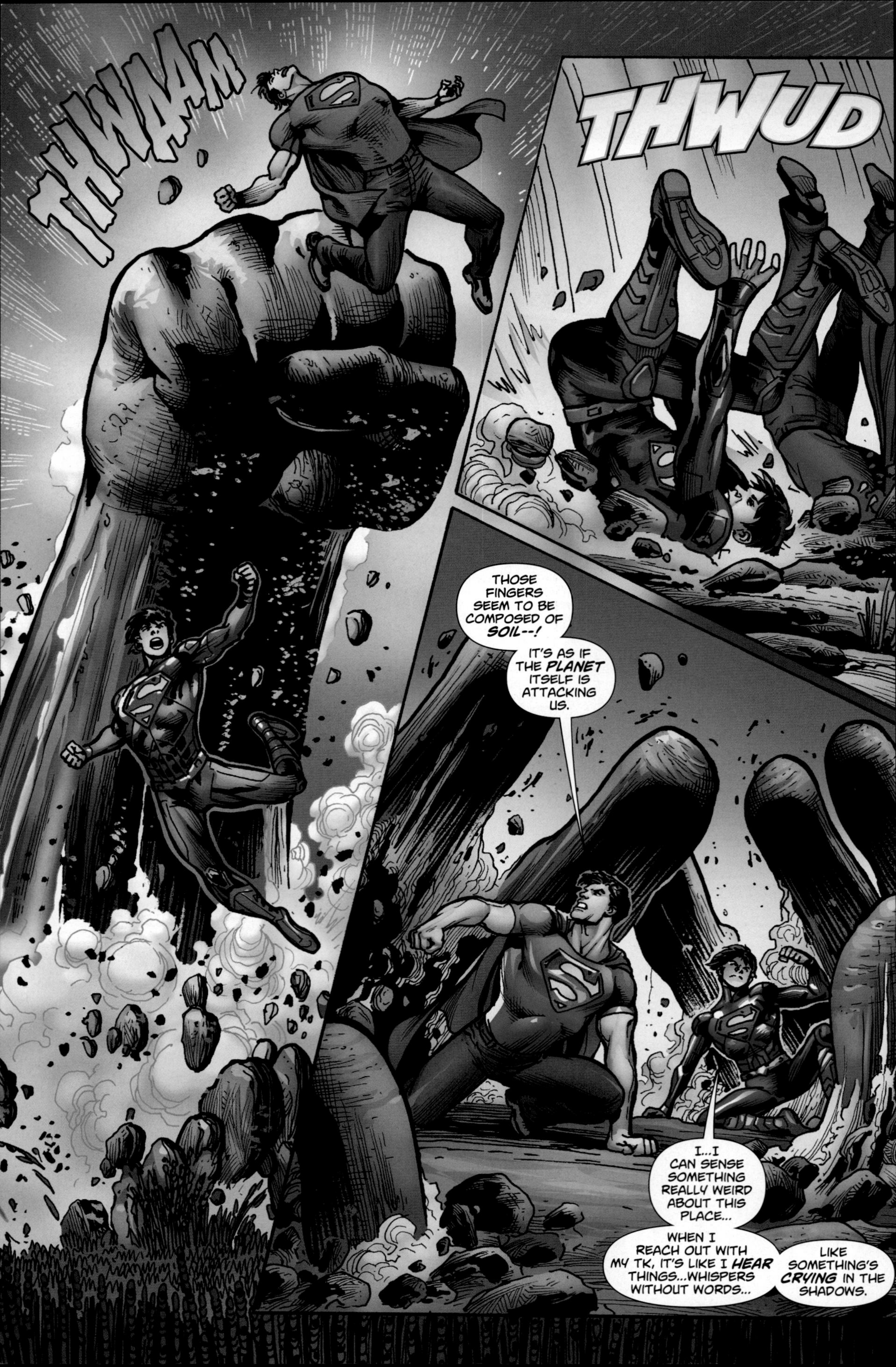
THWAM
THWUD
THOSE FINGERS SEEM TO BE COMPOSED OF SOIL--!
IT'S AS IF THE PLANET ITSELF IS ATTACKING US.
I...I CAN SENSE SOMETHING REALLY WEIRD ABOUT THIS PLACE...
WHEN I REACH OUT WITH MY TK, IT'S LIKE I HEAR THINGS...WHISPERS WITHOUT WORDS...
LIKE SOMETHING'S CRYING IN THE SHADOWS.

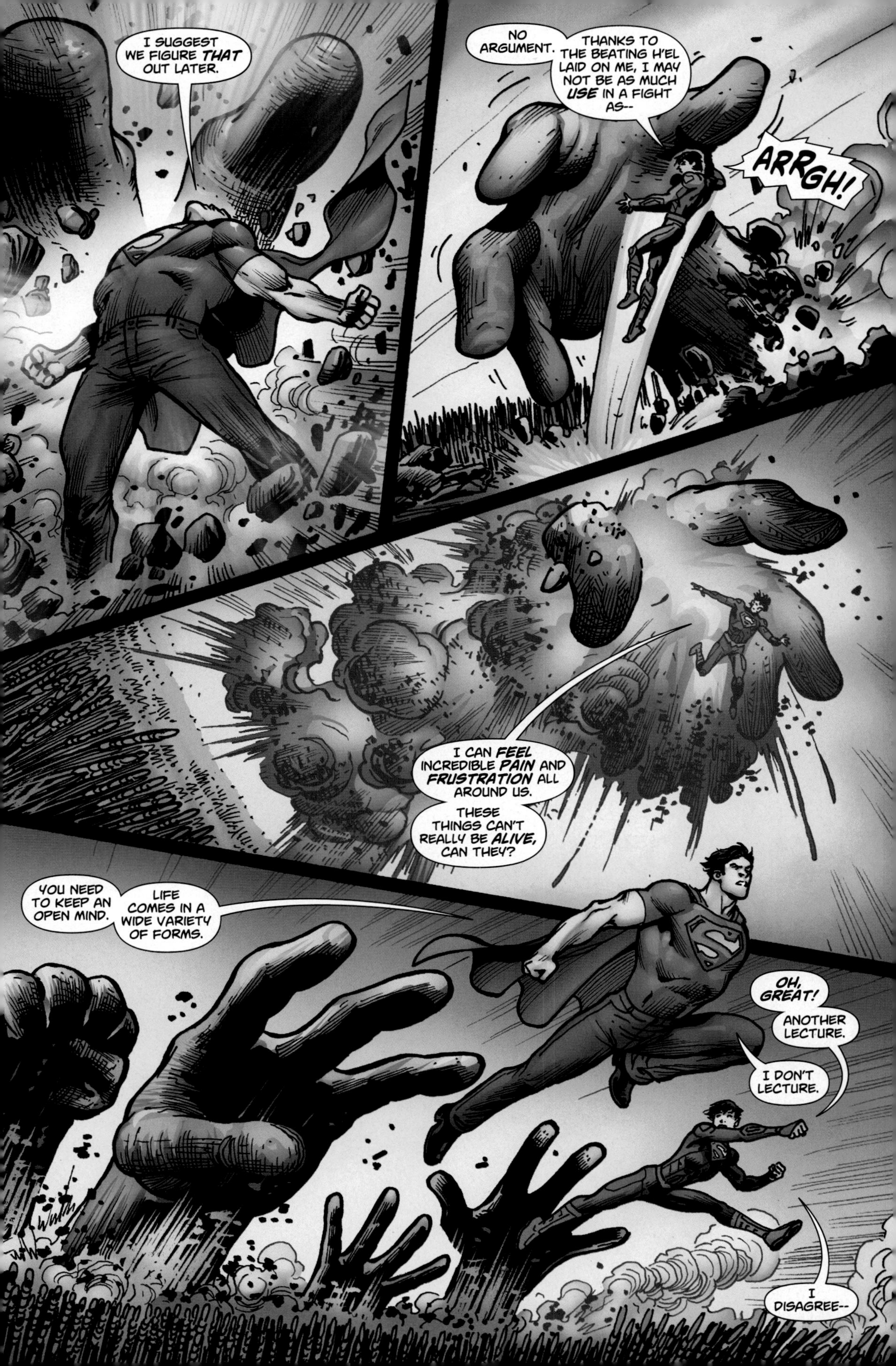
I SUGGEST WE FIGURE THAT OUT LATER.
NO ARGUMENT.
THANKS TO THE BEATING H'EL LAID ON ME, I MAY NOT BE AS MUCH USE IN A FIGHT AS--
ARRGH!
I CAN FEEL INCREDIBLE PAIN AND FRUSTRATION ALL AROUND US.
THESE THINGS CAN'T REALLY BE ALIVE, CAN THEY?
YOU NEED TO KEEP AN OPEN MIND.
LIFE COMES IN A WIDE VARIETY OF FORMS.
OH, GREAT!
ANOTHER LECTURE.
I DON'T LECTURE.
I DISAGREE--

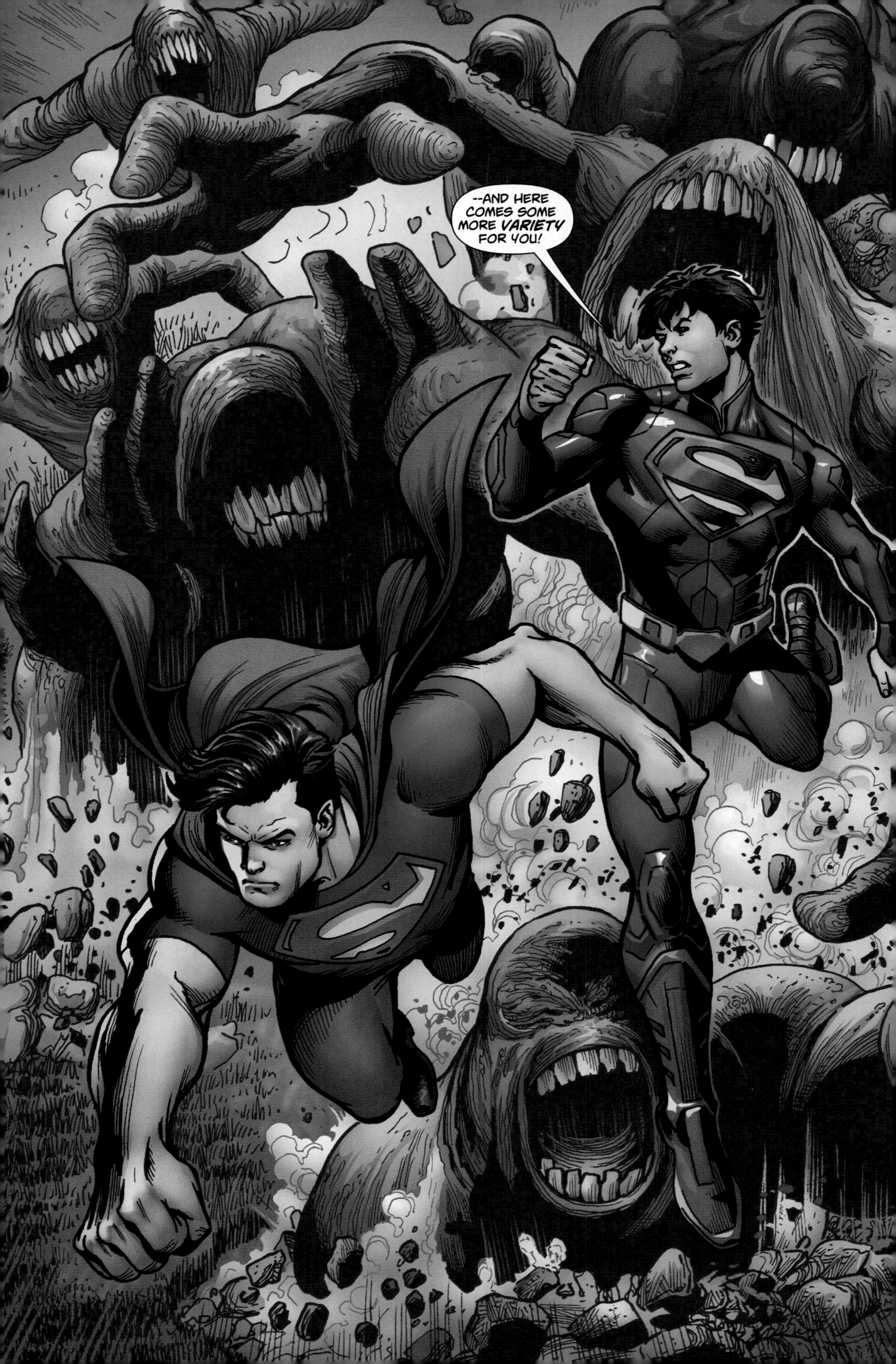
--AND HERE COMES SOME MORE *VARIETY* FOR YOU!

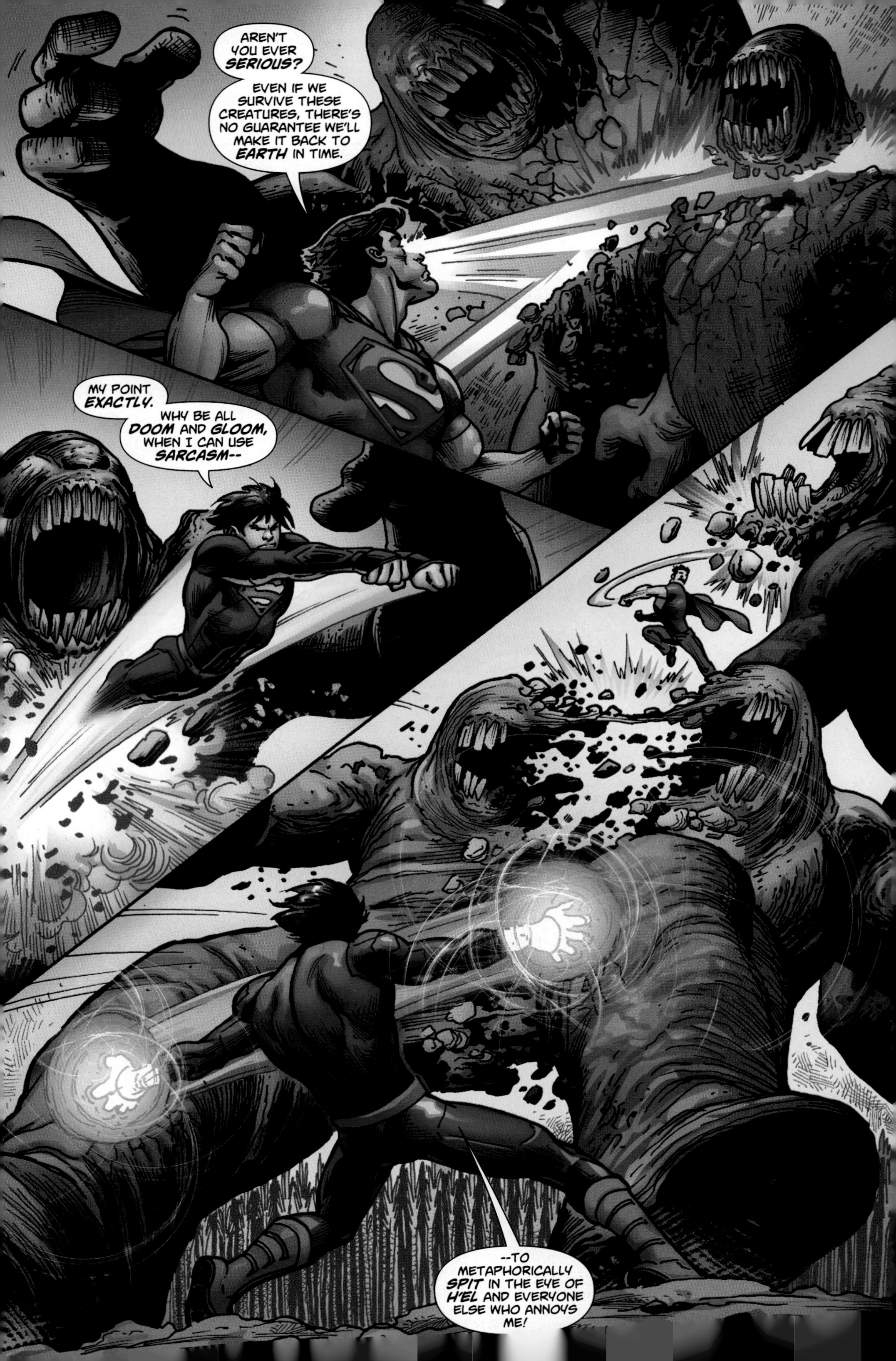
AREN'T YOU EVER SERIOUS?
EVEN IF WE SURVIVE THESE CREATURES, THERE'S NO GUARANTEE WE'LL MAKE IT BACK TO EARTH IN TIME.
MY POINT EXACTLY.
WHY BE ALL DOOM AND GLOOM, WHEN I CAN USE SARCASM--
--TO METAPHORICALLY SPIT IN THE EYE OF H'EL AND EVERYONE ELSE WHO ANNOYS ME!

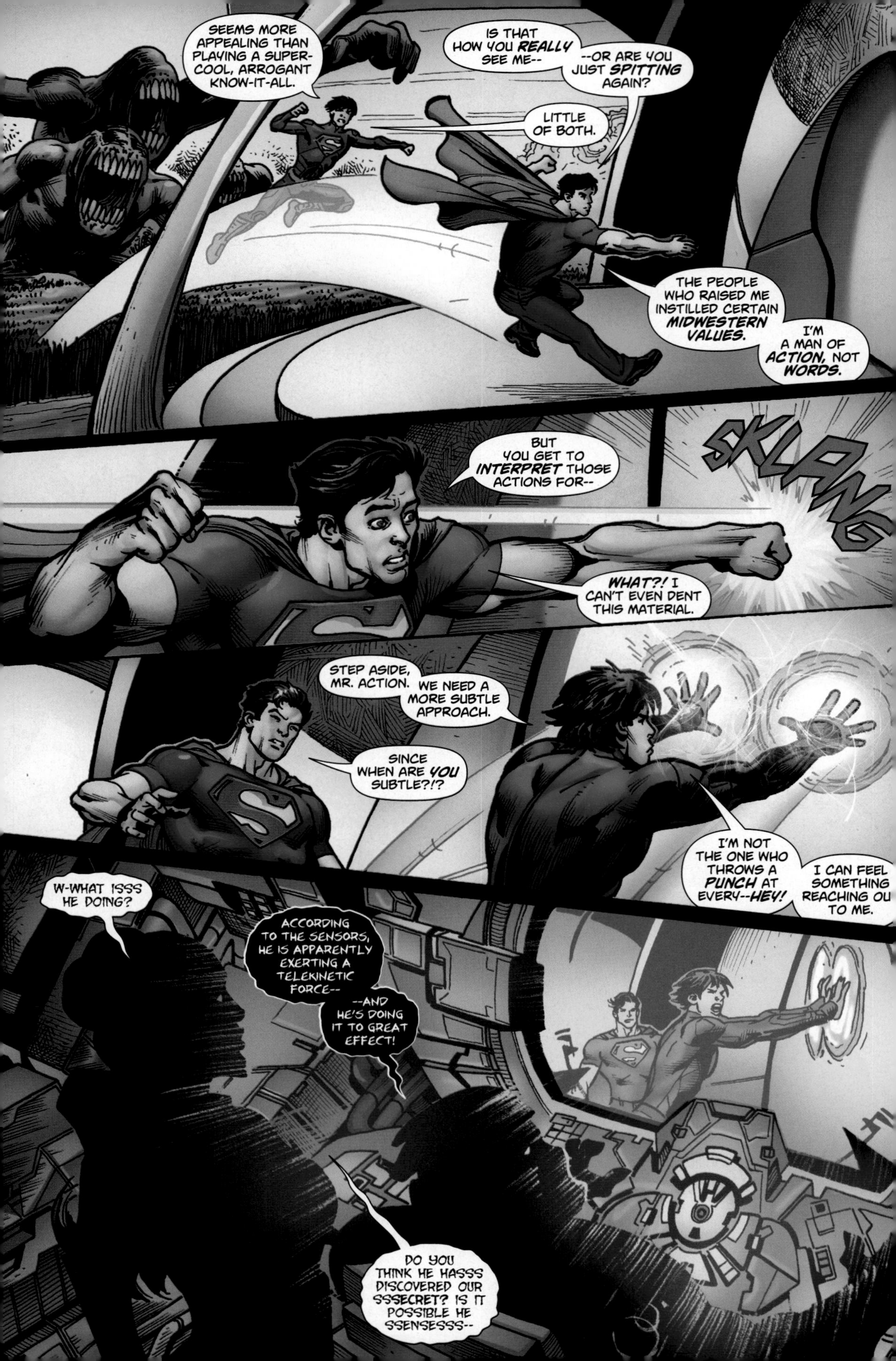
SEEMS MORE APPEALING THAN PLAYING A SUPER-COOL, ARROGANT KNOW-IT-ALL.
IS THAT HOW YOU REALLY SEE ME--
--OR ARE YOU JUST SPITTING AGAIN?
LITTLE OF BOTH.
THE PEOPLE WHO RAISED ME INSTILLED CERTAIN MIDWESTERN VALUES.
I'M A MAN OF ACTION, NOT WORDS.
BUT YOU GET TO INTERPRET THOSE ACTIONS FOR--
SKLANG
WHAT?! I CAN'T EVEN DENT THIS MATERIAL.
STEP ASIDE, MR. ACTION.
WE NEED A MORE SUBTLE APPROACH.
SINCE WHEN ARE YOU SUBTLE?!?
I'M NOT THE ONE WHO THROWS A PUNCH AT EVERY--HEY!
I CAN FEEL SOMETHING REACHING OU TO ME.
W-WHAT ISSS HE DOING?
ACCORDING TO THE SENSORS, HE IS APPARENTLY EXERTING A TELEKINETIC FORCE--
--AND HE'S DOING IT TO GREAT EFFECT!
DO YOU THINK HE HASSS DISCOVERED OUR SSSECRET? IS IT POSSIBLE HE SSENSESSS--

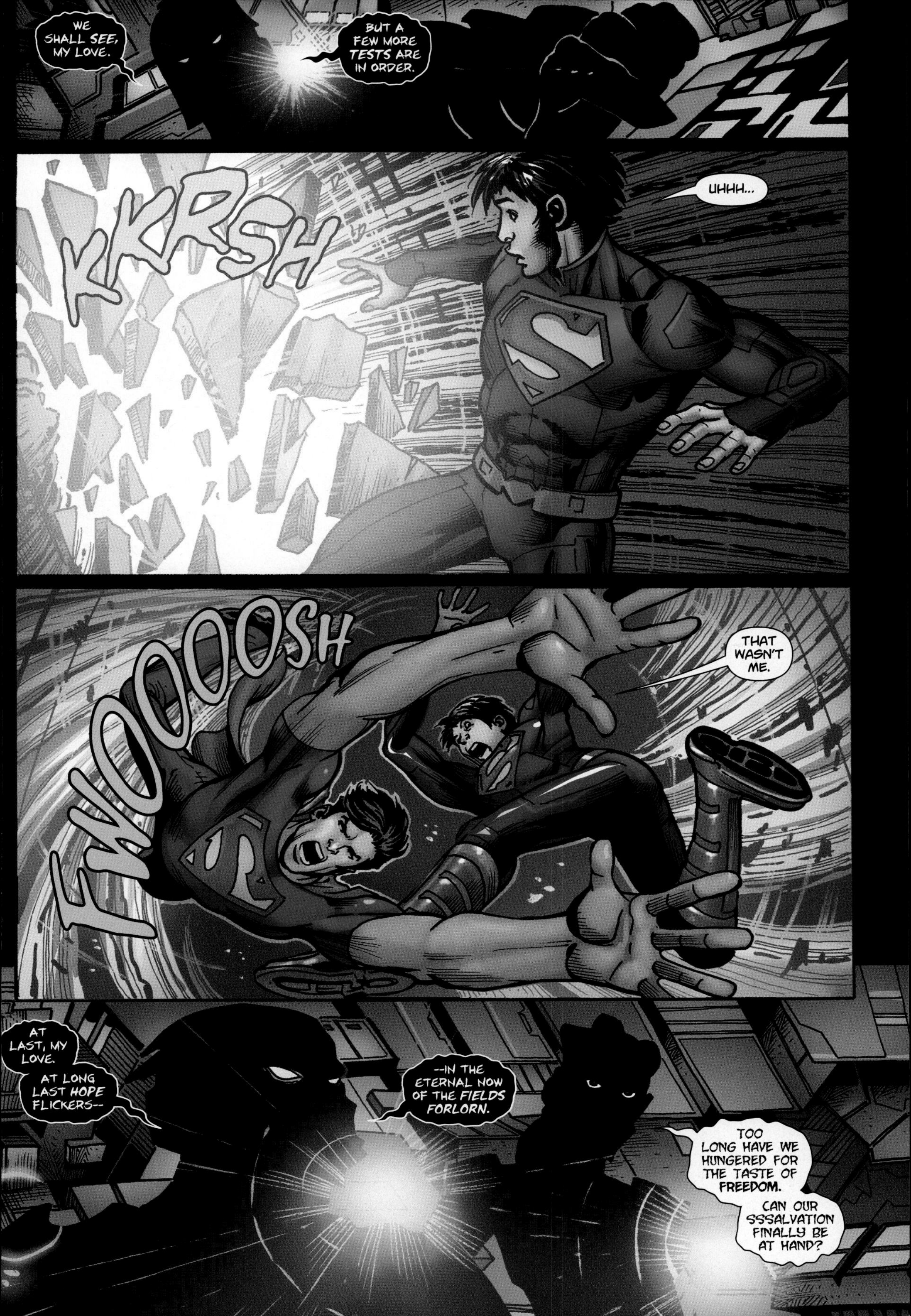
WE SHALL SEE, MY LOVE.
BUT A FEW MORE TESTS ARE IN ORDER.
KKRSH
UHHH...
FWOOOOSH
THAT WASN'T ME.
AT LAST, MY LOVE.
AT LONG LAST HOPE FLICKERS--
--IN THE ETERNAL NOW OF THE FIELDS FORLORN.
TOO LONG HAVE WE HUNGERED FOR THE TASTE OF FREEDOM.
CAN OUR SSSALVATION FINALLY BE AT HAND?

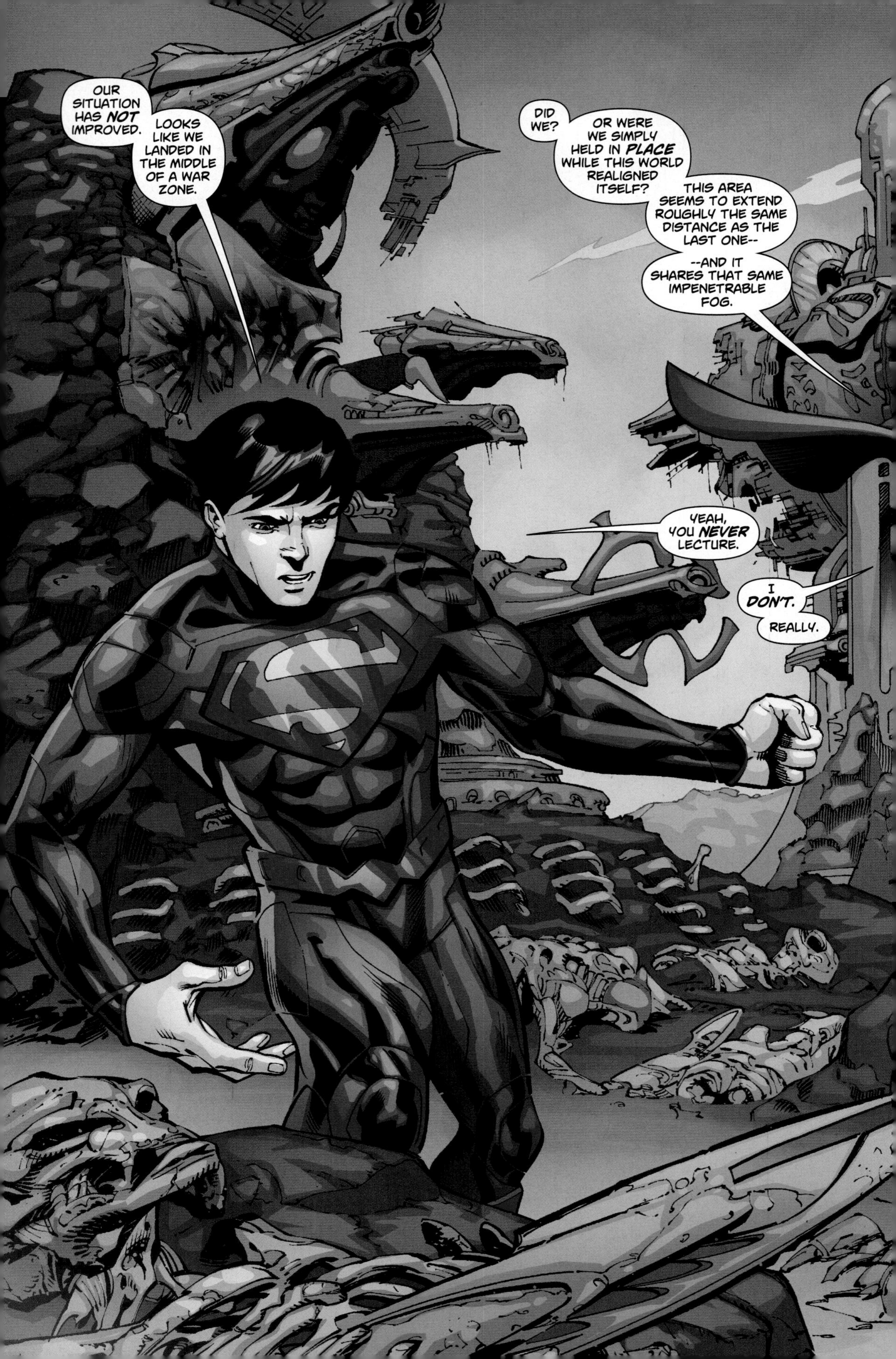
OUR SITUATION HAS NOT IMPROVED.
LOOKS LIKE WE LANDED IN THE MIDDLE OF A WAR ZONE.
DID WE?
OR WERE WE SIMPLY HELD IN PLACE WHILE THIS WORLD REALIGNED ITSELF?
THIS AREA SEEMS TO EXTEND ROUGHLY THE SAME DISTANCE AS THE LAST ONE--
--AND IT SHARES THAT SAME IMPENETRABLE FOG.
YEAH, YOU NEVER LECTURE.
I DON'T.
REALLY.

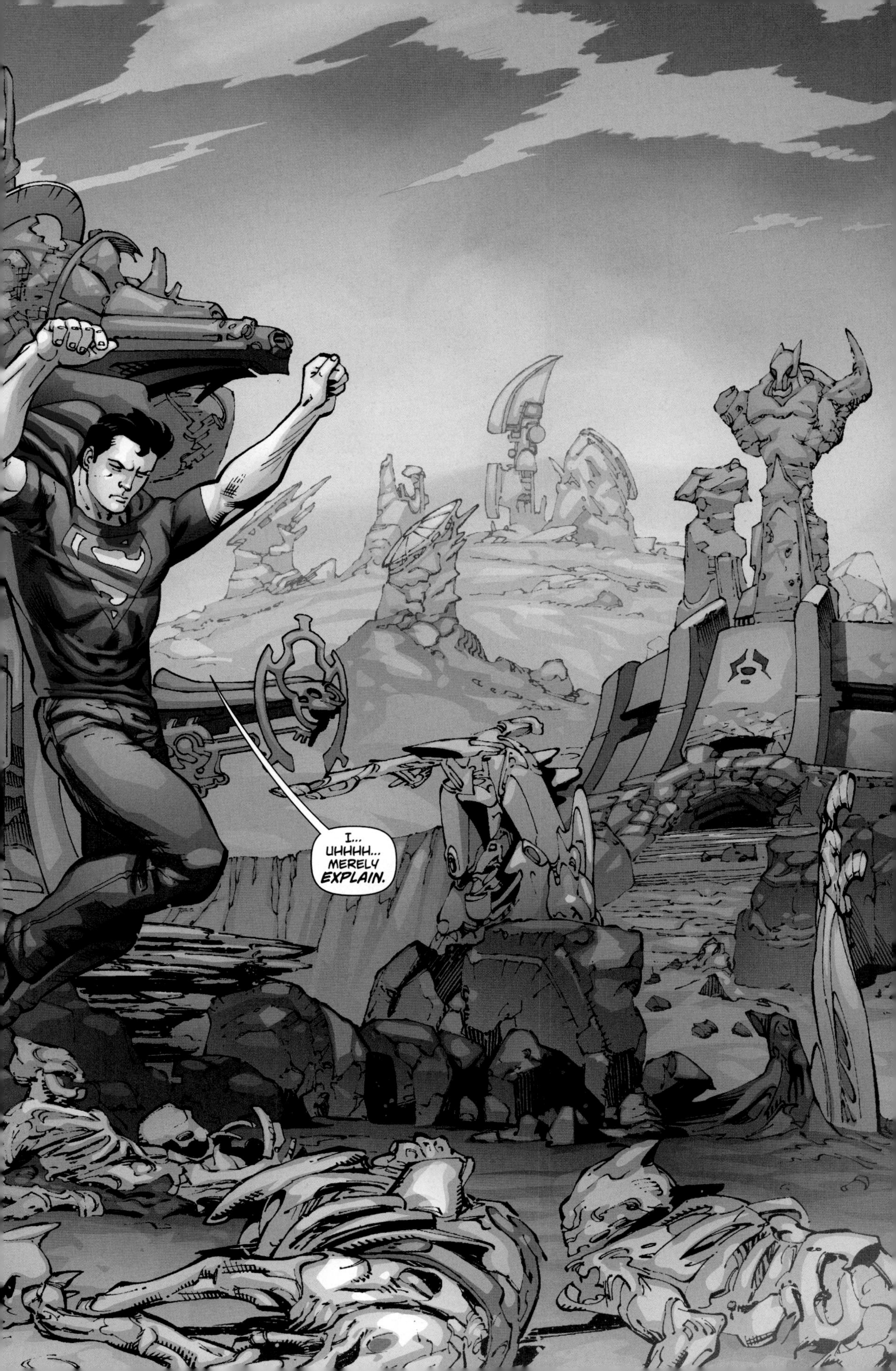
I... UHHHH... MERELY EXPLAIN.

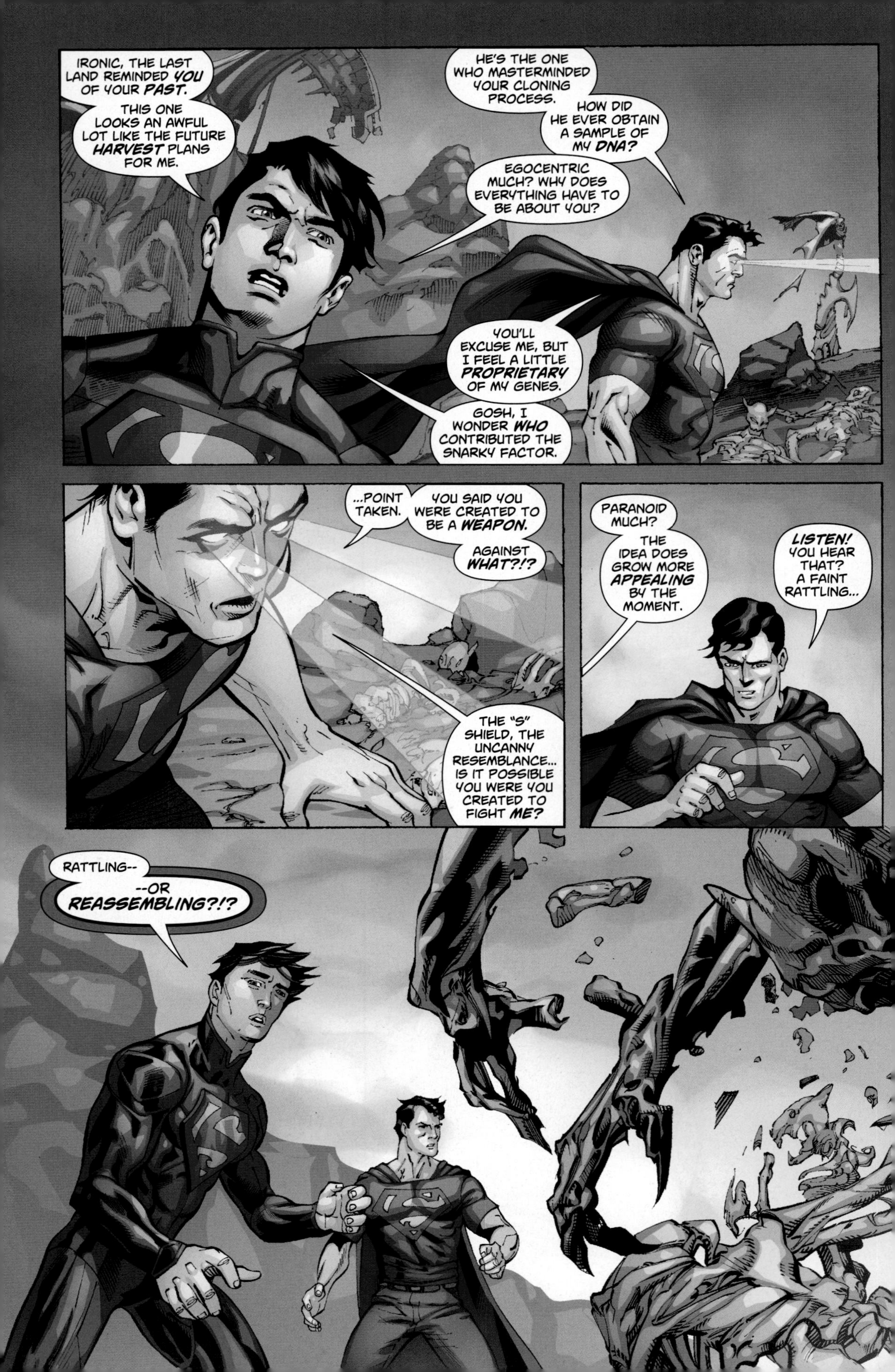
IRONIC, THE LAST LAND REMINDED YOU OF YOUR PAST.
THIS ONE LOOKS AN AWFUL LOT LIKE THE FUTURE HARVEST PLANS FOR ME.
HE'S THE ONE WHO MASTERMINDED YOUR CLONING PROCESS.
HOW DID HE EVER OBTAIN A SAMPLE OF MY DNA?
EGOCENTRIC MUCH? WHY DOES EVERYTHING HAVE TO BE ABOUT YOU?
YOU'LL EXCUSE ME, BUT I FEEL A LITTLE PROPRIETARY OF MY GENES.
GOSH, I WONDER WHO CONTRIBUTED THE SNARKY FACTOR.
...POINT TAKEN.
YOU SAID YOU WERE CREATED TO BE A WEAPON.
AGAINST WHAT?!?
THE "S" SHIELD, THE UNCANNY RESEMBLANCE... IS IT POSSIBLE YOU WERE YOU CREATED TO FIGHT ME?
PARANOID MUCH?
THE IDEA DOES GROW MORE APPEALING BY THE MOMENT.
LISTEN! YOU HEAR THAT? A FAINT RATTLING...
RATTLING--
--OR REASSEMBLING?!?

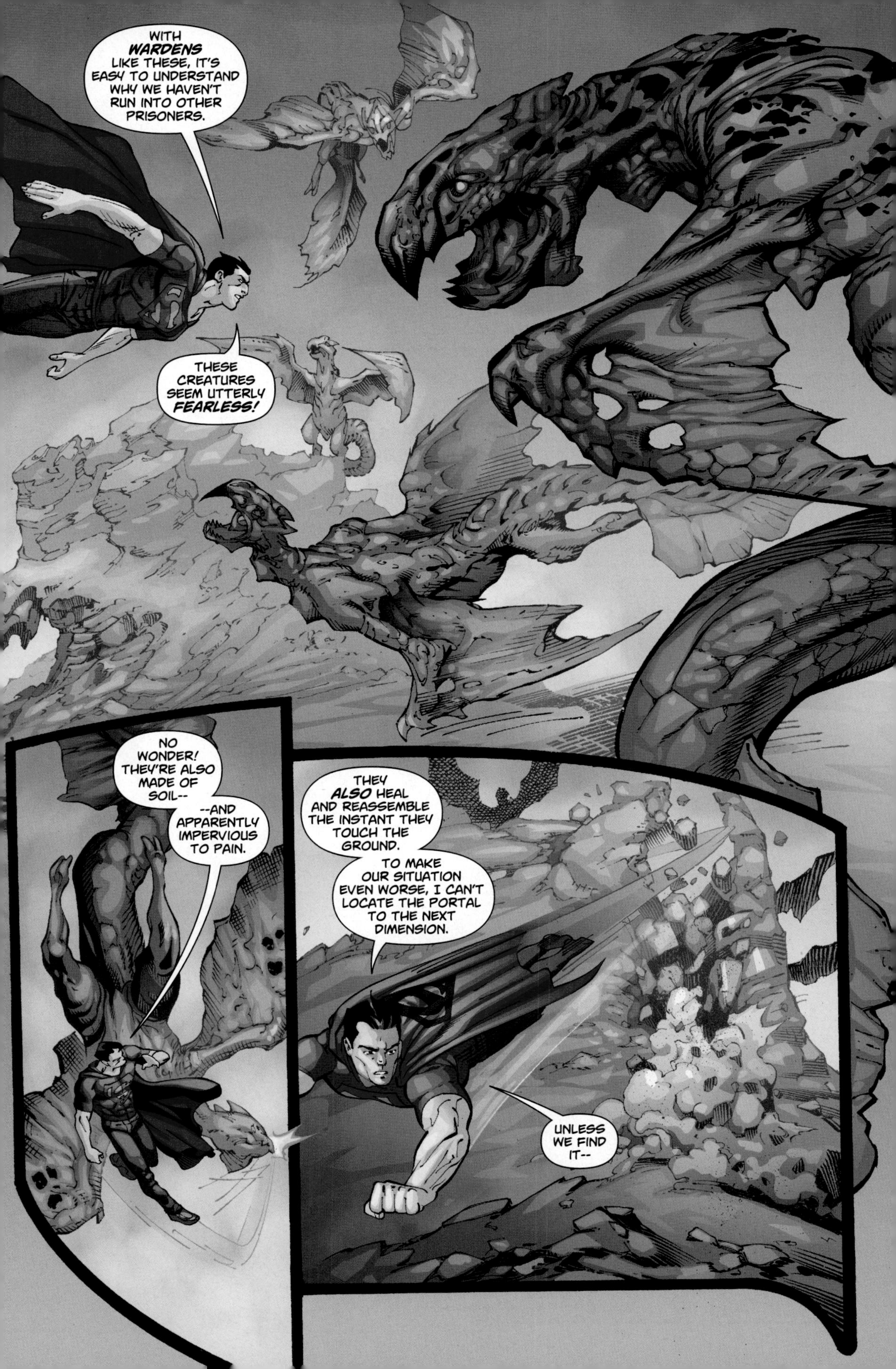
WITH WARDENS LIKE THESE, IT'S EASY TO UNDERSTAND WHY WE HAVEN'T RUN INTO OTHER PRISONERS.
THESE CREATURES SEEM UTTERLY FEARLESS!
NO WONDER! THEY'RE ALSO MADE OF SOIL--
--AND APPARENTLY IMPERVIOUS TO PAIN.
THEY ALSO HEAL AND REASSEMBLE THE INSTANT THEY TOUCH THE GROUND.
TO MAKE OUR SITUATION EVEN WORSE, I CAN'T LOCATE THE PORTAL TO THE NEXT DIMENSION.
UNLESS WE FIND IT--

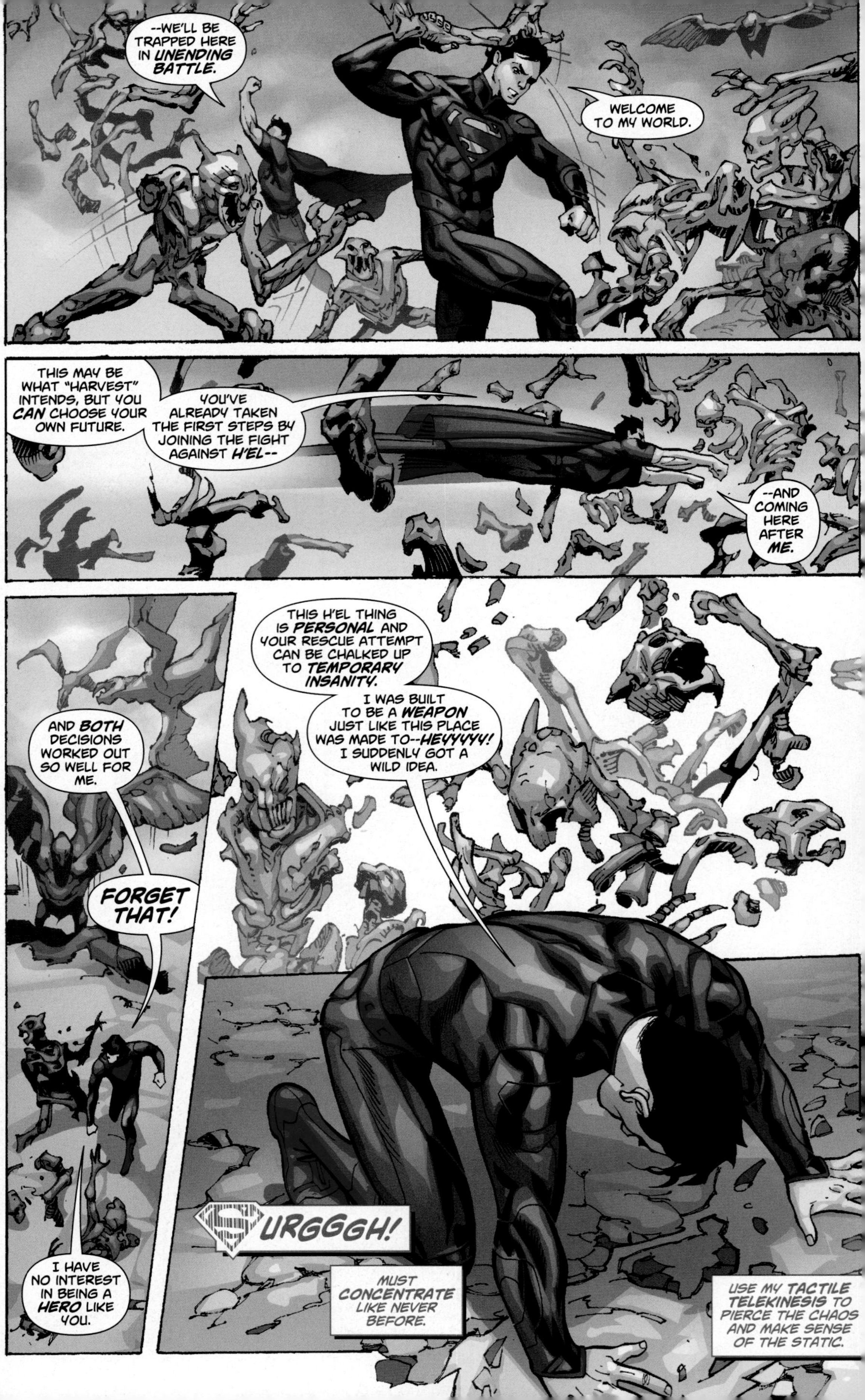

--WE'LL BE TRAPPED HERE IN *UNENDING BATTLE.*
WELCOME TO MY WORLD.
THIS MAY BE WHAT "HARVEST" INTENDS, BUT YOU *CAN* CHOOSE YOUR OWN FUTURE.
YOU'VE ALREADY TAKEN THE FIRST STEPS BY JOINING THE FIGHT AGAINST *H'EL--*
--AND COMING HERE AFTER *ME.*
AND *BOTH* DECISIONS WORKED OUT SO WELL FOR ME.
FORGET THAT!
I HAVE NO INTEREST IN BEING A *HERO* LIKE YOU.
THIS H'EL THING IS *PERSONAL* AND YOUR RESCUE ATTEMPT CAN BE CHALKED UP TO *TEMPORARY INSANITY.*
I WAS BUILT TO BE A *WEAPON* JUST LIKE THIS PLACE WAS MADE TO--*HEYYYYY!* I SUDDENLY GOT A WILD IDEA.
URGGGH!
MUST *CONCENTRATE* LIKE NEVER BEFORE.
USE MY *TACTILE TELEKINESIS* TO PIERCE THE CHAOS AND MAKE SENSE OF THE STATIC.

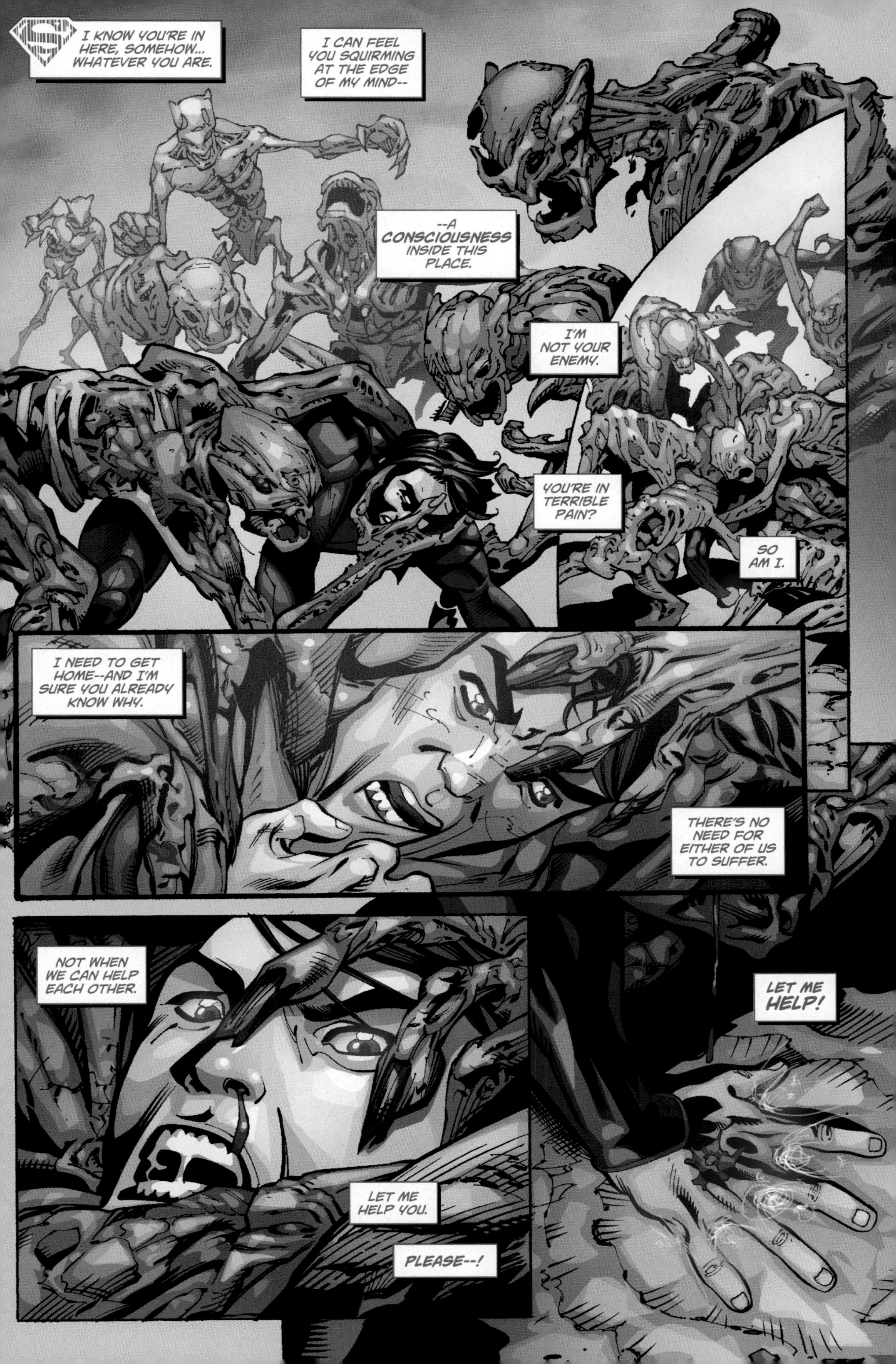

I KNOW YOU'RE IN HERE, SOMEHOW... WHATEVER YOU ARE.
I CAN FEEL YOU SQUIRMING AT THE EDGE OF MY MIND--
--A CONSCIOUSNESS INSIDE THIS PLACE.
I'M NOT YOUR ENEMY.
YOU'RE IN TERRIBLE PAIN?
SO AM I.
I NEED TO GET HOME--AND I'M SURE YOU ALREADY KNOW WHY.
THERE'S NO NEED FOR EITHER OF US TO SUFFER.
NOT WHEN WE CAN HELP EACH OTHER.
LET ME HELP YOU.
PLEASE--!
LET ME HELP!

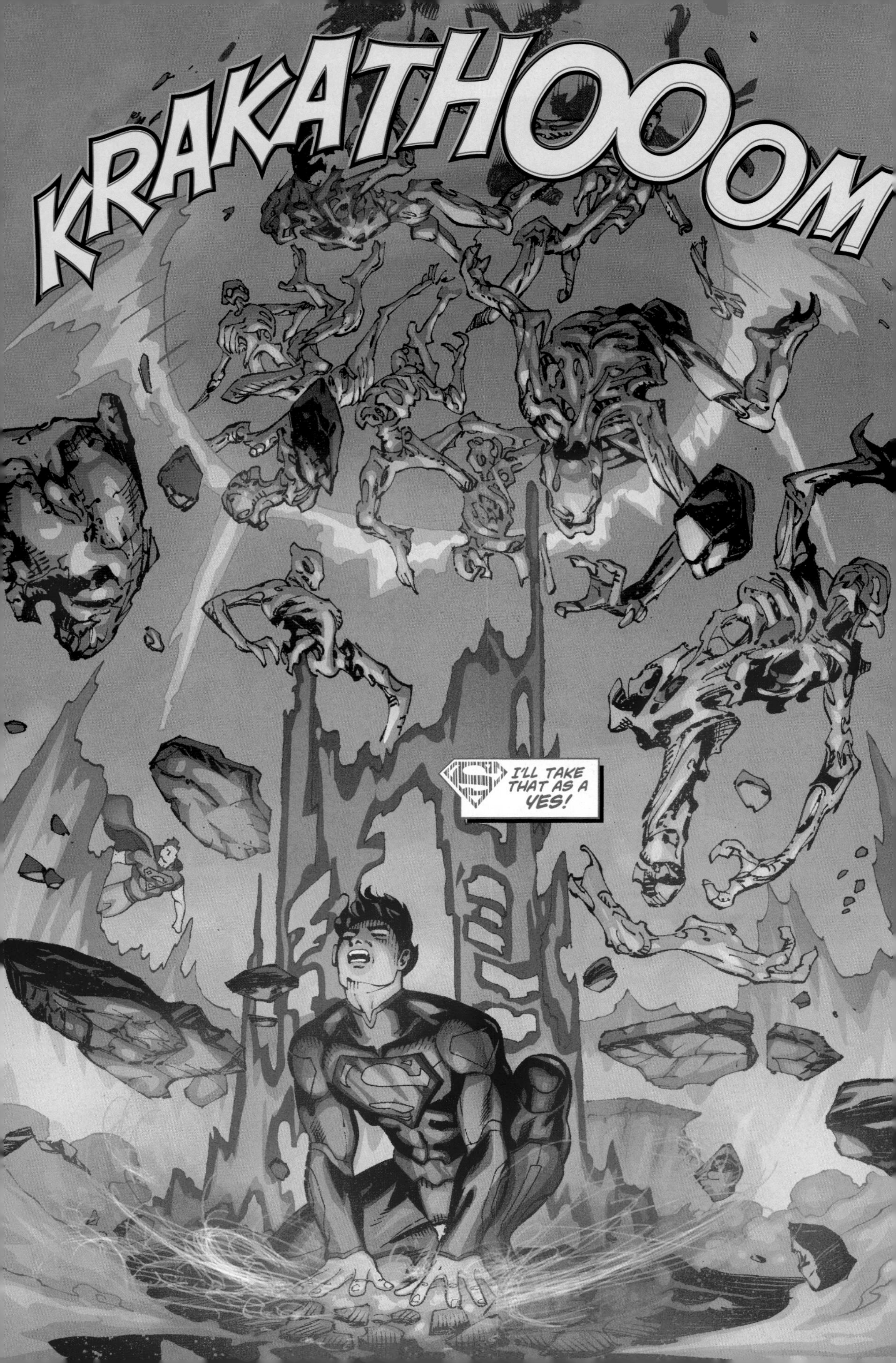
KRAKATHOOOOM
I'LL TAKE THAT AS A YES!

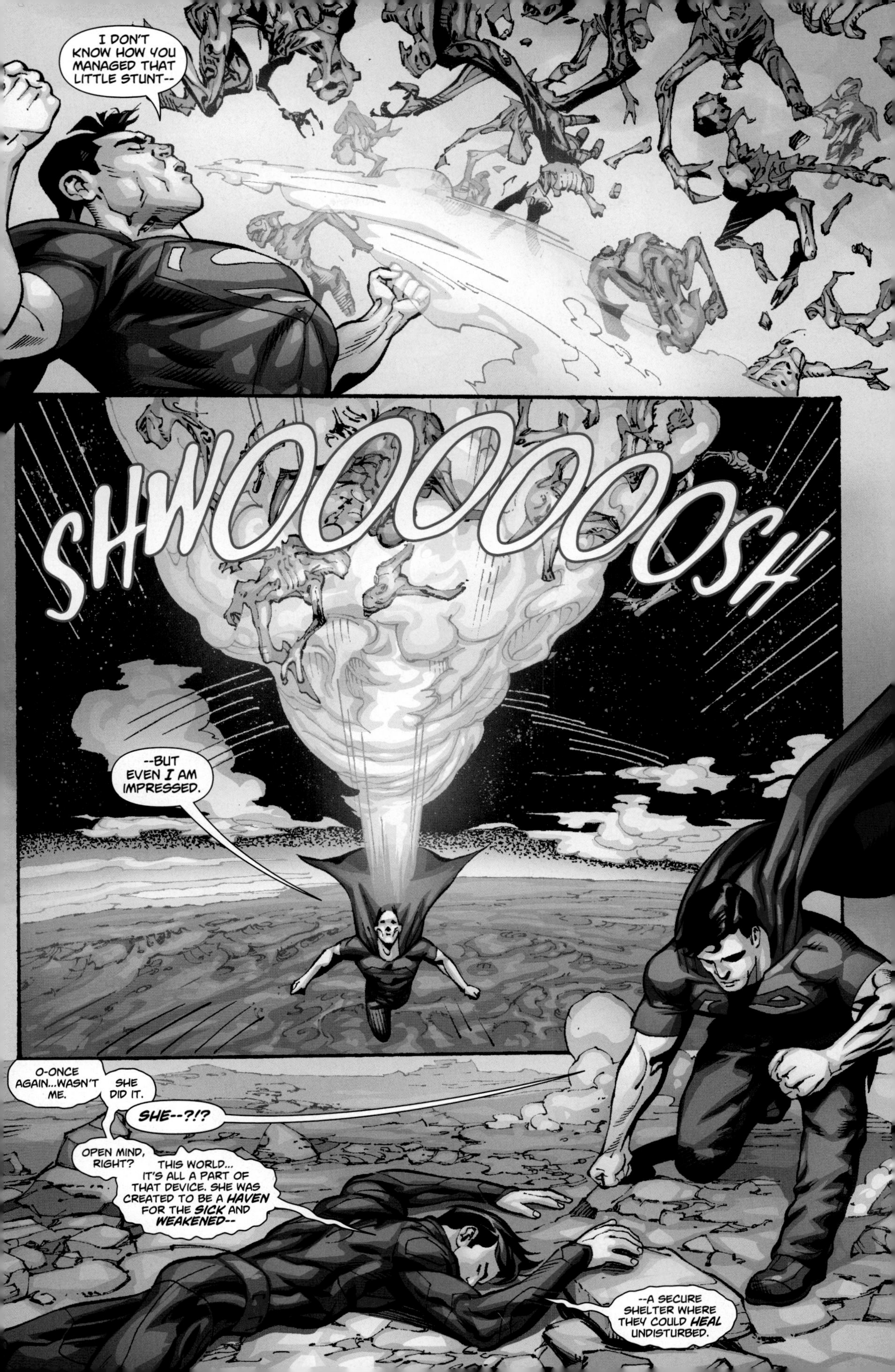

I DON'T KNOW HOW YOU MANAGED THAT LITTLE STUNT--
SHWOOOOOOOSH
--BUT EVEN *I* AM IMPRESSED.
O-ONCE AGAIN...WASN'T ME.
SHE DID IT.
SHE--?!?
OPEN MIND, RIGHT?
THIS WORLD... IT'S ALL A PART OF THAT DEVICE. SHE WAS CREATED TO BE A *HAVEN* FOR THE *SICK* AND *WEAKENED*--
--A SECURE SHELTER WHERE THEY COULD *HEAL* UNDISTURBED.

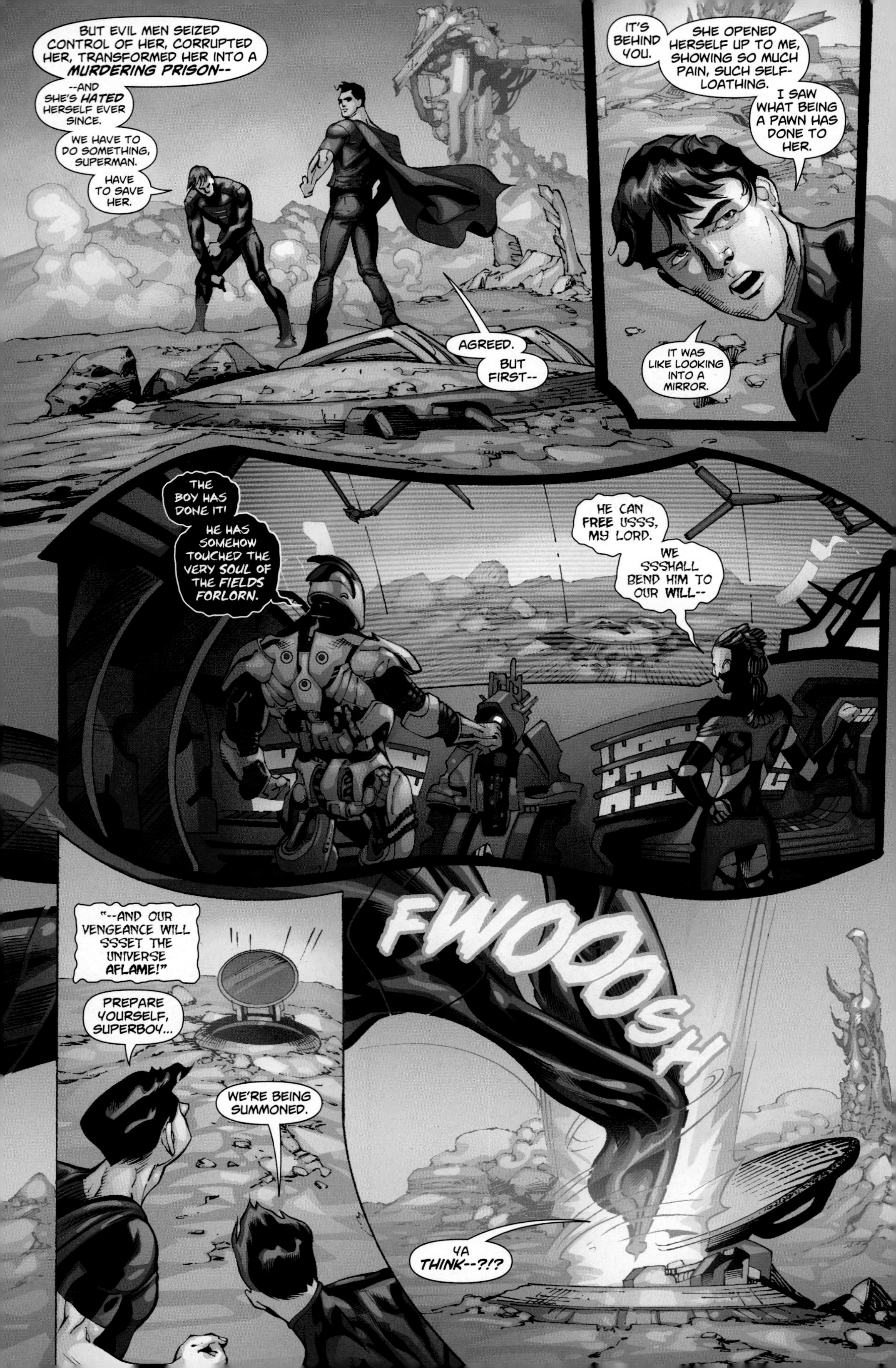
BUT EVIL MEN SEIZED CONTROL OF HER, CORRUPTED HER, TRANSFORMED HER INTO A MURDERING PRISON--
--AND SHE'S HATED HERSELF EVER SINCE.
WE HAVE TO DO SOMETHING, SUPERMAN.
HAVE TO SAVE HER.
AGREED.
BUT FIRST--
IT'S BEHIND YOU.
SHE OPENED HERSELF UP TO ME, SHOWING SO MUCH PAIN, SUCH SELF-LOATHING.
I SAW WHAT BEING A PAWN HAS DONE TO HER.
IT WAS LIKE LOOKING INTO A MIRROR.
THE BOY HAS DONE IT!
HE HAS SOMEHOW TOUCHED THE VERY SOUL OF THE FIELDS FORLORN.
HE CAN FREE USSS, MY LORD.
WE SSSHALL BEND HIM TO OUR WILL--
"--AND OUR VENGEANCE WILL SSSET THE UNIVERSE AFLAME!"
PREPARE YOURSELF, SUPERBOY...
WE'RE BEING SUMMONED.
FWOOOSH
YA THINK--?!?

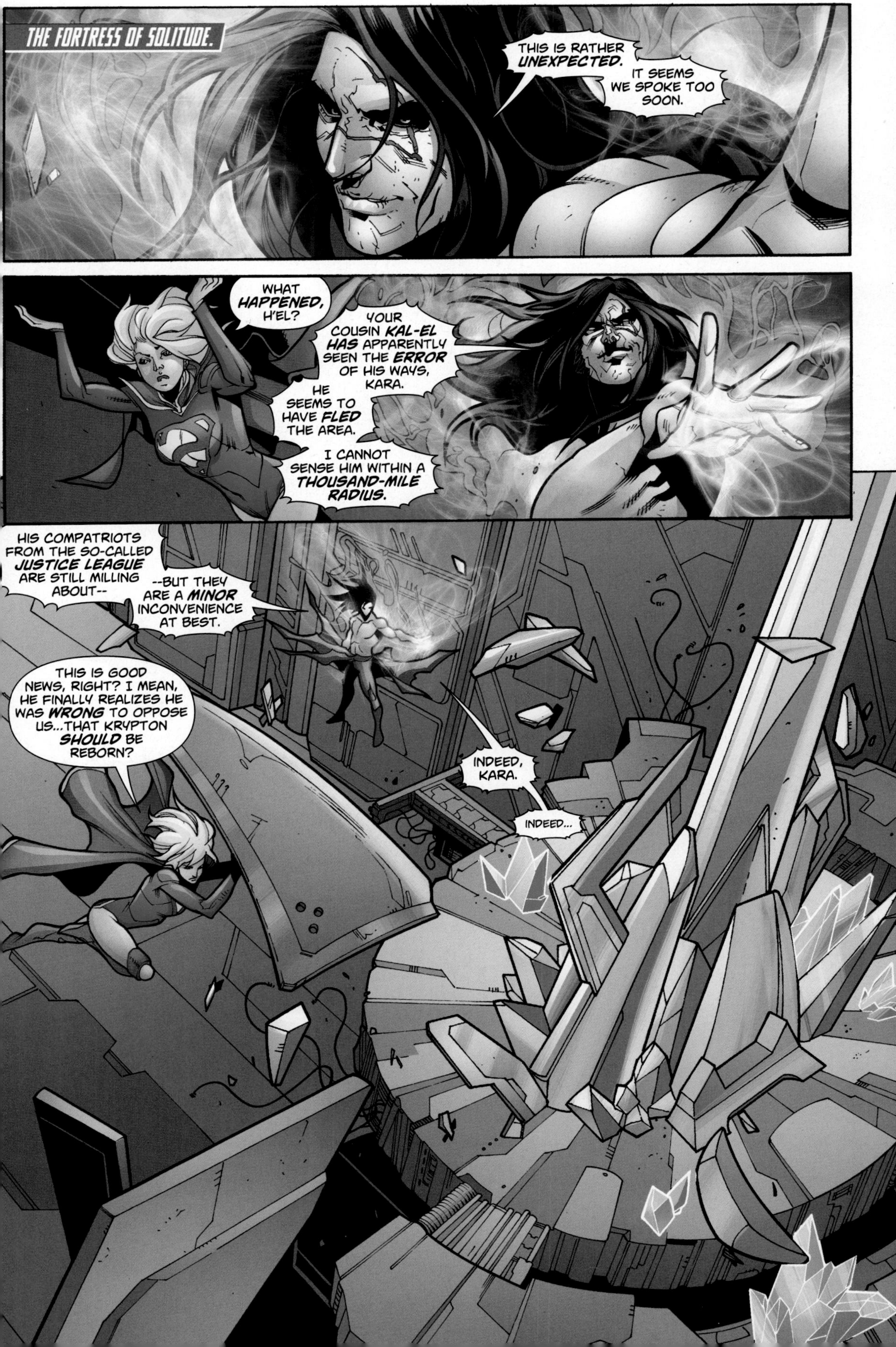
THE FORTRESS OF SOLITUDE.
THIS IS RATHER UNEXPECTED.
IT SEEMS WE SPOKE TOO SOON.
WHAT HAPPENED, H'EL?
YOUR COUSIN KAL-EL HAS APPARENTLY SEEN THE ERROR OF HIS WAYS, KARA.
HE SEEMS TO HAVE FLED THE AREA.
I CANNOT SENSE HIM WITHIN A THOUSAND-MILE RADIUS.
HIS COMPATRIOTS FROM THE SO-CALLED JUSTICE LEAGUE ARE STILL MILLING ABOUT--
--BUT THEY ARE A MINOR INCONVENIENCE AT BEST.
THIS IS GOOD NEWS, RIGHT? I MEAN, HE FINALLY REALIZES HE WAS WRONG TO OPPOSE US...THAT KRYPTON SHOULD BE REBORN?
INDEED, KARA.
INDEED...

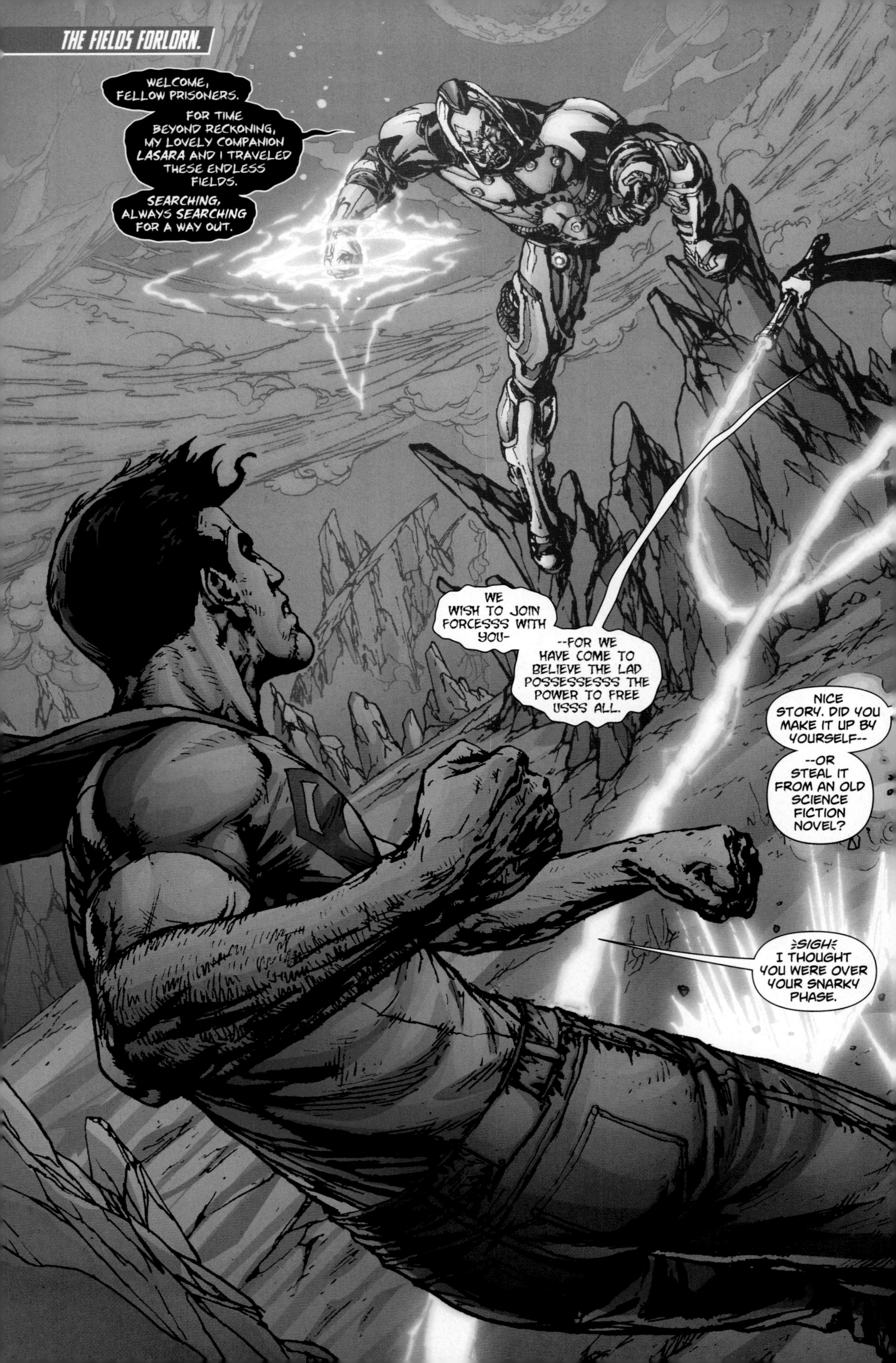
THE FIELDS FORLORN.
WELCOME, FELLOW PRISONERS.
FOR TIME BEYOND RECKONING, MY LOVELY COMPANION LASARA AND I TRAVELED THESE ENDLESS FIELDS.
SEARCHING, ALWAYS SEARCHING FOR A WAY OUT.
WE WISH TO JOIN FORCESSS WITH YOU-
--FOR WE HAVE COME TO BELIEVE THE LAD POSSESSESSS THE POWER TO FREE USSS ALL.
NICE STORY. DID YOU MAKE IT UP BY YOURSELF--
--OR STEAL IT FROM AN OLD SCIENCE FICTION NOVEL?
≡SIGH≡ I THOUGHT YOU WERE OVER YOUR SNARKY PHASE.

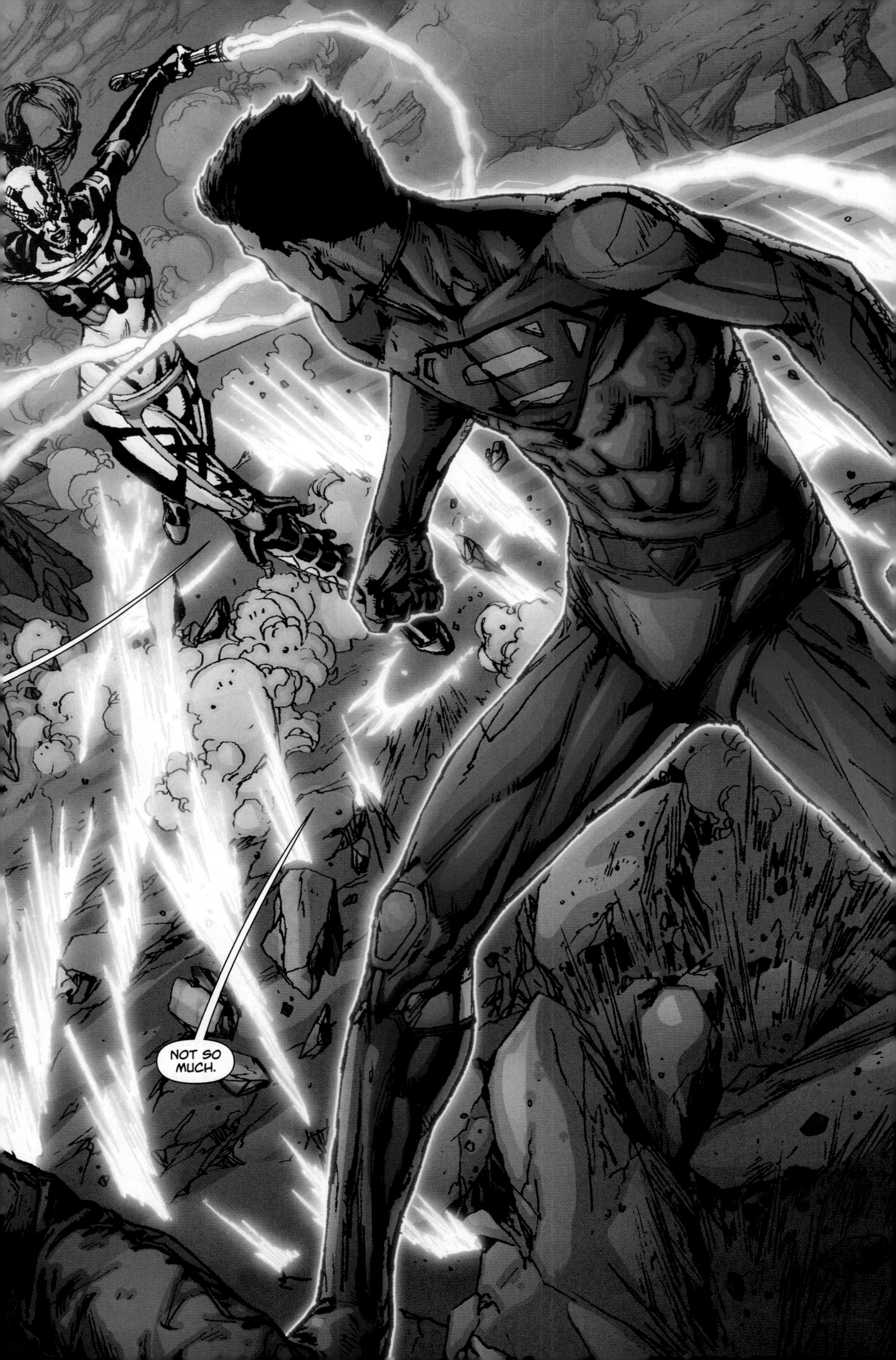
NOT SO MUCH.

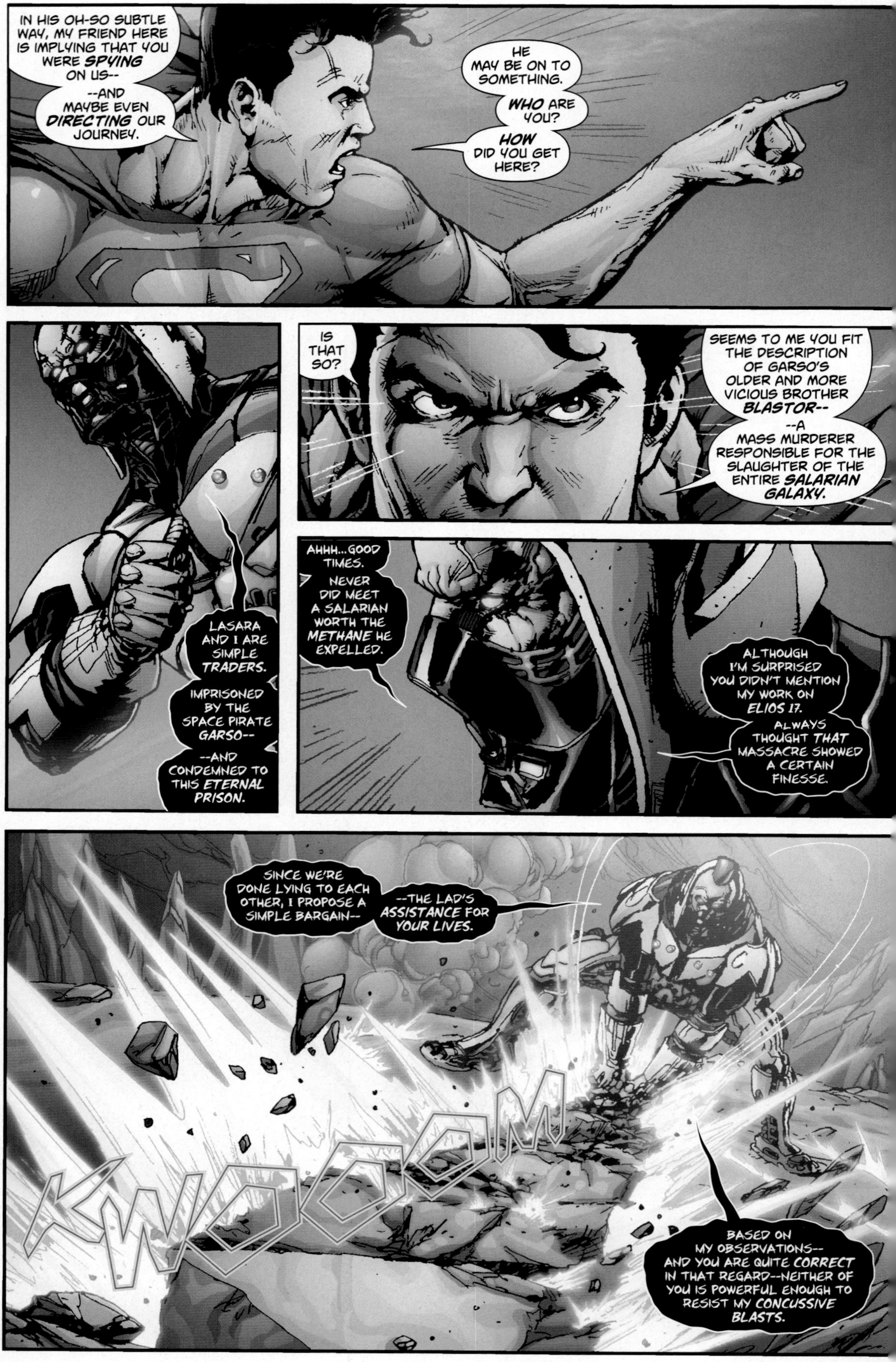
IN HIS OH-SO SUBTLE WAY, MY FRIEND HERE IS IMPLYING THAT YOU WERE SPYING ON US--
--AND MAYBE EVEN DIRECTING OUR JOURNEY.
HE MAY BE ON TO SOMETHING.
WHO ARE YOU?
HOW DID YOU GET HERE?
IS THAT SO?
SEEMS TO ME YOU FIT THE DESCRIPTION OF GARSO'S OLDER AND MORE VICIOUS BROTHER BLASTOR--
--A MASS MURDERER RESPONSIBLE FOR THE SLAUGHTER OF THE ENTIRE SALARIAN GALAXY.
LASARA AND I ARE SIMPLE TRADERS.
IMPRISONED BY THE SPACE PIRATE GARSO--
--AND CONDEMNED TO THIS ETERNAL PRISON.
AHHH...GOOD TIMES.
NEVER DID MEET A SALARIAN WORTH THE METHANE HE EXPELLED.
ALTHOUGH I'M SURPRISED YOU DIDN'T MENTION MY WORK ON ELIOS 17.
ALWAYS THOUGHT THAT MASSACRE SHOWED A CERTAIN FINESSE.
SINCE WE'RE DONE LYING TO EACH OTHER, I PROPOSE A SIMPLE BARGAIN--
--THE LAD'S ASSISTANCE FOR YOUR LIVES.
KWOOOOM
BASED ON MY OBSERVATIONS--AND YOU ARE QUITE CORRECT IN THAT REGARD--NEITHER OF YOU IS POWERFUL ENOUGH TO RESIST MY CONCUSSIVE BLASTS.

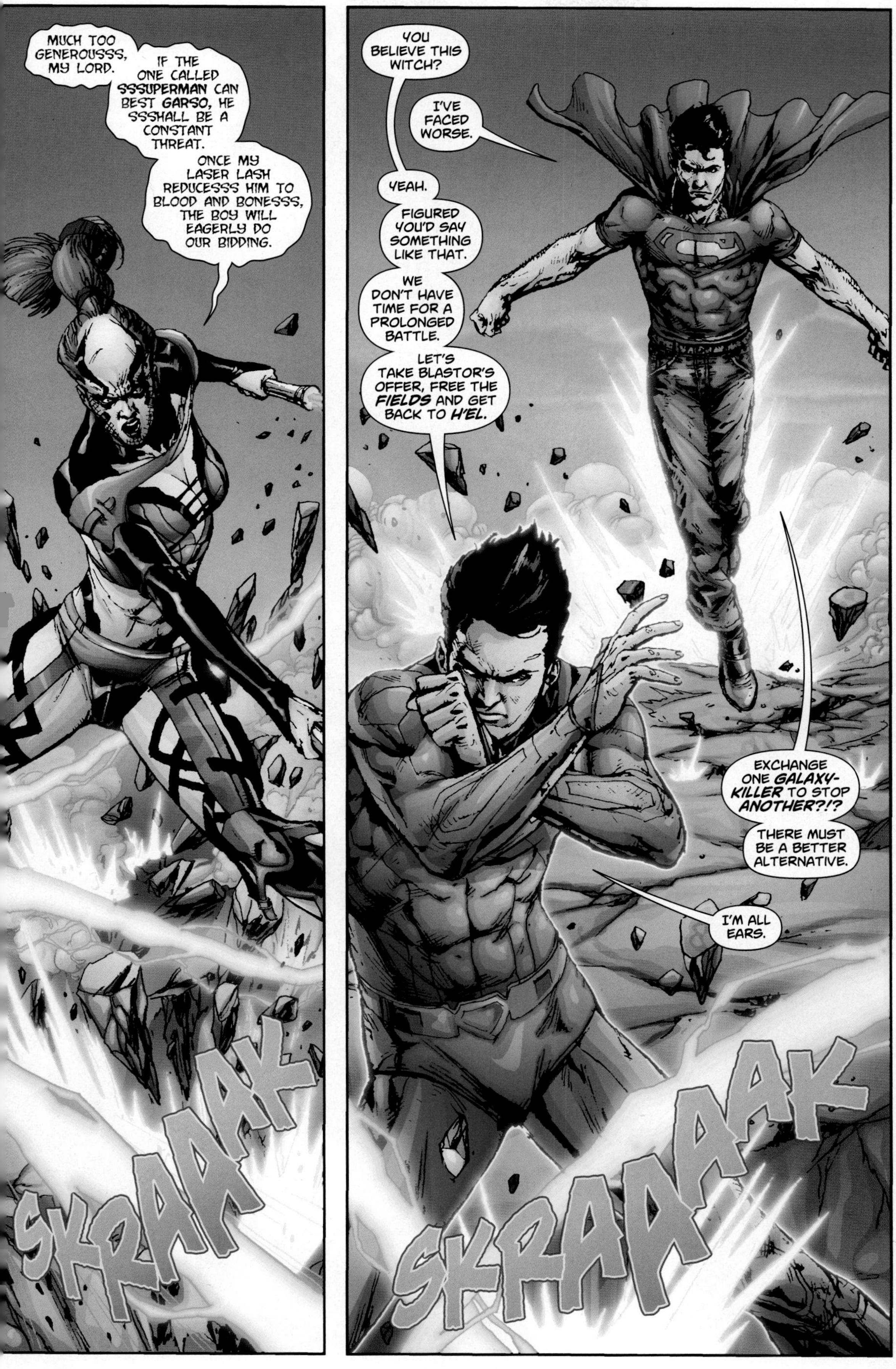

MUCH TOO GENEROUSSS, MY LORD.
IF THE ONE CALLED SSSUPERMAN CAN BEST GARSO, HE SSSHALL BE A CONSTANT THREAT.
ONCE MY LASER LASH REDUCESSS HIM TO BLOOD AND BONESSS, THE BOY WILL EAGERLY DO OUR BIDDING.
SKRAAK
YOU BELIEVE THIS WITCH?
I'VE FACED WORSE.
YEAH.
FIGURED YOU'D SAY SOMETHING LIKE THAT.
WE DON'T HAVE TIME FOR A PROLONGED BATTLE.
LET'S TAKE BLASTOR'S OFFER, FREE THE FIELDS AND GET BACK TO H'EL.
EXCHANGE ONE GALAXY-KILLER TO STOP ANOTHER?!?
THERE MUST BE A BETTER ALTERNATIVE.
I'M ALL EARS.
SKRAAAAK

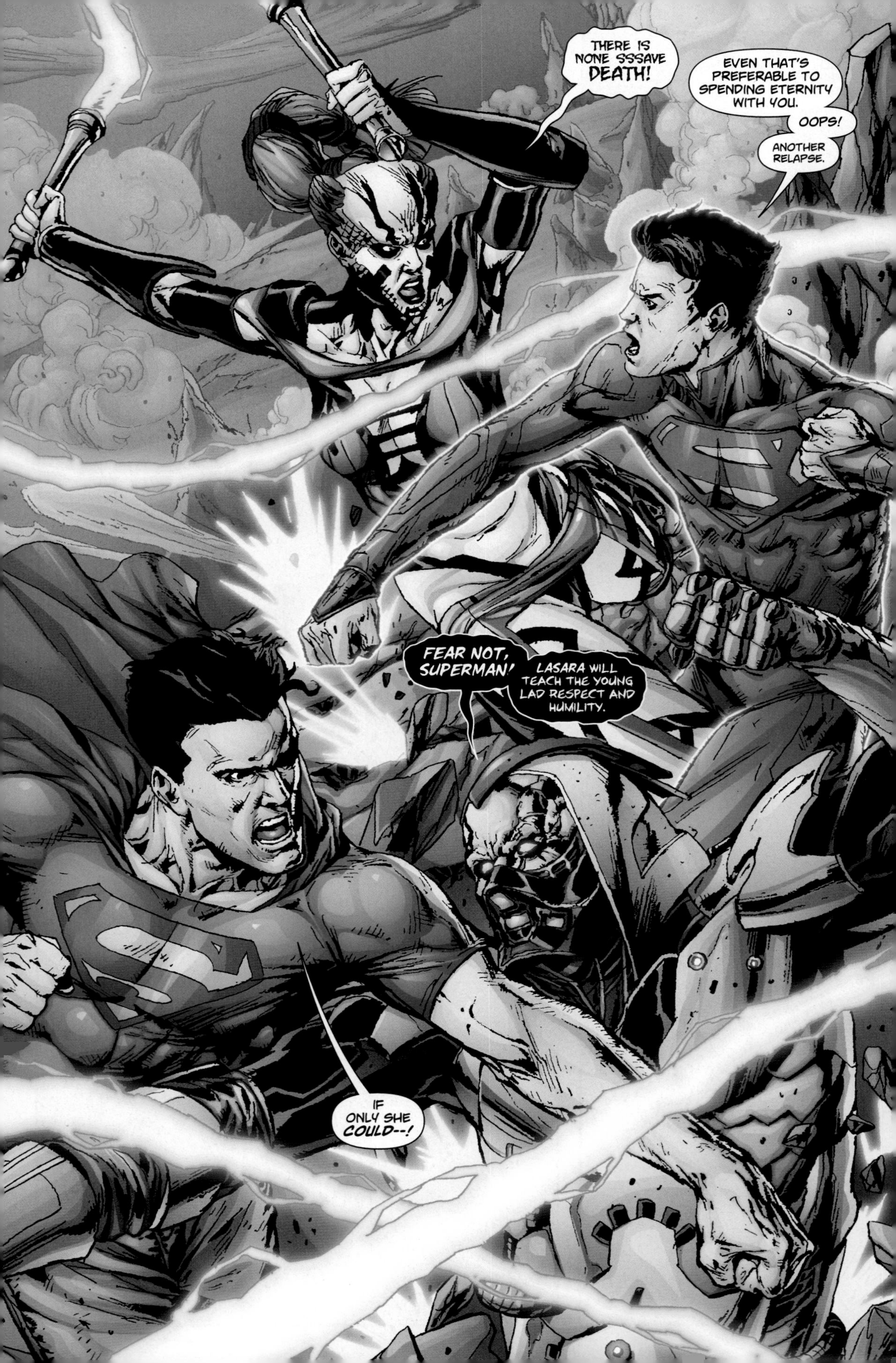
THERE IS NONE SSSAVE DEATH!
EVEN THAT'S PREFERABLE TO SPENDING ETERNITY WITH YOU.
OOPS!
ANOTHER RELAPSE.
FEAR NOT, SUPERMAN!
LASARA WILL TEACH THE YOUNG LAD RESPECT AND HUMILITY.
IF ONLY SHE COULD--!

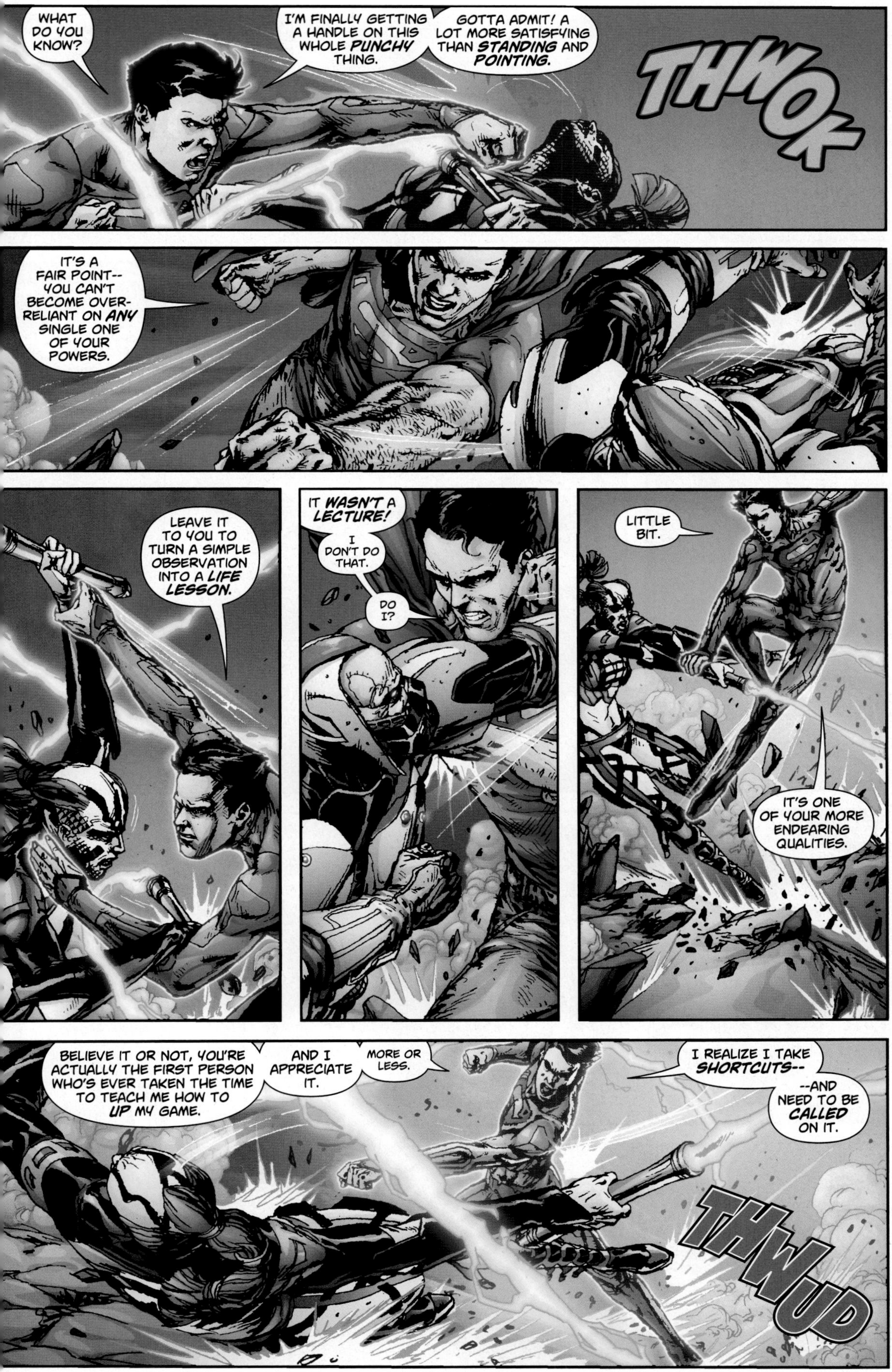
WHAT DO YOU KNOW?
I'M FINALLY GETTING A HANDLE ON THIS WHOLE PUNCHY THING.
GOTTA ADMIT! A LOT MORE SATISFYING THAN STANDING AND POINTING.
THWOK
IT'S A FAIR POINT-- YOU CAN'T BECOME OVER-RELIANT ON ANY SINGLE ONE OF YOUR POWERS.
LEAVE IT TO YOU TO TURN A SIMPLE OBSERVATION INTO A LIFE LESSON.
IT WASN'T A LECTURE!
I DON'T DO THAT.
DO I?
LITTLE BIT.
IT'S ONE OF YOUR MORE ENDEARING QUALITIES.
BELIEVE IT OR NOT, YOU'RE ACTUALLY THE FIRST PERSON WHO'S EVER TAKEN THE TIME TO TEACH ME HOW TO UP MY GAME.
AND I APPRECIATE IT.
MORE OR LESS.
I REALIZE I TAKE SHORTCUTS--
--AND NEED TO BE CALLED ON IT.
THWUD

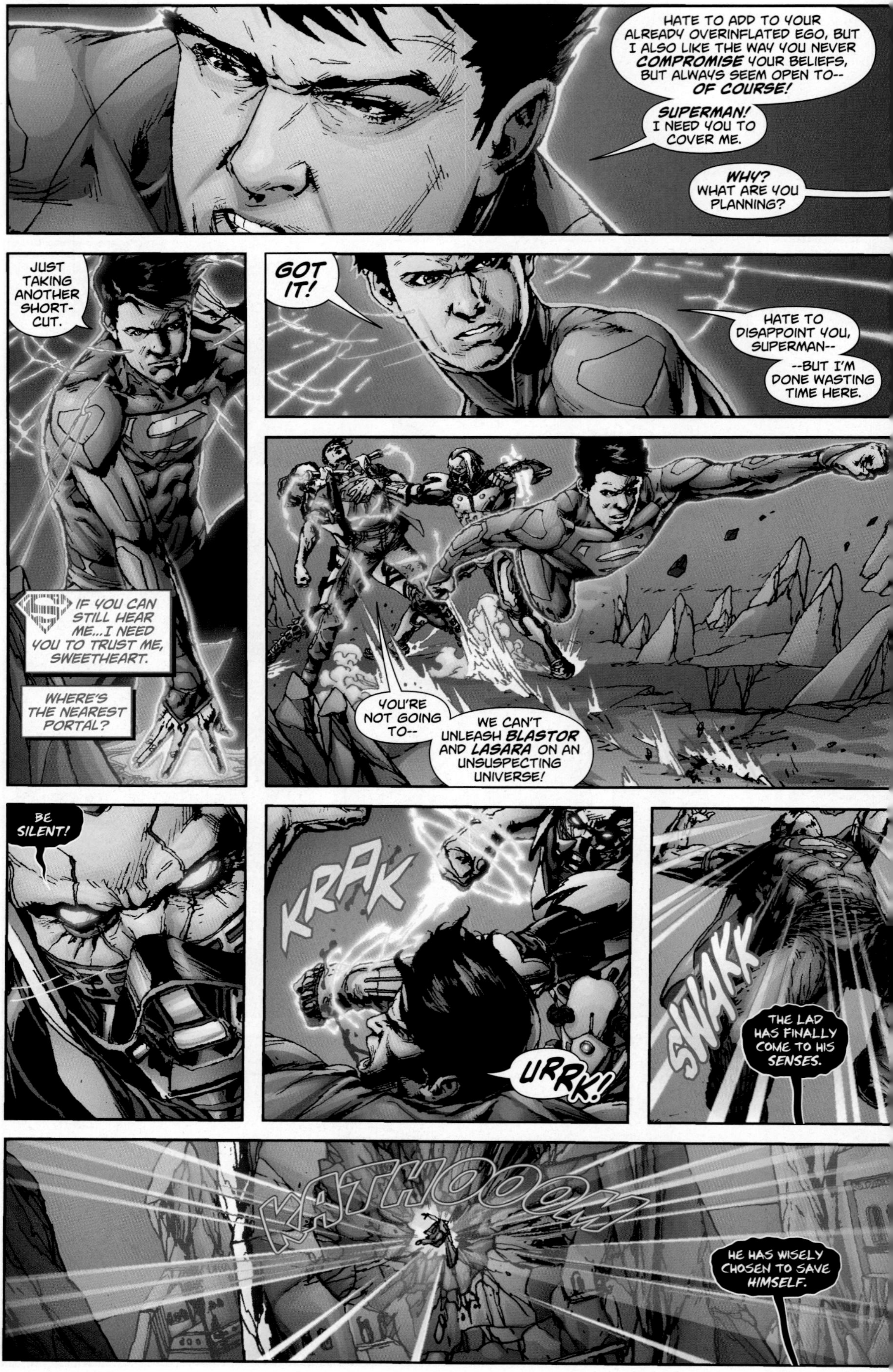
HATE TO ADD TO YOUR ALREADY OVERINFLATED EGO, BUT I ALSO LIKE THE WAY YOU NEVER COMPROMISE YOUR BELIEFS, BUT ALWAYS SEEM OPEN TO-- OF COURSE!
SUPERMAN! I NEED YOU TO COVER ME.
WHY? WHAT ARE YOU PLANNING?
JUST TAKING ANOTHER SHORT-CUT.
IF YOU CAN STILL HEAR ME...I NEED YOU TO TRUST ME, SWEETHEART.
WHERE'S THE NEAREST PORTAL?
GOT IT!
HATE TO DISAPPOINT YOU, SUPERMAN--
--BUT I'M DONE WASTING TIME HERE.
YOU'RE NOT GOING TO--
WE CAN'T UNLEASH BLASTOR AND LASARA ON AN UNSUSPECTING UNIVERSE!
BE SILENT!
KRAK
URRK!
SWAKK
THE LAD HAS FINALLY COME TO HIS SENSES.
KATHOOOM
HE HAS WISELY CHOSEN TO SAVE HIMSELF.

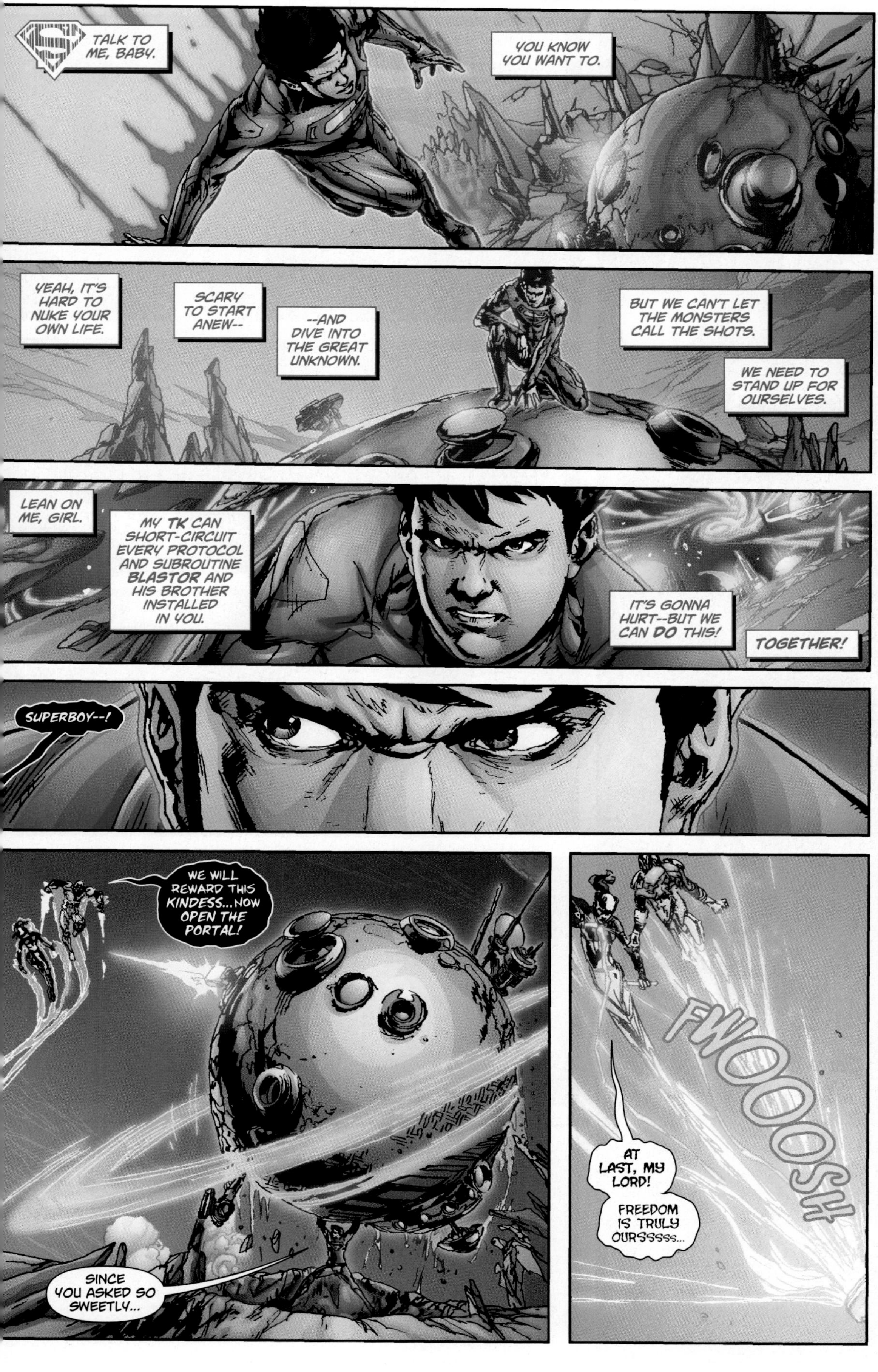

TALK TO ME, BABY.
YOU KNOW YOU WANT TO.
YEAH, IT'S HARD TO NUKE YOUR OWN LIFE.
SCARY TO START ANEW--
--AND DIVE INTO THE GREAT UNKNOWN.
BUT WE CAN'T LET THE MONSTERS CALL THE SHOTS.
WE NEED TO STAND UP FOR OURSELVES.
LEAN ON ME, GIRL.
MY TK CAN SHORT-CIRCUIT EVERY PROTOCOL AND SUBROUTINE BLASTOR AND HIS BROTHER INSTALLED IN YOU.
IT'S GONNA HURT--BUT WE CAN DO THIS!
TOGETHER!
SUPERBOY--!
WE WILL REWARD THIS KINDESS...NOW OPEN THE PORTAL!
SINCE YOU ASKED SO SWEETLY...
FWOOOSH
AT LAST, MY LORD!
FREEDOM IS TRULY OURSSSSS...

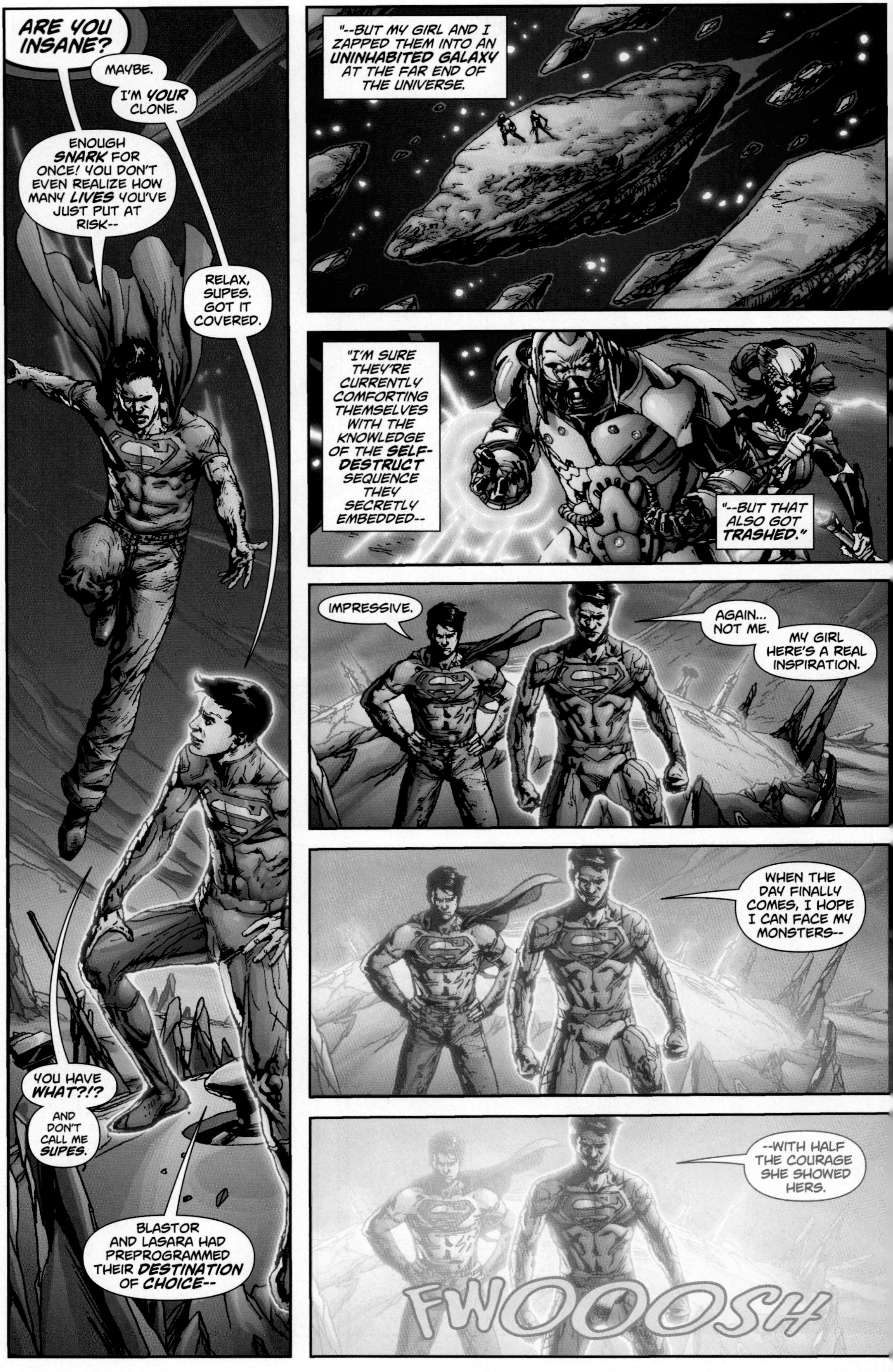

ARE YOU INSANE?
MAYBE.
I'M YOUR CLONE.
ENOUGH SNARK FOR ONCE! YOU DON'T EVEN REALIZE HOW MANY LIVES YOU'VE JUST PUT AT RISK--
RELAX, SUPES. GOT IT COVERED.
YOU HAVE WHAT?!?
AND DON'T CALL ME SUPES.
BLASTOR AND LASARA HAD PREPROGRAMMED THEIR DESTINATION OF CHOICE--
"--BUT MY GIRL AND I ZAPPED THEM INTO AN UNINHABITED GALAXY AT THE FAR END OF THE UNIVERSE.
"I'M SURE THEY'RE CURRENTLY COMFORTING THEMSELVES WITH THE KNOWLEDGE OF THE SELF-DESTRUCT SEQUENCE THEY SECRETLY EMBEDDED--
"--BUT THAT ALSO GOT TRASHED."
IMPRESSIVE.
AGAIN... NOT ME.
MY GIRL HERE'S A REAL INSPIRATION.
WHEN THE DAY FINALLY COMES, I HOPE I CAN FACE MY MONSTERS--
--WITH HALF THE COURAGE SHE SHOWED HERS.
FWOOOSH

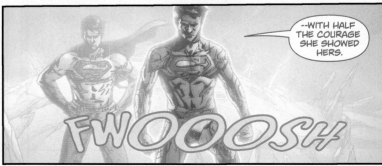

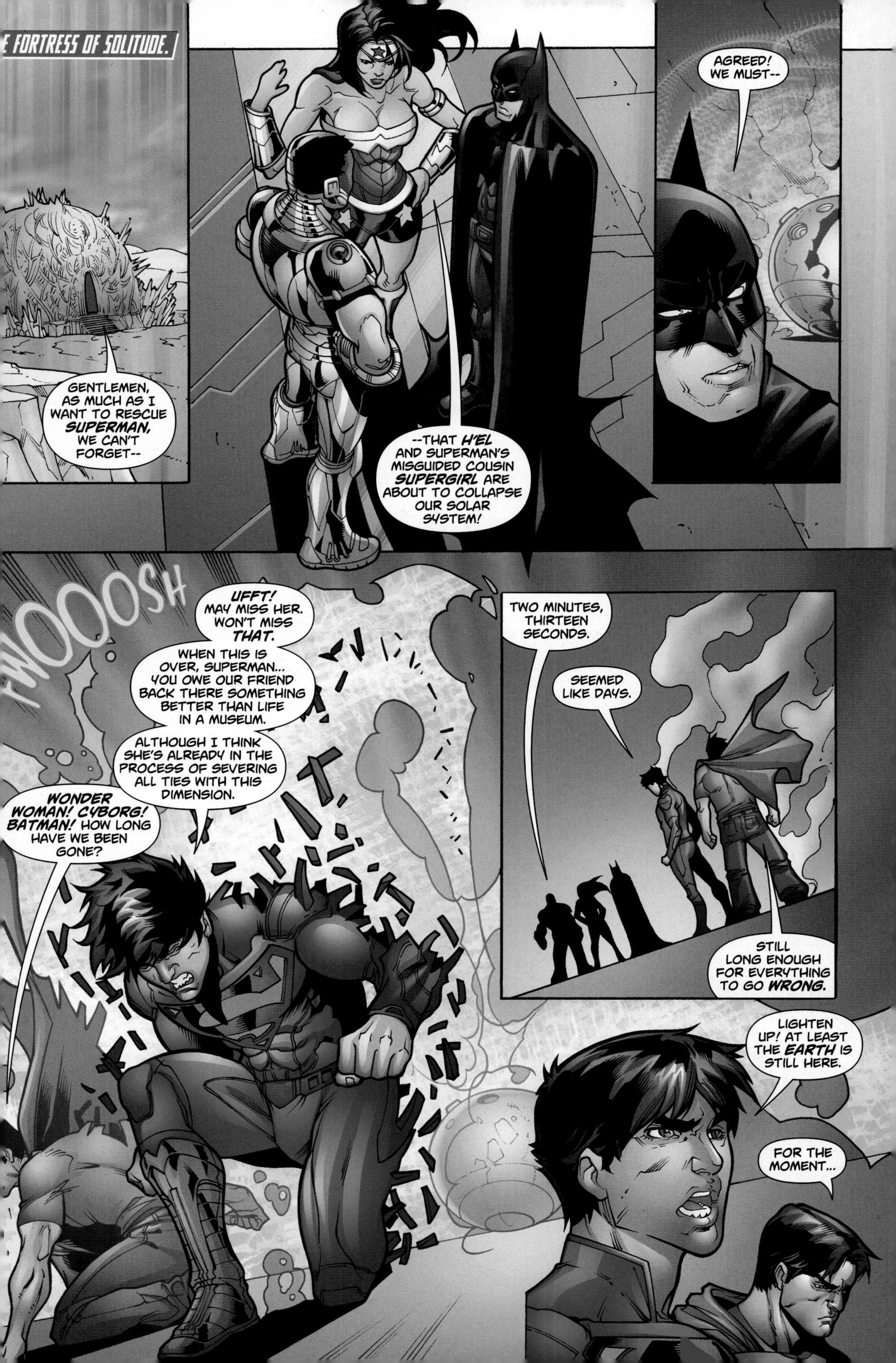

...THE FORTRESS OF SOLITUDE.
GENTLEMEN, AS MUCH AS I WANT TO RESCUE SUPERMAN, WE CAN'T FORGET--
--THAT H'EL AND SUPERMAN'S MISGUIDED COUSIN SUPERGIRL ARE ABOUT TO COLLAPSE OUR SOLAR SYSTEM!
AGREED! WE MUST--
FWOOOSH
UFFT! MAY MISS HER. WON'T MISS THAT.
WHEN THIS IS OVER, SUPERMAN... YOU OWE OUR FRIEND BACK THERE SOMETHING BETTER THAN LIFE IN A MUSEUM.
ALTHOUGH I THINK SHE'S ALREADY IN THE PROCESS OF SEVERING ALL TIES WITH THIS DIMENSION.
WONDER WOMAN! CYBORG! BATMAN! HOW LONG HAVE WE BEEN GONE?
TWO MINUTES, THIRTEEN SECONDS.
SEEMED LIKE DAYS.
STILL LONG ENOUGH FOR EVERYTHING TO GO WRONG.
LIGHTEN UP! AT LEAST THE EARTH IS STILL HERE.
FOR THE MOMENT...

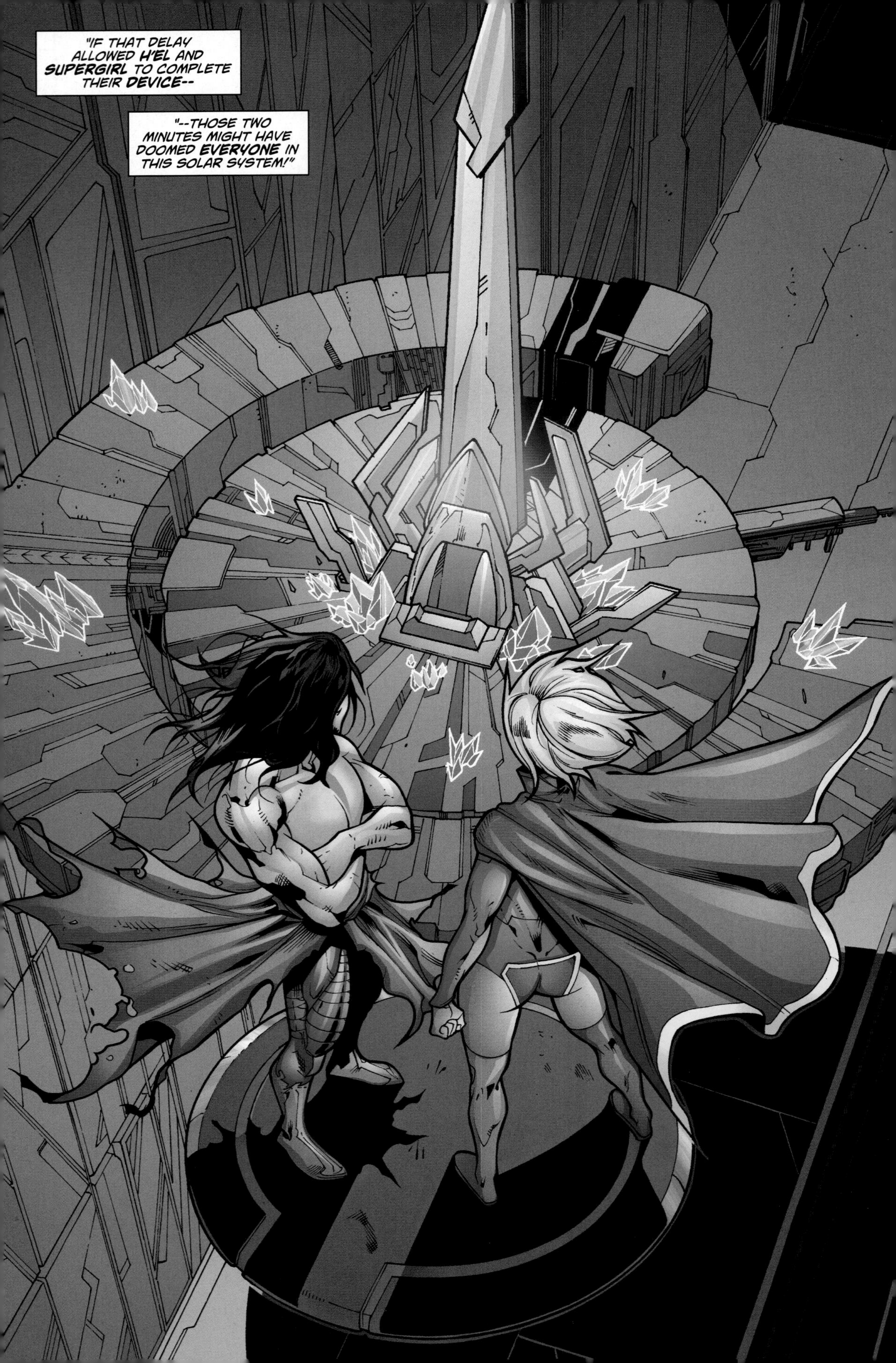
"IF THAT DELAY ALLOWED H'EL AND SUPERGIRL TO COMPLETE THEIR DEVICE--
"--THOSE TWO MINUTES MIGHT HAVE DOOMED EVERYONE IN THIS SOLAR SYSTEM!"

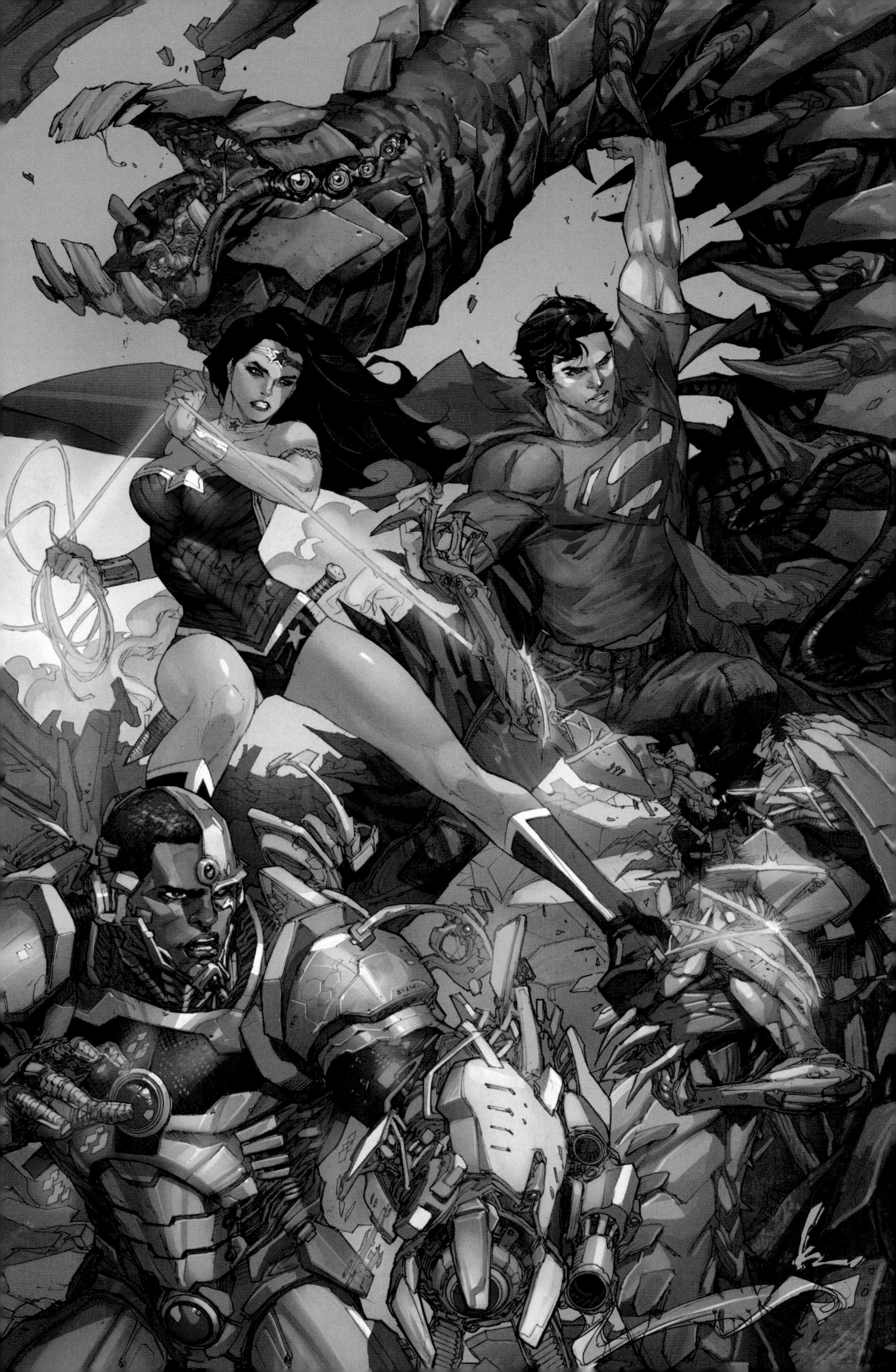

A FISTFUL OF STICKS

SCOTT LOBDELL writer **KENNETH ROCAFORT** artist cover art by **KENNETH ROCAFORT & SUNNY GHO**

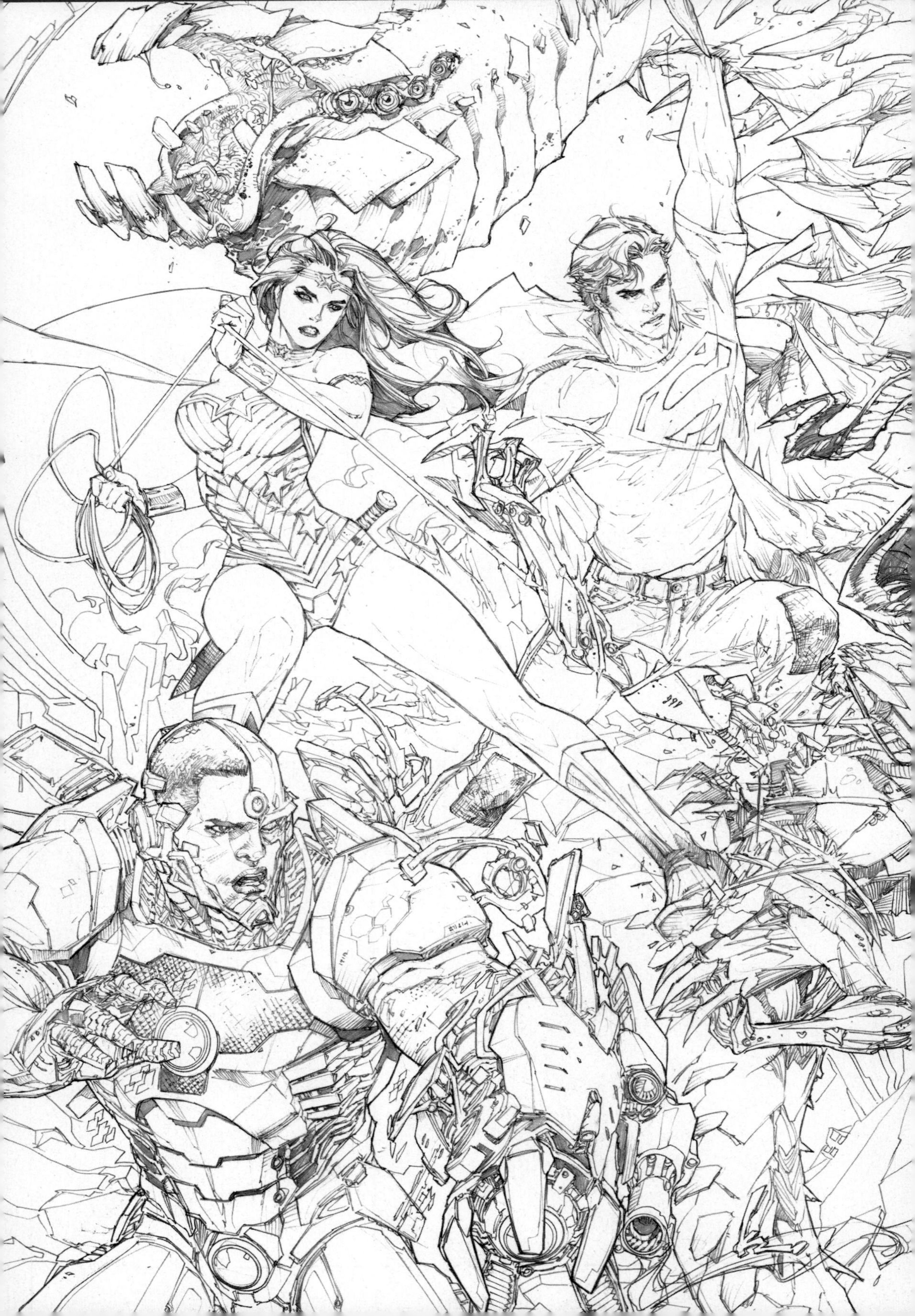

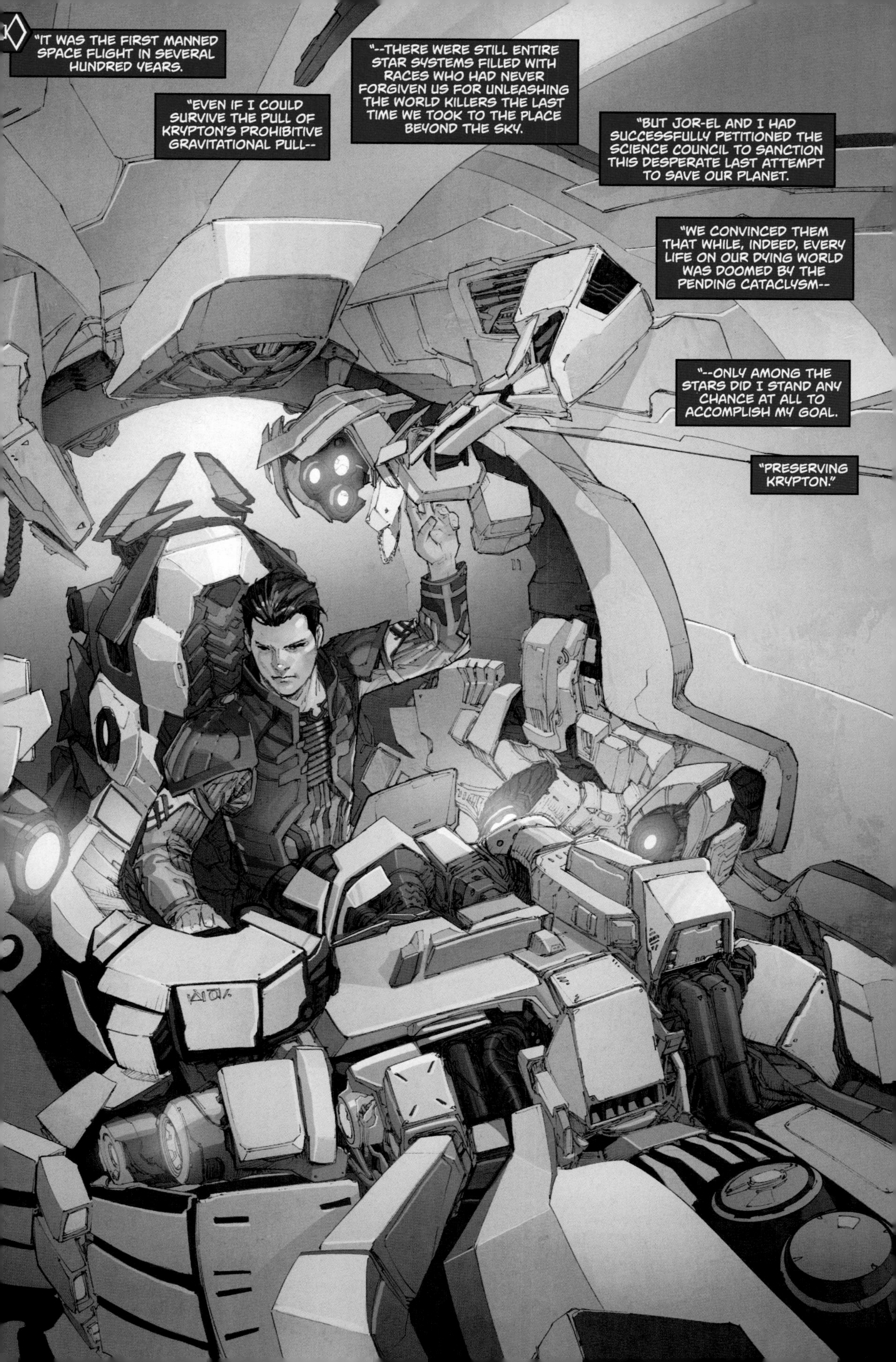
"IT WAS THE FIRST MANNED SPACE FLIGHT IN SEVERAL HUNDRED YEARS.
"EVEN IF I COULD SURVIVE THE PULL OF KRYPTON'S PROHIBITIVE GRAVITATIONAL PULL--
"--THERE WERE STILL ENTIRE STAR SYSTEMS FILLED WITH RACES WHO HAD NEVER FORGIVEN US FOR UNLEASHING THE WORLD KILLERS THE LAST TIME WE TOOK TO THE PLACE BEYOND THE SKY.
"BUT JOR-EL AND I HAD SUCCESSFULLY PETITIONED THE SCIENCE COUNCIL TO SANCTION THIS DESPERATE LAST ATTEMPT TO SAVE OUR PLANET.
"WE CONVINCED THEM THAT WHILE, INDEED, EVERY LIFE ON OUR DYING WORLD WAS DOOMED BY THE PENDING CATACLYSM--
"--ONLY AMONG THE STARS DID I STAND ANY CHANCE AT ALL TO ACCOMPLISH MY GOAL.
"PRESERVING KRYPTON."

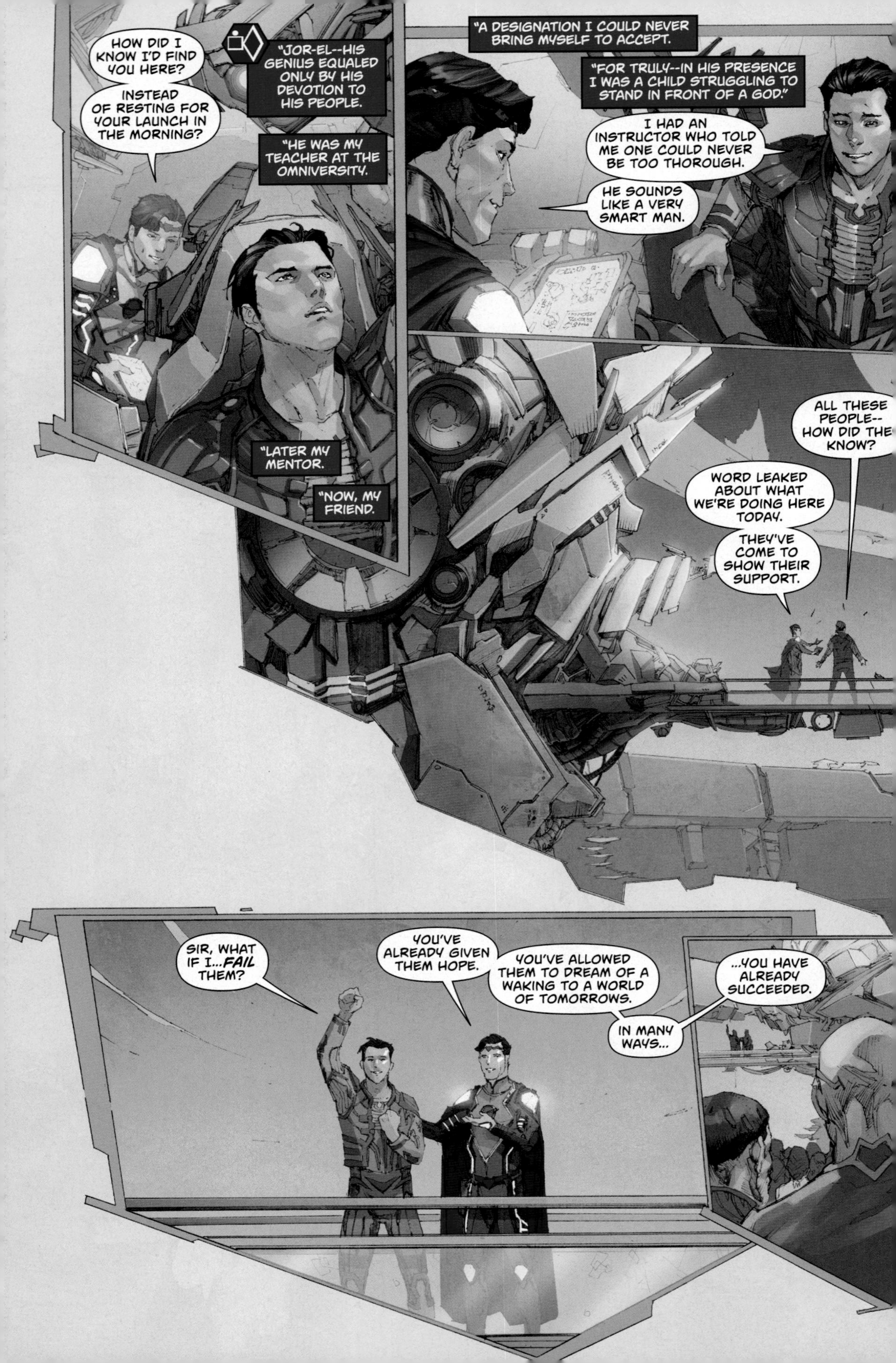
HOW DID I KNOW I'D FIND YOU HERE?
INSTEAD OF RESTING FOR YOUR LAUNCH IN THE MORNING?
"JOR-EL--HIS GENIUS EQUALED ONLY BY HIS DEVOTION TO HIS PEOPLE.
"HE WAS MY TEACHER AT THE OMNIVERSITY.
"LATER MY MENTOR.
"NOW, MY FRIEND.
"A DESIGNATION I COULD NEVER BRING MYSELF TO ACCEPT.
"FOR TRULY--IN HIS PRESENCE I WAS A CHILD STRUGGLING TO STAND IN FRONT OF A GOD."
I HAD AN INSTRUCTOR WHO TOLD ME ONE COULD NEVER BE TOO THOROUGH.
HE SOUNDS LIKE A VERY SMART MAN.
ALL THESE PEOPLE--HOW DID THE KNOW?
WORD LEAKED ABOUT WHAT WE'RE DOING HERE TODAY.
THEY'VE COME TO SHOW THEIR SUPPORT.
SIR, WHAT IF I...FAIL THEM?
YOU'VE ALREADY GIVEN THEM HOPE.
YOU'VE ALLOWED THEM TO DREAM OF A WAKING TO A WORLD OF TOMORROWS.
IN MANY WAYS...
...YOU HAVE ALREADY SUCCEEDED.

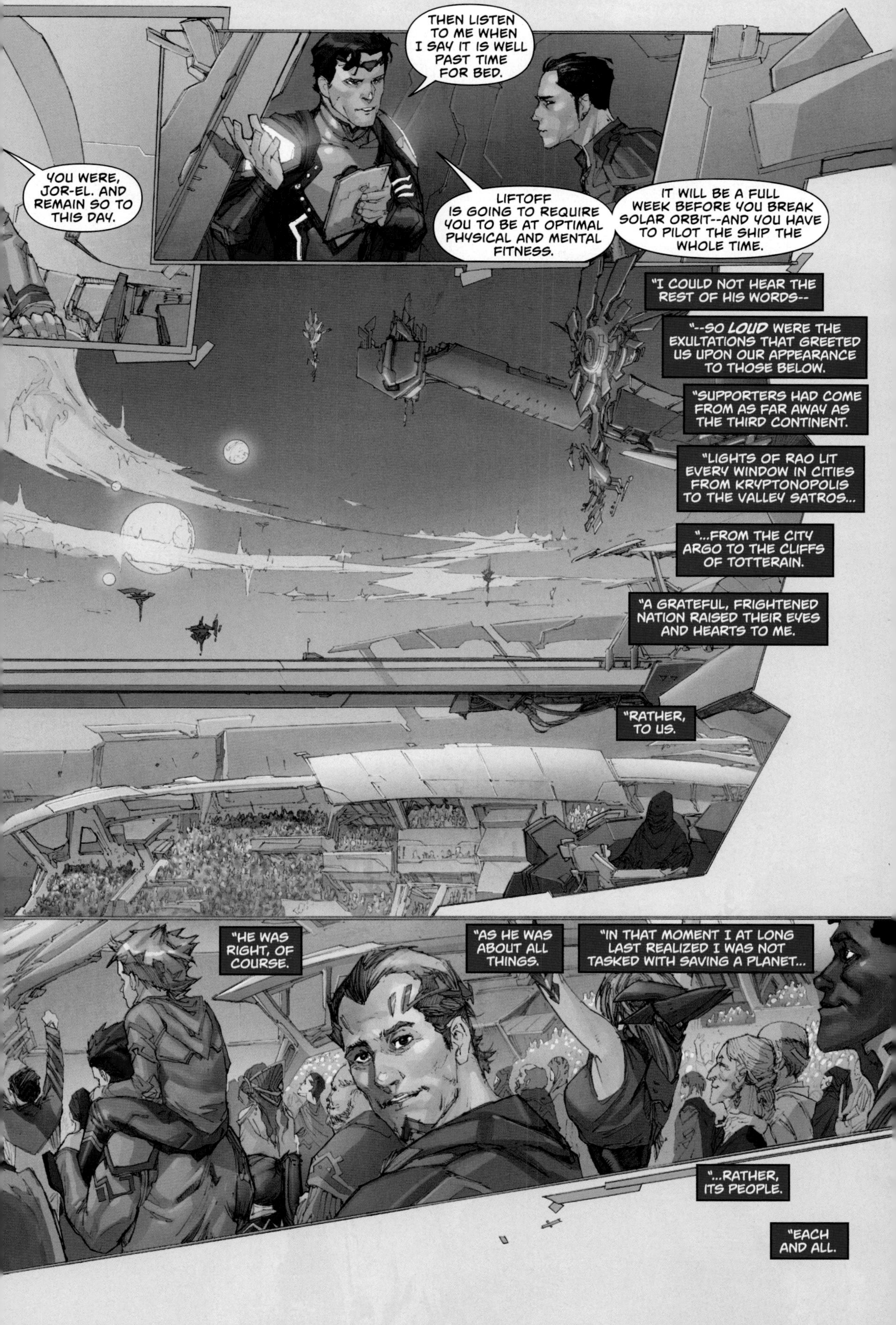
THEN LISTEN TO ME WHEN I SAY IT IS WELL PAST TIME FOR BED.
YOU WERE, JOR-EL. AND REMAIN SO TO THIS DAY.
LIFTOFF IS GOING TO REQUIRE YOU TO BE AT OPTIMAL PHYSICAL AND MENTAL FITNESS.
IT WILL BE A FULL WEEK BEFORE YOU BREAK SOLAR ORBIT--AND YOU HAVE TO PILOT THE SHIP THE WHOLE TIME.
"I COULD NOT HEAR THE REST OF HIS WORDS--
"--SO LOUD WERE THE EXULTATIONS THAT GREETED US UPON OUR APPEARANCE TO THOSE BELOW.
"SUPPORTERS HAD COME FROM AS FAR AWAY AS THE THIRD CONTINENT.
"LIGHTS OF RAO LIT EVERY WINDOW IN CITIES FROM KRYPTONOPOLIS TO THE VALLEY SATROS...
"...FROM THE CITY ARGO TO THE CLIFFS OF TOTTERAIN.
"A GRATEFUL, FRIGHTENED NATION RAISED THEIR EYES AND HEARTS TO ME.
"RATHER, TO US.
"HE WAS RIGHT, OF COURSE.
"AS HE WAS ABOUT ALL THINGS.
"IN THAT MOMENT I AT LONG LAST REALIZED I WAS NOT TASKED WITH SAVING A PLANET...
"...RATHER, ITS PEOPLE.
"EACH AND ALL.

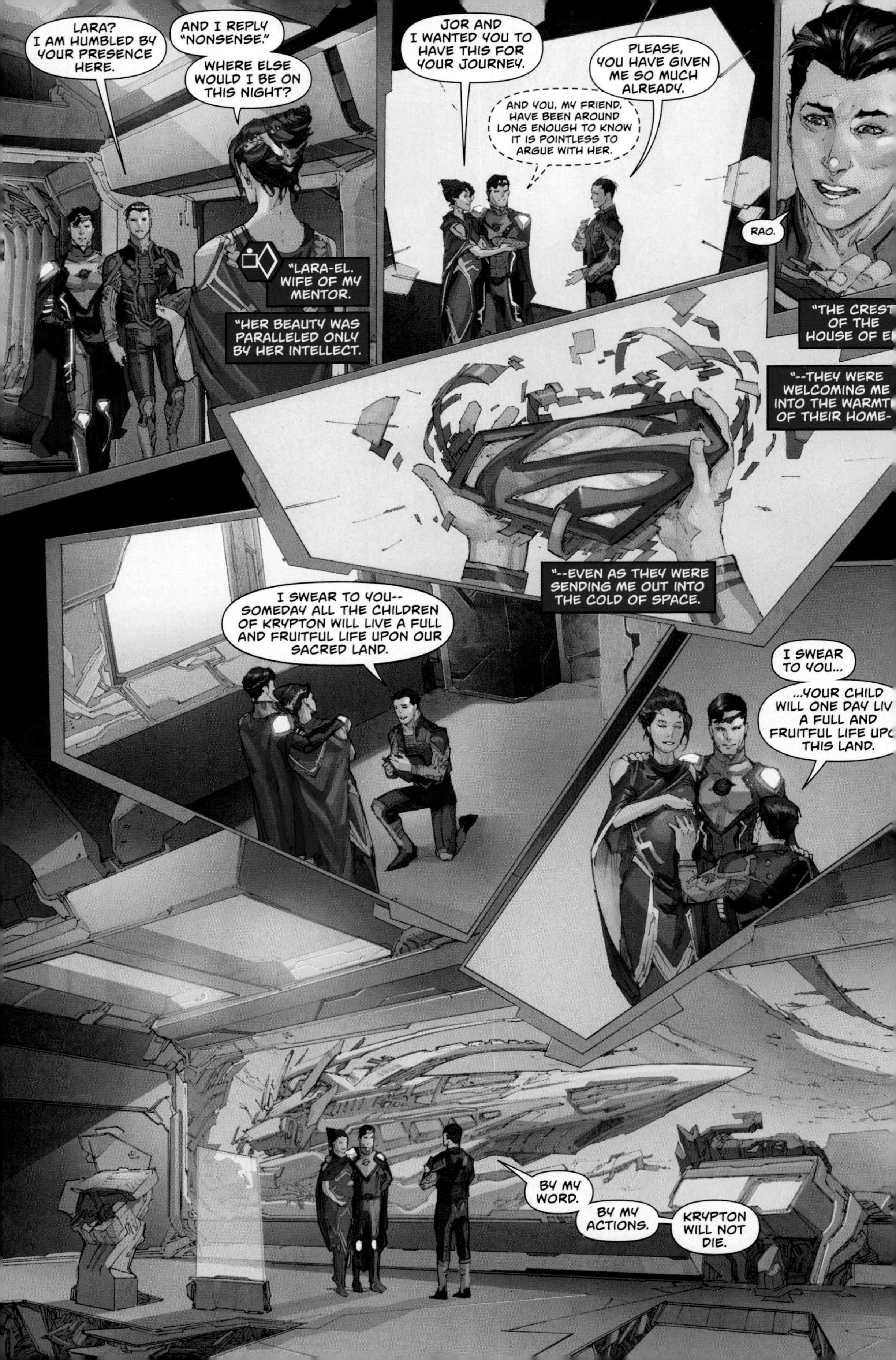
LARA? I AM HUMBLED BY YOUR PRESENCE HERE.
AND I REPLY "NONSENSE."
WHERE ELSE WOULD I BE ON THIS NIGHT?
"LARA-EL. WIFE OF MY MENTOR.
"HER BEAUTY WAS PARALLELED ONLY BY HER INTELLECT.
JOR AND I WANTED YOU TO HAVE THIS FOR YOUR JOURNEY.
PLEASE, YOU HAVE GIVEN ME SO MUCH ALREADY.
AND YOU, MY FRIEND, HAVE BEEN AROUND LONG ENOUGH TO KNOW IT IS POINTLESS TO ARGUE WITH HER.
RAO.
"THE CREST OF THE HOUSE OF E
"--THEY WERE WELCOMING ME INTO THE WARMT OF THEIR HOME-
"--EVEN AS THEY WERE SENDING ME OUT INTO THE COLD OF SPACE.
I SWEAR TO YOU-- SOMEDAY ALL THE CHILDREN OF KRYPTON WILL LIVE A FULL AND FRUITFUL LIFE UPON OUR SACRED LAND.
I SWEAR TO YOU...
...YOUR CHILD WILL ONE DAY LIV A FULL AND FRUITFUL LIFE UPO THIS LAND.
BY MY WORD.
BY MY ACTIONS.
KRYPTON WILL NOT DIE.

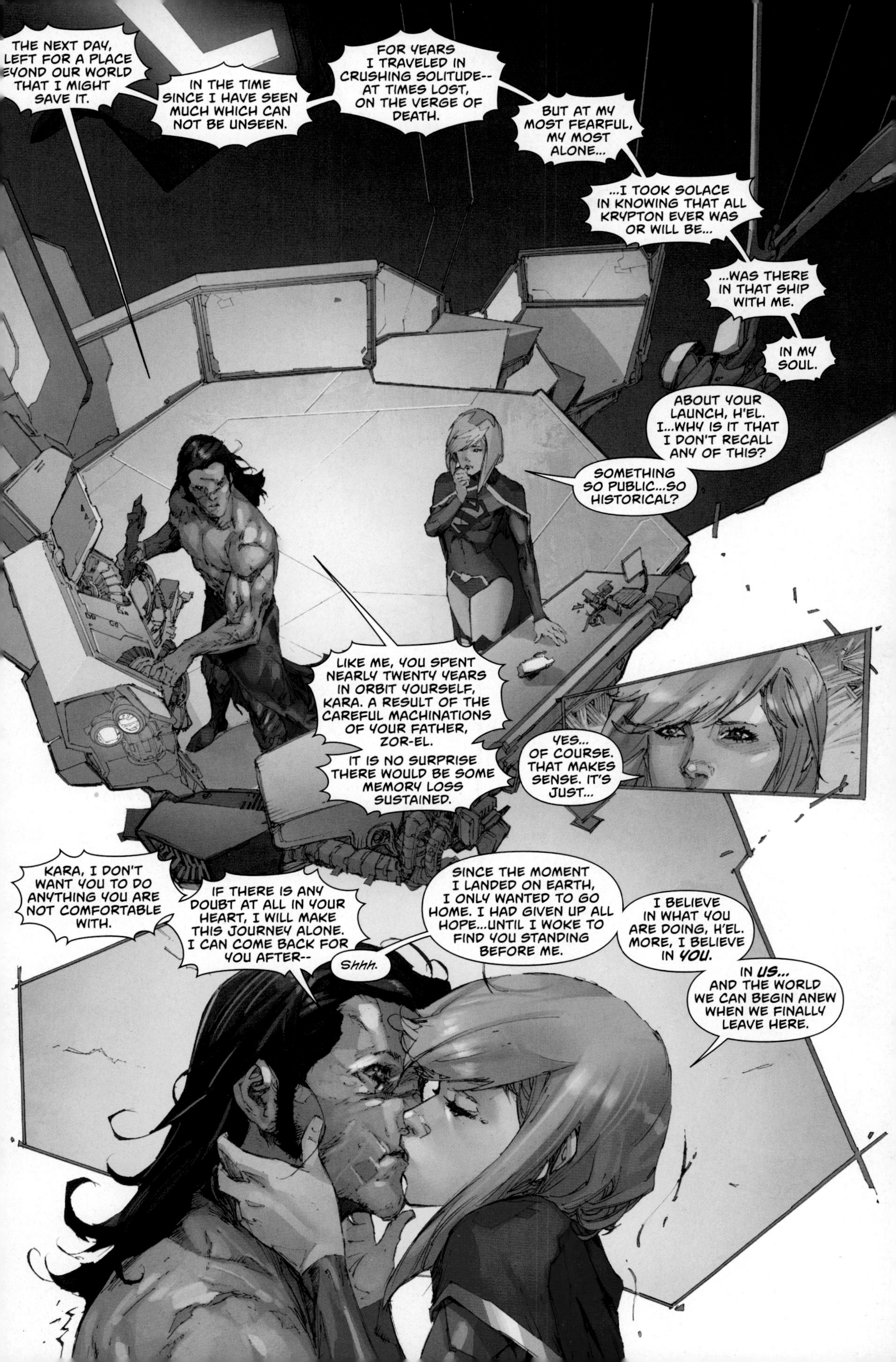
THE NEXT DAY, LEFT FOR A PLACE EYOND OUR WORLD THAT I MIGHT SAVE IT.
IN THE TIME SINCE I HAVE SEEN MUCH WHICH CAN NOT BE UNSEEN.
FOR YEARS I TRAVELED IN CRUSHING SOLITUDE-- AT TIMES LOST, ON THE VERGE OF DEATH.
BUT AT MY MOST FEARFUL, MY MOST ALONE...
...I TOOK SOLACE IN KNOWING THAT ALL KRYPTON EVER WAS OR WILL BE...
...WAS THERE IN THAT SHIP WITH ME.
IN MY SOUL.
ABOUT YOUR LAUNCH, H'EL. I...WHY IS IT THAT I DON'T RECALL ANY OF THIS?
SOMETHING SO PUBLIC...SO HISTORICAL?
LIKE ME, YOU SPENT NEARLY TWENTY YEARS IN ORBIT YOURSELF, KARA. A RESULT OF THE CAREFUL MACHINATIONS OF YOUR FATHER, ZOR-EL.
IT IS NO SURPRISE THERE WOULD BE SOME MEMORY LOSS SUSTAINED.
YES... OF COURSE. THAT MAKES SENSE. IT'S JUST...
KARA, I DON'T WANT YOU TO DO ANYTHING YOU ARE NOT COMFORTABLE WITH.
IF THERE IS ANY DOUBT AT ALL IN YOUR HEART, I WILL MAKE THIS JOURNEY ALONE. I CAN COME BACK FOR YOU AFTER--
Shhh.
SINCE THE MOMENT I LANDED ON EARTH, I ONLY WANTED TO GO HOME. I HAD GIVEN UP ALL HOPE...UNTIL I WOKE TO FIND YOU STANDING BEFORE ME.
I BELIEVE IN WHAT YOU ARE DOING, H'EL. MORE, I BELIEVE IN *YOU*.
IN *US*... AND THE WORLD WE CAN BEGIN ANEW WHEN WE FINALLY LEAVE HERE.

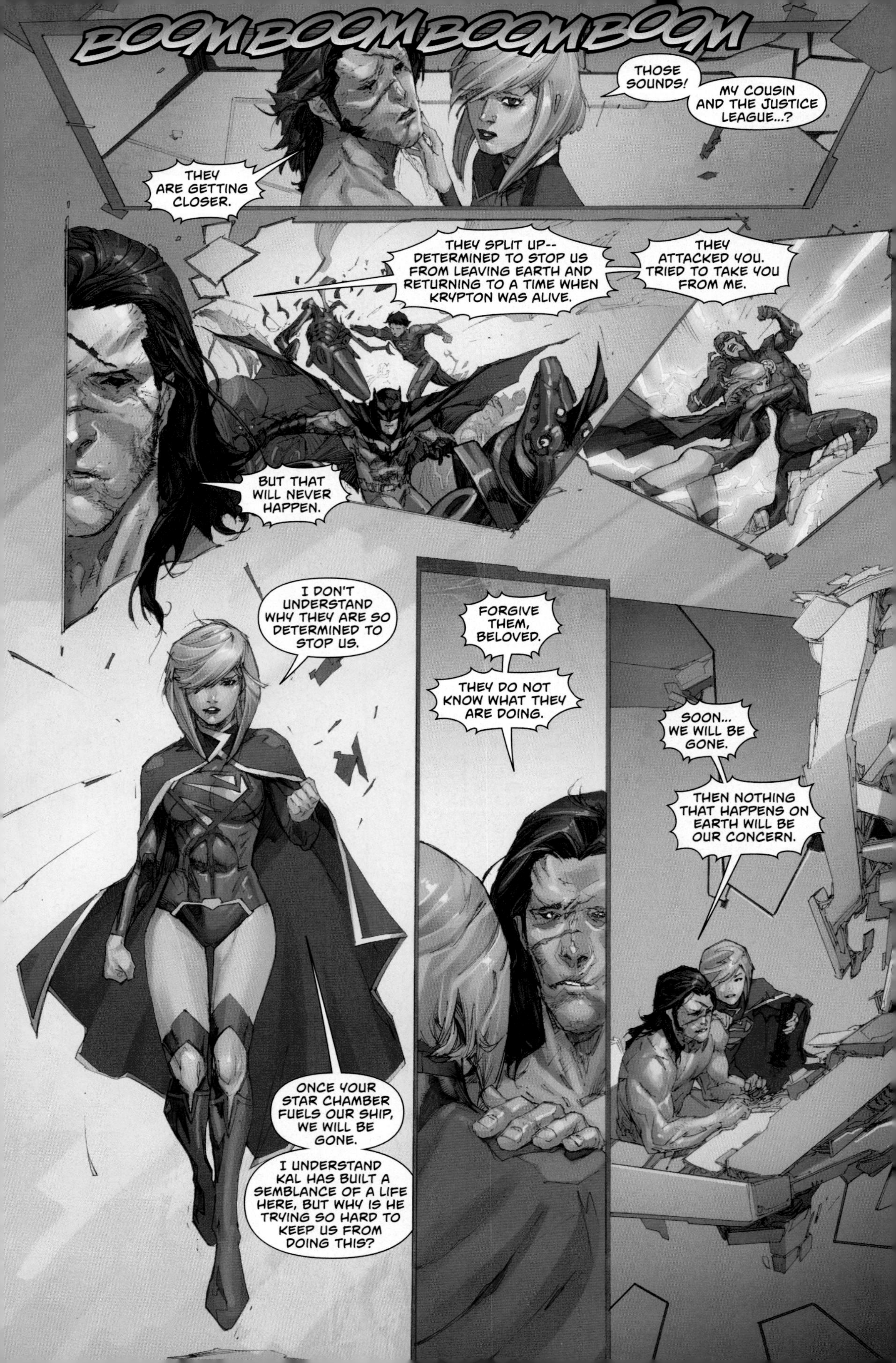
BOOM BOOM BOOM BOOM
THOSE SOUNDS!
MY COUSIN AND THE JUSTICE LEAGUE...?
THEY ARE GETTING CLOSER.
THEY SPLIT UP-- DETERMINED TO STOP US FROM LEAVING EARTH AND RETURNING TO A TIME WHEN KRYPTON WAS ALIVE.
THEY ATTACKED YOU. TRIED TO TAKE YOU FROM ME.
BUT THAT WILL NEVER HAPPEN.
I DON'T UNDERSTAND WHY THEY ARE SO DETERMINED TO STOP US.
ONCE YOUR STAR CHAMBER FUELS OUR SHIP, WE WILL BE GONE.
I UNDERSTAND KAL HAS BUILT A SEMBLANCE OF A LIFE HERE, BUT WHY IS HE TRYING SO HARD TO KEEP US FROM DOING THIS?
FORGIVE THEM, BELOVED.
THEY DO NOT KNOW WHAT THEY ARE DOING.
SOON... WE WILL BE GONE.
THEN NOTHING THAT HAPPENS ON EARTH WILL BE OUR CONCERN.

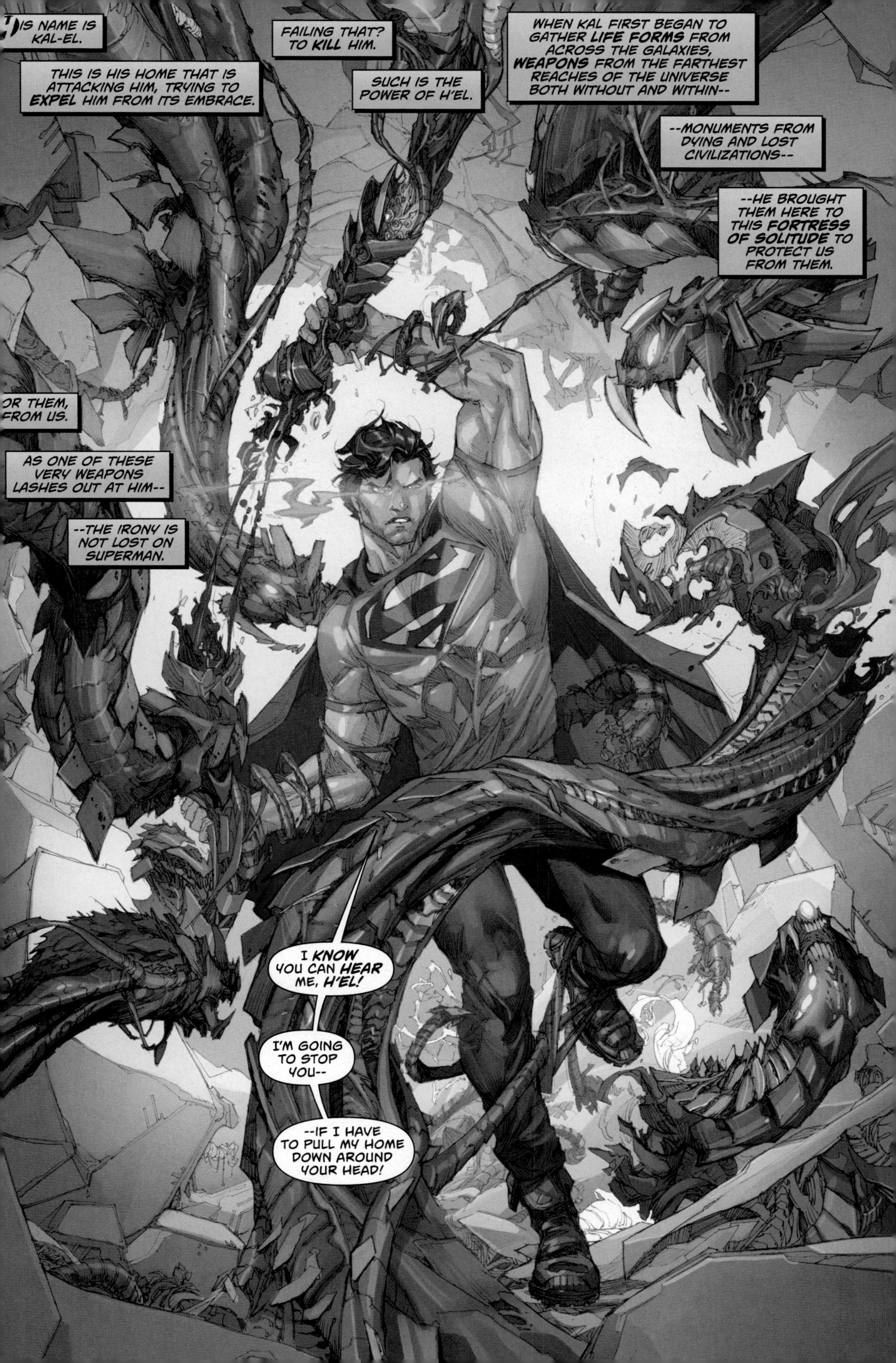

HIS NAME IS KAL-EL.
THIS IS HIS HOME THAT IS ATTACKING HIM, TRYING TO EXPEL HIM FROM ITS EMBRACE.
FAILING THAT? TO KILL HIM.
SUCH IS THE POWER OF H'EL.
WHEN KAL FIRST BEGAN TO GATHER LIFE FORMS FROM ACROSS THE GALAXIES, WEAPONS FROM THE FARTHEST REACHES OF THE UNIVERSE BOTH WITHOUT AND WITHIN--
--MONUMENTS FROM DYING AND LOST CIVILIZATIONS--
--HE BROUGHT THEM HERE TO THIS FORTRESS OF SOLITUDE TO PROTECT US FROM THEM.
OR THEM, FROM US.
AS ONE OF THESE VERY WEAPONS LASHES OUT AT HIM--
--THE IRONY IS NOT LOST ON SUPERMAN.
I KNOW YOU CAN HEAR ME, H'EL!
I'M GOING TO STOP YOU--
--IF I HAVE TO PULL MY HOME DOWN AROUND YOUR HEAD!

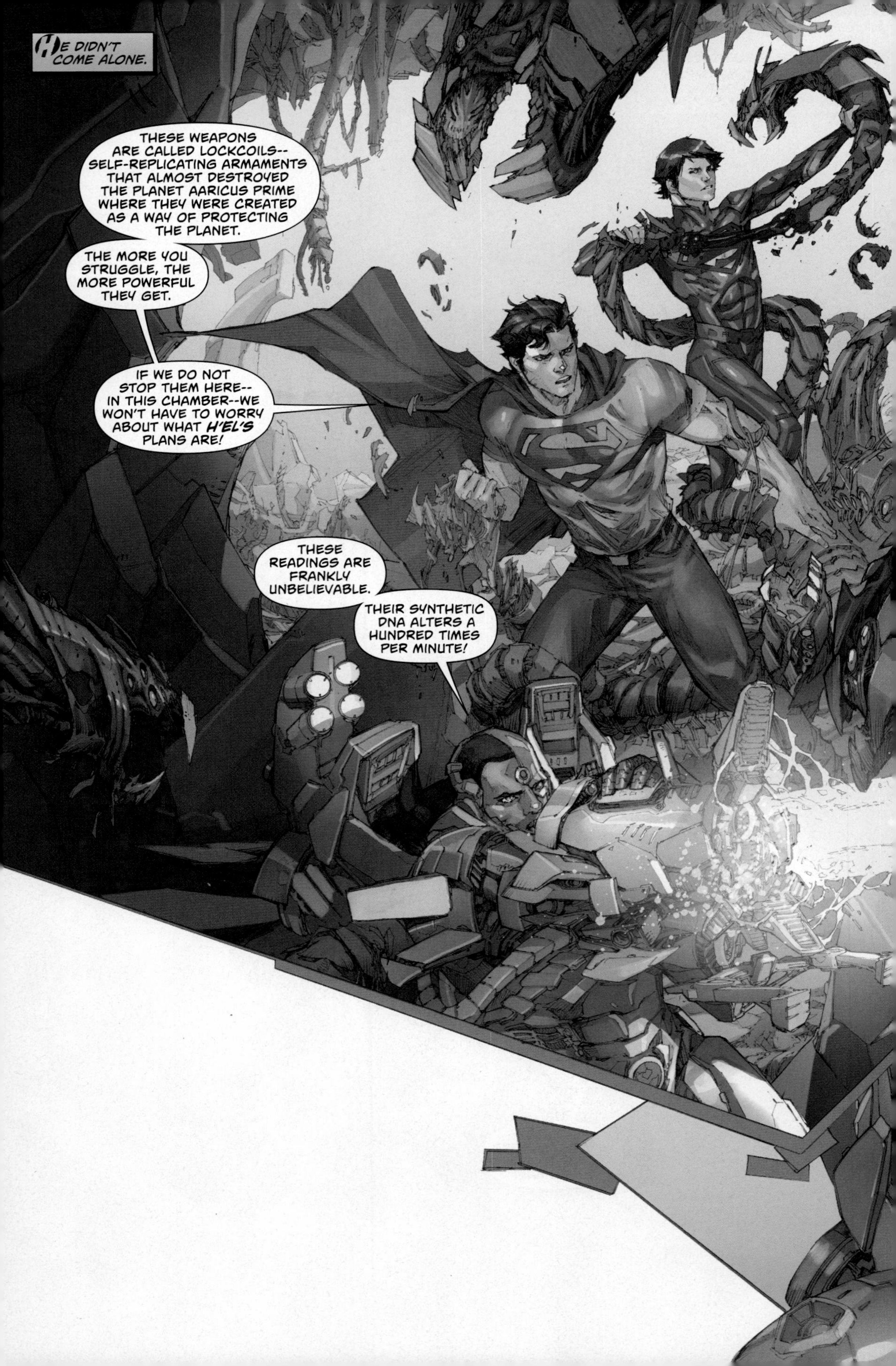
HE DIDN'T COME ALONE.
THESE WEAPONS ARE CALLED LOCKCOILS--SELF-REPLICATING ARMAMENTS THAT ALMOST DESTROYED THE PLANET AARICUS PRIME WHERE THEY WERE CREATED AS A WAY OF PROTECTING THE PLANET.
THE MORE YOU STRUGGLE, THE MORE POWERFUL THEY GET.
IF WE DO NOT STOP THEM HERE--IN THIS CHAMBER--WE WON'T HAVE TO WORRY ABOUT WHAT H'EL'S PLANS ARE!
THESE READINGS ARE FRANKLY UNBELIEVABLE.
THEIR SYNTHETIC DNA ALTERS A HUNDRED TIMES PER MINUTE!

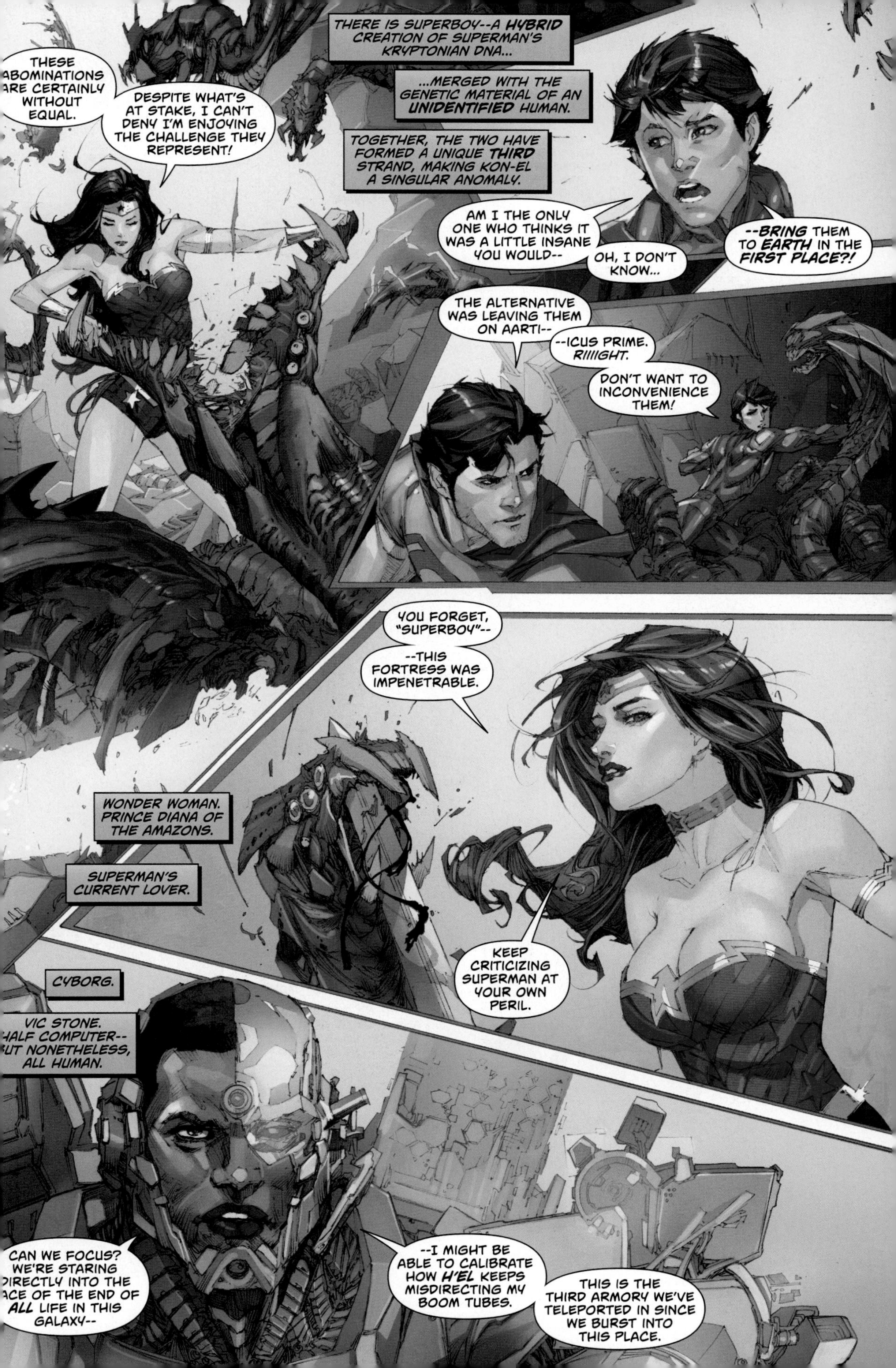
THERE IS SUPERBOY--A HYBRID CREATION OF SUPERMAN'S KRYPTONIAN DNA...
...MERGED WITH THE GENETIC MATERIAL OF AN UNIDENTIFIED HUMAN.
TOGETHER, THE TWO HAVE FORMED A UNIQUE THIRD STRAND, MAKING KON-EL A SINGULAR ANOMALY.
THESE ABOMINATIONS ARE CERTAINLY WITHOUT EQUAL.
DESPITE WHAT'S AT STAKE, I CAN'T DENY I'M ENJOYING THE CHALLENGE THEY REPRESENT!
AM I THE ONLY ONE WHO THINKS IT WAS A LITTLE INSANE YOU WOULD--
OH, I DON'T KNOW...
--BRING THEM TO EARTH IN THE FIRST PLACE?!
THE ALTERNATIVE WAS LEAVING THEM ON AARTI--
--ICUS PRIME. RIIIIGHT.
DON'T WANT TO INCONVENIENCE THEM!
YOU FORGET, "SUPERBOY"--
--THIS FORTRESS WAS IMPENETRABLE.
WONDER WOMAN. PRINCE DIANA OF THE AMAZONS.
SUPERMAN'S CURRENT LOVER.
KEEP CRITICIZING SUPERMAN AT YOUR OWN PERIL.
CYBORG.
VIC STONE. HALF COMPUTER-- BUT NONETHELESS, ALL HUMAN.
CAN WE FOCUS? WE'RE STARING DIRECTLY INTO THE FACE OF THE END OF ALL LIFE IN THIS GALAXY--
--I MIGHT BE ABLE TO CALIBRATE HOW H'EL KEEPS MISDIRECTING MY BOOM TUBES.
THIS IS THE THIRD ARMORY WE'VE TELEPORTED IN SINCE WE BURST INTO THIS PLACE.

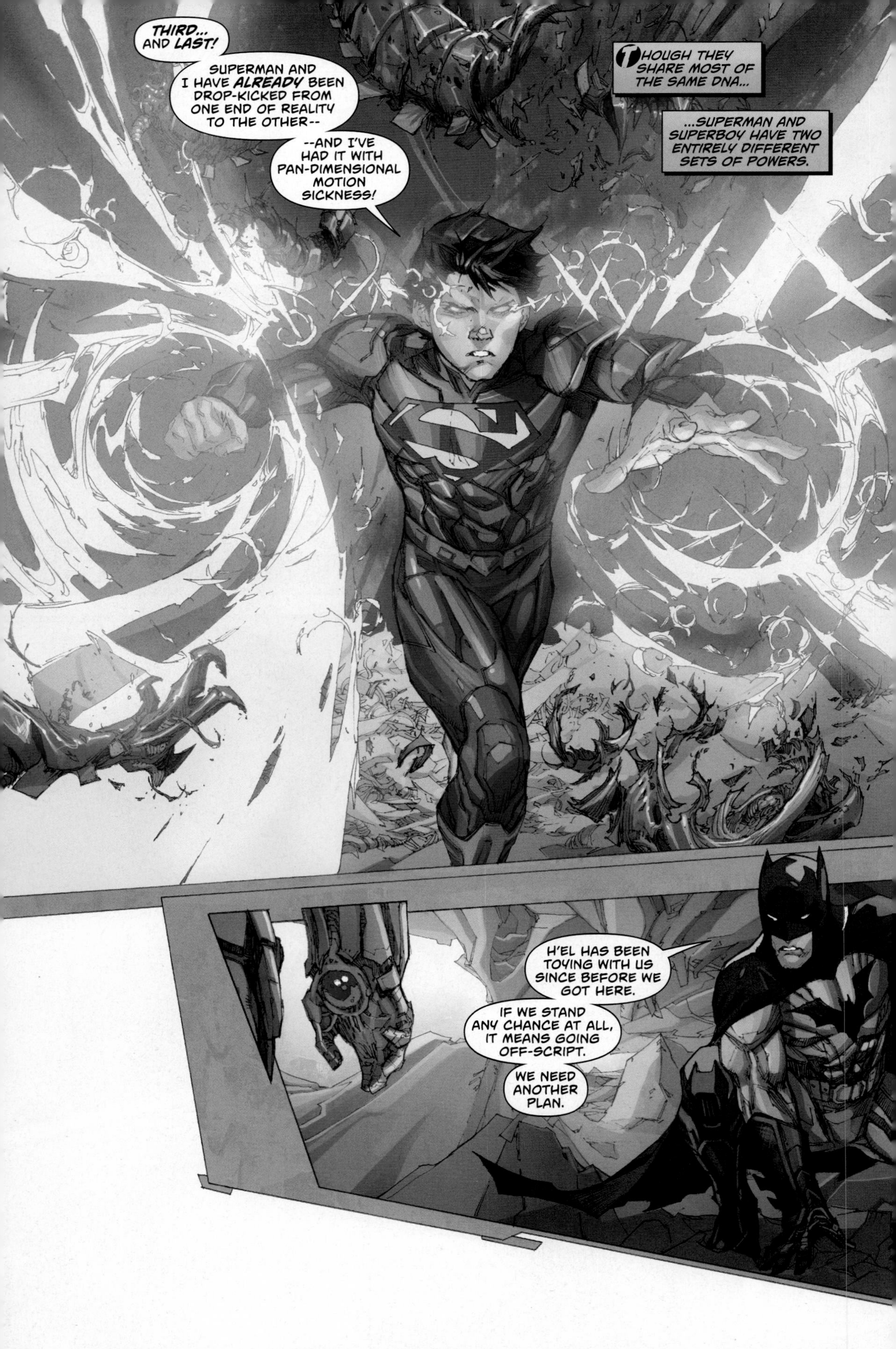

THIRD... AND LAST!
SUPERMAN AND I HAVE ALREADY BEEN DROP-KICKED FROM ONE END OF REALITY TO THE OTHER--
--AND I'VE HAD IT WITH PAN-DIMENSIONAL MOTION SICKNESS!
THOUGH THEY SHARE MOST OF THE SAME DNA...
...SUPERMAN AND SUPERBOY HAVE TWO ENTIRELY DIFFERENT SETS OF POWERS.
H'EL HAS BEEN TOYING WITH US SINCE BEFORE WE GOT HERE.
IF WE STAND ANY CHANCE AT ALL, IT MEANS GOING OFF-SCRIPT.
WE NEED ANOTHER PLAN.

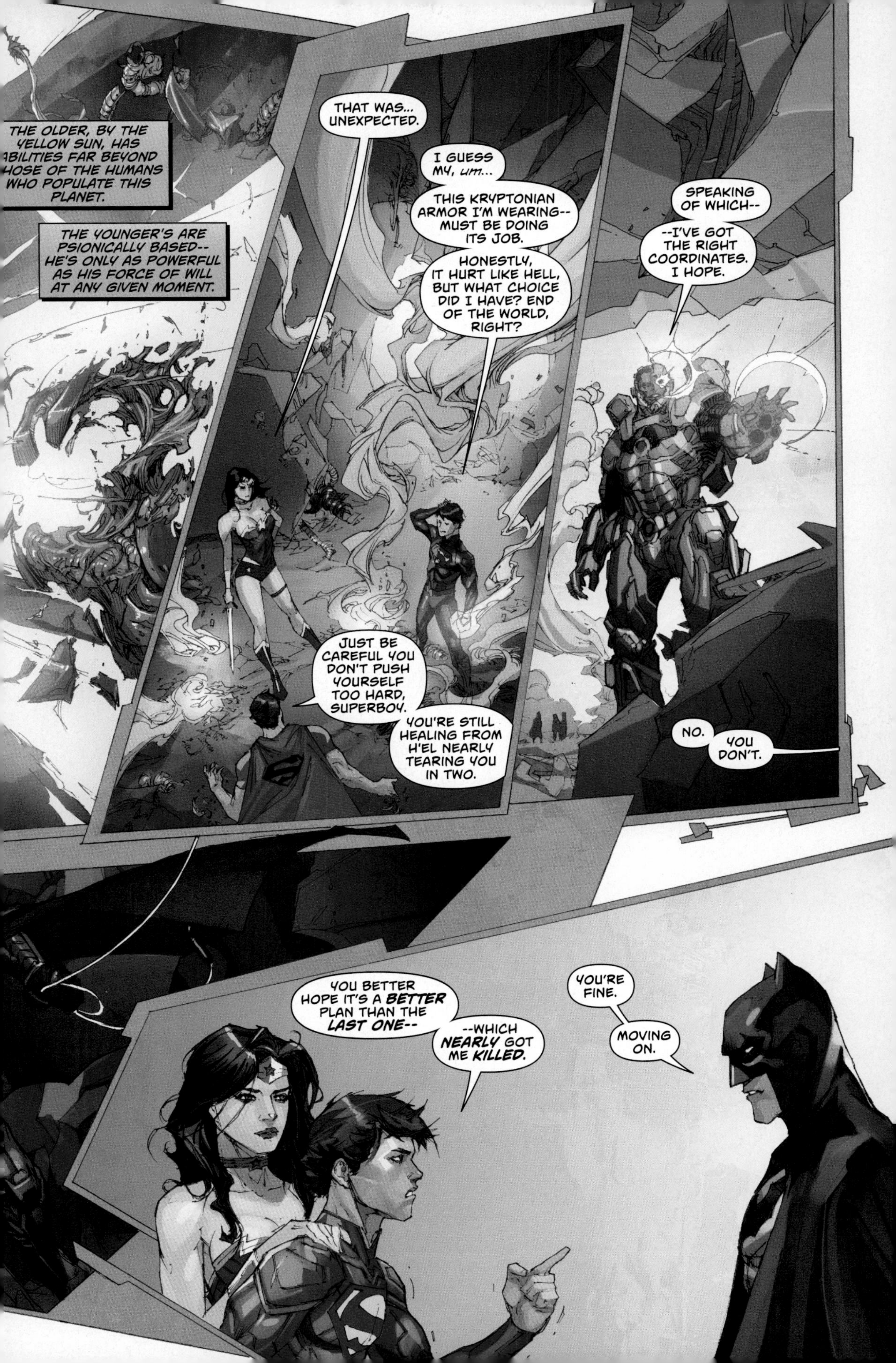

THE OLDER, BY THE YELLOW SUN, HAS ABILITIES FAR BEYOND THOSE OF THE HUMANS WHO POPULATE THIS PLANET.
THE YOUNGER'S ARE PSIONICALLY BASED-- HE'S ONLY AS POWERFUL AS HIS FORCE OF WILL AT ANY GIVEN MOMENT.
THAT WAS... UNEXPECTED.
I GUESS MY, *UM*...
THIS KRYPTONIAN ARMOR I'M WEARING-- MUST BE DOING ITS JOB.
HONESTLY, IT HURT LIKE HELL, BUT WHAT CHOICE DID I HAVE? END OF THE WORLD, RIGHT?
JUST BE CAREFUL YOU DON'T PUSH YOURSELF TOO HARD, SUPERBOY.
YOU'RE STILL HEALING FROM H'EL NEARLY TEARING YOU IN TWO.
SPEAKING OF WHICH--
--I'VE GOT THE RIGHT COORDINATES. I HOPE.
NO.
YOU DON'T.
YOU BETTER HOPE IT'S A **BETTER** PLAN THAN THE **LAST ONE**--
--WHICH **NEARLY** GOT ME **KILLED**.
YOU'RE FINE.
MOVING ON.

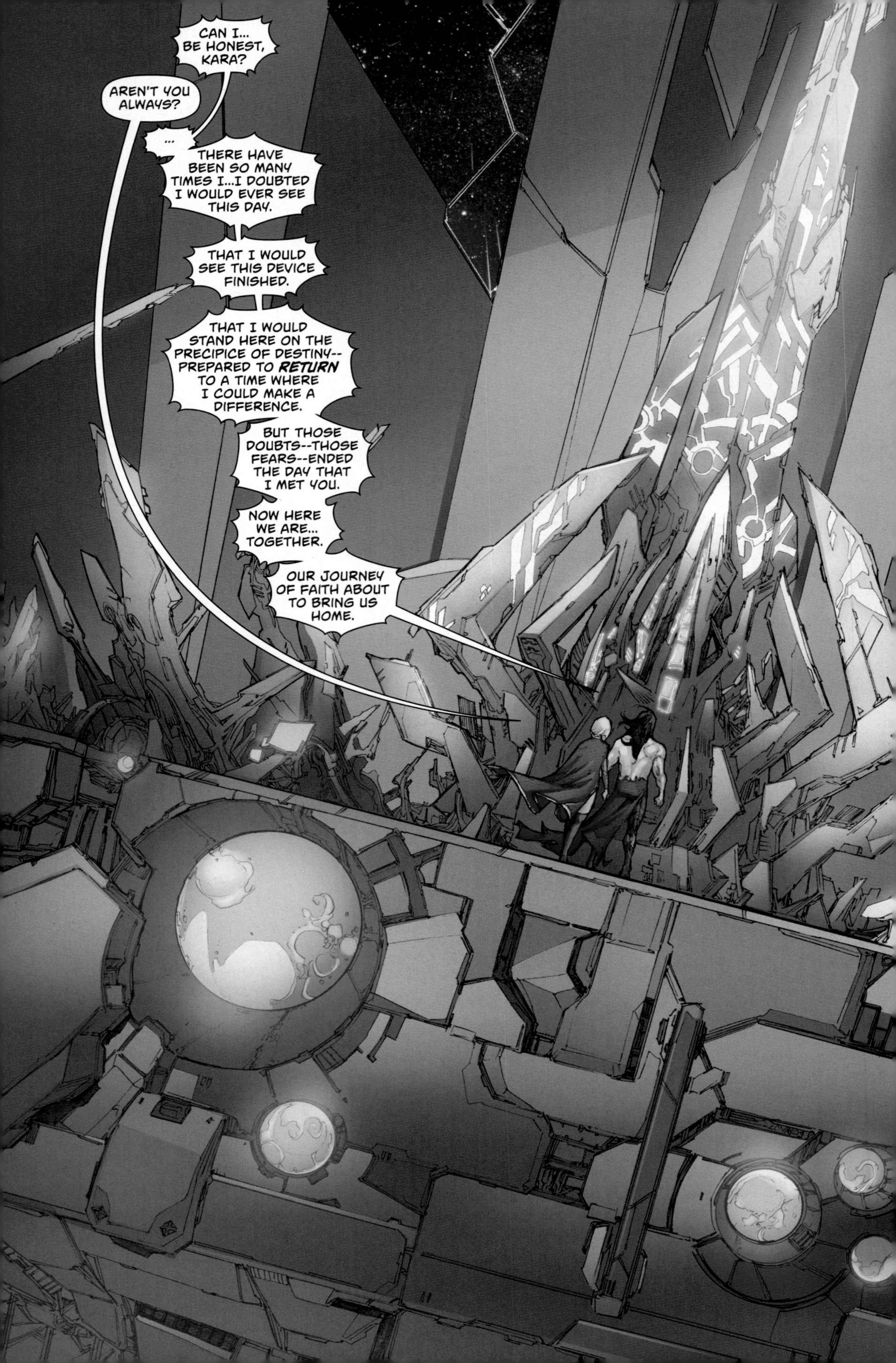
CAN I... BE HONEST, KARA?
AREN'T YOU ALWAYS?
...
THERE HAVE BEEN SO MANY TIMES I...I DOUBTED I WOULD EVER SEE THIS DAY.
THAT I WOULD SEE THIS DEVICE FINISHED.
THAT I WOULD STAND HERE ON THE PRECIPICE OF DESTINY-- PREPARED TO RETURN TO A TIME WHERE I COULD MAKE A DIFFERENCE.
BUT THOSE DOUBTS--THOSE FEARS--ENDED THE DAY THAT I MET YOU.
NOW HERE WE ARE... TOGETHER.
OUR JOURNEY OF FAITH ABOUT TO BRING US HOME.

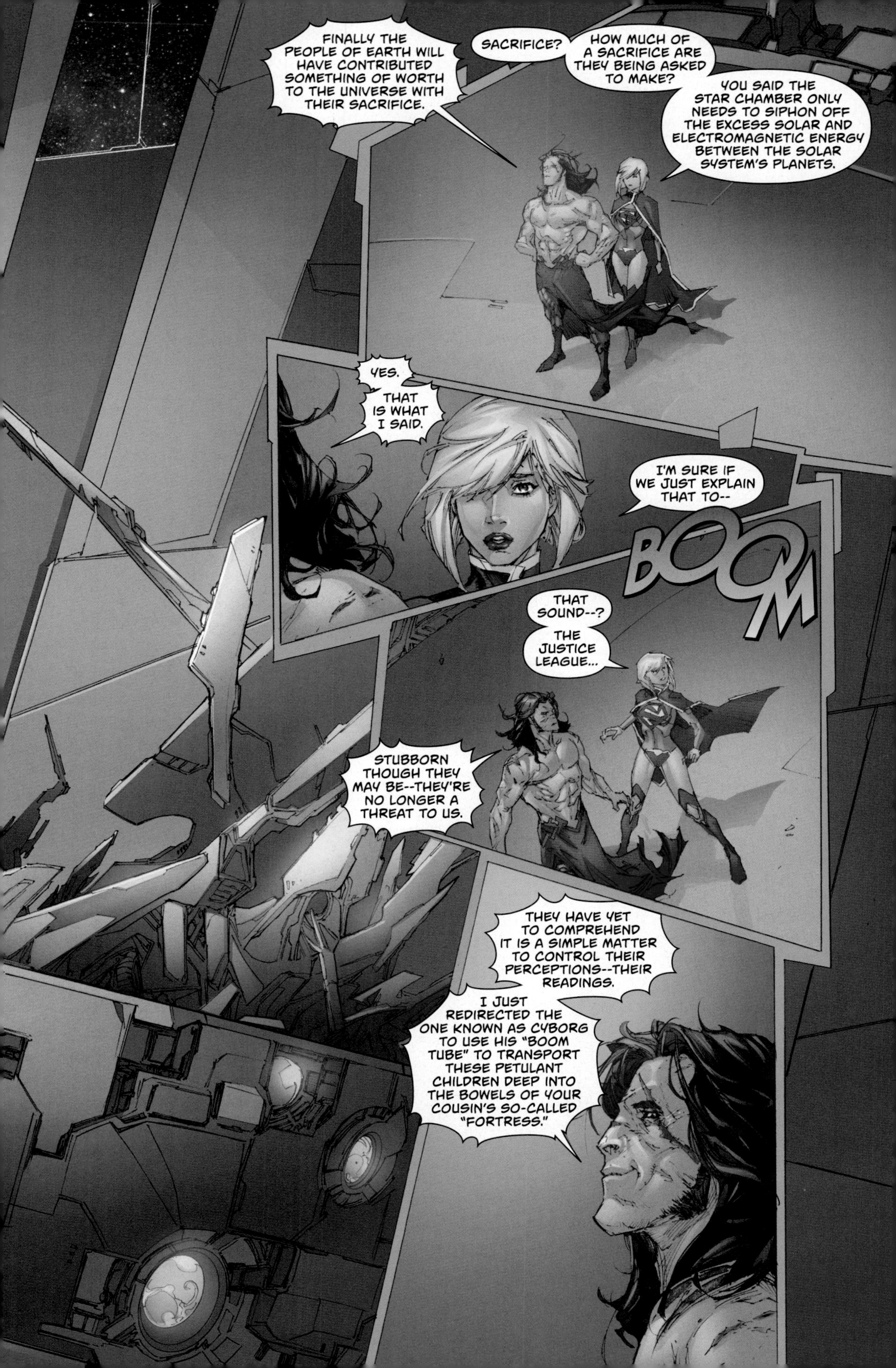
FINALLY THE PEOPLE OF EARTH WILL HAVE CONTRIBUTED SOMETHING OF WORTH TO THE UNIVERSE WITH THEIR SACRIFICE.
SACRIFICE?
HOW MUCH OF A SACRIFICE ARE THEY BEING ASKED TO MAKE?
YOU SAID THE STAR CHAMBER ONLY NEEDS TO SIPHON OFF THE EXCESS SOLAR AND ELECTROMAGNETIC ENERGY BETWEEN THE SOLAR SYSTEM'S PLANETS.
YES.
THAT IS WHAT I SAID.
I'M SURE IF WE JUST EXPLAIN THAT TO--
BOOM
THAT SOUND--?
THE JUSTICE LEAGUE...
STUBBORN THOUGH THEY MAY BE--THEY'RE NO LONGER A THREAT TO US.
THEY HAVE YET TO COMPREHEND IT IS A SIMPLE MATTER TO CONTROL THEIR PERCEPTIONS--THEIR READINGS.
I JUST REDIRECTED THE ONE KNOWN AS CYBORG TO USE HIS "BOOM TUBE" TO TRANSPORT THESE PETULANT CHILDREN DEEP INTO THE BOWELS OF YOUR COUSIN'S SO-CALLED "FORTRESS."

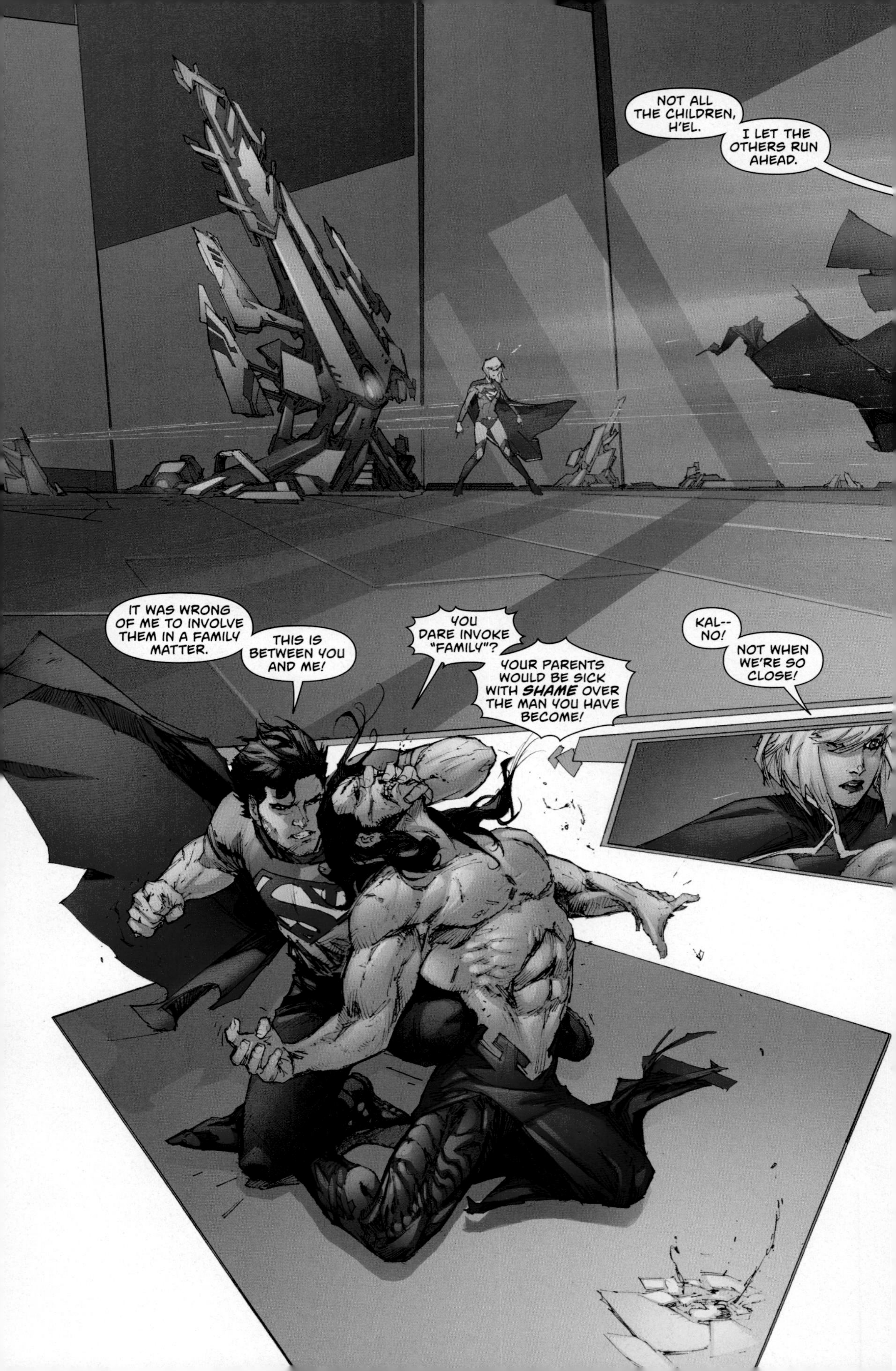
NOT ALL THE CHILDREN, H'EL.
I LET THE OTHERS RUN AHEAD.
IT WAS WRONG OF ME TO INVOLVE THEM IN A FAMILY MATTER.
THIS IS BETWEEN YOU AND ME!
YOU DARE INVOKE "FAMILY"?
YOUR PARENTS WOULD BE SICK WITH SHAME OVER THE MAN YOU HAVE BECOME!
KAL--NO!
NOT WHEN WE'RE SO CLOSE!

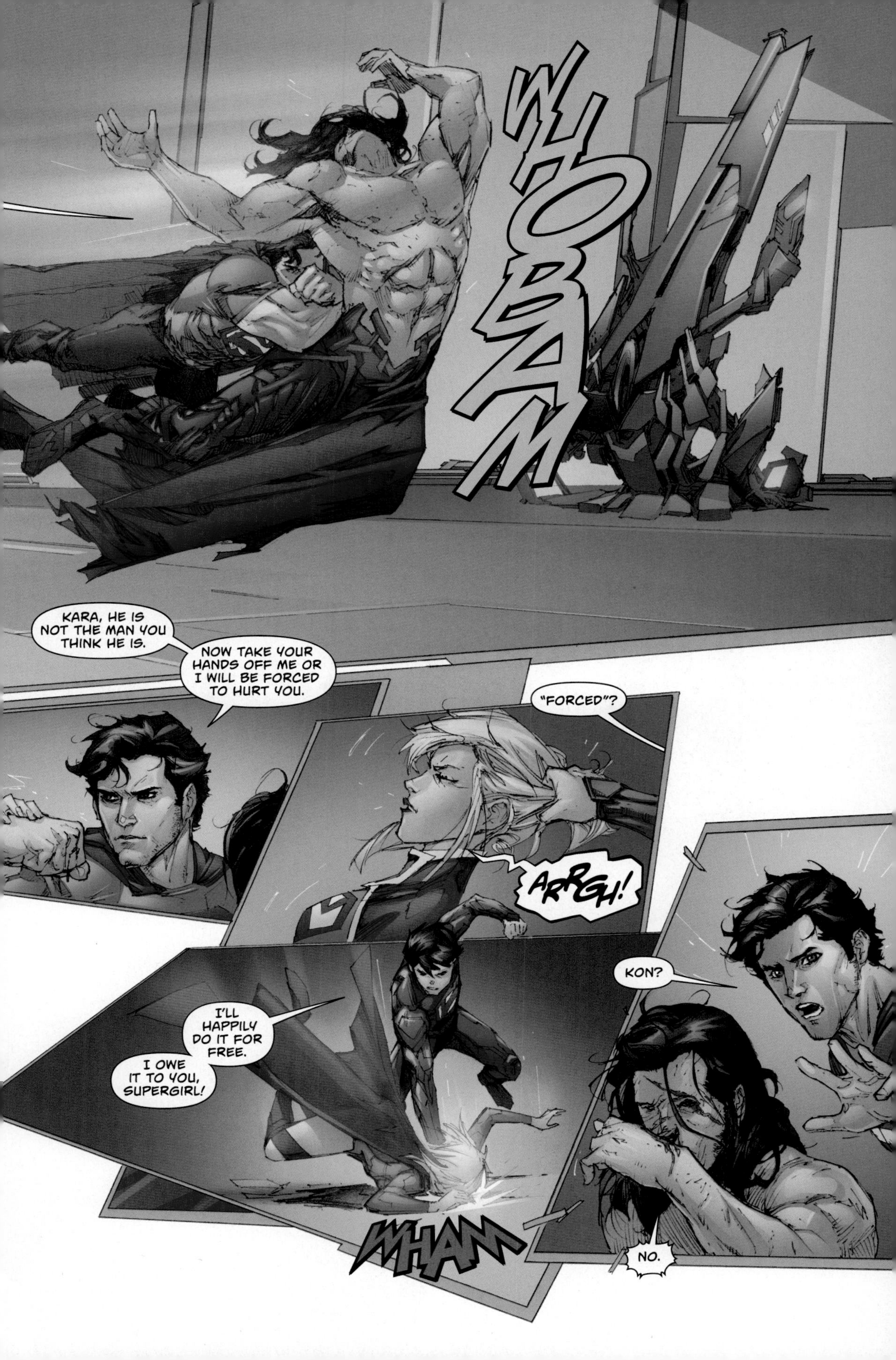
WHOBAM
KARA, HE IS NOT THE MAN YOU THINK HE IS.
NOW TAKE YOUR HANDS OFF ME OR I WILL BE FORCED TO HURT YOU.
"FORCED"?
ARRGH!
I'LL HAPPILY DO IT FOR FREE.
I OWE IT TO YOU, SUPERGIRL!
WHAM
KON?
NO.

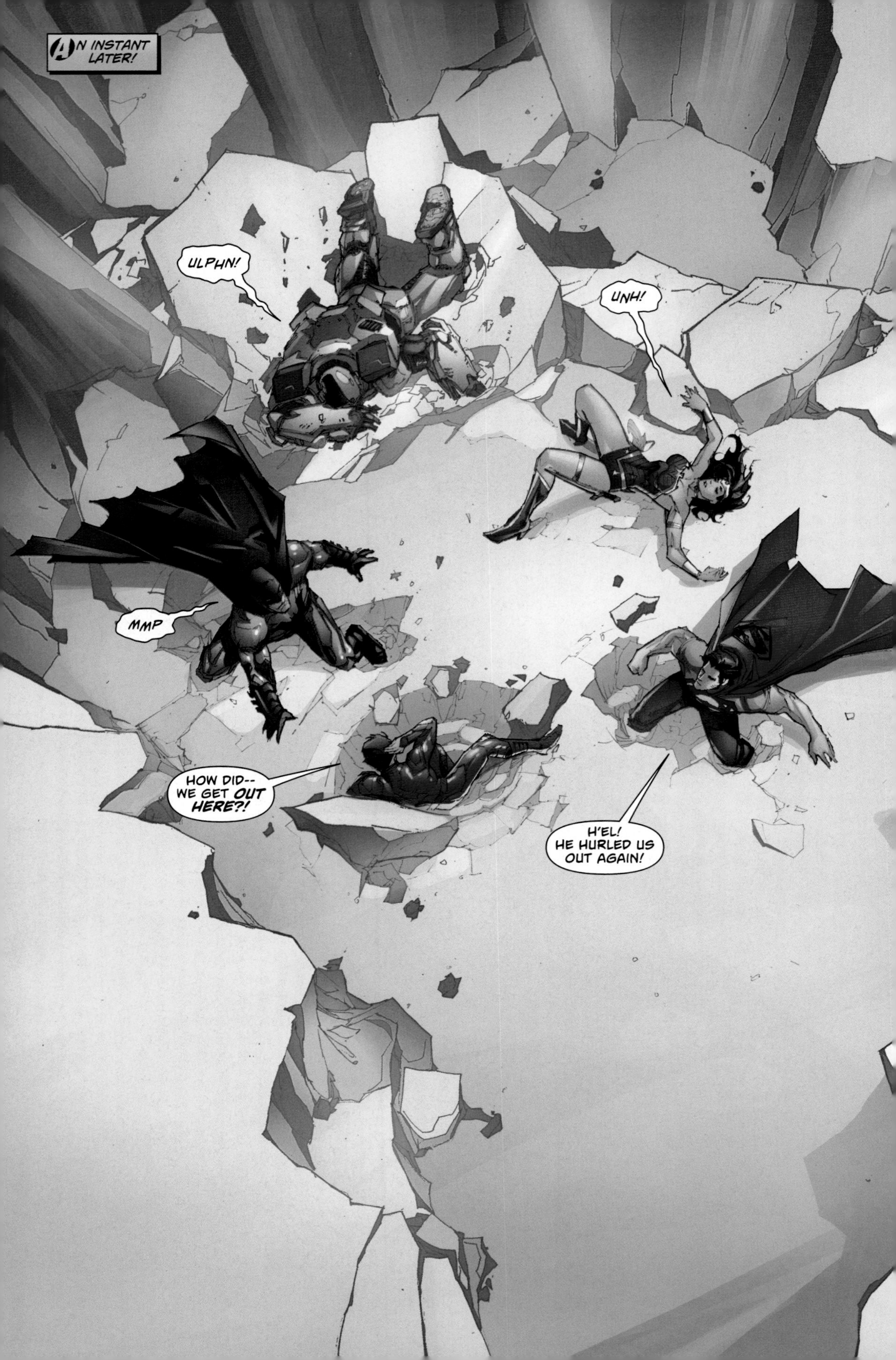
AN INSTANT LATER!
ULPHN!
UNH!
MMP
HOW DID-- WE GET OUT HERE?!
H'EL! HE HURLED US OUT AGAIN!

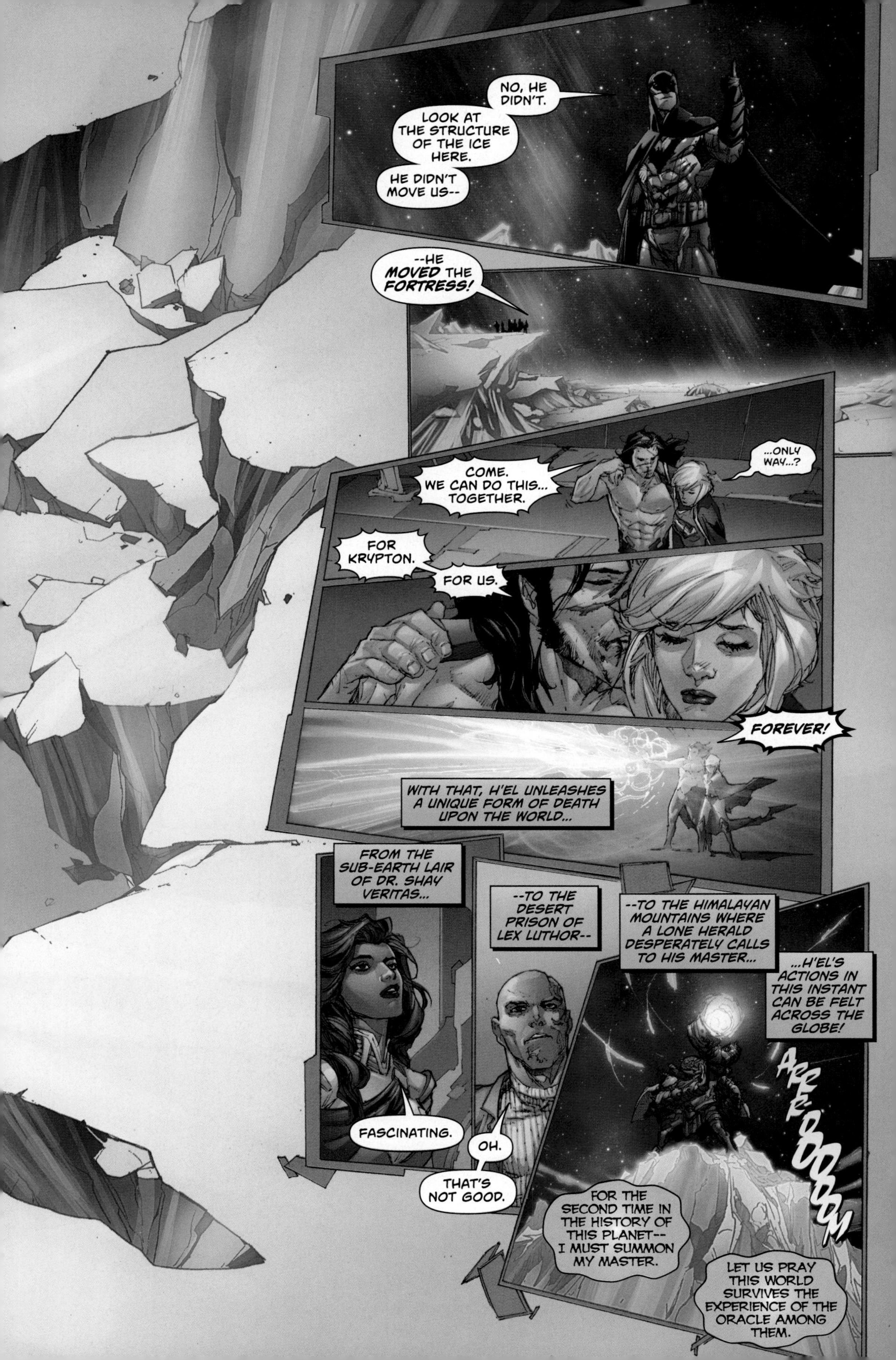
NO, HE DIDN'T.
LOOK AT THE STRUCTURE OF THE ICE HERE.
HE DIDN'T MOVE US--
--HE *MOVED* THE *FORTRESS!*
COME. WE CAN DO THIS... TOGETHER.
...ONLY WAY...?
FOR KRYPTON.
FOR US.
FOREVER!
WITH THAT, H'EL UNLEASHES A UNIQUE FORM OF DEATH UPON THE WORLD...
FROM THE SUB-EARTH LAIR OF DR. SHAY VERITAS...
FASCINATING.
--TO THE DESERT PRISON OF LEX LUTHOR--
OH.
THAT'S NOT GOOD.
--TO THE HIMALAYAN MOUNTAINS WHERE A LONE HERALD DESPERATELY CALLS TO HIS MASTER...
...H'EL'S ACTIONS IN THIS INSTANT CAN BE FELT ACROSS THE GLOBE!
AKKBOOOM
FOR THE SECOND TIME IN THE HISTORY OF THIS PLANET-- I MUST SUMMON MY MASTER.
LET US PRAY THIS WORLD SURVIVES THE EXPERIENCE OF THE ORACLE AMONG THEM.

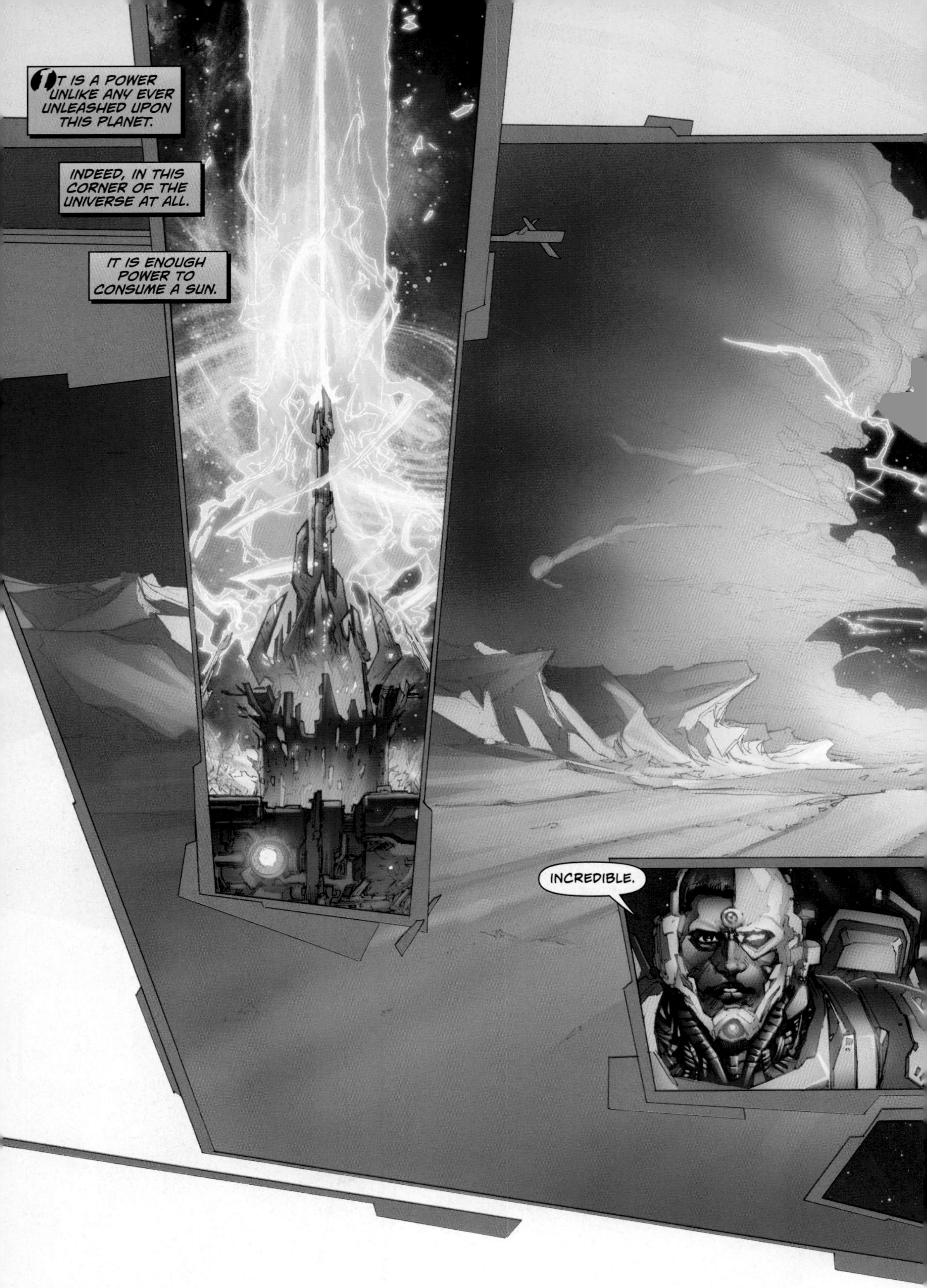
IT IS A POWER UNLIKE ANY EVER UNLEASHED UPON THIS PLANET.
INDEED, IN THIS CORNER OF THE UNIVERSE AT ALL.
IT IS ENOUGH POWER TO CONSUME A SUN.
INCREDIBLE.

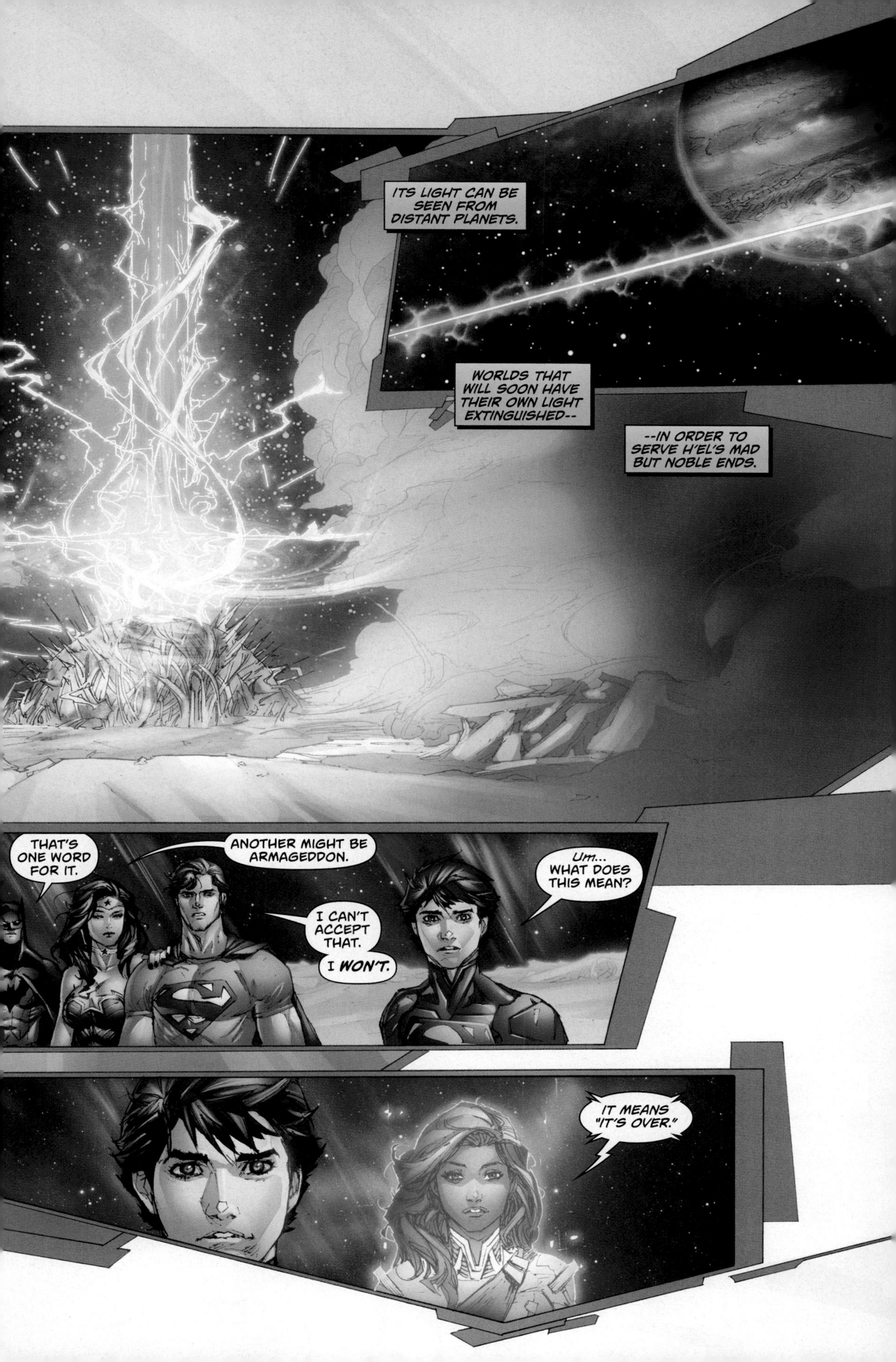
ITS LIGHT CAN BE SEEN FROM DISTANT PLANETS.
WORLDS THAT WILL SOON HAVE THEIR OWN LIGHT EXTINGUISHED--
--IN ORDER TO SERVE H'EL'S MAD BUT NOBLE ENDS.
THAT'S ONE WORD FOR IT.
ANOTHER MIGHT BE ARMAGEDDON.
Um... WHAT DOES THIS MEAN?
I CAN'T ACCEPT THAT.
I WON'T.
IT MEANS "IT'S OVER."

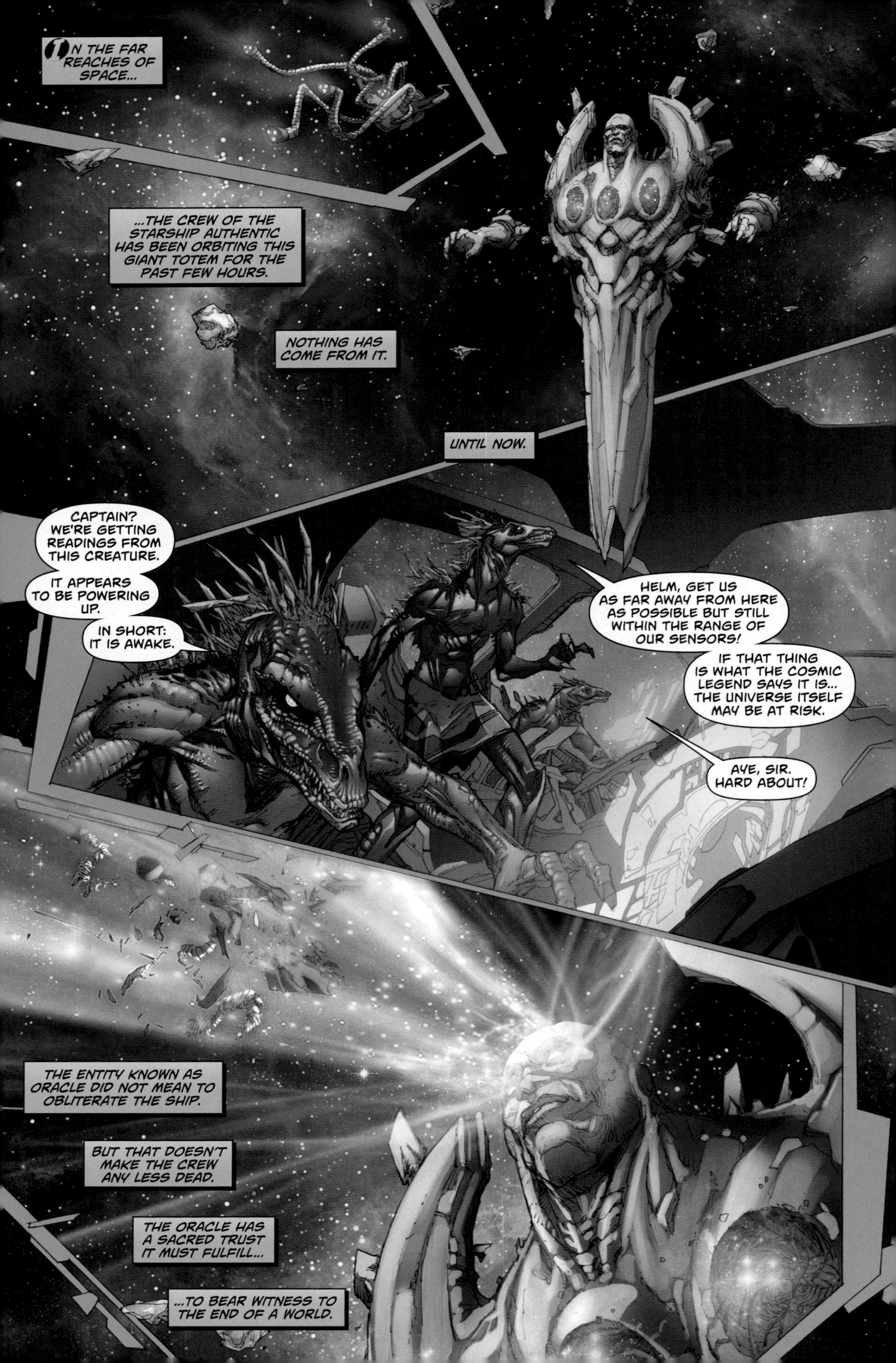
IN THE FAR REACHES OF SPACE...
...THE CREW OF THE STARSHIP AUTHENTIC HAS BEEN ORBITING THIS GIANT TOTEM FOR THE PAST FEW HOURS.
NOTHING HAS COME FROM IT.
UNTIL NOW.
CAPTAIN? WE'RE GETTING READINGS FROM THIS CREATURE.
IT APPEARS TO BE POWERING UP.
IN SHORT: IT IS AWAKE.
HELM, GET US AS FAR AWAY FROM HERE AS POSSIBLE BUT STILL WITHIN THE RANGE OF OUR SENSORS!
IF THAT THING IS WHAT THE COSMIC LEGEND SAYS IT IS... THE UNIVERSE ITSELF MAY BE AT RISK.
AYE, SIR. HARD ABOUT!
THE ENTITY KNOWN AS ORACLE DID NOT MEAN TO OBLITERATE THE SHIP.
BUT THAT DOESN'T MAKE THE CREW ANY LESS DEAD.
THE ORACLE HAS A SACRED TRUST IT MUST FULFILL...
...TO BEAR WITNESS TO THE END OF A WORLD.

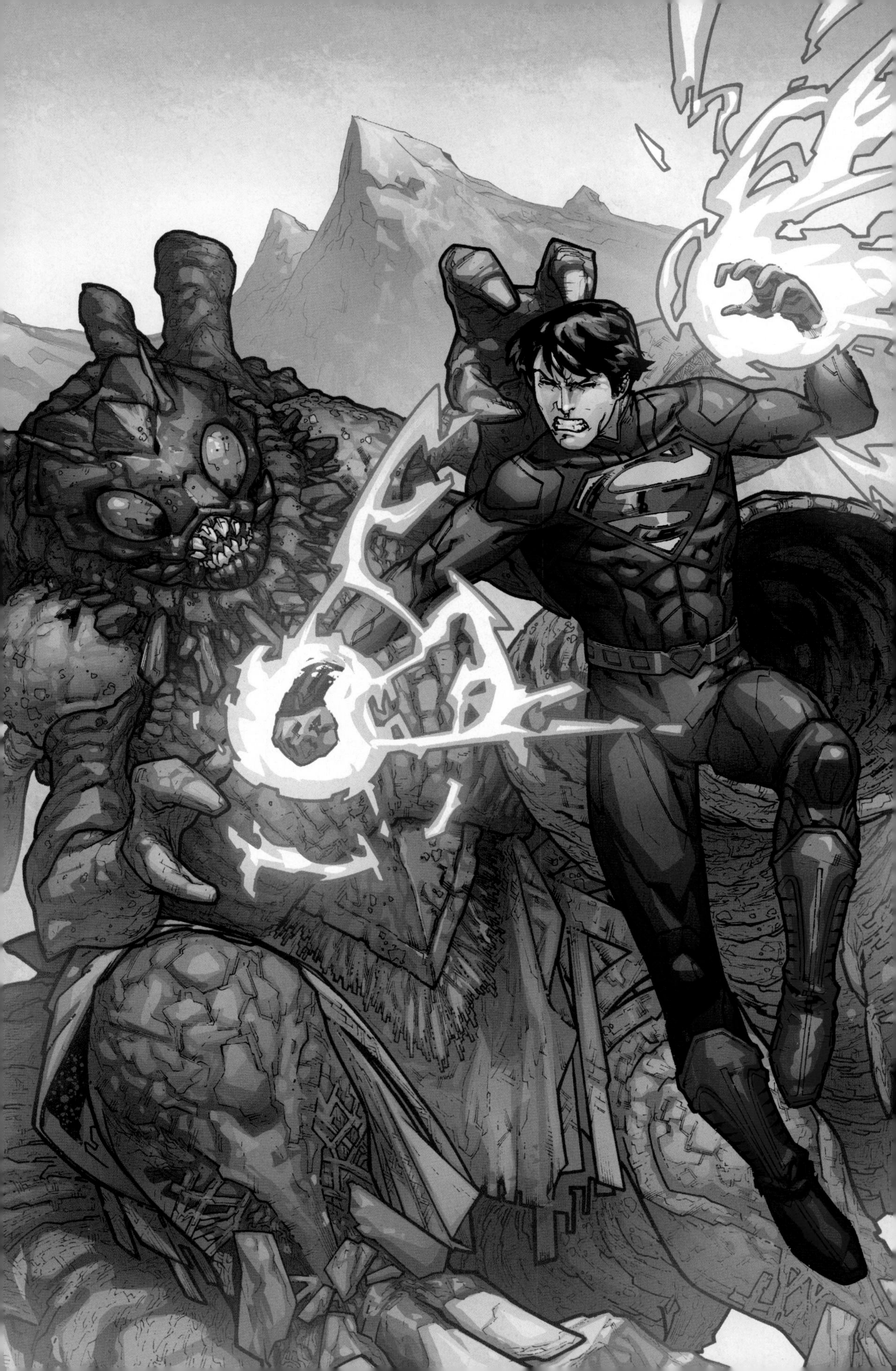

LOST CAUSE!

TOM DEFALCO writer **R.B. SILVA** penciller **ROB LEAN** inker cover art by **R.B. SILVA & JAVA TARTAGLIA**

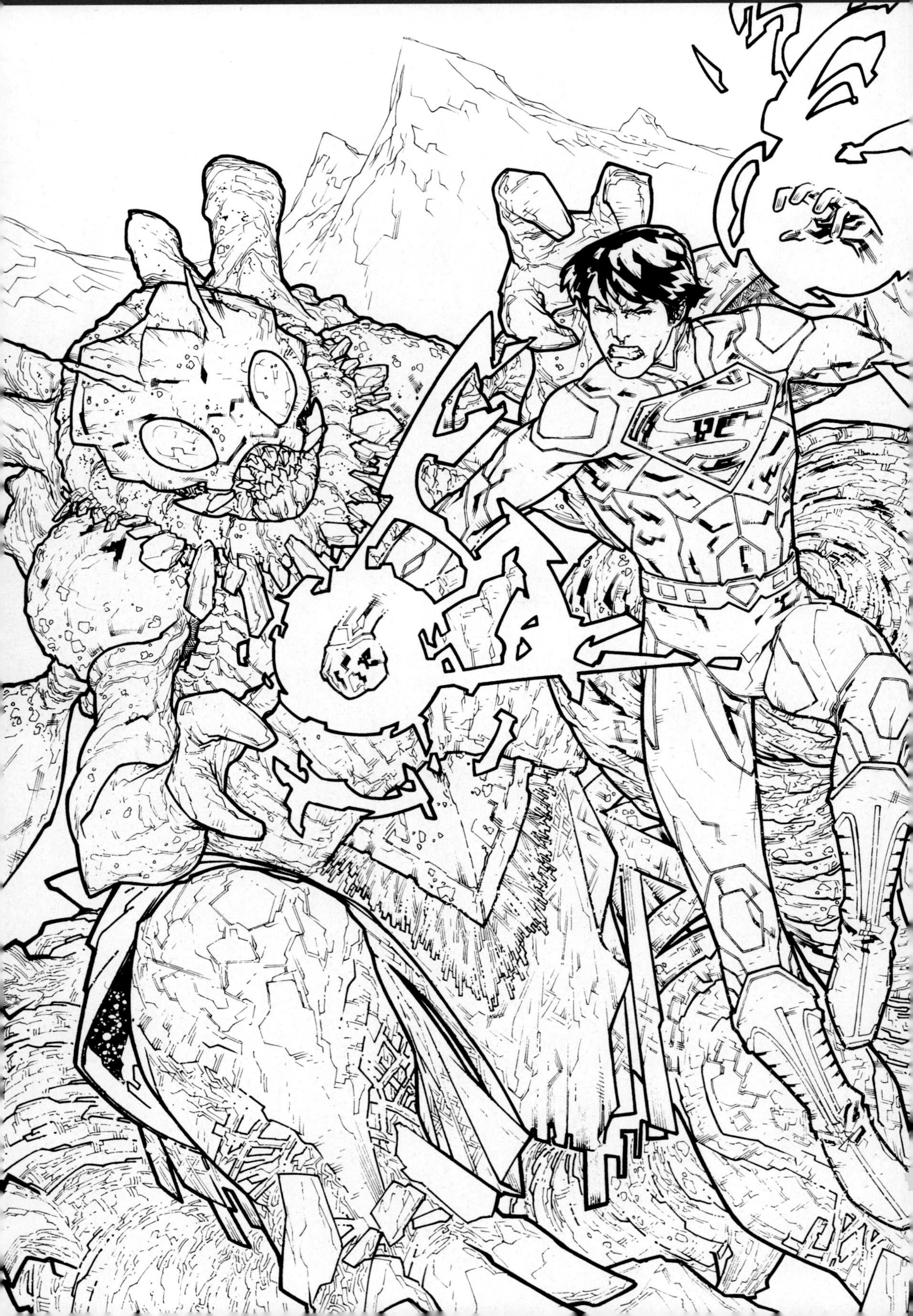

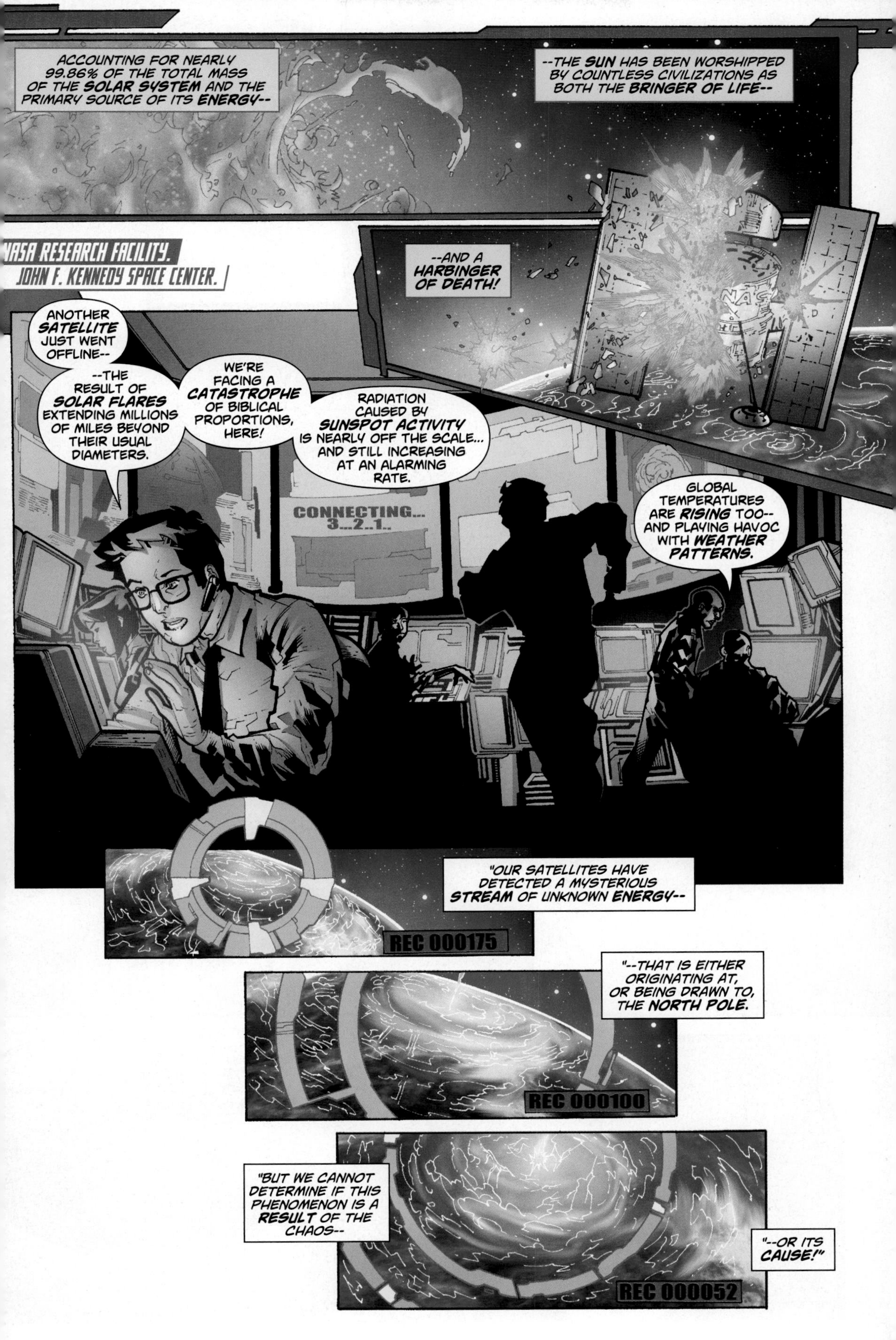
ACCOUNTING FOR NEARLY 99.86% OF THE TOTAL MASS OF THE SOLAR SYSTEM AND THE PRIMARY SOURCE OF ITS ENERGY--
--THE SUN HAS BEEN WORSHIPPED BY COUNTLESS CIVILIZATIONS AS BOTH THE BRINGER OF LIFE--
--AND A HARBINGER OF DEATH!
NASA RESEARCH FACILITY.
JOHN F. KENNEDY SPACE CENTER.
ANOTHER SATELLITE JUST WENT OFFLINE--
--THE RESULT OF SOLAR FLARES EXTENDING MILLIONS OF MILES BEYOND THEIR USUAL DIAMETERS.
WE'RE FACING A CATASTROPHE OF BIBLICAL PROPORTIONS, HERE!
RADIATION CAUSED BY SUNSPOT ACTIVITY IS NEARLY OFF THE SCALE... AND STILL INCREASING AT AN ALARMING RATE.
CONNECTING... 3...2...1...
GLOBAL TEMPERATURES ARE RISING TOO--AND PLAYING HAVOC WITH WEATHER PATTERNS.
"OUR SATELLITES HAVE DETECTED A MYSTERIOUS STREAM OF UNKNOWN ENERGY--
REC 000175
"--THAT IS EITHER ORIGINATING AT, OR BEING DRAWN TO, THE NORTH POLE.
REC 000100
"BUT WE CANNOT DETERMINE IF THIS PHENOMENON IS A RESULT OF THE CHAOS--
"--OR ITS CAUSE!"
REC 000052

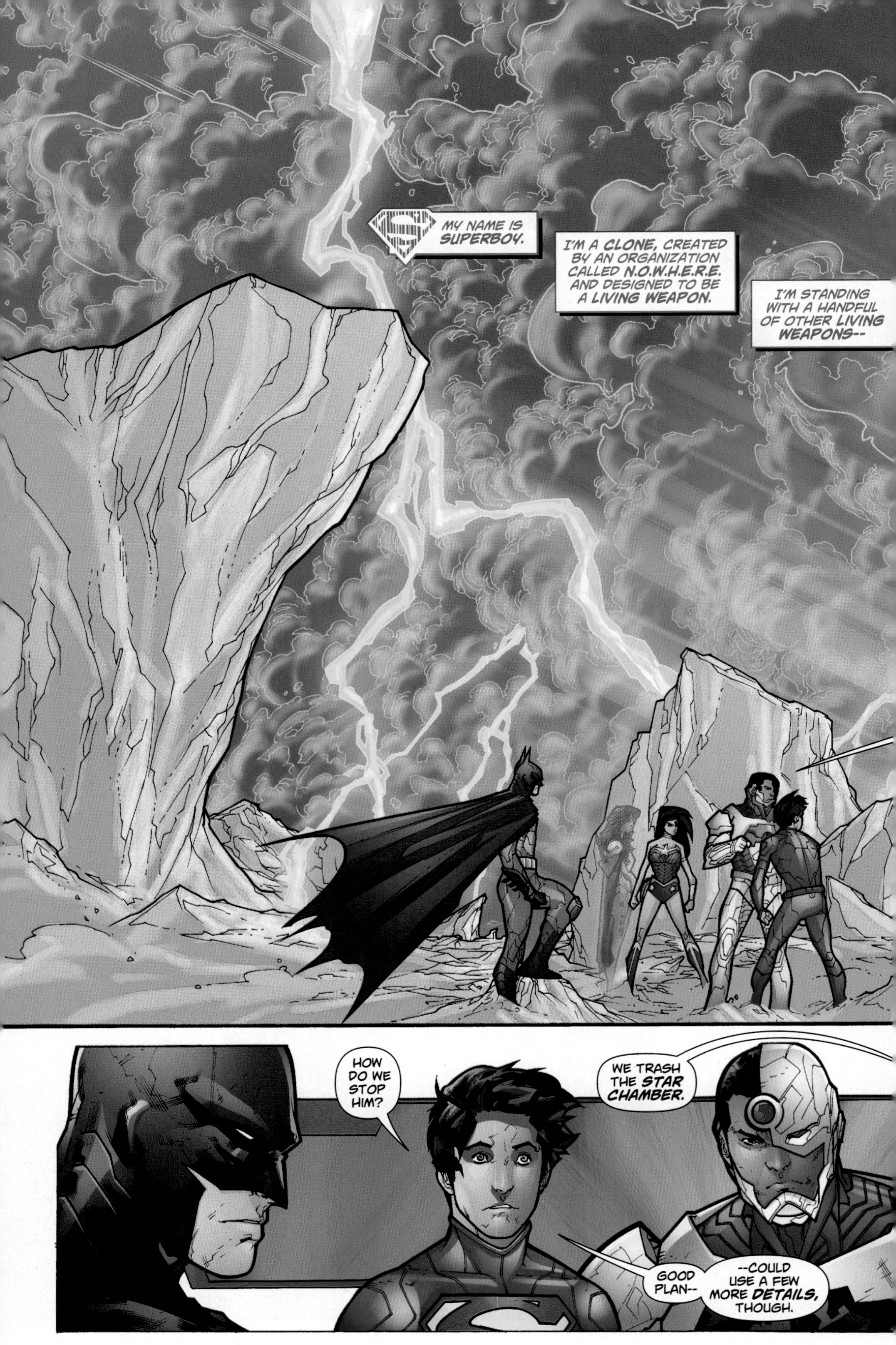

MY NAME IS SUPERBOY.
I'M A CLONE, CREATED BY AN ORGANIZATION CALLED N.O.W.H.E.R.E. AND DESIGNED TO BE A LIVING WEAPON.
I'M STANDING WITH A HANDFUL OF OTHER LIVING WEAPONS--
HOW DO WE STOP HIM?
WE TRASH THE STAR CHAMBER.
GOOD PLAN--
--COULD USE A FEW MORE DETAILS, THOUGH.

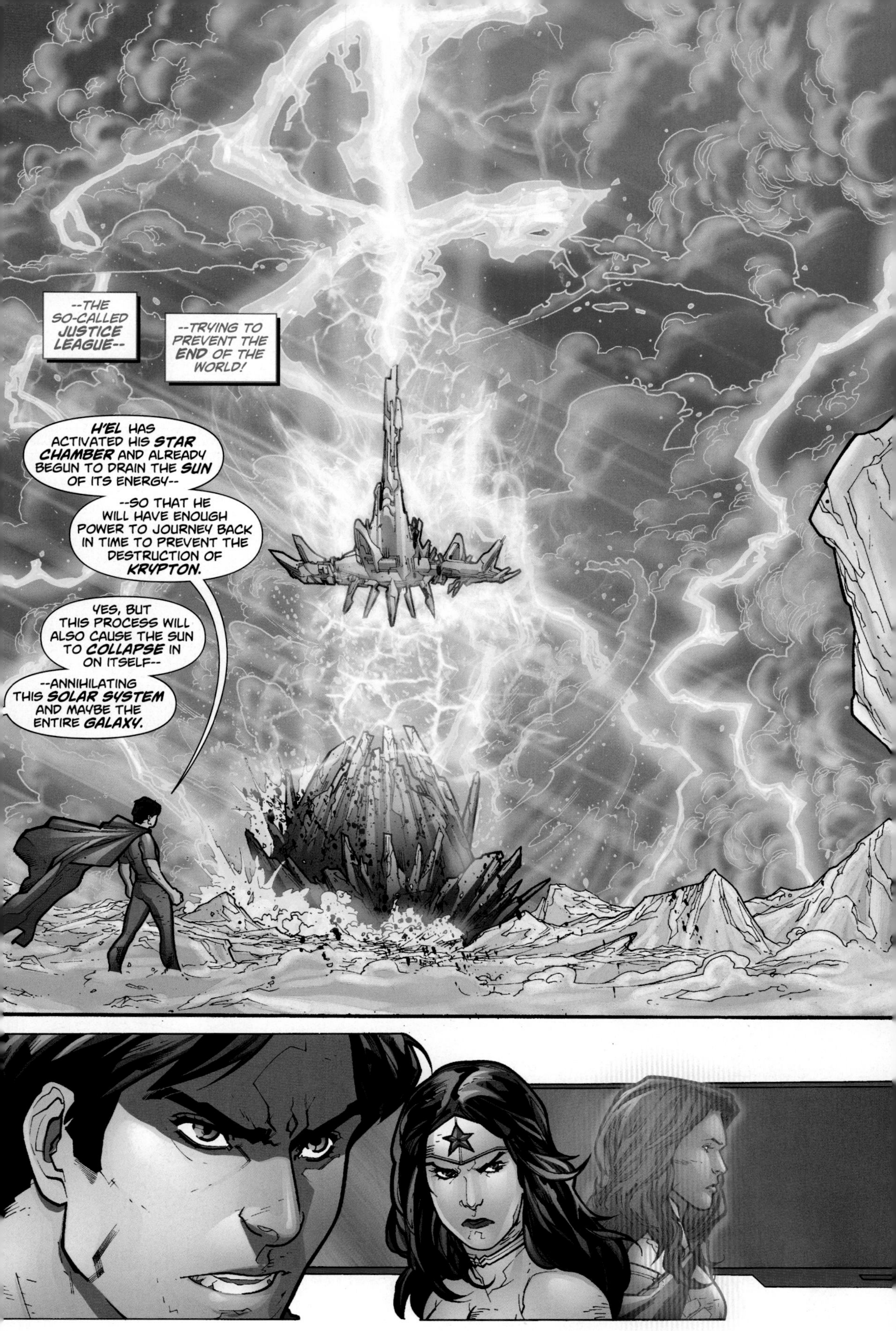
--THE SO-CALLED JUSTICE LEAGUE--
--TRYING TO PREVENT THE END OF THE WORLD!
H'EL HAS ACTIVATED HIS STAR CHAMBER AND ALREADY BEGUN TO DRAIN THE SUN OF ITS ENERGY--
--SO THAT HE WILL HAVE ENOUGH POWER TO JOURNEY BACK IN TIME TO PREVENT THE DESTRUCTION OF KRYPTON.
YES, BUT THIS PROCESS WILL ALSO CAUSE THE SUN TO COLLAPSE IN ON ITSELF--
--ANNIHILATING THIS SOLAR SYSTEM AND MAYBE THE ENTIRE GALAXY.

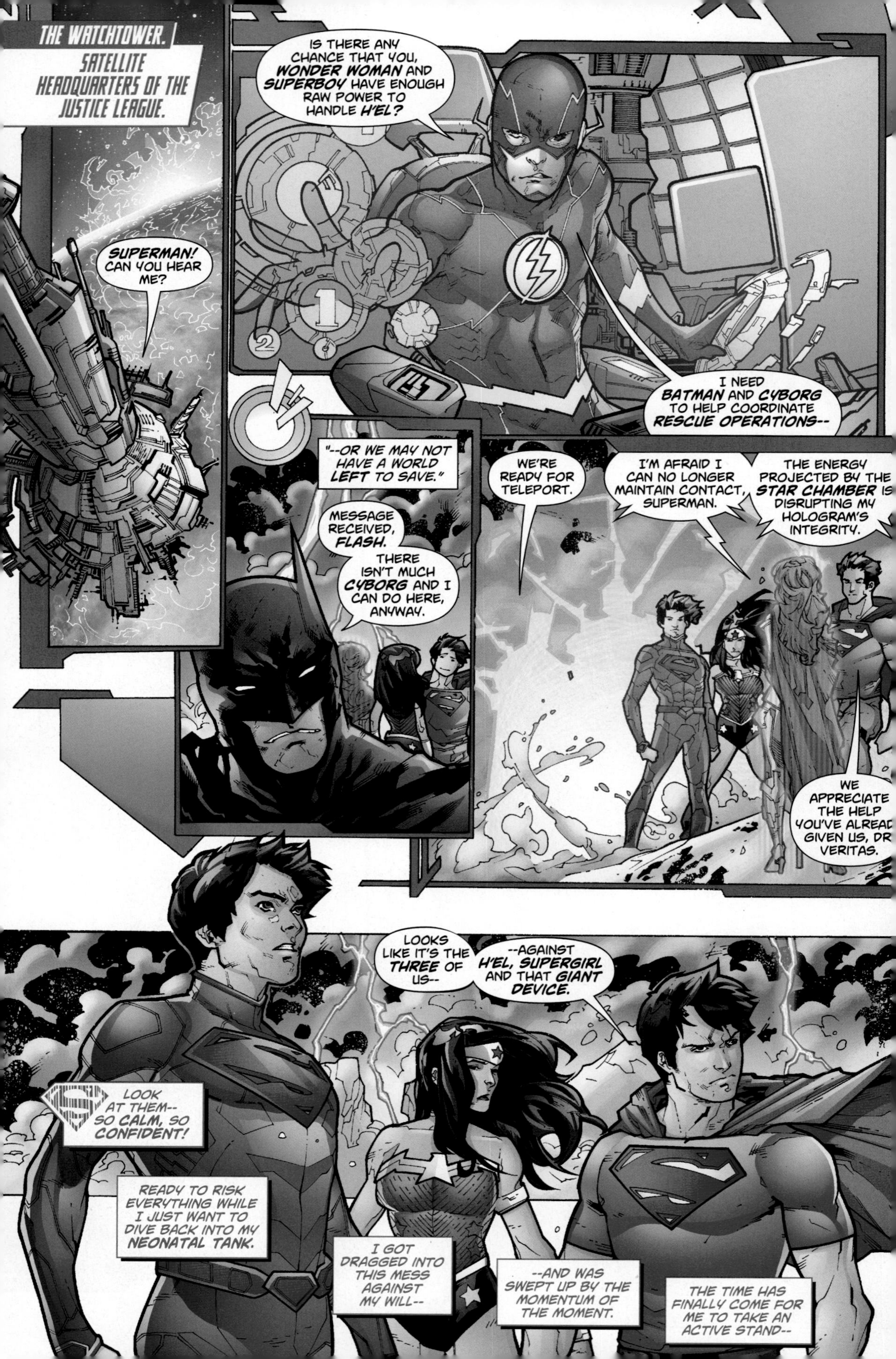
THE WATCHTOWER.
SATELLITE HEADQUARTERS OF THE JUSTICE LEAGUE.
SUPERMAN! CAN YOU HEAR ME?
IS THERE ANY CHANCE THAT YOU, WONDER WOMAN AND SUPERBOY HAVE ENOUGH RAW POWER TO HANDLE H'EL?
I NEED BATMAN AND CYBORG TO HELP COORDINATE RESCUE OPERATIONS--
"--OR WE MAY NOT HAVE A WORLD LEFT TO SAVE."
MESSAGE RECEIVED, FLASH.
THERE ISN'T MUCH CYBORG AND I CAN DO HERE, ANYWAY.
WE'RE READY FOR TELEPORT.
I'M AFRAID I CAN NO LONGER MAINTAIN CONTACT, SUPERMAN.
THE ENERGY PROJECTED BY THE STAR CHAMBER IS DISRUPTING MY HOLOGRAM'S INTEGRITY.
WE APPRECIATE THE HELP YOU'VE ALREAD GIVEN US, DR VERITAS.
LOOKS LIKE IT'S THE THREE OF US--
--AGAINST H'EL, SUPERGIRL AND THAT GIANT DEVICE.
LOOK AT THEM-- SO CALM, SO CONFIDENT!
READY TO RISK EVERYTHING WHILE I JUST WANT TO DIVE BACK INTO MY NEONATAL TANK.
I GOT DRAGGED INTO THIS MESS AGAINST MY WILL--
--AND WAS SWEPT UP BY THE MOMENTUM OF THE MOMENT.
THE TIME HAS FINALLY COME FOR ME TO TAKE AN ACTIVE STAND--

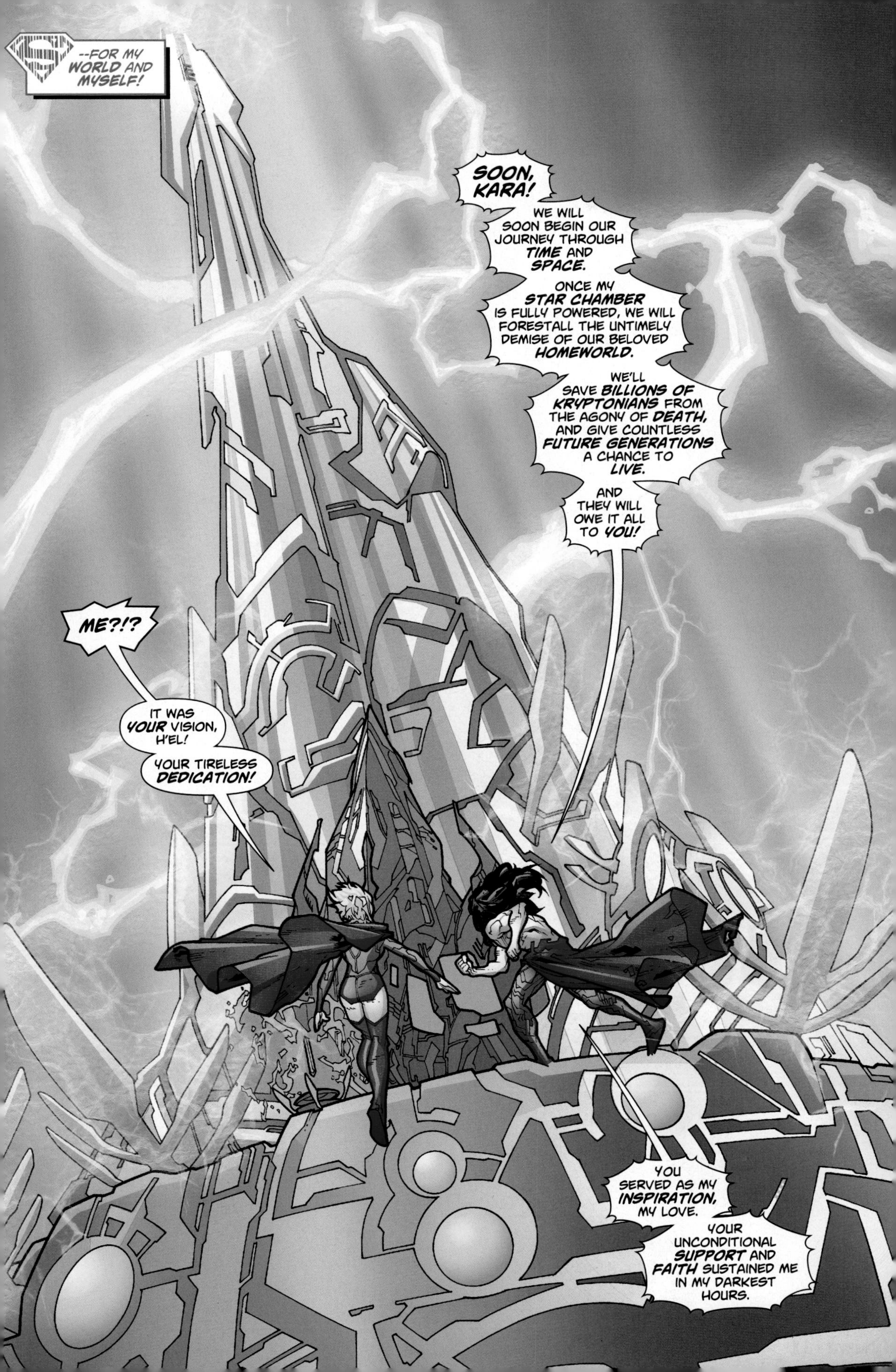
--FOR MY WORLD AND MYSELF!
SOON, KARA!
WE WILL SOON BEGIN OUR JOURNEY THROUGH TIME AND SPACE.
ONCE MY STAR CHAMBER IS FULLY POWERED, WE WILL FORESTALL THE UNTIMELY DEMISE OF OUR BELOVED HOMEWORLD.
WE'LL SAVE BILLIONS OF KRYPTONIANS FROM THE AGONY OF DEATH, AND GIVE COUNTLESS FUTURE GENERATIONS A CHANCE TO LIVE.
AND THEY WILL OWE IT ALL TO YOU!
ME?!?
IT WAS YOUR VISION, H'EL!
YOUR TIRELESS DEDICATION!
YOU SERVED AS MY INSPIRATION, MY LOVE.
YOUR UNCONDITIONAL SUPPORT AND FAITH SUSTAINED ME IN MY DARKEST HOURS.

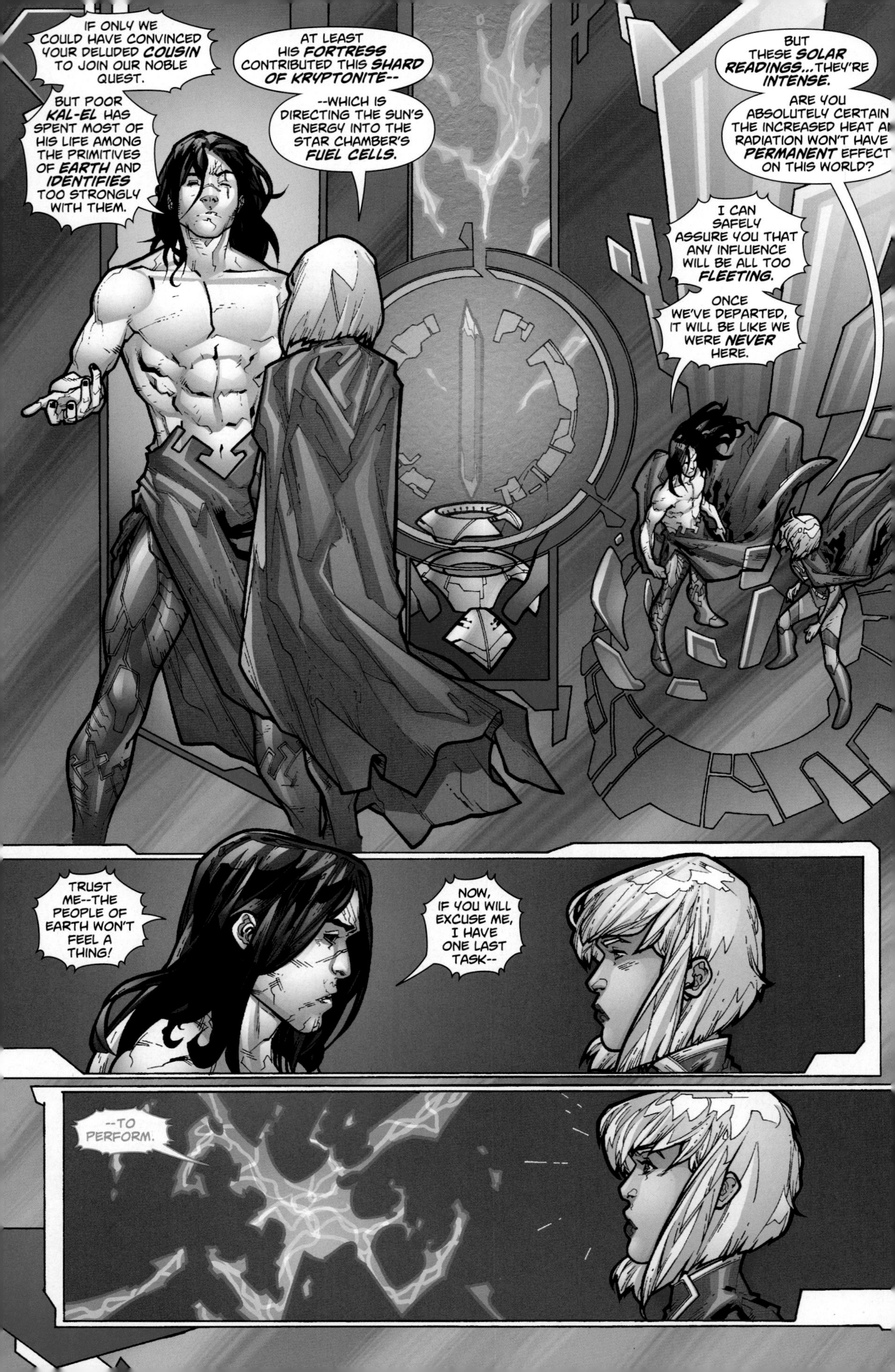
IF ONLY WE COULD HAVE CONVINCED YOUR DELUDED COUSIN TO JOIN OUR NOBLE QUEST.
BUT POOR KAL-EL HAS SPENT MOST OF HIS LIFE AMONG THE PRIMITIVES OF EARTH AND IDENTIFIES TOO STRONGLY WITH THEM.
AT LEAST HIS FORTRESS CONTRIBUTED THIS SHARD OF KRYPTONITE--
--WHICH IS DIRECTING THE SUN'S ENERGY INTO THE STAR CHAMBER'S FUEL CELLS.
BUT THESE SOLAR READINGS...THEY'RE INTENSE.
ARE YOU ABSOLUTELY CERTAIN THE INCREASED HEAT AN RADIATION WON'T HAVE PERMANENT EFFECT ON THIS WORLD?
I CAN SAFELY ASSURE YOU THAT ANY INFLUENCE WILL BE ALL TOO FLEETING.
ONCE WE'VE DEPARTED, IT WILL BE LIKE WE WERE NEVER HERE.
TRUST ME--THE PEOPLE OF EARTH WON'T FEEL A THING!
NOW, IF YOU WILL EXCUSE ME, I HAVE ONE LAST TASK--
--TO PERFORM.

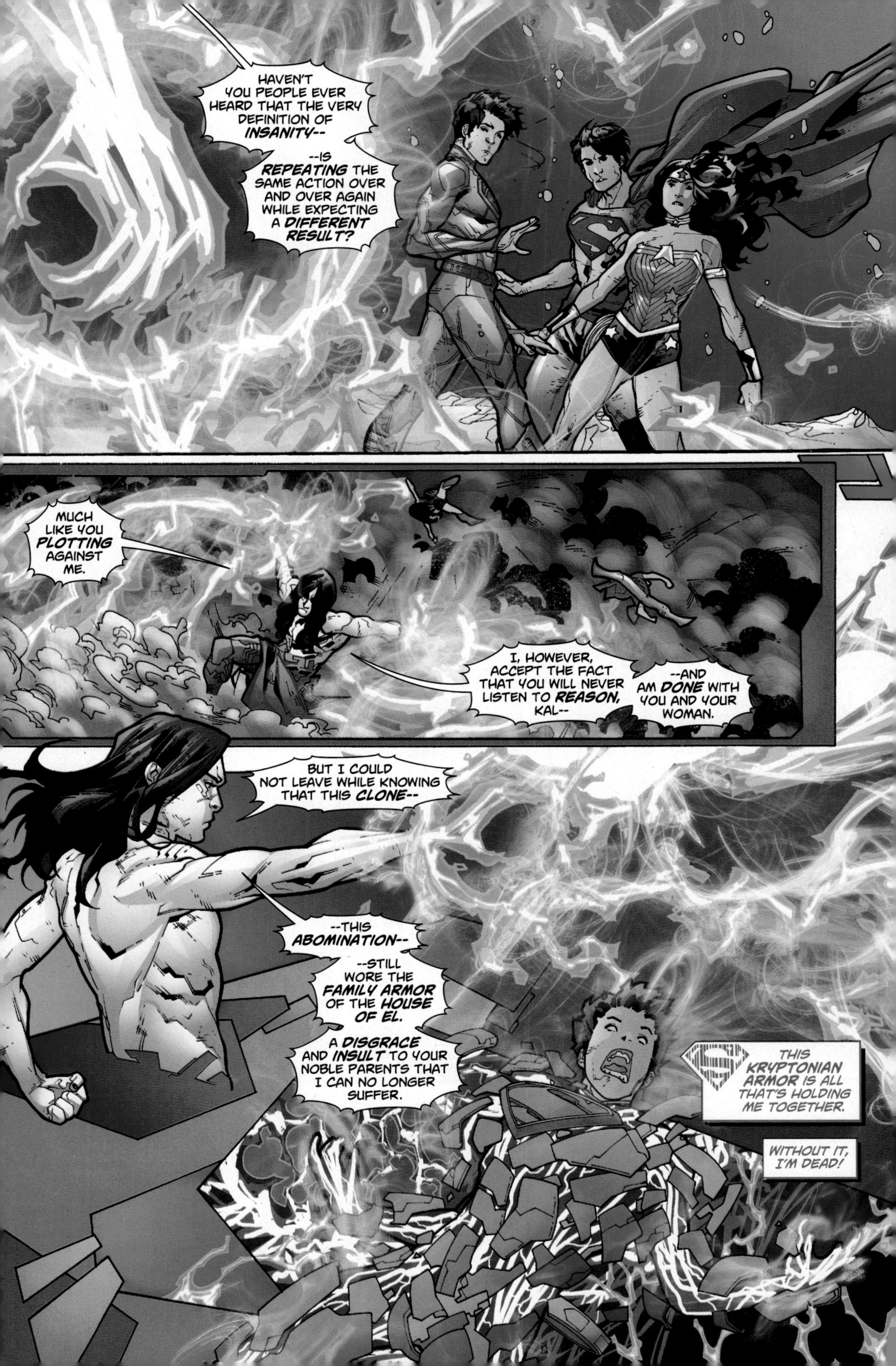
HAVEN'T YOU PEOPLE EVER HEARD THAT THE VERY DEFINITION OF INSANITY--
--IS REPEATING THE SAME ACTION OVER AND OVER AGAIN WHILE EXPECTING A DIFFERENT RESULT?
MUCH LIKE YOU PLOTTING AGAINST ME.
I, HOWEVER, ACCEPT THE FACT THAT YOU WILL NEVER LISTEN TO REASON, KAL--
--AND AM DONE WITH YOU AND YOUR WOMAN.
BUT I COULD NOT LEAVE WHILE KNOWING THAT THIS CLONE--
--THIS ABOMINATION--
--STILL WORE THE FAMILY ARMOR OF THE HOUSE OF EL.
A DISGRACE AND INSULT TO YOUR NOBLE PARENTS THAT I CAN NO LONGER SUFFER.
THIS KRYPTONIAN ARMOR IS ALL THAT'S HOLDING ME TOGETHER.
WITHOUT IT, I'M DEAD!

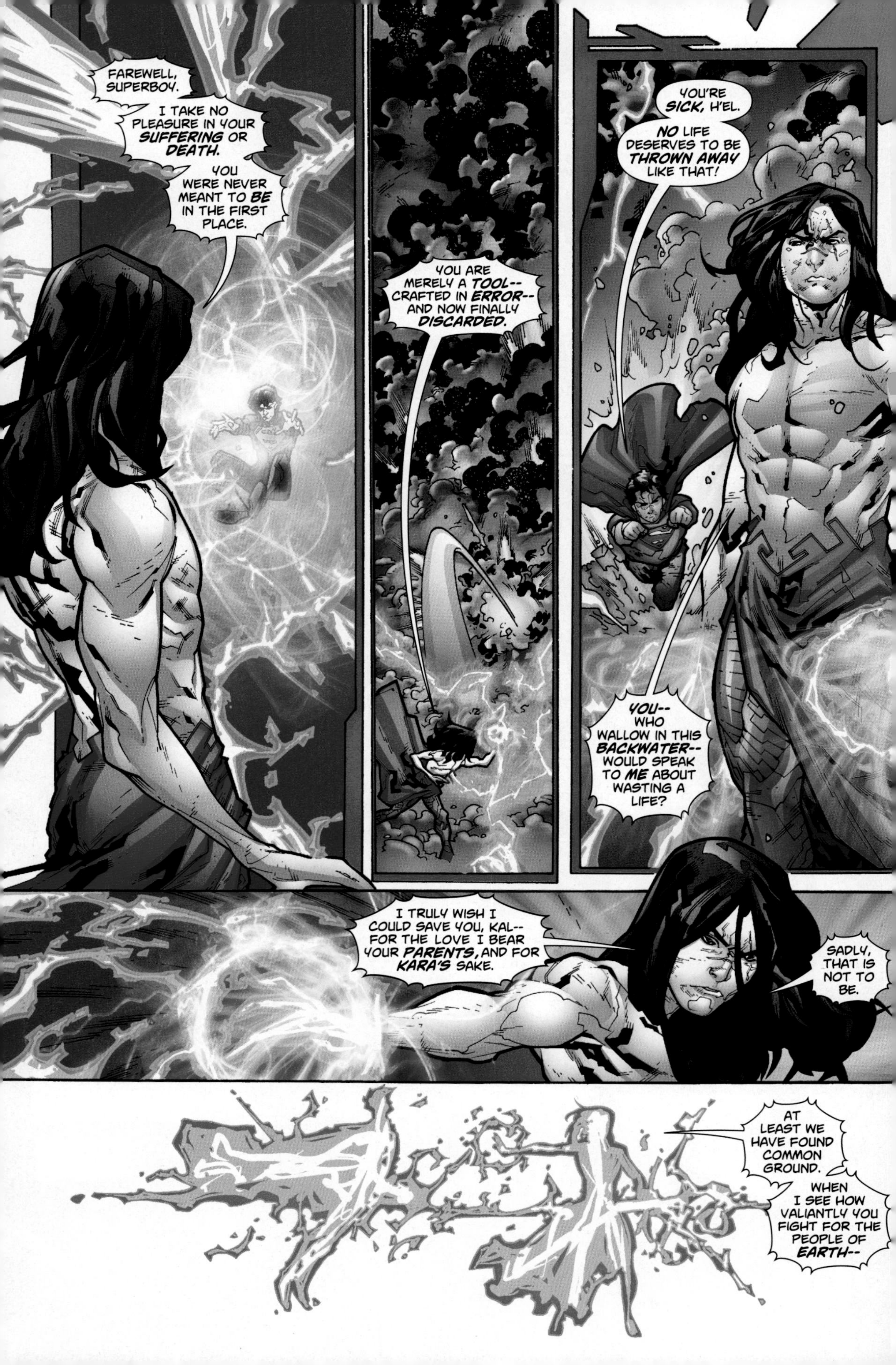
FAREWELL, SUPERBOY.
I TAKE NO PLEASURE IN YOUR SUFFERING OR DEATH.
YOU WERE NEVER MEANT TO BE IN THE FIRST PLACE.
YOU ARE MERELY A TOOL-- CRAFTED IN ERROR-- AND NOW FINALLY DISCARDED.
YOU'RE SICK, H'EL.
NO LIFE DESERVES TO BE THROWN AWAY LIKE THAT!
YOU-- WHO WALLOW IN THIS BACKWATER-- WOULD SPEAK TO ME ABOUT WASTING A LIFE?
I TRULY WISH I COULD SAVE YOU, KAL-- FOR THE LOVE I BEAR YOUR PARENTS, AND FOR KARA'S SAKE.
SADLY, THAT IS NOT TO BE.
AT LEAST WE HAVE FOUND COMMON GROUND.
WHEN I SEE HOW VALIANTLY YOU FIGHT FOR THE PEOPLE OF EARTH--

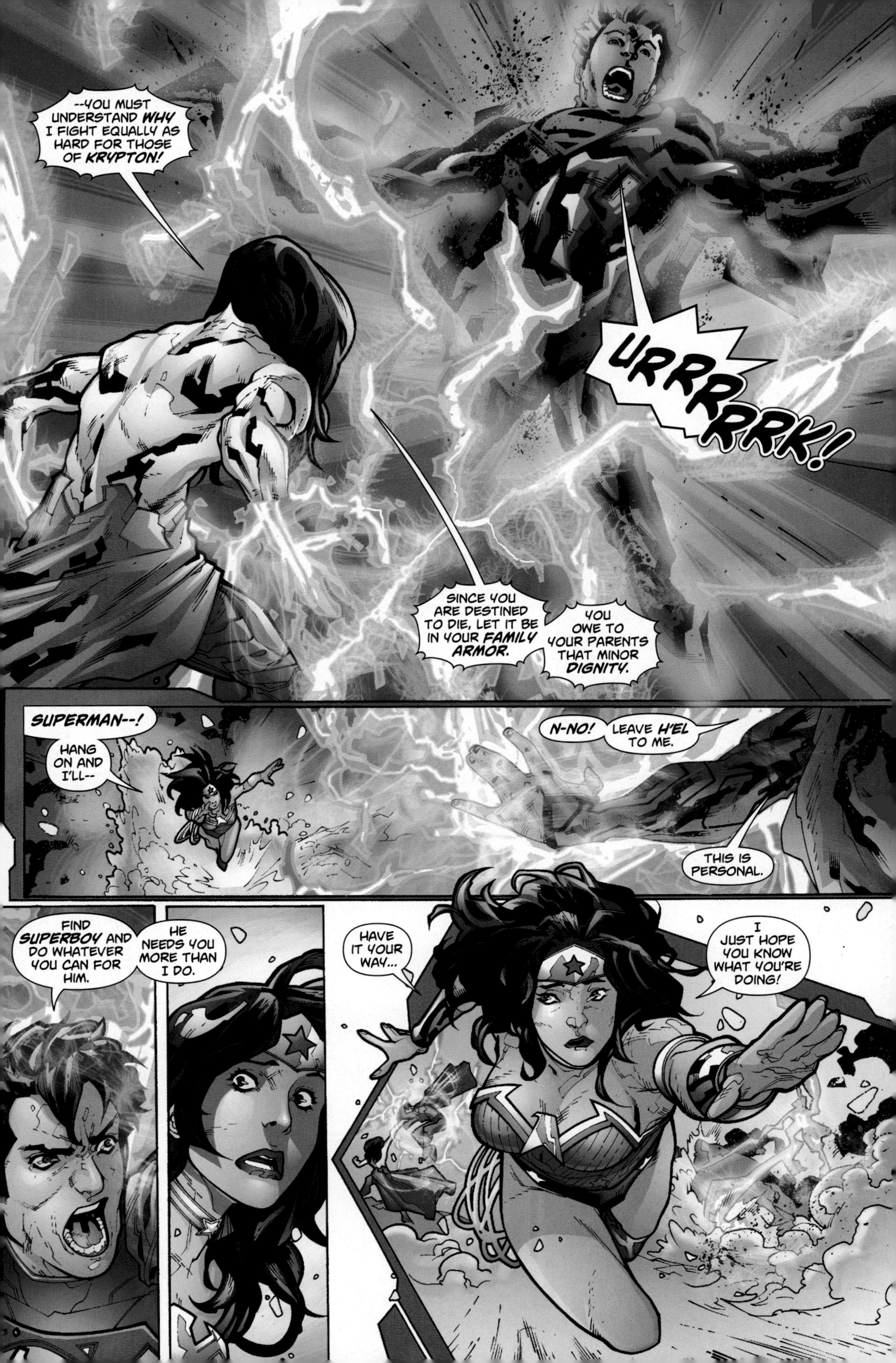
--YOU MUST UNDERSTAND WHY I FIGHT EQUALLY AS HARD FOR THOSE OF KRYPTON!
URRRRRK!
SINCE YOU ARE DESTINED TO DIE, LET IT BE IN YOUR FAMILY ARMOR.
YOU OWE TO YOUR PARENTS THAT MINOR DIGNITY.
SUPERMAN--!
HANG ON AND I'LL--
N-NO!
LEAVE H'EL TO ME.
THIS IS PERSONAL.
FIND SUPERBOY AND DO WHATEVER YOU CAN FOR HIM.
HE NEEDS YOU MORE THAN I DO.
HAVE IT YOUR WAY...
I JUST HOPE YOU KNOW WHAT YOU'RE DOING!

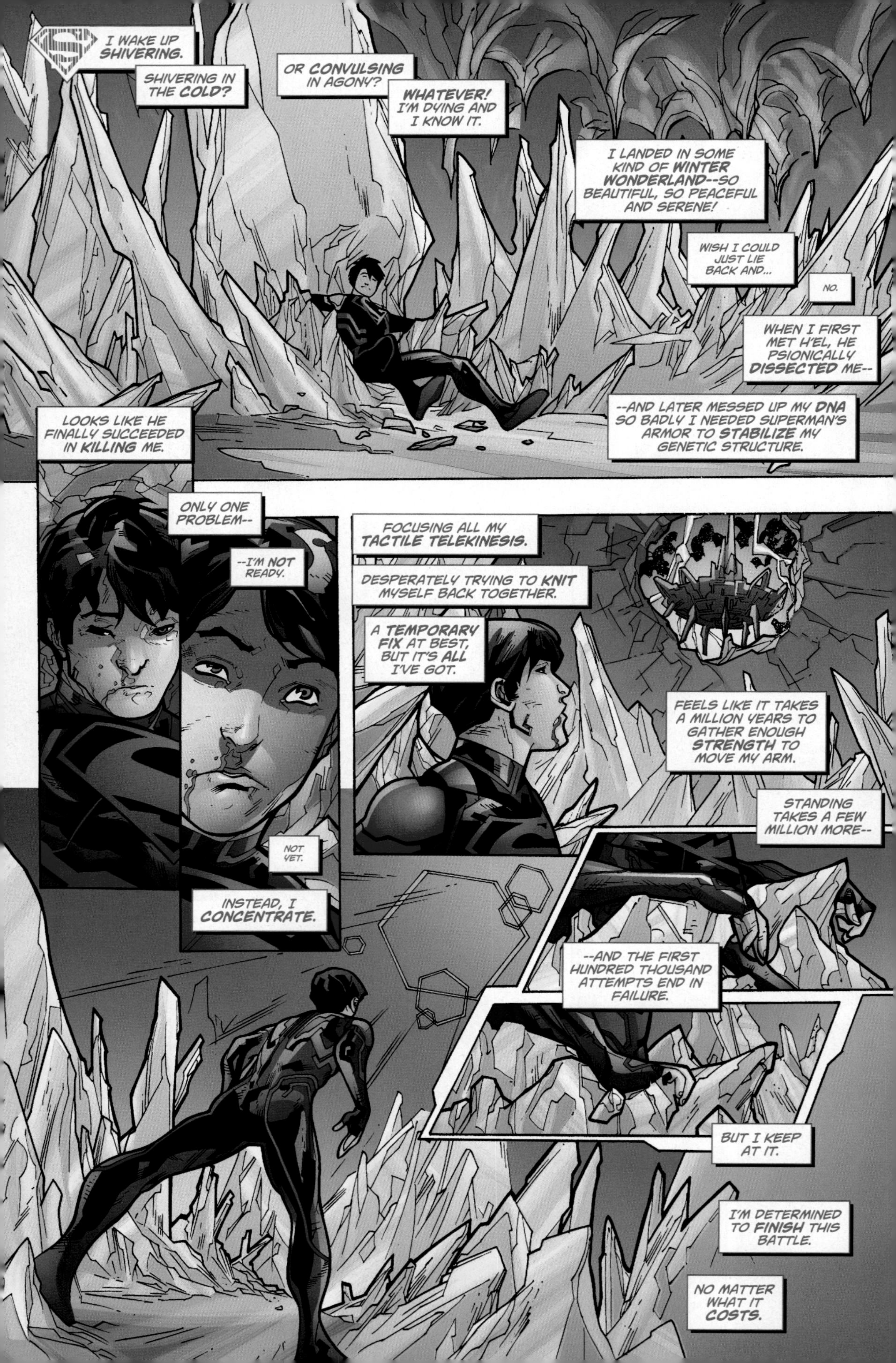
I WAKE UP SHIVERING.
SHIVERING IN THE COLD?
OR CONVULSING IN AGONY?
WHATEVER! I'M DYING AND I KNOW IT.
I LANDED IN SOME KIND OF WINTER WONDERLAND--SO BEAUTIFUL, SO PEACEFUL AND SERENE!
WISH I COULD JUST LIE BACK AND...
NO.
WHEN I FIRST MET H'EL, HE PSIONICALLY DISSECTED ME--
--AND LATER MESSED UP MY DNA SO BADLY I NEEDED SUPERMAN'S ARMOR TO STABILIZE MY GENETIC STRUCTURE.
LOOKS LIKE HE FINALLY SUCCEEDED IN KILLING ME.
ONLY ONE PROBLEM--
--I'M NOT READY.
NOT YET.
INSTEAD, I CONCENTRATE.
FOCUSING ALL MY TACTILE TELEKINESIS.
DESPERATELY TRYING TO KNIT MYSELF BACK TOGETHER.
A TEMPORARY FIX AT BEST, BUT IT'S ALL I'VE GOT.
FEELS LIKE IT TAKES A MILLION YEARS TO GATHER ENOUGH STRENGTH TO MOVE MY ARM.
STANDING TAKES A FEW MILLION MORE--
--AND THE FIRST HUNDRED THOUSAND ATTEMPTS END IN FAILURE.
BUT I KEEP AT IT.
I'M DETERMINED TO FINISH THIS BATTLE.
NO MATTER WHAT IT COSTS.

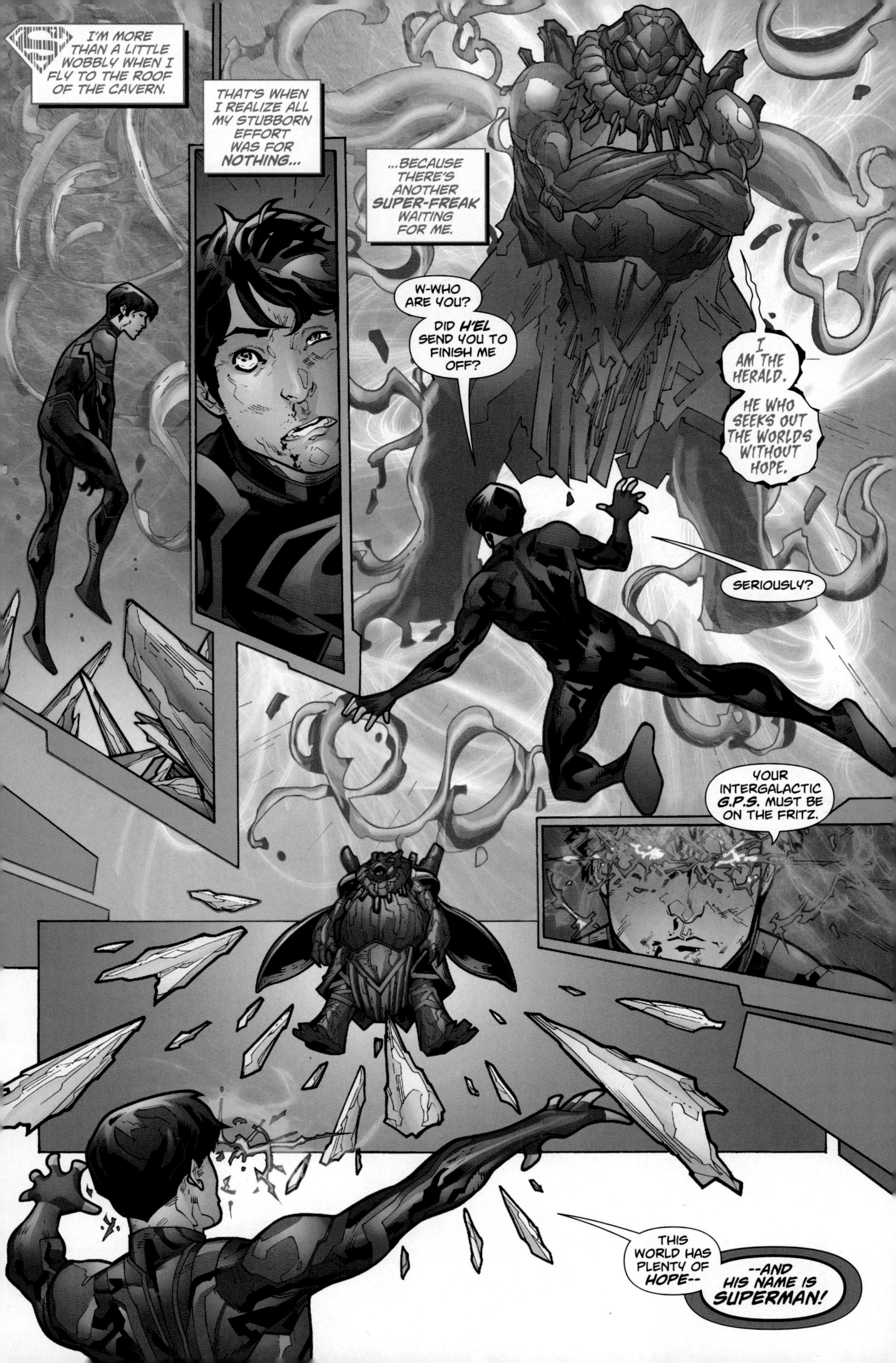
I'M MORE THAN A LITTLE WOBBLY WHEN I FLY TO THE ROOF OF THE CAVERN.
THAT'S WHEN I REALIZE ALL MY STUBBORN EFFORT WAS FOR NOTHING...
...BECAUSE THERE'S ANOTHER SUPER-FREAK WAITING FOR ME.
W-WHO ARE YOU?
DID H'EL SEND YOU TO FINISH ME OFF?
I AM THE HERALD.
HE WHO SEEKS OUT THE WORLDS WITHOUT HOPE.
SERIOUSLY?
YOUR INTERGALACTIC G.P.S. MUST BE ON THE FRITZ.
THIS WORLD HAS PLENTY OF HOPE--
--AND HIS NAME IS SUPERMAN!

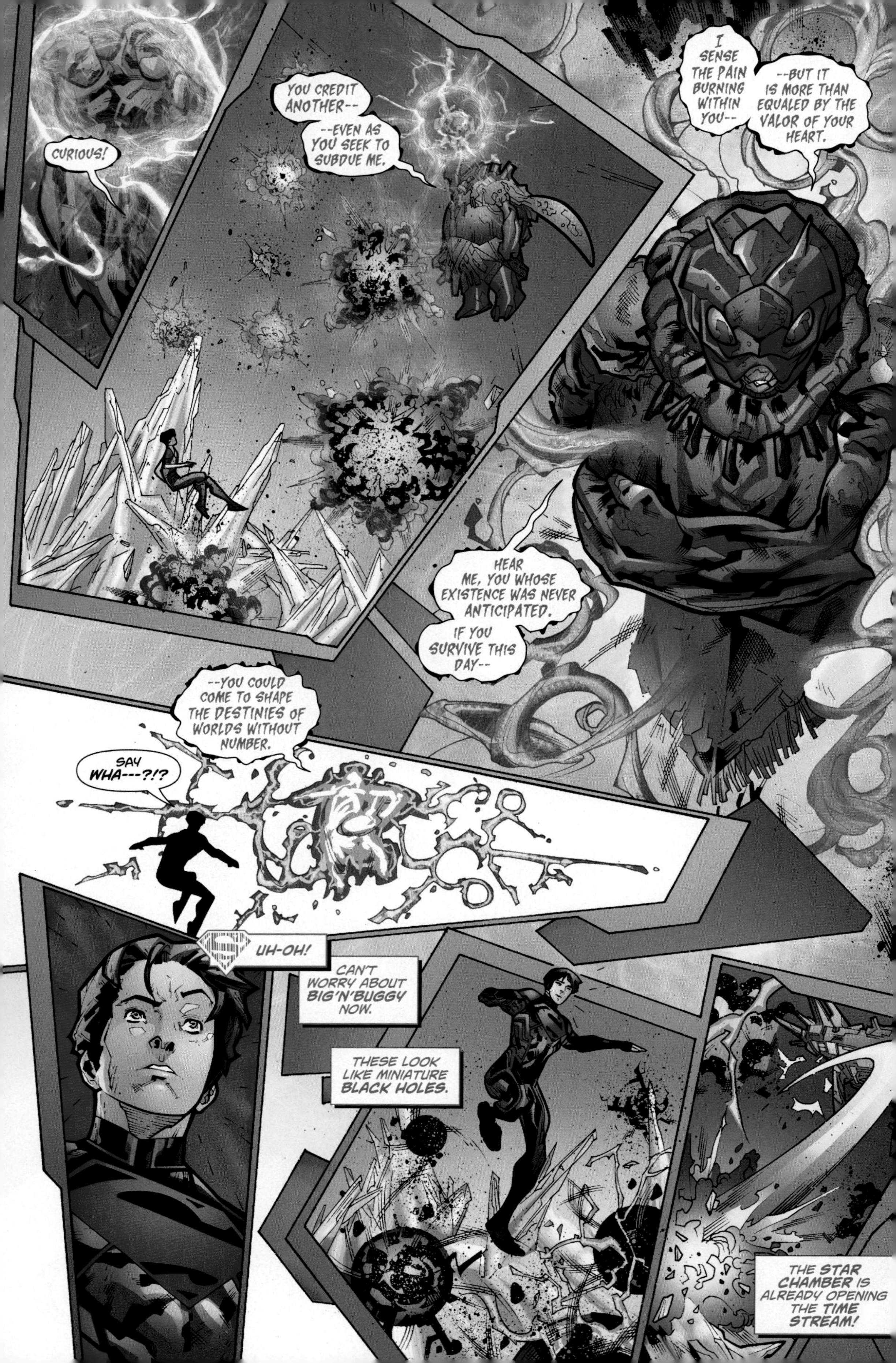
CURIOUS!
YOU CREDIT ANOTHER--
--EVEN AS YOU SEEK TO SUBDUE ME.
I SENSE THE PAIN BURNING WITHIN YOU--
--BUT IT IS MORE THAN EQUALED BY THE VALOR OF YOUR HEART.
HEAR ME, YOU WHOSE EXISTENCE WAS NEVER ANTICIPATED.
IF YOU SURVIVE THIS DAY--
--YOU COULD COME TO SHAPE THE DESTINIES OF WORLDS WITHOUT NUMBER.
SAY WHA---?!?
UH-OH!
CAN'T WORRY ABOUT BIG'N'BUGGY NOW.
THESE LOOK LIKE MINIATURE BLACK HOLES.
THE STAR CHAMBER IS ALREADY OPENING THE TIME STREAM!

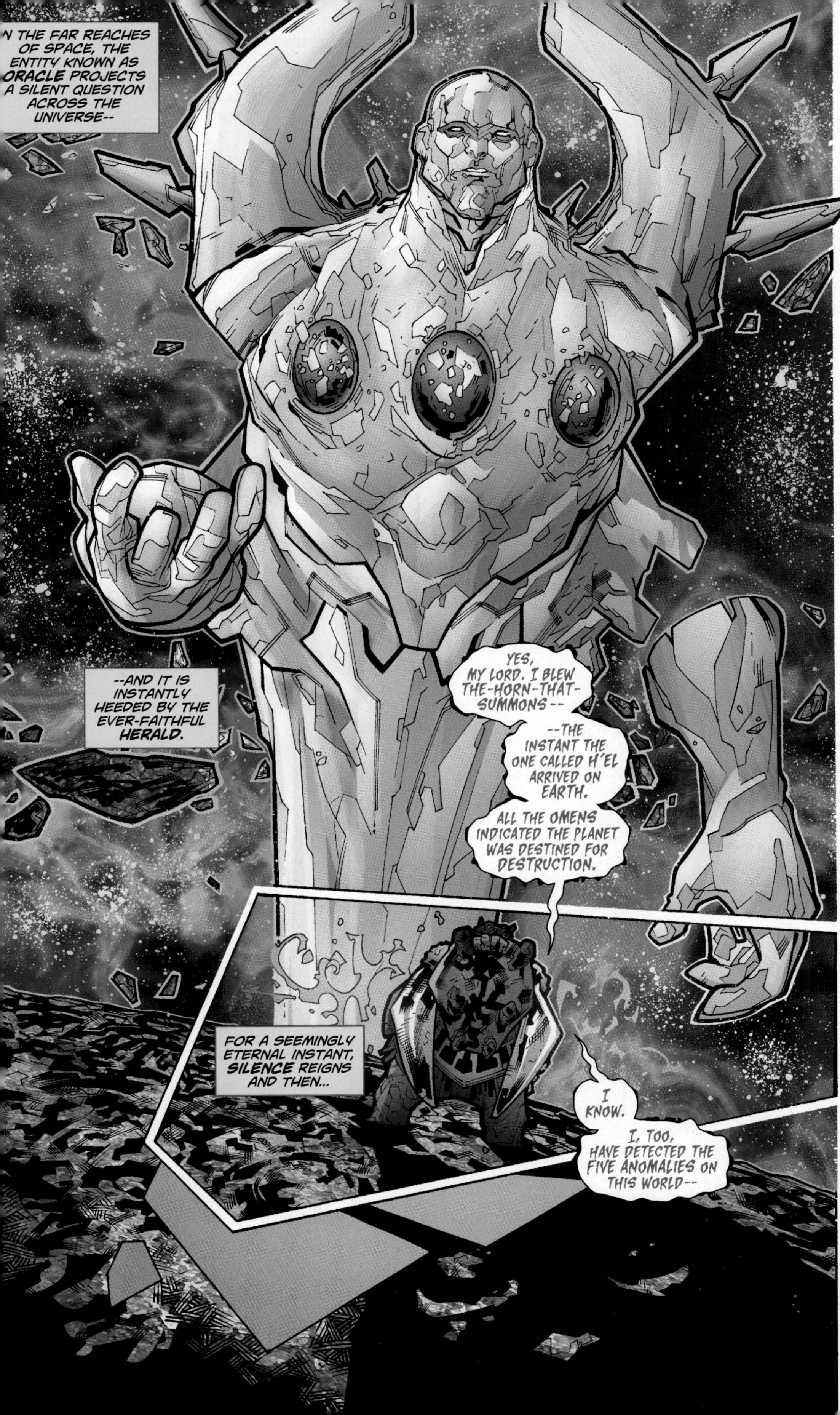
N THE FAR REACHES OF SPACE, THE ENTITY KNOWN AS ORACLE PROJECTS A SILENT QUESTION ACROSS THE UNIVERSE--
--AND IT IS INSTANTLY HEEDED BY THE EVER-FAITHFUL HERALD.
YES, MY LORD. I BLEW THE-HORN-THAT-SUMMONS--
--THE INSTANT THE ONE CALLED H'EL ARRIVED ON EARTH.
ALL THE OMENS INDICATED THE PLANET WAS DESTINED FOR DESTRUCTION.
FOR A SEEMINGLY ETERNAL INSTANT, SILENCE REIGNS AND THEN...
I KNOW.
I, TOO, HAVE DETECTED THE FIVE ANOMALIES ON THIS WORLD--

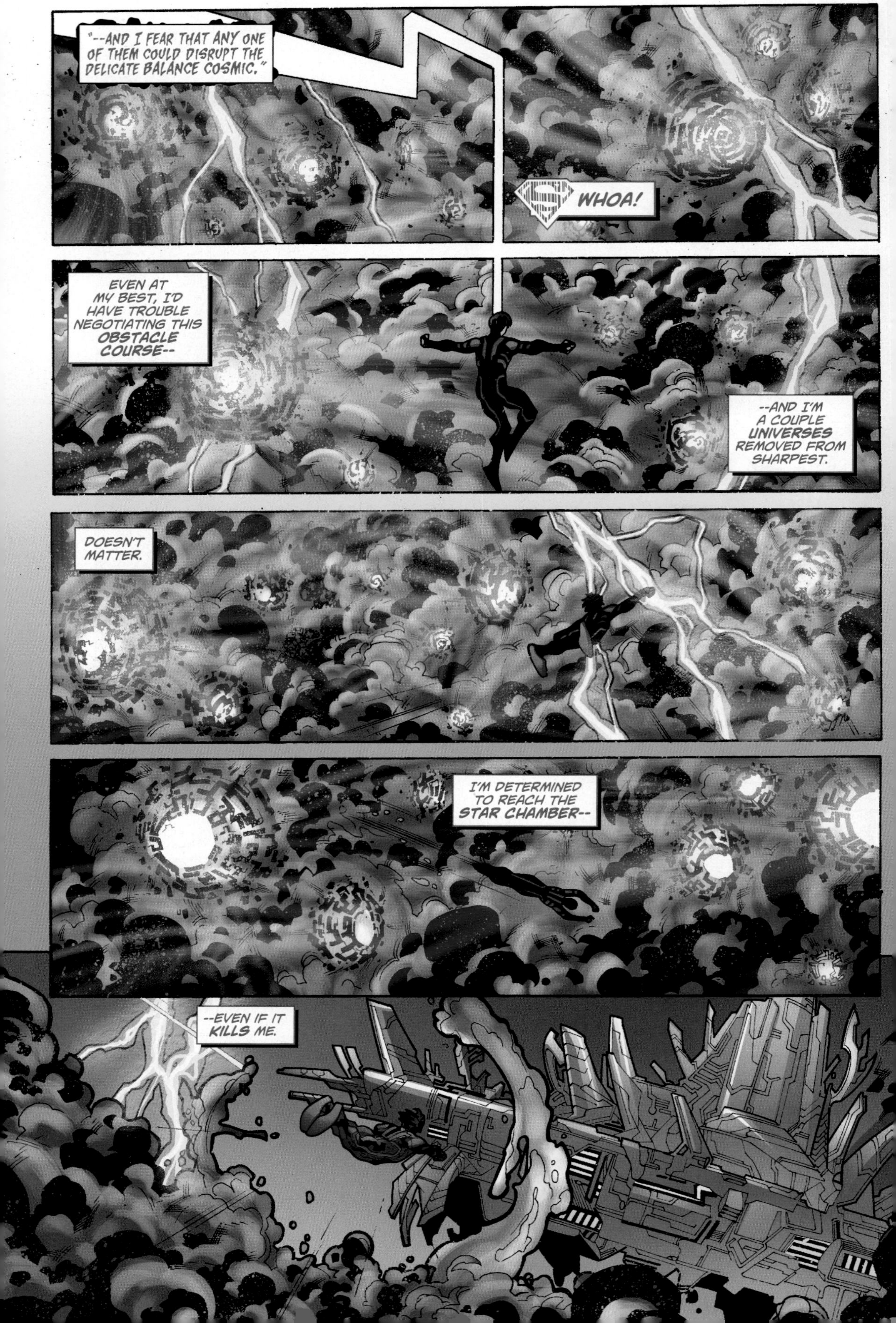
"--AND I FEAR THAT ANY ONE OF THEM COULD DISRUPT THE DELICATE BALANCE COSMIC."
WHOA!
EVEN AT MY BEST, I'D HAVE TROUBLE NEGOTIATING THIS OBSTACLE COURSE--
--AND I'M A COUPLE UNIVERSES REMOVED FROM SHARPEST.
DOESN'T MATTER.
I'M DETERMINED TO REACH THE STAR CHAMBER--
--EVEN IF IT KILLS ME.

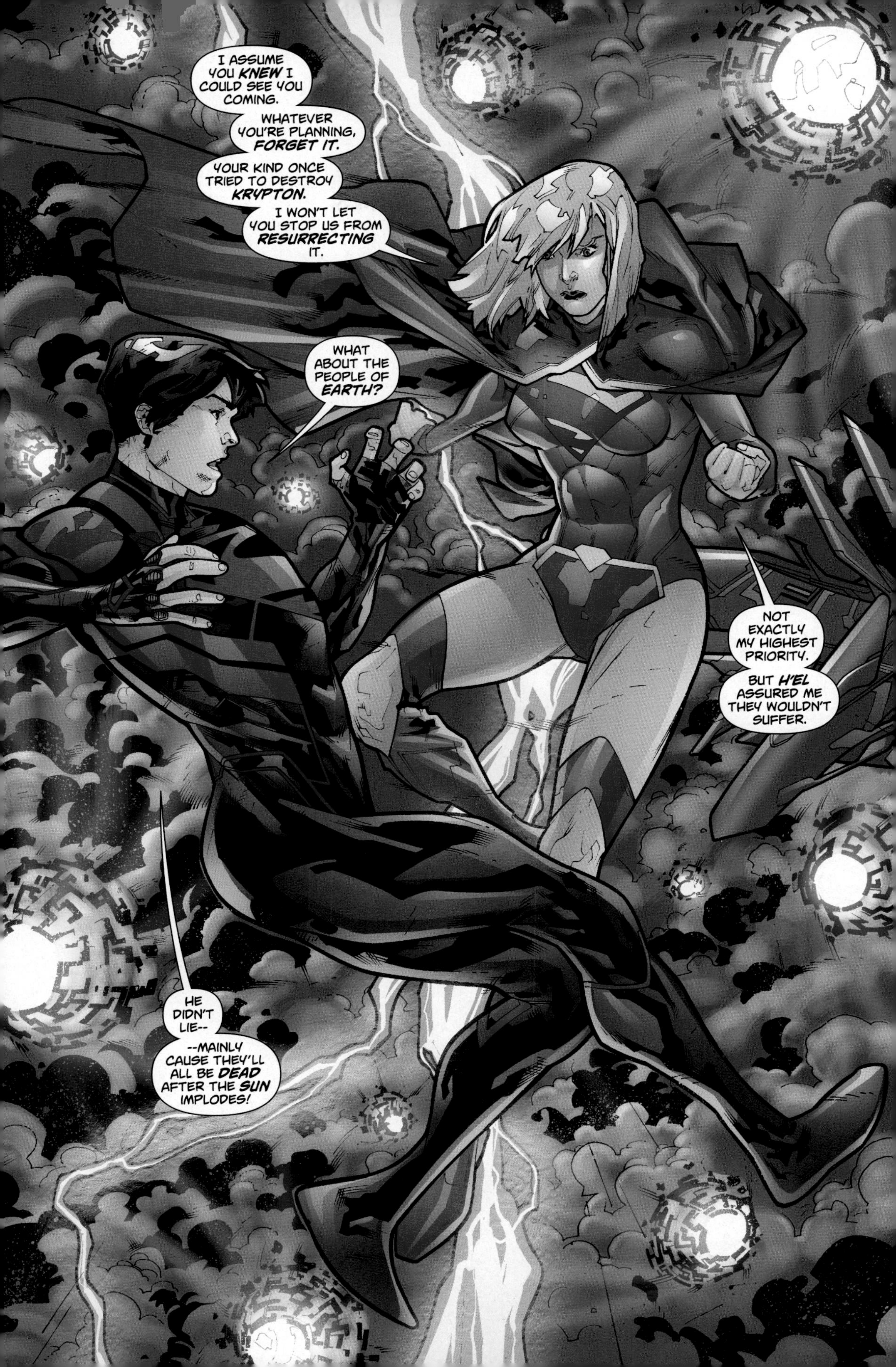
I ASSUME YOU **KNEW** I COULD SEE YOU COMING.
WHATEVER YOU'RE PLANNING, **FORGET IT.**
YOUR KIND ONCE TRIED TO DESTROY **KRYPTON.**
I WON'T LET YOU STOP US FROM **RESURRECTING** IT.
WHAT ABOUT THE PEOPLE OF **EARTH?**
NOT EXACTLY MY HIGHEST PRIORITY.
BUT **H'EL** ASSURED ME THEY WOULDN'T SUFFER.
HE DIDN'T LIE--
--MAINLY CAUSE THEY'LL ALL BE **DEAD** AFTER THE **SUN** IMPLODES!

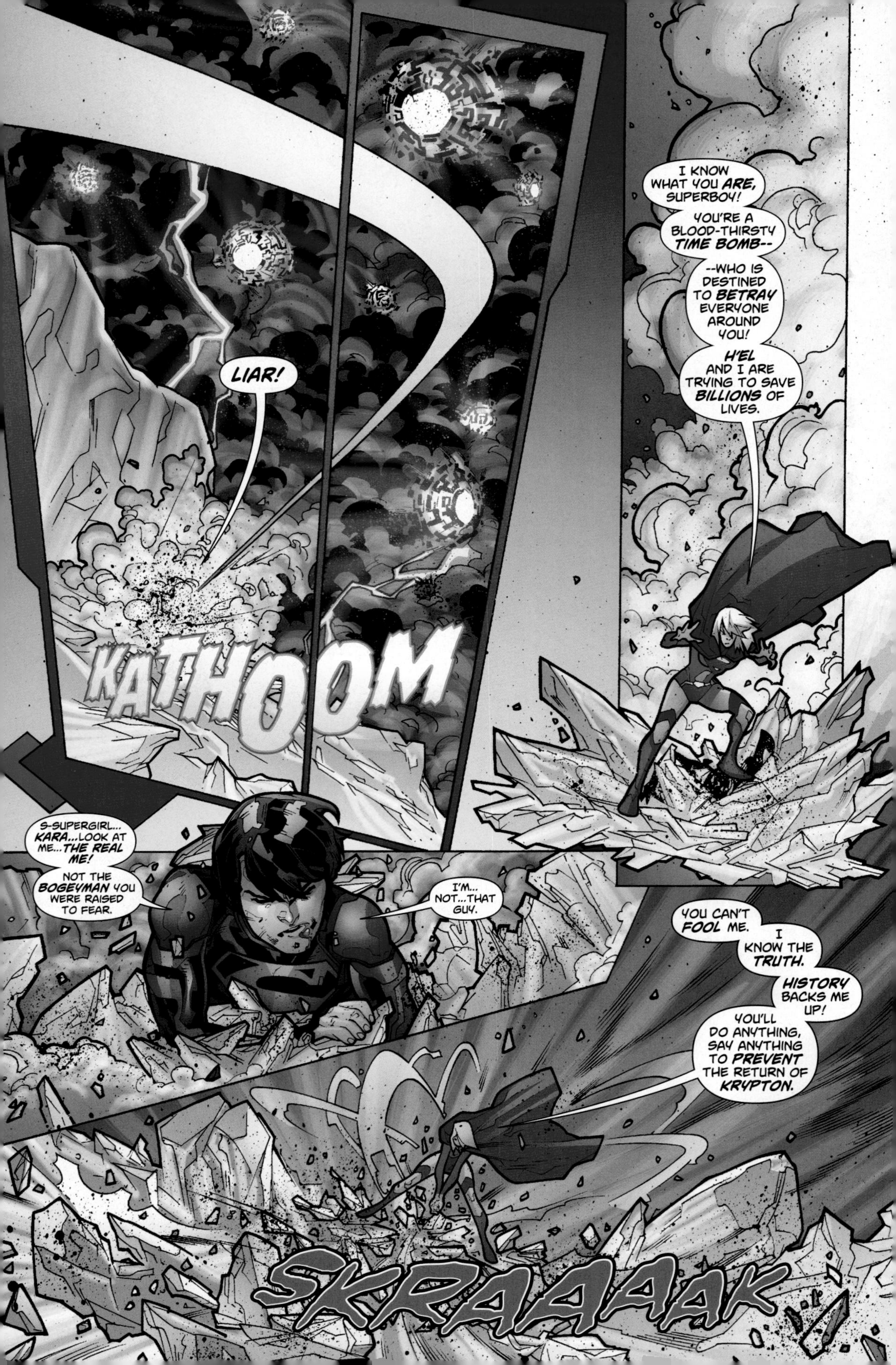
LIAR!
KATHOOM
I KNOW WHAT YOU ARE, SUPERBOY!
YOU'RE A BLOOD-THIRSTY TIME BOMB--
--WHO IS DESTINED TO BETRAY EVERYONE AROUND YOU!
H'EL AND I ARE TRYING TO SAVE BILLIONS OF LIVES.
S-SUPERGIRL... KARA...LOOK AT ME...THE REAL ME!
NOT THE BOGEYMAN YOU WERE RAISED TO FEAR.
I'M... NOT...THAT GUY.
YOU CAN'T FOOL ME.
I KNOW THE TRUTH.
HISTORY BACKS ME UP!
YOU'LL DO ANYTHING, SAY ANYTHING TO PREVENT THE RETURN OF KRYPTON.
SKRAAAAAK

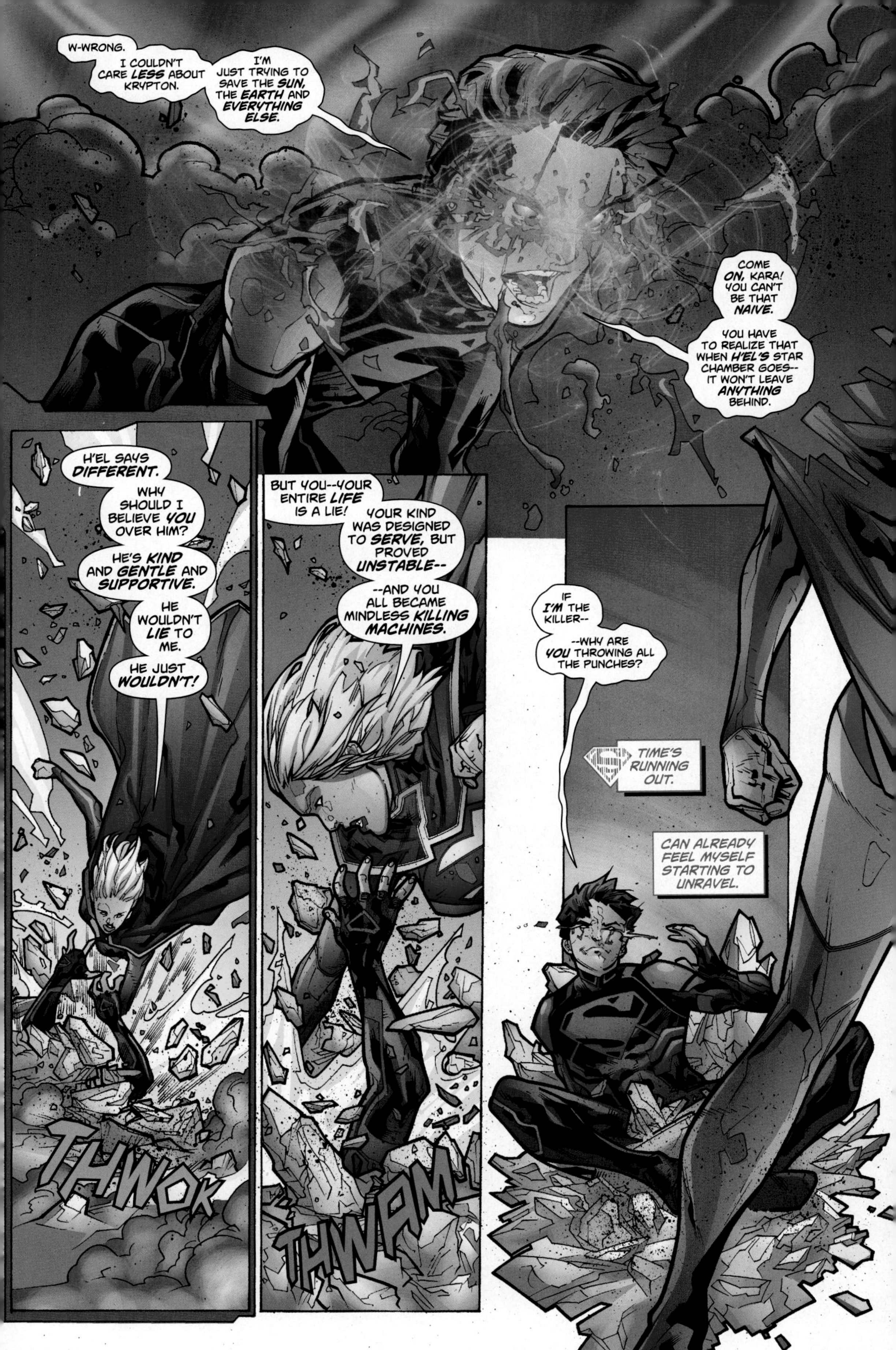
W-WRONG.
I COULDN'T CARE LESS ABOUT KRYPTON.
I'M JUST TRYING TO SAVE THE SUN, THE EARTH AND EVERYTHING ELSE.
COME ON, KARA! YOU CAN'T BE THAT NAIVE.
YOU HAVE TO REALIZE THAT WHEN H'EL'S STAR CHAMBER GOES-- IT WON'T LEAVE ANYTHING BEHIND.
H'EL SAYS DIFFERENT.
WHY SHOULD I BELIEVE YOU OVER HIM?
HE'S KIND AND GENTLE AND SUPPORTIVE.
HE WOULDN'T LIE TO ME.
HE JUST WOULDN'T!
THWOK
BUT YOU--YOUR ENTIRE LIFE IS A LIE!
YOUR KIND WAS DESIGNED TO SERVE, BUT PROVED UNSTABLE--
--AND YOU ALL BECAME MINDLESS KILLING MACHINES.
THWAM
IF I'M THE KILLER--
--WHY ARE YOU THROWING ALL THE PUNCHES?
TIME'S RUNNING OUT.
CAN ALREADY FEEL MYSELF STARTING TO UNRAVEL.

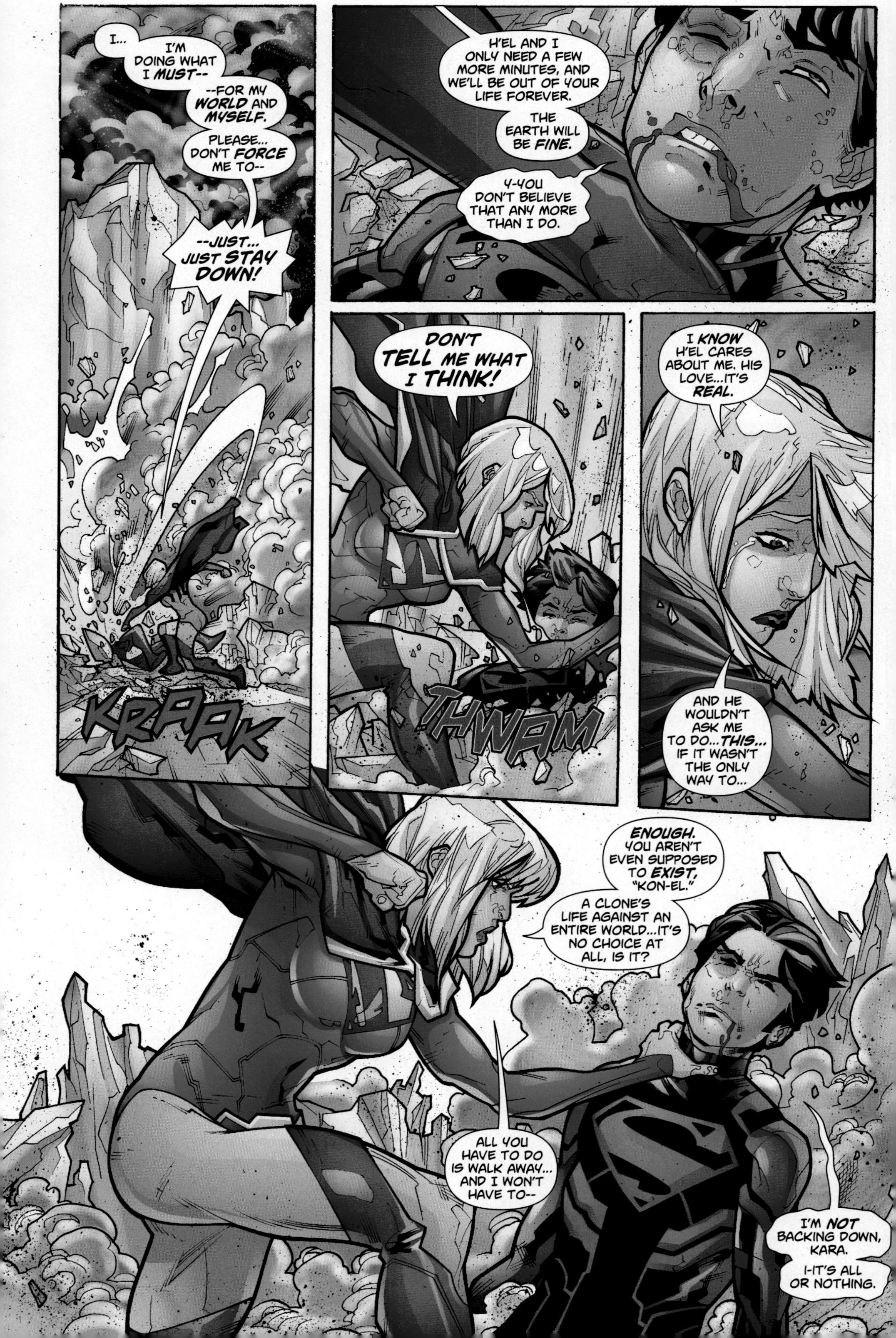
I...
I'M DOING WHAT I MUST--
--FOR MY WORLD AND MYSELF.
PLEASE... DON'T FORCE ME TO--
--JUST... JUST STAY DOWN!
KRAAAK
H'EL AND I ONLY NEED A FEW MORE MINUTES, AND WE'LL BE OUT OF YOUR LIFE FOREVER.
THE EARTH WILL BE FINE.
Y-YOU DON'T BELIEVE THAT ANY MORE THAN I DO.
DON'T TELL ME WHAT I THINK!
THWAM
I KNOW H'EL CARES ABOUT ME. HIS LOVE...IT'S REAL.
AND HE WOULDN'T ASK ME TO DO...THIS... IF IT WASN'T THE ONLY WAY TO...
ENOUGH. YOU AREN'T EVEN SUPPOSED TO EXIST, "KON-EL."
A CLONE'S LIFE AGAINST AN ENTIRE WORLD...IT'S NO CHOICE AT ALL, IS IT?
ALL YOU HAVE TO DO IS WALK AWAY... AND I WON'T HAVE TO--
I'M NOT BACKING DOWN, KARA.
I-IT'S ALL OR NOTHING.

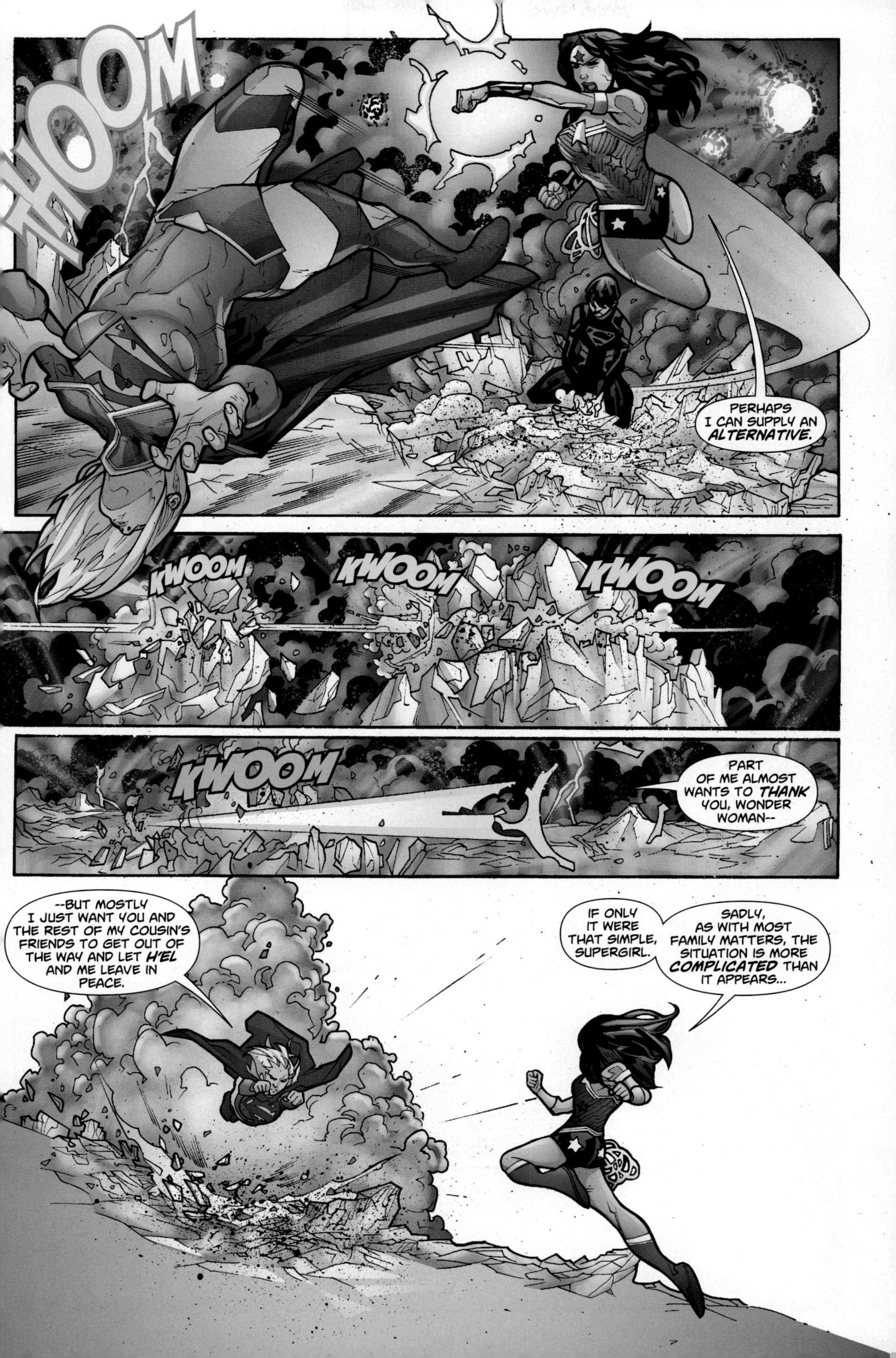
THOOM
PERHAPS I CAN SUPPLY AN ALTERNATIVE.
KWOOM
KWOOM
KWOOM
KWOOM
PART OF ME ALMOST WANTS TO THANK YOU, WONDER WOMAN--
--BUT MOSTLY I JUST WANT YOU AND THE REST OF MY COUSIN'S FRIENDS TO GET OUT OF THE WAY AND LET H'EL AND ME LEAVE IN PEACE.
IF ONLY IT WERE THAT SIMPLE, SUPERGIRL.
SADLY, AS WITH MOST FAMILY MATTERS, THE SITUATION IS MORE COMPLICATED THAN IT APPEARS...

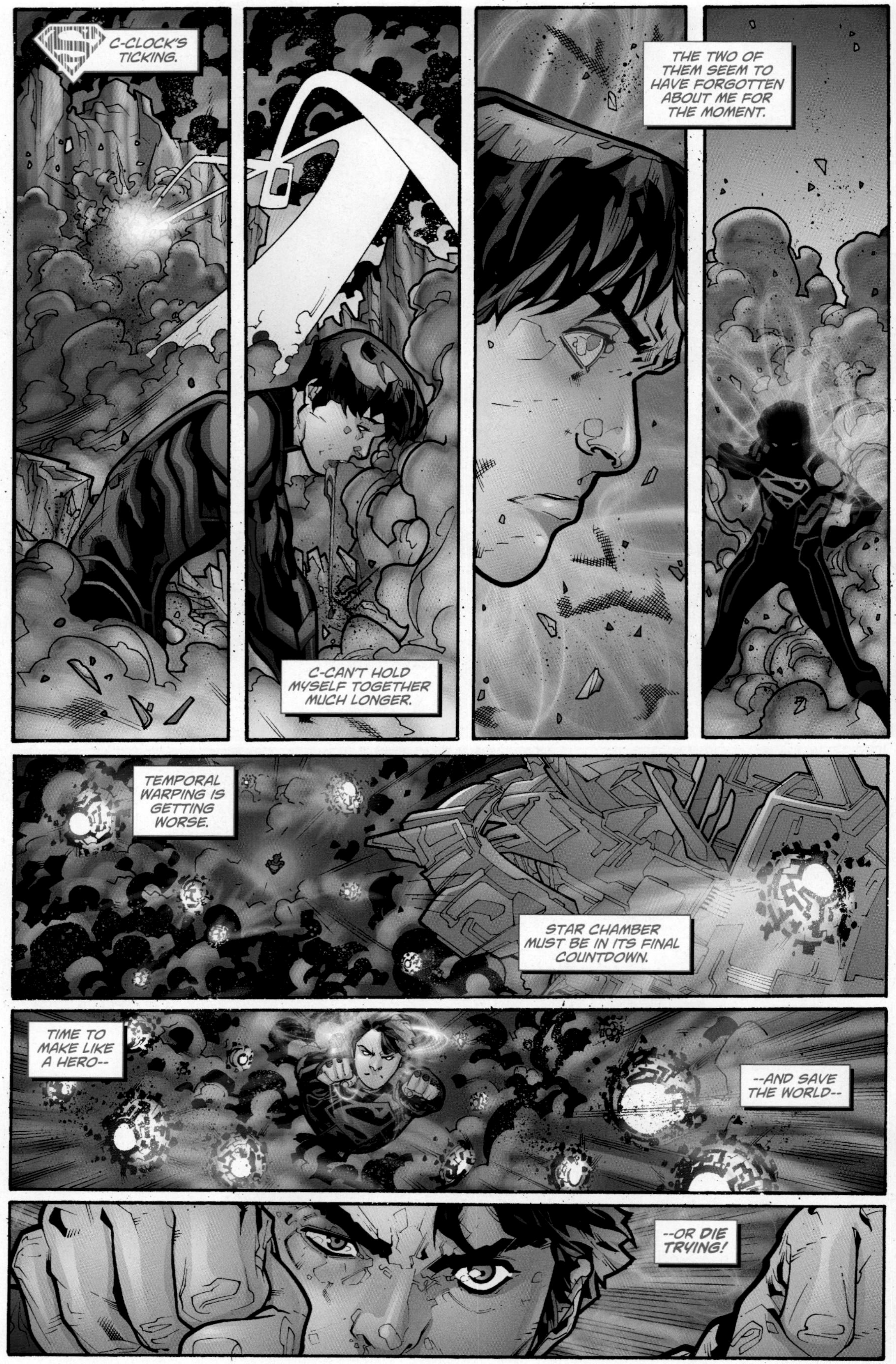
C-CLOCK'S TICKING.
C-CAN'T HOLD MYSELF TOGETHER MUCH LONGER.
THE TWO OF THEM SEEM TO HAVE FORGOTTEN ABOUT ME FOR THE MOMENT.
TEMPORAL WARPING IS GETTING WORSE.
STAR CHAMBER MUST BE IN ITS FINAL COUNTDOWN.
TIME TO MAKE LIKE A HERO--
--AND SAVE THE WORLD--
--OR DIE TRYING!

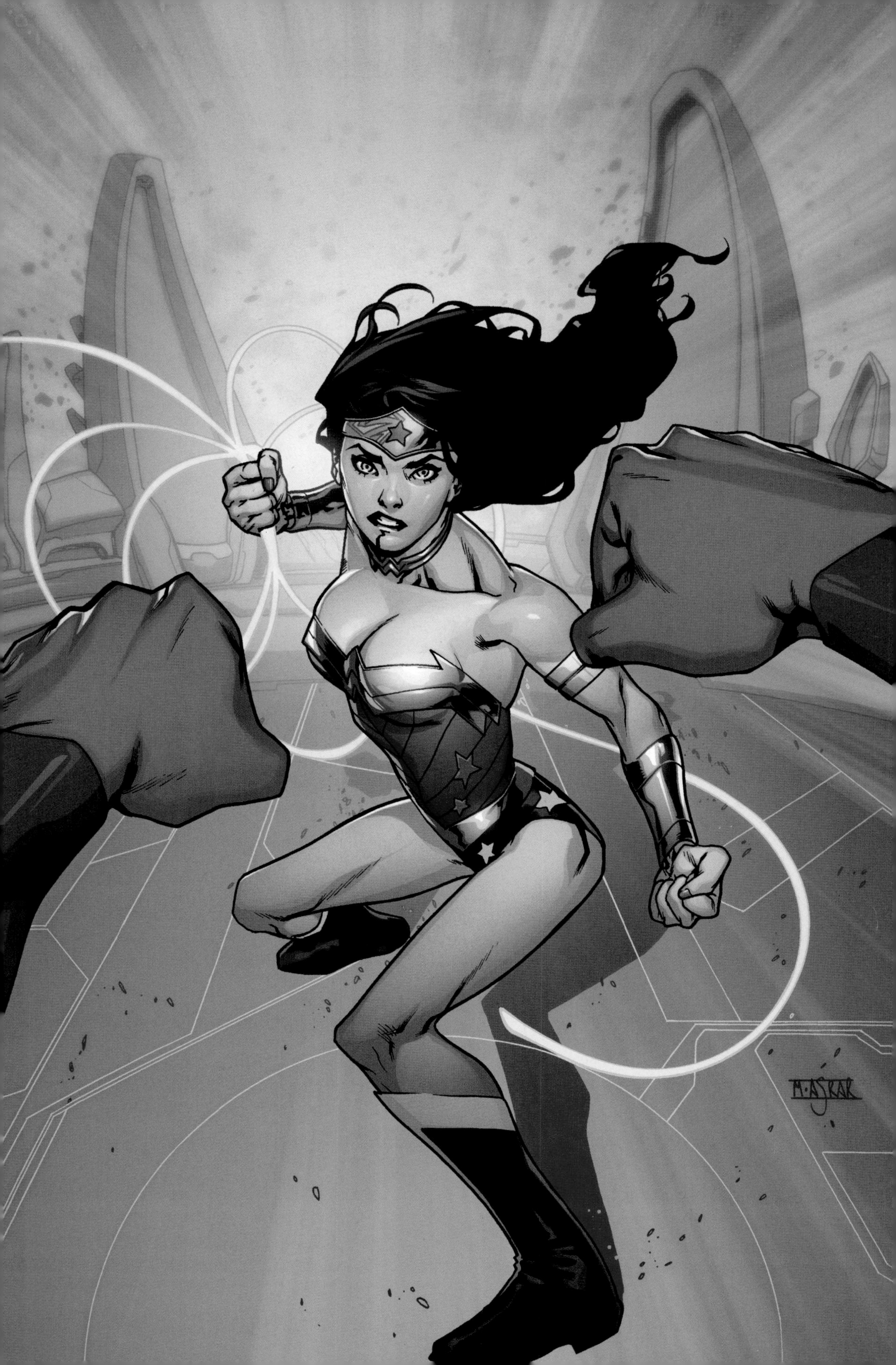
M.ASRAR

GIRL VS. GODDESS

MIKE JOHNSON writer **MAHMUD ASRAR** artist cover art by **MAHMUD ASRAR & DAVE MCCAIG**

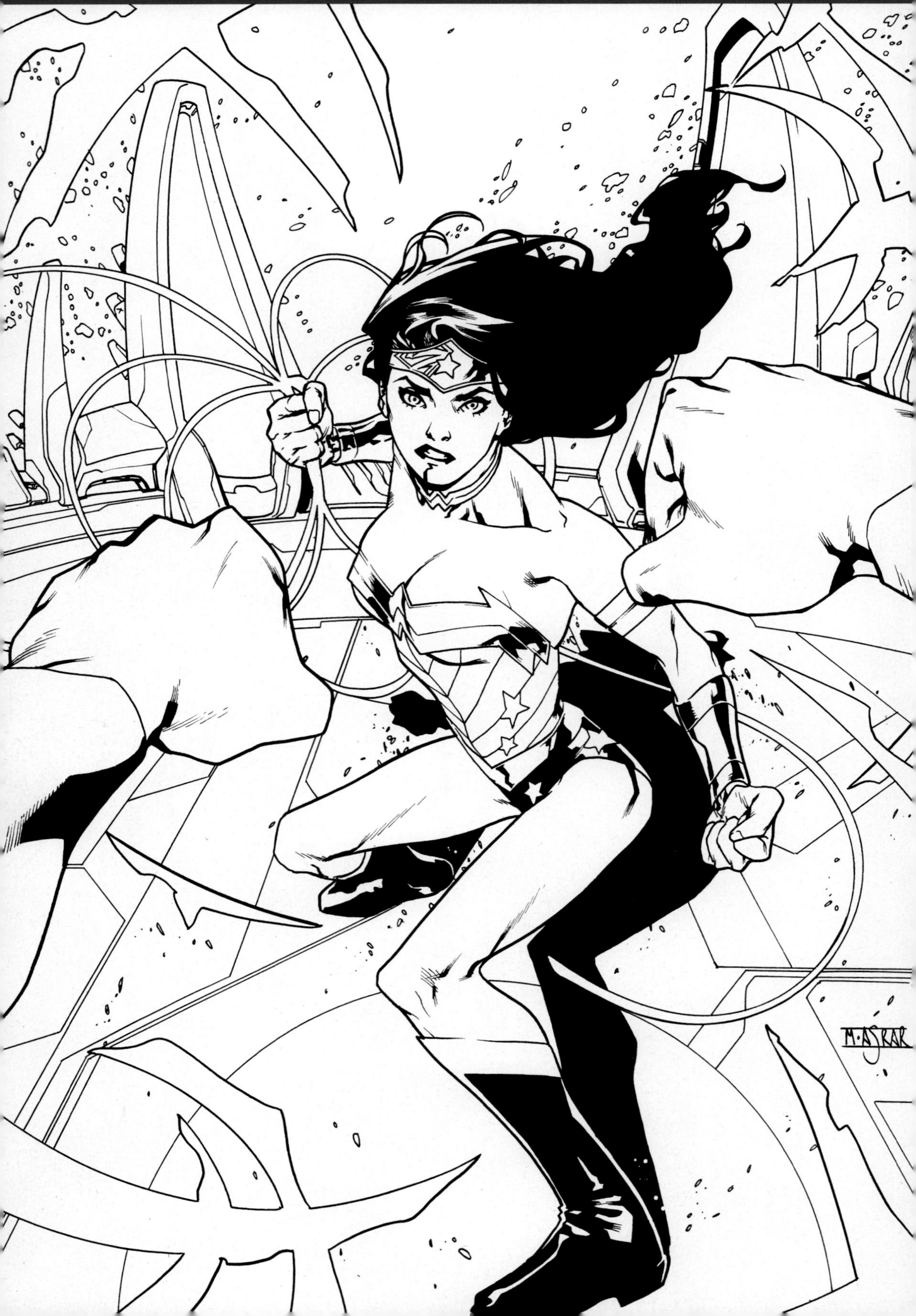

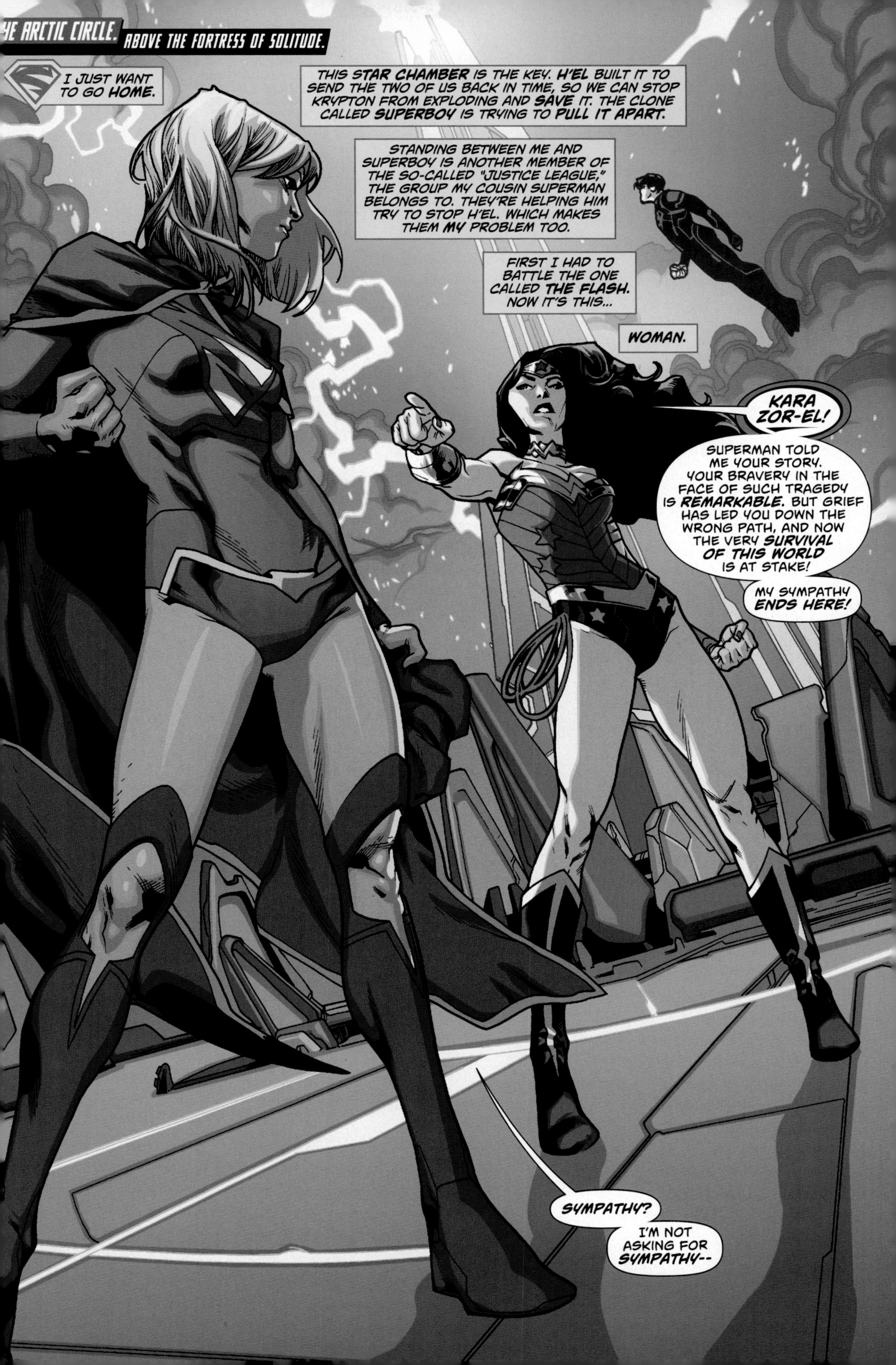
HE ARCTIC CIRCLE.
ABOVE THE FORTRESS OF SOLITUDE.
I JUST WANT TO GO HOME.
THIS STAR CHAMBER IS THE KEY. H'EL BUILT IT TO SEND THE TWO OF US BACK IN TIME, SO WE CAN STOP KRYPTON FROM EXPLODING AND SAVE IT. THE CLONE CALLED SUPERBOY IS TRYING TO PULL IT APART.
STANDING BETWEEN ME AND SUPERBOY IS ANOTHER MEMBER OF THE SO-CALLED "JUSTICE LEAGUE," THE GROUP MY COUSIN SUPERMAN BELONGS TO. THEY'RE HELPING HIM TRY TO STOP H'EL. WHICH MAKES THEM MY PROBLEM TOO.
FIRST I HAD TO BATTLE THE ONE CALLED THE FLASH. NOW IT'S THIS...
WOMAN.
KARA ZOR-EL!
SUPERMAN TOLD ME YOUR STORY. YOUR BRAVERY IN THE FACE OF SUCH TRAGEDY IS REMARKABLE. BUT GRIEF HAS LED YOU DOWN THE WRONG PATH, AND NOW THE VERY SURVIVAL OF THIS WORLD IS AT STAKE!
MY SYMPATHY ENDS HERE!
SYMPATHY?
I'M NOT ASKING FOR SYMPATHY--

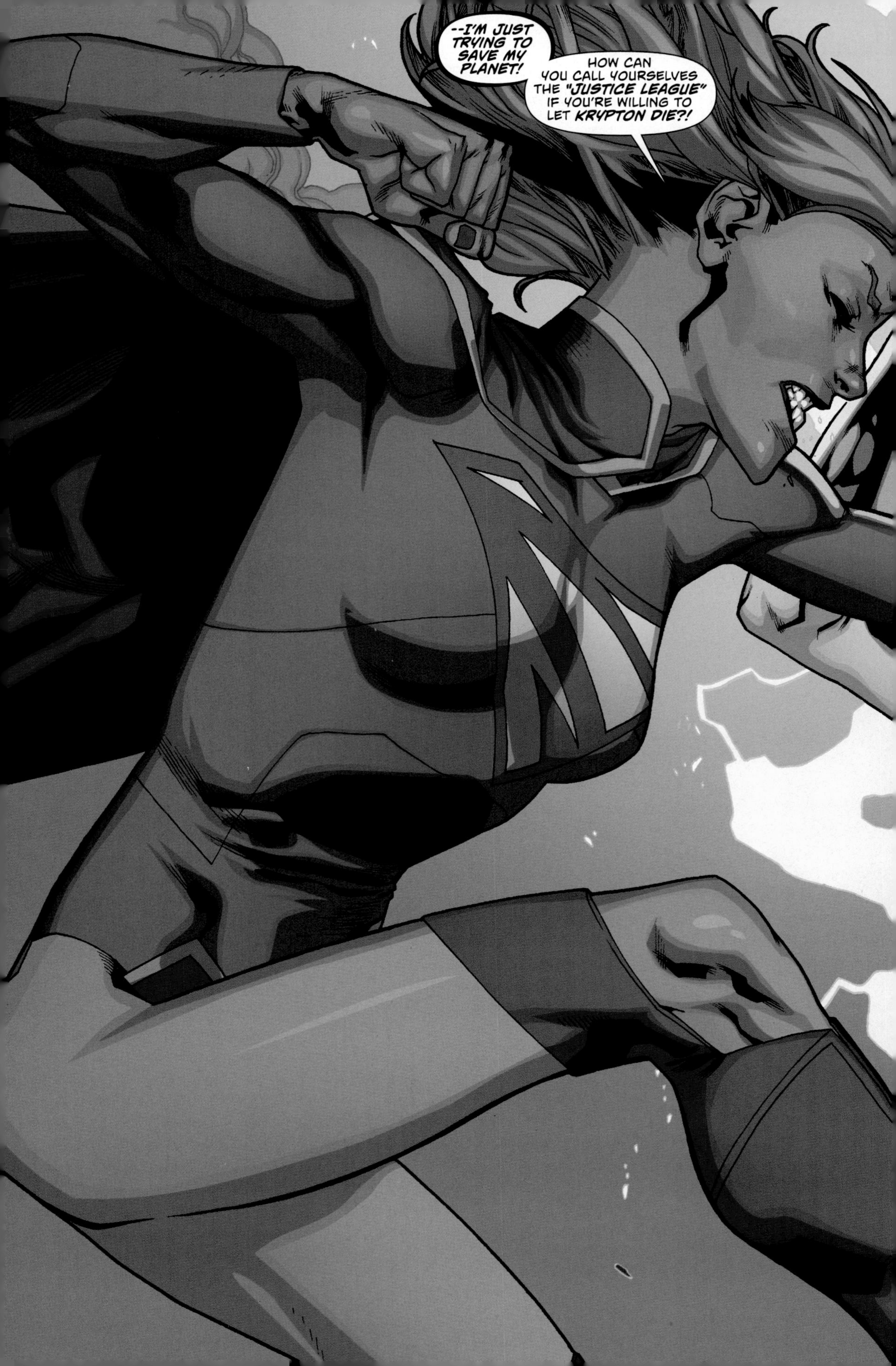
--I'M JUST TRYING TO SAVE MY PLANET!
HOW CAN YOU CALL YOURSELVES THE "JUSTICE LEAGUE" IF YOU'RE WILLING TO LET KRYPTON DIE?!

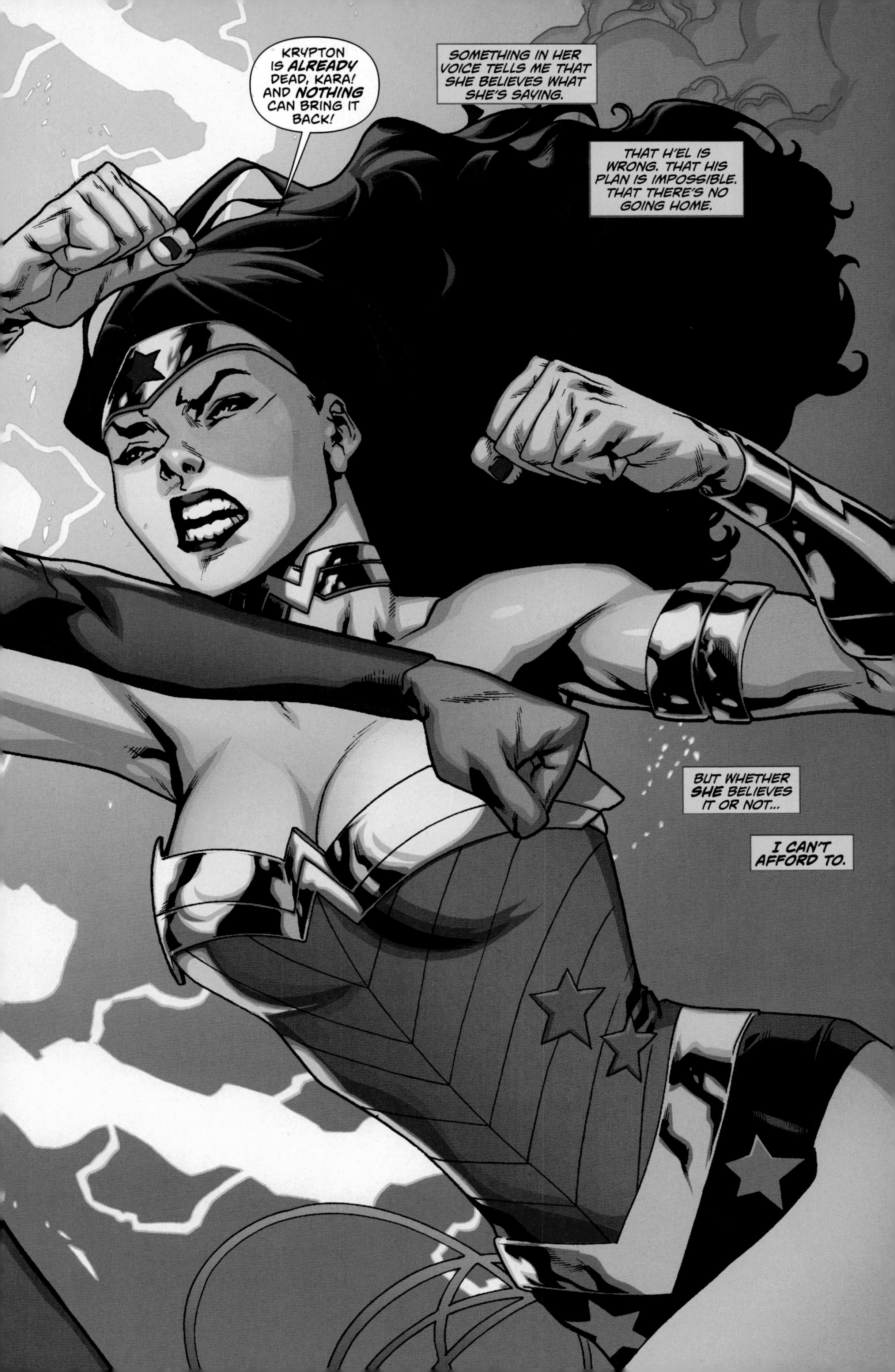
KRYPTON IS ALREADY DEAD, KARA! AND NOTHING CAN BRING IT BACK!
SOMETHING IN HER VOICE TELLS ME THAT SHE BELIEVES WHAT SHE'S SAYING.
THAT H'EL IS WRONG. THAT HIS PLAN IS IMPOSSIBLE. THAT THERE'S NO GOING HOME.
BUT WHETHER SHE BELIEVES IT OR NOT...
I CAN'T AFFORD TO.

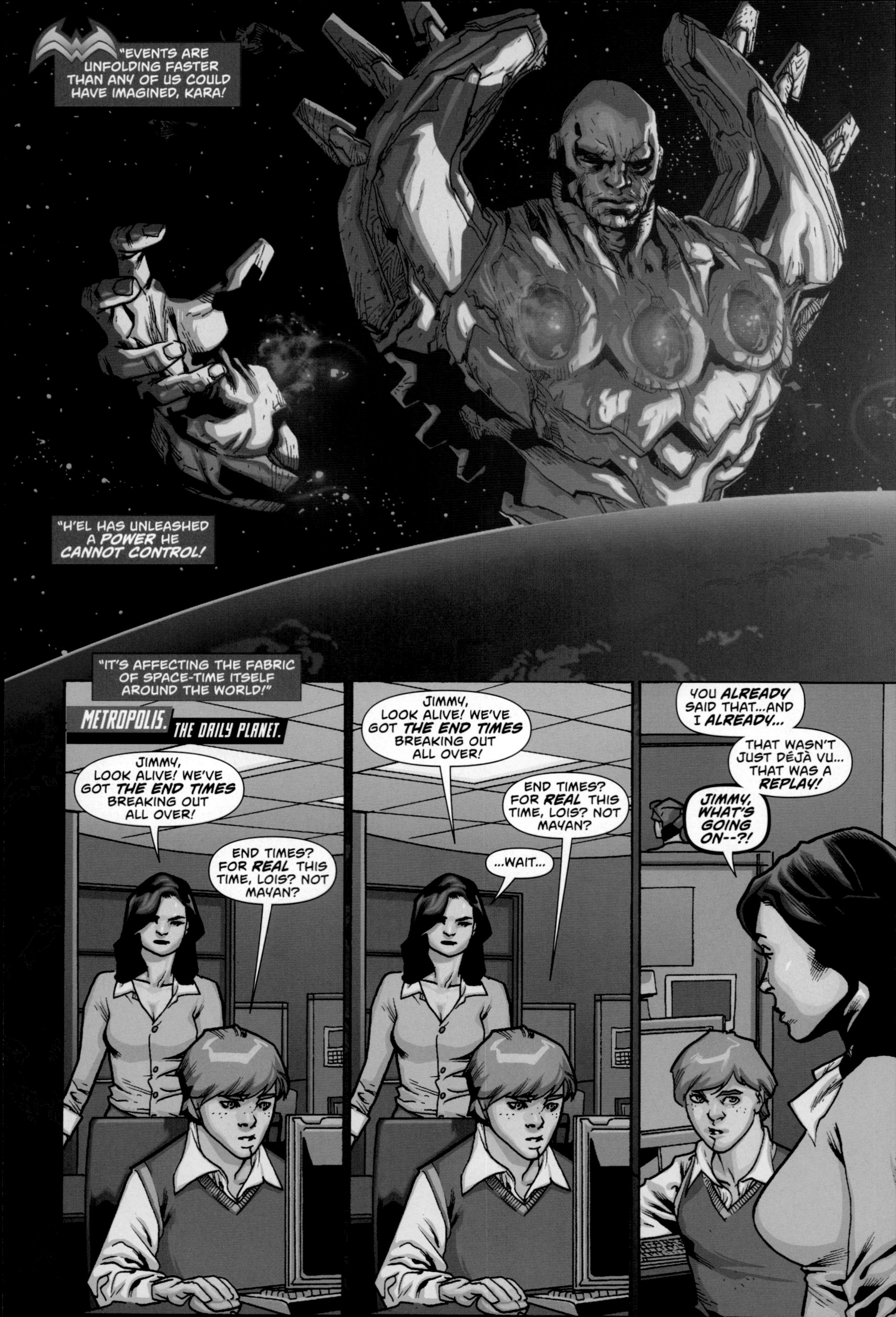
"EVENTS ARE UNFOLDING FASTER THAN ANY OF US COULD HAVE IMAGINED, KARA!
"H'EL HAS UNLEASHED A **POWER** HE **CANNOT CONTROL!**
"IT'S AFFECTING THE FABRIC OF SPACE-TIME ITSELF AROUND THE WORLD!"
METROPOLIS. THE DAILY PLANET.
JIMMY, LOOK ALIVE! WE'VE GOT **THE END TIMES** BREAKING OUT ALL OVER!
END TIMES? FOR **REAL** THIS TIME, LOIS? NOT MAYAN?
JIMMY, LOOK ALIVE! WE'VE GOT **THE END TIMES** BREAKING OUT ALL OVER!
END TIMES? FOR **REAL** THIS TIME, LOIS? NOT MAYAN?
...WAIT...
YOU **ALREADY** SAID THAT...AND I **ALREADY**...
THAT WASN'T JUST DÉJÀ VU... THAT WAS A **REPLAY!**
JIMMY, WHAT'S GOING ON--?!

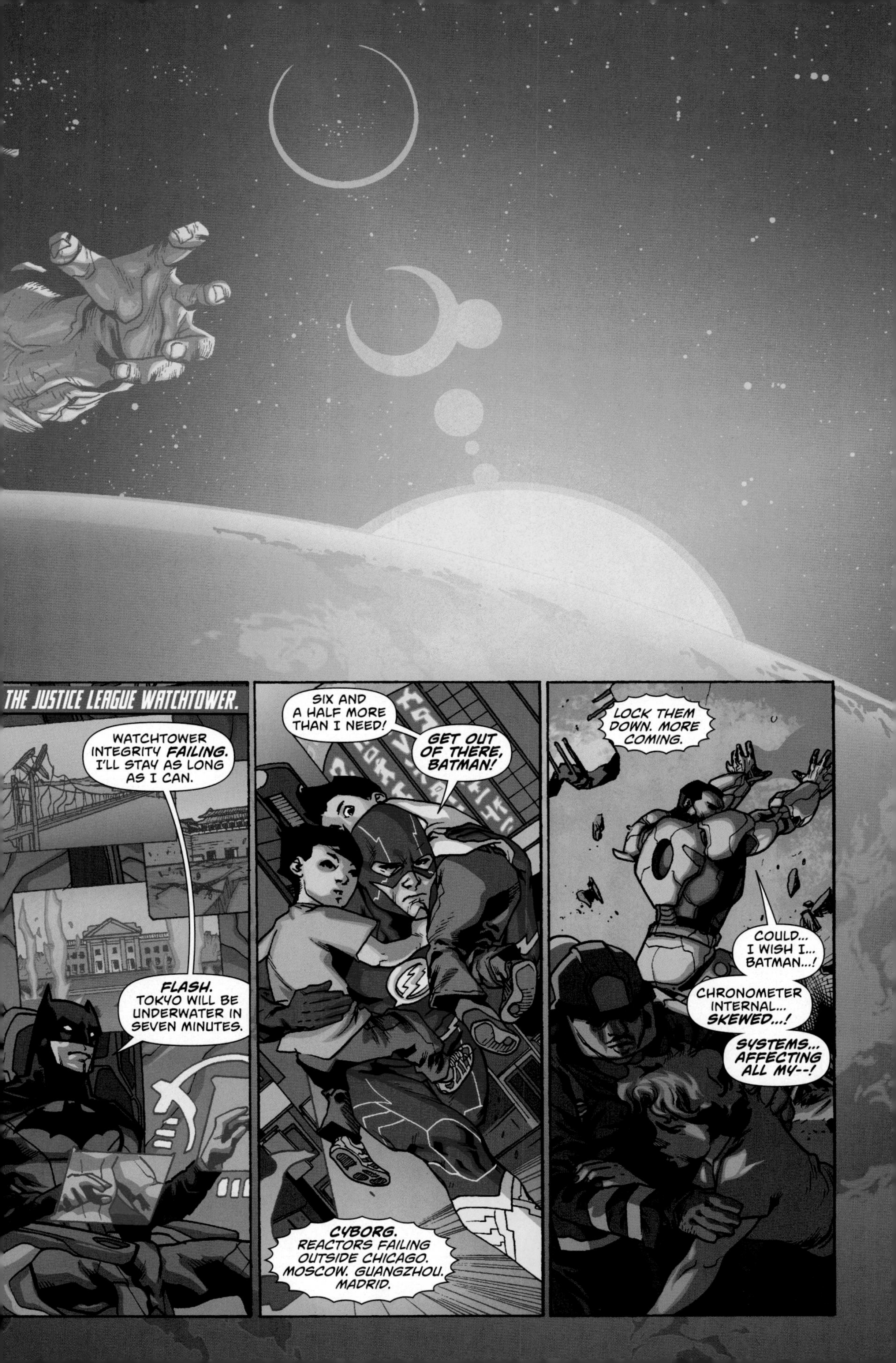
THE JUSTICE LEAGUE WATCHTOWER.
WATCHTOWER INTEGRITY FAILING. I'LL STAY AS LONG AS I CAN.
FLASH. TOKYO WILL BE UNDERWATER IN SEVEN MINUTES.
SIX AND A HALF MORE THAN I NEED!
GET OUT OF THERE, BATMAN!
CYBORG. REACTORS FAILING OUTSIDE CHICAGO. MOSCOW. GUANGZHOU. MADRID.
LOCK THEM DOWN. MORE COMING.
COULD... I WISH I... BATMAN...!
CHRONOMETER INTERNAL... SKEWED...!
SYSTEMS... AFFECTING ALL MY--!

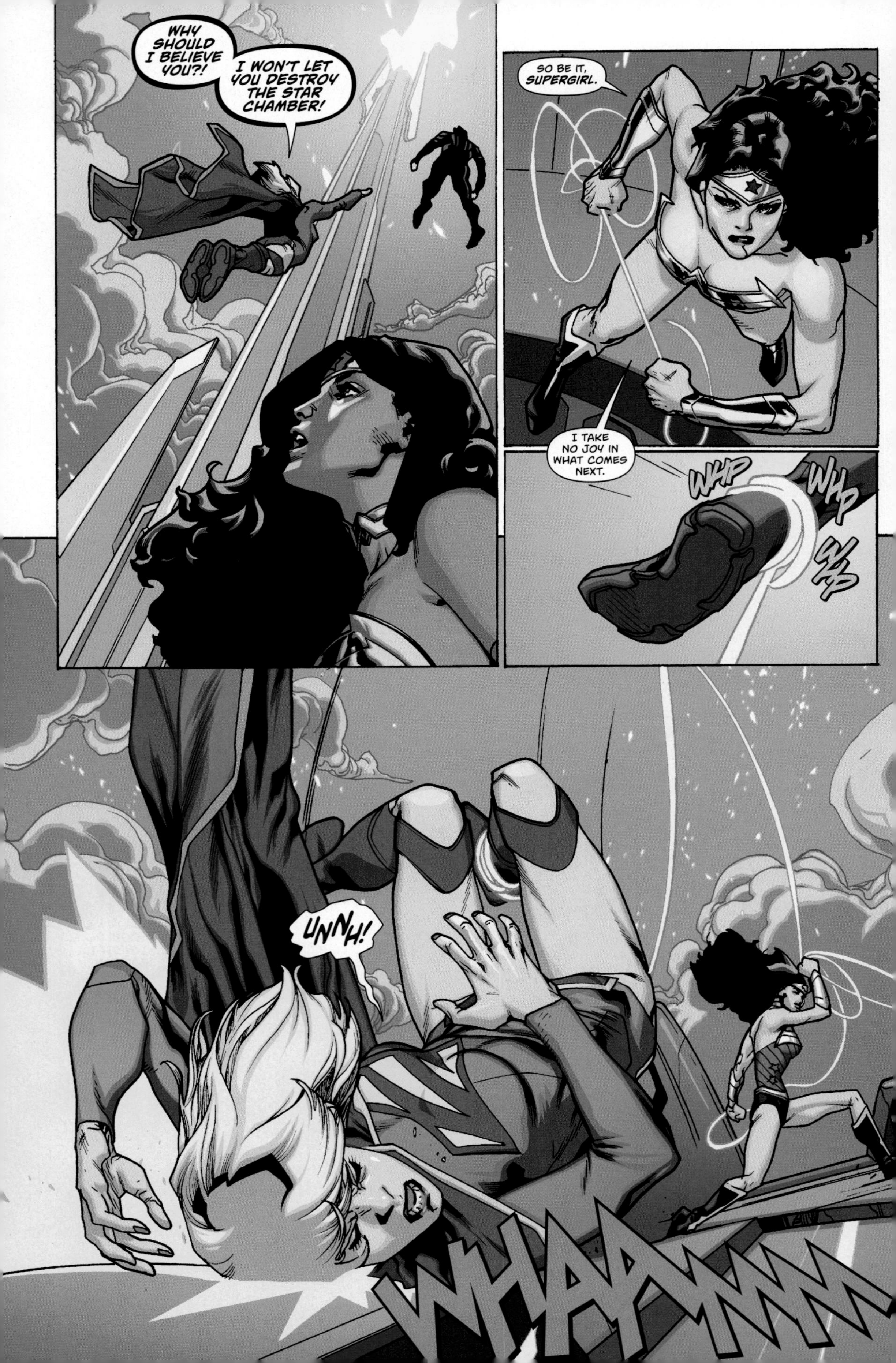
WHY SHOULD I BELIEVE YOU?!
I WON'T LET YOU DESTROY THE STAR CHAMBER!
SO BE IT, SUPERGIRL.
I TAKE NO JOY IN WHAT COMES NEXT.
WHP
WHP
WHP
UNNH!
WHAMM

WHAT IS THIS?

SOME KIND OF PRIMITIVE *ROPE?* YOU THINK A *ROPE* CAN STOP ME?!

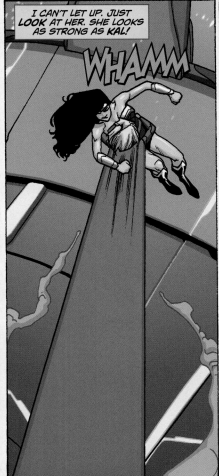

I CAN'T LET UP. JUST *LOOK* AT HER. SHE LOOKS AS STRONG AS *KAL!*

WHAMM

BUT IF I DON'T FIGHT BACK, I LOSE MY *ONLY* CHANCE TO SAVE MY FAMILY!

KRAANG

IN ANOTHER TIME, ANOTHER PLACE, MAYBE SHE AND I WOULD BE ALLIES...

BAAMMM

BUT NOT TODAY!

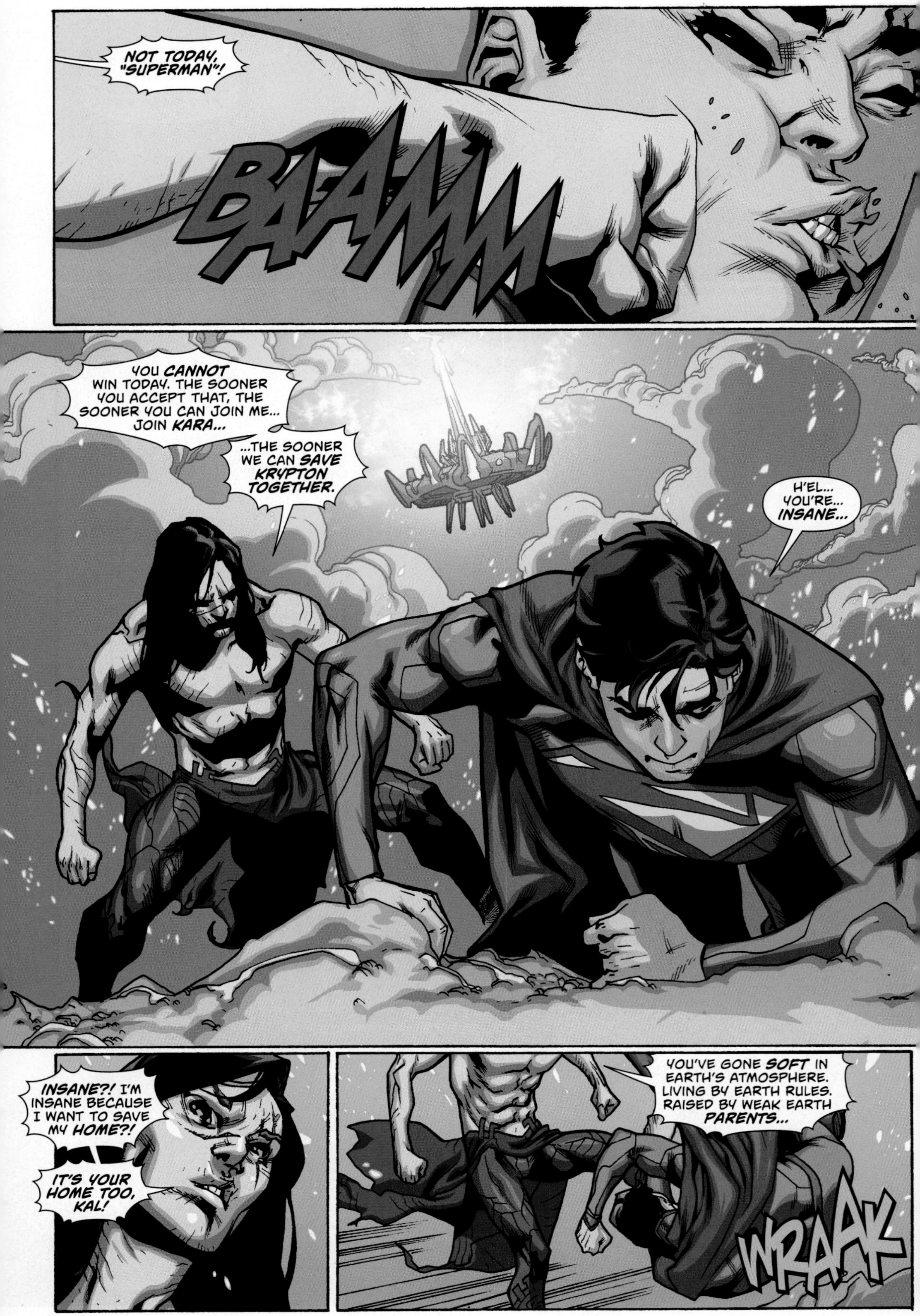
NOT TODAY, "SUPERMAN"!
BAAMM
YOU CANNOT WIN TODAY. THE SOONER YOU ACCEPT THAT, THE SOONER YOU CAN JOIN ME... JOIN KARA...
...THE SOONER WE CAN SAVE KRYPTON TOGETHER.
H'EL... YOU'RE... INSANE...
INSANE?! I'M INSANE BECAUSE I WANT TO SAVE MY HOME?!
IT'S YOUR HOME TOO, KAL!
YOU'VE GONE SOFT IN EARTH'S ATMOSPHERE. LIVING BY EARTH RULES. RAISED BY WEAK EARTH PARENTS...
WRAAK

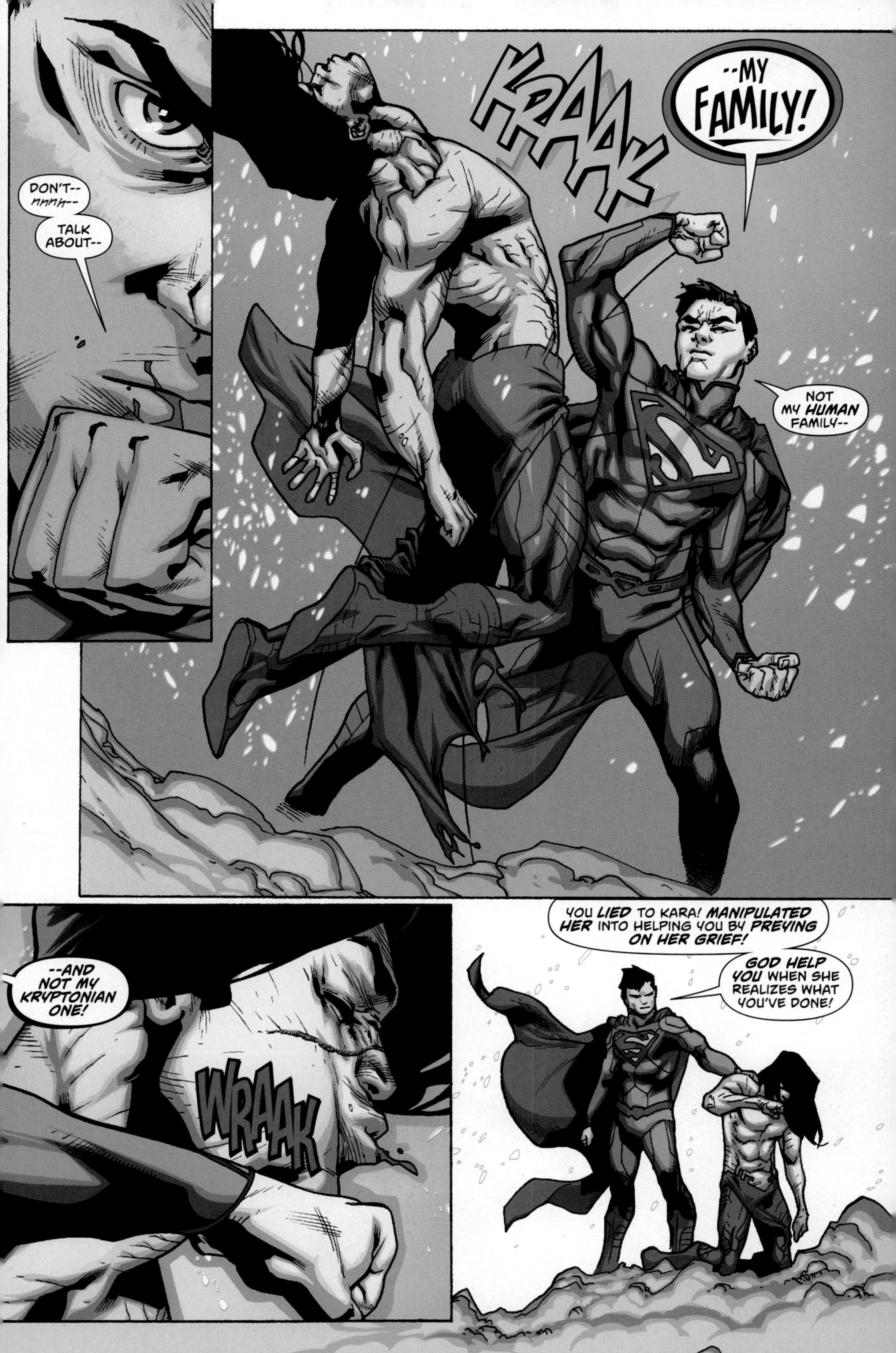
DON'T--
nnnh--
TALK ABOUT--
KRAAK
--MY FAMILY!
NOT MY HUMAN FAMILY--
--AND NOT MY KRYPTONIAN ONE!
WRAAK
YOU LIED TO KARA! MANIPULATED HER INTO HELPING YOU BY PREYING ON HER GRIEF!
GOD HELP YOU WHEN SHE REALIZES WHAT YOU'VE DONE!

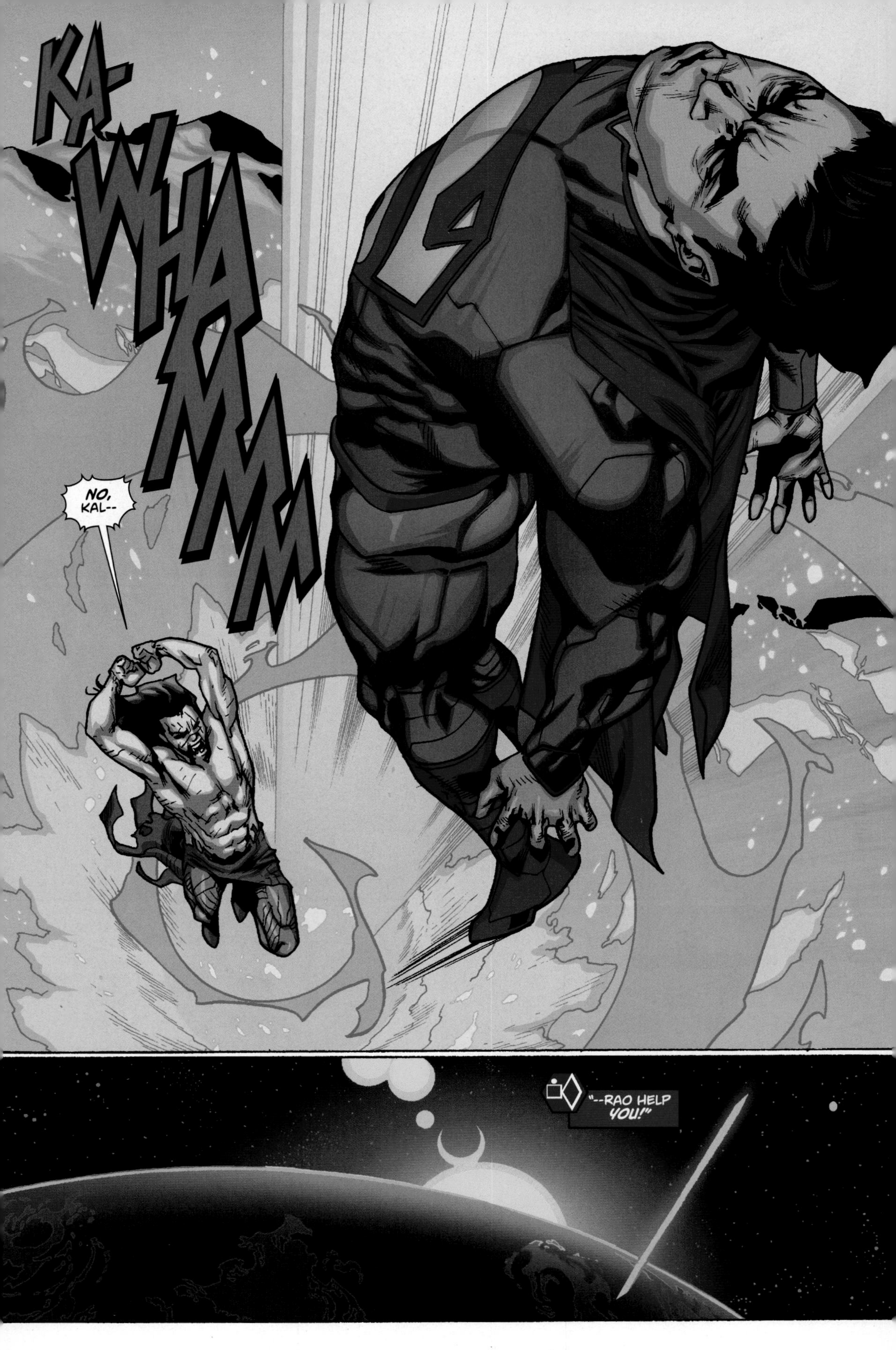
KA-WHAMMMM
NO, KAL--
"--RAO HELP YOU!"

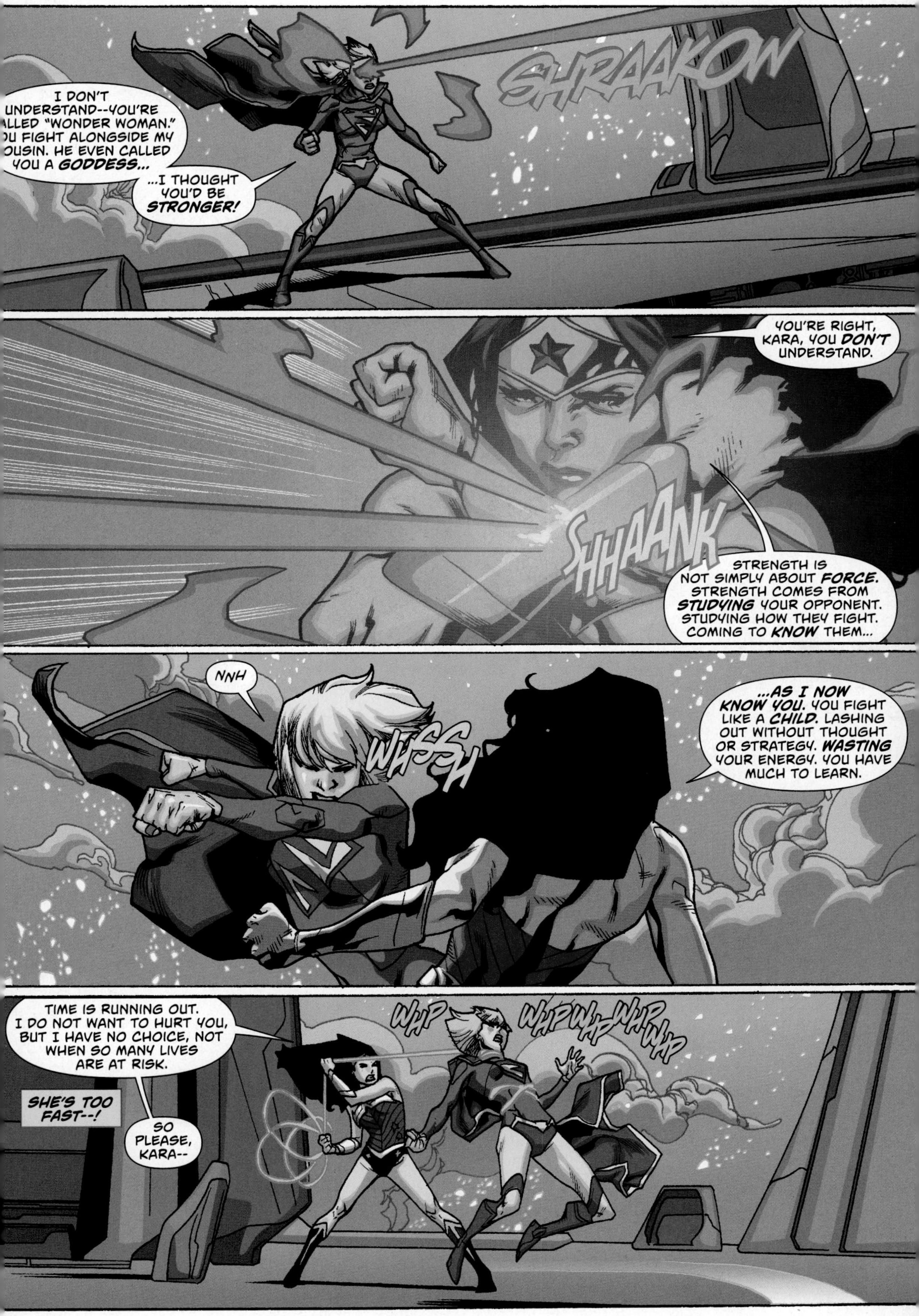

I DON'T UNDERSTAND--YOU'RE CALLED "WONDER WOMAN." YOU FIGHT ALONGSIDE MY COUSIN. HE EVEN CALLED YOU A GODDESS...
...I THOUGHT YOU'D BE STRONGER!
SHRAAKOW
YOU'RE RIGHT, KARA, YOU DON'T UNDERSTAND.
SHHAANK
STRENGTH IS NOT SIMPLY ABOUT FORCE. STRENGTH COMES FROM STUDYING YOUR OPPONENT. STUDYING HOW THEY FIGHT. COMING TO KNOW THEM...
NNH
WHSSH
...AS I NOW KNOW YOU. YOU FIGHT LIKE A CHILD. LASHING OUT WITHOUT THOUGHT OR STRATEGY. WASTING YOUR ENERGY. YOU HAVE MUCH TO LEARN.
TIME IS RUNNING OUT. I DO NOT WANT TO HURT YOU, BUT I HAVE NO CHOICE, NOT WHEN SO MANY LIVES ARE AT RISK.
SHE'S TOO FAST--!
SO PLEASE, KARA--
WHP
WHP WHP WHP WHP

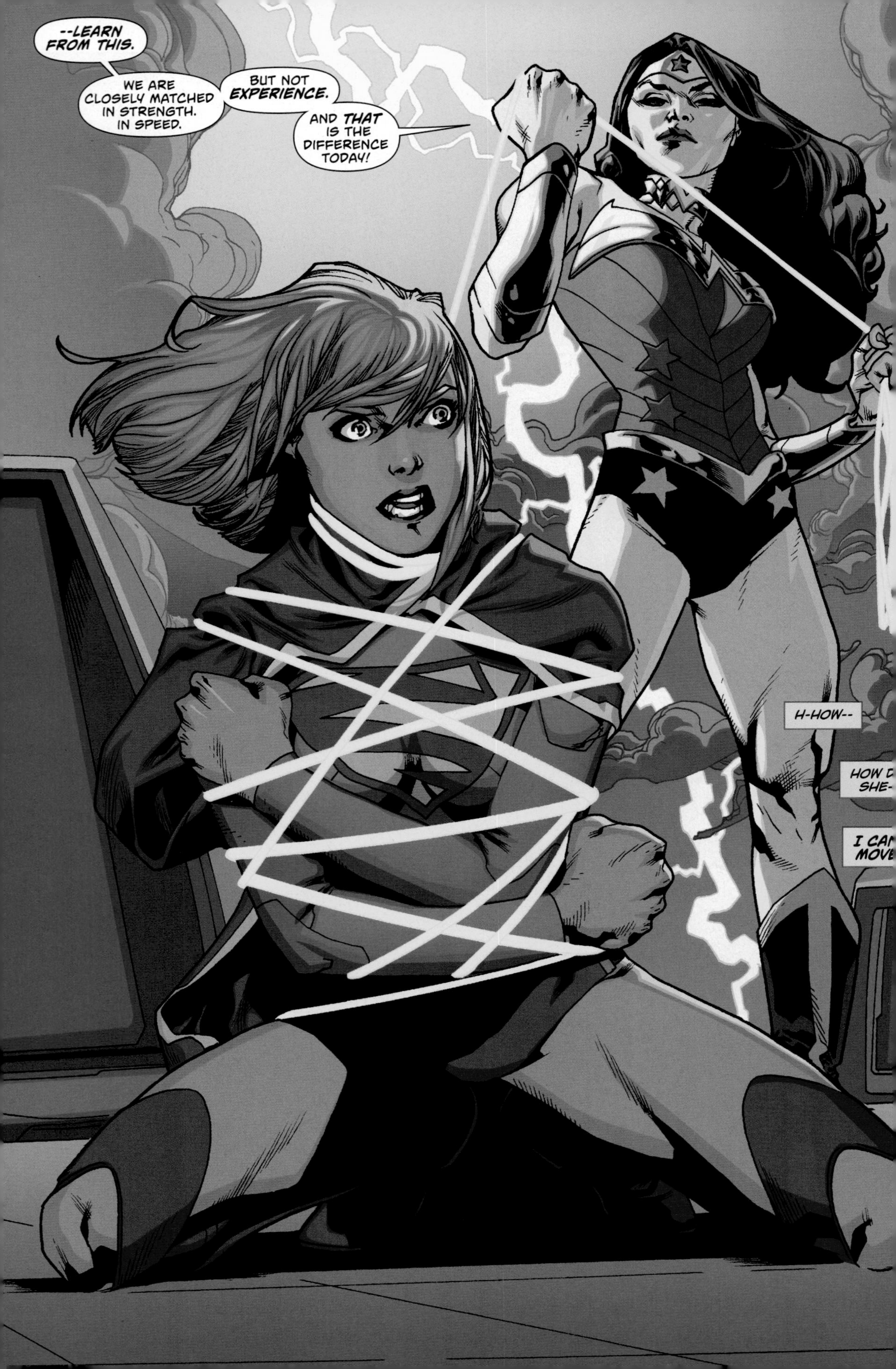
--LEARN FROM THIS.
WE ARE CLOSELY MATCHED IN STRENGTH. IN SPEED.
BUT NOT EXPERIENCE.
AND THAT IS THE DIFFERENCE TODAY!
H-HOW--

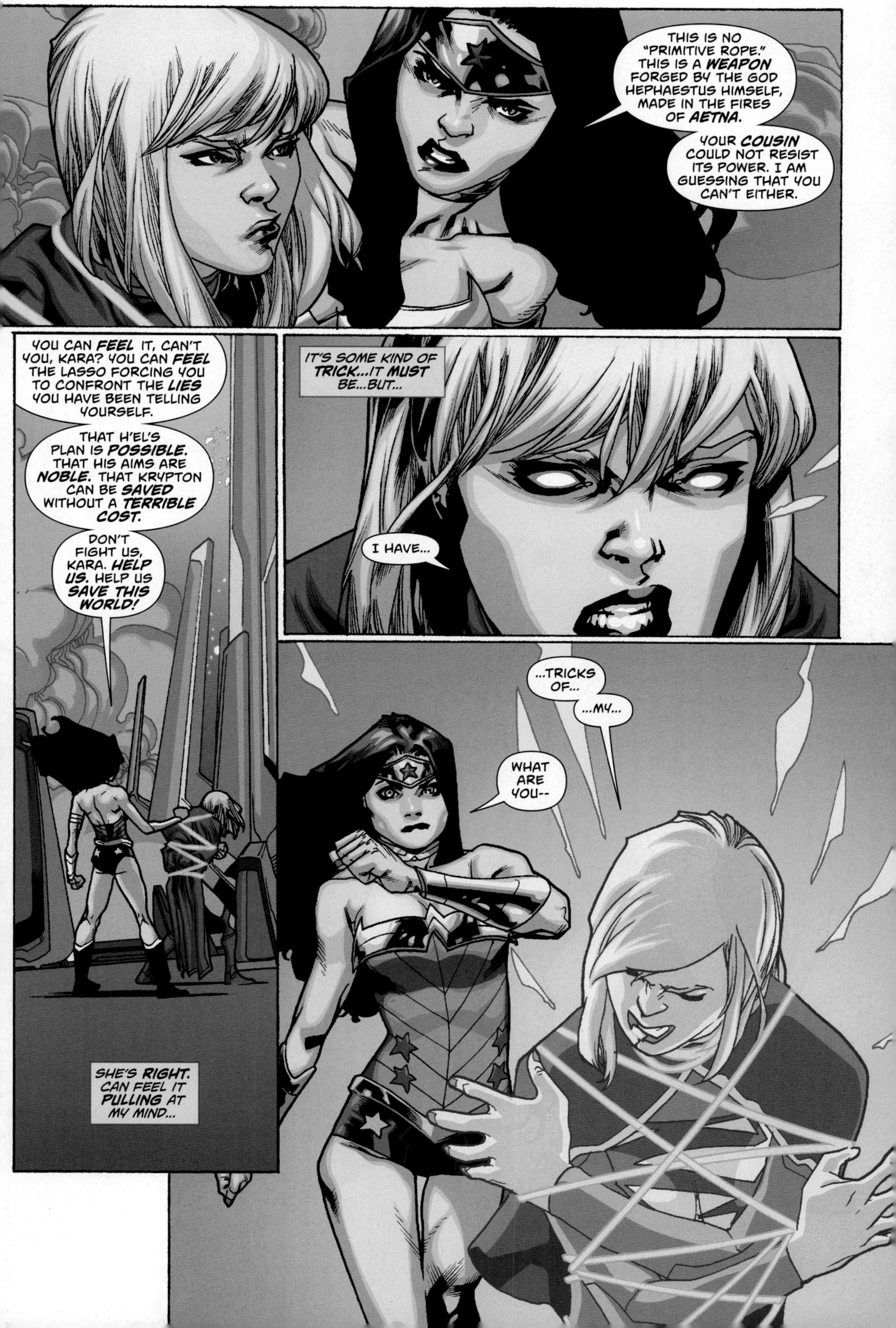
THIS IS NO "PRIMITIVE ROPE." THIS IS A WEAPON FORGED BY THE GOD HEPHAESTUS HIMSELF, MADE IN THE FIRES OF AETNA.
YOUR COUSIN COULD NOT RESIST ITS POWER. I AM GUESSING THAT YOU CAN'T EITHER.
YOU CAN FEEL IT, CAN'T YOU, KARA? YOU CAN FEEL THE LASSO FORCING YOU TO CONFRONT THE LIES YOU HAVE BEEN TELLING YOURSELF.
THAT H'EL'S PLAN IS POSSIBLE. THAT HIS AIMS ARE NOBLE. THAT KRYPTON CAN BE SAVED WITHOUT A TERRIBLE COST.
DON'T FIGHT US, KARA. HELP US. HELP US SAVE THIS WORLD!
SHE'S RIGHT. CAN FEEL IT PULLING AT MY MIND...
IT'S SOME KIND OF TRICK...IT MUST BE...BUT...
I HAVE...
...TRICKS OF...
...MY...
WHAT ARE YOU--

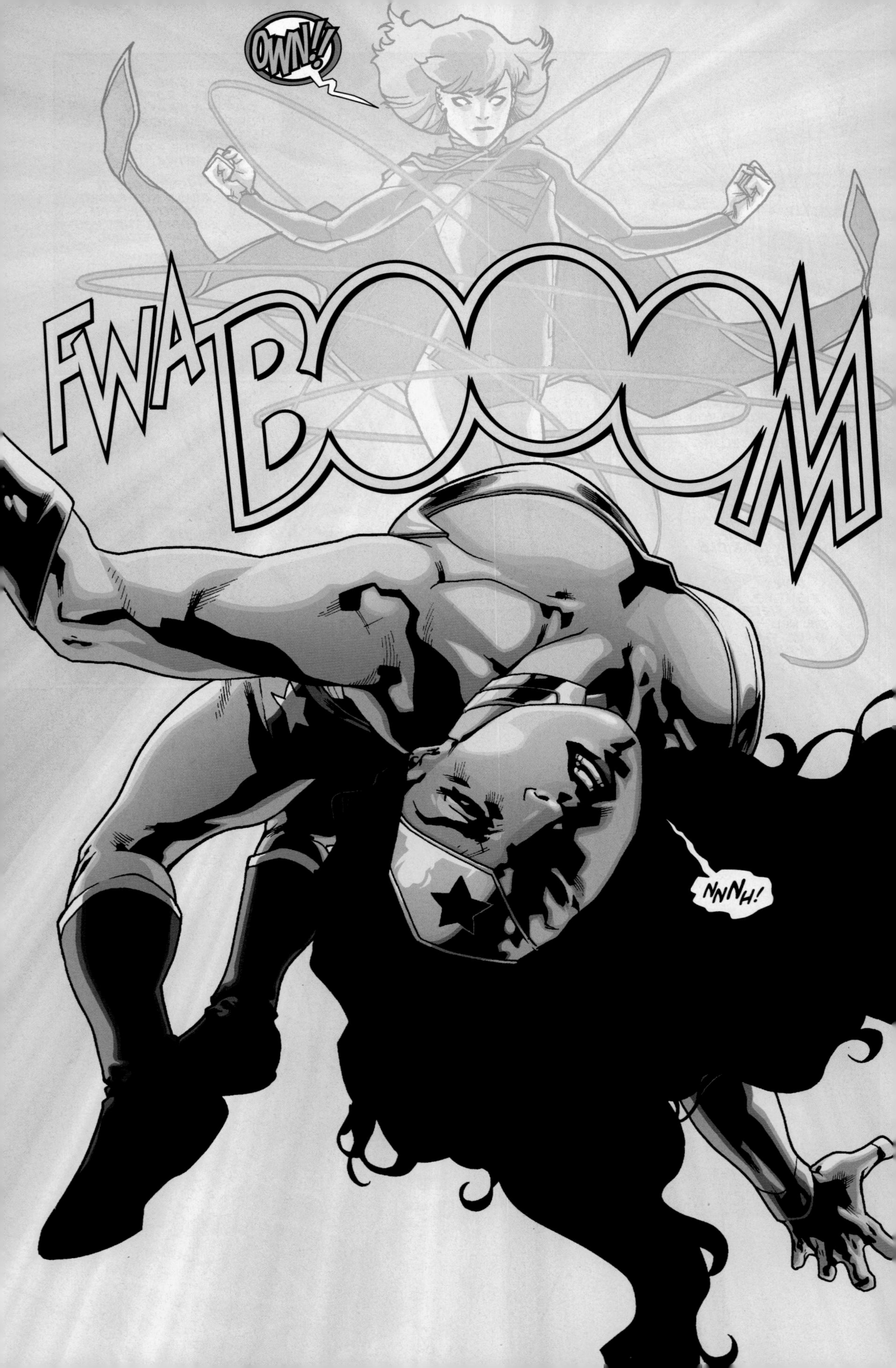
OWN!!
FWABOOOM
NNNH!

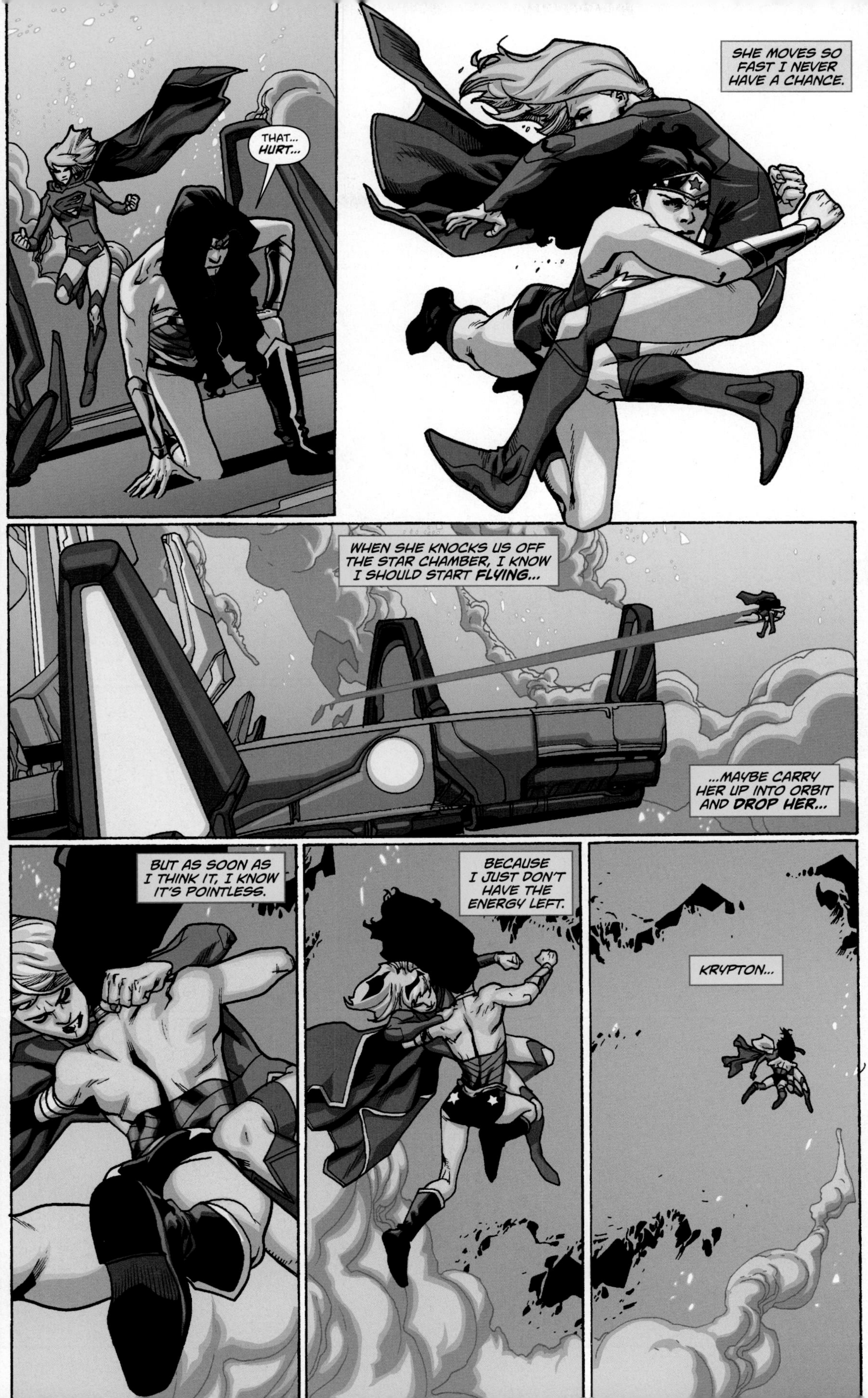
THAT... HURT...
SHE MOVES SO FAST I NEVER HAVE A CHANCE.
WHEN SHE KNOCKS US OFF THE STAR CHAMBER, I KNOW I SHOULD START FLYING...
...MAYBE CARRY HER UP INTO ORBIT AND DROP HER...
BUT AS SOON AS I THINK IT, I KNOW IT'S POINTLESS.
BECAUSE I JUST DON'T HAVE THE ENERGY LEFT.
KRYPTON...

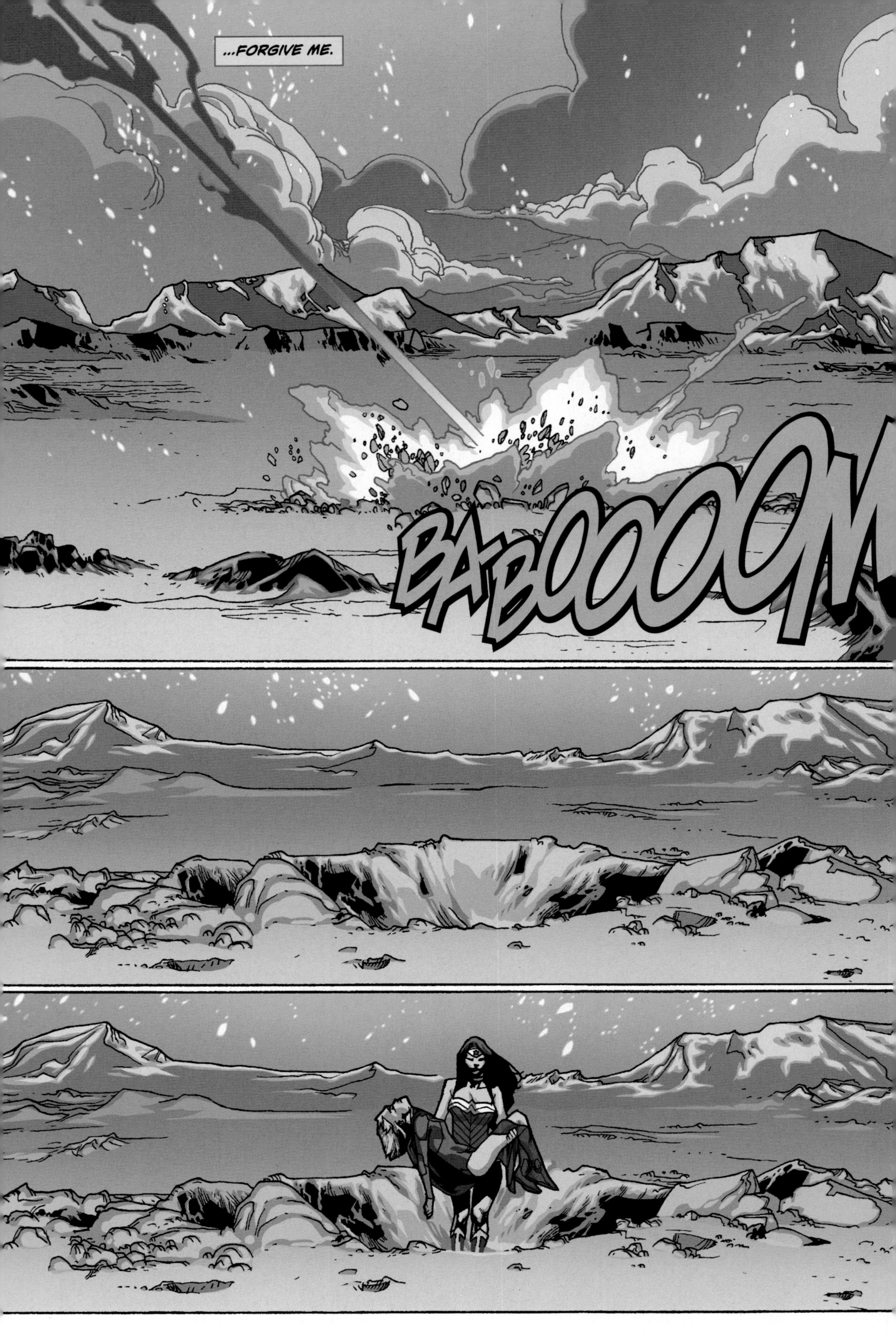
...FORGIVE ME.
BABOOOOM

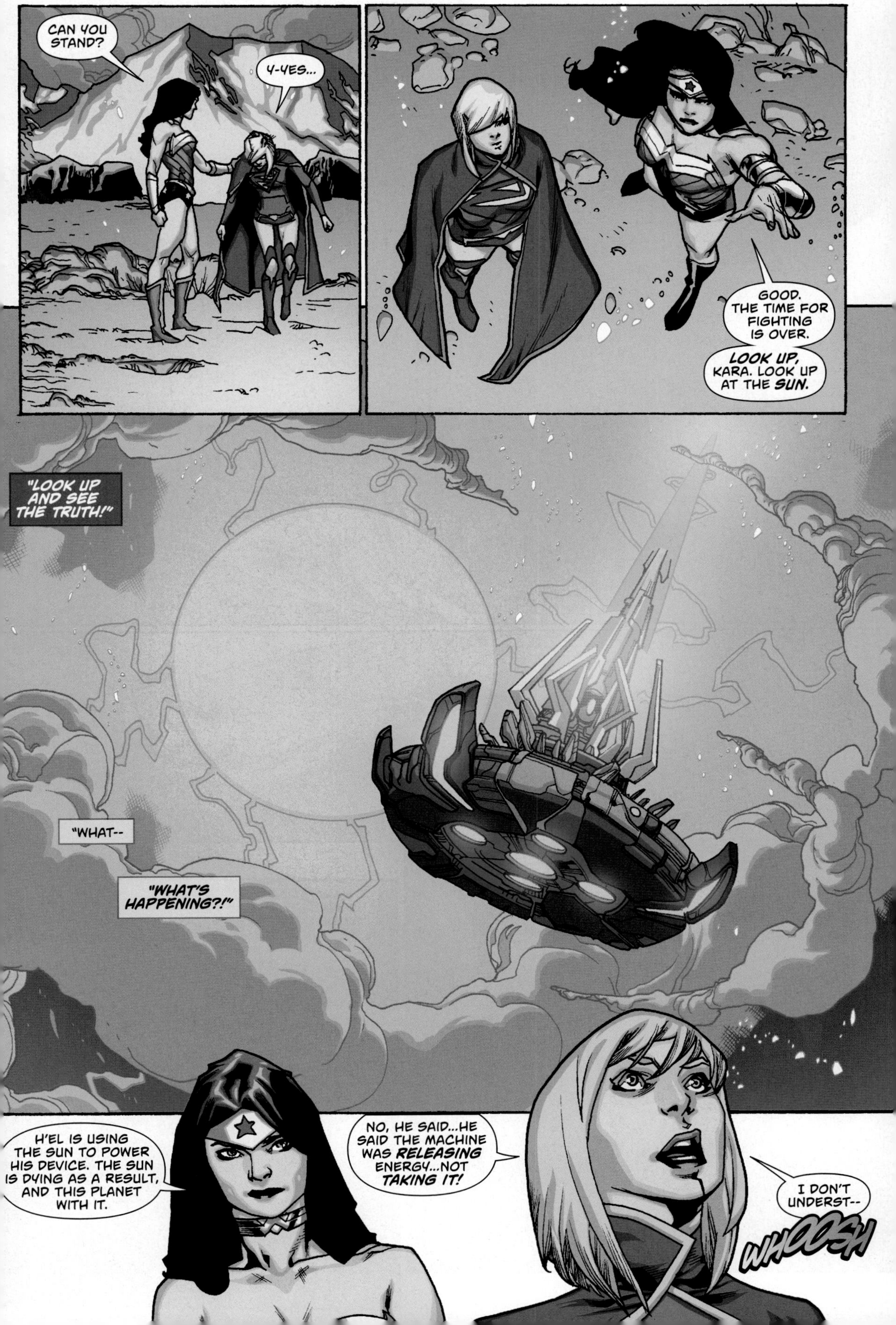
CAN YOU STAND?
Y-YES...
GOOD. THE TIME FOR FIGHTING IS OVER.
LOOK UP, KARA. LOOK UP AT THE SUN.
"LOOK UP AND SEE THE TRUTH!"
"WHAT--
"WHAT'S HAPPENING?!"
H'EL IS USING THE SUN TO POWER HIS DEVICE. THE SUN IS DYING AS A RESULT, AND THIS PLANET WITH IT.
NO, HE SAID...HE SAID THE MACHINE WAS RELEASING ENERGY...NOT TAKING IT!
I DON'T UNDERST--
WHOOSH

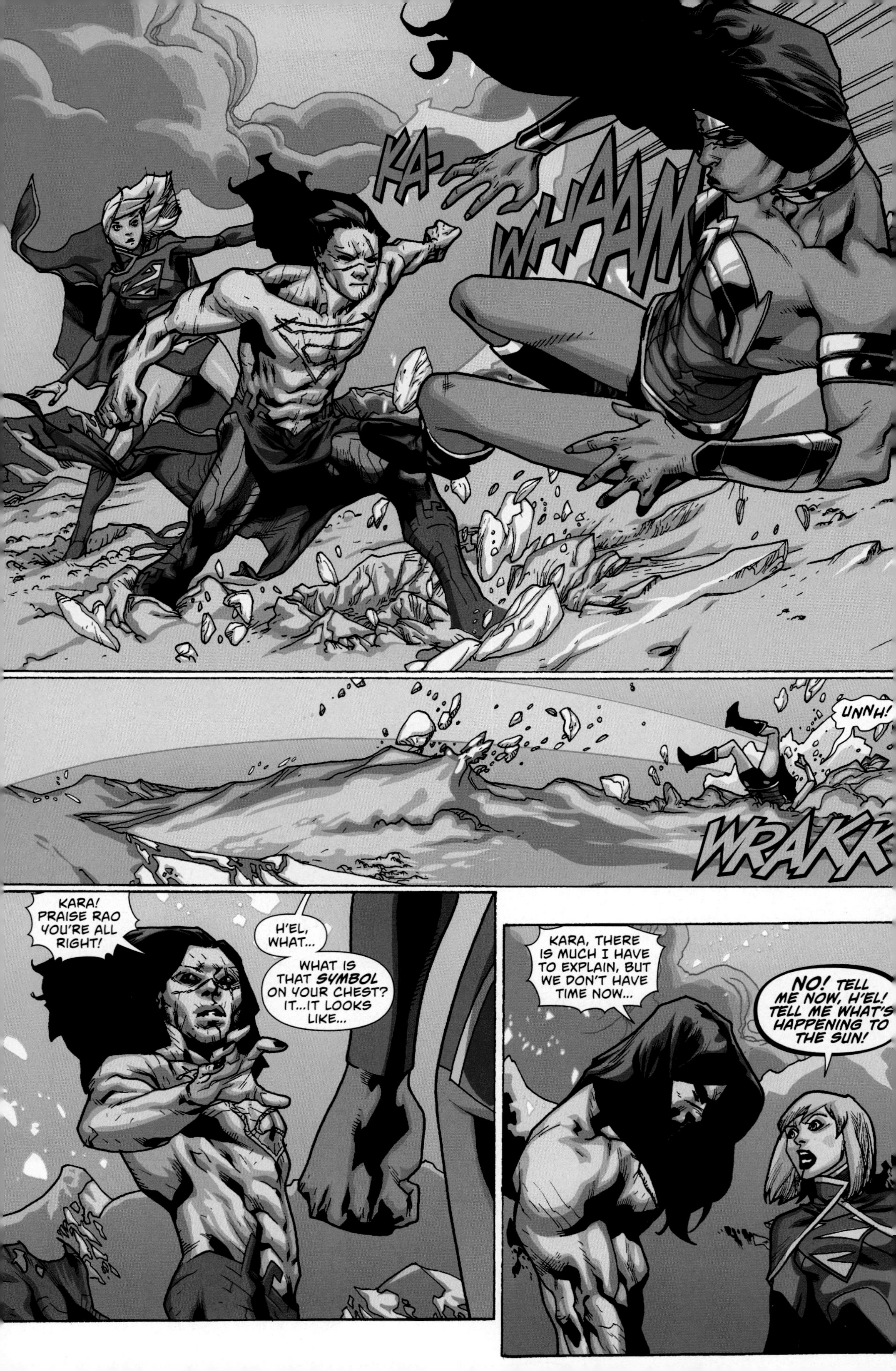
KA-
WHAAM
UNNH!
WRAKK
KARA! PRAISE RAO YOU'RE ALL RIGHT!
H'EL, WHAT...
WHAT IS THAT SYMBOL ON YOUR CHEST? IT...IT LOOKS LIKE...
KARA, THERE IS MUCH I HAVE TO EXPLAIN, BUT WE DON'T HAVE TIME NOW...
NO! TELL ME NOW, H'EL! TELL ME WHAT'S HAPPENING TO THE SUN!

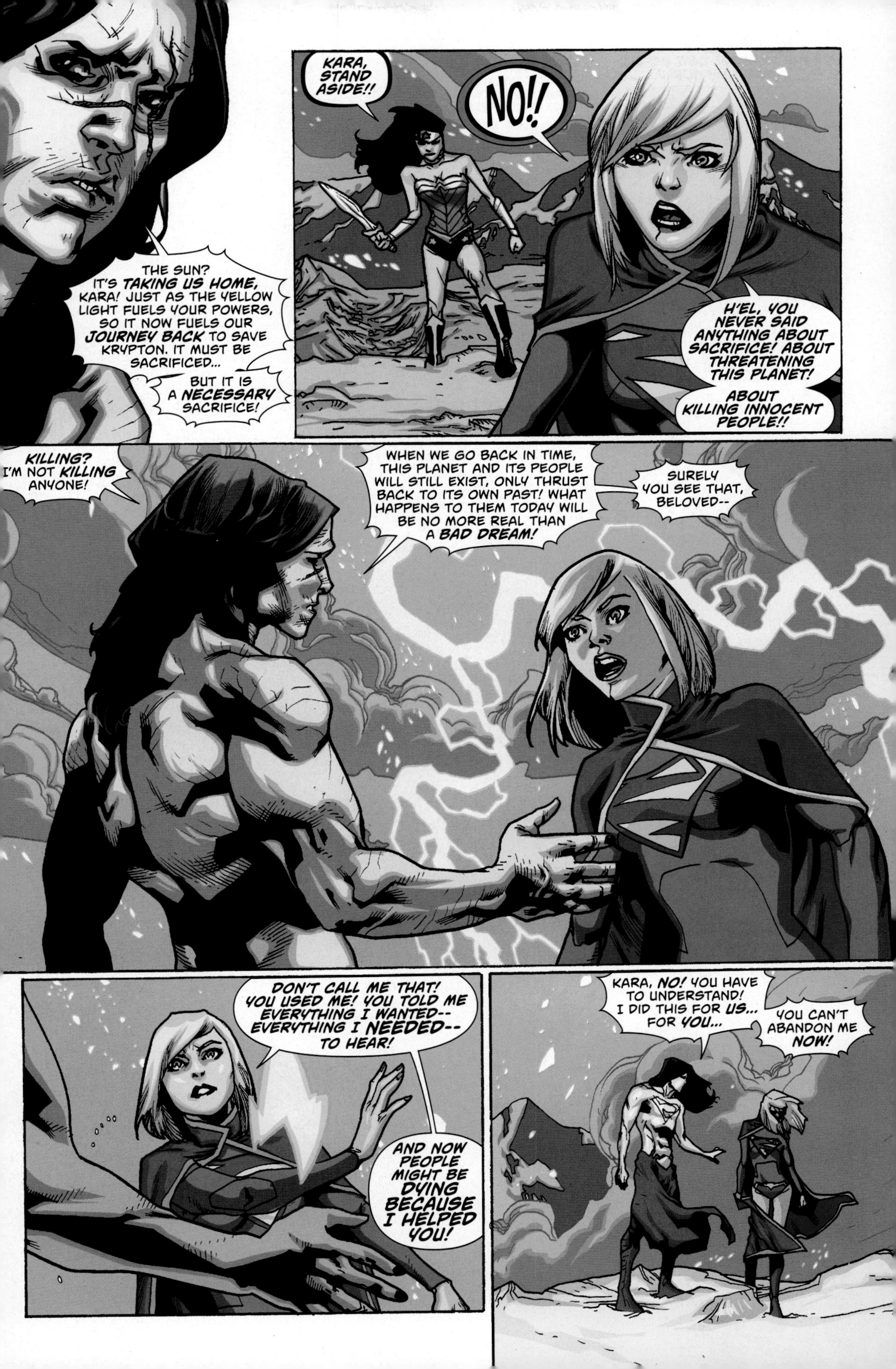
THE SUN? IT'S TAKING US HOME, KARA! JUST AS THE YELLOW LIGHT FUELS YOUR POWERS, SO IT NOW FUELS OUR JOURNEY BACK TO SAVE KRYPTON. IT MUST BE SACRIFICED...
BUT IT IS A NECESSARY SACRIFICE!
KARA, STAND ASIDE!!
NO!!
H'EL, YOU NEVER SAID ANYTHING ABOUT SACRIFICE! ABOUT THREATENING THIS PLANET!
ABOUT KILLING INNOCENT PEOPLE!!
KILLING? I'M NOT KILLING ANYONE!
WHEN WE GO BACK IN TIME, THIS PLANET AND ITS PEOPLE WILL STILL EXIST, ONLY THRUST BACK TO ITS OWN PAST! WHAT HAPPENS TO THEM TODAY WILL BE NO MORE REAL THAN A BAD DREAM!
SURELY YOU SEE THAT, BELOVED--
DON'T CALL ME THAT! YOU USED ME! YOU TOLD ME EVERYTHING I WANTED-- EVERYTHING I NEEDED-- TO HEAR!
AND NOW PEOPLE MIGHT BE DYING BECAUSE I HELPED YOU!
KARA, NO! YOU HAVE TO UNDERSTAND! I DID THIS FOR US... FOR YOU...
YOU CAN'T ABANDON ME NOW!

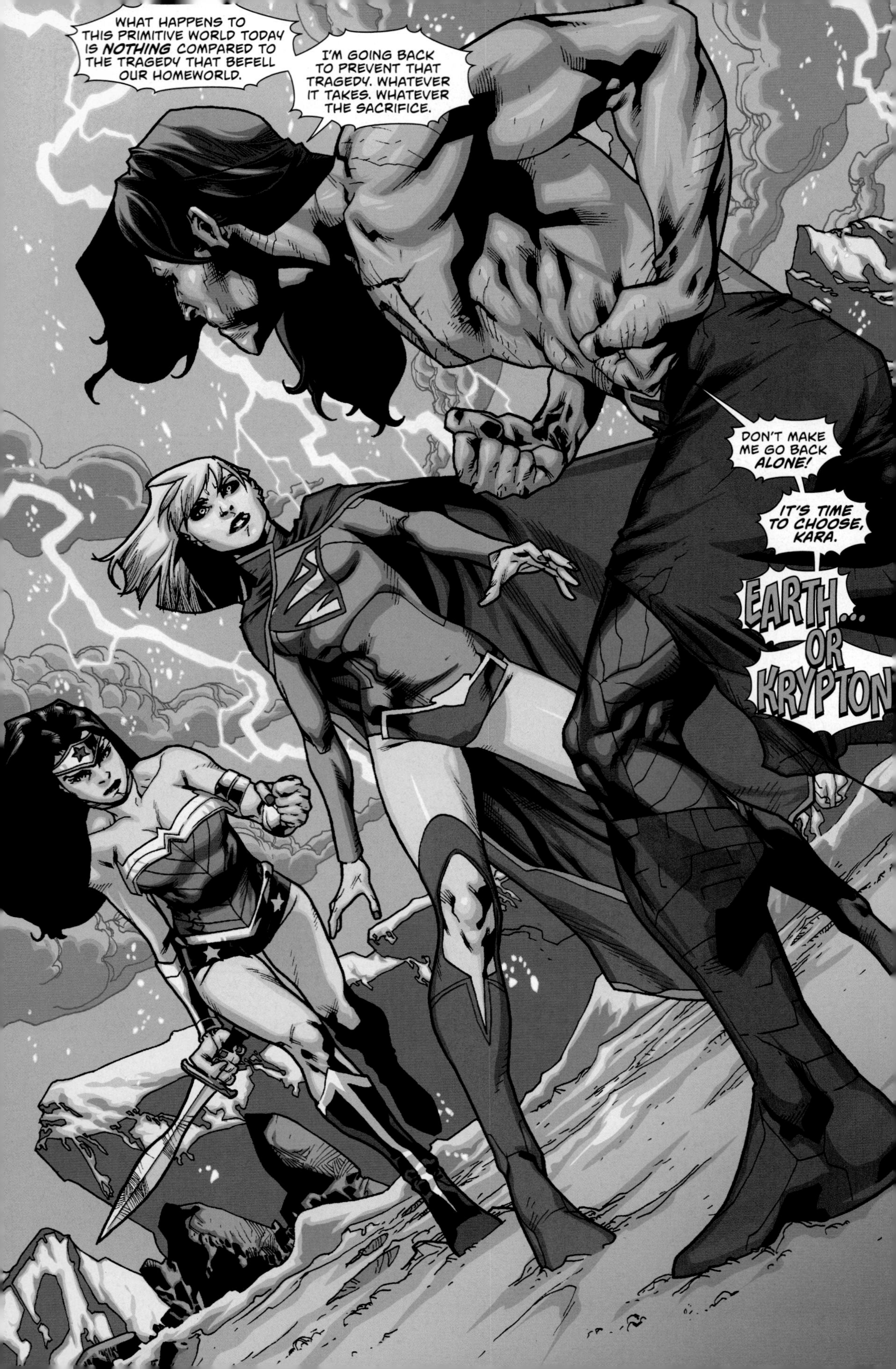
WHAT HAPPENS TO THIS PRIMITIVE WORLD TODAY IS NOTHING COMPARED TO THE TRAGEDY THAT BEFELL OUR HOMEWORLD.
I'M GOING BACK TO PREVENT THAT TRAGEDY. WHATEVER IT TAKES. WHATEVER THE SACRIFICE.
DON'T MAKE ME GO BACK ALONE!
IT'S TIME TO CHOOSE, KARA.
EARTH... OR KRYPTON

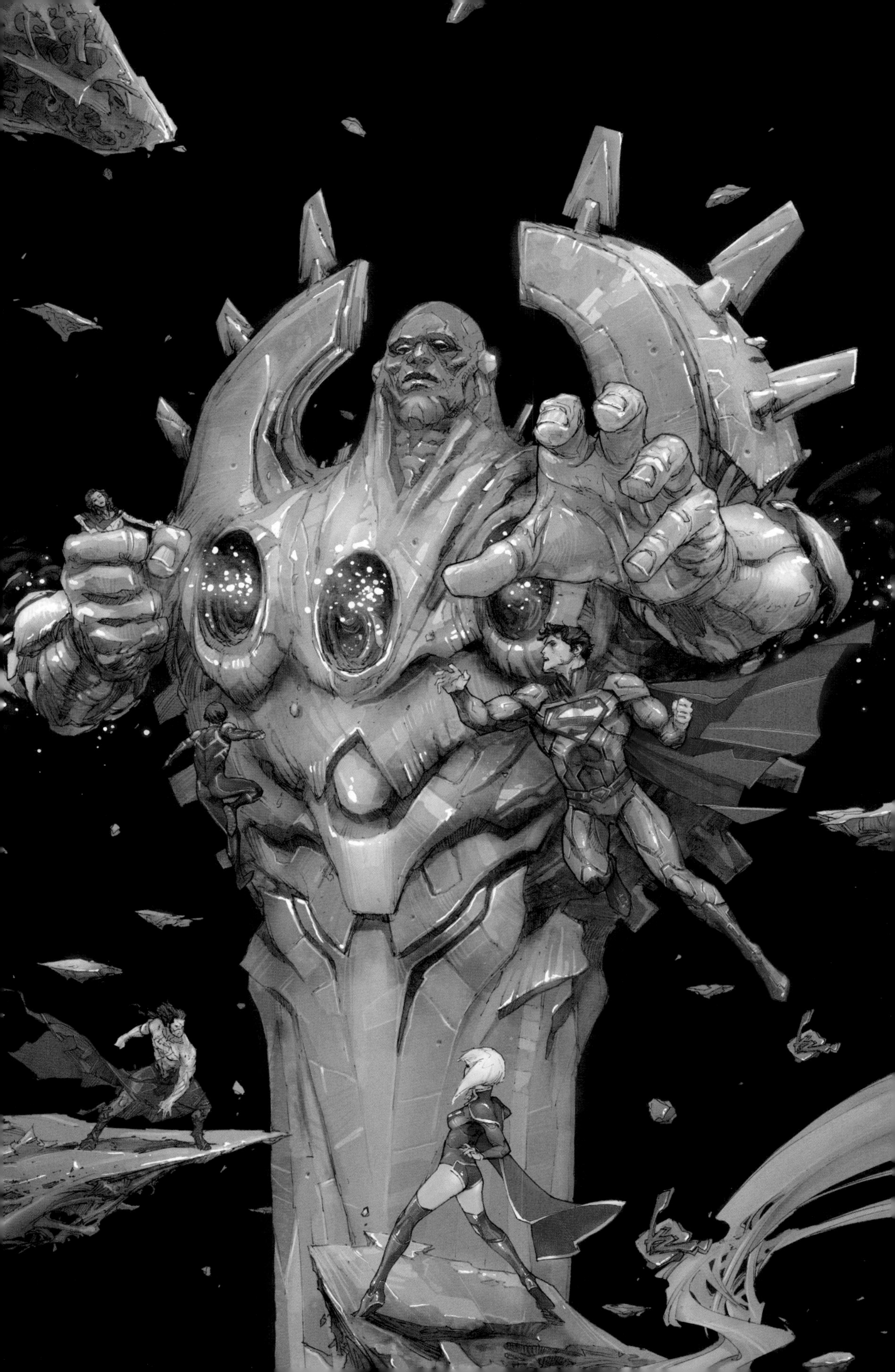

FURY AT WORLD'S END

SCOTT LOBDELL writer **KENNETH ROCAFORT** artist cover art by **KENNETH ROCAFORT**

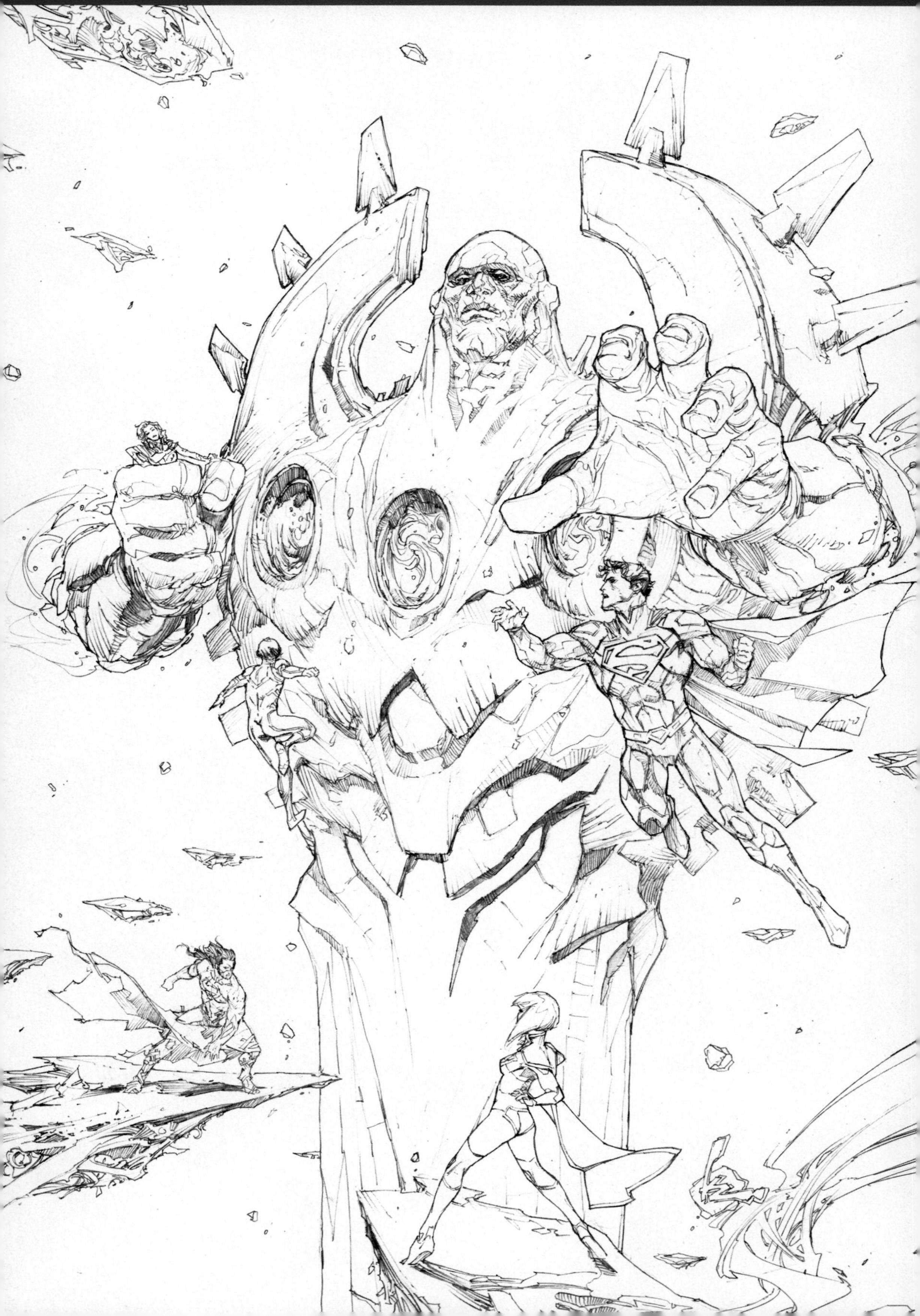

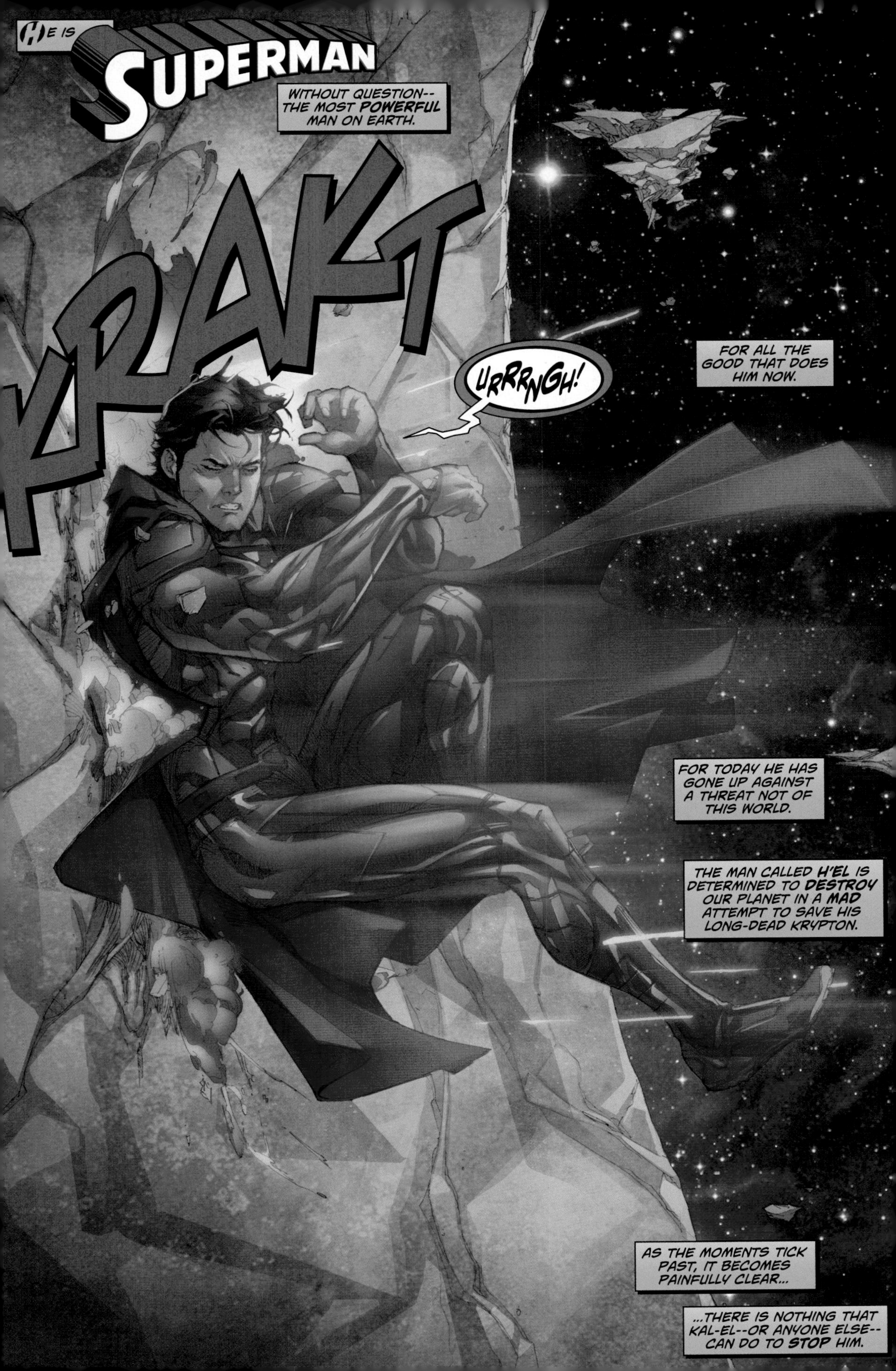
HE IS SUPERMAN
WITHOUT QUESTION-- THE MOST POWERFUL MAN ON EARTH.
KRAKT
URRRNGH!
FOR ALL THE GOOD THAT DOES HIM NOW.
FOR TODAY HE HAS GONE UP AGAINST A THREAT NOT OF THIS WORLD.
THE MAN CALLED H'EL IS DETERMINED TO DESTROY OUR PLANET IN A MAD ATTEMPT TO SAVE HIS LONG-DEAD KRYPTON.
AS THE MOMENTS TICK PAST, IT BECOMES PAINFULLY CLEAR...
...THERE IS NOTHING THAT KAL-EL--OR ANYONE ELSE-- CAN DO TO STOP HIM.

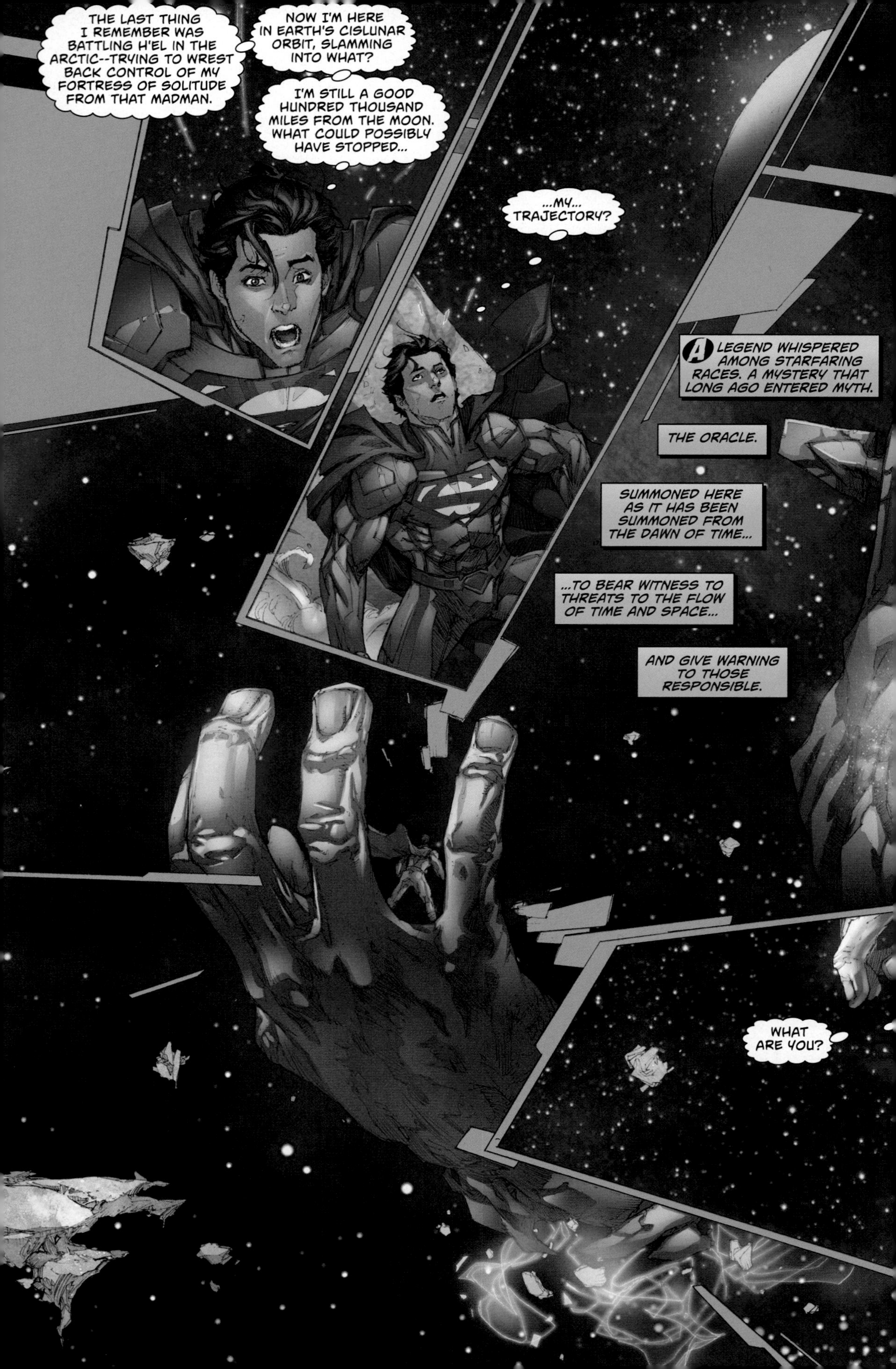
THE LAST THING I REMEMBER WAS BATTLING H'EL IN THE ARCTIC--TRYING TO WREST BACK CONTROL OF MY FORTRESS OF SOLITUDE FROM THAT MADMAN.
NOW I'M HERE IN EARTH'S CISLUNAR ORBIT, SLAMMING INTO WHAT?
I'M STILL A GOOD HUNDRED THOUSAND MILES FROM THE MOON. WHAT COULD POSSIBLY HAVE STOPPED...
...MY... TRAJECTORY?
A LEGEND WHISPERED AMONG STARFARING RACES. A MYSTERY THAT LONG AGO ENTERED MYTH.
THE ORACLE.
SUMMONED HERE AS IT HAS BEEN SUMMONED FROM THE DAWN OF TIME...
...TO BEAR WITNESS TO THREATS TO THE FLOW OF TIME AND SPACE...
AND GIVE WARNING TO THOSE RESPONSIBLE.
WHAT ARE YOU?

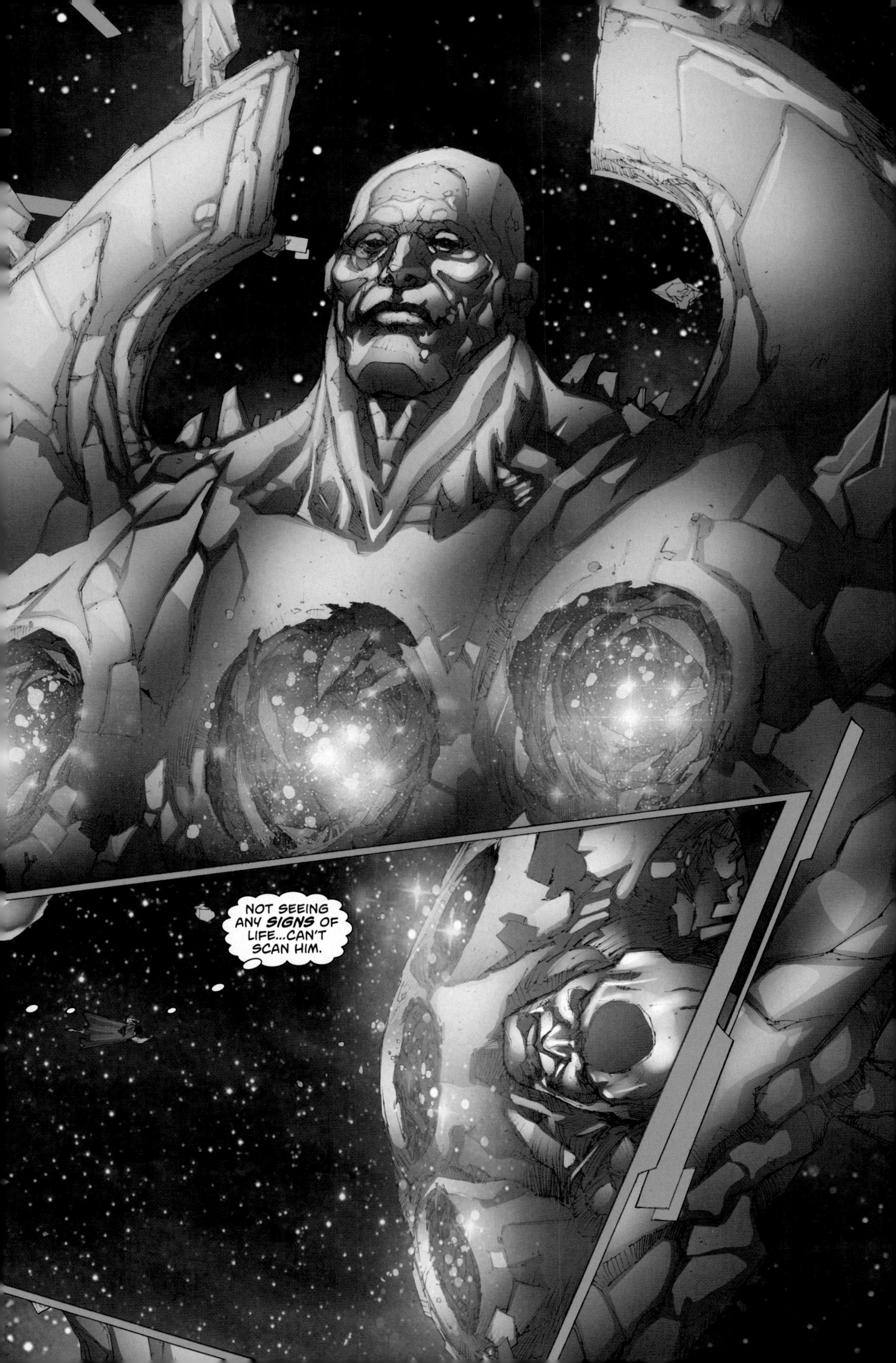
NOT SEEING ANY SIGNS OF LIFE...CAN'T SCAN HIM.

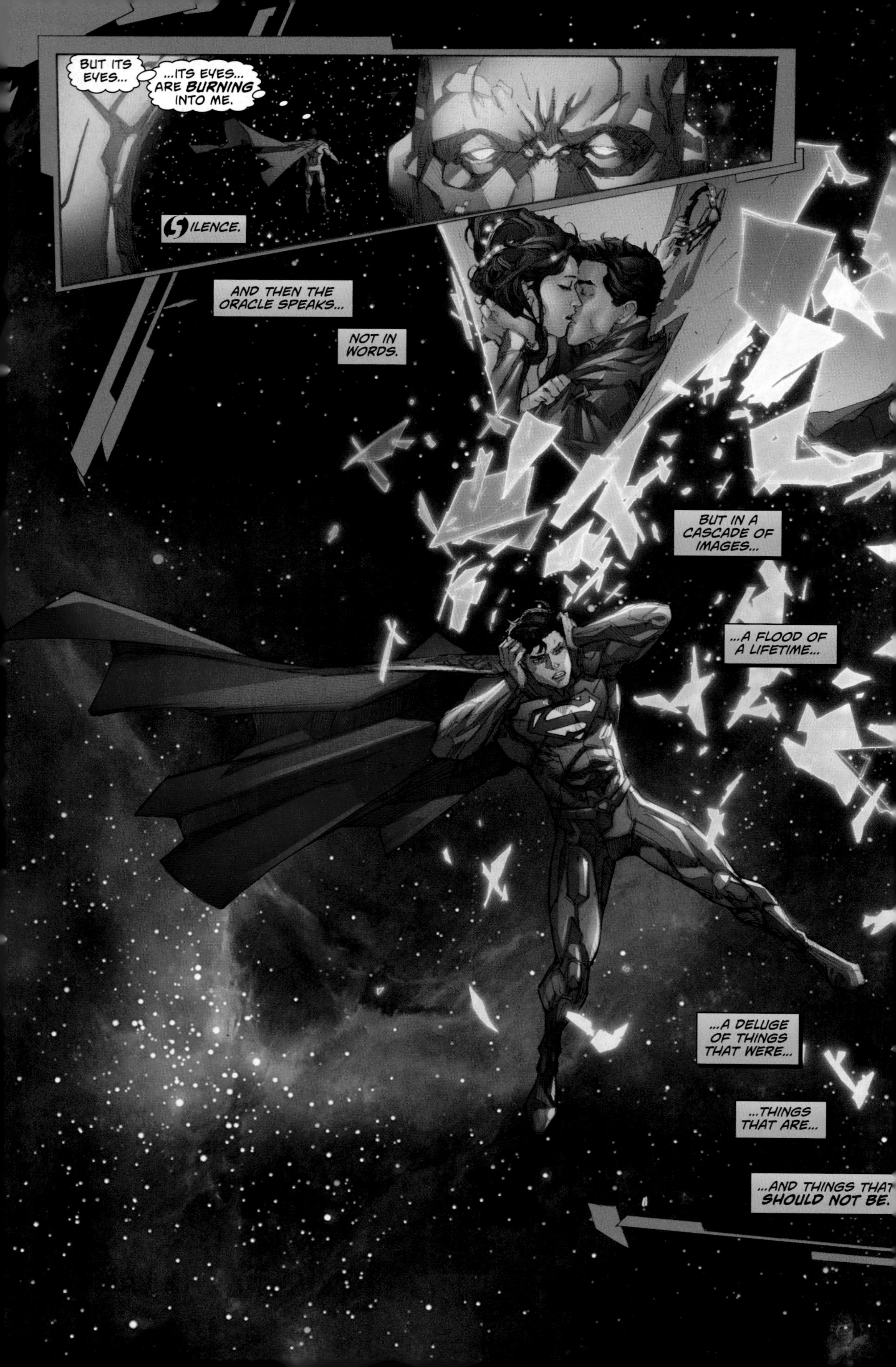

BUT ITS EYES...
...ITS EYES... ARE BURNING INTO ME.
SILENCE.
AND THEN THE ORACLE SPEAKS...
NOT IN WORDS.
BUT IN A CASCADE OF IMAGES...
...A FLOOD OF A LIFETIME...
...A DELUGE OF THINGS THAT WERE...
...THINGS THAT ARE...
...AND THINGS THAT SHOULD NOT BE.

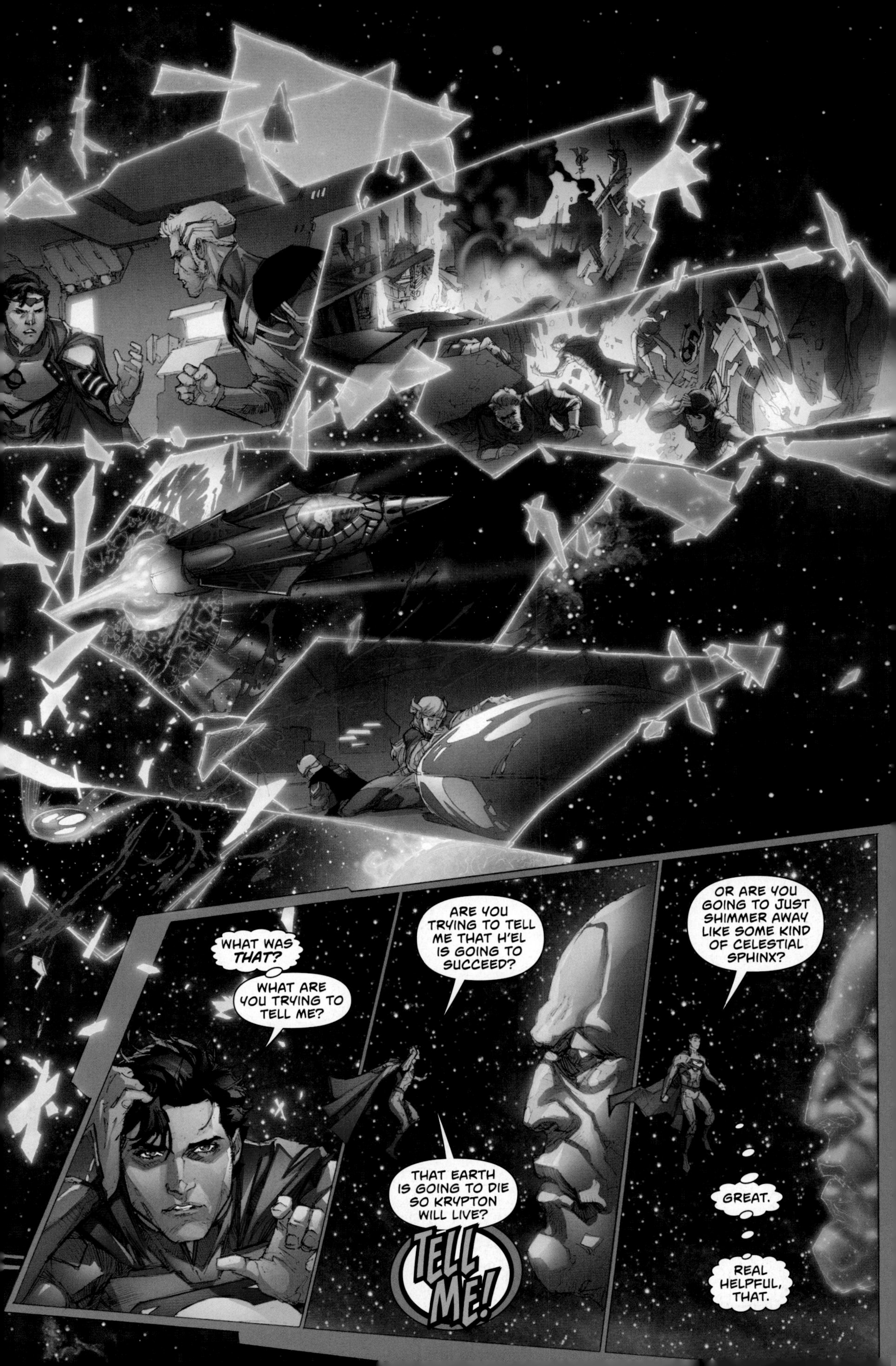
WHAT WAS THAT?
WHAT ARE YOU TRYING TO TELL ME?
ARE YOU TRYING TO TELL ME THAT H'EL IS GOING TO SUCCEED?
THAT EARTH IS GOING TO DIE SO KRYPTON WILL LIVE?
TELL ME!
OR ARE YOU GOING TO JUST SHIMMER AWAY LIKE SOME KIND OF CELESTIAL SPHINX?
GREAT.
REAL HELPFUL, THAT.

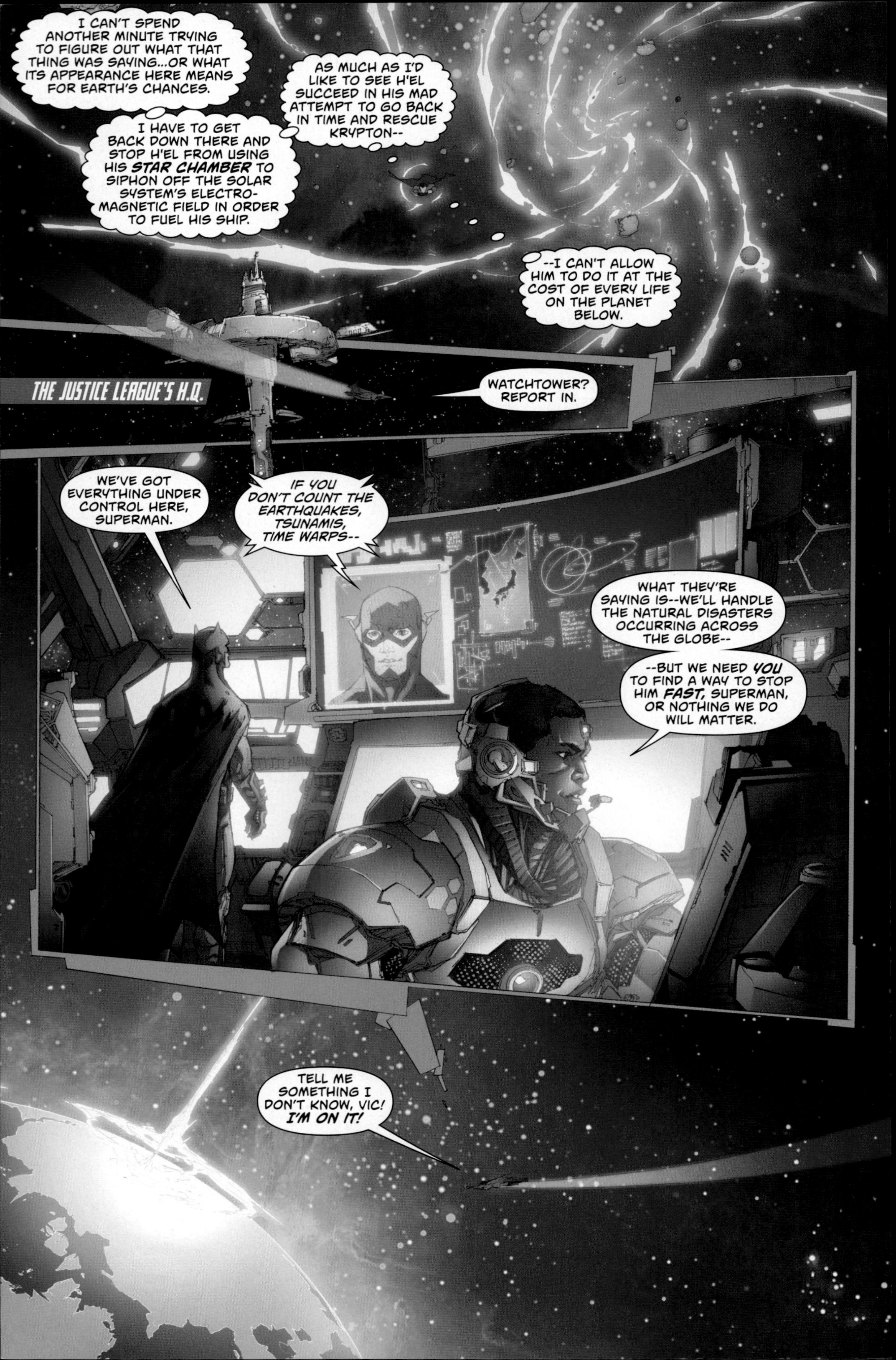

I CAN'T SPEND ANOTHER MINUTE TRYING TO FIGURE OUT WHAT THAT THING WAS SAYING...OR WHAT ITS APPEARANCE HERE MEANS FOR EARTH'S CHANCES.
I HAVE TO GET BACK DOWN THERE AND STOP H'EL FROM USING HIS **STAR CHAMBER** TO SIPHON OFF THE SOLAR SYSTEM'S ELECTRO-MAGNETIC FIELD IN ORDER TO FUEL HIS SHIP.
AS MUCH AS I'D LIKE TO SEE H'EL SUCCEED IN HIS MAD ATTEMPT TO GO BACK IN TIME AND RESCUE KRYPTON--
--I CAN'T ALLOW HIM TO DO IT AT THE COST OF EVERY LIFE ON THE PLANET BELOW.
THE JUSTICE LEAGUE'S H.Q.
WATCHTOWER? REPORT IN.
WE'VE GOT EVERYTHING UNDER CONTROL HERE, SUPERMAN.
IF YOU DON'T COUNT THE EARTHQUAKES, TSUNAMIS, TIME WARPS--
WHAT THEY'RE SAYING IS--WE'LL HANDLE THE NATURAL DISASTERS OCCURRING ACROSS THE GLOBE--
--BUT WE NEED ***YOU*** TO FIND A WAY TO STOP HIM ***FAST,*** SUPERMAN, OR NOTHING WE DO WILL MATTER.
TELL ME SOMETHING I DON'T KNOW, VIC! ***I'M ON IT!***

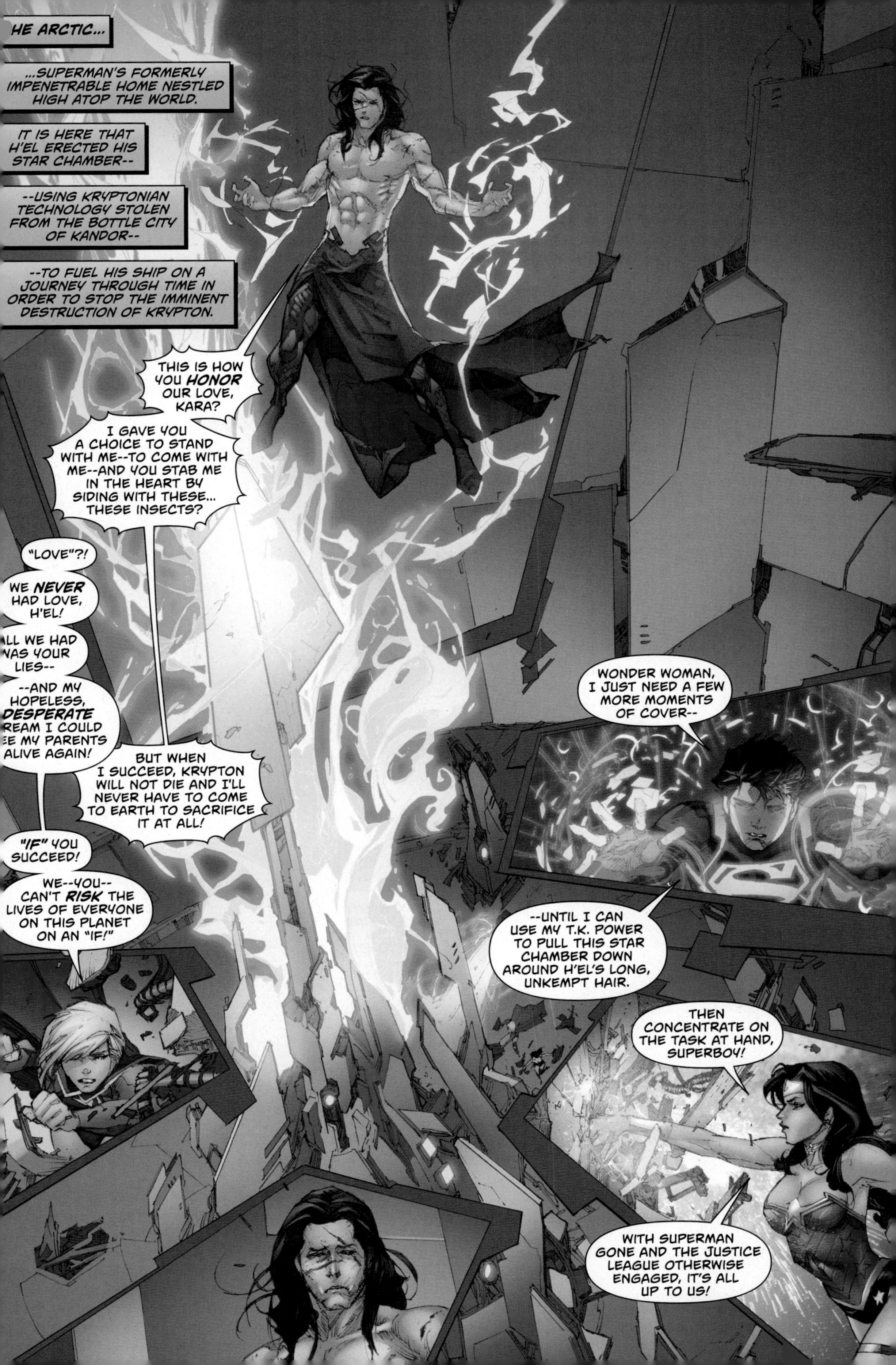
HE ARCTIC...
...SUPERMAN'S FORMERLY IMPENETRABLE HOME NESTLED HIGH ATOP THE WORLD.
IT IS HERE THAT H'EL ERECTED HIS STAR CHAMBER--
--USING KRYPTONIAN TECHNOLOGY STOLEN FROM THE BOTTLE CITY OF KANDOR--
--TO FUEL HIS SHIP ON A JOURNEY THROUGH TIME IN ORDER TO STOP THE IMMINENT DESTRUCTION OF KRYPTON.
THIS IS HOW YOU HONOR OUR LOVE, KARA?
I GAVE YOU A CHOICE TO STAND WITH ME--TO COME WITH ME--AND YOU STAB ME IN THE HEART BY SIDING WITH THESE... THESE INSECTS?
"LOVE"?!
WE NEVER HAD LOVE, H'EL!
LL WE HAD NAS YOUR LIES--
--AND MY HOPELESS, DESPERATE REAM I COULD EE MY PARENTS ALIVE AGAIN!
BUT WHEN I SUCCEED, KRYPTON WILL NOT DIE AND I'LL NEVER HAVE TO COME TO EARTH TO SACRIFICE IT AT ALL!
"IF" YOU SUCCEED!
WE--YOU--CAN'T RISK THE LIVES OF EVERYONE ON THIS PLANET ON AN "IF!"
WONDER WOMAN, I JUST NEED A FEW MORE MOMENTS OF COVER--
--UNTIL I CAN USE MY T.K. POWER TO PULL THIS STAR CHAMBER DOWN AROUND H'EL'S LONG, UNKEMPT HAIR.
THEN CONCENTRATE ON THE TASK AT HAND, SUPERBOY!
WITH SUPERMAN GONE AND THE JUSTICE LEAGUE OTHERWISE ENGAGED, IT'S ALL UP TO US!

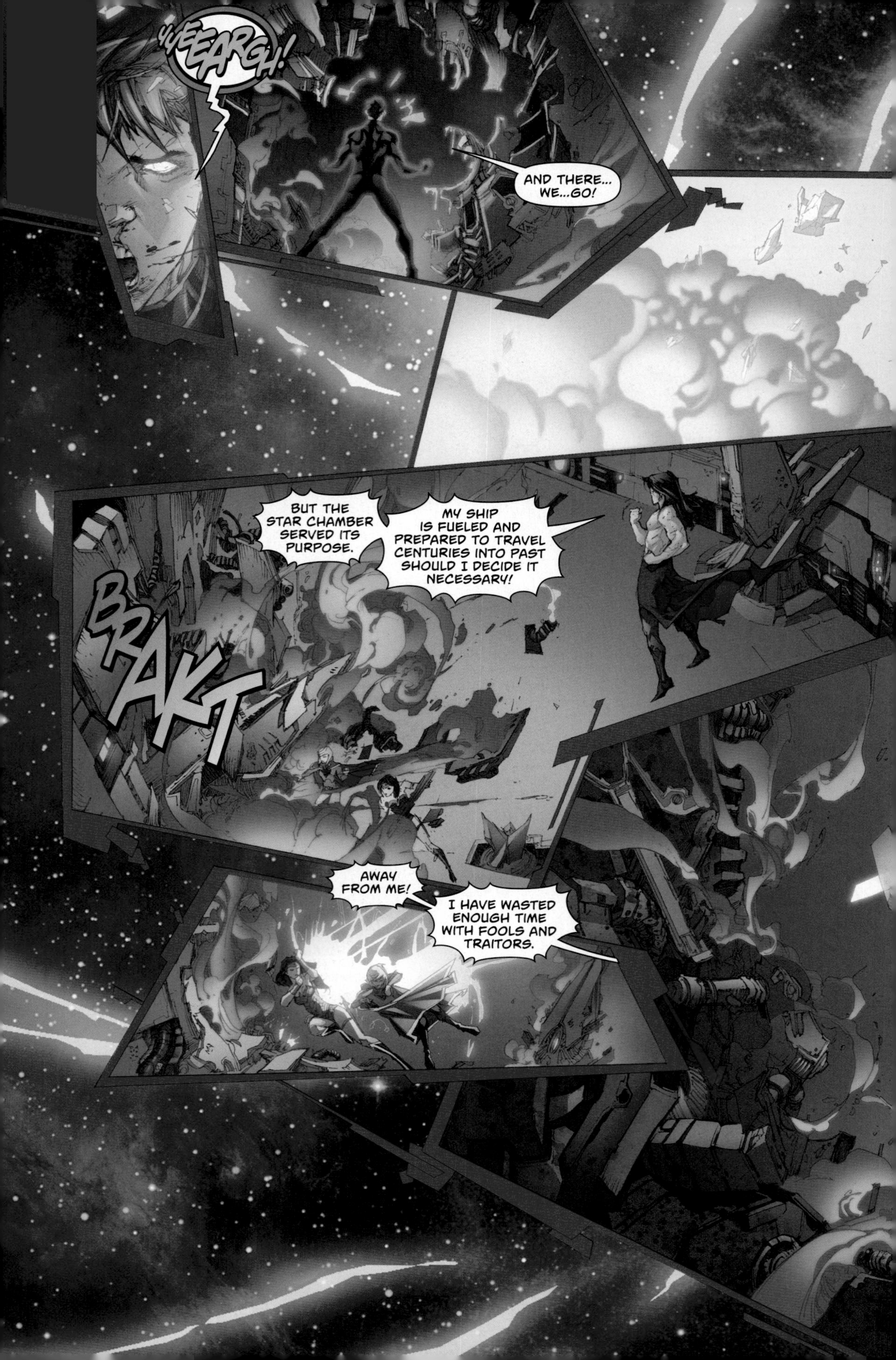
YUEEEARGH!
AND THERE... WE...GO!
BRAKT
BUT THE STAR CHAMBER SERVED ITS PURPOSE.
MY SHIP IS FUELED AND PREPARED TO TRAVEL CENTURIES INTO PAST SHOULD I DECIDE IT NECESSARY!
AWAY FROM ME!
I HAVE WASTED ENOUGH TIME WITH FOOLS AND TRAITORS.

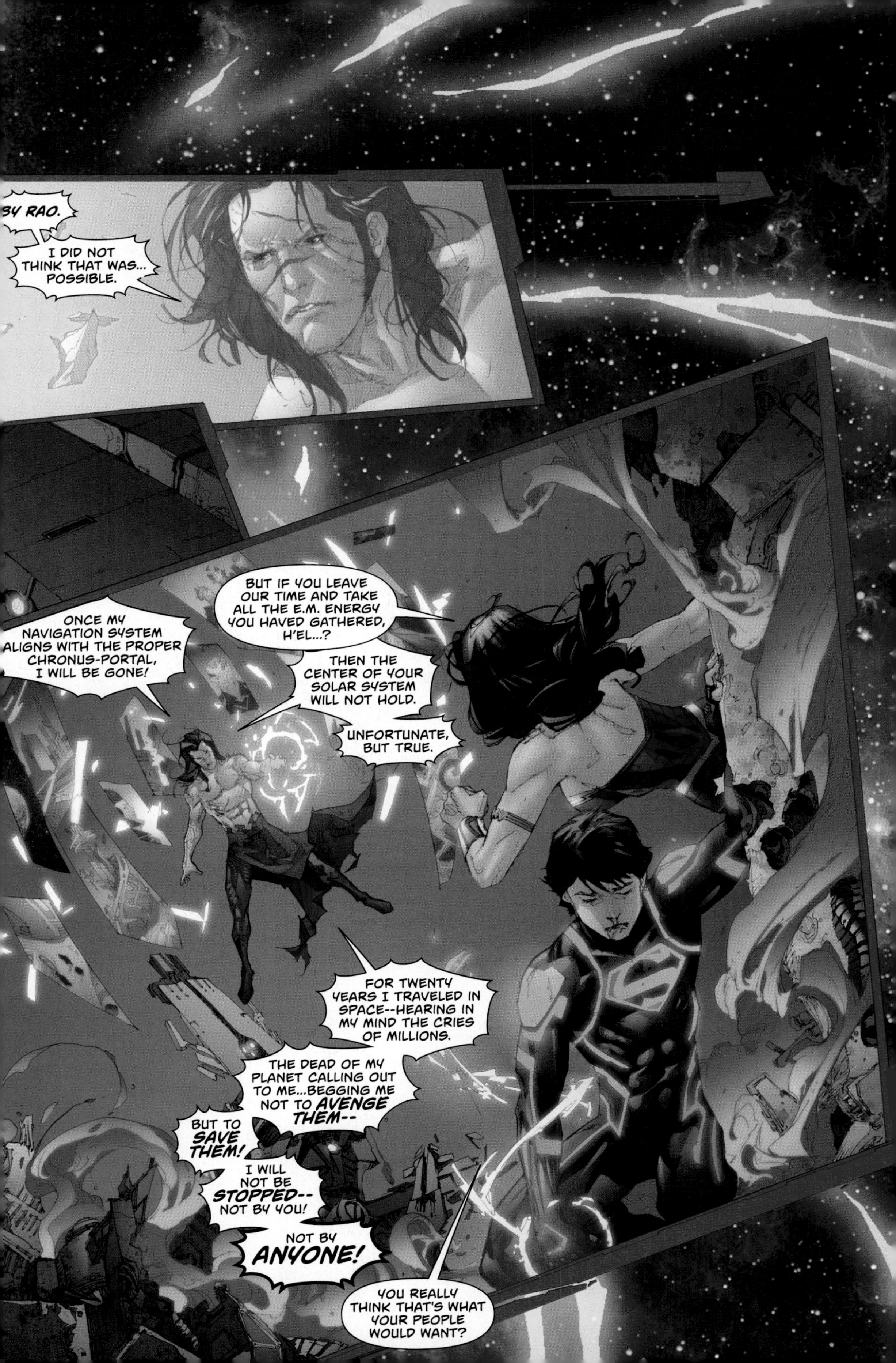
BY RAO.
I DID NOT THINK THAT WAS... POSSIBLE.
BUT IF YOU LEAVE OUR TIME AND TAKE ALL THE E.M. ENERGY YOU HAVED GATHERED, H'EL...?
ONCE MY NAVIGATION SYSTEM ALIGNS WITH THE PROPER CHRONUS-PORTAL, I WILL BE GONE!
THEN THE CENTER OF YOUR SOLAR SYSTEM WILL NOT HOLD.
UNFORTUNATE, BUT TRUE.
FOR TWENTY YEARS I TRAVELED IN SPACE--HEARING IN MY MIND THE CRIES OF MILLIONS.
THE DEAD OF MY PLANET CALLING OUT TO ME...BEGGING ME NOT TO AVENGE THEM--
BUT TO SAVE THEM!
I WILL NOT BE STOPPED-- NOT BY YOU!
NOT BY ANYONE!
YOU REALLY THINK THAT'S WHAT YOUR PEOPLE WOULD WANT?

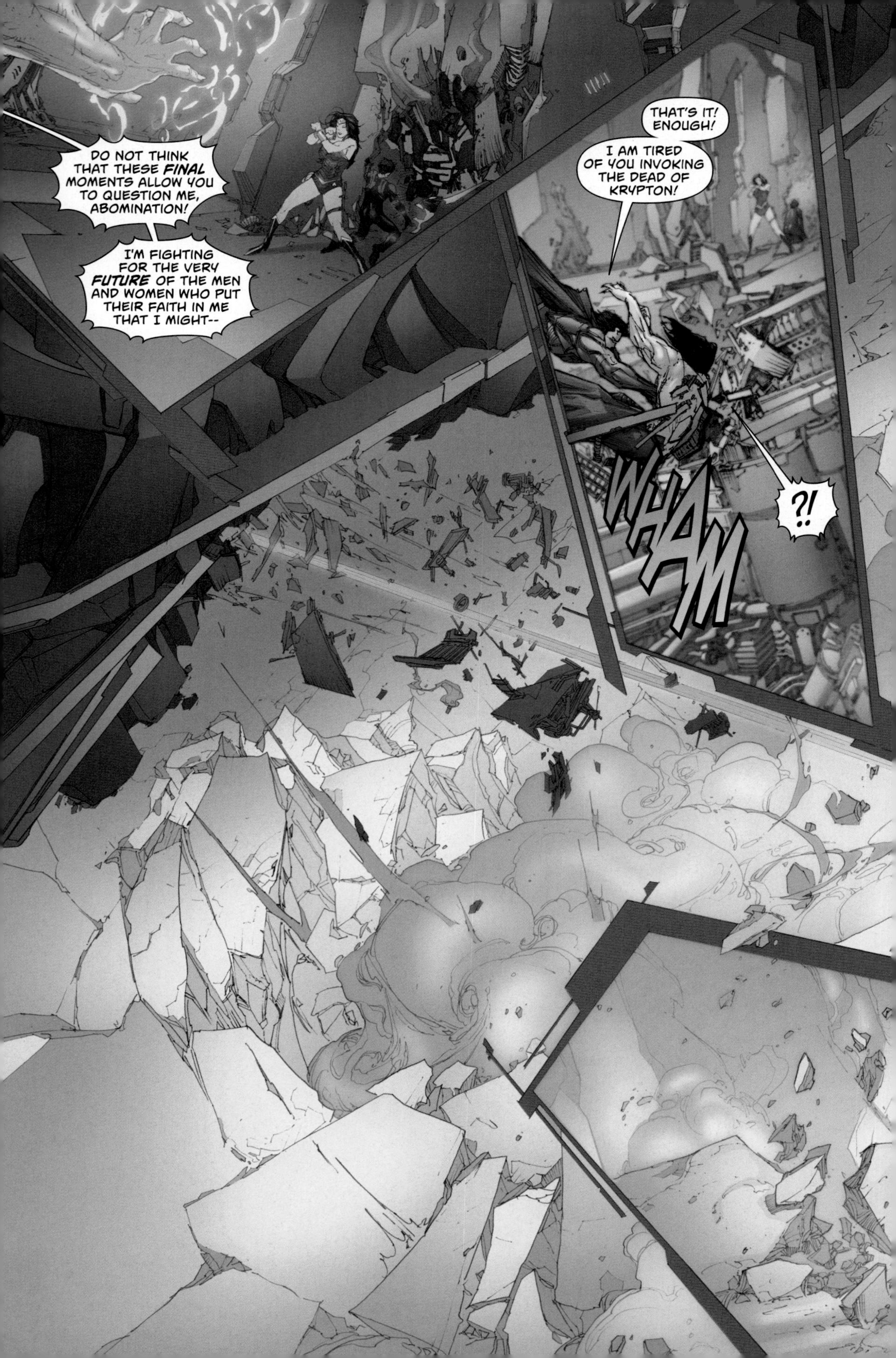
DO NOT THINK THAT THESE FINAL MOMENTS ALLOW YOU TO QUESTION ME, ABOMINATION!
I'M FIGHTING FOR THE VERY FUTURE OF THE MEN AND WOMEN WHO PUT THEIR FAITH IN ME THAT I MIGHT--
THAT'S IT! ENOUGH!
I AM TIRED OF YOU INVOKING THE DEAD OF KRYPTON!
WHAM
?!

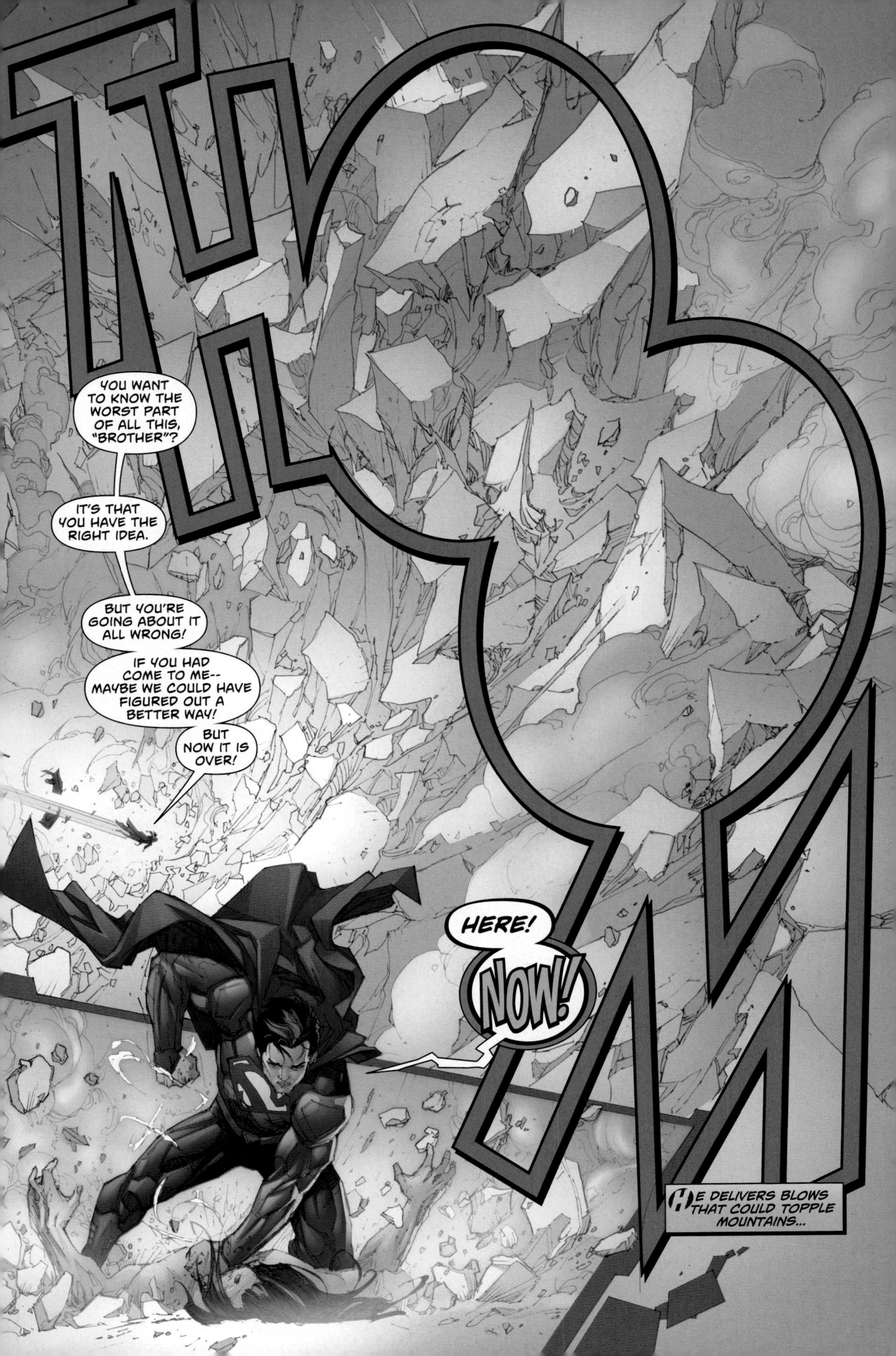
THOOM
YOU WANT TO KNOW THE WORST PART OF ALL THIS, "BROTHER"?
IT'S THAT YOU HAVE THE RIGHT IDEA.
BUT YOU'RE GOING ABOUT IT ALL WRONG!
IF YOU HAD COME TO ME-- MAYBE WE COULD HAVE FIGURED OUT A BETTER WAY!
BUT NOW IT IS OVER!
HERE!
NOW!
HE DELIVERS BLOWS THAT COULD TOPPLE MOUNTAINS...

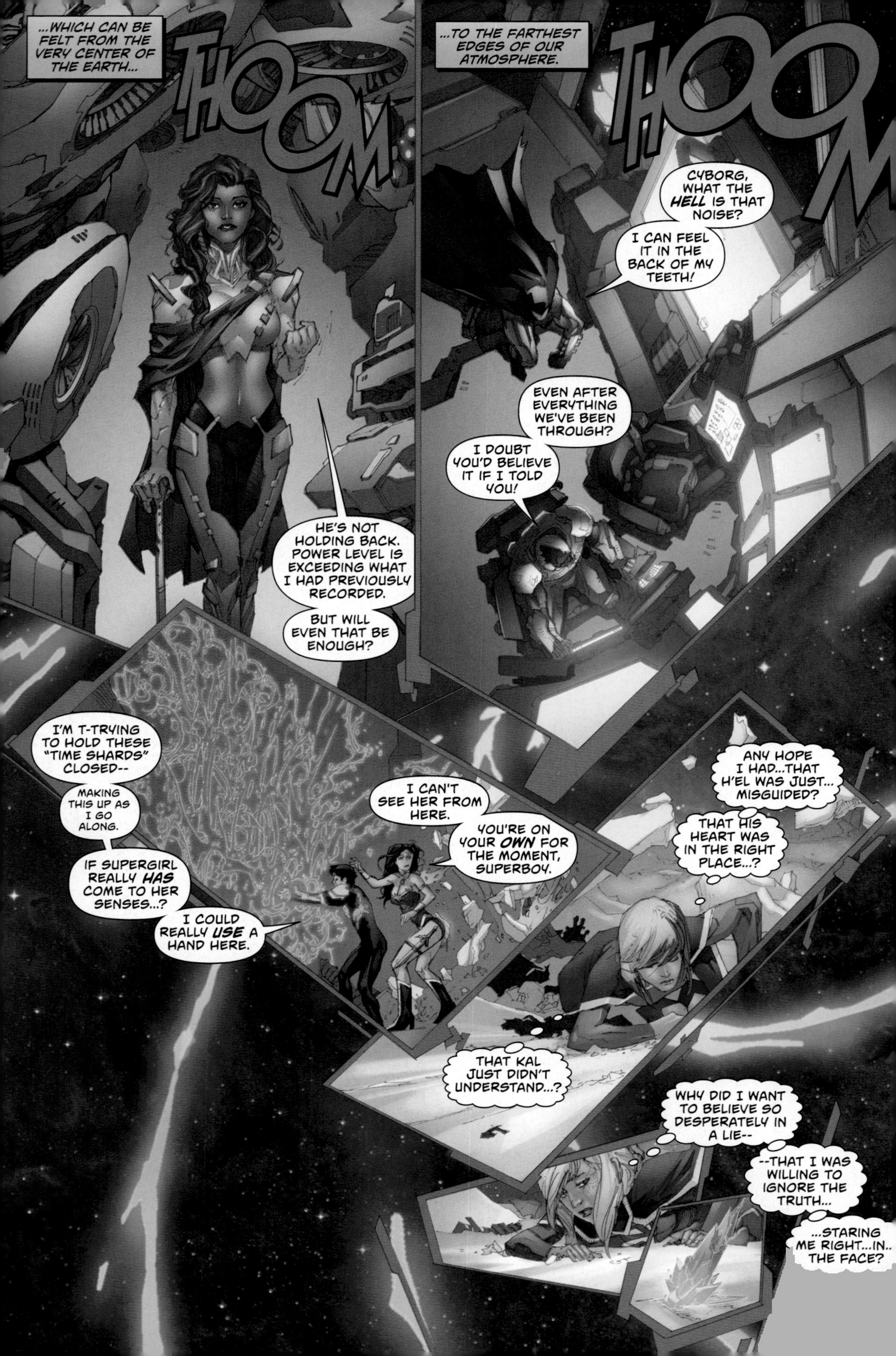
...WHICH CAN BE FELT FROM THE VERY CENTER OF THE EARTH...
THOOM
...TO THE FARTHEST EDGES OF OUR ATMOSPHERE.
THOOM
CYBORG, WHAT THE HELL IS THAT NOISE?
I CAN FEEL IT IN THE BACK OF MY TEETH!
EVEN AFTER EVERYTHING WE'VE BEEN THROUGH?
I DOUBT YOU'D BELIEVE IT IF I TOLD YOU!
HE'S NOT HOLDING BACK. POWER LEVEL IS EXCEEDING WHAT I HAD PREVIOUSLY RECORDED.
BUT WILL EVEN THAT BE ENOUGH?
I'M T-TRYING TO HOLD THESE "TIME SHARDS" CLOSED--
MAKING THIS UP AS I GO ALONG.
IF SUPERGIRL REALLY HAS COME TO HER SENSES...?
I COULD REALLY USE A HAND HERE.
I CAN'T SEE HER FROM HERE.
YOU'RE ON YOUR OWN FOR THE MOMENT, SUPERBOY.
ANY HOPE I HAD...THAT H'EL WAS JUST... MISGUIDED?
THAT HIS HEART WAS IN THE RIGHT PLACE...?
THAT KAL JUST DIDN'T UNDERSTAND...?
WHY DID I WANT TO BELIEVE SO DESPERATELY IN A LIE--
--THAT I WAS WILLING TO IGNORE THE TRUTH...
...STARING ME RIGHT...IN... THE FACE?

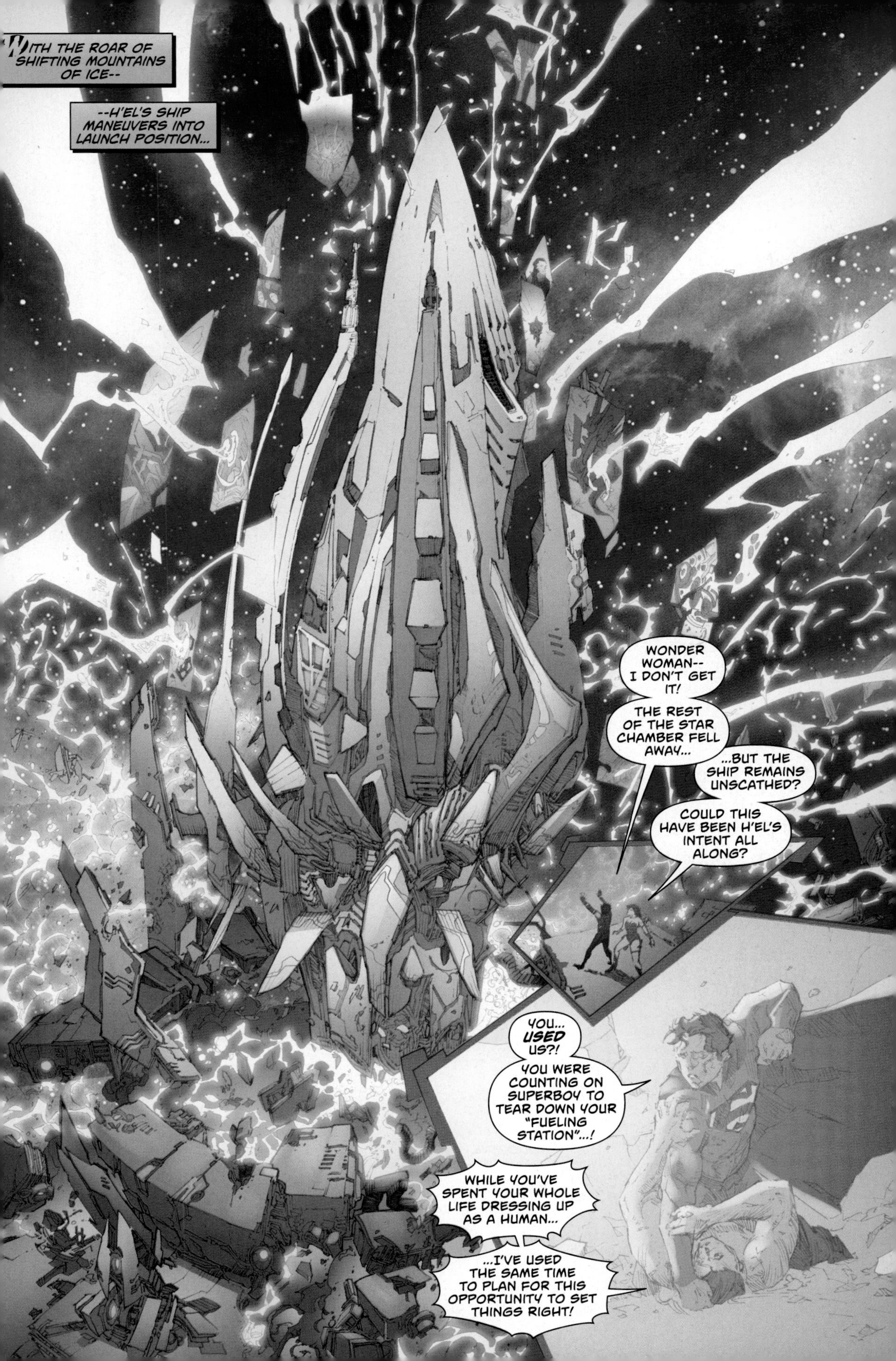
WITH THE ROAR OF SHIFTING MOUNTAINS OF ICE--
--H'EL'S SHIP MANEUVERS INTO LAUNCH POSITION...
WONDER WOMAN-- I DON'T GET IT!
THE REST OF THE STAR CHAMBER FELL AWAY...
...BUT THE SHIP REMAINS UNSCATHED?
COULD THIS HAVE BEEN H'EL'S INTENT ALL ALONG?
YOU... USED US?!
YOU WERE COUNTING ON SUPERBOY TO TEAR DOWN YOUR "FUELING STATION"...!
WHILE YOU'VE SPENT YOUR WHOLE LIFE DRESSING UP AS A HUMAN...
...I'VE USED THE SAME TIME TO PLAN FOR THIS OPPORTUNITY TO SET THINGS RIGHT!

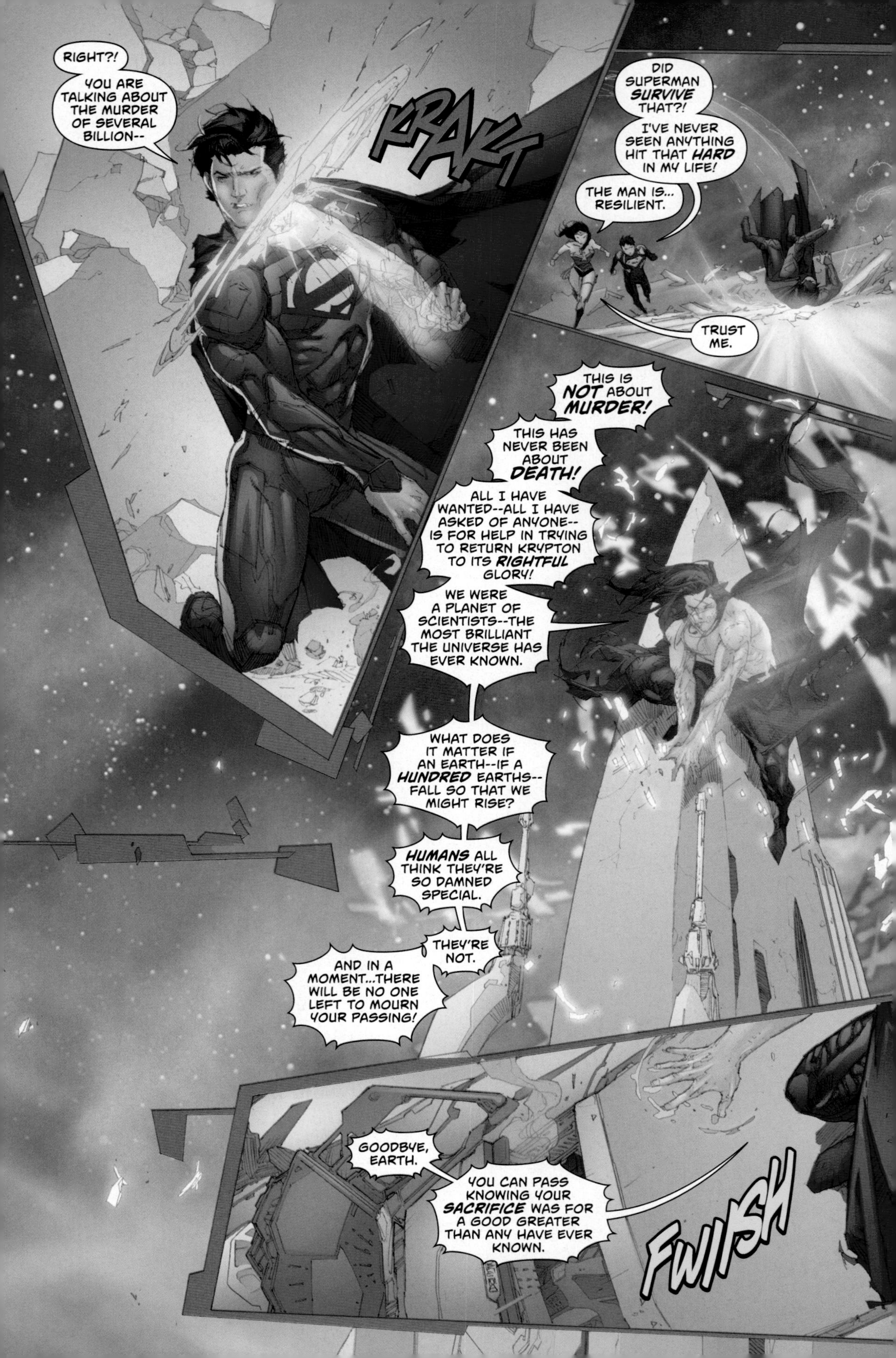
RIGHT?!
YOU ARE TALKING ABOUT THE MURDER OF SEVERAL BILLION--
KRAKT
DID SUPERMAN SURVIVE THAT?!
I'VE NEVER SEEN ANYTHING HIT THAT HARD IN MY LIFE!
THE MAN IS... RESILIENT.
TRUST ME.
THIS IS NOT ABOUT MURDER!
THIS HAS NEVER BEEN ABOUT DEATH!
ALL I HAVE WANTED--ALL I HAVE ASKED OF ANYONE--IS FOR HELP IN TRYING TO RETURN KRYPTON TO ITS RIGHTFUL GLORY!
WE WERE A PLANET OF SCIENTISTS--THE MOST BRILLIANT THE UNIVERSE HAS EVER KNOWN.
WHAT DOES IT MATTER IF AN EARTH--IF A HUNDRED EARTHS--FALL SO THAT WE MIGHT RISE?
HUMANS ALL THINK THEY'RE SO DAMNED SPECIAL.
THEY'RE NOT.
AND IN A MOMENT...THERE WILL BE NO ONE LEFT TO MOURN YOUR PASSING!
GOODBYE, EARTH.
YOU CAN PASS KNOWING YOUR SACRIFICE WAS FOR A GOOD GREATER THAN ANY HAVE EVER KNOWN.
FWISH

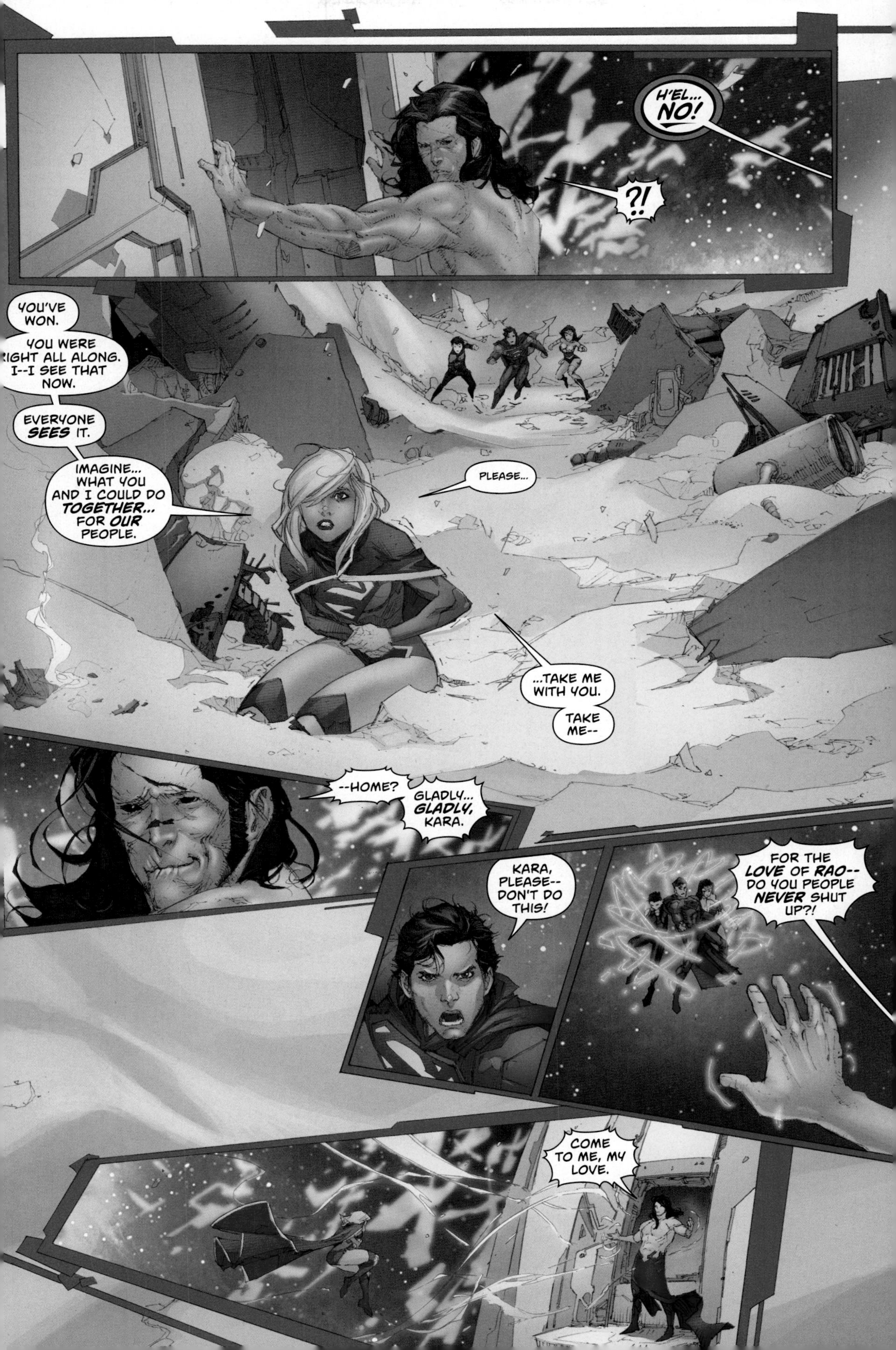
H'EL... NO!
?!
YOU'VE WON.
YOU WERE RIGHT ALL ALONG. I--I SEE THAT NOW.
EVERYONE SEES IT.
IMAGINE... WHAT YOU AND I COULD DO TOGETHER... FOR OUR PEOPLE.
PLEASE...
...TAKE ME WITH YOU.
TAKE ME--
--HOME?
GLADLY... GLADLY, KARA.
KARA, PLEASE-- DON'T DO THIS!
FOR THE LOVE OF RAO-- DO YOU PEOPLE NEVER SHUT UP?!
COME TO ME, MY LOVE.

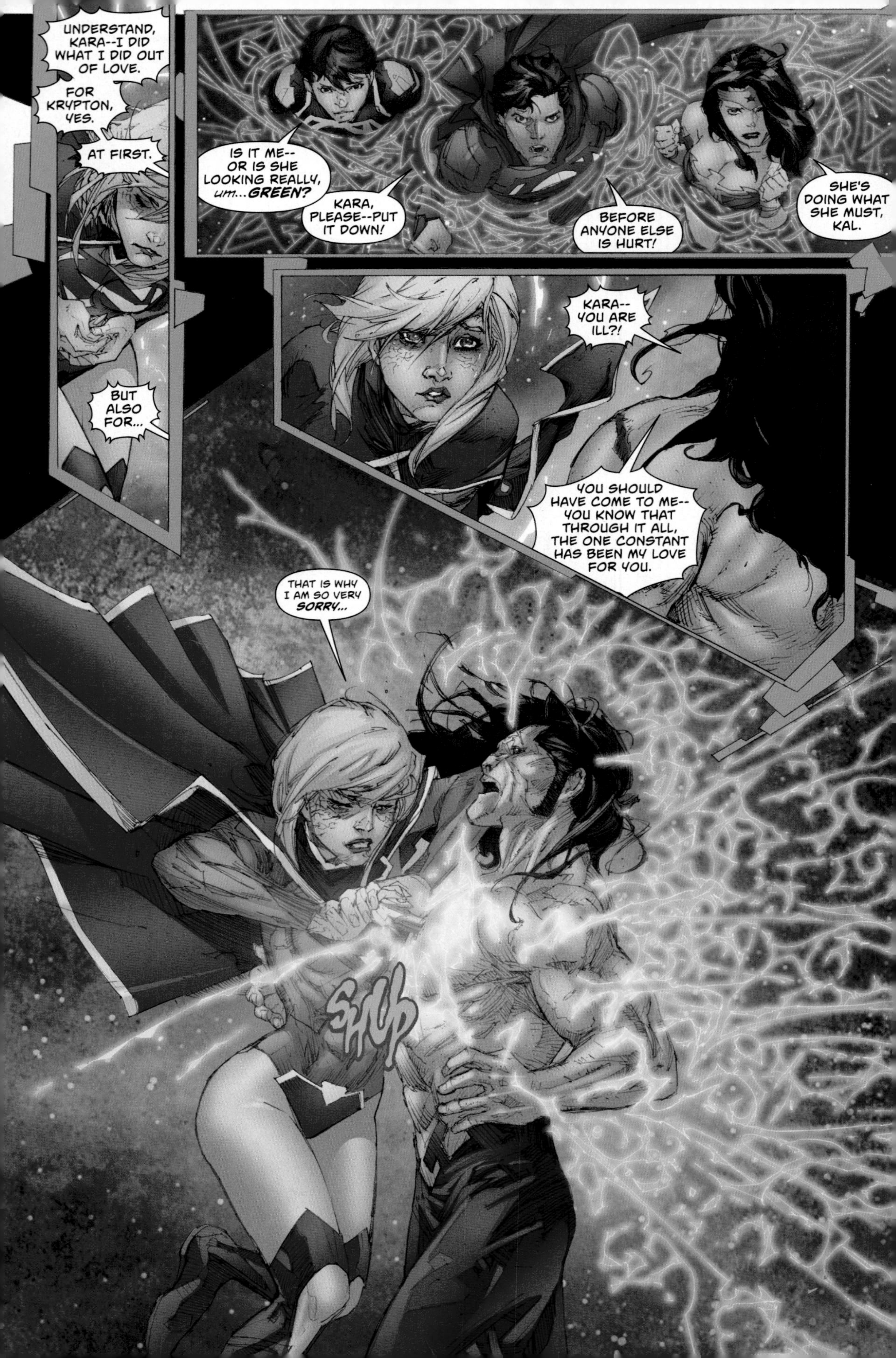

UNDERSTAND, KARA--I DID WHAT I DID OUT OF LOVE.
FOR KRYPTON, YES.
AT FIRST.
IS IT ME-- OR IS SHE LOOKING REALLY, um...GREEN?
KARA, PLEASE--PUT IT DOWN!
BEFORE ANYONE ELSE IS HURT!
SHE'S DOING WHAT SHE MUST, KAL.
BUT ALSO FOR...
KARA-- YOU ARE ILL?!
YOU SHOULD HAVE COME TO ME-- YOU KNOW THAT THROUGH IT ALL, THE ONE CONSTANT HAS BEEN MY LOVE FOR YOU.
THAT IS WHY I AM SO VERY SORRY...
SHUK

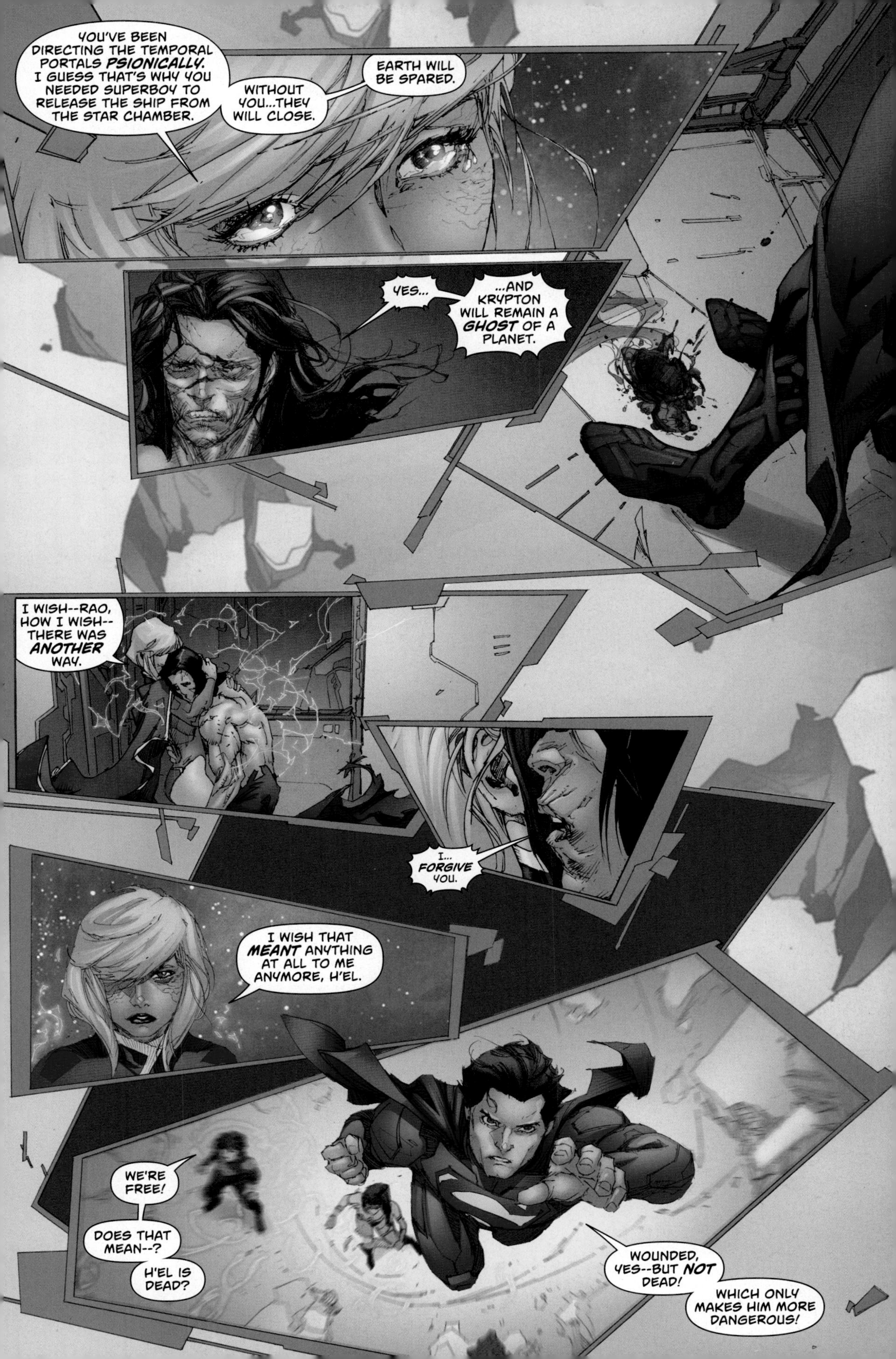
YOU'VE BEEN DIRECTING THE TEMPORAL PORTALS PSIONICALLY. I GUESS THAT'S WHY YOU NEEDED SUPERBOY TO RELEASE THE SHIP FROM THE STAR CHAMBER.
WITHOUT YOU...THEY WILL CLOSE.
EARTH WILL BE SPARED.
YES...
...AND KRYPTON WILL REMAIN A GHOST OF A PLANET.
I WISH--RAO, HOW I WISH--THERE WAS ANOTHER WAY.
I... FORGIVE YOU.
I WISH THAT MEANT ANYTHING AT ALL TO ME ANYMORE, H'EL.
WE'RE FREE!
DOES THAT MEAN--?
H'EL IS DEAD?
WOUNDED, YES--BUT NOT DEAD!
WHICH ONLY MAKES HIM MORE DANGEROUS!

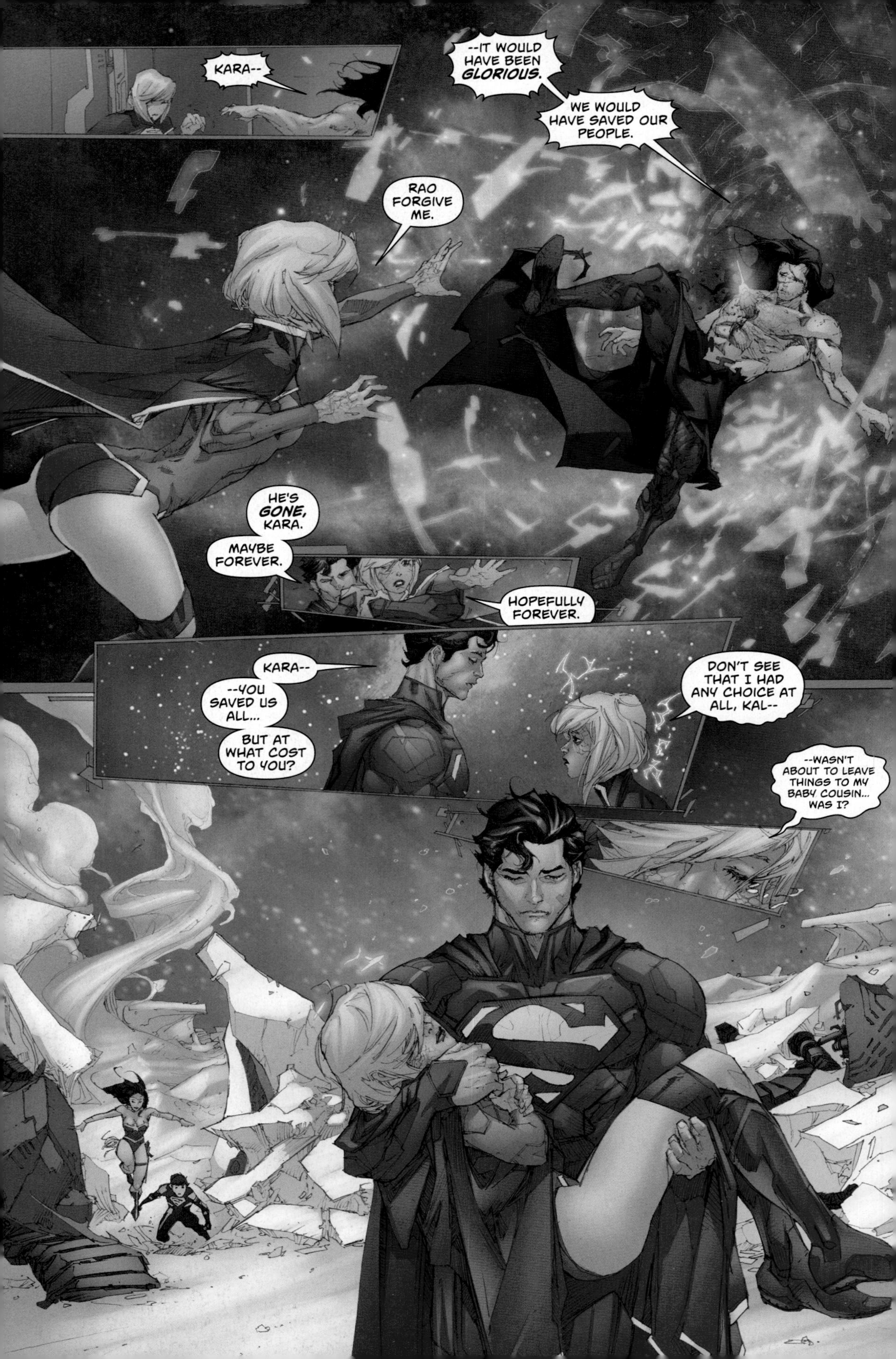
KARA--
--IT WOULD HAVE BEEN GLORIOUS.
WE WOULD HAVE SAVED OUR PEOPLE.
RAO FORGIVE ME.
HE'S GONE, KARA.
MAYBE FOREVER.
HOPEFULLY FOREVER.
KARA--
--YOU SAVED US ALL...
BUT AT WHAT COST TO YOU?
DON'T SEE THAT I HAD ANY CHOICE AT ALL, KAL--
--WASN'T ABOUT TO LEAVE THINGS TO MY BABY COUSIN... WAS I?

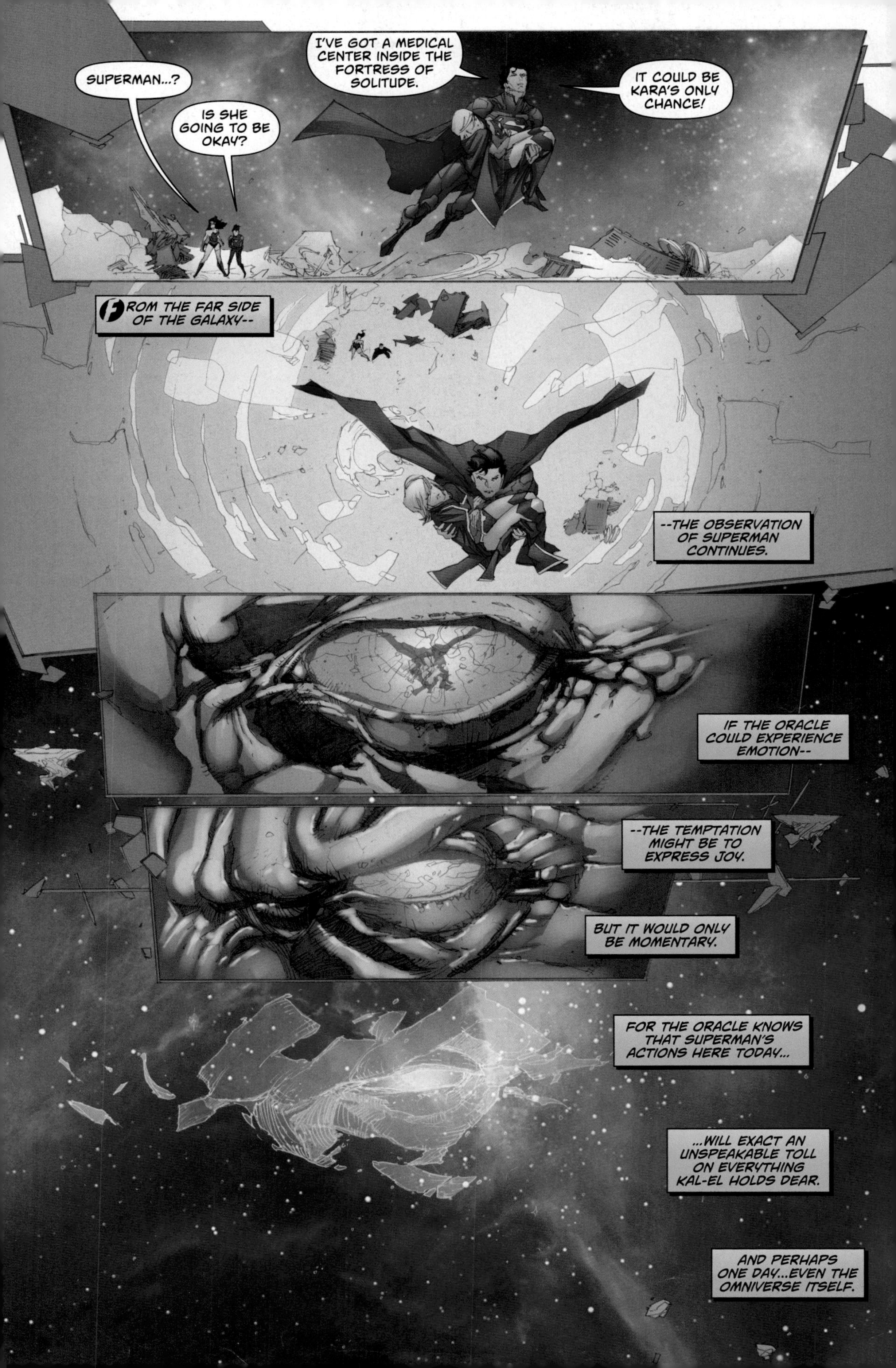
SUPERMAN...?
IS SHE GOING TO BE OKAY?
I'VE GOT A MEDICAL CENTER INSIDE THE FORTRESS OF SOLITUDE.
IT COULD BE KARA'S ONLY CHANCE!
FROM THE FAR SIDE OF THE GALAXY--
--THE OBSERVATION OF SUPERMAN CONTINUES.
IF THE ORACLE COULD EXPERIENCE EMOTION--
--THE TEMPTATION MIGHT BE TO EXPRESS JOY.
BUT IT WOULD ONLY BE MOMENTARY.
FOR THE ORACLE KNOWS THAT SUPERMAN'S ACTIONS HERE TODAY...
...WILL EXACT AN UNSPEAKABLE TOLL ON EVERYTHING KAL-EL HOLDS DEAR.
AND PERHAPS ONE DAY...EVEN THE OMNIVERSE ITSELF.

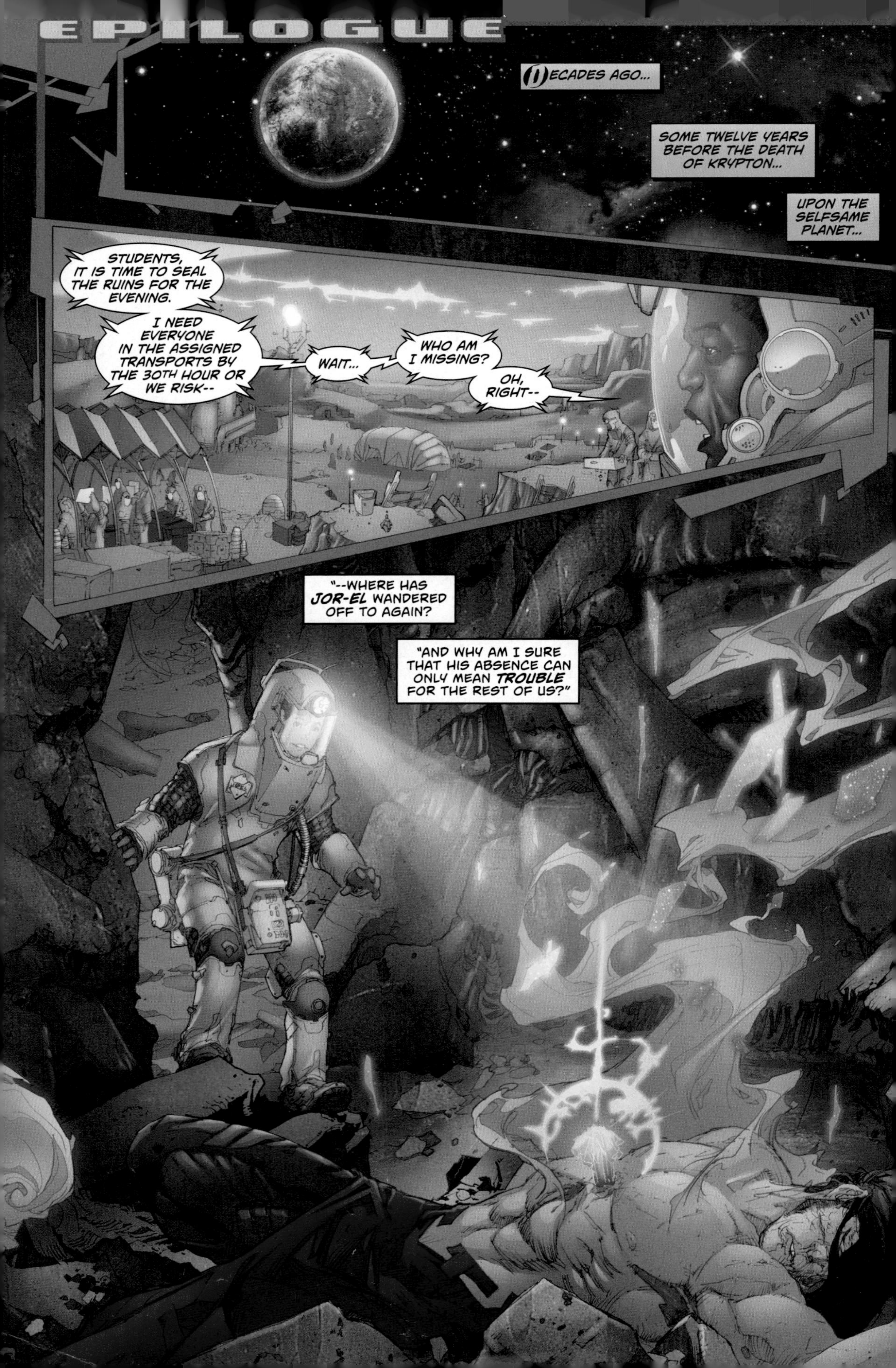
EPILOGUE
DECADES AGO...
SOME TWELVE YEARS BEFORE THE DEATH OF KRYPTON...
UPON THE SELFSAME PLANET...
STUDENTS, IT IS TIME TO SEAL THE RUINS FOR THE EVENING.
I NEED EVERYONE IN THE ASSIGNED TRANSPORTS BY THE 30TH HOUR OR WE RISK--
WAIT...
WHO AM I MISSING?
OH, RIGHT--
"--WHERE HAS JOR-EL WANDERED OFF TO AGAIN?
"AND WHY AM I SURE THAT HIS ABSENCE CAN ONLY MEAN TROUBLE FOR THE REST OF US?"